DETECTIVE FICTION
Crime and Compromise

DETECTIVE FICTION
Crime and Compromise

Edited by
Dick Allen and David Chacko
University of Bridgeport

Harcourt Brace Jovanovich, Inc.
New York / Chicago / San Francisco / Atlanta

ISBN: 0–15–517408–8

Library of Congress Catalog Card Number: 73–17632

Printed in the United States of America

Copyrights and Acknowledgments

COVER PHOTO courtesy Sue Green

BRANDT & BRANDT for "The Possibility of Evil" by Shirley Jackson, copyright © 1965
by Stanley Edgar Hyman. Reprinted by permission of Brandt & Brandt.
DODD, MEAD & COMPANY, INC., for "The Blue Cross" by G. K. Chesterton. Reprinted
by permission of Dodd, Mead & Company, Inc., from *The Innocence of Father
Brown* by G. K. Chesterton. Copyright 1910, 1911 by The Curtis Publishing Com-
pany. Copyright 1911 by Dodd, Mead & Company. Copyright renewed 1938 by
Gilbert K. Chesterton.
FARRAR, STRAUS & GIROUX, INC., for "Views of My Father Weeping" by Donald Barthelme. Reprinted with the permission of Farrar, Straus & Giroux, Inc., from *City
Life* by Donald Barthelme. Copyright © 1968, 1969, 1970 by Donald Barthelme.
THOMAS FLANAGAN for permission to reprint his "The Cold Winds of Adesta." Copy-
right © 1952 by Mercury Publications, Inc.
HELGA GREENE LITERARY AGENCY for "The Curtain" by Raymond Chandler from *Killer
in the Rain*. Copyright © 1964 by Helga Greene Literary Agency. Reprinted by
permission of Houghton Mifflin Company and the Helga Greene Literary Agency.
GEORGE GRELLA for permission to reprint his "Murder in the Mean Streets: The Hard-
Boiled Detective Novel." First published in *Contempora*, March 1970.
GROVE PRESS, INC., for "Death and the Compass" by Jorge Luis Borges from *Ficciones*
by Jorge Luis Borges. Reprinted by permission of Grove Press, Inc. Copyright ©
1962 by Grove Press, Inc.
HARPER & ROW, INC., for "The Stolen White Elephant" from *Tom Sawyer Abroad*
by Mark Twain.

Preface

Detective Fiction: Crime and Compromise deals with a form of popular fiction that is forever concerned with the basic questions of "right" and "wrong" in human behavior. Most of the fiction in this genre assumes that solutions, even if only partial or "compromised," can be found by those who are dedicated to seeking out truth. Mysteries, Poe's Monsieur C. Auguste Dupin knew, can almost always be solved through a combination of deduction and induction. A brave and honest person in search of truth might be a protector of what is noble in mankind. Secrets involving cover-ups of criminal actions must not be ignored or excused. The truth, whether it concerns the bodies stuffed up the chimney by the gorilla in "The Murders in the Rue Morgue" or the files in a psychiatrist's office, must be faced. It is the unknown or the only half-known that is most dangerous. Once in the open, exposed to rational examination, the mystery of crime is able to be at least confronted. Motivations can be understood. Punishment can be cleansing. Forgiveness depends upon understanding. Existential psychologists of the twentieth century, such as Rollo May, in his study Power and Innocence, have maintained that there is really no such thing as an innocent victim. Innocence is dangerous to us; it renders us powerless. Much better is the full facing of criminality, even horror, and all its implications. Raymond Chandler wrote: "Down these mean streets a man must go."

The sourcebook at hand is an open-ended one, which can be used as a basis for the exploration of many fascinating issues and side issues related to what we have called "detective fiction." We have, in fact, tried to raise questions rather than answer them. We have purposely avoided giving hard and fast definitions, "definitive" histories, and conclusions. These we leave to the writers in Part 4 on "Theories"—and to those readers who enjoy the research and controversy that aids them to form their own opinions.

To those familiar with only some of the most popular detective stories, movies, and TV dramas, the book may provide an introduction to the genre. Throughout, we have taken pains to choose selections for their literary merit as well as for their treatment of major issues.

The genre as a whole has too long been ignored in the classroom. The student and instructor will, we hope, find that they can discuss fully questions of social and individual import while also focusing upon questions of literature, writing style, and relationship of author and audience. What, the student of detective fiction might ask, are the differences among detective fiction, mystery fiction, suspense fiction, spy fiction, and gangster or criminal fiction? What distinctions can or should be made? How does British detective fiction differ from American detective fiction? What does the difference reveal about the two societies? Why has the basic genre proved to be so overwhelmingly popular for so long? What about the role of the hero in detective fiction? Is he generally a stereotyped romantic? Is he almost always a "cardboard" figure? How does detective fiction differ from "quality" fiction? Is plot so overwhelmingly important in the genre that it makes fine characterization impossible or perhaps even undesirable? How does the "hard-boiled" style of writing help form or reflect the American idiom? Is there such a thing as "the criminal mind"?

We begin the sourcebook with a section designed to provide the reader with an overall perspective on some of the metaphysical questions related to the genre. Robert Frost's poem "Design" poses an initial question concerning the presence of evil and horror in the world. In Ernest Hemingway's "The Killers," Nick Adams comes face to face with problems of human action he cannot yet understand and from which he seeks to run. Graham Greene's "The Destructors" compels us to explore the possible good as well as evil aspects of using force to eliminate a past seemingly no longer appropriate to the present. "Markheim" by Robert Louis Stevenson is an early kind of "inverted" criminal story. In the inverted mystery, we already know who did it; the excitement is in finding out why or how and in waiting for the crime's discovery and punishment by the authorities. There is a murder, also, in Robert Browning's "My Last Duchess." Here, as in "Markheim," we are asked to comprehend the motives behind the criminal act. Shirley Jackson's "The Possibility of Evil" deals with a malignancy possible even in the most innocent-seeming characters, in what appears to be an "innocent" small town. The final paragraphs of Agatha Christie's "The Dressmaker's Doll" may bring us up short.

Part 2, "The Detective," gives a representative selection of noted stories in the genre. In this section the reader can examine matters such as the role of detective as hero, compare varying detective "types," follow the use and possible misuse of reason and free will, note the serious or nonserious treatment of crime, and see how the detective achieves a working "compromise" within his element of work.

We begin Part 2 with the introduction and first section of Edgar Allan Poe's "The Murders in the Rue Morgue," which many students of the genre consider the first detective story ever written. In it, both Poe and his character Dupin explain their methods of "ratiocination," or detecting. Following it is a full example of the method—Poe's "The Purloined Letter." Sherlock Holmes is represented by what is essentially a "locked room" mystery, "The Adventure of the Speckled Band" by A. Conan Doyle. Another story concerning a sort of room, Jacques Futrelle's "The Problem of Cell 13," is an example of the reasoning mind triumphing over a seemingly insoluble problem. The heroes of these first stories illustrate those characteristics that have done so much to create the traditional stereotype of the quasi-aristocratic detective: snobbishness, supercilious actions, eccentricities, and even effeteness.

"The Blue Cross," by G. K. Chesterton, illustrates some of Chesterton's observations in his short essay in the part on "Theories." Chesterton's London—as Doyle's and indeed as the cities of Baudelaire and T. S. Eliot—is a city seething with clues, one almost designed to induce paranoia. Father Brown, however, is considerably different from the detectives created by the "Black Mask" school. The "hard-boiled" detective is seen in stories by Dashiell Hammett, Raymond Chandler, and Ross Macdonald. Notable in the so-called "hard-boiled" fiction is the development of a new "tough" style in American fiction, a style allied to that of Ernest Hemingway: hard, accurate, terse, avoiding a certain kind of sentiment while provoking perhaps a different kind.

There are many variations on the standard type of detective. Georges Simenon's Inspector Maigret is one of the most famous—an official detective of patience, determination, compassion. He is the most secret of men, who nonetheless can observe with pure fascination the moods of his city, the criminals he tracks, his own being.

In Thomas Flanagan's "The Cold Winds of Adesta" we see how the military and the detective story can merge across borders of international intrigue. "The Stolen White Elephant," which closes this part, is Mark Twain's spoof of the whole genre—a good corrective.

Part 3, "The Genre Extended," demonstrates how the "detection" element operates in the fiction of some highly regarded masters of quality literature. Students can ask, for instance, what characteristics Peter Brench, in Henry James's "The Tree of Knowledge," shares with the detective. They can see how the mystery in this story is unraveled in a manner quite like that used in traditional detective literature. The difference is perhaps that James writes a "psychological" mystery story, focusing on how truth affects its seeker. Stories by Borges, Burroughs, and Barthelme also concentrate on psychological mysteries—revelations of hidden truth and the effects of the revelations. Donald Barthelme's "Views of My Father Weeping," for instance, makes us ask if any final truth will ever be found and points out the ultimate absurdity of our presuming that there is any single solution to any crime, real or imagined. Chapters from Ross Macdonald's novel *The Far Side of the Dollar* and Dashiell Hammett's *The Maltese Falcon* demonstrate how the gap between pure detection stories and "literary" fiction is narrowed by writers concerned exclusively with the genre figure of the detective.

Part 4 begins with Dorothy L. Sayers's extensive examination of the genre's history. Articles by G. K. Chesterton and W. H. Auden go a long way toward explaining why detective fiction has always fascinated so many intellectuals. Raymond Chandler's "The Simple Art of Murder" explains much of the importance and popularity of the form. In his essay, "Murder and the Mean Streets: The Hard-Boiled Detective Novel," George Grella looks at the detective hero as he popularizes the fantasies and actualities of twentieth-century Americans. This part concludes with articles that provide factual information related to both the detective and modern crime. Robert Daley watches his television screen and compares fact and fancy in "Police Report on TV Cop Shows." Fred P. Graham's article "A Contemporary History of American Crime" reminds us that the problems of modern crime are enormous, and by implication we may feel that detective fiction—at least if taken as mainly fantasy and entertainment—might be only a way in which we suppress a full understanding of the contemporary crime problem. Do we prefer to think that individuals can, alone, solve what is essentially a problem burst out of all proportions? What of the "drug problem" and the steady increase in "crimes of major proportion" in America? Are we victims of our own bourgeois morality, creating criminals by prosecuting "victimless" crimes? How does pornography affect the so-called "criminal mind"? Should there be more police? Fewer? Is capital punishment justified? A deterrent to crime? Should more American streets be placed under twenty-four-hour TV surveillance? Are the courts too lenient? What about the prison system? Are criminals "made" or "born"? Could a knight in dusty armor, Constitution of the United States under one arm, have prevented the conception of such an attitude as that which fostered the Watergate scandal? Are not seemingly trivial, ordinary crimes microcosms of the massive ones?

Concluding the book, we provide suggestions for research or critical papers. Basic detective fiction materials are staples of public libraries and bookstores. Because most students will naturally supplement this book with such materials, a selective bibliography closes the volume.

We would particularly like to express our gratitude to William A. Pullin of Harcourt Brace Jovanovich for encouraging us to construct this sourcebook; to Gail Goldey, our patient editor, whose suggestions and admonitions have been invaluable; to David Madden, whose advice we have not always followed but whose careful readings and manuscript comments have helped us better define our own concerns; and especially to Jacques Barzun and Wendell Hertig Taylor, whose monumental *A Catalogue of Crime* is a gift to all fans, critics, and scholars of the genre, and without which we might have become lost.

Dick Allen
David Chacko

Contents

4   THEORIES   347

Introduction

I

Detective fiction, this strange child of Edgar Allan Poe, has since its birth been acclaimed by a wide and avid following, boasting addicts matched only by a stranger child—science fiction. Addiction is a leveler. Economic and social barriers are circumvented by both detective and science fiction, attracting the rising and the risen and the set, intellectuals and non-intellectuals. It would seem that both genres fulfill the needs and expectations of the modern reader. We crave a vision of the future-present, a craving science fiction attempts to satisfy. At the same time, we want to know where we have been, what we said and did there, what the past-present can tell us. Detective fiction attempts to satisfy some of these needs.

We demand in detective fiction a concern for reality. Verisimilitude—the strong sense of reality—is perhaps the detective story's primary concern, either appealing to our sense of logic, as do the civilized writers of detection from Conan Doyle to Harry Kemelman, or combining that appeal with another, as do the hard-boiled dicks of Hammett, Chandler, and Macdonald, men who seem to echo in their speech the real intonations of violence.

But the detectives of fiction are a fantasy, rarer in reality than the club of moonwalkers. Their real-life counterparts are the failed insurance salesmen, eavesdropping on grocery lists and assignations, by anyone's estimate light years from the conception of Macdonald's Lew Archer—knight-errant, father confessor, psychologist, owner of one of the more chaste couches in the vicinity of Hollywood. It seems that the reader of detective fiction, although demanding a high level of reality in some respects, is rolling his own with the figure of the fictional detective.

G. K. Chesterton sees our imaginations ignited by the figure of the detective. "No one can have failed to notice that in these stories the hero crosses cities with something of the loneliness and liberty of a prince in a tale of elfland, that in the course of that incalculable journey the casual automobile assumes the primal colors of a fairy ship." Clearly we allow our detective a generous range of possibilities. Furthermore, we seem willing to do this for the detective while being stingy with other, more likely, heroes.

Perhaps one of the reasons the detective has become a familiar example of the modern hero is that, unlike many other contemporary protagonists, he can move easily between various economic and social levels in an increasingly stratified and complex society. Although we are surely the most mobile people ever to inhabit the earth, our lives are as much pigeon-holed by this mobility as expanded by it: we can travel from Alaska to Tierra del Fuego without leaving the family camper; motels everywhere seem designed to achieve that blandness which is readily taken for familiarity; the suburbs of Atlanta, Georgia, look indistinguishable from those of Columbus, Ohio. The detective shares our mobility; yet at the same time he is allowed access to the various physical and psychological cubicles in which so many of us lead our lives—the office, the apartment, the car. By his actions he transforms the nuclear family into an extended one. The detective is the connector, the man who can link the cubicles together. His role requires that he meet people on a personal, in some ways intimate, basis, that he probe their pasts and possible sins, that he evaluate their character, and that he do these things in a relatively unrestricted manner, moving from townhouse to country cottage, from Hollywood to Watts. Put another way, the detective enacts the fantasies that our insular mobility denies us.

The same civilization that creates our wide access to space, and the paradoxical contraction that often accompanies this access, causes us to prize time while we squander it, to seek clarity as we rapidly displace the future. In the twentieth century many fiction writers have made increasing demands on the reader, shunting from the novel of social interaction to the novel of interior consciousness, from the structure of plot to the structure of theme and idea, from mature characters of some repose to the fragmentations of the anti-hero. These emphases place a heavy burden on the reader, even the determined and intelligent reader. The detective story meets this sometimes difficult fiction with relatively simple language, intricate plots, sound characterizations, and examples of how the rational mind can decipher truths through the use of inductive and deductive logic. Underlying these conditions is a belief in free will, a belief that is reflected in the figure of the detective as well as in the figure of the villain.

Still more sweeping claims have been put forth to explain the continuing appeal of detective fiction. Marjorie Nicolson has written that reading detective works "is a revolt from a smart and easy pessimism which interprets the universe in terms of relativity and purposelessness." She sees as inherent in detective fiction a "return to an older and more primitive conception of cosmic order."

> Perhaps we are protesting against a conception of the universe as governed—if governed at all—by chance, by haphazard circumstance;

against a conception of men and women as purposeless, aimless, impotent; against a theory of the world as wandering, devoid of purpose or meaning, in unlimited space. In our detective stories we find with relief a return to an older ethics and metaphysics: an Hebraic insistence upon justice as the measure of all things—an eye for an eye; a Greek feeling of inevitability, for man as the victim of circumstance and fate, to be sure, but a fate brought upon him by his own carelessness, his own ignorance, or his own choice; a Calvinistic insistence, if you will, upon destiny, but a Calvinistic belief also in the need for intense and constant activity on the part of man; last of all, a scientific insistence upon the inevitable operation of cause and effect.

We also see reflected in the detective some of our own curious and at times ambivalent attitudes toward the law. The ostensible failure of police methods in bringing criminals to justice, especially those criminals who use financial or social position, political influence, or illicit power to escape retribution, undoubtedly encourages our wish to see the freelance detective, or the official detective of uncommon ability, succeed. In fact we seem overly generous in permitting the detective a certain amorality in his pursuit of the truth or criminal. The detective can use people, abuse some, bend or break laws, suppress evidence, and on rare occasions even murder. We insist only that at length the truth or criminal be found out. Do we forgive the detective too much? The criminal too little?

II

Dorothy Sayers notes in her "Ominibus of Crime" that the detective story, "though it deals with the most desperate effects of rage, jealousy, and revenge . . . rarely touches the heights and depths of human passion. It presents us only with the *fait accompli*, and looks upon death and mutilation with a dispassionate eye. It does not show the inner workings of the murderer's mind." Sayers' statement indicates that the detective story often omits, as one of its working premises, comprehension of the criminal's motivation and environment. We see, in the typical story of detection, only the aftermath, the deed, the palpable manifestation of evil that is too real to ignore. It is the manifestation that we are more than willing to have passed on to the courts and prisons.

Since the detective story has flourished most in England and America (and to a lesser extent France), where democratic systems of government prevail, we may see some relation between the hero-figure of the detective and the pressure democracy can exert on its participants. Theoretically, citizens of a democracy govern themselves. Furthermore, one of the cornerstones of any democracy is the belief and confidence in an impartial system of justice, free from corruption by concentrations of power. Democracy assumes, not only that men may govern themselves, but that they must judge other men. A vote is a judgment. An accused man is, or can be, judged by his peers. A jury must weigh facts, evaluate character, and use precedent as a guide. If we look back to the beginnings of the Western conception of democratic justice, to our first precedents in the ancient Greece of Athens, we can see in the *Oresteia*, Aeschylus' trilogy, an illustration of the problems of vengeance, justice, and trial.

The House of Atreus has been cursed, fated forever to consume itself in violence. The first play of the trilogy deals with King Agamemnon's return from the Trojan War and his death at the hands of his wife, Clytemnestra. In the second play Clytemnestra is murdered by her son, Orestes. He, in turn, though thinking himself free of the curse, since his action was justified by the previous murder, is pursued by the ancient Furies, hideous, snake-haired creatures who wish to drive Orestes to insanity and death. The Furies want—simply—revenge. Even the god Apollo, as rational and civilized as the Furies are blunt and barbarous, cannot help Orestes deflect their wrath. When Orestes is finally driven to Athens, the aid of the goddess Athena is enlisted. She arranges a compromise, a jury of Athenian men to decide Orestes' fate. With Athena casting the swing vote, Orestes is acquitted, while at the same time the Furies are accorded a place of honor in the city. These creatures will live in caves under the city, their spirit will be venerated, and their name changed to the Eumenides—"The Kindly Ones."

The symbolism of the Eumenides has as much significance for us as for the ancient Athenians. Calling the Furies "The Kindly Ones" belies the unchanged ferocity of their natures, yet these creatures will inhabit the earth under the city, forming the foundation of democratic justice. The meaning is apparent, as Richmond Lattimore notes: "Man cannot obliterate, and should not repress, the unintelligible emotions. Or again, in different terms, man's nature being what it is and Fury being a part of it, Justice must go armed with Terror before it can work." The ancient Athenians did well to call these wretches The Kindly Ones. We may only placate the Furies and honor them with euphemisms. If the Furies are cast out, disregarded as a part of us, or regarded only as owned by others, a most dangerous kind of innocence, one that has little to do with the presumption of innocence, will victimize democratic justice.

There are some ways in which the detective performs as our benevolent Fury; the detective-hero, whether he is Jacques Futrelle's "Thinking Machine" or Dashiell Hammett's two-fisted Continental Op, relieves by means of fantasy some of the pressures exerted by the contradictions of modern life and the responsibilities of democratic government. Even the most genteel sort of amateur detective, a Miss Marple or a Father Brown, exposes the criminal so thoroughly that in essence it acts as our surrogate. The guilt of the perpetrator, finally, is incontestable. All detectives in their work, particularly those professionals of the hard-boiled and official schools, operate on the assumption that there is always, to borrow Shirley Jackson's title, "The Possibility of Evil." The two basic categories of detective fiction, the "genteel" and "realistic" schools, recognize this potential in human beings, the former with a sense of shock and outraged innocence, the latter with a sense of resignation and loss. To some extent the detectives of the realistic school see this tendency in themselves: though at heart they may be romantics, they are never innocents.

A man like Raymond Chandler's Philip Marlowe may "hear voices crying in the night," he may "go see what's the matter," but he also knows the range of human behavior—the heights and shortfalls—only too well.

> Twenty-four hours a day somebody is running, somebody else is trying to catch him. Out there in the night of a thousand crimes people are dying, being maimed, cut by flying glass, crushed against steering wheels or under heavy tires. People were being beaten, robbed, strangled, raped and murdered. People were hungry, sick, bored, desperate with loneliness or remorse or fear, angry, cruel, feverish, shaken by sobs. A city no worse than others, a city rich and vigorous and full of pride, a city lost and beaten and full of emptiness.

Marlowe, or any fictional detective, assumes an absurdly romantic burden for all of us. He is the individual man who solves dilemmas that seem insoluble, who searches the chaos of cities both "vigorous" and "lost," who comes up with connections that inevitably reveal the "pride" and "emptiness" of our life.

The fictional detective in his own way stands for the possibilities of the individual mind informed by intelligence and experience. He knows the Furies that inhabit man's nature and makes no attempt to deny them. But the detective's existence is a representation of the intelligence that ultimately settles disputes such as the fate of Orestes. Justice, armed with terror, must also go armed with the rational acumen of the goddess of Athens, the spirit chosen by the people to represent them as a proud and vigorous citizenry; the spirit too that must hover over every jury. Anyone who has ever served on a jury, who has seen or heard actual trials broadcast, or has watched a day's complement of the Senate Watergate Hearings, knows the intractable ways of truth. Every vector of evidence must be followed. Every strobe of intelligence must be brought to bear on the problem. Not many alternatives exist.

part 1

Manifestations

We would live without a sense of evil. Yet the news is consumed by it. In fear of it, some suburban communities, newly built, have erected palisades reminiscent of feudal cities, the walls scanned electronically, the gates opened by guards who permit passage only to residents who themselves have been screened by the most scrupulous computers. Inside these walls the environment will be as uncorrupted as technology permits. Love, understanding, conditioning, legislation, education, measured doses perhaps of bucolic living—all these will mitigate the sap of aggression in the young, the rancor that curdles in the older ones. Man is perfectible. Shown the most reasonable course, he will choose it. He will not flee New Cannan for the East Village. He will not sympathize with the wrong half of a morality play. The office of the Presidency will transform him. Or so we wish to believe.

The "Manifestations" section of this text should cause us to question man's goodness and access to perfection. Without a realistic assessment of the influence of the irrational or super-rational in the conduct of human beings, we may find ourselves badly equipped to face life, or even to sample vicariously the milieu of the detective. His world is, of course, an exaggerated one where violence is common. The following stories, written by some of the most widely read and respected authors of English and American literature's last century, will show us the roots of crime as they occur in our more mundane world. We will be asked to explore motivations and the boundaries of morality. Can anything account for our basest impulses? We cannot deny the presence of such impulses without being true hypocrites, but what causes some to enact their lusts while others forbear? Is the fear of detection the only difference between a criminal and a good citizen?

We may come to grips with an elusive thing here—character. In his study of mass-murderers, Murder for Profit, *William Bolitho made the following observation: "In the mental life of most men there are no free thoughts, for each as it gets up is hooked by the foot in the piled accumulation of the past. Memory, with the background of punishments, fatigues, partings, regrets, breaks our actions, as it hampers all our thoughts and its weight produces the prevalent mood we call character." No one can deny the past; it has made us what we are. Every act we perform is a manifestation of our lives in totality. Certain evil acts, such as the destruction of an historic house by young vandals, are explicable only by reference to the nature of man and his capacity for harm, while others, such as the murder of a young duchess, are understandable in the specific context of one man's conscious pride and egotism. Perhaps we will see things revealed in these stories that are best revealed, recognized, and accepted with distaste. We would also do well to recognize the simultaneous creative acts that accompany each revelation of character and evil—acts of the writers as well as protagonists.*

The metaphysical question is a strange one. Is Earth some gigantic testing ground? Are we all in a training camp? Why do tensions pull us so mightily? Is there, as Frost questions, some "design of darkness to appall"—a design to life that is evil in its very nature, a design that runs from microcosm to macrocosm, from insect and flower to statesman and nation?

We cannot avoid a confrontation with evil. It may come in the guise of "The Killers," as we innocently work in a small town diner. What do we do—seek to avoid it, compromise with it, or run from our realization that it exists? It seems likely that Hemingway means us to see that Nick Adams is not ready to comprehend it, and because he is not ready, he is not yet "initiated."

Old women can be wicked, too, as in Shirley Jackson's "The Possibility of Evil." What created this pure maliciousness? Would her wickedness have been at least muted if she had been sent to live in a rocking chair in some Miami leisure village? And witness how Jackson shows evil creating a kind of "evil" retribution. We might be reminded of how William Blake, in his poem "A Poison Tree," suggests that the very acts of anger and retribution poison those who would strike back at their enemies.

Is there some kind of inborn impulse that compels those confident of their power to begin eliminating, killing those they cannot bend to their will? An arrogance against which those who live quiet and smiling lives must protect themselves or be protected by others? Who could have aided or saved the duchess in Browning's famous dramatic monologue?

In the mysterious figure of the boy who controls his friends in Graham Greene's "The Destructors" there is another figure of power and domination. The old house, that which is beautiful and has survived, must be eliminated completely. Its reminder of another time is too painful to tolerate. Yet while we understand the motives behind the destruction, we nonetheless must question the value of a wasteland. Out of a completely shattered civilization can anything grow up beautiful again? Will anyone have the impulse or memory to build again?

Robert Louis Stevenson's "Markheim" compels us to explore the element of the irrational, the spur-of-the-moment factor that so strongly contributes to crime. The murder is committed, but what happens to the murderer? Can a man, confessing to himself, hope for even a partial forgiveness?

"The Dressmaker's Doll" is a story near to the supernatural. What wickedness have these women done to be so subjected to the terror of unexplained incidents? Could, as the ending of Agatha Christie's story suggests, simple acts of caring and kindness have prevented the desire for attention that so often is the

root of *callous actions? Who and what have we ignored? The bum on the street who only wanted a quarter? How much punishment do we subconsciously wish to bring upon ourselves? Does our forgetting to lock the door indicate that we really wish to be burglarized? Does the flare-up at our employer really indicate that we want to be fired, even though our conscious mind cannot admit this desire and is terrified of its initial consequences?*

The questions of crime, evil, and motivations—indeed, of the nature of man—are certainly too many and too complex to answer simply. At best, they provide a pattern we can endlessly explore. It is into this kind of world that the detective is plunged. How he deals with these manifestations of deeper issues defines him; how deeply the author of the detective story is able to relate to at least a few of these questions may indicate the relative quality and importance of his fiction. Upon backgrounds and questions such as those related above, and with these stories and poems in mind, we can better consider the treatment of crime, the hero figure, the fiction of detective literature in the section that follows this one.

Design

Robert Frost

I found a dimpled spider, fat and white,
On a white heal-all, holding up a moth
Like a white piece of rigid satin cloth—
Assorted characters of death and blight
Mixed ready to begin the morning right,
Like the ingredients of a witches' broth—
A snow-drop spider, a flower like a froth,
And dead wings carried like a paper kite.

What had that flower to do with being white,
The wayside blue and innocent heal-all?
What brought the kindred spider to that height,
Then steered the white moth thither in the night?
What but design of darkness to appall?—
If design govern in a thing so small.

QUESTIONS

1. Is the word "evil" applicable to this poem? What is your definition of evil? Would an "uncaring" universe be as appalling as a universe "designed" for death and blight? Discuss how these two conceptions of the nature of the universe could affect one's approach to life.

2. Which lines reveal a feeling of either anger or despair? How?

3. Imagine the poem being written in an unrhymed, unmetrical form. How might this have changed the effect?

4. If "design govern in a thing so small," must it necessarily (or logically) govern in all larger encounters, aspects of life? Discuss.

5. Analyze the color imagery in the poem.

The Killers

Ernest Hemingway

The door of Henry's lunch-room opened and two men came in. They sat down at the counter.

"What's yours?" George asked them.

"I don't know," one of the men said. "What do you want to eat, Al?"

"I don't know," said Al. "I don't know what I want to eat."

Outside it was getting dark. The street-light came on outside the window. The two men at the counter read the menu. From the other end of the counter Nick Adams watched them. He had been talking to George when they came in.

"I'll have a roast pork tenderloin with apple sauce and mashed potatoes," the first man said.

"It isn't ready yet."

"What the hell do you put it on the card for?"

"That's the dinner," George explained. "You can get that at six o'clock."

George looked at the clock on the wall behind the counter.

"It's five o'clock."

"The clock says twenty minutes past five," the second man said.

"It's twenty minutes fast."

"Oh, to hell with the clock," the first man said. "What have you got to eat?"

"I can give you any kind of sandwiches," George said. "You can have ham and eggs, bacon and eggs, liver and bacon, or a steak."

"Give me chicken croquettes with green peas and cream sauce and mashed potatoes."

"That's the dinner."

"Everything we want's the dinner, eh? That's the way you work it."

"I can give you ham and eggs, bacon and eggs, liver—"

"I'll take ham and eggs," the man called Al said. He wore a derby hat and a black overcoat buttoned across the chest. His face was small and white and he had tight lips. He wore a silk muffler and gloves.

"Give me bacon and eggs," said the other man. He was about the same size as Al. Their faces were different, but they were dressed like twins.

Both wore overcoats too tight for them. They sat leaning forward, their elbows on the counter.

"Got anything to drink?" Al asked.

"Silver beer, bevo, ginger-ale," George said.

"I mean you got anything to *drink?*"

"Just those I said."

"This is a hot town," said the other. "What do they call it?"

"Summit."

"Ever hear of it?" Al asked his friend.

"No," said the friend.

"What do you do here nights?" Al asked.

"They eat the dinner," his friend said. "They all come here and eat the big dinner."

"That's right," George said.

"So you think that's right?" Al asked George.

"Sure."

"You're a pretty bright boy, aren't you?"

"Sure," said George.

"Well, you're not," said the other little man. "Is he, Al?"

"He's dumb," said Al. He turned to Nick. "What's your name?"

"Adams."

"Another bright boy," Al said. "Ain't he a bright boy, Max?"

"The town's full of bright boys," Max said.

George put the two platters, one of ham and eggs, the other of bacon and eggs, on the counter. He set down two side-dishes of fried potatoes and closed the wicket into the kitchen.

"Which is yours?" he asked Al.

"Don't you remember?"

"Ham and eggs."

"Just a bright boy," Max said. He leaned forward and took the ham and eggs. Both men ate with their gloves on. George watched them eat.

"What are *you* looking at?" Max looked at George.

"Nothing."

"The hell you were. You were looking at me."

"Maybe the boy meant it for a joke, Max," Al said.

George laughed.

"*You* don't have to laugh," Max said to him. "*You* don't have to laugh at all, see?"

"All right," said George.

"So he thinks it's all right." Max turned to Al. "He thinks it's all right. That's a good one."

"Oh, he's a thinker," Al said. They went on eating.

"What's the bright boy's name down the counter?" Al asked Max.

"Hey, bright boy," Max said to Nick. "You go around on the other side of the counter with your boy friend."

"What's the idea?" Nick asked.

"There isn't any idea."

"You better go around, bright boy," Al said. Nick went around behind the counter.

"What's the idea?" George asked.

"None of your damn business," Al said. "Who's out in the kitchen?"

"The nigger."

"What do you mean the nigger?"

"The nigger that cooks."

"Tell him to come in."

"What's the idea?"

"Tell him to come in."

"Where do you think you are?"

"We know damn well where we are," the man called Max said. "Do we look silly?"

"You talk silly," Al said to him. "What the hell do you argue with this kid for? Listen," he said to George, "tell the nigger to come out here."

"What are you going to do to him?"

"Nothing. Use your head, bright boy. What would we do to a nigger?"

George opened the slit that opened back into the kitchen. "Sam," he called. "Come in here a minute."

The door to the kitchen opened and the nigger came in. "What was it?" he asked. The two men at the counter took a look at him.

"All right, nigger. You stand right there," Al said.

Sam, the nigger, standing in his apron, looked at the two men sitting at the counter. "Yes, sir," he said. Al got down from his stool.

"I'm going back to the kitchen with the nigger and bright boy," he said. "Go on back to the kitchen, nigger. You go with him, bright boy." The little man walked after Nick and Sam, the cook, back into the kitchen. The door shut after them. The man called Max sat at the counter opposite George. He didn't look at George but looked in the mirror that ran along back of the counter. Henry's had been made over from a saloon into a lunch-counter.

"Well, bright boy," Max said, looking into the mirror, "why don't you say something?"

"What's it all about?"

"Hey, Al," Max called, "bright boy wants to know what it's all about."

"Why don't you tell him?" Al's voice came from the kitchen.

"What do you think it's all about?"

"I don't know."

"What do you think?"

Max looked into the mirror all the time he was talking.

"I wouldn't say."

"Hey, Al, bright boy says he wouldn't say what he thinks it's all about."

"I can hear you, all right," Al said from the kitchen. He had propped open the slit that dishes passed through into the kitchen with a catsup bottle. "Listen, bright boy," he said from the kitchen to George. "Stand a little further along the bar. You move a little to the left, Max." He was like a photographer arranging for a group picture.

"Talk to me, bright boy," Max said. "What do you think's going to happen?"

George did not say anything.

"I'll tell you," Max said. "We're going to kill a Swede. Do you know a big Swede named Ole Andreson?"

"Yes."

"He comes here to eat every night, don't he?"

"Sometimes he comes here."

"He comes here at six o'clock, don't he?"

"If he comes."

"We know all that, bright boy," Max said. "Talk about something else. Ever go to the movies?"

"Once in a while."

"You ought to go to the movies more. The movies are fine for a bright boy like you."

"What are you going to kill Ole Andreson for? What did he ever do to you?"

"He never had a chance to do anything to us. He never even seen us."

"And he's only going to see us once," Al said from the kitchen.

"What are you going to kill him for, then?" George asked.

"We're killing him for a friend. Just to oblige a friend, bright boy."

"Shut up," said Al from the kitchen. "You talk too goddam much."

"Well, I got to keep bright boy amused. Don't I, bright boy?"

"You talk too damn much," Al said. "The nigger and my bright boy are amused by themselves. I got them tied up like a couple of girl friends in the convent."

"I suppose you were in a convent."

"You never know."

"You were in a kosher convent. That's where you were."

George looked up at the clock.

"If anybody comes in you tell them the cook is off, and if they keep after it, you tell them you'll go back and cook yourself. Do you get that, bright boy?"

"All right," George said. "What you going to do with us afterward?"

"That'll depend," Max said. "That's one of those things you never know at the time."

George looked up at the clock. It was a quarter past six. The door from the street opened. A street-car motorman came in.

"Hello, George," he said. "Can I get supper?"

"Sam's gone out," George said. "He'll be back in about half an hour."

"I'd better go up the street," the motorman said. George looked at the clock. It was twenty minutes past six.

"That was nice, bright boy," Max said. "You're a regular little gentleman."

"He knew I'd blow his head off," Al said from the kitchen.

"No," said Max. "It ain't that. Bright boy is nice. He's a nice boy. I like him."

At six-fifty-five George said: "He's not coming."

Two other people had been in the lunch-room. Once George had gone out to the kitchen and made a ham-and-egg sandwich "to go" that a man wanted to take with him. Inside the kitchen he saw Al, his derby hat tipped back, sitting on a stool beside the wicket with the muzzle of a sawed-off shotgun resting on the ledge. Nick and the cook were back to back in the corner, a towel tied in each of their mouths. George had cooked the sandwich, wrapped it up in oiled paper, put it in a bag, brought it in, and the man had paid for it and gone out.

"Bright boy can do everything," Max said. "He can cook and everything. You'd make some girl a nice wife, bright boy."

"Yes?" George said. "Your friend, Ole Andreson, isn't going to come."

"We'll give him ten minutes," Max said.

Max watched the mirror and the clock. The hands of the clock marked seven o'clock, and then five minutes past seven.

"Come on, Al," said Max. "We better go. He's not coming."

"Better give him five minutes," Al said from the kitchen.

In the five minutes a man came in, and George explained that the cook was sick.

"Why the hell don't you get another cook?" the man asked. "Aren't you running a lunch-counter?" He went out.

"Come on, Al," Max said.

"What about the two bright boys and the nigger?"

"They're all right."

"You think so?"

"Sure. We're through with it."

"I don't like it," said Al. "It's sloppy. You talk too much."

"Oh, what the hell," said Max. "We got to keep amused, haven't we?"

"You talk too much, all the same," Al said. He came out from the kitchen. The cut-off barrels of the shotgun made a slight bulge under the waist of his too tight-fitting overcoat. He straightened his coat with his gloved hands.

"So long, bright boy," he said to George. "You got a lot of luck."

"That's the truth," Max said. "You ought to play the races, bright boy."

The two of them went out the door. George watched them, through the window, pass under the arc-light and cross the street. In their tight overcoats and derby hats they looked like a vaudeville team. George went back through the swinging-door into the kitchen and untied Nick and the cook.

"I don't want any more of that," said Sam, the cook. "I don't want any more of that."

Nick stood up. He had never had a towel in his mouth before.

"Say," he said. "What the hell?" He was trying to swagger it off.

"They were going to kill Ole Andreson," George said. "They were going to shoot him when he came in to eat."

"Ole Andreson?"

"Sure."

The cook felt the corners of his mouth with his thumbs.

"They all gone?" he asked.

"Yeah," said George. "They're gone now."

"I don't like it," said the cook. "I don't like any of it at all."

"Listen," George said to Nick. "You better go see Ole Andreson."

"All right."

"You better not have anything to do with it at all," Sam, the cook, said. "You better stay way out of it."

"Don't go if you don't want to," George said.

"Mixing up in this ain't going to get you anywhere," the cook said. "You stay out of it."

"I'll go see him," Nick said to George. "Where does he live?"

The cook turned away.

"Little boys always know what they want to do," he said.

"He lives up at Hirsch's rooming-house," George said to Nick.

"I'll go up there."

Outside the arc-light shone through the bare branches of a tree. Nick walked up the street beside the car-tracks and turned at the next arc-light down a side-street. Three houses up the street was Hirsch's rooming-house. Nick walked up the two steps and pushed the bell. A woman came to the door.

"Is Ole Andreson here?"

"Do you want to see him?"

"Yes, if he's in."

Nick followed the woman up a flight of stairs and back to the end of a corridor. She knocked on the door.

"Who is it?"

"It's somebody to see you, Mr. Andreson," the woman said.

"It's Nick Adams."

"Come in."

Nick opened the door and went into the room. Ole Andreson was lying on the bed with all his clothes on. He had been a heavyweight prizefighter and he was too long for the bed. He lay with his head on two pillows. He did not look at Nick.

"What was it?" he asked.

"I was up at Henry's," Nick said, "and two fellows came in and tied up me and the cook, and they said they were going to kill you."

It sounded silly when he said it. Ole Andreson said nothing.

"They put us out in the kitchen," Nick went on. "They were going to shoot you when you came in to supper."

Ole Andreson looked at the wall and did not say anything.

"George thought I better come and tell you about it."

"There isn't anything I can do about it," Ole Andreson said.

"I'll tell you what they were like."

"I don't want to know what they were like," Ole Andreson said. He looked at the wall. "Thanks for coming to tell me about it."

"That's all right."

Nick looked at the big man lying on the bed.

"Don't you want me to go and see the police?"

"No," Ole Andreson said. "That wouldn't do any good."

"Isn't there something I could do?"

"No. There ain't anything to do."

"Maybe it was just a bluff."

"No. It ain't just a bluff."

Ole Andreson rolled over toward the wall.

"The only thing is," he said, talking toward the wall, "I just can't make up my mind to go out. I been in here all day."

"Couldn't you get out of town?"

"No," Ole Andreson said. "I'm through with all that running around." He looked at the wall.

"There ain't anything to do now."

"Couldn't you fix it up some way?"

"No. I got in wrong." He talked in the same flat voice. "There ain't anything to do. After a while I'll make up my mind to go out."

"I better go back and see George," Nick said.

"So long," said Ole Andreson. He did not look toward Nick. "Thanks for coming around."

Nick went out. As he shut the door he saw Ole Andreson with all his clothes on, lying on the bed looking at the wall.

"He's been in his room all day," the landlady said downstairs. "I guess he don't feel well. I said to him: 'Mr. Andreson, you ought to go out and take a walk on a nice fall day like this,' but he didn't feel like it."

"He doesn't want to go out."

"I'm sorry he don't feel well," the woman said. "He's an awfully nice man. He was in the ring, you know."

"I know it."

"You'd never know it except from the way his face is," the woman said. They stood talking just inside the street door. "He's just as gentle."

"Well, good-night, Mrs. Hirsch," Nick said.

"I'm not Mrs. Hirsch," the woman said. "She owns the place. I just look after it for her. I'm Mrs. Bell."

"Well, good-night, Mrs. Bell," Nick said.

"Good-night," the woman said.

Nick walked up the dark street to the corner under the arc-light, and then along the car-tracks to Henry's eating-house. George was inside, back of the counter.

"Did you see Ole?"

"Yes," said Nick. "He's in his room and he won't go out."

The cook opened the door from the kitchen when he heard Nick's voice.

"I don't even listen to it," he said and shut the door.

"Did you tell him about it?" George asked.

"Sure. I told him but he knows what it's all about."

"What's he going to do?"

"Nothing."

"They'll kill him."

"I guess they will."

"He must have got mixed up in something in Chicago."

"I guess so," said Nick.

"It's a hell of a thing."

"It's an awful thing," Nick said.

They did not say anything. George reached down for a towel and wiped the counter.

"I wonder what he did?" Nick said.

"Double-crossed somebody. That's what they kill them for."

"I'm going to get out of this town," Nick said.

"Yes," said George. "That's a good thing to do."

"I can't stand to think about him waiting in the room and knowing he's going to get it. It's too damned awful."

"Well," said George, "you better not think about it."

QUESTIONS

1. How is the style of this story like and different from the style used by Dashiell Hammett, Raymond Chandler, Ross MacDonald?

2. How does Hemingway make the two killers so terrifying?

3. What do the three reactions of the diner's workers reveal about their understanding of life?

4. Does the story present a problem that nothing ultimately could solve, or does it suggest that answers might be found?

5. Why does Ole wait in his room? Is he an admirable character?

6. In every Hemingway story, the smallest detail can be

revealing. Why, for instance, does Nick call the woman at the boarding house by the wrong name?

7. Is this story more "violent" than stories in which actual "on stage" violence occurs? Why or why not?

8. Ole Andreson says that he does not want to know what the killers are "like." What similies does Hemingway use to describe the two killers? Do the similies add anything more than a descriptive element to the killers? Are these what Hemingway sees evil as being "like"?

9. Discuss any thematic similarities between "Design" and "The Killers."

The Possibility of Evil

Shirley Jackson

Miss Adela Strangeworth came daintily along Main Street on her way to the grocery. The sun was shining, the air was fresh and clear after the night's heavy rain, and everything in Miss Strangeworth's little town looked washed and bright. Miss Strangeworth took deep breaths and thought that there was nothing in the world like a fragrant summer day.

She knew everyone in town, of course; she was fond of telling strangers—tourists who sometimes passed through the town and stopped to admire Miss Strangeworth's roses—that she had never spent more than a day outside this town in all her long life. She was seventy-one, Miss Strangeworth told the tourists, with a pretty little dimple showing by her lip, and she sometimes found herself thinking that the town belonged to her. "My grandfather built the first house on Pleasant Street," she would say, opening her blue eyes wide with the wonder of it. "This house, right here. My family has lived here for better than a hundred years. My grandmother planted these roses, and my mother tended them, just as I do. I've watched my town grow; I can remember when Mr. Lewis, Senior, opened the grocery store, and the year the river flooded out the shanties on the low road, and the excitement when some young folks wanted to move the park over to the space in front of where the new post office is today. They wanted to put up a statue of Ethan Allen"—Miss Strangeworth would frown a little and sound stern—"but it should have been a statue of my grandfather. There wouldn't have been a town here at all if it hadn't been for my grandfather and the lumber mill."

Miss Strangeworth never gave away any of her roses, although the tourists often asked her. The roses belonged on Pleasant Street, and it bothered Miss Strangeworth to think of people wanting to carry them away, to take them into strange towns and down strange streets. When the new minister came, and the ladies were gathering flowers to decorate the church, Miss Strangeworth sent over a great basket of gladioli; when she picked the roses at all, she set them in bowls and vases around the inside of the house her grandfather had built.

Walking down Main Street on a summer morning, Miss Strangeworth had to stop every minute or so to say good morning to someone or to ask after someone's health. When she came into the grocery, half a dozen people turned away from the shelves and the counters to wave at her or call out good morning.

"And good morning to you, too, Mr. Lewis," Miss Strangeworth said at last. The Lewis family had been in the town almost as long as the Strangeworths; but the day young Lewis left high school and went to work in the grocery, Miss Strangeworth had stopped calling him Tommy and started calling him Mr. Lewis, and he had stopped calling her Addie and started calling her Miss Strangeworth. They had been in high school together, and had gone to picnics together, and to high-school dances and basketball games; but now Mr. Lewis was behind the counter in the grocery, and Miss Strangeworth was living alone in the Strangeworth house on Pleasant Street.

"Good morning," Mr. Lewis said, and added politely, "Lovely day."

"It is a very nice day," Miss Strangeworth said, as though she had only just decided that it would do after all. "I would like a chop, please, Mr. Lewis, a small, lean veal chop. Are those strawberries from Arthur Parker's garden? They're early this year."

"He brought them in this morning," Mr. Lewis said.

"I shall have a box," Miss Strangeworth said. Mr. Lewis looked worried, she thought, and for a minute she hesitated, but then she decided that he surely could not be worried over the strawberries. He looked very tired indeed. He was usually so chipper, Miss Strangeworth thought, and almost commented, but it was far too personal a subject to be introduced to Mr. Lewis, the grocer, so she only said, "And a can of cat food and, I think, a tomato."

Silently, Mr. Lewis assembled her order on the counter, and waited. Miss Strangeworth looked at him curiously and then said, "It's Tuesday, Mr. Lewis. You forgot to remind me."

"Did I? Sorry."

"Imagine your forgetting that I always buy my tea on Tuesday," Miss Strangeworth said gently. "A quarter pound of tea, please, Mr. Lewis."

"Is that all, Miss Strangeworth?"

"Yes, thank you, Mr. Lewis. Such a lovely day, isn't it?"

"Lovely," Mr. Lewis said.

Miss Strangeworth moved slightly to make room for Mrs. Harper at the counter. "Morning, Adela," Mrs. Harper said, and Miss Strangeworth said, "Good morning, Martha."

"Lovely day," Mrs. Harper said, and Miss Strangeworth said, "Yes, lovely," and Mr. Lewis, under Mrs. Harper's glance, nodded.

"Ran out of sugar for my cake frosting," Mrs. Harper explained. Her hand shook slightly as she opened her pocketbook. Miss Strangeworth wondered, glancing at her quickly, if she had been taking proper care of herself. Martha Harper was not as young as she used to be, Miss Strangeworth thought. She probably could use a good strong tonic.

"Martha," she said, "you don't look well."

"I'm perfectly all right," Mrs. Harper said shortly. She handed her money to Mr. Lewis, took her change and her sugar, and went out without speaking again. Looking after her, Miss Strangeworth shook her head slightly. Martha definitely did *not* look well.

Carrying her little bag of groceries, Miss Strangeworth came out of the store into the bright sunlight and stopped to smile down on the Crane baby. Don and Helen Crane were really the two most infatuated young parents she had ever known, she thought indulgently, looking at the delicately embroidered baby cap and the lace-edged carriage cover.

"That little girl is going to grow up expecting luxury all her life," she said to Helen Crane.

Helen laughed. "That's the way we want her to feel," she said. "Like a princess."

"A princess can see a lot of trouble sometimes," Miss Strangeworth said dryly. "How old is Her Highness now?"

"Six months next Tuesday," Helen Crane said, looking down with rapt wonder at her child. "I've been worrying, though, about her. Don't you think she ought to move around more? Try to sit up, for instance?"

"For plain and fancy worrying," Miss Strangeworth said, amused, "give me a new mother every time."

"She just seems—slow," Helen Crane said.

"Nonsense. All babies are different. Some of them develop much more quickly than others."

"That's what my mother says." Helen Crane laughed, looking a little bit ashamed.

"I suppose you've got young Don all upset about the fact that his daughter is already six months old and hasn't yet begun to learn to dance?"

"I haven't mentioned it to him. I suppose she's just so precious that I worry about her all the time."

"Well, apologize to her right now," Miss Strangeworth said. "*She* is probably worrying about why you keep jumping around all the time." Smiling to herself and shaking her old head, she went on down the sunny street, stopping once to ask little Billy Moore why he wasn't out riding in his daddy's shiny new car, and talking for a few minutes outside the library with Miss Chandler, the librarian, about the new novels to be ordered and paid for by the annual library appropriation. Miss Chandler seemed absent-minded and very much as though she were thinking about something else. Miss Strangeworth noticed that Miss Chandler had not taken much trouble with her hair that morning, and sighed. Miss Strangeworth hated sloppiness.

Many people seemed disturbed recently, Miss Strangeworth thought. Only yesterday the Stewarts' fifteen-year-old Linda had run crying down her own front walk and all the way to school, not caring who saw her. People around town thought she might have had a fight with the Harris boy, but they showed up together at the soda shop after school as usual, both of them looking grim and bleak. Trouble at home, people concluded, and sighed over the problems of trying to raise kids right these days.

From halfway down the block Miss Strangeworth could catch the heavy scent of her roses, and she moved a little more quickly. The perfume of roses meant home, and home meant the Strangeworth House on Pleasant Street. Miss Strangeworth stopped at her own front gate, as she always did, and looked with deep pleasure at her house, with the red and pink and white roses massed along the narrow lawn, and the rambler going up along the porch; and the neat, the unbelievably trim lines of the house itself, with its slimness and its washed white look. Every window sparkled, every curtain hung stiff and straight, and even the stones of the front walk were swept and clear. People around town wondered how old Miss Strangeworth managed to keep the house looking the way it did, and there was a legend about a tourist once mistaking it for the local museum and going all through the place without finding out about his mistake. But the town was proud of Miss Strangeworth and her roses and her house. They had all grown together.

Miss Strangeworth went up her front steps, unlocked her front door with her key, and went into the kitchen to put away her groceries. She debated about having a cup of tea and then decided that it was too close to midday dinnertime; she would not have the appetite for her little chop if she had tea now. Instead she went into the light, lovely sitting room, which still glowed from the hands of her mother and her grandmother, who had covered the chairs with bright chintz and hung the curtains. All the furniture was spare and shining, and the round hooked rugs on the floor had been the work of Miss Strangeworth's grandmother and her mother. Miss Strangeworth had put a bowl of her red roses on the low table before the window, and the room was full of their scent.

Miss Strangeworth went to the narrow desk in the corner and unlocked it with her key. She never knew when she might feel like writing letters, so she kept her notepaper inside and the desk locked. Miss Strangeworth's usual stationery was heavy and cream-colored, with STRANGEWORTH HOUSE engraved across the top, but, when she felt like writing her other letters, Miss Strangeworth used a pad of various-colored paper bought from the local newspaper shop. It was almost a town joke, that colored paper, layered in pink and green and blue and yellow; everyone in town bought it and used it for odd, informal notes and shopping lists. It was usual to remark, upon receiving a note written on a blue page, that so-and-so would be needing a new pad soon—here she was, down to the blue already. Everyone used the matching envelopes for tucking away recipes, or keeping odd little things in, or even to hold cookies in the school lunchboxes. Mr. Lewis sometimes gave them to the children for carrying home penny candy.

Although Miss Strangeworth's desk held a trimmed quill pen which had belonged to her grandfather, and a gold-frosted fountain pen which had belonged to her father, Miss Strangeworth always used a dull stub of pencil when she wrote her letters, and she printed them in a childish block print. After thinking for a minute, although she had been phrasing the letter in the back of her mind all the way home, she wrote on a pink sheet: DIDN'T YOU EVER SEE AN IDIOT CHILD BEFORE? SOME PEOPLE JUST SHOULDN'T HAVE CHILDREN SHOULD THEY?

She was pleased with the letter. She was fond of doing things exactly right. When she made a mistake, as she sometimes did, or when the letters were not spaced nicely on the page, she had to take the discarded page to the kitchen stove and burn it at once. Miss Strangeworth never delayed when things had to be done.

After thinking for a minute, she decided that she would like to write another letter, perhaps to go to Mrs. Harper, to follow up the ones she had already mailed. She selected a green sheet this time and wrote quickly: HAVE YOU FOUND OUT YET WHAT THEY WERE ALL LAUGHING ABOUT AFTER YOU LEFT THE BRIDGE CLUB ON THURSDAY? OR IS THE WIFE REALLY ALWAYS THE LAST ONE TO KNOW?

Miss Strangeworth never concerned herself with facts; her letters all dealt with the more negotiable stuff of suspicion. Mr. Lewis would never have imagined for a minute that his grandson might be lifting petty cash from the store register if he had not had one of Miss Strangeworth's letters. Miss Chandler, the librarian, and Linda Stewart's parents would have gone unsuspectingly ahead with their lives, never aware of possible evil lurking nearby, if Miss Strangeworth had not sent letters opening their eyes. Miss Strangeworth would have been genuinely shocked if there *had* been anything between Linda Stewart and the Harris boy, but, as long as evil existed unchecked in the world, it was Miss Strangeworth's duty to keep her town alert to it. It was far more sensible for Miss Chandler to wonder what Mr. Shelley's first wife had really died of than to take a chance on not knowing. There were so many wicked people in the world and only one Strangeworth left in the town. Besides, Miss Strangeworth liked writing her letters.

She addressed an envelope to Don Crane after a moment's thought, wondering curiously if he would show the letter to his wife, and using a pink envelope to match the pink paper. Then she addressed a second envelope, green, to Mrs. Harper. Then an idea came to her and she selected a blue sheet and wrote: YOU NEVER KNOW ABOUT DOCTORS. REMEMBER THEY'RE ONLY HUMAN AND NEED MONEY LIKE THE REST OF US.

SUPPOSE THE KNIFE SLIPPED ACCIDENTALLY. WOULD DR. BURNS GET HIS FEE AND A LITTLE EXTRA FROM THAT NEPHEW OF YOURS?

She addressed the blue envelope to old Mrs. Foster, who was having an operation next month. She had thought of writing one more letter, to the head of the school board, asking how a chemistry teacher like Billy Moore's father could afford a new convertible, but, all at once, she was tired of writing letters. The three she had done would do for one day. She could write more tomorrow; it was not as though they all had to be done at once.

She had been writing her letters—sometimes two or three every day for a week, sometimes no more than one in a month—for the past year. She never got any answers, of course, because she never signed her name. If she had been asked, she would have said that her name, Adela Strangeworth, a name honored in the town for so many years, did not belong on such trash. The town where she lived had to be kept clean and sweet, but people everywhere were lustful and evil and degraded, and needed to be watched; the world was so large, and there was only one Strangeworth left in it. Miss Strangeworth sighed, locked her desk, and put the letters into her big black leather pocketbook, to be mailed when she took her evening walk.

She broiled her little chop nicely, and had a sliced tomato and a good cup of tea ready when she sat down to her midday dinner at the table in her dining room, which could be opened to seat twenty-two, with a second table, if necessary, in the hall. Sitting in the warm sunlight that came through the tall windows of the dining room, seeing her roses massed outside, handling the heavy, old silverware and the fine, translucent china, Miss Strangeworth was pleased; she would not have cared to be doing anything else. People must live graciously, after all, she thought, and sipped her tea. Afterward, when her plate and cup and saucer were washed and dried and put back onto the shelves where they belonged, and her silverware was back in the mahogany silver chest, Miss Strangeworth went up the graceful staircase and into her bedroom, which was the front room overlooking the roses, and had been her mother's and her grandmother's. Their Crown Derby dresser set and furs had been kept here, their fans and silver-backed brushes and their own bowls of roses; Miss Strangeworth kept a bowl of white roses on the bed table.

She drew the shades, took the rose satin spread from the bed, slipped out of her dress and her shoes, and lay down tiredly. She knew that no doorbell or phone would ring; no one in town would dare to disturb Miss Strangeworth during her afternoon nap. She slept, deep in the rich smell of roses.

After her nap she worked in her garden for a little while, sparing herself because of the heat; then she came in to her supper. She ate asparagus from her own garden, with sweet-butter sauce and a soft-boiled egg, and, while she had her supper, she listened to a late-evening news broadcast and then to a program of classical music on her small radio. After her dishes were done and her kitchen set in order, she took up her hat—Miss Strangeworth's hats were proverbial in the town; people believed that she had inherited them from her mother and her grandmother—and, locking the front door of her house behind her, set off on her evening walk, pocketbook under her arm. She nodded to Linda Stewart's father, who was washing his car in the pleasantly cool evening. She thought that he looked troubled.

There was only one place in town where she could mail her letters, and that was the new post office, shiny with red brick and silver letters. Although Miss Strangeworth had never given the matter any particular thought, she had always made a point of mailing her letters very secretly; it would, of course, not have been wise to let anyone see her mail them. Consequently, she timed her walk so she could reach the post office just as darkness was starting to dim the outlines of the trees and the shapes of people's faces, although no one could ever mistake Miss Strangeworth, with her dainty walk and her rustling skirts.

There was always a group of young people around the post office, the very youngest roller-skating upon its driveway, which went all the way around the building and was the only smooth road in town; and the slightly older ones already knowing how to gather in small groups and chatter and laugh and make great, excited plans for going across the street to the soda shop in a minute or two. Miss Strangeworth had never had any self-consciousness before the children. She did not feel that any of them were staring at her unduly or longing to laugh at her; it would have been most reprehensible for their parents to permit their children to mock Miss Strangeworth of Pleasant Street. Most of the children stood back respectfully as Miss Strangeworth passed, silenced briefly in her presence, and some of the older children greeted her, saying soberly, "Hello, Miss Strangeworth."

Miss Strangeworth smiled at them and quickly went on. It had been a long time since she had known the name of every child in town. The mail slot was in the door of the post office. The children stood away as Miss Strangeworth approached it, seemingly surprised that anyone should want to use the post office after it had been officially closed up for the night and turned over to the children. Miss Strangeworth stood by the door, opening her black pocketbook to take out the letters, and heard a voice which she knew at once to be Linda Stewart's. Poor little Linda was crying again, and Miss Strangeworth listened carefully. This was, after all, her town, and these were her people; if one of them was in trouble she ought to know about it.

"I can't tell you, Dave," Linda was saying—so she *was* talking to the Harris boy, as Miss Strangeworth had supposed—"I just *can't*. It's just *nasty*."

"But why won't your father let me come around any more? What on earth did I do?"

"I can't tell you. I just wouldn't tell you for *any*thing. You've got to have a dirty, dirty mind for things like that."

"But something's happened. You've been crying and crying, and your father is all upset. Why can't *I* know about it, too? Aren't I like one of the family?"

"Not any more, Dave, not any more. You're not to come near our house again; my father said so. He said he'd horsewhip you. That's all I can tell you: You're not to come near our house any more."

"But I didn't *do* anything."

"Just the same, my father said . . ."

Miss Strangeworth sighed and turned away. There was so much evil in people. Even in a charming little town like this one, there was still so much evil in people.

She slipped her letters into the slot, and two of them fell inside. The third caught on the edge and fell outside, onto the ground at Miss Strangeworth's feet. She did not notice it because she was wondering whether a letter to the Harris boy's father might not be of some service in wiping out this potential badness. Wearily Miss Strangeworth turned to go home to her quiet bed in her lovely house, and never heard the Harris boy calling to her to say that she had dropped something.

"Old lady Strangeworth's getting deaf," he said, looking after her and holding in his hand the letter he had picked up.

"Well, who cares?" Linda said. "Who cares any more, anyway?"

"It's for Don Crane," the Harris boy said, "this letter. She dropped a letter addressed to Don Crane. Might as well take it on over. We pass his house anyway." He laughed. "Maybe it's got a check or something in it and he'd be just as glad to get it tonight instead of tomorrow."

"Catch old lady Strangeworth sending anybody a check," Linda said. "Throw it in the post office. Why do anyone a favor?" She sniffled. "Doesn't seem to me anybody around here cares about us," she said. "Why should we care about them?"

"I'll take it over anyway," the Harris boy said. "Maybe it's good news for them. Maybe they need something happy tonight, too. Like us."

Sadly, holding hands, they wandered off down the dark street, the Harris boy carrying Miss Strangeworth's pink envelope in his hand.

Miss Strangeworth awakened the next morning with a feeling of intense happiness and, for a minute wondered why, and then remembered that this morning three people would open her letters. Harsh, perhaps, at first, but wickedness was never easily banished, and a clean heart was a scoured heart. She washed her soft old face and brushed her teeth, still sound in spite of her seventy-one years, and dressed herself carefully in her sweet, soft clothes and buttoned shoes. Then, coming downstairs and reflecting that perhaps a little waffle would be agreeable for breakfast in the sunny dining room, she found the mail on the hall floor and bent to pick it up. A bill, the morning paper, a letter in a green envelope that looked oddly familiar. Miss Strangeworth stood perfectly still for a minute, looking down at the green envelope with the penciled printing, and thought: It looks like one of my letters. Was one of my letters sent back? No, because no one would know where to send it. How did this get here?

Miss Strangeworth was a Strangeworth of Pleasant Street. Her hand did not shake as she opened the envelope and unfolded the sheet of green paper inside. She began to cry silently for the wickedness of the world when she read the words: LOOK OUT AT WHAT USED TO BE YOUR ROSES.

QUESTIONS

1. The key to this story's meaning may well lie in the several ways the final sentence can be interpreted. What, for instance, do the roses symbolize? What other uses of symbolism or symbolic objects do you find in the story?

2. Could the theme of this story be summed up in one sentence? Why or why not?

3. Note how Shirley Jackson slowly builds up the mood of the story. When did you first begin to suspect Miss Strangeworth was other than what she first appeared to be?

4. Discuss the story as it relates to the role of the public censor (say, of movies, books, television) in society. Take recent court decisions into consideration.

5. What is accomplished by our noting that Miss Strangeworth calls her old high school classmate by his last name?

6. What reasons might Miss Strangeworth give as evidence of her good and moral character?

Markheim

Robert Louis Stevenson

"Yes," said the dealer, "our windfalls are of various kinds. Some customers are ignorant, and then I touch a dividend on my superior knowledge. Some are dishonest," and here he held up the candle, so that the light fell strongly on his visitor, "and in that case," he continued, "I profit by my virtue."

Markheim had but just entered from the daylight streets, and his eyes had not yet grown familiar with the mingled shine and darkness in the shop. At these pointed words, and before the near presence of the flame, he blinked painfully and looked aside.

The dealer chuckled. "You come to me on Christmas Day," he resumed, "when you know that I am alone in my house, put up my shutters and make a point of refusing business. Well, you will have to pay for that; you will have to pay for my loss of time, when I should be balancing my books; you will have to pay, besides, for a kind of manner that I remark in you to-day very strongly. I am the essence of discretion, and ask no awkward questions; but when a customer cannot look me in the eye, he has to pay for it."

The dealer once more chuckled; and then, changing to his usual business voice, though still with a note of irony, "You can give, as usual, a clear account of how you came into the possession of the object?" he continued. "Still your uncle's cabinet? A remarkable collector, sir!"

And the little pale, round-shouldered dealer stood almost on tip-toe, looking over the top of his gold spectacles, and nodding his head with every mark of disbelief. Markheim returned his gaze with one of infinite pity, and a touch of horror.

"This time," said he, "you are in error. I have not come to sell, but to buy. I have no curios to dispose of; my uncle's cabinet is bare to the wainscot; even were it still intact, I have done well on the Stock Exchange, and should more likely add to it than otherwise, and my errand to-day is simplicity itself. I seek a Christmas present for a lady," he continued, waxing more fluent as he struck into the speech he had prepared; "and certainly I owe you every excuse for thus disturbing you upon so small a matter. But the thing was neglected yesterday; I must produce my little compliment at dinner; and, as you very well know, a rich marriage is not a thing to be neglected."

There followed a pause, during which the dealer seemed to weigh this statement incredulously. The ticking of many clocks among the curious lumber of the shop, and the faint rushing of the cabs in a near thoroughfare, filled up the interval of silence.

"Well, sir," said the dealer, "be it so. You are an old customer after all; and if, as you say, you have the chance of a good marriage, far be it from me to be an obstacle. Here is a nice thing for a lady now," he went on, "this hand glass—fifteenth century, warranted; comes from a good collection, too; but I reserve the name, in the interests of my customer, who was just like yourself, my dear sir, the nephew and sole heir of a remarkable collector."

The dealer, while he thus ran on in his dry and biting voice, had stooped to take the object from its place; and, as he had done so, a shock had passed through Markheim, a start both of hand and foot, a sudden leap of many tumultuous passions to the face. It passed as swiftly as it came, and left no trace beyond a certain trembling of the hand that now received the glass.

"A glass," he said hoarsely, and then paused, and repeated it more clearly. "A glass? For Christmas? Surely not?"

"And why not?" cried the dealer. "Why not a glass?"

Markheim was looking upon him with an indefinable expression. "You ask me why not?" he said. "Why, look here—look in it—look at yourself! Do you like to see it? No! nor—nor any man."

The little man had jumped back when Markheim had so suddenly confronted him with the mirror; but now, perceiving there was nothing worse on hand, he chuckled. "Your future lady, sir, must be pretty hard-favoured," said he.

"I ask you," said Markheim, "for a Christmas present, and you give me this—this damned reminder of years, and sins and follies—this hand-conscience? Did you mean it? Had you a thought in your mind? Tell me. It will be better for you if you do. Come, tell me about yourself. I hazard a guess now, that you are in secret a very charitable man?"

The dealer looked closely at his companion. It was very odd, Markheim did not appear to be laughing; there was something in his face like an eager sparkle of hope, but nothing of mirth.

"What are you driving at?" the dealer asked.

"Not charitable?" returned the other gloomily. "Not charitable; not pious; not scrupulous; unloving, unbeloved; a hand to get money, a safe to keep it. Is that all? Dear God, man, is that all?"

"I will tell you what it is," began the dealer, with some sharpness, and then broke off again into a chuckle. "But I see this is a love match of yours, and you have been drinking the lady's health."

"Ah!" cried Markheim, with a strange curiosity. "Ah, have you been in love? Tell me about that."

"I," cried the dealer. "I in love! I never had the time, nor have I the time to-day for all this nonsense. Will you take the glass?"

"Where is the hurry?" returned Markheim. "It is very pleasant to stand here talking; and life is so short and insecure that I would not hurry away from any pleasure—no, not even from so mild a one as this. We should rather cling, cling to what little we can get, like a man at a cliff's edge. Every second is a cliff, if you think upon it—a cliff a mile high—high enough, if we fall, to dash us out of every feature of humanity. Hence it is best to talk pleasantly. Let us talk of each other: why should we wear this mask? Let us be confidential. Who knows, we might become friends?"

"I have just one word to say to you," said the dealer. "Either make your purchase, or walk out of my shop!"

"True, true," said Markheim. "Enough fooling. To business. Show me something else."

The dealer stooped once more, this time to replace the glass upon the shelf, his thin blond hair falling over his eyes as he did so. Markheim moved a little nearer, with one hand in the pocket of his greatcoat; he drew himself up and filled his lungs; at the same time many different emotions were depicted together on his face—terror, horror, and resolve, fascination and a physical repulsion; and through a haggard lift of his upper lip, his teeth looked out.

"This, perhaps, may suit," observed the dealer; and then, as he began to re-arise, Markheim bounded from behind upon his victim. The long, skewerlike dagger flashed and fell. The dealer struggled like a hen, striking his temple on the shelf, and then tumbled on the floor in a heap.

Time had some score of small voices in that shop, some stately and slow as was becoming to their great age; others garrulous and hurried. All these told out the seconds in an intricate chorus of tickings. Then the passage of a lad's feet, heavily running on the pavement, broke in upon these smaller voices and startled Markheim into the consciousness of his surroundings.

He looked about him awfully. The candle stood on the counter, its flame solemnly wagging in a draught; and by that inconsiderable movement, the whole room was filled with noiseless bustle and kept heaving like a sea: the tall shadows nodding, the gross blots of darkness swelling and dwindling as with respiration, the faces of the portraits and the china gods changing and wavering like images in water. The inner door stood ajar, and peered into that leaguer of shadows with a long slit of daylight like a pointing finger.

From these fear-stricken rovings, Markheim's eyes returned to the body of his victim, where it lay both humped and sprawling, incredibly small and strangely meaner than in life. In these poor, miserly clothes, in that ungainly attitude, the dealer lay like so much sawdust. Markheim had feared to see it, and, lo! it was nothing. And yet, as he gazed, this bundle of old clothes and pool of blood began to find eloquent voices. There it must lie; there was none to work the cunning hinges or direct the miracle of locomotion—there it must lie till it was found. Found! ay, and then? Then would this dead flesh lift up a cry that would ring over England, and fill the world with the echoes of pursuit. Ay, dead or not, this was still the enemy.

"Time was that when the brains were out," he thought; and the first word struck into his mind. Time, now that the deed was accomplished—time, which had closed for the victim, had become instant and momentous for the slayer.

The thought was yet in his mind, when, first one and then another, with every variety of pace and voice—one deep as the bell from a cathedral turret, another ringing on its treble notes the prelude of a waltz—the clocks began to strike the hour of three in the afternoon.

The sudden outbreak of so many tongues in that dumb chamber staggered him. He began to bestir himself, going to and fro with the candle, beleaguered by moving shadows, and startled to the soul by chance reflections. In many rich mirrors, some of home designs, some from Venice or Amsterdam, he saw his face repeated and repeated, as it were an army of spies; his own eyes met and detected him; and the sound of his own steps, lightly as they fell, vexed the surrounding quiet.

And still, as he continued to fill his pockets, his mind accused him with a sickening iteration, of the thousand faults of his design. He should have chosen a more quiet hour; he should have prepared an alibi; he should not have used a knife; he should have been more cautious, and only bound and gagged the dealer, and not killed him; he should have been more bold, and killed the servant also; he should have done all things otherwise—poignant regrets, weary, incessant toiling of the mind to change what was unchangeable, to plan what was now useless, to be the architect of the irrevocable past.

Meanwhile, and behind all this activity, brute terrors, like the scurrying of rats in a deserted attic, filled the more remote chambers of his brain with riot; the hand of the constable would fall heavy on his shoulder, and his nerves would jerk like a hooked fish; or he beheld, in galloping defile, the dock, the prison, the gallows, and the black coffin.

Terror of the people in the street sat down before his mind like a besieging army. It was impossible, he thought, but that some rumour of the struggle must have reached their ears and set on edge their curiosity; and now, in all the neighbouring houses, he divined them sitting motionless and with uplifted ear—solitary people, condemned to spend Christmas dwelling alone on memories of the past, and now startingly recalled from that tender exercise; happy family parties, struck into silence round the table, the mother still with raised finger: every degree and age and humour, but all, by their own hearths, prying and hearkening and weaving the rope that was to hang him.

Sometimes it seemed to him he could not move too softly; the clink of the tall Bohemian goblets rang out loudly like a bell; and alarmed by the bigness of the ticking, he was tempted to stop the clocks. And then, again, with a swift transition of his terrors, the very silence of the place appeared a source of peril, and a thing to strike and freeze the passer-by; and he would step more boldly, and bustle aloud among the contents of the shop, and imitate, with elaborate bravado, the movements of a busy man at ease in his own house.

But he was now so pulled about by different alarms that, while one portion of his mind was still alert and cunning, another trembled on the brink of lunacy. One hallucination in particular took a strong hold on his credulity. The neighbour hearkening with white face beside his window, the passer-by arrested by a horrible surmise on the pavement—these could at worst suspect, they could not know; through the brick walls and shuttered windows only sounds could penetrate.

But here, within the house, was he alone? He knew he was; he had watched the servant set forth sweet-hearting, in her poor best, "out for the day" written in every ribbon and smile. Yes, he was alone, of course; and yet, in the bulk of empty house above him, he could surely hear a stir of delicate footing—he was surely conscious, inexplicably conscious of some presence. Ay, surely; to every room and corner of the house his imagination followed it; and now it was a faceless thing, and yet had eyes to see with; and again it was a shadow of himself; and yet again behold the image of the dead dealer, reinspired with cunning and hatred.

At times, with a strong effort, he would glance at the open door which still seemed to repel his eyes. The house was tall, the skylight small and dirty, the day blind with fog; and the light that filtered down to the ground story was exceedingly faint, and showed dimly on the threshold of the shop. And yet, in that strip of doubtful brightness, did there not hang wavering a shadow?

Suddenly, from the street outside, a very jovial gentleman began to beat with a staff on the shop-door, accompanying his blows with shouts and railleries in which the dealer was continually called upon by name. Markheim, smitten into ice, glanced at the dead man. But no! he lay quite still; he was fled away far beyond earshot of these blows and shoutings; he was sunk beneath seas of silence; and his name, which would once have caught his notice above the howling of a storm, had become an empty sound. And presently the jovial gentleman desisted from his knocking and departed.

Here was a broad hint to hurry what remained to be done, to get forth from this accusing neighbourhood, to plunge into a bath of London multitudes, and to reach, on the other side of day, that haven of safety and apparent innocence—his bed. One visitor had come; at any moment another might follow and be more obstinate. To have done the deed, and yet not to reap the profit, would be too abhorrent a failure. The money, that was now Markheim's concern; and as a means to that, the keys.

He glanced over his shoulder at the open door, where the shadow was still lingering and shivering; and with no conscious repugnance of the mind, yet with a tremor of the belly, he drew near the body of his victim. The human character had quite departed. Like a suit half-stuffed with bran, the limbs lay scattered, the trunk doubled, on the floor, and yet the thing repelled him. Although so dingy and inconsiderable to the eye, he feared it might have more significance to the touch.

He took the body by the shoulders, and turned it on its back. It was strangely light and supple, and the limbs, as if they had been broken, fell into the oddest postures. The face was robbed of all expression; but it was as pale as wax, and shockingly smeared with blood about one temple. That was, for Markheim, the one displeasing circumstance. It carried him back, upon the instant, to a certain fair-day in a fisher's village: a gray day, a piping wind, a crowd upon the street, the blare of the brasses, the booming of drums, the nasal voice of a ballad singer; and a boy going to and fro, buried over head in the crowd and divided between interest and fear, until, coming out upon the chief place of concourse, he beheld a booth and a great screen with pictures, dismally designed, garishly coloured: Brownrigg with her apprentice; the Mannings with their murdered guest; Weare in the death-grip of Thurtell; and a score besides of famous crimes.

The thing was as clear as an illusion; he was once again that little boy; he was looking once again, and with the same sense of physical revolt, at these vile pictures; he was still stunned by the thumping of the drums. A bar of that day's music returned upon his memory; and at that, for the first time, a qualm came over him, a breath of nausea, a sudden weakness of the joints, which he must instantly resist and conquer.

He judged it more prudent to confront than to flee from these considerations; looking the more hardily in the dead face, bending his mind to realise the nature and greatness of his crime. So little a while ago that face had moved with every change of sentiment, that pale mouth had spoken, that body had been on fire with governable energies; and now, and by his act, that piece of life had been arrested, as the horologist, with interjected finger, arrests the beating of the clock. So he reasoned in vain; he could rise to no more remorseful consciousness; the same heart which had shuddered before the painted effigies of crime, looked on its reality unmoved. At best, he felt a gleam of pity for one who had been endowed in vain with all those faculties that can make the world a garden of enchantment, one who had never lived and who was now dead. But of penitence, no, not a tremor.

With that, shaking himself clear of these considerations, he found the keys and advanced towards the open door of the shop. Outside, it had begun to rain smartly; and the sound of the shower upon the roof had banished silence. Like some dripping cavern, the chambers of the house were haunted by an incessant echoing, which filled the ear and mingled with the ticking of the clocks. And, as Markheim approached the door, he seemed to hear, in answer to his own cautious tread, the steps of another foot withdrawing up the stair. The shadow still palpitated loosely on the threshold. He threw a ton's weight of resolve upon his muscles, and drew back the door.

The faint, foggy daylight glimmered dimly on the bare floor and stairs; on the bright suit of armour posted, halberd in hand, upon the landing; and on the dark woodcarvings, and framed pictures that hung against the yellow panels of the wainscot. So loud was the beating of the rain through all the house that, in Markheim's ears, it began to be distinguished into many different sounds. Footsteps and sighs, the tread of regiments marching in the distance, the chink of money in the counting, and the creaking of doors held stealthily ajar, appeared to mingle with the patter of the drops upon the cupola and the gushing of the water in the pipes.

The sense that he was not alone grew upon him to the verge of madness. On every side he was haunted and begirt by presences. He heard them moving in the upper chambers; from the shop, he heard the dead man getting to his legs; and as he began with a great effort to mount the stairs, feet fled quietly before him and followed stealthily behind. If he were but deaf, he thought, how tranquilly he would possess his soul! And then again, and hearkening with ever fresh attention, he blessed himself for that unresting sense which held the outposts and stood a trusty sentinel upon his life. His head turned continually on his neck; his eyes, which seemed starting from their orbits, scouted on every side, and on every side were half-rewarded as with the tail of something nameless vanishing. The four-and-twenty steps to the first floor were four-and-twenty agonies.

On that first story, the doors stood ajar, three of them like three ambushes, shaking his nerves like the throats of cannon. He could never again, he felt, be sufficiently immured and fortified from men's observing eyes; he longed to be home, girt in by walls, buried among bed-clothes, and invisible to all but God. And at that thought he wondered a little, recollecting tales of other murderers and the fear they were said to entertain of heavenly avengers. It was not so, at least, with him. He feared the laws of nature, lest, in their callous and immutable procedure, they should preserve some damning evidence of his crime. He feared tenfold more, with a slavish, superstitious terror, some scission in the continuity of man's experience, some wilful illegality of nature. He played a game of skill, depending on the rules, calculating consequence from cause; and what if nature, as the defeated tyrant overthrew the chessboard, should break the mould of their succession?

The like had befallen Napoleon (so writers said) when the winter changed the time of its appearance. The like might befall Markheim: the solid walls might become transparent and reveal his doings like those of bees in a glass hive; the stout planks might yield under his foot like quicksands and detain him in their clutch; ay, and there were soberer accidents that might destroy him: if, for instance, the house should fall and imprison him beside the body of his victim; or the house next door should fly on fire, and the firemen invade him from all sides. These things he feared; and, in a sense, these things might be called the hands of God reached forth against sin. But about God Himself he was at ease; his act was doubtless exceptional, but so were his excuses, which God knew; it was there, and not among men, that he felt sure of justice.

When he had got safe into the drawing-room, and shut the door behind him, he was aware of a respite from alarms. The room was quite dismantled, uncarpeted besides, and strewn with packing cases and incongruous furniture; several great pier glasses, in which he beheld himself at various angles, like an actor on a stage; many pictures, framed and unframed, standing, with their faces to the wall, a fine Sheraton sideboard, a cabinet of marquetry, and a great old bed, with tapestry hangings. The windows opened to the floors; but by great good fortune the lower part of the shutters had been closed, and this concealed him from the neighbors. Here, then, Markheim drew in a packing case before the cabinet, and began to search among the keys.

It was a long business, for there were many; and it was irksome, besides; for, after all there might be nothing in the cabinet, and time was on the wing. But the closeness of the occupation sobered him. With the tail of his eye he saw the door—even glanced at it from time to time directly, like a besieged commander pleased to verify the good estate of his defences. But in truth he was at peace. The rain falling in the street sounded natural and pleasant. Presently, on the other side, the notes of a piano were wakened to the music of a hymn, and the voices of many children took up the air and words. How stately, how comfortable was the melody! How fresh the youthful voices!

Markheim gave ear to it smilingly, as he sorted out the keys; and his mind was thronged with answerable ideas and images; church-going children and the pealing of the high organ; children afield, bathers by the brookside, ramblers on the brambly common, kite-flyers in the windy and cloud-navigated sky; and then, at another cadence of the hymn, back again to church, and the somnolence of summer Sundays, and the high genteel voice of the parson (which he smiled a little to recall) and the painted Jacobean tombs, and the dim lettering of the Ten Commandments in the chancel.

And as he sat thus, at once busy and absent, he was startled to his feet. A flash of ice, a flash of fire, a bursting gush of blood, went over him, and then he stood transfixed and thrilling. A step mounted the stair slowly and steadily and presently a hand was laid upon the knob, and the lock clicked, and the door opened.

Fear held Markheim in a vice. What to expect he knew not, whether the dead man walking, or the official ministers of human justice, or some chance witness blindly stumbling in to consign him to the gallows. But when a face thrust into the aperture, glanced round the room, looked at him, nodded and smiled as if in friendly recognition, and then withdrew again, and the door closed behind it, his fear broke loose from his control in a hoarse cry. At the sound of this the visitant returned.

"Did you call me?" he asked pleasantly, and with that he entered the room and closed the door behind him.

Markheim stood and gazed at him with all his eyes. Perhaps there was a film upon his sight, but the outlines of the newcomer seemed to change and waver like those of the idols in the wavering candlelight of the shop; and at times he thought he knew him; and at times he thought he bore a likeness to himself; and always, like a lump of living terror, there lay in his bosom the conviction that this thing was not of the earth and not of God.

And yet the creature had a strange air of the commonplace, as he stood looking on Markheim with a smile; and when he added: "You are looking for the money, I believe?" it was in the tones of everyday politeness.

Markheim made no answer.

"I should warn you," resumed the other, "that the maid has left her sweetheart earlier than usual and will soon be here. If Mr. Markheim be found in this house, I need not describe to him the consequences."

"You know me?" cried the murderer.

The visitor smiled. "You have long been a favourite of mine," he said; "and I have long observed and often sought to help you."

"What are you?" cried Markheim; "the devil?"

"What I may be," returned the other, "cannot affect the service I propose to render you."

"It can," cried Markheim; "it does! Be helped by you? No, never; not by you! You do not know me yet; thank God, you do not know me!"

"I know you," replied the visitant, with a sort of kind severity or rather firmness. "I know you to the soul."

"Know me!" cried Markheim. "Who can do so? My life is but a travesty and slander on myself. I have lived to belie my nature. All men do, all men are better than this disguise that grows about and stifles them. You see each dragged away by life, like one whom bravos have seized and muffled in a cloak. If they had their own control—if you could see their faces, they would be altogether different, they would shine out for heroes and saints! I am worse than most; myself is more overlaid; my excuse is known to men and God. But, had I the time, I could disclose myself."

"To me?" inquired the visitant.

"To you before all," returned the murderer. "I supposed you were intelligent. I thought—since you exist—you could prove a reader of the heart. And yet you would propose to judge me by my acts! Think of it; my acts! I was born and I have lived in a land of giants; giants have dragged me by the wrists since I was born out of my mother—the giants of circumstance. And you would judge me by my acts! But can you not look within? Can you not understand that evil is hateful to me? Can you not see within me the clear writing of conscience, never blurred by any wilful sophistry, although too often disregarded? Can you not read me for a thing that surely must be common as humanity—the unwilling sinner?"

"All this is very feelingly expressed," was the reply, "but it regards me not. These points of consistency are beyond my province, and I care not in the least by what compulsion you may have been dragged away, so as you are but carried in the right direction. But time flies; the servant delays, looking in the faces of the crowd and at the pictures on the hoardings, but still she keeps moving nearer; and remember, it is as if the gallows itself was striding towards you through the Christmas streets! Shall I help you; I, who know all? Shall I tell you where to find the money?"

"For what price?" asked Markheim.

"I offer you the service for a Christmas gift," returned the other.

Markheim could not refrain from smiling with a kind of bitter triumph. "No," said he, "I will take nothing at your hands; if I were dying of thirst, and it was your hand that put the pitcher to my lips, I should find the courage to refuse. It may be credulous, but I will do nothing to commit myself to evil."

"I have no objection to a deathbed repentance," observed the visitant.

"Because you disbelieve their efficacy!" Markheim cried.

"I do not say so," returned the other; "but I look on these things from a different side, and when the life is done my interest falls. The man has lived to serve me, to spread black looks under colour of religion, or to sow tares in the wheatfield, as you do, in a course of weak compliance with desire. Now that he draws so near to his deliverance, he can add but one act of service—to repent, to die smiling, and thus to build up in confidence and hope the more timorous of my surviving followers. I am not so hard a master. Try me. Accept my help. Please yourself in life as you have done hitherto; please yourself more amply, spread your elbows at the board; and when the night begins to fall and the curtains to be drawn, I tell you, for your greater comfort, that you will find it even easy to compound your quarrel with your conscience, and to make a truckling peace with God. I came but now from such a deathbed, and the room was full of sincere mourners, listening to the man's last words; and when I looked into that face, which had been set as a flint against mercy, I found it smiling with hope."

"And do you, then, suppose me such a creature?" asked Markheim. "Do you think I have no more generous aspirations than to sin, and sin, and sin, and, at the last, sneak into heaven? My heart rises at the thought. Is this, then, your experience of mankind? Or is it because you find me with red hands that you presume such baseness? And is this crime of murder indeed so impious as to dry up the very springs of good?"

"Murder is to me no special category," replied the other. "All sins are murder, even as all life is war. I behold your race, like starving mariners on a raft, plucking crusts out of the hands of famine and feeding on each other's lives. I follow sins beyond the moment of their acting; I find in all that the last consequence is death; and to my eyes, the pretty maid who thwarts her mother with such taking graces on a question of a ball, drips no less visibly with human gore than such a murderer as yourself. Do I say that I follow sins? I follow virtues also; they differ not by the thickness of a nail, they are both scythes for the reaping angel of Death. Evil, for which I live, consists not in action but in character. The bad man is dear to me; not the bad act, whose fruits, if we could follow them far enough down the hurtling cataract of the ages, might yet be found more blessed than those of the rarest virtues. And it is not because you have killed a dealer, but because you are Markheim, that I offer to forward your escape."

"I will lay my heart open to you," answered Markheim. "This crime on which you find me is my last. On my way to it I have learned many lessons; itself is a lesson, a momentous lesson. Hitherto I have been driven with revolt to what I would not; I was a bond-slave to poverty, driven and scourged. There are robust virtues that can stand in these temptations; mine are not so: I had a thirst of pleasure. But to-day, and out of this deed, I pluck both warning and riches—both the power and a fresh resolve to be myself. I become in all things a free actor in the world; I begin to see myself all changed, hands the agents of good, this heart at peace. Something comes over me out of the past; something of what I have dreamed on Sabbath evenings to the sound of the church organ, of what I forecast when I shed tears over noble books, or talked, an innocent child, with my mother. There lies my life; I have wandered a few years, but now I see once more my city of destination."

"You are to use this money on the Stock Exchange, I think?" remarked the visitor; "and there, if I mistake not, you have already lost some thousands?"

"Ah," said Markheim, "but this time I have a sure thing."

"This time, again, you will lose," replied the visitor quietly.

"Ah, but I keep back the half!" cried Markheim.

"That also you will lose," said the other.

The sweat started upon Markheim's brow. "Well, then, what matter?" he exclaimed. "Say it be lost, say I am plunged again in poverty, shall one part of me, and that the worst, continue until the end to override the better? Evil and good run strong in me, haling me both ways. I do not love the one thing, I love all. I can conceive great deeds, renunciations, martyrdoms; and though I be fallen to such a crime as murder, pity is no stranger to my thoughts. I pity the poor; who knows their trials better than myself? I pity and help them; I prize love, I love honest laughter; there is no good thing nor true thing on earth but I love it from my heart. And are my vices only to direct my life, and my virtues without effect, like some passive lumber of the mind? Not so; good, also, is a spring of acts."

But the visitant raised his finger. "For six-and-thirty years that you have been in this world," said he, "through many changes of fortune and varieties of humour, I have watched you steadily fall. Fifteen years ago you would have started at a theft. Three years back you would have blenched at the name of murder. Is there any crime, is there any cruelty or meanness, from which you still recoil?—five years from now I shall detect you in the fact! Downward, downward, lies your way; nor can anything but death avail to stop you."

"It is true," Markheim said huskily, "I have in some degree complied with evil. But it is so with all; the very saints, in the mere exercise of living, grow less dainty, and take on the tone of their surroundings."

"I will propound to you one simple question," said the other; "and as you answer, I shall read to you your moral horoscope. You have grown in many things more lax; possibly you do right to be so; and at any account, it is the same with all men. But granting that, are you in any one particular, however trifling, more difficult to please with your own conduct, or do you go in all things with a looser rein?"

"In any one?" repeated Markheim, with an anguish of consideration. "No," he added, with despair, "in none! I have gone down in all."

"Then," said the visitor, "content yourself with what you are, for you will never change; and the words of your part on this stage are irrevocably written down."

Markheim stood for a long while silent, and indeed it was the visitor who first broke the silence. "That being so," he said, "shall I show you the money?"

"And grace?" cried Markheim.

"Have you not tried it?" returned the other. "Two or three years ago did I not see you on the platform of revival meetings, and was not your voice the loudest in the hymn?"

"It is true," said Markheim; "and I see clearly what remains for me by way of duty. I thank you for these lessons from my soul; my eyes are opened, and I behold myself at last for what I am."

At this moment, the sharp note of the door-bell rang through the house; and the visitant, as though this were some concerted signal for which he had been waiting, changed at once in his demeanour.

"The maid!" he cried. "She has returned, as I forewarned you, and there is now before you one more difficult passage. Her master, you must say, is ill; you must let her in, with an assured but rather serious countenance—no smiles, no over-acting, and I promise you success! Once the girl within, and the door closed, the same dexterity that has already rid you of the dealer will relieve you of this last danger in your path. Thenceforward you have the whole evening—the whole night, if needful—to ransack the treasures of the house and to make good your safety. This is help that comes to you with the mask of danger. Up!" he cried; "up, friend; your life hangs trembling in the scales: up, and act!"

Markheim steadily regarded his counsellor. "If I be condemned to evil acts," he said, "there is still one door of freedom open—I can cease from action. If my life be an ill thing, I can lay it down. Though I be, as you say truly, at the beck of every small temptation, I can yet, by one decisive gesture, place myself beyond the reach of all. My love of good is damned to barrenness; it may, and let it be! But I have still my hatred of evil; and from that, to your galling disappointment, you shall see that I can draw both energy and courage."

The features of the visitor began to undergo a wonderful and lovely change: they brightened and softened with a tender triumph, and, even as they brightened, faded and dislimned. But Markheim did not pause to watch or understand the transformation. He opened the door and went downstairs very slowly, thinking to himself. His past went soberly before him; he beheld it as it was, ugly and strenuous like a dream, random as chance-medley—a scene of defeat. Life, as he thus reviewed it, tempted him no longer; but on the farther side he perceived a quiet haven for his bark.

He paused in the passage, and looked into the shop, where the candle still burned by the dead body. It was strangely silent. Thoughts of the dealer swarmed into his mind, as he stood gazing. And then the bell once more broke out into impatient clamour.

He confronted the maid upon the threshold with something like a smile.

"You had better go for the police," said he. "I have killed your master."

QUESTIONS

1. Who is the visitor? Is he really "the devil"?

2. There seems to be an extreme slowing down of time in this story. How does Stevenson accomplish this?

3. Discuss this story in terms of rationalization. Does every criminal seek to justify his crime and life in a manner similar to Markheim?

4. Markheim asks his visitor, "Can you not read me for a thing that surely must be common as humanity—the unwilling sinner?" Do you feel that most "sinners" are "unwilling"?

5. The visitor says, "Evil, for which I live, consists not in action but in character." Do you agree?

6. Describe the concept of free will presented in "Markheim," especially in the idea of ceasing from action.

7. Must one be a criminal of some sort to understand crime? Or poor to pity the poor?

8. Markheim says that "the very saints, in the mere exercise of living, grow less dainty, and take on the tone of their surroundings." Do you agree? Must this inevitably happen to those who, like detectives and policemen, live and work in an atmosphere of crime?

My Last Duchess

Robert Browning

FERRARA

That's my last Duchess painted on the wall,
Looking as if she were alive. I call
That piece a wonder, now: Frà Pandolf's hands
Worked busily a day, and there she stands.
Will't please you sit and look at her? I said
"Frà Pandolf" by design, for never read
Strangers like you that pictured countenance,
The depth and passion of its earnest glance,
But to myself they turned (since none puts by
The curtain I have drawn for you, but I)
And seemed as they would ask me, if they durst,
How such a glance came there; so, not the first
Are you to turn and ask thus. Sir, 'twas not
Her husband's presence only, called that spot
Of joy into the Duchess' cheek: perhaps
Frà Pandolf chanced to say, "Her mantle laps
Over my lady's wrist too much," or "Paint
Must never hope to reproduce the faint
Half-flush that dies along her throat:" such stuff
Was courtesy, she thought, and cause enough
For calling up that spot of joy. She had
A heart—how shall I say?—too soon made glad,
Too easily impressed; she liked whate'er
She looked on, and her looks went everywhere.
Sir, 'twas all one! My favor at her breast,
The dropping of the daylight in the West,
The bough of cherries some officious fool
Broke in the orchard for her, the white mule
She rode with round the terrace—all and each
Would draw from her alike the approving speech,

Or blush, at least. She thanked men,—good! but thanked
Somehow—I know not how—as if she ranked
My gift of a nine-hundred-years-old name
With anybody's gift. Who'd stoop to blame
This sort of trifling? Even had you skill
In speech—(which I have not)—to make your will
Quite clear to such an one, and say, "Just this
Or that in you disgusts me; here you miss,
Or there exceed the mark"—and if she let
Herself be lessoned so, nor plainly set   40
Her wits to yours, forsooth, and made excuse,
—E'en then would be some stooping; and I choose
Never to stoop. Oh sir, she smiled, no doubt,
Whene'er I passed her; but who passed without
Much the same smile? This grew; I gave commands;
Then all smiles stopped together. There she stands
As if alive. Will't please you rise? We'll meet
The company below, then. I repeat,
The Count your master's known munificence
Is ample warrant that no just pretence   50
Of mine for dowry will be disallowed;
Though his fair daughter's self, as I avowed
At starting, is my object. Nay, we'll go
Together down, sir. Notice Neptune, though,
Taming a sea-horse, thought a rarity,
Which Claus of Innsbruck cast in bronze for me!

QUESTIONS

1. The poem is a dramatic monologue. Put yourself in the
courier's place and relate what you have discovered about the Duke. His
wife? Has the speaker revealed anything he did not wish or choose to
reveal?

2. Do you feel that the Duke's justifications for his order to
murder are typical of those who commit (or order committed) acts of
this sort?

3. Discuss this poem as regards the connections between power
and evil and between egotism and self-gratification.

4. What of innocence? Was the Duchess punished for her own
innocence, her lack of knowledge of how corrupt the world might be?

5. What does the Duke value? Do the things he values

constitute a definition of evil in themselves? Do the Duke's values comment upon the innate amorality of political acts, or upon his character? Or both?

6. Compare the Duke with Miss Strangeworth. Why is overbearing pride in one's own ancestry so often associated with less than admirable characters?

7. Notice all the Duke's parenthetical remarks. How do these and other technical devices serve to evoke his duplicity?

The Destructors

Graham Greene

I

It was on the eve of August Bank Holiday that the latest recruit became the leader of the Wormsley Common Gang. No one was surprised except Mike, but Mike at the age of nine was surprised by everything. "If you don't shut your mouth," somebody once said to him, "you'll get a frog down it." After that Mike had kept his teeth tightly clamped except when the surprise was too great.

The new recruit had been with the gang since the beginning of the summer holidays, and there were possibilities about his brooding silence that all recognized. He never wasted a word even to tell his name until that was required of him by the rules. When he said "Trevor" it was a statement of fact, not as it would have been with the others a statement of shame or defiance. Nor did anyone laugh except Mike, who finding himself without support and meeting the dark gaze of the newcomer opened his mouth and was quiet again. There was every reason why T., as he was afterwards referred to, should have been an object of mockery—there was his name (and they substituted the initial because otherwise they had no excuse not to laugh at it), the fact that his father, a former architect and present clerk, had "come down in the world" and that his mother considered herself better than the neighbours. What but an odd quality of danger, of the unpredictable, established him in the gang without any ignoble ceremony of initiation?

The gang met every morning in an impromptu car-park, the site of the last bomb of the first blitz. The leader, who was known as Blackie, claimed to have heard it fall, and no one was precise enough in his dates to point out that he would have been one year old and fast asleep on the down platform of Wormsley Common Underground Station. On one side of the car-park leant the first occupied house, number 3, of the shattered Northwood Terrace—literally leant, for it had suffered from the blast of the bomb and the side walls were supported on wooden struts. A smaller bomb and some incendiaries had fallen beyond, so that the house stuck up like a jagged tooth and carried on the further wall relics of its neighbour, a dado, the remains of a fireplace. T., whose words were almost confined to voting "Yes" or "No" to the plan of operations proposed each day by Blackie, once startled the whole gang by saying broodingly, "Wren built that house, father says."

"Who's Wren?"

"The man who built St. Paul's."

"Who cares?" Blackie said. "It's only old Misery's."

Old Misery—whose real name was Thomas—had once been a builder and decorator. He lived alone in the crippled house, doing for himself: once a week you could see him coming back across the common with bread and vegetables, and once as the boys played in the car-park he put his head over the smashed wall of his garden and looked at them.

"Been to the loo," one of the boys said, for it was common knowledge that since the bombs fell something had gone wrong with the pipes of the house and Old Misery was too mean to spend money on the property. He could do the redecorating himself at cost price, but he had never learnt plumbing. The loo was a wooden shed at the bottom of the narrow garden with a star-shaped hole in the door: it had escaped the blast which had smashed the house next door and sucked out the window-frames of No. 3.

The next time the gang became aware of Mr. Thomas was more surprising. Blackie, Mike, and a thin yellow boy, who for some reason was called by his surname Summers, met him on the common coming back from the market. Mr. Thomas stopped them. He said glumly, "You belong to the lot that play in the car-park?"

Mike was about to answer when Blackie stopped him. As the leader he had responsibilities. "Suppose we are?" he said ambiguously.

"I got some chocolates," Mr. Thomas said. "Don't like 'em myself. Here you are. Not enough to go round, I don't suppose. There never is," he added with sombre conviction. He handed over three packets of Smarties.

The gang were puzzled and perturbed by this action and tried to explain it away. "Bet someone dropped them and he picked 'em up," somebody suggested.

"Pinched 'em and then got in a bleeding funk," another thought aloud.

"It's a bribe," Summers said. "He wants us to stop bouncing balls on his wall."

"We'll show him we don't take bribes," Blackie said, and they sacrificed the whole morning to the game of bouncing that only Mike was young enough to enjoy. There was no sign from Mr. Thomas.

Next day T. astonished them all. He was late at the rendezvous, and the voting for that day's exploit took place without him. At Blackie's suggestion the gang was to disperse in pairs, take buses at random, and see how many free rides could be snatched from unwary conductors (the operation was to be carried out in pairs to avoid cheating). They were drawing lots for their companions when T. arrived.

"Where you been, T.?" Blackie asked. "You can't vote now. You know the rules."

"I've been *there*," T. said. He looked at the ground, as though he had thoughts to hide.

"Where?"

"At Old Misery's." Mike's mouth opened and then hurriedly closed again with a click. He had remembered the frog.

"At Old Misery's?" Blackie said. There was nothing in the rules against it, but he had a sensation that T. was treading on dangerous ground. He asked hopefully, "Did you break in?"

"No. I rang the bell."

"And what did you say?"

"I said I wanted to see his house."

"What did he do?"

"He showed it me."

"Pinch anything?"

"No."

"What did you do it for then?"

The gang had gathered round: it was as though an impromptu court were about to form and try some case of deviation. T. said, "It's a beautiful house," and still watching the ground, meeting no one's eyes, he licked his lips first one way, then the other.

"What do you mean, a beautiful house?" Blackie asked with scorn.

"It's got a staircase two hundred years old like a corkscrew. Nothing holds it up."

"What do you mean, nothing holds it up. Does it float?"

"It's to do with opposite forces, Old Misery said."

"What else?"

"There's panelling."

"Like in the Blue Boar?"

"Two hundred years old."

"Is Old Misery two hundred years old?"

Mike laughed suddenly and then was quiet again. The meeting was in a serious mood. For the first time since T. had strolled into the car-park on the first day of the holidays his position was in danger. It only needed a single use of his real name and the gang would be at his heels.

"What did you do it for?" Blackie asked. He was just, he had no jealousy, he was anxious to retain T. in the gang if he could. It was the word "beautiful" that worried him—that belonged to a class world that you could still see parodied at the Wormsley Common Empire by a man wearing a top hat and a monocle, with a haw-haw accent. He was tempted to say, "My dear Trevor, old chap," and unleash his hell hounds. "If you'd broken in," he said sadly—that indeed would have been an exploit worthy of the gang.

"This was better," T. said. "I found out things." He continued to stare at his feet, not meeting anybody's eye, as though he were absorbed in some dream he was unwilling—or ashamed—to share.

"What things?"

"Old Misery's going to be away all tomorrow and Bank Holiday."

Blackie said with relief, "You mean we could break in?"

"And pinch things?" somebody asked.

Blackie said, "Nobody's going to pinch things. Breaking in—that's good enough, isn't it? We don't want any court stuff."

"I don't want to pinch anything," T. said. "I've got a better idea."

"What is it?"

T. raised eyes, as grey and disturbed as the drab August day. "We'll pull it down," he said. "We'll destroy it."

Blackie gave a single hoot of laughter and then, like Mike, fell quiet, daunted by the serious implacable gaze. "What'd the police be doing all the time?" he said.

"They'd never know. We'd do it from inside. I've found a way in." He said with a sort of intensity, "We'd be like worms, don't you see, in an apple. When we came out again there'd be nothing there, no staircase, no panels, nothing but just walls, and then we'd make the walls fall down—somehow."

"We'd go to jug," Blackie said.

"Who's to prove? And anyway we wouldn't have pinched anything." He added without the smallest flicker of glee, "There wouldn't be anything to pinch after we'd finished."

"I've never heard of going to prison for breaking things," Summers said.

"There wouldn't be time," Blackie said. "I've seen housebreakers at work."

"There are twelve of us," T. said. "We'd organize."

"None of us know how—"

"I know," T. said. He looked across at Blackie, "Have you got a better plan?"

"Today," Mike said tactlessly, "we're pinching free rides—"

"Free rides," T. said. "You can stand down, Blackie, if you'd rather. . . ."

"The gang's got to vote."

"Put it up then."

Blackie said uneasily, "It's proposed that tomorrow and Monday we destroy Old Misery's house."

"Here, here," said a fat boy called Joe.

"Who's in favour?"

T. said, "It's carried."

"How do we start?" Summers asked.

"He'll tell you," Blackie said. It was the end of his leadership. He went away to the back of the car-park and began to kick a stone, dribbling it this way and that. There was only one old Morris in the park, for few cars were left there except lorries: without an attendant there was no safety. He took a flying kick at the car and scraped a little paint off the rear mudguard. Beyond, paying no more attention to him than to a stranger, the gang had gathered round T.; Blackie was dimly aware of the fickleness of favour. He thought of going home, of never returning, of letting them all discover the hollowness of T.'s leadership, but suppose after all what T. proposed was possible—nothing like it had ever been done before. The fame of the Wormsley Common car-park gang would surely reach around London. There would be headlines in the papers. Even the grown-up gangs who ran the betting at the all-in wrestling and the barrow-boys would hear with respect of how Old Misery's house had been destroyed. Driven by the pure, simple, and altruistic ambition of fame for the gang, Blackie came back to where T. stood in the shadow of Misery's wall.

T. was giving his orders with decision: it was as though his plan had been with him all his life, pondered through the seasons, now in his fifteenth year crystallized with the pain of puberty. "You," he said to Mike, "bring some big nails, the biggest you can find, and a hammer. Anyone else who can better bring a hammer and a screwdriver. We'll need plenty of them. Chisels too. We can't have too many chisels. Can anybody bring a saw?"

"I can," Mike said.

"Not a child's saw," T. said. "A real saw."

Blackie realized he had raised his hand like any ordinary member of the gang.

"Right, you bring one, Blackie. But now there's a difficulty. We want a hacksaw."

"What's a hacksaw?" someone asked.

"You can get 'em at Woolworth's," Summers said.

The fat boy called Joe said gloomily, "I knew it would end in a collection."

"I'll get one myself," T. said. "I don't want your money. But I can't buy a sledge-hammer."

Blackie said, "They are working on number fifteen. I know where they'll leave their stuff for Bank Holiday."

"Then that's all," T. said. "We meet here at nine sharp."

"I've got to go to church," Mike said.

"Come over the wall and whistle. We'll let you in."

II

On Sunday morning all were punctual except Blackie, even Mike. Mike had had a stroke of luck. His mother felt ill, his father was tired after Saturday night, and he was told to go to church alone with many warnings of what would happen if he strayed. Blackie had had difficulty in smuggling out the saw, and then in finding the sledge-hammer at the back of number 15. He approached the house from a lane at the rear of the garden, for fear of the policeman's beat along the main road. The tired evergreens kept off a stormy sun: another wet Bank Holiday was being prepared over the Atlantic, beginning in swirls of dust under the trees. Blackie climbed the wall into Misery's garden.

There was no sign of anybody anywhere. The loo stood like a tomb in a neglected graveyard. The curtains were drawn. The house slept. Blackie lumbered nearer with the saw and the sledge-hammer. Perhaps after all nobody had turned up: the plan had been a wild invention: they had woken wiser. But when he came close to the back door he could hear a confusion of sound, hardly louder than a hive in a swarm: a clickety-clack, a bang bang bang, a scraping, a creaking, a sudden painful crack. He thought. It's true, and whistled.

They opened the back door to him and he came in. He had at once the impression of organization, very different from the old happy-go-lucky ways under his leadership. For a while he wandered up and down stairs looking for T. Nobody addressed him: he had a sense of great urgency, and already he could begin to see the plan. The interior of the old house was being carefully demolished without touching the outer walls. Summers with hammer and chisel was ripping out the skirting-boards in the ground floor dining room: he had already smashed the panels of the door. In the same room Joe was heaving up the parquet blocks, exposing the soft wood floor-boards over the cellar. Coils of wire came out of the damaged skirting and Mike sat happily on the floor, clipping the wires.

On the curved stairs two of the gang were working hard with an inadequate child's saw on the banisters—when they saw Blackie's big saw they signalled for it wordlessly. When he next saw them a quarter of the banisters had been dropped into the hall. He found T. at last in the bathroom—he sat moodily in the least cared-for room in the house, listening to the sounds coming up from below.

"You've really done it," Blackie said with awe. "What's going to happen?"

"We've only just begun," T. said. He looked at the sledge-hammer and gave his instructions. "You stay here and break the bath and the wash-basin. Don't bother about the pipes. They come later."

Mike appeared at the door. "I've finished the wire, T.," he said.

"Good. You've just got to go wandering round now. The kitchen's in the basement. Smash all the china and glass and bottles you can lay hold of. Don't turn on the taps—we don't want a flood—yet. Then go into all the rooms and turn out drawers. If they are locked get one of the others to break them open. Tear up any papers you find and smash all the ornaments. Better take a carving-knife with you from the kitchen. The bedroom's opposite here. Open the pillows and tear up the sheets. That's enough for the moment. And you, Blackie, when you've finished in here crack the plaster in the passage up with your sledge-hammer."

"What are you going to do?" Blackie asked.

"I'm looking for something special," T. said.

It was nearly lunch-time before Blackie had finished and went in search of T. Chaos had advanced. The kitchen was a shambles of broken glass and china. The dining-room was stripped of parquet, the skirting was up, the door had been taken off its hinges, and the destroyers had moved up a floor. Streaks of light came in through the closed shutters where they worked with the seriousness of creators—and destruction after all is a form of creation. A kind of imagination had seen this house as it had now become.

Mike said, "I've got to go home for dinner."

"Who else?" T. asked, but all the others on one excuse or another had brought provisions with them.

They squatted in the ruins of the room and swapped unwanted sandwiches. Half an hour for lunch and they were at work again. By the time Mike returned, they were on the top floor, and by six the superficial damage was completed. The doors were all off, all the skirtings raised, the furniture pillaged and ripped and smashed—no one could have slept in the house except on a bed of broken plaster. T. gave his orders—eight o'clock next morning—and to escape notice they climbed singly over the garden wall, into the car-park. Only Blackie and T. were left; the light had nearly gone, and when they touched a switch, nothing worked— Mike had done his job thoroughly.

"Did you find anything special?" Blackie asked.

T. nodded. "Come over here," he said, "and look." Out of both pockets he drew bundles of pound notes. "Old Misery's savings," he said. "Mike ripped out the mattress, but he missed them."

"What are you going to do? Share them?"

"We aren't thieves," T. said. "Nobody's going to steal anything from this house. I kept these for you and me—a celebration." He knelt down on the floor and counted them out—there were seventy in all. "We'll burn them," he said, "one by one," and taking it in turns they held a note upwards and lit the top corner, so that the flame burnt slowly towards their fingers. The grey ash floated above them and fell on their heads like age. "I'd like to see Old Misery's face when we are through," T. said.

"You hate him a lot?" Blackie asked.

"Of course I don't hate him," T. said. "There'd be no fun if I hated him." The last burning note illuminated his brooding face. "All this hate and love," he said, "it's soft, it's hooey. There's only things, Blackie," and he looked round the room crowded with the unfamiliar shadows of half things, broken things, former things. "I'll race you home, Blackie," he said.

III

Next morning the serious destruction started. Two were missing —Mike and another boy whose parents were off to Southend and Brighton in spite of the slow warm drops that had begun to fall and the rumble of thunder in the estuary like the first guns of the old blitz. "We've got to hurry," T. said.

Summers was restive. "Haven't we done enough?" he said. "I've been given a bob for slot machines. This is like work."

"We've hardly started," T. said. "Why, there's all the floors left, and the stairs. We haven't taken out a single window. You voted like the others. We are going to *destroy* this house. There won't be anything left when we've finished."

They began again on the first floor picking up the top floor-boards next the outer wall, leaving the joists exposed. Then they sawed through the joists and retreated into the hall, as what was left of the floor heeled and sank. They had learnt with practise, and the second floor collapsed more easily. By the evening an odd exhilaration seized them as they looked down the great hollow of the house. They ran risks and made mistakes: when they thought of the windows it was too late to reach them. "Cor," Joe said, and dropped a penny down into the dry rubble-filled well. It cracked and span among the broken glass.

"Why did we start this?" Summers asked with astonishment; T. was already on the ground, digging at the rubble, clearing a space along the outer wall. "Turn on the taps," he said. "It's too dark for anyone to see now, and in the morning it won't matter." The water overtook them on the stairs and fell through the floorless rooms.

It was then they heard Mike's whistle at the back. "Something's wrong," Blackie said. They could hear his urgent breathing as they unlocked the door.

"The bogies?" Summers asked.

"Old Misery," Mike said. "He's on his way." He put his head between his knees and retched. "Ran all the way," he said with pride.

"But why?" T. said. "He told me . . ." He protested with the fury of the child he had never been, "It isn't fair."

"He was down at Southend," Mike said, "and he was on the train coming back. Said it was too cold and wet." He paused and gazed at the water. "My, you've had a storm here. Is the roof leaking?"

"How long will he be?"

"Five minutes. I gave Ma the slip and ran."

"We better clear," Summers said. "We've done enough, anyway."

"Oh, no, we haven't. Anybody could do this—" "this" was the shattered hollowed house with nothing left but the walls. Yet walls could be preserved. Façades were valuable. They could build inside again more beautifully than before. This could again be a home. He said angrily, "We've got to finish. Don't move. Let me think."

"There's no time," a boy said.

"There's got to be a way," T. said. "We couldn't have got thus far . . ."

"We've done a lot," Blackie said.

"No. No, we haven't. Somebody watch the front."

"We can't do any more."

"He may come in at the back."

"Watch the back too." T. began to plead. "Just give me a minute and I'll fix it. I swear I'll fix it." But his authority had gone with his ambiguity. He was only one of the gang. "Please," he said.

"Please," Summers mimicked him, and then suddenly struck home with the fatal name. "Run along home, Trevor."

T. stood with his back to the rubble like a boxer knocked groggy against the ropes. He had no words as his dreams shook and slid. Then Blackie acted before the gang had time to laugh, pushing Summers backward. "I'll watch the front, T.," he said, and cautiously he opened the shutters of the hall. The grey wet common stretched ahead, and the lamps gleamed in the puddles. "Someone's coming, T. No, it's not him. What's your plan, T.?"

"Tell Mike to go out to the loo and hide close beside it. When he hears me whistle he's got to count ten and start to shout."

"Shout what?"

"Oh, 'Help,' anything."

"You hear, Mike," Blackie said. He was the leader again. He took a quick look between the shutters. "He's coming, T."

"Quick, Mike. The loo. Stay here, Blackie, all of you till I yell."

"Where are you going, T.?"

"Don't worry. I'll see to this. I said I would, didn't I?"

Old Misery came limping off the common. He had mud on his shoes and he stopped to scrape them on the pavement's edge. He didn't want to soil his house, which stood jagged and dark between the bomb-sites, saved so narrowly, as he believed, from destruction. Even the fan-light had been left unbroken by the bomb's blast. Somewhere somebody whistled. Old Misery looked sharply round. He didn't trust whistles. A child was shouting: it seemed to come from his own garden. Then a boy ran into the road from the car-park. "Mr. Thomas," he called, "Mr. Thomas."

"What is it?"

"I'm terribly sorry, Mr. Thomas. One of us got taken short, and we thought you wouldn't mind, and now he can't get out."

"What do you mean, boy?"

"He's got stuck in your loo."

"He'd no business— Haven't I seen you before?"

"You showed me your house."

"So I did. So I did. That doesn't give you the right to—"

"Do hurry, Mr. Thomas. He'll suffocate."

"Nonsense. He can't suffocate. Wait till I put my bag in."

"I'll carry your bag."

"Oh, no, you don't. I carry my own."

"This way, Mr. Thomas."

"I can't get in the garden that way. I've got to go through the house."

"But you *can* get in the garden this way, Mr. Thomas. We often do."

"You often do?" He followed the boy with a scandalized fascination. "When? What right . . ."

"Do you see . . . ? The wall's low."

"I'm not going to climb walls into my own garden. It's absurd."

"This is how we do it. One foot here, one foot there, and over." The boy's face peered down, an arm shot out, and Mr. Thomas found his bag taken and deposited on the other side of the wall.

"Give me back my bag," Mr. Thomas said. From the loo a boy yelled and yelled. "I'll call the police."

"Your bag's all right, Mr. Thomas. Look. One foot there. On your right. Now just above. To your left." Mr. Thomas climbed over his own garden wall. "Here's your bag, Mr. Thomas."

"I'll have the wall built up," Mr. Thomas said, "I'll not have you boys coming over here, using my loo." He stumbled on the path, but the boy caught his elbow and supported him. "Thank you, thank you, my boy," he murmured automatically. Somebody shouted again through the dark. "I'm coming, I'm coming," Mr. Thomas called. He said to the boy beside him, "I'm not unreasonable. Been a boy myself. As long as things are done regular. I don't mind you playing round the place Saturday mornings. Sometimes I like company. Only it's got to be regular. One of you asks leave and I say Yes. Sometimes I'll say No. Won't feel like it. And you come in at the front door and out at the back. No garden walls."

"Do get him out, Mr. Thomas."

"He won't come to any harm in my loo," Mr. Thomas said, stumbling slowly down the garden. "Oh, my rheumatics," he said. "Always get 'em on Bank Holiday. I've got to go careful. There's loose stones here. Give me your hand. Do you know what my horoscope said yesterday? 'Abstain from any dealings in first half of week. Danger of serious crash.' That might be on this path," Mr. Thomas said. "They speak in parables and double meanings." He paused at the door of the loo. "What's the matter in there?" he called. There was no reply.

"Perhaps he's fainted," the boy said.

"Not in my loo. Here, you, come out," Mr. Thomas said, and giving a great jerk at the door he nearly fell on his back when it swung easily open. A hand first supported him and then pushed him hard. His head hit the opposite wall and he sat heavily down. His bag hit his feet. A hand whipped the key out of the lock and the door slammed. "Let me out," he called, and heard the key turn in the lock. "A serious crash," he thought, and felt dithery and confused and old.

A voice spoke to him softly through the star-shaped hole in the door. "Don't worry, Mr. Thomas," it said, "we won't hurt you, not if you stay quiet."

Mr. Thomas put his head between his hands and pondered. He had noticed that there was only one lorry in the car-park, and he felt certain that the driver would not come for it before the morning. Nobody could hear him from the road in front, and the lane at the back was seldom used. Anyone who passed there would be hurrying home and would not pause for what they would certainly take to be drunken cries. And if he did call "Help," who, on a lonely Bank Holiday evening, would have the courage to investigate? Mr. Thomas sat on the loo and pondered with the wisdom of age.

After a while it seemed to him that there were sounds in the silence—they were faint and came from the direction of his house. He stood up and peered through the ventilation hole—between the cracks in one of the shutters he saw a light, not the light of a lamp, but the wavering light that a candle might give. Then he thought he heard the sound of hammering and scraping and chipping. He thought of burglars—perhaps they had employed the boy as a scout, but why should burglars engage in what sounded more and more like a stealthy form of carpentry? Mr. Thomas let out an experimental yell, but nobody answered. The noise could not even have reached his enemies.

IV

Mike had gone home to bed, but the rest stayed. The question of leadership no longer concerned the gang. With nails, chisels, screwdrivers, anything that was sharp and penetrating they moved around the inner walls worrying at the mortar between the bricks. They started too high, and it was Blackie who hit on the damp course and realized the work could be halved if they weakened the joists immediately above. It was a long, tiring, unamusing job, but at last it was finished. The gutted house stood there balanced on a few inches of mortar between the damp course and the bricks.

There remained the most dangerous task of all, out in the open at the edge of the bomb-site. Summers was sent to watch the road for passers-by, and Mr. Thomas, sitting in the loo, heard clearly now the sound of sawing. It no longer came from his house, and that a little reassured him. He felt less concerned. Perhaps the other noises too had no significance.

A voice spoke to him through the hole. "Mr. Thomas."

"Let me out," Mr. Thomas said sternly.

"Here's a blanket," the voice said, and a long grey sausage was worked through the hole and fell in swathes over Mr. Thomas's head.

"There's nothing personal," the voice said. "We want you to be comfortable tonight."

"Tonight," Mr. Thomas repeated incredulously.

"Catch," the voice said. "Penny buns—we've buttered them, and sausage-rolls. We don't want you to starve, Mr. Thomas."

Mr. Thomas pleaded desperately. "A joke's a joke, boy. Let me out and I won't say a thing. I've got rheumatics. I got to sleep comfortable."

"You wouldn't be comfortable, not in your house, you wouldn't. Not now."

"What do you mean, boy?" but the footsteps receded. There was only the silence of night: no sound of sawing. Mr. Thomas tried one more yell, but he was daunted and rebuked by the silence—a long way off an owl hooted and made away again on its muffled flight through the soundless world.

At seven next morning the driver came to fetch his lorry. He climbed into the seat and tried to start the engine. He was vaguely aware of a voice shouting, but it didn't concern him. At last the engine responded and he backed the lorry until it touched the great wooden shore that supported Mr. Thomas's house. That way he could drive right out and down the street without reversing. The lorry moved forward, was momentarily checked as though something were pulling it from behind, and then went on to the sound of a long rumbling crash. The driver was astonished to see bricks bouncing ahead of him, while stones hit the roof of his cab. He put on his brakes. When he climbed out the whole landscape had suddenly altered. There was no house beside the car-park, only a hill of rubble. He went round and examined the back of his car for damage, and found a rope tied there that was still twisted at the other end round part of a wooden strut.

The driver again became aware of somebody shouting. It came from the wooden erection which was the nearest thing to a house in that desolation of broken brick. The driver climbed the smashed wall and unlocked the door. Mr. Thomas came out of the loo. He was wearing a grey blanket to which flakes of pastry adhered. He gave a sobbing cry. "My house," he said. "Where's my house?"

"Search me," the driver said. His eye lit on the remains of a bath and what had once been a dresser and he began to laugh. There wasn't anything left anywhere.

"How dare you laugh," Mr. Thomas said. "It was my house. My house."

"I'm sorry," the driver said, making heroic efforts, but when he remembered the sudden check to his lorry, the crash of bricks falling, he became convulsed again. One moment the house had stood there with such dignity between the bomb-sites like a man in a top hat, and then, bang, crash, there wasn't anything left—not anything. He said, "I'm sorry. I can't help it, Mr. Thomas. There's nothing personal, but you got to admit it's funny."

QUESTIONS

1. Discuss the statement that "destruction after all is a form of creation."

2. What does Trevor mean when he says, "All this hate and love . . . it's soft, it's hooey. There's only things, Blackie"? In what way is Trevor not a child? What does his father's career have to do with his wanting to destroy the house?

3. The story is symbolic. Can "The Destructors" also be said to have major aspects of allegory and parable? Explain.

4. The story ends with the word "funny." Discuss the element of humor in the story. What purpose does it serve?

5. What about the power struggle between Trevor and Blackie? Could Trevor's use of imagination be related to the deference to the "mastermind" found in many crime stories?

6. What part does World War II play in the story's meaning?

7. Look up the origin of the word "holiday." How is it significant that the destruction takes place on a Bank [secular] Holiday?

The Dressmaker's Doll

Agatha Christie

A mess of limp rags, bits of velvet and silk, with a painted face, and origin unknown—but it was (and this was the haunting and horrifying part) a peripatetic creature . . .

The doll lay in the big velvet-covered chair. There was not much light in the room; the London skies were dark. In the gentle, grayish-green gloom, the sage-green coverings and the curtains and the rugs all blended with each other. The doll blended too. She lay long and limp and sprawled in her green-velvet clothes and her velvet cap and the painted mask of her face. She was not a doll as children understand dolls. She was the Puppet Doll, the whim of Rich Women, the doll who lolls beside the telephone, or among the cushions of the divan. She sprawled there, eternally limp and yet strangely alive. She looked a decadent product of the twentieth century.

Sybil Fox, hurrying in with some patterns and a sketch, looked at the doll with a faint feeling of surprise and bewilderment. She wondered—but whatever she wondered did not get to the front of her mind. Instead, she thought to herself, "Now, what's happened to the pattern of the blue velvet? Wherever have I put it? I'm sure I had it here just now." She went out on the landing and called up to the workroom.

"Elspeth. Elspeth, have you the blue pattern up there? Mrs. Fellows-Brown will be here any minute now."

She went in again, switching on the lights. Again she glanced at the doll. "Now where on earth—ah, there it is." She picked the pattern up from where it had fallen from her hand. There was the usual creak outside on the landing as the elevator came to a halt, and in a minute or two Mrs. Fellows-Brown, accompanied by her Pekinese, came puffing into the room rather like a fussy local train arriving at a wayside station.

"It's going to pour," she said, "simply *pour!*"

She threw off gloves and a fur. Alicia Coombe came in. She didn't always come in nowadays, only when special customers arrived, and Mrs. Fellows-Brown was such a customer.

Elspeth, the forewoman of the workroom, came down with the frock and Sybil pulled it over Mrs. Fellows-Brown's head.

"There," she said. "It really does suit you. It's a lovely color, isn't it."

Alicia Coombe sat back a little in her chair, studying it.

"Yes," she said, "I think it's good. Yes, it's definitely a success."

Mrs. Fellows-Brown turned sideways and looked in the mirror.

"I must say," she said, "your clothes do *do* something to my behind."

"You're much thinner than you were three months ago," Sybil assured her.

"I'm really not," said Mrs. Fellows-Brown, "though I must say I *look* it in this. There's something about the way you cut, it really does minimize my behind. I almost look as though I hadn't got one—I mean only the usual kind that most people have." She sighed and gingerly smoothed the troublesome portion of her anatomy. "It's always been a bit of a trial to me," she said. "Of course, for years I could pull it in, you know, by sticking out my front. Well, I can't do that any longer because I've got a stomach now as well as a behind. And I mean—well, you can't pull it in both ways, can you?"

Alicia Coombe said, "You should see some of my customers!"

Mrs. Fellows-Brown experimented to and fro.

"A stomach is worse than a behind," she said. "It shows more. Or perhaps you think it does, because, I mean, when you're talking to people you're facing them and that's the moment they can't see your behind but they can notice your stomach. Anyway, I've made it a rule to pull in my stomach and let my behind look after itself." She craned her neck round still farther, then said suddenly, "Oh, that doll of yours! She gives me the creeps. How long have you had her?"

Sybil glanced uncertainly at Alicia Coombe who looked puzzled but vaguely distressed.

"I don't know exactly . . . some time I think—I never *can* remember things. It's awful nowadays—I simply *cannot* remember. Sybil, how long have we had her?"

Sybil said shortly, "I don't know."

"Well," said Mrs. Fellows-Brown, "she gives *me* the creeps. Uncanny! She looks, you know, as though she was watching us all, and perhaps laughing in that velvet sleeve of hers. I'd get rid of her if I were you." She gave a little shiver. Then she plunged once more into dressmaking details. Should she or should she not have the sleeves an inch shorter? And what about the length? When all these important points were settled satisfactorily, Mrs. Fellows-Brown resumed her own garments and prepared to leave. As she passed the doll, she turned her head again.

"No," she said, "I *don't* like that doll. She looks too much as though she *belonged* here. It isn't healthy."

"Now what did she mean by that?" demanded Sybil, as Mrs. Fellows-Brown departed down the stairs.

Before Alicia Coombe could answer, Mrs. Fellows-Brown returned, poking her head round the door.

"Good gracious, I forgot all about Fou-Ling. Where are you, ducksie? Well I never!"

She stared and the other two women stared too. The Pekinese was sitting by the green-velvet chair, staring up at the limp doll sprawled on it. There was no expression, either of pleasure or resentment, on his small popeyed face. He was merely looking.

"Come along, mum's darling," said Mrs. Fellows-Brown.

Mum's darling paid no attention whatever.

"He gets more disobedient every day," said Mrs. Fellows-Brown, with the air of one cataloguing a virtue. "Come *on*, Fou-Ling. Din-dins. Luffly liver."

Fou-Ling turned his head about an inch and a half toward his mistress, then with disdain resumed his appraisal of the doll.

"She certainly made an impression on him," said Mrs. Fellows-Brown. "I don't think he's ever noticed her before. *I* haven't either. Was she here last time I came?"

The two other women looked at each other. Sybil now had a frown on her face, and Alicia Coombe said, wrinkling up her forehead, "I told you—I simply can't remember anything nowadays. How long *have* we had her, Sybil?"

"Where did she come from?" demanded Mrs. Fellows-Brown. "Did you buy her?"

"Oh, no." Somehow Alicia Coombe was shocked at the idea. "Oh no. I suppose—I suppose someone gave her to me." She shook her head. "Maddening!" she exclaimed. "Absolutely maddening, when everything goes out of your head the very moment after it's happened."

"Now don't be stupid, Fou-Ling," said Mrs. Fellows-Brown sharply. "Come on. I'll have to pick you up."

She picked him up. Fou-Ling uttered a short bark of agonized protest. They went out of the room with Fou-Ling's popeyed face turned over his fluffy shoulder, still staring with enormous attention at the doll on the chair. . . .

"That there doll," said Mrs. Groves, "fair gives me the creeps, it does."

Mrs. Groves was the cleaner. She had just finished a crablike progress backward along the floor. Now she was standing up and working slowly round the room with a duster.

"Funny thing," said Mrs. Groves, "never noticed it really until yesterday. And then it hit me all of a sudden, as you might say."

"You don't like it?" asked Sybil.

"I tell you, Mrs. Fox, it gives me the creeps," said the cleaning woman. "It ain't natural, if you know what I mean. All those long hanging legs and the way she's slouched down there and the cunning look she has in her eye. It doesn't look healthy, that's what I say."

"You've never said anything about her before," said Sybil.

"I tell you, I never noticed her—not till this morning . . . Of course I know she's been here some time but—" She stopped and a puzzled expression flitted across her face. "Sort of thing you might dream of at night," she said, and gathering up various cleaning implements she departed from the fitting room and walked across the landing to the room on the other side.

Sybil stared at the relaxed doll. An expression of bewilderment was growing on her face. Alicia Coombe entered and Sybil turned sharply.

"Miss Coombe, how long *have* you had this creature?"

"What, the doll? My dear, you know I can't remember things. Yesterday—why, it's too silly! I was going out to that lecture and I hadn't gone halfway down the street when I suddenly found I couldn't remember where I was going. I thought and I thought. Finally I told myself it *must* be Fortnums. I knew there was something I wanted to get at Fortnums. Well, you won't believe me, it wasn't till I actually got home and was having some tea that I remembered about the lecture. Of course, I've always heard that people go gaga as they get on in life, but it's happening to me much too fast. I've forgotten now where I've put my handbag—and my spectacles too. Where did I put those spectacles? I had them just now—I was reading something in the *Times.*"

"The spectacles are on the mantelpiece here," said Sybil, handing them to her. "How did you get the doll? Who gave her to you?"

"That's a blank, too," said Alicia Coombe. "*Somebody* gave her to me or sent her to me, I suppose. . . . However she does seem to match the room very well, doesn't she?"

"Rather too well, I think," said Sybil. "Funny thing is, *I* can't remember when I first noticed her here."

"Now don't you get the same way as I am," Alicia Coombe admonished her. "After all, you're young still."

"But really, Miss Coombe, I don't remember. I mean, I looked at her yesterday and thought there was something—well, Mrs. Grove is quite right—something creepy about her. And then I thought I'd already thought so, and then I tried to remember when I first thought so and—well, I just couldn't remember anything! In a way, it was as if I'd never seen her before—only it didn't feel like that. It felt as though she'd been here a long time but I'd only just noticed her."

"Perhaps she flew in through the window one day on a broomstick," said Alicia Coombe. "Anyway, she belongs here now all right." She looked round. "You could hardly imagine the room without her, could you?"

"No," said Sybil, with a slight shiver, "but I rather wish I could."

"Could what?"

"Imagine the room without her."

"Are we all going barmy about this doll?" demanded Alicia Coombe impatiently. "What's wrong with the poor thing? Looks like a decayed cabbage to me, but perhaps," she added, "that's because I haven't got my spectacles on." She put them on her nose and looked firmly at the doll. "Yes," she said, "I see what you mean. She *is* a little creepy. . . . Sad-looking but—well, sly and rather determined, too."

"Funny," said Sybil, "Mrs. Fellows-Brown taking such a violent dislike to her."

"She's one who never minds speaking her mind," said Alicia Coombe.

"But it's odd," persisted Sybil, "that this doll should make such an impression on her."

"Well, people do take dislikes very suddenly sometimes."

"Perhaps," said Sybil, with a little laugh, "that doll never *was* here until yesterday. . . . Perhaps she just—flew in through the window as you say and settled herself here."

"No," said Alicia Coombe, "I'm sure she's been here some time. Perhaps she only became visible yesterday."

"That's what I feel, too," said Sybil, "that she's been here some time . . . but all the same I *don't* remember really seeing her till yesterday."

"Now, dear," said Alicia Coombe briskly, "do stop it. You're making me feel quite peculiar with shivers running up and down my spine. You're not going to work up a great deal of supernatural hoo-hah about that creature, are you?" She picked up the doll, shook it out, rearranged its shoulders, and sat it down again on another chair. Immediately the doll flopped slightly and relaxed.

"It's not a bit lifelike," said Alicia Coombe, staring at the doll. "And yet, in a funny way, she does seem alive, doesn't she?"

"Oo, it did give me a turn," said Mrs. Groves, as she went round the showroom, dusting. "Such a turn as I hardly like to go into the fitting room any more."

"What's given you a turn?" demanded Miss Coombe, who was sitting at a writing table in the corner, busy with various accounts. "This woman," she added more for her own benefit than that of Mrs. Groves, "thinks she can have two evening dresses, three cocktail dresses, and a suit every year without ever paying me a penny for them! Really, some people!"

"It's that doll," said Mrs. Groves.

"What, our doll again?"

"Yes, sitting up there at the desk, like a human. Oo, it didn't half give me a turn!"

"What are you talking about?"

Alicia Coombe got up, strode across the room, across the little landing outside, and into the room opposite—the fitting room. There was a small Sheraton desk in one corner of it, and there, sitting in a chair drawn up to it, her long floppy arms on the desk, sat the doll.

"Somebody seems to have been having fun," said Alicia Coombe. "Fancy sitting her up like that. Really, she looks quite natural."

Sybil Fox came down the stairs at this moment carrying a dress that was to be tried on that morning.

"Come here, Sybil. Look at our doll sitting at my private desk and writing letters now."

The two women looked.

"Really," said Alicia Coombe, "it's too ridiculous! I wonder who propped her up there. Did you?"

"No, I didn't," said Sybil. "It must have been one of the girls from upstairs."

"A silly sort of joke, really," said Alicia Coombe. She picked up the doll from the desk and threw her back on the sofa.

Sybil laid the dress over a chair carefully, then she went out and up the stairs to the workroom.

"You know the doll," she said, "the velvet doll in Miss Coombe's room downstairs—in the fitting room?"

The forewoman and three of the girls looked up.

"Yes, miss, of course we know."

"Who sat her up at the desk this morning for a joke?"

The three girls looked at her, then Elspeth, the forewoman, said, "Sat her up at the desk? *I* didn't."

"Nor did I," said one of the girls. "Did you, Marlene?"

Marlene shook her head.

"This your bit of fun, Elspeth?"

"No, indeed," said Elspeth, a stern woman who looked as though her mouth should always be full of pins. "I've more to do than going about playing with dolls and sitting them up at desks."

"Look here," said Sybil, and to her surprise her voice shook slightly. "It was—it was quite a good joke, only I'd just like to know who did it."

The three girls bristled.

"We've told you, Mrs. Fox. None of us did it, did we, Marlene?"

"I didn't," said Marlene, "and if Nellie and Margaret say they didn't, well then none of us did."

"You've heard what *I* had to say," said Elspeth. "What's this all about anyway, Mrs. Fox?"

Sybil said slowly, "It just seemed so odd."

"Perhaps it was Mrs. Groves?" said Elspeth.

Sybil shook her head. "It wouldn't be Mrs. Groves. It gave *her* quite a turn."

"I'll come down and see for myself," said Elspeth.

"She's not there now," said Sybil. "Miss Coombe took her away from the desk and threw her back on the sofa. Well—" she paused, "what I mean is, someone must have stuck her up there in the chair at the writing desk—thinking it was funny, I suppose. And—and I don't see why they won't say so."

"I've told you twice, Mrs. Fox," said Margaret. "I don't see why you should go on accusing us of telling lies. None of us would do a silly thing like that."

"I'm sorry," said Sybil, "I didn't mean to upset you. But—but who else could possibly have done it?"

"Perhaps she got up and walked there herself," said Marlene, and giggled.

For some reason Sybil didn't like the suggestion.

"Oh, it's all a lot of nonsense, anyway," she said, and went down the stairs again.

Alicia Coombe was humming quite cheerfully. She looked around the room.

"I've lost my spectacles again," she said, "but it doesn't really matter. I don't want to see anything this moment. The trouble is, of course, when you're as blind as I am, that when you have lost your spectacles, unless you've got another pair to put on and find them with, well then you can't find them because you can't see to find them."

"I'll look round for you," said Sybil. "You had them just now."

"I went into the other room when you went upstairs. I expect I took them back in there."

She went across to the other room.

"It's such a bother," said Alicia Coombe. "I want to get on with these accounts. How can I if I haven't my spectacles?"

"I'll go up and get your second pair from the bedroom," said Sybil.

"I haven't got a second pair at present," said Alicia Coombe.

"Why, what's happened to them?"

"Well, I think I left them yesterday when I was out at lunch. I've rung up there, and I've rung up the two shops I went into, too."

"Oh, dear," said Sybil, "you'll have to get *three* pairs, I suppose."

"If I had three pairs of spectacles," said Alicia Coombe, "I should spend my whole life looking for one or the other of them. I really think it's best to have only *one*. Then you've *got* to look till you find it."

"Well, they must be somewhere," said Sybil. "You haven't been out of these two rooms. They're certainly not here, so you must have laid them down in the fitting room."

She went back, walking round, looking quite closely. Finally, as a last idea, she took up the doll from the sofa.

"I've got them," she called.

"Oh, where were they, Sybil?"

"Under our precious doll. I suppose you must have thrown them down when you put her back on the sofa."

"I didn't. I'm sure I didn't."

"Oh," said Sybil with exasperation. "Then I suppose the doll took them and was hiding them from you!"

"Really, you know," said Alicia, looking thoughtfully at the doll, "I wouldn't put it past her. She looks very intelligent, don't you think, Sybil?"

"I don't think I like her face," said Sybil. "She looks as though she knew something that we didn't."

"You don't think she looks sort of sad and sweet?" said Alicia Coombe, pleadingly, but without conviction.

"I don't think she's in the least sweet," said Sybil.

"No . . . perhaps you're right. . . . Oh, well, let's get on with things. Lady Lee will be here in another ten minutes. I just want to get these invoices done and posted."

"Mrs. Fox. Mrs. Fox."

"Yes, Margaret?" said Sybil. "What is it?"

Sybil was busy leaning over a table, cutting a piece of satin material.

"Oh, Mrs. Fox, it's that doll again. I took down the brown dress like you said, and there's that doll sitting up at the desk again. And it wasn't me—it wasn't any of us. Please, Mrs. Fox, we really wouldn't do such a thing."

Sybil's scissors slid a little.

"There," she said angrily, "look what you've made me do. Oh, well, it'll be all right, I suppose. Now, what's this about the doll?"

"She's sitting at the desk again."

Sybil went down and walked into the fitting room. The doll was sitting at the desk exactly as she had sat there before.

"You're very determined, aren't you?" said Sybil, speaking to the doll.

She picked her up unceremoniously and put her back on the sofa.

"That's your place, my girl," she said. "You stay there."

She walked across to the other room.

"Miss Coombe."

"Yes, Sybil?"

"Somebody is having a game with us, you know. That doll was sitting at the desk again."

"Who do you think it is?"

"It must be one of those three upstairs," said Sybil. "Thinks it's funny, I suppose. Of course they all swear to high heaven it wasn't them."

"Who do you think it is—Margaret?"

"No, I don't think it's Margaret. She looked quite queer when she came in and told me. I expect it's that giggling Marlene."

"Anyway, it's a very silly thing to do."

"Of course it is—idiotic," said Sybil. "However," she added grimly, "I'm going to put a stop to it."

"What are you going to do?"

"You'll see," said Sybil.

That night when she left, she locked the fitting-room door from the outside.

"I'm locking this door," she said, "and I'm taking the key with me."

"Oh, I see," said Alicia Coombe, with a faint air of amusement. "You're beginning to think it's me, are you? You think I'm so absent-minded that I go in there and think I'll write at the desk, but instead I pick the doll up and put her there to write for me. Is that the idea? And then I forget all about it?"

"Well, it's a possibility," Sybil admitted. "Anyway, I'm going to be quite sure that no silly practical joke is played tonight."

The following morning, her lips set grimly, the first thing Sybil did on arrival was to unlock the door of the fitting room and march in. Mrs. Groves, with an aggrieved expression and mop and duster in hand, had been waiting on the landing.

"*Now* we'll see!" said Sybil.

Then she drew back with a slight gasp.

The doll was sitting at the desk.

"Coo!" said Mrs. Groves behind her. "It's uncanny! That's what it is. Oh, there, Mrs. Fox, you look quite pale, as though you've come over queer. You need a little drop of something. Has Miss Coombe got a drop upstairs, do you know?"

"I'm quite all right," said Sybil.

She walked over to the doll, lifted her carefully, and crossed the room with her.

"Somebody's been playing a trick on you again," said Mrs. Groves.

"I don't see how they could have played a trick on me this time," said Sybil slowly. "I locked that door last night. You know yourself that no one could get in."

"Somebody's got another key, maybe," said Mrs. Groves, helpfully.

"I don't think so," said Sybil. "We've never bothered to lock this door before. It's one of those old-fashioned keys and there's only one of them."

"Perhaps the other key fits it—the one to the door opposite."

In due course they tried all the keys in the shop, but none fitted the door of the fitting room.

"It *is* odd, Miss Coombe," said Sybil later, as they were having lunch together.

Alicia Coombe was looking rather pleased.

"My dear," she said. "I think it's simply extraordinary. I think we ought to write to the psychical research people about it. You know, they might send an investigator—a medium or someone—to see if there's anything peculiar about the room."

"You don't seem to mind at all," said Sybil.

"Well, I rather enjoy it in a way," said Alicia Coombe. "I mean, at my age, it's rather fun when things happen! All the same—no," she added thoughtfully, "I don't think I do quite like it. I mean, that doll's getting rather above herself, isn't she?"

On that evening Sybil and Alicia Coombe locked the door once more on the outside.

"I still think," said Sybil, "that somebody might be playing a practical joke, though really, I don't see why. . . ."

"Do you think she'll be at the desk again tomorrow morning?" demanded Alicia.

"Yes," said Sybil, "I do."

But they were wrong. The doll was not at the desk. Instead, she was on the window sill, looking out into the street. And again there was an extraordinary naturalness about her position.

"It's all frightfully silly, isn't it?" said Alicia Coombe, as they were snatching a quick cup of tea that afternoon. By common consent they were not having it in the fitting room, as they usually did, but in Alicia Coombe's own room opposite.

"Silly in what way?"

"Well, I mean, there's nothing you can get hold of. Just a doll that's always in a different place."

As day followed day it seemed a more and more apt observation. It was not only at night that the doll now moved. At any moment when they came into the fitting room, after they had been absent even a few minutes, they might find the doll in a different place. They could have left her on the sofa and find her on a chair. Then she'd be on a different chair. Sometimes she'd be in the window seat, sometimes at the desk again.

"She just moves about as she likes," said Alicia Coombe. "And I think, Sybil, I *think* it's amusing her."

The two women stood looking down at the inert sprawling figure in its limp, soft velvet, with its painted silk face.

"Some old bits of velvet and silk and a lick of paint, that's all it is," said Alicia Coombe. Her voice was strained. "I suppose, you know, we could—er—we could dispose of her."

"What do you mean, dispose of her?" asked Sybil. Her voice sounded almost shocked.

"Well," said Alicia Coombe, "we could put her in the fire, if there was a fire. Burn her, I mean, like a witch. . . . Or of course," she added matter-of-factly, "we could just put her in the dustbin."

"I don't think that would do," said Sybil. "Somebody would probably take her out of the dustbin and bring her back to us."

"Or we could send her somewhere," said Alicia Coombe. "You know, to one of those societies who are always writing and asking for something—for a sale or a bazaar. I think that's the best idea."

"I don't know . . ." said Sybil. "I'd be almost afraid to do that."

"Afraid?"

"Well, I think she'd come back," said Sybil.

"You mean, she'd come back *here?*"

"Yes."

"Like a homing pigeon?"

"Yes, that's what I mean."

"I suppose we're not going off our heads, are we?" said Alicia Coombe.

"Perhaps I've really gone gaga and perhaps you're just humoring me, is that it?"

"No," said Sybil. "But I've got a nasty frightened feeling—a horrid feeling that she's too strong for us."

"What? That mess of rags?"

"Yes, that horrible limp mess of rags. Because, you see, she's so determined."

"Determined?"

"To have her own way. This is *her* room now!"

"Yes," said Alicia Coombe, looking round, "it is, isn't it? Of course, it always was, when you come to think of it—the colors and everything . . . I thought she fitted in here, but it's the room that fits her. I must say," added the dressmaker, with a touch of briskness in her voice, "it's rather absurd when a doll comes and takes possession of things like this. You know, Mrs. Groves won't come in here any longer and clean."

"Does she say she's frightened of the doll?"

"No. She just makes excuses of some kind or other." Then Alicia added with a hint of panic, "What are we going to do, Sybil? It's getting me down, you know. I haven't been able to design anything for weeks."

"I can't keep my mind on cutting out properly," Sybil confessed. "I make all sorts of silly mistakes. Perhaps," she said uncertainly, "your idea of writing to the psychical research people might do some good."

"Just make us look like a couple of fools," said Alicia Coombe. "I didn't seriously mean it. No, I suppose we'll just have to go on until—"

"Until what?"

"Oh, I don't know," said Alicia, and she laughed uncertainly.

On the following day Sybil, when she arrived, found the door of the fitting room locked.

"Miss Coombe, have you got the key? Did you lock this last night?"

"Yes," said Alicia Coombe, "I locked it and it's going to stay locked."

"What do you mean?"

"I just mean I've given up the room. The doll can have it. We don't need two rooms. We can fit in here."

"But it's your own private sitting room."

"Well, I don't want it any more. I've got a very nice bedroom. I can make a bed-sitting room out of that, can't I?"

"Do you mean you're really not going into that fitting room ever again?" said Sybil incredulously.

"That's exactly what I mean."

"But—what about cleaning? It'll get in a terrible state."

"Let it!" said Alicia Coombe. "If this place is suffering from some kind of possession by a doll, all right—let her keep possession. And clean the room herself." And she added, "She hates us, you know."

"What do you mean?" said Sybil. "The doll *hates* us?"

"Yes," said Alicia. "Didn't you know? You must have known. You must have seen it when you looked at her."

"Yes," said Sybil thoughtfully, "I suppose I did. I suppose I felt like that all along—that she hated us and wanted to get us out of there."

"She's a malicious little thing," said Alicia Coombe. "Anyway, she ought to be satisfied now."

Things went on rather more peacefully after that. Alicia Coombe announced to her staff that she was giving up the use of the fitting room for the present—it made too many rooms to dust and clean, she explained.

But it hardly helped her to overhear one of the work girls saying to another on the evening of the same day, "She really is batty, Miss Coombe is now. I always thought she was a bit queer—the way she lost things and forgot things. But it's really beyond anything now, isn't it? She's got a sort of thing about that doll downstairs."

"Ooo, you don't think she'll go really bats, do you?" said the other girl. "That she might knife us or something?"

They passed, chattering, and Alicia sat up indignantly in her chair. Going bats indeed! Then she added ruefully, to herself, "I suppose, if it wasn't for Sybil, I should think myself that I was going bats. But with me and Sybil and Mrs. Groves too, well, it does look as though there was *something* in it. But what I don't see is, how is it going to end?"

Three weeks later, Sybil said to Alicia Coombe, "We've got to go into that room *sometime*."

"Why?"

"Well, I mean, it must be in a filthy state. Moths will be getting into things, and all that. We ought just to dust and sweep it and then lock it up again."

"I'd much rather keep it shut up and not go back in there," said Alicia Coombe.

Sybil said, "Really, you know, you're even more superstitious than I am."

"I suppose I am," said Alicia Coombe. "I was much more ready to believe in all this than you were, but to begin with, you know—I—well, I found it exciting in an odd sort of way. I don't know. I'm just scared, and I'd rather not go into that room again."

"Well, I want to," said Sybil, "and I'm going to."

"You know what's the matter with you?" said Alicia Coombe. "You're simply curious, that's all."

"All right, then I'm curious. I want to see what the doll's done."

"I still think it's much better to leave her alone," said Alicia. "Now we've got out of that room, she's satisfied. You'd better leave her satisfied." She gave an exasperated sigh. "What nonsense we are talking!"

"Yes, I know we're talking nonsense, but if you tell me of any way of *not* talking nonsense—come on, now, give me that key."

"All right, all right."

"I believe you're afraid I'll let her out or something. I should think she was the kind that could pass through doors or windows."

Sybil unlocked the door and went in.

"How terribly odd," she said.

"What's odd?" said Alicia Coombe, peering over her shoulder.

"The room hardly seems dusty at all, does it? You'd think, after being shut up all this time—"

"Yes, it is odd."

"There she is," said Sybil.

The doll was on the sofa. She was not lying in her usual limp position. She was sitting upright, a cushion behind her back. She had the air of the mistress of the house, waiting to receive people.

"Well," said Alicia Coombe, "she seems at home all right, doesn't she? I almost feel I ought to apologize for coming in."

"Let's go," said Sybil.

She backed out, pulled the door to, and locked it again.

The two women gazed at each other.

"I wish I knew," said Alicia Coombe, "why it scares us so much . . ."

"My goodness, who wouldn't be scared?"

"Well, I mean, what *happens*, after all? It's nothing really—just a kind of puppet that gets moved around the room. I expect it isn't the puppet itself—it's a poltergeist."

"Now that *is* a good idea."

"Yes, but I don't really believe it. I think it's—it's that doll."

"Are you *sure* you don't know where she really came from?"

"I haven't the faintest idea," said Alicia. "And the more I think of it the more I'm perfectly certain that I didn't buy her, and that nobody gave her to me. I think she—well, she just came."

"Do you think she'll—ever go?"

"Really," said Alicia, "I don't see why she should. . . . She's got all she wants."

But it seemed that the doll had not got all she wanted. The next day, when Sybil went into the showroom, she drew in her breath with a sudden gasp. Then she called up the stairs.

"Miss Coombe, Miss Coombe, come down here."

"What's the matter?"

Alicia Coombe, who had got up late, came down the stairs, hobbling a little precariously for she had rheumatism in her right knee.

"What is the matter with you, Sybil?"

"Look. Look what's happened now."

They stood in the doorway of the showroom. Sitting on a sofa, sprawled easily over the arm of it, was the doll.

"She's got out," said Sybil. "*She's got out of that room!* She wants this room as well."

Alicia Coombe sat down by the door. "In the end," she said, "I suppose she'll want the whole shop."

"She might," said Sybil.

"You nasty, sly, malicious brute," said Alicia, addressing the doll. "What do you want to come and pester us so? We don't want you."

It seemed to her, and to Sybil too, that the doll moved very slightly. It was as though its limbs relaxed still further. A long limp arm was lying on the arm of the sofa and the half-hidden face looked as if it were peering from under the arm. And it was a sly, malicious look.

"Horrible creature," said Alicia. "I can't bear it! I can't bear it any longer."

Suddenly, taking Sybil completely by surprise, she dashed across the room, picked up the doll, ran to the window, opened it, and flung the doll out into the street. There was a gasp and a half cry of fear from Sybil.

"Oh, Alicia, you shouldn't have done that! I'm sure you shouldn't have done that!"

"I had to do something," said Alicia Coombe. "I just couldn't stand it any more."

Sybil joined her at the window. Down below on the pavement the doll lay, loose-limbed, face down.

"You've *killed* her," said Sybil.

"Don't be absurd. . . . How can I kill something that's made of velvet and silk, bits and pieces. It's not real."

"It's horribly real," said Sybil.

Alicia caught her breath.

"Good heavens. That child—"

A small ragged girl was standing over the doll on the pavement. She looked up and down the street—a street that was not unduly crowded at this time of the morning though there was some automobile traffic; then, as though satisfied, the child bent, picked up the doll, and ran across the street.

"Stop, stop!" called Alicia.

She turned to Sybil.

"That child mustn't take the doll. She *mustn't!* That doll is dangerous—it's evil. We've got to stop her."

It was not they who stopped her. It was the traffic. At that moment three taxis came down one way and two tradesmen's vans in the other direction. The child was marooned on an island in the middle of the road. Sybil rushed down the stairs, Alicia Coombe following her. Dodging between a tradesman's van and a private car, Sybil, with Alicia Coombe directly behind her, arrived on the island before the child could get through the traffic on the opposite side.

"You can't take that doll," said Alicia Coombe. "Give her back to me."

The child looked at her. She was a skinny little girl about eight years old, with a slight squint. Her face was defiant.

"Why should I give 'er to you?" she said. "Pitched her out of the window, you did—I saw you. If you pushed her out of the window you don't want her, so now she's mine."

"I'll buy you another doll," said Alicia frantically. "We'll go to a toy shop—anywhere you like—and I'll buy you the best doll we can find. But give me back this one."

"Shan't," said the child.

Her arms went protectingly round the velvet doll.

"You *must* give her back," said Sybil. "She isn't yours."

She stretched out to take the doll from the child and at that moment the child stamped her foot, turned, and screamed at them.

"Shan't! Shan't! Shan't! She's my very own. I love her. *You* don't love her. You hate her. If you didn't hate her you wouldn't of pushed her out of the window. I love her, I tell you, and that's what she wants. She *wants* to be loved."

And then like an eel, sliding through the vehicles, the child ran across the street, down an alleyway, and out of sight before the two older women could decide to dodge the cars and follow.

"She's gone," said Alicia.

"She said the doll wanted to be loved," said Sybil.

"Perhaps," said Alicia, "perhaps that's what she wanted all along . . . to be loved. . . ."

In the middle of the London traffic the two frightened women stared at each other.

QUESTIONS

1. Describe how the effect of horror builds in this story. How does it compare to the horror effects in the previous stories?

2. Why do the women start to dislike the doll?

3. Does the doll in any way reflect the personalities of the women?

4. How would the story have been affected if the women were considerably younger?

5. In what sense is the story symbolic? Can the doll, for instance, be compared to a human who is deprived, disadvantaged? How does the doll's determination fit in? Why do the women think that the doll "hates" them and wants to take over the whole shop?

6. How convincing is the explanation that the doll wishes to be loved? Relate your answer to your discussion of question five.

7. Were you disappointed that the author did not supply a rational explanation of the mystery? Or was the suggested solution in its own way "rational"?

part 2
The Detective

A crime has been committed. The detective is called in. He is the specialist, the expert in the field, the man who can read clues and find solutions. Grudgingly, we give him our trust. We follow his activities, trying to outguess him, testing our acumen against his. The very nature of the detective story assures us there will be answers—that, in fact, the answers are here before us, if only we knew where, or more importantly how, to look properly. We are asked to present hypotheses, draw analogies, assume that this is a causal universe. At the end of the story the solution is explained to us. We nod our heads, seldom angry at having been baffled. In a way our experience is like having been at the horse races. We almost bet on the horse that won; the notion slipped through our minds. The next time we will arrive at the solution before the detective. We will win.

Ratiocination, Inspector C. Auguste Dupin calls it. The grand solution, appearing almost miraculous, is the end result of the use of our powers of observation and of reason. We are humbled to find that in the seemingly insignificant may lie the entire answer. The purloined letter could have been spotted immediately. It is a measure of the story-teller's art that he has led us both toward and away from the truth. How do we learn to read life, experience, accurately? What scars tell? Are someone's eyes, his way of holding his body, the callouses on his hands the real indicators of his deepest character?

In this section, Edgar Allan Poe, A. Conan Doyle, and G. K. Chesterton lead their readers through confusing clues toward solutions to what have seemed unfathomable crimes. The solution to Doyle's story hinges on words of horror. G. K. Chesterton, in "The Blue Cross," asks us to observe everything. The reader becomes the actual detective in Jacques Futrelle's "The Problem of Cell 13." How were the messages written? How could a man escape from such a cell? Would it truly take a "Thinking Machine" or could we have figured it out for ourselves?

The detection elements are strong, also, in the stories by Dashiell Hammett and Raymond Chandler. Yet the timbre, the tone, the writing style of the stories has changed. Hammett and Chandler are members of what has been called "The Black Mask" or "hard-boiled" school of American detective-story writing. Unlike the British school of detective and mystery writing, this school enrolled detectives who were barely, themselves, out of the lower classes of society. Their *environment was not one of teacups and mansions, drawing rooms and white-skinned ladies. Rather, it was the environment of the docks, the slums, the rough, crude world of crime itself. The influences on their style were those of realism and naturalism. The detective himself—most often the shamus, or private-eye—can be corrupted in some ways. More important, he can sympathize with or at least understand the victims and the criminals with whom he was thrown in contact. These detectives are in the world, as grubby as the things they touch, real heroes with dirty hands. They seek, they solve, but they never rise completely above their element. They are not metaphysicians. They achieve workable compromises, retain their most essential idealism while discarding idealistic thoughts that are obviously not applicable to the society in which they move.*

Ross Macdonald is the leading contemporary practitioner of the hard-boiled school of detective writing. His Lew Archer is as rumpled, as disillusioned as any. Archer finds always causes rooted deeply in the past, in an area of secrets, mistaken ancestry, crimes for which no payment has yet been made. Macdonald's work might be called curiously Puritanical. One might live a lie for ten or fifteen years, but sooner or later he will be discovered; he will pay. In the meantime, his suffering will be enormous. The crime committed in the past will have informed his entire life.

If it isn't Lew Archer in pursuit, it might be George Simenon's Inspector Maigret. There is no ultimate escape. Inspector Maigret is relentless. What he is really seeking is not so much the criminal as an understanding of him. Perhaps Inspector Maigret ultimately always pursues Inspector Maigret.

"The Cold Winds of Adesta" places us in a setting of international intrigue. This time a repressive government is involved, making a muck of easy morality, causing us to question the motives of men who live without a belief in justice, without hope for the future—men who seem capable only of pity.

Finally, Mark Twain's "The Stolen White Elephant" pokes fun at the whole detective story genre. If there are clues everywhere, if the truth is smack in front of our faces, what fools we are to be caught up by false leads; how ridiculous the convention of the detective story can seem to some.

from The Murders in the Rue Morgue

Edgar Allan Poe

What song the Syrens sang, or what name Achilles assumed when he hid himself among women, although puzzling questions, are not beyond all conjecture.

Sir Thomas Browne

The mental features discoursed of as the analytical, are, in themselves, but little susceptible of analysis. We appreciate them only in their effects. We know of them, among other things, that they are always to their possessor, when inordinately possessed, a source of the liveliest enjoyment. As the strong man exults in his physical ability, delighting in such exercises as call his muscles into action, so glories the analyst in that moral activity which *disentangles*. He derives pleasure from even the most trivial occupations bringing his talent into play. He is fond of enigmas, of conundrums, hieroglyphics; exhibiting in his solutions of each a degree of *acumen* which appears to the ordinary apprehension præternatural. His results, brought about by the very soul and essence of method, have, in truth, the whole air of intuition.

The faculty of re-solution is possibly much invigorated by mathematical study, and especially by that highest branch of it which, unjustly, and merely on account of its retrograde operations, has been called, as if *par excellence*, analysis. Yet to calculate is not in itself to analyze. A chess-player, for example, does the one, without effort at the other. It follows that the game of chess, in its effects upon mental character, is greatly misunderstood. I am not now writing a treatise, but simply prefacing a somewhat peculiar narrative by observations very much at random; I will, therefore, take occasion to assert that the higher powers of the reflective intellect are more decidedly and more usefully tasked by the unostentatious game of draughts than by all the elaborate frivolity of chess. In this latter, where the pieces have different and *bizarre* motions, with various and variable values, what is only complex, is mistaken (a not unusual error) for what is profound. The *attention* is here called powerfully into play. If it flag for an instant, an oversight is committed, resulting in injury or defeat. The possible moves being not only manifold, but involute, the chances of such oversights are multiplied; and in nine cases out of ten, it is the more concentrative rather than the more acute player who conquers. In draughts, on the contrary, where the moves are *unique* and have but little variation, the probabilities of inadvertence are diminished, and the mere attention being left comparatively unemployed, what advantages are obtained by either party are obtained by superior *acumen*. To be less abstract, let us suppose a game of draughts where the pieces are reduced to four kings, and where, of course, no oversight is to be expected. It is obvious that here the victory can be decided (the players being at all equal) only by some *recherché* movement, the result of some strong exertion of the intellect. Deprived of ordinary resources, the analyst throws himself into the spirit of his opponent, identifies himself therewith, and not unfrequently sees thus, at a glance, the sole methods (sometimes indeed absurdly simple ones) by which he may seduce into error or hurry into miscalculation.

Whist has long been known for its influence upon what is termed the calculating power; and men of the highest order of intellect have been known to take an apparently unaccountable delight in it, while eschewing chess as frivolous. Beyond doubt there is nothing of a similar nature so greatly tasking the faculty of analysis. The best chess-player in Christendom *may* be little more than the best player of chess; but proficiency in whist implies capacity for success in all these more important undertakings where mind struggles with mind. When I say proficiency, I mean that perfection in the game which includes a comprehension of *all* the sources whence legitimate advantage may be derived. These are not only manifold, but multiform, and lie frequently among recesses of thought altogether inaccessible to the ordinary understanding. To observe attentively is to remember distinctly; and, so far, the concentrative chess-player will do very well at whist; while the rules of Hoyle (themselves based upon the mere mechanism of the game) are sufficiently and generally comprehensible. Thus to have a retentive memory, and proceed by "the book" are points commonly regarded as the sum total of good playing. But it is in matters beyond the limits of mere rule that the skill of the analyst is evinced. He makes, in silence, a host of observations and inferences. So, perhaps, do his companions; and the difference in the extent of the information obtained, lies not so much in the validity of the inference as in the quality of the observation. The necessary knowledge is that of *what* to observe. Our player confines himself not at all; nor, because the game is the object, does he reject deductions from things external to the game. He examines the countenance of his partner, comparing it carefully with that of each of his opponents. He considers the mode of assorting the cards in each hand; often counting trump by trump, and honor by honor, through the glances bestowed by their holders upon each. He notes every variation of face as the play progresses, gathering a fund of thought from the differences in the expression of certainty, of surprise, of triumph, or chagrin. From the manner of gathering up a trick he judges whether the person taking it, can make another in the suit. He recognizes what is played through feint, by the manner with which it is thrown upon the table. A casual or inadvertent word; the accidental dropping or turning of a card, with the accompanying anxiety or carelessness in regard to its concealment; the counting of the tricks, with the order of their arrangement; embarrassment, hesitation, eagerness, or trepidation—all afford, to his apparently intuitive perception, indications of the true state of affairs. The first two or three rounds having been played, he is in full possession of the contents of each hand, and thenceforward puts down his cards with as absolute a precision of purpose as if the rest of the party had turned outward the faces of their own.

The analytical power should not be confounded with simple ingenuity; for while the analyst is necessarily ingenious, the ingenious man is often remarkably incapable of analysis. The constructive or combining power, by which ingenuity is usually manifested, and to which the phrenologists (I believe erroneously) have assigned a separate organ, supposing it a primitive faculty, has been so frequently seen in those whose intellect bordered otherwise upon idiocy, as to have attracted general observation among writers on morals. Between ingenuity and the analytic ability there exists a difference far greater, indeed, than that between the fancy and the imagination, but of a character very strictly analogous. It will be found, in fact, that the ingenious are always fanciful, and the *truly* imaginative never otherwise than analytic.

The narrative which follows will appear to the reader somewhat in the light of a commentary upon the propositions just advanced.

Residing in Paris during the spring and part of the summer of 18—, I there became acquainted with a Monsieur C. Auguste Dupin. This young gentleman was of an excellent, indeed of an illustrious family, but, by a variety of untoward events, had been reduced to such poverty that the energy of his character succumbed beneath it, and he ceased to bestir himself in the world, or to care for the retrieval of his fortunes. By courtesy of his creditors, there still remained in his possession a small remnant of his patrimony; and, upon the income arising from this, he managed, by means of a rigorous economy, to procure the necessities of life, without troubling himself about its superfluities. Books, indeed, were his sole luxuries, and in Paris these are easily obtained.

Our first meeting was at an obscure library in the Rue Montmartre, where the accident of our both being in search of the same very rare and very remarkable volume, brought us into closer communion. We saw each other again and again. I was deeply interested in the little family history which he detailed to me with all that candor which a Frenchman indulges whenever mere self is the theme. I was astonished, too, at the vast extent of his reading; and, above all, I felt my soul enkindled within me by the wild fervor, and the vivid freshness of his imagination. Seeking in Paris the objects I then sought, I felt that the society of such a man would be to me a treasure beyond price; and this feeling I frankly confided to him. It was at length arranged that we should live together during my stay in the city; and as my worldly circumstances were somewhat less embarrassed than his own, I was permitted to be at the expense of renting, and furnishing in a style which suited the rather fantastic gloom of our common temper, a time-eaten and grotesque mansion, long deserted through superstitions into which we did not inquire, and tottering to its fall in a retired and desolate portion of the Faubourg St. Germain.

Had the routine of our life at this place been known to the world, we should have been regarded as madmen—although, perhaps, as madmen of a harmless nature. Our seclusion was perfect. We admitted no visitors. Indeed the locality of our retirement had been carefully kept a secret from my own former associates; and it had been many years since Dupin had ceased to know or be known in Paris. We existed within ourselves alone.

It was a freak of fancy in my friend (for what else shall I call it?) to be enamored of the night for her own sake; and into this *bizarrerie*, as into all his others, I quietly fell; giving myself up to his wild whims with a perfect *abandon*. The sable divinity would not herself dwell with us always; but we could counterfeit her presence. At the first dawn of the morning we closed all the massy shutters of our old building; lighted a couple of tapers which, strongly perfumed, threw out only the ghastliest and feeblest of rays. By the aid of these we then busied our souls in dreams—reading, writing, or conversing, until warned by the clock of the advent of the true Darkness. Then we sallied forth into the streets, arm in arm, continuing the topics of the day, or roaming far and wide until a late hour, seeking, amid the wild lights and shadows of the populous city, that infinity of mental excitement which quiet observation can afford.

At such times I could not help remarking and admiring (although from his rich ideality I had been prepared to expect it) a peculiar analytic ability in Dupin. He seemed, too, to take an eager delight in its exercise—if not exactly in its display—and did not hesitate to confess the pleasure thus derived. He boasted to me, with a low chuckling laugh, that most men, in respect to himself, wore windows in their bosoms, and was wont to follow up such assertions by direct and very startling proofs of his intimate knowledge of my own. His manner at these moments was frigid and abstract; his eyes were vacant in expression; while his voice, usually a rich tenor, rose into a treble which would have sounded petulant but for the deliberateness and entire distinctness of the enunciation. Observing him in these moods, I often dwelt meditatively upon the old philosophy of the Bi-Part Soul, and amused myself with the fancy of a double Dupin—the creative and the resolvent.

Let it not be supposed, from what I have just said, that I am detailing any mystery, or penning any romance. What I have described in the Frenchman was merely the result of an excited, or perhaps of a diseased, intelligence. But of the character of his remarks at the periods in question an example will best convey the idea.

We were strolling one night down a long dirty street, in the vicinity of the Palais Royal. Being both, apparently, occupied with thought, neither of us had spoken a syllable for fifteen minutes at least. All at once Dupin broke forth with these words:

"He is a very little fellow, that's true, and would do better for the *Théâtre des Variétés*."

"There can be no doubt of that," I replied, unwittingly, and not at first observing (so much had I been absorbed in reflection) the extraordinary manner in which the speaker had chimed in with my meditations. In an instant afterward I recollected myself, and my astonishment was profound.

"Dupin," said I, gravely, "this is beyond my comprehension. I do not hesitate to say that I am amazed, and can scarcely credit my senses. How was it possible you should know I was thinking of—?" Here I paused, to ascertain beyond a doubt whether he really knew of whom I thought.

"—— of Chantilly," said he, "why do you pause? You were remarking to yourself that his diminutive figure unfitted him for tragedy."

This was precisely what had formed the subject of my reflections. Chantilly was a *quondam* cobbler of the Rue St. Denis, who, becoming stage-mad, had attempted the *rôle* of Xerxes, in Crébillon's tragedy so called, and been notoriously Pasquinaded for his pains.

"Tell me, for Heaven's sake," I exclaimed, "the method—if method there is—by which you have been enabled to fathom my soul in this matter." In fact, I was even more startled than I would have been willing to express.

"It was the fruiterer," replied my friend, "who brought you to the conclusion that the mender of soles was not of sufficient height for Xerxes *et id genus omne*."

"The fruiterer!—you astonish me—I know no fruiterer whomsoever."

"The man who ran up against you as we entered the street—it may have been fifteen minutes ago."

I now remembered that, in fact, a fruiterer, carrying upon his head a large basket of apples, had nearly thrown me down, by accident, as we passed from the Rue C—— into the thoroughfare where we stood; but what this had to do with Chantilly I could not possibly understand.

There was not a particle of *charlatânerie* about Dupin. "I will explain," he said, "and that you may comprehend all clearly, we will first retrace the course of your meditations, from the moment in which I spoke to you until that of the *rencontre* with the fruiterer in question. The larger links of the chain run thus—Chantilly, Orion, Dr. Nichols, Epicurus, Stereotomy, the street stones, the fruiterer."

There are few persons who have not, at some period of their lives amused themselves in retracing the steps by which particular conclusions of their own minds have been attained. The occupation is often full of interest; and he who attempts it for the first time is astonished by the apparently illimitable distance and incoherence between the starting-point and the goal. What, then, must have been my amazement, when I heard the Frenchman speak what he had just spoken, and when I could not help acknowledging that he had spoken the truth. He continued:

"We had been talking of horses, if I remember aright, just before leaving the Rue C——. This was the last subject we discussed. As we crossed into this street, a fruiterer, with a large basket upon his head, brushing quickly past us, thrust you upon a pile of paving-stones collected at a spot where the causeway is undergoing repair. You stepped upon one of the loose fragments, slipped, slightly strained your ankle, appeared vexed or sulky, muttered a few words, turned to look at the pile, and then proceeded in silence. I was not particularly attentive to what you did; but observation has become with me, of late, a species of necessity.

"You kept your eyes upon the ground—glancing, with a petulant expression, at the holes and ruts in the pavement (so that I saw you were still thinking of the stones), until we reached the little alley called Lamartine, which has been paved, by way of experiment, with the overlapping and riveted blocks. Here your countenance brightened up, and, perceiving your lips move, I could not doubt that you murmured the word 'stereotomy,' a term very affectedly applied to this species of pavement. I knew that you could not say to yourself 'stereotomy' without being brought to think of atomies, and thus of the theories of Epicurus; and since, when we discussed this subject not very long ago, I mentioned to you how singularly, yet with how little notice, the vague guesses of that noble Greek had met with confirmation in the late nebular cosmogony, I felt that you could not avoid casting your eyes upward to the great *nebula* in Orion, and I certainly expected that you would do so. You did look up; and I was now assured that I had correctly followed your steps. But in that bitter *tirade* upon Chantilly, which appeared in yesterday's '*Musée*,' the satirist, making some disgraceful allusions to the cobbler's change of name upon assuming the buskin, quoted a Latin line about which we have often conversed. I mean the line

Perdidit antiquum litera prima sonum.

I had told you that this was in reference to Orion, formerly written Urion; and, from certain pungencies connected with this explanation, I was aware that you could not have forgotten it. It was clear, therefore, that you would not fail to combine the two ideas of Orion and Chantilly. That you did combine them I saw by the character of the smile which passed over your lips. You thought of the poor cobbler's immolation. So far, you had been stooping in your gait; but now I saw you draw yourself up to your full height. I was then sure that you reflected upon the diminutive figure of Chantilly. At this point I interrupted your meditations to remark that as, in fact, he *was* a very little fellow—that Chantilly—he would do better at the *Théâtre des Variétés*."

QUESTIONS

1. Poe advances a number of propositions about the reasoning process. Discuss these, especially in light of literary genres other than the detective story. Is the detective story itself a kind of game?

2. The basic characteristics of many detectives were first established by Poe's portrayal of Monsieur C. Auguste Dupin. Why, do you think, does Dupin so love the darkness? Why are so many detectives—compare Sherlock Holmes—given eccentric characteristics?

3. Discuss point of view in "The Murders in the Rue Morgue" and "The Purloined Letter." Are there any significant differences from point of view in "The Adventure of the Speckled Band"?

4. Are you convinced by Dupin's explanation of how he accomplished what first appeared to be mind-reading? How might this explanation also explain many instances of what seems to be telepathy?

5. What about the tone of this section from "The Murders in the Rue Morgue"? Is it supercilious? Do you resent the lecturing aspect, the self-assurance of Dupin?

The Purloined Letter

Edgar Allan Poe

Nil sapientiae odiosius acumine nimio.

[Nothing is more odious to good sense than too much cleverness.]
Seneca

At Paris, just after dark one gusty evening in the autumn of 18——, I was enjoying the twofold luxury of meditation and a meerschaum, in company with my friend C. Auguste Dupin, in his little back library, or book-closet, *au troisième, No. 33, Rue Dunôt, Faubourg St. Germain.* For one hour at least we had maintained a profound silence; while each, to any casual observer, might have seemed intently and exclusively occupied with the curling eddies of smoke that oppressed the atmosphere of the chamber. For myself, however, I was mentally discussing certain topics which had formed matter for conversation between us at an earlier period of the evening; I mean the affair of the Rue Morgue, and the mystery attending the murder of Marie Rogêt. I looked upon it, therefore, as something of a coincidence, when the door of our apartment was thrown open and admitted our old acquaintance, Monsieur G——, the Prefect of the Parisian police.

We gave him a hearty welcome; for there was nearly half as much of the entertaining as of the contemptible about the man, and we had not seen him for several years. We had been sitting in the dark, and Dupin now arose for the purpose of lighting a lamp, but sat down again, without doing so, upon G——'s saying that he had called to consult us, or rather to ask the opinion of my friend, about some official business which had occasioned a great deal of trouble.

"If it is any point requiring reflection," observed Dupin, as he forebore to enkindle the wick, "we shall examine it to better purpose in the dark."

"That is another of your odd notions," said the Prefect, who had a fashion of calling every thing "odd" that was beyond his comprehension, and thus lived amid an absolute legion of "oddities."

"Very true," said Dupin, as he supplied his visitor with a pipe, and rolled towards him a comfortable chair.

"And what is the difficulty now?" I asked. "Nothing more in the assassination way, I hope?"

"Oh no; nothing of that nature. The fact is, the business is *very* simple indeed, and I make no doubt that we can manage it sufficiently well ourselves; but then I thought Dupin would like to hear the details of it, because it is so excessively *odd.*"

"Simple and odd," said Dupin.

"Why, yes; and not exactly that, either. The fact is, we have all been a good deal puzzled because the affair *is* so simple, and yet baffles us altogether."

"Perhaps it is the very simplicity of the thing which puts you at fault," said my friend.

"What nonsense you *do* talk!" replied the Prefect, laughing heartily.

"Perhaps the mystery is a little *too* plain," said Dupin.

"Oh, good heavens! who ever heard of such an idea?"

"A little *too* self-evident."

"Ha! ha! ha!—ha! ha! ha!—ho! ho! ho!"—roared our visitor, profoundly amused, "oh, Dupin, you will be the death of me yet!"

"And what, after all, *is* the matter on hand?" I asked.

"Why, I will tell you," replied the Prefect, as he gave a long, steady, and contemplative puff, and settled himself in his chair. "I will tell you in a few words; but, before I begin, let me caution you that this is an affair demanding the greatest secrecy, and that I should most probably lose the position I now hold, were it known that I confided it to any one."

"Proceed," said I.

"Or not," said Dupin.

"Well, then; I have received personal information, from a very high quarter, that a certain document of the last importance has been purloined from the royal apartments. The individual who purloined it is known; this beyond a doubt; he was seen to take it. It is known, also, that it still remains in his possession."

"How is this known?" asked Dupin.

"It is clearly inferred," replied the Prefect, "from the nature of the document, and from the non-appearance of certain results which would at once arise from its passing *out* of the robber's possession;—that is to say, from his employing it as he must design in the end to employ it."

"Be a little more explicit," I said.

"Well, I may venture so far as to say that the paper gives its holder a certain power in a certain quarter where such power is immensely valuable." The Prefect was fond of the cant of diplomacy.

"Still I do not quite understand," said Dupin.

"No? Well; the disclosure of the document to a third person who shall be nameless would bring in question the honor of a personage of most exalted station; and this fact gives the holder of the document an ascendancy over the illustrious personage whose honor and peace are so jeopardized."

"But this ascendancy," I interposed, "would depend upon the robber's knowledge of the loser's knowledge of the robber. Who would dare—"

"The thief," said G——, "is the Minister D——, who dares all things, those unbecoming as well as those becoming a man. The method of the theft was not less ingenious than bold. The document in question—a letter, to be frank—had been received by the personage robbed while alone in the royal *boudoir*. During its perusal she was suddenly interrupted by the entrance of the other exalted personage from whom especially it was her wish to conceal it. After a hurried and vain endeavor to thrust it in a drawer, she was forced to place it, open as it was, upon a table. The address, however, was uppermost, and, the contents thus unexposed, the letter escaped notice. At this juncture enters the Minister D——. His lynx eye immediately perceives the paper, recognizes the handwriting of the address, observes the confusion of the personage addressed, and fathoms her secret. After some business transactions, hurried through in his ordinary manner, he produces a letter somewhat similar to the one in question, opens it, pretends to read it, and then places it in close juxtaposition to the other. Again he converses, for some fifteen minutes, upon the public affairs. At length, in taking leave, he takes also from the table the letter to which he had no claim. Its rightful owner saw, but, of course, dared not call attention to the act, in the presence of the third personage who stood at her elbow. The Minister decamped; leaving his own letter—one of no importance—upon the table."

"Here, then," said Dupin to me, "you have precisely what you demand to make the ascendancy complete—the robber's knowledge of the loser's knowledge of the robber."

"Yes," replied the Prefect; "and the power thus attained has, for some months past, been wielded, for political purposes, to a very dangerous extent. The personage robbed is more thoroughly convinced, every day, of the necessity of reclaiming her letter. But this, of course, cannot be done openly. In fine, driven to despair, she has committed the matter to me."

"Than whom," said Dupin, amid a perfect whirlwind of smoke, "no more sagacious agent could, I suppose, be desired, or even imagined."

"You flatter me," replied the Prefect; "but it is possible that some such opinion may have been entertained."

"It is clear," said I, "as you observe, that the letter is still in possession of the Minister; since it is this possession, and not any employment of the letter, which bestows the power. With the employment the power departs."

"True," said G——; "and upon this conviction I proceeded. My first care was to make thorough search of the Minister's hotel; and here my chief embarrassment lay in the necessity of searching without his knowledge. Beyond all things, I have been warned of the danger which would result from giving him reason to suspect our design."

"But," said I, "you are quite *au fait* in these investigations. The Parisian police have done this thing often before."

"Oh yes; and for this reason I did not despair. The habits of the

Minister gave me, too, a great advantage. He is frequently absent from home all night. His servants are by no means numerous. They sleep at a distance from their master's apartment, and, being chiefly Neapolitans, are readily made drunk. I have keys, as you know, with which I can open any chamber or cabinet in Paris. For three months a night has not passed, during the greater part of which I have not been engaged, personally, in ransacking the D—— Hôtel. My honor is interested, and, to mention a great secret, the reward is enormous. So I did not abandon the search until I had become fully satisfied that the thief is a more astute man than myself. I fancy that I have investigated every nook and corner of the premises in which it is possible that the paper can be concealed."

"But is it not possible," I suggested, "that although the letter may be in the possession of the Minister, as it unquestionably is, he may have concealed it elsewhere than upon his own premises?"

"This is barely possible," said Dupin. "The present peculiar condition of affairs at court, and especially of those intrigues in which D—— is known to be involved, would render the instant availability of the document—its susceptibility of being produced at a moment's notice—a point of nearly equal importance with its possession."

"Its susceptibility of being produced?" said I.

"That is to say, of being *destroyed*," said Dupin.

"True," I observed; "the paper is clearly then upon the premises. As for its being upon the person of the Minister, we may consider that as out of the question."

"Entirely," said the Prefect. "He has been twice waylaid, as if by footpads, and his person rigorously searched under my own inspection."

"You might have spared yourself this trouble," said Dupin. "D——, I presume, is not altogether a fool, and, if not, must have anticipated these waylayings, as a matter of course."

"Not *altogether* a fool," said G——, "but then he's a poet, which I take to be only one remove from a fool."

"True," said Dupin, after a long and thoughtful whiff from his meerschaum, "although I have been guilty of certain doggerel myself."

"Suppose you detail," said I, "the particulars of your search."

"Why the fact is, we took our time, and we searched *every where*. I have had long experience in these affairs. I took the entire building, room by room; devoting the nights of a whole week to each. We examined, first, the furniture of each apartment. We opened every possible drawer; and I presume you know that, to a properly trained police agent, such a thing as a *secret* drawer is impossible. Any man is a dolt who permits a 'secret' drawer to escape him in a search of this kind. The thing is *so* plain. There is a certain amount of bulk—a space—to be accounted for in every cabinet. Then we have accurate rules. The fiftieth part of a line could not escape us. After the cabinets we took the chairs. The cushions we probed with the fine long needles you have seen me employ. From the tables we removed the tops."

"Why so?"

"Sometimes the top of a table, or other similarly arranged piece of furniture, is removed by the person wishing to conceal an article; then the leg is excavated, the article deposited within the cavity, and the top replaced. The bottoms and tops of bed-posts are employed in the same way."

"But could not the cavity be detected by sounding?" I asked.

"By no means, if, when the article is deposited, a sufficient wadding of cotton be placed around it. Besides, in our case, we were obliged to proceed without noise."

"But you could not have removed—you could not have taken to pieces *all* articles of furniture in which it would have been possible to make a deposit in the manner you mention. A letter may be compressed into a thin spiral roll, not differing much in shape or bulk from a large knitting-needle, and in this form it might be inserted into the rung of a chair, for example. You did not take to pieces all the chairs?"

"Certainly not; but we did better—we examined the rungs of every chair in the hotel, and, indeed, the jointings of every description of furniture, by the aid of a most powerful microscope. Had there been any traces of recent disturbance we should not have failed to detect it instantly. A single grain of gimlet-dust, for example, would have been as obvious as an apple. Any disorder in the glueing—any unusual gaping in the joints—would have sufficed to insure detection."

"I presume you looked to the mirrors, between the boards and the plates, and you probed the beds and the bed-clothes, as well as the curtains and carpets."

"That of course; and when we had absolutely completed every particle of the furniture in this way, then we examined the house itself. We divided its entire surface into compartments, which we numbered, so that none might be missed; then we scrutinized each individual square inch throughout the premises, including the two houses immediately adjoining, with the microscope, as before."

"The two houses adjoining!" I exclaimed; "you must have had a great deal of trouble."

"We had; but the reward offered is prodigious."

"You include the *grounds* about the houses?"

"All the grounds are paved with brick. They gave us comparatively little trouble. We examined the moss between the bricks, and found it undisturbed."

"You looked among D——'s papers, of course, and into the books of the library?"

"Certainly; we opened every package and parcel; we not only opened every book, but we turned over every leaf in each volume, not contenting ourselves with a mere shake, according to the fashion of some of our police officers. We also measured the thickness of every book-*cover*, with the most accurate admeasurement, and applied to each the most jealous scrutiny of the microscope. Had any of the bindings been recently meddled with, it would have been utterly impossible that the fact should have escaped observation. Some five or six volumes, just from the hands of the binder, we carefully probed, longitudinally, with the needles."

"You explored the floors beneath the carpets?"

"Beyond doubt. We removed every carpet, and examined the boards with the microscope."

"And the paper on the walls?"

"Yes."

"You looked into the cellars?"

"We did."

"Then," I said, "you have been making a miscalculation, and the letter is *not* upon the premises, as you suppose."

"I fear you are right there," said the Prefect. "And now, Dupin, what would you advise me to do?"

"To make a thorough re-search of the premises."

"That is absolutely needless," replied G——. "I am not more sure that I breathe than I am that the letter is not at the Hôtel."

"I have no better advice to give you," said Dupin. "You have, of course, an accurate description of the letter?"

"Oh yes!"—And here the Prefect, producing a memorandum-book, proceeded to read aloud a minute account of the internal, and especially of the external appearance of the missing document. Soon after finishing the perusal of this description, he took his departure, more entirely depressed in spirits than I had ever known the good gentleman before.

In about a month afterwards he paid us another visit, and found us occupied very nearly as before. He took a pipe and a chair and entered into some ordinary conversation. At length I said,—

"Well, but G——, what of the purloined letter? I presume you have at last made up your mind that there is no such thing as overreaching the Minister?"

"Confound him, say I—yes; I made the re-examination, however, as Dupin suggested—but it was all labor lost, as I knew it would be."

"How much was the reward offered, did you say?" asked Dupin.

"Why, a very great deal—a *very* liberal reward—I don't like to say how much, precisely; but one thing I *will* say, that I wouldn't mind giving my individual check for fifty thousand francs to any one who could obtain me that letter. The fact is, it is becoming of more and more importance every day; and the reward has been lately doubled. If it were trebled, however, I could do no more than I have done."

"Why, yes," said Dupin, drawlingly, between the whiffs of his meerschaum, "I really—think, G——, you have not exerted yourself—to the utmost in this matter. You might—do a little more, I think, eh?"

"How?—in what way?"

"Why—puff, puff—you might—puff, puff—employ counsel in the matter, eh?—puff, puff, puff. Do you remember the story they tell of Abernethy?"

"No; hang Abernethy!"

"To be sure! hang him and welcome. But, once upon a time, a certain rich miser conceived the design of sponging upon this Abernethy for a medical opinion. Getting up, for this purpose, an ordinary conversation in a private company, he insinuated his case to his physician, as that of an imaginary individual.

" 'We will suppose,' said the miser, 'that his symptoms are such and such; now, doctor, what would *you* have directed him to take?' "

" 'Take!' said Abernethy, 'why, take *advice*, to be sure.' "

"But," said the Prefect, a little discomposed, "*I am perfectly* willing to take advice, and to pay for it. I would *really* give fifty thousand francs to any one who would aid me in the matter."

"In that case," replied Dupin, opening a drawer, and producing a check-book, "you may as well fill me up a check for the amount mentioned. When you have signed it, I will hand you the letter."

I was astounded. The Prefect appeared absolutely thunder-stricken. For some minutes he remained speechless and motionless, looking incredulously at my friend with open mouth, and eyes that seemed starting from their sockets; then, apparently recovering himself in some measure, he seized a pen, and after several pauses and vacant stares, finally filled up and signed a check for fifty thousand francs, and handed it across the table to Dupin. The latter examined it carefully and deposited it in his pocket-book; then, unlocking an *escritoire*, took thence a letter and gave it to the Prefect. This functionary grasped it in a perfect agony of joy, opened it with a trembling hand, cast a rapid glance at its contents, and then, scrambling and struggling to the door, rushed at length unceremoniously from the room and from the house, without having uttered a syllable since Dupin had requested him to fill up the check.

When he had gone, my friend entered into some explanations.

"The Parisian police," he said, "are exceedingly able in their way. They are persevering, ingenious, cunning, and thoroughly versed in the knowledge which their duties seem chiefly to demand. Thus, when G—— detailed to us his mode of searching the premises at the Hôtel D——, I felt entire confidence in his having made a satisfactory investigation—so far as his labors extended."

"So far as his labors extended?" said I.

"Yes," said Dupin. "The measures adopted were not only the best of their kind, but carried out to absolute perfection. Had the letter been deposited within the range of their search, these fellows would, beyond a question, have found it."

I merely laughed—but he seemed quite serious in all that he said.

"The measures, then," he continued, "were good in their kind, and well executed; their defect lay in their being inapplicable to the case, and to the man. A certain set of highly ingenious resources are, with the Prefect, a sort of Procrustean bed, to which he forcibly adapts his designs. But he perpetually errs by being too deep or too shallow, for the matter in hand; and many a schoolboy is a better reasoner than he. I knew one about eight years of age, whose success at guessing in the game of 'even and odd' attracted universal admiration. This game is simple, and is played with marbles. One player holds in his hand a number of these toys, and demands of another whether that number is even or odd. If the guess is right, the guesser wins one; if wrong, he loses one. The boy to whom I allude won all the marbles of the school. Of course he had some principle of guessing; and this lay in mere observation and admeasurement of the astuteness of his opponents. For example, an arrant simpleton is his opponent, and, holding up his closed hand, asks, 'are they even or odd?' Our schoolboy replies, 'odd,' and loses; but upon the second trial he wins, for he then says to himself, 'the simpleton had them even upon the first trial, and his amount of cunning is just sufficient to make him have them odd upon the second; I will therefore guess odd';—he guesses odd, and wins. Now, with a simpleton a degree above the first, he would have reasoned thus: 'This fellow finds that in the first instance I guessed odd, and, in the second, he will propose to himself upon the first impulse, a simple variation from even to odd, as did the first simpleton; but then a second thought will suggest that this is too simple a variation, and finally he will decide upon putting it even as before. I will therefore guess even';—he guesses even, and wins. Now this mode of reasoning in the schoolboy, whom his fellows termed 'lucky,'— what, in its last analysis, is it?"

"It is merely," I said, "an identification of the reasoner's intellect with that of his opponent."

"It is," said Dupin; "and, upon inquiring of the boy by what means he effected the *thorough* identification in which his success consisted, I received answer as follows: 'When I wish to find out how wise, or how stupid, or how good, or how wicked is any one, or what are his thoughts at the moment, I fashion the expression of my face, as accurately as possible, in accordance with the expression of his, and then wait to see what thoughts or sentiments arise in my mind or heart, as if to match or correspond with the expression.' This response of the schoolboy lies at the bottom of all the spurious profundity which has been attributed to Rochefoucauld, to La Bougive, to Machiavelli, and to Campanella."

"And the identification," I said, "of the reasoner's intellect with that of his opponent, depends, if I understand you aright, upon the accuracy with which the opponent's intellect is admeasured."

"For its practical value it depends upon this," replied Dupin; "and the Prefect and his cohort fail so frequently, first, by default of this identification, and, secondly, by ill-admeasurement, or rather through non-admeasurement of the intellect with which they are engaged. They consider only their *own* ideas of ingenuity; and, in searching for anything hidden, advert only to the modes in which *they* would have hidden it. They are right in this much—that their own ingenuity is a faithful representative of that of *the mass*; but when the cunning of the individual felon is diverse in character from their own, the felon foils them, of course. This always happens when it is above their own, and very usually when it is below. They have no variation of principle in their investigations; at best, when urged by some unusual emergency—by some extraordinary reward—they extend or exaggerate their old modes of *practice*, without touching their principles. What, for example, in this case of D——, has been done to vary the principle of action? What is all this boring, and probing, and sounding, and scrutinizing with the microscope, and dividing the surface of the building into registered square inches—what is it all but an exaggeration *of the application* of the one principle or set of principles of search, which are based upon the one set of notions regarding human ingenuity, to which the Prefect, in the long routine of his duty, has been accustomed? Do you not see he has taken it for granted that *all* men proceed to conceal a letter—not exactly in a gimlet-hole bored in a chair-leg—but, at least, in *some* out-of-the-way hole or corner suggested by the same tenor of thought which would urge a man to secrete a letter in a gimlet-hole bored in a chair-leg? And do you not see also, that such *recherchés* nooks for concealment are adopted only for ordinary occasions, and would be adopted only by ordinary intellects; for, in all cases of concealment, a disposal of the article concealed—a disposal of it in this *recherché* manner—is, in the very first instance, presumable and presumed; and thus its discovery depends, not at all upon the acumen, but altogether upon the mere care, patience, and determination of the seekers; and where the case is of importance—or, what amounts to the same thing in the policial eyes, when the reward is of magnitude,—the qualities in question have *never* been known to fail? You will now understand what I meant in suggesting that, had the purloined letter been hidden any where within the limits of the Prefect's examination—in other words, had the principle of its concealment been comprehended within the principles of the Prefect—its discovery would have been a matter altogether beyond question. This functionary, however, has been thoroughly mystified; and the remote source of his defeat lies in the supposition that the Minister is a fool, because he has acquired renown as a poet. All fools are poets; this the Prefect *feels*; and he is merely guilty of a *non distributio medii* [undistributed middle] in thence inferring that all poets are fools."

"But is this really the poet?" I asked. "There are two brothers, I know; and both have attained reputation in letters. The Minister I believe has written learnedly on the Differential Calculus. He is a mathematician, and no poet."

"You are mistaken; I know him well; he is both. As poet *and* mathematician, he would reason well; as mere mathematician, he could not have reasoned at all, and thus would have been at the mercy of the Prefect."

"You surprise me," I said, "by these opinions, which have been contradicted by the voice of the world. You do not mean to set at naught the well-digested idea of centuries. The mathematical reason has long been regarded as *the* reason *par excellence.*"

" '*Il y a à parier,*' " replied Dupin, quoting from Chamfort, " '*que toute idée publique, toute convention reçue, est une sottise, car elle a convenu au plus grand nombre.*' [I'll bet that every popular idea, every set convention, is an idiocy, because it has suited the majority.] The mathematicians, I grant you, have done their best to promulgate the popular error to which you allude, and which is none the less an error for its promulgation as truth. With an art worthy a better cause, for example, they have insinuated the term 'analysis' into application to algebra. The French are the originators of this particular deception; but if a term is of any importance—if words derive any value from applicability—then 'analysis' conveys 'algebra' about as much as, in Latin, '*ambitus*' implies 'ambition,' '*religio*' 'religion,' or '*homines honesti*' a set of *honorable* men."

"You have a quarrel on hand, I see," said I, "with some of the algebraists of Paris; but proceed."

"I dispute the availability, and thus the value, of that reason which is cultivated in any especial form other than the abstractly logical. I dispute, in particular, the reason educed by mathematical study. The mathematics are the science of form and quantity; mathematical reasoning is merely logic applied to observation upon form and quantity. The great error lies in supposing that even the truths of what is called *pure* algebra, are abstract or general truths. And this error is so egregious that I am confounded at the universality with which it has been received. Mathematical axioms are *not* axioms of general truth. What is true of *relation*—of form and quantity—is often grossly false in regard to morals, for example. In this latter science it is very usually *un*true that the aggregated parts are equal to the whole. In chemistry also the axiom fails. In the consideration of motive it fails; for two motives, each of a given value, have not, necessarily, a value when united, equal to the sum of their values apart. There are numerous other mathematical truths which are only truths within the limits of *relation*. But the mathematician argues, from his *finite truths*, through habit, as if they were of an absolutely general applicability—as the world indeed imagines them to be. Bryant, in his very learned 'Mythology,' mentions an analogous source of error, when he says that 'although the Pagan fables are not believed, yet we forget ourselves continually, and make inferences from them as existing realities.' With the algebraists, however, who are Pagans themselves, the 'Pagan fables' *are* believed, and the inferences are made, not so much through lapse of memory, as through an unaccountable addling of the brains. In short, I never yet encountered the mere mathematician who could be trusted out of equal roots, or one who did not clandestinely hold it as a point of his faith that $x^2 + px$ was absolutely and unconditionally equal to q. Say to one of these gentlemen, by way of experiment, if you please, that you believe occasions may occur where $x^2 + px$ is *not* altogether equal to q, and, having made him understand what you mean, get out of his reach as speedily as convenient, for, beyond doubt, he will endeavor to knock you down.

"I mean to say," continued Dupin, while I merely laughed at his last observations, "that if the Minister had been no more than a mathematician, the Prefect would have been under no necessity of giving me this check. I knew him, however, as both mathematician and poet, and my measures were adapted to his capacity, with reference to the circumstances by which he was surrounded. I knew him as a courtier, too, and as a bold *intriguant*. Such a man, I considered, could not fail to be aware of the ordinary policial modes of action. He could not have failed to anticipate—and events have proved that he did not fail to anticipate—the waylayings to which he was subjected. He must have foreseen, I reflected, the secret investigations of his premises. His frequent absences from home at night, which were hailed by the Prefect as certain aids to his success, I regarded only as *ruses*, to afford opportunity for thorough search to the police, and thus the sooner to impress them with the conviction to which G——, in fact, did finally arrive—the conviction that the letter was not upon the premises. I felt, also, that the whole train of thought, which I was at some pains in detailing to you just now, concerning the invariable principle of policial action in searches for articles concealed—I felt that this whole train of thought would necessarily pass through the mind of the Minister. It would imperatively lead him to despise all the ordinary *nooks* of concealment. *He* could not, I reflected, be so weak as not to see that the most intricate and remote recess of his hotel would be as open as his commonest closets to the eyes, to the probes, to the gimlets, and to the microscopes of the Prefect. I saw, in fine, that he would be driven, as a matter of course, to *simplicity*, if not deliberately induced to it as a matter of choice. You will remember, perhaps, how desperately the Prefect laughed when I suggested, upon our first interview, that it was just possible this mystery troubled him so much on account of its being so *very* self-evident."

"Yes," said I, "I remember his merriment well. I really thought he would have fallen into convulsions."

"The material world," continued Dupin, "abounds with the very strict analogies to the immaterial; and thus some color of truth has been given to the rhetorical dogma, that metaphor, or simile, may be made to strengthen an argument, as well as to embellish a description. The principle of the *vis inertiæ* [force of inertia], for example, seems to be identical in physics and metaphysics. It is not more true in the former, that a large body is with more difficulty set in motion than a smaller one, and that its subsequent *momentum* is commensurate with this difficulty, than it is, in the latter, that intellects of the vaster capacity, while more forcible, more constant, and more eventful in their movements than those of inferior grade, are yet the less readily moved, and more embarrassed and full of hesitation in the first few steps of their progress. Again: have you ever noticed which of the street signs, over the shop doors, are the most attractive of attention?"

"I have never given the matter a thought," I said.

"There is a game of puzzles," he resumed, "which is played upon a map. One party playing requires another to find a given word—the name of town, river, state or empire—any word, in short, upon the motley and perplexed surface of the chart. A novice in the game generally seeks to embarrass his opponents by giving them the most minutely lettered names; but the adept selects such words as stretch, in large characters, from one end of the chart to the other. These, like the over-largely lettered signs and placards of the street, excape observation by dint of being excessively obvious; and here the physical oversight is precisely analogous with the moral inapprehension by which the intellect suffers to pass unnoticed those considerations which are too obtrusively and too palpably self-evident. But this is a point, it appears, somewhat above or beneath the understanding of the Prefect. He never once thought it probable, or possible, that the Minister had deposited the letter immediately beneath the nose of the whole world, by way of best preventing any portion of that world from perceiving it.

"But the more I reflected upon the daring, dashing, and discriminating ingenuity of D——; upon the fact that the document must always have been *at hand*, if he intended to use it to good purpose; and upon the decisive evidence, obtained by the Prefect, that it was not hidden within the limits of that dignitary's ordinary search—the more satisfied I became that, to conceal this letter, the Minister had resorted to the comprehensive and sagacious expedient of not attempting to conceal it at all.

"Full of these ideas, I prepared myself with a pair of green spectacles, and called one fine morning, quite by accident, at the Ministerial hotel. I found D—— at home, yawning, lounging, and dawdling, as usual, and pretending to be in the last extremity of *ennui*. He is, perhaps, the most really energetic human being now alive—but that is only when nobody sees him.

"To be even with him, I complained of my weak eyes, and lamented the necessity of the spectacles, under cover of which I cautiously and thoroughly surveyed the apartment, while seemingly intent only upon the conversation of my host.

"I paid especial attention to a large writing-table near which he sat, and upon which lay confusedly some miscellaneous letters and other papers, with one or two musical instruments and a few books. Here, however, after a long and very deliberate scrutiny, I saw nothing to excite particular suspicion.

"At length my eyes, in going the circuit of the room, fell upon a trumpery filigree card-rack of pasteboard, that hung dangling by a dirty blue ribbon, from a little brass knob just beneath the middle of the mantel-piece. In this rack, which had three or four compartments, were five or six visiting cards and a solitary letter. This last was much soiled and crumpled. It was torn nearly in two, across the middle—as if a design, in the first instance, to tear it entirely up as worthless, had been altered, or stayed, in the second. It had a large black seal, bearing the D—— cipher *very* conspicuously, and was addressed, in a diminutive female hand, to D——, the Minister, himself. It was thrust carelessly, and even, as it seemed, contemptuously, into one of the upper divisions of the rack.

"No sooner had I glanced at this letter, than I concluded it to be that of which I was in search. To be sure, it was, to all appearance, radically different from the one of which the Prefect had read us so minute a description. Here the seal was large and black, with the D—— cipher; there it was small and red, with the ducal arms of the S—— family. Here, the address, to the Minister, was diminutive and feminine; there the superscription, to a certain royal personage, was markedly bold and decided; the size alone formed a point of correspondence. But, then, the *radicalness* of these differences, which was excessive; the dirt; the soiled and torn condition of the paper, so inconsistent with the *true* methodical habits of D——, and so suggestive of a design to delude the beholder into an idea of the worthlessness of the document;—these things, together with the hyperobtrusive situation of this document, full in the view of every visitor, and thus exactly in accordance with the conclusions to which I had previously arrived; these things, I say, were strongly corroborative of suspicion, in one who came with the intention to suspect.

"I protracted my visit as long as possible, and, while I maintained a most animated discussion with the Minister, on a topic which I knew well had never failed to interest and excite him, I kept my attention really riveted upon the letter. In this examination, I committed to memory its external appearance and arrangement in the rack; and also fell, at length, upon a discovery which set at rest whatever trivial doubt I might have entertained. In scrutinizing the edges of the paper, I observed them to be more *chafed* than seemed necessary. They presented the *broken* appearance which is manifested when a stiff paper, having been once folded and pressed with a folder, is refolded in a reversed direction, in the same creases or edges which had formed the original fold. This discovery was sufficient. It was clear to me that the letter had been turned, as a glove, inside out, re-directed, and resealed. I bade the Minister good morning, and took my departure at once, leaving a gold snuff-box upon the table.

"The next morning I called for the snuff-box, when we resumed, quite eagerly, the conversation of the preceding day. While thus engaged, however, a loud report, as if of a pistol, was heard immediately beneath the windows of the hotel, and was succeeded by a series of fearful screams, and the shoutings of a mob. D—— rushed to a casement, threw it open, and looked out. In the meantime, I stepped to the card-rack, took the letter, and put it in my pocket, and replaced it by a *fac-simile* (so far as regards externals), which I had carefully prepared at my lodgings; imitating the D—— cipher, very readily, by means of a seal formed of bread.

"The disturbance in the street had been occasioned by the frantic behavior of a man with a musket. He had fired it among a crowd of women and children. It proved, however, to have been without ball, and the fellow was suffered to go his way as a lunatic or a drunkard. When he had gone, D—— came from the window, whither I had followed him immediately upon securing the object in view. Soon afterwards I bade him farewell. The pretended lunatic was a man in my own pay."

"But what purpose had you," I asked, "in replacing the letter by a *fac-simile*? Would it not have been better, at the first visit, to have seized it openly, and departed?"

"D——," replied Dupin, "is a desperate man, and a man of nerve. His hotel, too, is not without attendants devoted to his interests. Had I made the wild attempt you suggest, I might never have left the Ministerial presence alive. The good people of Paris might have heard of me no more. But I had an object apart from these considerations. You know my political prepossessions. In this matter, I act as a partisan of the lady concerned. For eighteen months the Minister has had her in his power. She has now him in hers—since, being unaware that the letter is not in his possession, he will proceed with his exactions as if it was. Thus will he inevitably commit himself, at once, to his political destruction. His downfall, too, will not be more precipitate than awkward. It is all very well to talk about the *facilis descensus Averni* [facile descent to Hades]; but in all kinds of climbing, as Catalani said of singing, it is far more easy to get up than to come down. In the present instance I have no sympathy—at least no pity—for him who descends. He is that *monstrum horrendum* [horrendous monster], an unprincipled man of genius. I confess, however, that I should like very well to know the precise character of his thoughts, when, being defied by her whom the Prefect terms 'a certain personage,' he is reduced to opening the letter which I left for him in the card-rack."

"How? did you put any thing particular in it?"

"Why—it did not seem altogether right to leave the interior blank— that would have been insulting. D——, at Vienna once, did me an evil turn, which I told him, quite good-humoredly, that I should remember. So, as I knew he would feel some curiosity in regard to the identity of the person who had outwitted him, I thought it a pity not to give him a clue. He is well acquainted with my MS., and I just copied into the middle of the blank sheet the words—

"–Un dessein si funeste,
S'il n'est digne d'Atrée, est digne de Thyeste.

[A plan so deadly is worthy of Thyestes, if not of Atreus.]

They are to be found in Crébillon's 'Atrée.'"

QUESTIONS

1. Discuss the way Monsieur G——, the Prefect of the Parisian police, is characterized. How is he like the stereotype of many other policemen in detective stories?

2. If you had never read this story before, did you find yourself trying to guess where the letter was? Did you want to be fooled? Did you feel impatience, a desire to skip to the end of the story in order to find the solution quickly?

3. Is the story allegorical? Is the truth often right before us? Can the *big* lie often fool people more effectively than the small lie?

4. How strong is the element of revenge in detective stories?

5. Why do readers so often wish for the individual, rather than the police, to solve the crime or mystery?

6. Compare the styles of Poe and Stevenson. How is the sentence structure and vocabulary different from that of Hemingway, Jackson, and Greene? Does the lack of authorial intrusion in the more modern writers affect your perception of the theme or moral of the story? Explain.

The Adventure of
the Speckled Band

A. Conan Doyle

In glancing over my notes of the seventy-odd cases in which I have, during the last eight years, studied the methods of my friend, Sherlock Holmes, I find many tragic, some comic, a large number merely strange, but none commonplace; for, working as he did rather for the love of his art than for the acquirement of wealth, he refused to associate himself with any investigation which did not tend toward the unusual, and even the fantastic. Of all these varied cases, however, I cannot recall any which presented more singular features than that which was associated with the well-known Surrey family of the Roylott of Stoke Moran. The events in question occurred in the early days of my association with Holmes, when we were sharing rooms as bachelors in Baker Street. It is possible that I might have placed them upon record before, but a promise of secrecy was made at the time, from which I have only been freed during the last month by the untimely death of the lady to whom the pledge was given. It is perhaps as well that the facts should now come to light, for I have reasons to know that there are wide-spread rumors as to the death of Dr. Grimesby Roylott which tend to make the matter even more terrible than the truth.

It was early in April in the year '83 that I woke one morning to find Sherlock Holmes standing, fully dressed, by the side of my bed. He was a late riser as a rule, and as the clock on the mantel-piece showed me that it was only a quarter past seven, I blinked up at him in some surprise, and perhaps just a little resentment, for I was myself regular in my habits.

"Very sorry to knock you up, Watson," said he, "but it's the common lot this morning. Mrs. Hudson has been knocked up; she retorted upon me; and I on you."

"What is it, then—a fire?"

"No; a client. It seems that a young lady has arrived in a considerable state of excitement, who insists upon seeing me. She is waiting now in the sitting-room. Now, when young ladies wander about the metropolis at this hour of the morning, and knock sleepy people up out of their beds, I presume that it is something very pressing which they have to communicate. Should it prove to be an interesting case, you would, I am sure, wish to follow it from the outset. I thought, at any rate, that I should call you and give you the chance."

"My dear fellow, I would not miss it for anything."

I had no keener pleasure than in following Holmes in his professional investigations, and in admiring the rapid deductions, as swift as intuitions, and yet always founded on a logical basis, with which he unraveled the problems which were submitted to him. I rapidly threw on my clothes, and was ready in a few minutes to accompany my friend down to the sitting-room. A lady dressed in black and heavily veiled, who had been sitting in the window, rose as we entered.

"Good-morning, madam," said Holmes, cheerily. "My name is Sherlock Holmes. This is my intimate friend and associate, Dr. Watson, before whom you can speak as freely as before myself. Ha!—I am glad to see that Mrs. Hudson has had the good sense to light the fire. Pray draw up to it, and I shall order you a cup of hot coffee, for I observe that you are shivering."

"It is not cold which makes me shiver," said the woman, in a low voice, changing her seat as requested.

"What then?"

"It is fear, Mr. Holmes. It is terror." She raised her veil as she spoke, and we could see that she was indeed in a pitiable state of agitation, her face all drawn and gray, with restless, frightened eyes, like those of some hunted animal. Her features and figure were those of a woman of thirty, but her hair was shot with premature gray, and her expression was weary and haggard. Sherlock Holmes ran her over with one of his quick, all-comprehensive glances.

"You must not fear," said he, soothingly, bending forward and patting her forearm. "We shall soon set matters right, I have no doubt. You have come in by train this morning, I see."

"You know me, then?"

"No, but I observe the second half of a return ticket in the palm of your left glove. You must have started early, and yet you had a good drive in a dog-cart, along heavy roads, before you reached the station."

The lady gave a violent start, and stared in bewilderment at my companion.

"There is no mystery, my dear madam," said he, smiling.

"The left arm of your jacket is spattered with mud in no less than seven places. The marks are perfectly fresh. There is no vehicle save a dog-cart which throws up mud in that way, and then only when you sit on the left-hand side of the driver."

"Whatever your reasons may be, you are perfectly correct," said she. "I started from home before six, reached Leatherhead at twenty past, and came in by the first train to Waterloo. Sir, I can stand this strain no longer; I shall go mad if it continues. I have no one to turn to—none, save only one, who cares for me, and he, poor fellow, can be of little aid.

I have heard of you, Mr. Holmes; I have heard of you from Mrs. Farintosh, whom you helped in the hour of her sore need. It was from her that I had your address. Oh, sir, do you not think that you could help me, too, and at least throw a little light through the dense darkness which surrounds me? At present it is out of my power to reward you for your services, but in a month or six weeks I shall be married, with the control of my own income, and then at least you shall not find me ungrateful."

Holmes turned to his desk, and unlocking it, drew out a small casebook, which he consulted.

"Farintosh," said he. "Ah, yes, I recall the case; it was concerned with an opal tiara. I think it was before your time, Watson. I can only say, madam, that I shall be happy to devote the same care to your case as I did to that of your friend. As to reward, my profession is its own reward; but you are at liberty to defray whatever expenses I may be put to, at the time which suits you best. And now I beg that you will lay before us everything that may help us in forming an opinion upon the matter."

"Alas!" replied our visitor, "the very horror of my situation lies in the fact that my fears are so vague, and my suspicions depend so entirely upon small points, which might seem trivial to another, that even he to whom of all others I have a right to look for help and advice, looks upon all that I tell him about it as the fancies of a nervous woman. He does not say so, but I can read it from his soothing answers and averted eyes. But I have heard, Mr. Holmes, that you can see deeply into the manifold wickedness of the human heart. You may advise me how to walk amid the dangers which encompass me."

"I am all attention, madam."

"My name is Helen Stoner, and I am living with my step-father, who is the last survivor of one of the oldest Saxon families in England, the Roylotts of Stoke Moran, on the western border of Surrey."

Holmes nodded his head. "The name is familiar to me," said he.

"The family was at one time among the richest in England, and the estates extended over the borders into Berkshire in the north, and Hampshire in the west. In the last century, however, four successive heirs were of a dissolute and wasteful disposition, and the family ruin was eventually completed by a gambler in the days of the Regency. Nothing was left save a few acres of ground, and the two-hundred-year-old house, which is itself crushed under a heavy mortgage. The last squire dragged out his existence there, living the horrible life of an aristocratic pauper; but his only son, my step-father, seeing that he must adapt himself to the new conditions, obtained an advance from a relative, which enabled him to take a medical degree, and went out to Calcutta, where, by his professional skill and his force of character, he established a large practice. In a fit of anger, however, caused by some robberies which had been perpetrated in the house, he beat his native butler to death, and narrowly escaped a capital sentence. As it was, he suffered a long term of imprisonment, and afterward returned to England a morose and disappointed man.

"When Dr. Roylott was in India he married my mother, Mrs. Stoner, the young widow of Major-General Stoner, of the Bengal Artillery. My sister Julia and I were twins, and we were only two years old at the time of my mother's remarriage. She had a considerable sum of money—not less than 1,000 pounds a year—and this she bequeathed to Dr. Roylott entirely while we resided with him, with a provision that a certain annual sum should be allowed to each of us in the event of our marriage. Shortly after our return to England my mother died—she was killed eight years ago in a railway accident near Crewe. Dr. Roylott then abandoned his attempts to establish himself in practice in London, and took us to live with him in the old ancestral house at Stoke Moran. The money which my mother had left was enough for all our wants, and there seemed to be no obstacle to our happiness.

"But a terrible change came over our step-father about this time. Instead of making friends and exchanging visits with our neighbors, who had at first been overjoyed to see a Roylott of Stoke Moran back in the old family seat, he shut himself up in his house, and seldom came out save to indulge in ferocious quarrels with whoever might cross his path. Violence of temper approaching to mania has been hereditary in the men of the family, and in my step-father's case it had, I believe, been increased by his long residence in the tropics. A series of disgraceful brawls took place, two of which ended in the police-court, until at last he became the terror of the village, and the folks would fly at his approach, for he is a man of immense strength, and absolutely uncontrollable in his anger.

"Last week he hurled the local blacksmith over a parapet into a stream; and it was only by paying over all the money which I could gather together that I was able to avert another public exposure. He had no friends at all save the wandering gypsies, and he would give these vagabonds leave to encamp upon the few acres of bramble-covered land which represent the family estate, and would accept in return the hospitality of their tents, wandering away with them sometimes for weeks on end. He has a passion also for Indian animals, which are sent over to him by a correspondent, and he has at this moment a cheetah and a baboon, which wander freely over his grounds, and are feared by the villagers almost as much as their master.

"You can imagine from what I say that my poor sister Julia and I had no great pleasure in our lives. No servant would stay with us, and for a long time we did all the work of the house. She was but thirty at the time of her death, and yet her hair had already begun to whiten, even as mine has."

"Your sister is dead, then?"

"She died just two years ago, and it is of her death that I wish to speak to you. You can understand that, living the life which I have described, we were little likely to see anyone of our own age and position. We had, however, an aunt, my mother's maiden sister, Miss Honoria Westphail, who lives near Harrow, and we were occasionally allowed to pay short visits at this lady's house. Julia went there at Christmas two years ago, and met there a half-pay major of marines, to whom she became engaged. My step-father learned of the engagement when my sister returned, and offered no objection to the marriage; but within a fortnight of the day which had been fixed for the wedding, the terrible event occurred which has deprived me of my only companion."

Sherlock Holmes had been leaning back in his chair with his eyes closed and his head sunk in a cushion, but he half opened his lids now and glanced at his visitor.

"Pray be precise as to details," said he.

"It is easy for me to be so, for every event of that dreadful time is seared into my memory. The manorhouse is, as I have already said, very old, and only one wing is now inhabited. The bedrooms in this wing are on the ground floor, the sitting-rooms being in the central block of the buildings. Of these bedrooms the first is Dr. Roylott's, the second my sister's, and the third my own. There is no communication between them, but they all open out into the same corridor. Do I make myself plain?"

"Perfectly so."

"The windows of the three rooms open out upon the lawn. That fatal night Dr. Roylott had gone to his room early, though we knew that he had not retired to rest, for my sister was troubled by the smell of the strong Indian cigars which it was his custom to smoke. She left her room, therefore, and came into mine, where she sat for some time, chatting about her approaching wedding. At eleven o'clock she rose to leave me, but she paused at the door and looked back.

" 'Tell me, Helen,' said she, 'have you ever heard any one whistle in the dead of the night?'

" 'Never,' said I.

" 'I suppose that you could not possibly whistle, yourself, in your sleep?'

" 'Certainly not. But why?'

" 'Because during the last few nights I have always, about three in the morning, heard a low, clear whistle. I am a light sleeper, and it has awakened me. I cannot tell where it came from—perhaps from the next room, perhaps from the lawn. I thought that I would just ask you whether you had heard it.'

" 'No, I have not. It must be those wretched gypsies in the plantation.'

" 'Very likely. And yet if it were on the lawn, I wonder that you did not hear it also.'

" 'Ah, but I sleep more heavily than you.'

" 'Well, it is of no great consequence, at any rate.' She smiled back at me, closed my door, and a few moments later I heard her key turn in the lock."

"Indeed," said Holmes. "Was it your custom always to lock yourselves in at night?"

"Always."

"And why?"

"I think that I mentioned to you that the doctor kept a cheetah and a baboon. We had no feeling of security unless our doors were locked."

"Quite so. Pray proceed with your statement."

"I could not sleep that night. A vague feeling of impending misfortune impressed me. My sister and I, you will recollect, were twins, and you know how subtle are the links which bind two souls which are so closely allied. It was a wild night. The wind was howling outside, and the rain was beating and splashing against the windows. Suddenly, amid all the hubbub of the gale, there burst forth the wild scream of a terrified woman. I knew that it was my sister's voice. I sprang from my bed, wrapped a shawl round me, and rushed into the corridor. As I opened my door I seemed to hear a low whistle, such as my sister described, and a few moments later a clanging sound, as if a mass of metal had fallen. As I ran down the passage my sister's door was unlocked, and revolved slowly upon its hinges. I stared at it horror-stricken, not knowing what was about to issue from it. By the light of the corridor-lamp I saw my sister appear at the opening, her face blanched with terror, her hands groping for help, her whole figure swaying to and fro like that of a drunkard. I ran to her and threw my arms round her, but at that moment her knees seemed to give way and she fell to the ground. She writhed as one who is in terrible pain, and her limbs were dreadfully convulsed. At first I thought that she had not recognized me, but as I bent over her, she suddenly shrieked out, in a voice which I shall never forget: 'Oh, my God! Helen! It was the band! The speckled band!' There was something else which she would fain have said, and she stabbed with her finger into the air in the direction of the doctor's room, but a fresh convulsion seized her and choked her words. I rushed out, calling loudly for my step-father, and I met him hastening from his room in his dressing-gown. When he reached my sister's side she was unconscious, and though he poured brandy down her throat and sent for medical aid from the village, all efforts were in vain, for she slowly sank and died without having recovered her consciousness. Such was the dreadful end of my beloved sister."

"One moment," said Holmes; "are you sure about this whistle and metallic sound? Could you swear to it?"

"That was what the county coroner asked me at the inquiry. It is my strong impression that I heard it, and yet, among the crash of the gale and the creaking of an old house, I may possibly have been deceived."

"Was your sister dressed?"

"No, she was in her night-dress. In her right hand was found the charred stump of a match, and in her left a match-box."

"Showing that she had struck a light and looked about her when the alarm took place. That is important. And what conclusions did the coroner come to?"

"He investigated the case with great care, for Dr. Roylott's conduct had long been notorious in the county, but he was unable to find any satisfactory cause of death. My evidence showed that the door had been fastened upon the inner side, and the windows were blocked by old-fashioned shutters with broad iron bars, which were secured every night. The walls were carefully sounded, and were shown to be quite solid all round, and the flooring as also thoroughly examined, with the same result. The chimney is wide, but is barred up by four large staples. It is certain, therefore, that my sister was quite alone when she met her end. Besides, there were no marks of any violence upon her."

"How about poison?"

"The doctors examined her for it, but without success."

"What do you think that this unfortunate lady died of, then?"

"It is my belief that she died of pure fear and nervous shock, though what it was that frightened her I cannot imagine."

"Were there gypsies in the plantation at the time?"

"Yes, there are nearly always some there."

"Ah, and what did you gather from this allusion to a band—a speckled band?"

"Sometimes I have thought that it was merely the wild talk of delirium, sometimes that it may have referred to some band of people, perhaps to these very gypsies in the plantation. I do not know whether the spotted handkerchiefs which so many of them wear over their heads might have suggested the strange adjective which she used."

Holmes shook his head like a man who is far from being satisfied.

"These are very deep waters," said he; "pray go on with your narrative."

"Two years have passed since then, and my life had been until lately lonelier than ever. A month ago, however, a dear friend, whom I have known for many years, has done me the honor to ask my hand in marriage. His name is Armitage—Percy Armitage—the second son of Mr. Armitage, of Crane Water, near Reading. My step-father has offered no opposition to the match, and we are to be married in the course of the spring. Two days ago some repairs were started in the west wing of the building, and my bedroom wall has been pierced, so that I have had to move into the chamber in which my sister died, and to sleep in the very bed in which she slept.

"Imagine, then, my thrill of terror when last night, as I lay awake, thinking over her terrible fate, I suddenly heard in the silence of the night the low whistle which had been the herald of her own death. I sprang up and lit the lamp, but nothing was to be seen in the room. I was too shaken to go to bed again, however; so I dressed, and as soon as it was daylight I slipped down, got a dog-cart at the 'Crown Inn,' which is opposite, and drove to Leatherhead, from whence I have come on this morning with the one object of seeing you and asking your advice."

"You have done wisely," said my friend. "But have you told me all?"

"Yes, all."

"Miss Roylott, you have not. You are screening your step-father."

"Why, what do you mean?"

For answer Holmes pushed back the frill of black lace which fringed the hand that lay upon our visitor's knee. Five little livid spots, the marks of four fingers and a thumb, were printed upon the white wrist.

"You have been cruelly used," said Holmes.

The lady colored deeply and covered over her injured wrist. "He is a hard man," she said, "and perhaps he hardly knows his own strength."

There was a long silence, during which Holmes leaned his chin upon his hands and stared into the crackling fire.

"This is a very deep business," he said, at last. "There are a thousand details which I should desire to know before I decide upon our course of action. Yet we have not a moment to lose. If we were to come to Stoke Moran today, would it be possible for us to see over these rooms without the knowledge of your step-father?"

"As it happens, he spoke of coming into town today upon some most important business. It is probable that he will be away all day, and that there would be nothing to disturb you. We have a housekeeper now, but she is old and foolish, and I could easily get her out of the way."

"Excellent. You are not averse to this trip, Watson?"

"By no means."

"Then we shall both come. What are you going to do yourself?"

"I have one or two things which I would wish to do now that I am in town. But I shall return by the twelve o'clock train, so as to be there in time for your coming."

"And you may expect us early in the afternoon. I have myself some small business matters to attend to. Will you not wait and breakfast?"

"No, I must go. My heart is lightened already since I have confided my trouble to you. I shall look forward to seeing you again this afternoon." She dropped her thick black veil over her face and glided from the room.

"And what do you think of it all, Watson?" asked Sherlock Holmes, leaning back in his chair.

"It seems to me to be a most dark and sinister business."

"Dark enough and sinister enough."

"Yet if the lady is correct in saying that the flooring and walls are sound, and that the door, window, and chimney are impassable, then her sister must have been undoubtedly alone when she met her mysterious end."

"What becomes, then, of these nocturnal whistles, and what of the very peculiar words of the dying woman?"

"I cannot think."

"When you combine the ideas of whistles at night, the presence of a band of gypsies who are on intimate terms with this old doctor, the fact that we have every reason to believe the doctor has an interest in preventing his step-daughter's marriage, the dying allusion to a band, and, finally, the fact that Miss Helen Stoner heard a metallic clang, which might have been caused by one of those metal bars which secured the shutters falling back into its place, I think that there is good ground to think that the mystery may be cleared along those lines."

"But what, then, did the gypsies do?"

"I cannot imagine."

"I see many objections to any such theory."

"And so do I. It is precisely for that reason that we are going to Stoke Moran this day. I want to see whether the objections are fatal, or if they may be explained away. But what, in the name of the devil!"

The ejaculation had been drawn from my companion by the fact that our door had been suddenly dashed open, and that a huge man had framed himself in the aperture. His costume was a peculiar mixture of the professional and of the agricultural, having a black top-hat, a long frock-coat, and a pair of high gaiters, with a hunting-crop swinging in his hand. So tall was he that his hat actually brushed the cross-bar of the doorway, and his breadth seemed to span it across from side to side. A large face, seared with a thousand wrinkles, burned yellow with the sun, and marked with every evil passion, was turned from one to the other of us, while his deep-set, bile-shot eyes, and his high, thin, fleshless nose, gave him somewhat the resemblance to a fierce old bird of prey.

"Which of you is Holmes?" asked this apparition.

"My name, sir; but you have the advantage of me," said my companion, quietly.

"I am Dr. Grimesby Roylott, of Stoke Moran."

"Indeed, doctor," said Holmes, blandly. "Pray take a seat."

"I will do nothing of the kind. My step-daughter has been here. I have traced her. What has she been saying to you?"

"It is a little cold for the time of the year," said Holmes.

"What has she been saying to you?" screamed the old man, furiously.

"But I have heard that the crocuses promise well," continued my companion, imperturbably.

"Ha! You put me off, do you?" said our new visitor, taking a step forward and shaking his hunting-crop. "I know you, you scoundrel! I have heard of you before. You are Holmes, the meddler."

My friend smiled.

"Holmes, the busybody!"

His smile broadened.

"Holmes, the Scotland-yard Jack-in-office!"

Holmes chuckled heartily. "Your conversation is most entertaining," said he. "When you go out, close the door, for there is a decided draught."

"I will go when I have said my say. Don't you dare to meddle with my affairs. I know that Miss Stoner has been here. I traced her! I am a dangerous man to fall foul of! See here." He stepped swiftly forward, seized the poker, and bent it into a curve with his huge brown hands.

"See that you keep yourself out of my grip," he snarled; and hurling the twisted poker into the fireplace, he strode out of the room.

"He seems a very amiable person," said Holmes, laughing. "I am not quite so bulky, but if he had remained I might have shown him that my grip was not much more feeble than his own." As he spoke he picked up the steel poker, and with a sudden effort straightened it out again.

"Fancy his having the insolence to confound me with the official detective force! This incident gives zest to our investigation, however, and I only trust that our little friend will not suffer from her imprudence in allowing this brute to trace her. And now, Watson, we shall order breakfast, and afterward I shall walk down to Doctors' Commons, where I hope to get some data which may help us in this matter."

It was nearly one o'clock when Sherlock Holmes returned from his excursion. He held in his hand a sheet of blue paper, scrawled over with notes and figures.

"I have seen the will of the deceased wife," said he. "To determine its exact meaning I have been obliged to work out the present prices of the investments with which it is concerned. The total income, which at the time of the wife's death was little short of 1,100 pounds, is now, through the fall in agricultural prices, not more than 750 pounds. Each daughter can claim an income of 250 pounds, in case of marriage. It is evident, therefore, that if both girls had married, this beauty would have had a mere pittance, while even one of them would cripple him to a very serious extent. My morning's work has not been wasted, since it has proved that he had the very strongest motives for standing in the way of anything of the sort. And now, Watson, this is too serious for dawdling, especially as the old man is aware that we are interesting ourselves in his affairs; so if you are ready, we shall call a cab and drive to Waterloo. I should be very much obliged if you would slip your revolver into your pocket. An Eley's No. 2 is an excellent argument with gentlemen who can twist steel pokers into knots. That and a toothbrush are, I think, all that we need."

At Waterloo, we were fortunate in catching a train for Leatherhead, where we hired a trap at the station inn, and drove for four or five miles through the lovely Surrey lanes. It was a perfect day, with a bright sun and a few fleecy clouds in the heavens. The trees and wayside hedges were just throwing out their first green shoots, and the air was full of the pleasant smell of the moist earth. To me at least there was a strange contrast between the sweet promise of the spring and the sinister quest upon which we were engaged. My companion sat in front of the trap, his arms folded, his hat pulled down over his eyes, and his chin sunk upon his breast, buried in the deepest thought. Suddenly, however, he started, tapped me on the shoulder, and pointed over the meadows.

"Look there!" said he.

A heavily timbered park stretched up in a gentle slope, thickening into a grove at the highest point. From amid the branches there jutted out the gray gables and high roof-tree of a very old mansion.

"Stoke Moran?" said he.

"Yes, sir, that be the house of Dr. Grimesby Roylott," remarked the driver.

"There is some building going on there," said Holmes; "that is where we are going."

"There's the village," said the driver, pointing to a cluster of roofs some distance to the left; "but if you want to get to the house, you'll find it shorter to get over this stile, and so by the foot-path over the fields. There it is, where the lady is walking."

"And the lady, I fancy, is Miss Stoner," observed Holmes, shading his eyes. "Yes, I think we had better do as you suggest."

We got off, paid our fare, and the trap rattled back on its way to Leatherhead.

"I thought it as well," said Holmes, as we climbed the stile, "that this fellow should think we had come here as architects or on some definite business. It may stop his gossip. Good-afternoon, Miss Stoner. You see that we have been as good as our word."

Our client of the morning had hurried forward to meet us with a face which spoke her joy. "I have been waiting so eagerly for you!" she cried, shaking hands with us warmly. "All has turned out splendidly. Dr. Roylott has gone to town, and it is unlikely that he will be back before evening."

"We have had the pleasure of making the doctor's acquaintance," said Holmes, and in a few words he sketched out what had occurred. Miss Stoner turned white to the lips as she listened.

"Good heavens!" she cried, "he has followed me, then."

"So it appears."

"He is so cunning that I never know when I am safe from him. What will he say when he returns?"

"He must guard himself, for he may find that there is some one more cunning than himself upon his track. You must lock yourself up from him tonight. If he is violent, we shall take you away to your aunt's at Harrow. Now, we must make the best use of our time, so kindly take us at once to the rooms which we are to examine."

The building was of gray, lichen-blotched stone, with a high central portion, and two curving wings, like the claws of a crab, thrown out on each side. In one of these wings the windows were broken, and blocked with wooden boards, while the roof was partly caved in, a picture of ruin. The central portion was in little better repair, but the right-hand block was comparatively modern, and the blinds in the windows, with the blue smoke curling up from the chimneys, showed that this was where the family resided. Some scaffolding had been erected against the end wall, and the stone-work had been broken into, but there were no signs of any workmen at the moment of our visit. Holmes walked slowly up and down the ill-trimmed lawn, and examined with deep attention the outsides of the windows.

"This, I take it, belongs to the room in which you used to sleep, the center one to your sister's, and the one next to the main building to Dr. Roylott's chamber?"

"Exactly so. But I am now sleeping in the middle one."

"Pending the alterations, as I understand. By-the-way, there does not seem to be any very pressing need for repairs at that end wall."

"There were none. I believe that it was an excuse to move me from my room."

"Ah! that is suggestive. Now, on the other side of this narrow wing runs the corridor from which these three rooms open. There are windows in it, of course?"

"Yes, but very small ones. Too narrow for any one to pass through."

"As you both locked your doors at night, your rooms were unapproachable from that side. Now, would you have the kindness to go into your room and bar your shutters."

Miss Stoner did so, and Holmes, after a careful examination through the open window, endeavored in every way to force the shutter open, but without success. There was no slit through which a knife could be passed to raise the bar. Then with his lens he tested the hinges, but they were of solid iron, built firmly into the massive masonry. "Hum!" said he, scratching his chin in some perplexity; "my theory certainly presents some difficulties. No one could pass these shutters if they were bolted. Well, we shall see if the inside throws any light upon the matter."

A small side door led into the whitewashed corridor from which the three bedrooms opened. Holmes refused to examine the third chamber, so we passed at once to the second, that in which Miss Stoner was now sleeping, and in which her sister had met with her fate. It was a homely little room, with a low ceiling and a gaping fireplace, after the fashion of old country-houses. A brown chest of drawers stood in one corner, a narrow white-counterpaned bed in another, and a dressing-table on the left-hand side of the window. These articles, with two small wicker-work chairs, made up all the furniture in the room, save for a square of Wilton carpet in the center. The boards round and the paneling of the walls were of brown, worm-eaten oak, so old and discolored that it may have dated from the original building of the house. Holmes drew one of the chairs into a corner and sat silent, while his eyes traveled round and round and up and down, taking in every detail of the apartment.

"Where does that bell communicate with?" he asked, at last, pointing to a thick bell-rope which hung down beside the bed, the tassel actually lying upon the pillow.

"It goes to the housekeeper's room."

"It looks newer than the other things?"

"Yes, it was only put there a couple of years ago."

"Your sister asked for it, I suppose?"

"No, I never heard of her using it. We used always to get what we wanted for ourselves."

"Indeed, it seemed unnecessary to put so nice a bell-pull there. You will excuse me for a few minutes while I satisfy myself as to this floor." He threw himself down upon his face with his lens in his hand, and crawled swiftly backward and forward, examining minutely the cracks between the boards. Then he did the same with the wood-work with which the chamber was paneled. Finally he walked over to the bed, and spent some time in staring at it, and in running his eye up and down the wall. Finally he took the bell-rope in his hand and gave it a brisk tug.

"Why, it's a dummy," said he.

"Won't it ring?"

"No, it is not even attached to a wire. This is very interesting. You can see now that it is fastened to a hook just above where the little opening for the ventilator is."

"How very absurd! I never noticed that before."

"Very strange!" muttered Holmes, pulling at the rope. "There are one or two very singular points about this room. For example, what a fool a builder must be to open a ventilator into another room, when, with the same trouble, he might have communicated with the outside air!"

"That is also quite modern," said the lady.

"Done about the same time as the bell-rope?" remarked Holmes.

"Yes, there were several little changes carried out about that time."

"They seem to have been of a most interesting character—dummy bell-ropes, and ventilators which do not ventilate. With your permission, Miss Stoner, we shall now carry our researches into the inner apartment."

Dr. Grimesby Roylott's chamber was larger than that of his stepdaughter, but was as plainly furnished. A camp-bed, a small wooden shelf full of books, mostly of a technical character, an arm-chair beside the bed, a plain wooden chair against the wall, a round table, and a large iron safe were the principal things which met the eye.

Holmes walked slowly round and examined each and all of them with the keenest interest.

"What's in here?" he asked, tapping the safe.

"My step-father's business papers."

"Oh, you have seen inside, then?"

"Only once, some years ago. I remember that it was full of papers."

"There isn't a cat in it, for example?"

"No. What a strange idea!"

"Well, look at this!" He took up a small saucer of milk which stood on the top of it.

"No; we don't keep a cat. But there is a cheetah and a baboon."

"Ah, yes, of course! Well, a cheetah is just a big cat, and yet a saucer of milk does not go very far in satisfying its wants, I dare say. There is one point which I should wish to determine." He squatted down in front of the wooden chair, and examined the seat of it with the greatest attention.

"Thank you. That is quite settled," said he, rising and putting his lens in his pocket. "Hello!—Here is something interesting!"

The object which had caught his eye was a small doglash hung on one corner of the bed. The lash, however, was curled upon itself, and tied so as to make a loop of whip-cord.

"What do you make of that, Watson?"

"It's a common enough lash. But I don't know why it should be tied."

"That is not quite so common, is it? Ah, me! it's a wicked world, and when a clever man turns his brains to crime it is the worst of all. I think that I have seen enough now, Miss Stoner, and with your permission we shall walk out upon the lawn."

I had never seen my friend's face so grim or his brow so dark as it was when we turned from the scene of this investigation. We had walked several times up and down the lawn, neither Miss Stoner nor myself liking to break in upon his thoughts before he roused himself from his reverie.

"It is very essential, Miss Stoner," said he, "that you should absolutely follow my advice in every respect."

"I shall most certainly do so."

"The matter is too serious for any hesitation. Your life may depend upon your compliance."

"I assure you that I am in your hands."

"In the first place, both my friend and I must spend the night in your room."

Both Miss Stoner and I gazed at him in astonishment.

"Yes, it must be so. Let me explain. I believe that that is the village inn over there?"

"Yes, that is the 'Crown.' "

"Very good. Your windows would be visible from there?"

"Certainly."

"You must confine yourself to your room, on pretense of a headache, when your step-father comes back. Then when you hear him retire for the night, you must open the shutters of your window, undo the hasp, put your lamp there as a signal to us, and then withdraw quietly with everything which you are likely to want into the room which you used to occupy. I have no doubt that, in spite of the repairs, you could manage there for one night."

"Oh, yes, easily."

"The rest you will leave in our hands."

"But what will you do?"

"We shall spend the night in your room, and we shall investigate the cause of this noise which has disturbed you."

"I believe, Mr. Holmes, that you have already made up your mind," said Miss Stoner, laying her hand upon my companion's sleeve.

"Perhaps I have."

"Then, for pity's sake, tell me what was the cause of my sister's death."

"I should prefer to have clearer proofs before I speak."

"You can at least tell me whether my own thought is correct, and if she died from some sudden fright."

"No, I do not think so. I think that there was probably some more tangible cause. And now, Miss Stoner, we must leave you, for if Dr. Roylott returned and saw us, our journey would be in vain. Goodbye, and be brave, for if you will do what I have told you, you may rest assured that we shall soon drive away the dangers that threaten you."

Sherlock Holmes and I had no difficulty in engaging a bedroom and sitting-room at the "Crown Inn." They were on the upper floor, and from our window we could command a view of the avenue gate, and of the inhabited wing of Stoke Moran Manor-House. At dusk we saw Dr. Grimesby Roylott drive past, his huge form looming up beside the little figure of the lad who drove him. The boy had some slight difficulty in undoing the heavy iron gates, and we heard the hoarse roar of the doctor's voice, and saw the fury with which he shook his clenched fists at him. The trap drove on, and a few minutes later we saw a sudden light spring up among the trees as the lamp was lit in one of the sitting-rooms.

"Do you know, Watson," said Holmes, as we sat together in the gathering darkness, "I have really some scruples as to taking you tonight. There is a distinct element of danger."

"Can I be of assistance?"

"Your presence might be invaluable."

"Then I shall certainly come."

"It is very kind of you."

"You speak of danger. You have evidently seen more in these rooms than was visible to me."

"No, but I fancy that I may have deduced a little more. I imagine that you saw all that I did."

"I saw nothing remarkable save the bell-rope, and what purpose that could answer I confess is more than I can imagine."

"You saw the ventilator, too?"

"Yes, but I do not think that it is such a very unusual thing to have a small opening between two rooms. It was so small that a rat could hardly pass through."

"I knew that we should find a ventilator before ever we came to Stoke Moran."

"My dear Holmes!"

"Oh, yes, I did. You remember in her statement she said that her sister could smell Dr. Roylott's cigar. Now, of course, that suggested at once that there must be a communication between the two rooms. It could only be a small one, or it would have been remarked upon at the coroner's inquiry. I deduced a ventilator."

But what harm can there be in that?"

"Well, there is at least a curious coincidence of dates. A ventilator is made, a cord is hung, and a lady who sleeps in the bed dies. Does not that strike you?"

"I cannot as yet see any connection."

"Did you observe anything very peculiar about that bed?"

"No."

"It was clamped to the floor. Did you ever see a bed fastened like that before?"

"I cannot say that I have."

"The lady could not move her bed. It must always be in the same relative position to the ventilator and to the rope—for so we may call it, since it was clearly never meant for a bell-pull."

"Holmes," I cried, "I seem to see dimly what you are hinting at! We are only just in time to prevent some subtle and horrible crime."

"Subtle enough and horrible enough. When a doctor does go wrong, he is the first of criminals. He has nerve, and he has knowledge. Palmer and Pritchard were among the heads of their profession. This man strikes even deeper; but I think, Watson, that we shall be able to strike deeper still. But we shall have horrors enough before the night is over; for goodness' sake let us have a quiet pipe, and turn our minds for a few hours to something more cheerful."

About nine o'clock the light among the trees was extinguished, and all was dark in the direction of the Manor-House. Two hours passed slowly away, and then, suddenly, just at the stroke of eleven, a single bright light shone out in front of us.

"That is our signal," said Holmes, springing to his feet; "it comes from the middle window."

As we passed out he exchanged a few words with the landlord, explaining that we were going on a late visit to an acquaintance, and that it was possible that we might spend the night there. A moment later we were out on the dark road, a chill wind blowing in our faces, and one yellow light twinkling in front of us through the gloom to guide us on our somber errand.

There was little difficulty in entering the grounds, for unrepaired breaches gaped in the park wall. Making our way among the trees, we reached the lawn, crossed it, and were about to enter through the window, when out from a clump of laurel-bushes there darted what seemed to be a hideous and distorted child, who threw itself upon the grass with writhing limbs, and then ran swiftly across the lawn into the darkness.

"My God!" I whispered; "did you see it?"

Holmes was for the moment as startled as I. His hand closed like a vise upon my wrist in his agitation. Then he broke into a low laugh, and put his lips to my ear.

"It is a nice household," he murmured. "That is the baboon."

I had forgotten the strange pets which the doctor affected. There was a cheetah, too; perhaps we might find it upon our shoulders at any moment. I confess that I felt easier in my mind when, after following Holmes' example and slipping off my shoes, I found myself inside the bedroom. My companion noiselessly closed the shutters, moved the lamp onto the table, and cast his eyes round the room. All was as we had seen it in the daytime. Then creeping up to me and making a trumpet of his hand, he whispered into my ear again so gently that it was all that I could do to distinguish the words:

"The least sound would be fatal to our plans."

I nodded to show that I had heard.

"We must sit without light. He would see it through the ventilator."

I nodded again.

"Do not go asleep; your very life may depend upon it. Have your pistol ready in case we should need it. I will sit on the side of the bed, and you in that chair."

I took out my revolver and laid it on the corner of the table.

Holmes had brought up a long, thin cane, and this he placed upon the bed beside him. By it he laid the box of matches and the stump of a candle. Then he turned down the lamp, and we were left in darkness.

How shall I ever forget that dreadful vigil? I could not hear a sound, not even the drawing of a breath, and yet I knew that my companion sat open-eyed, within a few feet of me, in the same state of nervous tension in which I was myself. The shutters cut off the least ray of light, and we waited in absolute darkness. From outside came the occasional cry of a night-bird, and once at our very window a long-drawn, cat-like whine, which told us that the cheetah was indeed at liberty. Far away we could hear the deep tones of the parish clock, which boomed out every quarter of an hour. How long they seemed, those quarters! Twelve struck, and one and two and three, and still we sat waiting silently for whatever might befall.

Suddenly there was the momentary gleam of a light up in the direction of the ventilator, which vanished immediately, but was succeeded by a strong smell of burning oil and heated metal. Some one in the next room had lit a dark-lantern. I heard a gentle sound of movement, and then all was silent once more, though the smell grew stronger. For half an hour I sat with straining ears. Then suddenly another sound became audible—a very gentle, soothing sound, like that of a small jet of steam escaping continually from a kettle. The instant that we heard it, Holmes sprang from the bed, struck a match, and lashed furiously with his cane at the bell-pull.

"You see it, Watson?" he yelled. "You see it?"

But I saw nothing. At the moment when Holmes struck the light I heard a low, clear whistle, but the sudden glare flashing into my weary eyes made it impossible for me to tell what it was at which my friend lashed so savagely. I could, however, see that his face was deadly pale, and filled with horror and loathing.

He had ceased to strike, and was gazing up at the ventilator, when suddenly there broke from the silence of the night the most horrible cry to which I have ever listened. It swelled up louder and louder, a hoarse yell of pain and fear and anger all mingled in the one dreadful shriek. They say that away down in the village, and even in the distant parsonage, that cry raised the sleepers from their beds. It struck cold to our hearts, and I stood gazing at Holmes, and he at me, until the last echoes of it had died away into the silence from which it rose.

"What can it mean?" I gasped.

"It means that it is all over," Holmes answered. "And perhaps, after all, it is for the best. Take your pistol, and we will enter Dr. Roylott's room."

With a grave face he lit the lamp and led the way down the corridor. Twice he struck at the chamber door without any reply from within. Then he turned the handle and entered, I at his heels, with the cocked pistol in my hand.

It was a singular sight which met our eyes. On the table stood a dark-lantern with the shutter half open, throwing a brilliant beam of light upon the iron safe, the door of which was ajar. Beside this table, on the wooden chair, sat Dr. Grimesby Roylott, clad in a long gray dressing gown, his bare ankles protruding beneath, and his feet thrust into red heelless Turkish slippers. Across his lap lay the short stock with the long lash which we had noticed during the day. His chin was cocked upward and his eyes were fixed in a dreadful, rigid stare at the corner of the ceiling. Round his brow he had a peculiar yellow band, with brownish speckles, which seemed to be bound tightly round his head. As we entered he made neither sound nor motion.

"The band! the speckled band!" whispered Holmes.

I took a step forward. In an instant his strange headgear began to move, and there reared itself from among his hair the squat diamond-shaped head and puffed neck of a loathsome serpent.

"It is a swamp adder!" cried Holmes; "the deadliest snake in India. He has died within ten seconds of being bitten. Violence does, in truth, recoil upon the violent, and the schemer falls into the pit which he digs for another. Let us thrust this creature back into its den, and we can then remove Miss Stoner to some place of shelter, and let the county police know what has happened."

As he spoke he drew the dog-whip swiftly from the dead man's lap, and throwing the noose round the reptile's neck, he drew it from its horrid perch, and carrying it at arm's-length, threw it into the iron safe, which he closed upon it.

Such are the true facts of the death of Dr. Grimesby Roylott, of Stoke Moran. It is not necessary that I should prolong a narrative which has already run to too great a length, by telling how we broke the sad news to the terrified girl, how we conveyed her by the morning train to the care of her good aunt at Harrow, of how the slow process of official inquiry came to the conclusion that the doctor met his fate while indiscreetly playing with a dangerous pet. The little which I had yet to learn of the case was told me by Sherlock Holmes as we traveled back next day.

"I had," said he, "come to an entirely erroneous conclusion, which shows, my dear Watson, how dangerous it always is to reason from insufficient data. The presence of the gypsies, and the use of the word 'band,' which was used by the poor girl, no doubt to explain the appearance which she had caught a hurried glimpse of by the light of her match, were sufficient to put me upon an entirely wrong scent. I can only claim the merit that I instantly reconsidered my position when, however, it became clear to me that whatever danger threatened an occupant of the room could not come either from the window or the door. My attention was speedily drawn, as I have already remarked to you, to this ventilator, and to the bell-rope which hung down to the bed. The discovery that this was a dummy, and that the bed was clamped to the floor, instantly gave rise to the suspicion that the rope was there as bridge for something passing through the hole and coming to the bed. The idea of a snake instantly occurred to me, and when I coupled it with my knowledge that the doctor was furnished with a supply of creatures from

India, I felt that I was probably on the right track. The idea of using a form of poison which could not possibly be discovered by any chemical test was just such a one as would occur to a clever and ruthless man who had had an Eastern training. The rapidity with which such a poison would take effect would also, from his point of view, be an advantage. It would be a sharp-eyed coroner, indeed, who could distinguish the two little dark punctures which would show where the poison fangs had done their work. Then I thought of the whistle. Of course he must recall the snake before the morning light revealed it to the victim. He had trained it, probably by the use of the milk which we saw, to return to him when summoned. He would put it through this ventilator at the hour that he thought best, with the certainty that it would crawl down the rope and land on the bed. It might not bite the occupant, perhaps she might escape every night for a week, but sooner or later she must fall a victim.

"I had come to these conclusions before ever I had entered his room. An inspection of his chair showed me that he had been in the habit of standing on it, which of course would be necessary in order that he should reach the ventilator. The sight of the safe, the saucer of milk, and the loop of whip-cord were enough to finally dispel any doubts which may have remained. The metallic clang heard by Miss Stoner was obviously caused by her step-father hastily closing the door of his safe upon its terrible occupant. Having once made up my mind, you know the steps which I took in order to put the matter to the proof. I heard the creature hiss, as I have no doubt that you did also, and I instantly lit the light and attacked it."

"With the result of driving it through the ventilator."

"And also with the result of causing it to turn upon its master at the other side. Some of the blows of my cane came home, and roused its snakish temper, so that it flew upon the first person it saw. In this way I am no doubt indirectly responsible for Dr. Grimesby Roylott's death, and I cannot say that it is likely to weigh very heavily upon my conscience."

QUESTIONS

1. The typical Sherlock Holmes story generally follows a formula. First there is a scene of the Baker Street rooms, then a visitor arrives to tell his or her story. Holmes makes some preliminary hypothesis, visits the scene of the crime, solves the mystery (with or without an attendant adventure), and explains how he came to the solution. Does the use of formula in fiction annoy you, or does it provide a certain kind of joyful relaxation? Discuss the use of formulas in other forms of popular entertainment.

2. "The Adventure of the Speckled Band" is a locked room

mystery. This type of story is one of the most famous of the genre. What do you think accounts for the locked room story's tremendous popularity?

3. How are suspense and tension created in "The Adventure of the Speckled Band"?

4. Mrs. Stoner says she has heard that Sherlock Holmes "can see deeply into the manifold wickedness of the human heart." But from your reading of this and other conventional detective stories, are you convinced that the usual detective has this ability? Would the popular detective story be so popular if it provided deep explorations of such things as "wickedness"?

5. Over a hundred movies featuring Holmes have been made. What makes him so special? Why is Sherlock Holmes so much more popular than any other fictional detective?

6. Examine the use of description and atmosphere in this story. What, for instance, is the function of the "hideous and distorted child"? Is there ghoulishness in this tale?

7. Sherlock Holmes feels he is "indirectly responsible" for Dr. Roylott's death, and yet the matter is not "likely to weigh very heavily upon" his conscience. Does this lack of feeling reveal a shallowness on the part of Holmes, or do we feel that his lack of concern is justified and even, perhaps, admirable?

The Problem of Cell 13

Jacques Futrelle

I

Practically all those letters remaining in the alphabet after Augustus S. F. X. Van Dusen was named were afterwards acquired by that gentleman in the course of a brilliant scientific career, and, being honorably acquired, were tacked on to the other end. His name, therefore, taken with all that belonged to it, was a wonderfully imposing structure. He was a Ph.D., an LL.D., an F.R.S., an M.D., and an M.D.S. He was also some other things—just what he himself couldn't say— through recognition of his ability by various foreign educational and scientific institutions.

In appearance he was no less striking than in nomenclature. He was slender with the droop of the student in his thin shoulders and the pallor of a close, sedentary life on his clean-shaven face. His eyes wore a perpetual, forbidding squint—the squint of a man who studies little things—and when they could be seen at all through his thick spectacles, were mere slits of watery blue. But above his eyes was his most striking feature. This was a tall, broad brow, almost abnormal in height and width, crowned by a heavy shock of bushy, yellow hair. All these things conspired to give him a peculiar, almost grotesque, personality.

Professor Van Dusen was remotely German. For generations his ancestors had been noted in the sciences; he was the logical result, the master mind. First and above all he was a logician. At least thirty-five years of the half-century or so of his existence had been devoted exclusively to proving that two and two always equal four, except in unusual cases, where they equal three or five, as the case may be. He stood broadly on the general proposition that all things that start must go somewhere, and was able to bring the concentrated mental force of his forefathers to bear on a given problem. Incidentally it may be remarked that Professor Van Dusen wore a No. 8 hat.

The world at large had heard vaguely of Professor Van Dusen as The Thinking Machine. It was a newspaper catch-phrase applied to him at the time of a remarkable exhibition at chess; he had demonstrated then that a stranger to the game might, by the force of inevitable logic, defeat a champion who had devoted a lifetime to its study. The Thinking Machine! Perhaps that more nearly described him than all his honorary initials, for he spent week after week, month after month, in the seclusion of his small laboratory from which had gone forth thoughts that staggered scientific associates and deeply stirred the world at large.

It was only occasionally that The Thinking Machine had visitors, and these were usually men who, themselves high in the sciences, dropped in to argue a point and perhaps convince themselves. Two of these men, Dr Charles Ransome and Alfred Fielding, called one evening to discuss some theory which is not of consequence here.

'Such a thing is possible,' declared Dr Ransome emphatically, in the course of the conversation.

'Nothing is impossible,' declared The Thinking Machine with equal emphasis. He always spoke petulantly. 'The mind is master of all things. When science fully recognizes that fact a great advance will have been made.'

'How about the airship?' asked Dr Ransome.

'That's not impossible at all,' asserted The Thinking Machine. 'It will be invented some time. I'd do it myself, but I'm busy.'

Dr Ransome laughed tolerantly.

'I've heard you say such things before,' he said. 'But they mean nothing. Mind may be master of matter, but it hasn't yet found a way to apply itself. There are some things that can't be *thought* out of existence, or rather which would not yield to any amount of thinking.'

'What, for instance?' demanded The Thinking Machine.

Dr Ransome was thoughtful for a moment as he smoked.

'Well, say prison walls,' he replied. 'No man can *think* himself out of a cell. If he could, there would be no prisoners.'

'A man can so apply his brain and ingenuity that he can leave a cell, which is the same thing,' snapped The Thinking Machine.

Dr Ransome was slightly amused.

'Let's suppose a case,' he said, after a moment. 'Take a cell where prisoners under sentence of death are confined—men who are desperate and, maddened by fear, would take any chance to escape—suppose you were locked in such a cell. Could you escape?'

'Certainly,' declared The Thinking Machine.

'Of course,' said Mr Fielding, who entered the conversation for the first time, 'you might wreck the cell with an explosive—but inside, a prisoner, you couldn't have that.'

'There would be nothing of that kind,' said The Thinking Machine. 'You might treat me precisely as you treated prisoners under sentence of death, and I would leave the cell.'

'Not unless you entered it with tools prepared to get out,' said Dr Ransome.

The Thinking Machine was visibly annoyed and his blue eyes snapped.

'Lock me in any cell in any prison anywhere at any time, wearing only what is necessary, and I'll escape in a week,' he declared, sharply.

Dr Ransome sat up straight in the chair, interested. Mr Fielding lighted a new cigar.

'You mean you could actually *think* yourself out?' asked Dr Ransome.

'I would get out,' was the response.

'Are you serious?'

'Certainly I am serious.'

Dr Ransome and Mr Fielding were silent for a long time.

'Would you be willing to try it?' asked Mr Fielding, finally.

'Certainly,' said Professor Van Dusen, and there was a trace of irony in his voice. 'I have done more asinine things than that to convince other men of less important truths.'

The tone was offensive and there was an under-current strongly resembling anger on both sides. Of course it was an absurd thing, but Professor Van Dusen reiterated his willingness to undertake the escape and it was decided upon.

'To begin now,' added Dr Ransome.

'I'd prefer that it begin to-morrow,' said The Thinking Machine, 'because—'

'No, now,' said Mr Fielding, flatly. 'You are arrested, figuratively, of course, without any warning locked in a cell with no chance to communicate with friends, and left there with identically the same care and attention that would be given to a man under sentence of death. Are you willing?'

'All right, now, then,' said The Thinking Machine, and he arose.

'Say, the death-cell in Chisholm Prison.'

'The death-cell in Chisholm Prison.'

'And what will you wear?'

'As little as possible,' said The Thinking Machine. 'Shoes, stockings, trousers and a shirt.'

'You will permit yourself to be searched, of course?'

'I am to be treated precisely as all prisoners are treated,' said The Thinking Machine. 'No more attention and no less.'

There were some preliminaries to be arranged in the matter of obtaining permission for the test, but all three were influential men and everything was done satisfactorily by telephone, albeit the prison commissioners, to whom the experiment was explained on purely scientific grounds, were sadly bewildered. Professor Van Dusen would be the most distinguished prisoner they had ever entertained.

When The Thinking Machine had donned those things which he was to wear during his incarceration he called the little old woman who was his housekeeper, cook and maid-servant all in one.

'Martha,' he said, 'it is now twenty-seven minutes past nine o'clock. I am going away. One week from to-night, at half-past nine, these gentlemen and one, possibly two, others will take supper with me here. Remember Dr Ransome is very fond of artichokes.'

The three men were driven to Chisholm Prison, where the Warden was awaiting them, having been informed of the matter by telephone. He understood merely that the eminent Professor Van Dusen was to be his prisoner, if he could keep him, for one week; that he had committed no crime, but that he was to be treated as all other prisoners were treated.

'Search him,' instructed Dr Ransome.

The Thinking Machine was searched. Nothing was found on him; the pockets of the trousers were empty; the white, stiff-bosomed shirt had no pocket. The shoes and stockings were removed, examined, then replaced. As he watched all these preliminaries—the rigid search and noted the pitiful, childlike physical weakness of the man, the colourless face, and the thin, white hands—Dr Ransome almost regretted his part in the affair.

'Are you sure you want to do this?' he asked.

'Would you be convinced if I did not?' inquired The Thinking Machine in turn.

'No.'

'All right. I'll do it.'

What sympathy Dr Ransome had was dissipated by the tone. It nettled him, and he resolved to see the experiment to the end; it would be a stinging reproof to egotism.

'It will be impossible for him to communicate with anyone outside?' he asked.

'Absolutely impossible,' replied the warden. 'He will not be permitted writing materials of any sort.'

'And your jailers, would they deliver a message from him?'

'Not one word, directly or indirectly,' said the warden. 'You may rest assured of that. They will report anything he might say or turn over to me anything he might give them.'

'That seems entirely satisfactory,' said Mr Fielding, who was frankly interested in the problem.

'Of course, in the event he fails,' said Dr Ransome, 'and asks for his liberty, you understand you are to set him free?'

'I understand,' replied the warden.

The Thinking Machine stood listening, but had nothing to say until this was all ended, then:

'I should like to make three small requests. You may grant them or not, as you wish.'

'No special favours, now,' warned Mr Fielding.

'I am asking none,' was the stiff response. 'I would like to have some tooth powder—buy it yourself to see that it is tooth powder—and I should like to have one five-dollar and two ten-dollar bills.'

Dr Ransome, Mr Fielding and the warden exchanged astonished glances. They were not surprised at the request for tooth powder, but were at the request for money.

'Is there any man with whom our friend would come in contact that he could bribe with twenty-five dollars?' asked Dr Ransome of the warden.

'Not for twenty-five hundred dollars,' was the positive reply.

'Well, let him have them,' said Mr Fielding. 'I think they are harmless enough.'

'And what is the third request?' asked Dr Ransome.

'I should like to have my shoes polished.'

Again the astonished glances were exchanged. This last request was the height of absurdity, so they agreed to it. These things all being attended to, The Thinking Machine was led back into the prison from which he had undertaken to escape.

'Here is Cell 13,' said the warden, stopping three doors down the steel corridor. 'This is where we keep condemned murderers. No one can leave it without my permission; and no one in it can communicate with the outside. I'll stake my reputation on that. It's only three doors back of my office and I can readily hear any unusual noise.'

'Will this cell do, gentlemen?' asked The Thinking Machine. There was a touch of irony in his voice.

Admirably,' was the reply.

The heavy steel door was thrown open, there was a great scurrying and scampering of tiny feet, and The Thinking Machine passed into the gloom of the cell. Then the door was closed and double locked by the warden.

'What is that noise in there?' asked Dr Ransome, through the bars.

'Rats—dozens of them,' replied The Thinking Machine, tersely.

The three men, with final good-nights, were turning away when The Thinking Machine called:

'What time is it exactly, warden?'

'Eleven seventeen,' replied the warden.

'Thanks. I will join you gentlemen in your office at half-past eight o'clock one week from tonight,' said The Thinking Machine.

'And if you do not?'

'There is no "if" about it.'

II

Chisholm Prison was a great, spreading structure of granite, four stories in all, which stood in the centre of acres of open space. It was surrounded by a wall of solid masonry eighteen feet high, and so smoothly finished inside and out as to offer no foothold to a climber, no matter how expert. Atop of this fence, as a further precaution, was a five-foot fence of steel rods, each terminating in a keen point. This fence in itself marked an absolute deadline between freedom and imprisonment, for, even if a man escaped from his cell, it would seem impossible for him to pass the wall.

The yard, which on all sides of the prison building was twenty-five feet wide, that being the distance from the building to the wall, was by day an exercise ground for those prisoners to whom was granted the boon of occasional semi-liberty. But that was not for those in Cell 13. At all times of the day there were armed guards in the yard, four of them, one patrolling each side of the prison building.

By night the yard was almost as brilliantly lighted as by day. On each of the four sides was a great arc light which rose above the prison wall and gave to the guards a clear sight. The lights, too, brightly illuminated the spiked top of the wall. The wires which fed the arc lights ran up the side of the prison building on insulators and from the top storey led out to the poles supporting the arc lights.

All these things were seen and comprehended by The Thinking Machine, who was only enabled to see out of his closely barred cell window by standing on his bed. This was on the morning following his incarceration. He gathered, too, that the river lay over there beyond the wall somewhere, because he heard faintly the pulsation of a motor boat and high up in the air saw a river bird. From that same direction came the shouts of boys at play and the occasional crack of a batted ball. He knew then that between the prison wall and the river was an open space, a playground.

Chisholm Prison was regarded as absolutely safe. No man had ever escaped from it. The Thinking Machine, from his perch on the bed, seeing what he saw, could readily understand why. The walls of the cell, though built, he judged, twenty years before, were perfectly solid, and the window bars of new iron had not a shadow of rust on them. The window itself, even with the bars out, would be a difficult mode of egress because it was small.

Yet, seeing these things, The Thinking Machine was not discouraged. Instead, he thoughtfully squinted at the great arc light—there was bright sunlight now—and traced with his eyes the wire which led from it to the building. That electric wire, he reasoned, must come down the side of the building not a great distance from his cell. That might be worth knowing.

Cell 13 was on the same floor with the offices of the prison—that is, not in the basement, nor yet upstairs. There were only four steps up to the office floor, therefore the level of the floor must be only three or four feet above the ground. He couldn't see the ground directly beneath his window, but he could see it further out toward the wall. It would be an easy drop from the window. Well and good.

Then The Thinking Machine fell to remembering how he had come to the cell. First, there was the outside guard's booth, a part of the wall. There were two heavily barred gates, both of steel. At this gate was one man always on guard. He admitted persons to the prison after much clanking of keys and locks, and let them out when ordered to do so. The warden's office was in the prison building, and in order to reach that official from the prison yard one had to pass a gate of solid steel with only a peep-hole in it. Then coming from that inner office to Cell 13, where he was now, one must pass a heavy wooden door and two steel doors into the corridors of the prison; and always there was the double-locked door of Cell 13 to reckon with.

There were then, The Thinking Machine recalled, seven doors to be overcome before one could pass from Cell 13 into the outer world, a free man. But against this was the fact that he was rarely interrupted. A jailer appeared at his cell door at six in the morning with a breakfast of prison fare; he would come again at noon, and again at six in the afternoon. At nine o'clock at night would come the inspection tour. That would be all.

'It's admirably arranged, this prison system,' was the mental tribute paid by The Thinking Machine. 'I'll have to study it a little when I get out. I had no idea there was such great care exercised in the prisons.'

There was nothing, positively nothing, in his cell, except his iron bed, so firmly put together that no man could tear it to pieces save with sledges or a file. He had neither of these. There was not even a chair, or a small table, or a bit of tin or crockery. Nothing! The jailer stood by when he ate, then took away the wooden spoon and bowl which he had used.

One by one these things sank into the brain of The Thinking Machine. When the last possibility had been considered he began an examination of his cell. From the roof, down the walls on all sides, he examined the stones and the cement between them. He stamped over the floor carefully time after time, but it was cement, perfectly solid. After the examination he sat on the edge of the iron bed and was lost in thought for a long time. For Professor Augustus S. F. X. Van Dusen, The Thinking Machine, had something to think about.

He was disturbed by a rat, which ran across his foot, then scampered away into a dark corner of the cell, frightened at its own daring. After a while The Thinking Machine, squinting steadily into the darkness of the corner where the rat had gone, was able to make out in the gloom many little beady eyes staring at him. He counted six pair, and there were perhaps others; he didn't see very well.

Then The Thinking Machine, from his seat on the bed, noticed for the first time the bottom of his cell door. There was an opening there of two inches between the steel bar and the floor. Still looking steadily at this opening, The Thinking Machine backed suddenly into the corner where he had seen the beady eyes. There was a great scampering of tiny feet, several squeaks of frightened rodents, and then silence.

None of the rats had gone out the door, yet there were none in the cell. Therefore there must be another way out of the cell, however small. The Thinking Machine, on hands and knees, started a search for this spot, feeling in the darkness with his long, slender fingers.

At last his search was rewarded. He came upon a small opening in the floor, level with the cement. It was perfectly round and somewhat larger than a silver dollar. This was the way the rats had gone. He put his fingers deep into the opening; it seemed to be a disused drainage pipe and was dry and dusty.

Having satisfied himself on this point, he sat on the bed again for an hour, then made another inspection of his surroundings through the small cell window. One of the outside guards stood directly opposite, beside the wall, and happened to be looking at the window of Cell 13 when the head of The Thinking Machine appeared. But the scientist didn't notice the guard.

Noon came and the jailer appeared with the prison dinner of repulsively plain food. At home The Thinking Machine merely ate to live; here he took what was offered without comment. Occasionally he spoke to the jailer who stood outside the door watching him.

'Any improvements made here in the last few years?' he asked.

'Nothing particularly,' replied the jailer. 'New wall was built four years ago.'

'Anything done to the prison proper?'

'Painted the woodwork outside, and I believe about seven years ago a new system of plumbing was put in.'

'Ah!' said the prisoner. 'How far is the river over there?'

'About three hundred feet. The boys have a baseball ground between the wall and the river.'

The Thinking Machine had nothing further to say just then, but when the jailer was ready to go he asked for some water.

'I get very thirsty here,' he explained. 'Would it be possible for you to leave a little water in a bowl for me?'

'I'll ask the warden,' replied the jailer, and he went away.

Half an hour later he returned with water in a small earthenware bowl.

'The warden says you may keep this bowl,' he informed the prisoner. 'But you must show it to me when I ask for it. If it is broken, it will be the last.'

'Thank you,' said The Thinking Machine. 'I shan't break it.'

The jailer went on about his duties. For just the fraction of a second it seemed that The Thinking Machine wanted to ask a question, but he didn't.

Two hours later this same jailer, in passing the door of Cell 13, heard a noise inside and stopped. The Thinking Machine was down on his hands and knees in a corner of the cell, and from that same corner came several frightened squeaks. The jailer looked on interestedly.

'Ah, I've got you,' he heard the prisoner say.

'Got what?' he asked, sharply.

'One of these rats,' was the reply. 'See?' And between the scientist's long fingers the jailer saw a small gray rat struggling. The prisoner brought it over to the light and looked at it closely. 'It's a water rat,' he said.

'Ain't you got anything better to do than to catch rats?' asked the jailer.

'It's disgraceful that they should be here at all,' was the irritated reply. 'Take this one away and kill it. There are dozens more where it came from.'

The jailer took the wriggling, squirmy rodent and flung it down on the floor violently. It gave one squeak and lay still. Later he reported the incident to the warden, who only smiled.

Still later that afternoon the outside armed guard on Cell 13 side of the prison looked up again at the window and saw the prisoner looking out. He saw a hand raised to the barred window and then something white fluttered to the ground, directly under the window of Cell 13. It was a little roll of linen, evidently of white shirting material, and tied around it was a five-dollar bill. The guard looked up at the window again, but the face had disappeared.

With a grim smile he took the little linen roll and the five-dollar bill to the warden's office. There together they deciphered something which was written on it with a queer sort of ink, frequently blurred. On the outside was this:

'Finder of this please deliver to Dr Charles Ransome.'

'Ah,' said the warden, with a chuckle. 'Plan of escape number one has gone wrong.' Then, as an afterthought: 'But why did he address it to Dr Ransome?'

'And where did he get the pen and ink to write with?' asked the guard.

The warden looked at the guard and the guard looked at the warden. There was no apparent solution of that mystery. The warden studied the writing carefully, then shook his head.

'Well, let's see what he was going to say to Dr Ransome,' he said at length, still puzzled, and he unrolled the inner piece of linen.

'Well, if that—what—what do you think of that?' he asked, dazed.

The guard took the bit of linen and read this:

'*Epa cseot d'net niiy awe htto n'si sih. "T." '*

III

The warden spent an hour wondering what sort of a cipher it was, and half an hour wondering why his prisoner should attempt to communicate with Dr Ransome, who was the cause of him being there. After this the warden devoted some thought to the question of where the prisoner got writing materials, and what sort of writing materials he had. With the idea of illuminating this point, he examined the linen again. It was a torn part of a white shirt and had ragged edges.

Now it was possible to account for the linen, but what the prisoner had used to write with was another matter. The warden knew it would have been impossible for him to have either pen or pencil, and, besides, neither pen nor pencil had been used in this writing. What, then? The warden decided to personally investigate. The Thinking Machine was his prisoner; he had orders to hold his prisoners; if this one sought to escape by sending cipher messages to persons outside, he would stop it, as he would have stopped it in the case of any other prisoner.

The warden went back to Cell 13 and found The Thinking Machine on his hands and knees on the floor, engaged in nothing more alarming than catching rats. The prisoner heard the warden's step and turned to him quickly.

'It's disgraceful,' he snapped, 'these rats. There are scores of them.'

Other men have been able to stand them,' said the warden. 'Here is another shirt for you—let me have the one you have on.'

'Why?' demanded The Thinking Machine, quickly. His tone was hardly natural, his manner suggested actual perturbation.

'You have attempted to communicate with Dr Ransome,' said the warden severely. 'As my prisoner, it is my duty to put a stop to it.'

The Thinking Machine was silent for a moment.

'All right,' he said, finally, 'Do your duty.'

The warden smiled grimly. The prisoner arose from the floor and removed the white shirt, putting on instead a striped convict shirt the warden had brought. The warden took the white shirt eagerly, and then and there compared the pieces of linen on which was written the cipher with certain torn places in the shirt. The Thinking Machine looked on curiously.

'The guard brought *you* those, then?' he asked.

'He certainly did,' replied the warden triumphantly. 'And that ends your first attempt to escape.'

The Thinking Machine watched the warden as he, by comparison, established to his own satisfaction that only two pieces of linen had been torn from the white shirt.

'What did you write this with?' demanded the warden.

'I should think it a part of your duty to find out,' said The Thinking Machine, irritably.

The warden started to say some harsh things, then restrained himself and made a minute search of the cell and of the prisoner instead. He found absolutely nothing; not even a match or toothpick which might have been used for a pen. The same mystery surrounded the fluid with which the cipher had been written. Although the warden left Cell 13 visibly annoyed, he took the torn shirt in triumph.

'Well, writing notes on a shirt won't get him out, that's certain,' he told himself with some complacency. He put the linen scraps into his desk to await developments. 'If that man escapes from that cell I'll—hang it—I'll resign.'

On the third day of his incarceration The Thinking Machine openly attempted to bribe his way out. The jailer had brought his dinner and was leaning against the barred door, waiting, when The Thinking Machine began the conversation.

'The drainage pipes of the prison lead to the river, don't they?' he asked.

'Yes,' said the jailer.

'I suppose they are very small?'

'Too small to crawl through, if that's what you're thinking about,' was the grinning response.

There was silence until The Thinking Machine finished his meal. Then:

'You know I'm not a criminal, don't you?'

'Yes.'

'And that I've a perfect right to be freed if I demand it?'

'Yes.'

'Well, I came here believing that I could make my escape,' said the prisoner, and his squint eyes studied the face of the jailer. 'Would you consider a financial reward for aiding me to escape?'

The jailer, who happened to be an honest man, looked at the slender, weak figure of the prisoner, at the large head with its mass of yellow hair, and was almost sorry.

'I guess prisons like these were not built for the likes of you to get out of,' he said, at last.

'But would you consider a proposition to help me get out?' the prisoner insisted, almost beseechingly.

'No,' said the jailer, shortly.

'Five hundred dollars,' urged The Thinking Machine. 'I am not a criminal.'

'No,' said the jailer.

'A thousand?'

'No,' again said the jailer, and he started away hurriedly to escape further temptation. Then he turned back. 'If you should give me ten thousand dollars I couldn't let you out. You'd have to pass through seven doors, and I only have the keys to two.'

Then he told the warden all about it.

'Plan number two fails,' said the warden, smiling grimly. 'First a cipher, then bribery.'

When the jailer was on his way to Cell 13 at six o'clock, again bearing food to The Thinking Machine, he paused, startled by the unmistakable scrape, scrape of steel against steel. It stopped at the sound of his steps, then craftily the jailer, who was beyond the prisoner's range of vision, resumed his tramping, the sound being apparently that of a man going away from Cell 13. As a matter of fact he was in the same spot.

After a moment there came again the steady scrape, scrape, and the jailer crept cautiously on tip-toes to the door and peered between the bars. The Thinking Machine was standing on the iron bed working at the bars of the little window. He was using a file, judging from the backward and forward swing of his arms.

Cautiously the jailer crept back to the office, summoned the warden in person, and they returned to Cell 13 on tip-toes. The steady scrape was still audible. The warden listened to satisfy himself and then suddenly appeared at the door.

'Well?' he demanded, and there was a smile on his face.

The Thinking Machine glanced back from his perch on the bed and leaped suddenly to the floor, making frantic efforts to hide something. The warden went in, with hand extended.

'Give it up,' he said.

'No,' said the prisoner, sharply.

'Come, give it up,' urged the warden. 'I don't want to have to search you again.'

'No,' repeated the prisoner.

'What was it, a file?' asked the warden.

The Thinking Machine was silent and stood squinting at the warden with something very nearly approaching disappointment on his face— nearly, but not quite. The warden was almost sympathetic.

'Plan number three fails, eh?' he asked, good-naturedly. 'Too bad, isn't it?'

The prisoner didn't say.

'Search him,' instructed the warden.

The jailer searched the prisoner carefully. At last, artfully concealed in the waist band of the trousers, he found a piece of steel about two inches long, with one side curved like a half moon.

'Ah,' said the warden, as he received it from the jailer. 'From your shoe heel,' and he smiled pleasantly.

The jailer continued his search and on the other side of the trouser's waist band found another piece of steel identical with the first. The edges showed where they had been worn against the bars of the window.

'You couldn't saw a way through those bars with these,' said the warden.

'I could have,' said The Thinking Machine firmly.

'In six months, perhaps,' said the warden, good-naturedly.

The warden shook his head slowly as he gazed into the slightly flushed face of his prisoner.

'Ready to give it up?' he asked.

'I haven't started yet,' was the prompt reply.

Then came another exhaustive search of the cell. Carefully the two men went over it, finally turning out the bed and searching that. Nothing. The warden in person climbed upon the bed and examined the bars of the window where the prisoner had been sawing. When he looked he was amused.

'Just made it a little bright by hard rubbing,' he said to the prisoner, who stood looking on with a somewhat crestfallen air. The warden grasped the iron bars in his strong hands and tried to shake them. They were immovable, set firmly in the solid granite. He examined each in turn and found them all satisfactory. Finally he climbed down from the bed.

'Give it up, professor,' he advised.

The Thinking Machine shook his head and the warden and jailer passed on again. As they disappeared down the corridor The Thinking Machine sat on the edge of the bed with his head in his hands.

'He's crazy to try to get out of that cell,' commented the jailer.

'Of course he can't get out,' said the warden. 'But he's clever. I would like to know what he wrote that cipher with.'

* * *

It was four o'clock next morning when an awful, heartracking shriek of terror resounded through the great prison. It came from a cell, somewhere about the centre, and its tone told a tale of horror, agony, terrible fear. The warden heard and with three of his men rushed into the long corridor leading to Cell 13.

IV

As they ran there came again that awful cry. It died away in a sort of wail. The white faces of prisoners appeared at cell doors upstairs and down, staring out wonderingly, frightened.

'It's that fool in Cell 13,' grumbled the warden.

He stopped and stared in as one of the jailers flashed a lantern. 'That fool in Cell 13' lay comfortably on his cot, flat on his back with his mouth open, snoring. Even as they looked there came again the piercing cry, from somewhere above. The warden's face blanched a little as he started up the stairs. There on the top floor he found a man in Cell 43, directly above Cell 13, but two floors higher, cowering in a corner of his cell.

'What's the matter?' demanded the warden.

'Thank God you've come,' exclaimed the prisoner, and he cast himself against the bars of his cell.

'What is it?' demanded the warden again.

He threw open the door and went in. The prisoner dropped on his knees and clasped the warden about the body. His face was white with terror, his eyes were widely distended, and he was shuddering. His hands, icy cold, clutched at the warden's.

'Take me out of this cell, please take me out,' he pleaded.

'What's the matter with you, anyhow?' insisted the warden impatiently.

'I heard something—something,' said the prisoner, and his eyes roved nervously around the cell.

'What did you hear?'

'I—I can't tell you,' stammered the prisoner. Then, in a sudden burst of terror: 'Take me out of this cell—put me anywhere—but take me out of here.'

The warden and the three jailers exchanged glances.

'Who is this fellow? What's he accused of?' asked the warden.

'Joseph Ballard,' said one of the jailers. 'He's accused of throwing acid in a woman's face. She died from it.'

'But they can't prove it,' gasped the prisoner. 'They can't prove it. Please put me in some other cell.'

He was still clinging to the warden, and that official threw his arms off roughly. Then for a time he stood looking at the cowering wretch, who seemed possessed of all the wild, unreasoning terror of a child.

'Look here, Ballard,' said the warden, finally, 'if you heard anything, I want to know what it was. Now tell me.'

'I can't, I can't,' was the reply. He was sobbing.

'Where did it come from?'

'I don't know. Everywhere—nowhere. I just heard it.'

'What was it—a voice?'

'Please don't make me answer,' pleaded the prisoner.

'You must answer,' said the warden, sharply.

'It was a voice—but—but it wasn't human,' was the sobbing reply.

'Voice, but not human?' repeated the warden, puzzled.

'It sounded muffled and—and far away—and ghostly,' explained the man.

'Did it come from inside or outside the prison?'

'It didn't seem to come from anywhere—it was just here, here, everywhere. I heard it. I heard it.'

For an hour the warden tried to get the story, but Ballard had become suddenly obstinate and would say nothing—only pleaded to be placed in another cell, or to have one of the jailers remain near him until daylight. These requests were gruffly refused.

'And see here,' said the warden, in conclusion, 'if there's any more of this screaming I'll put you in the padded cell.'

Then the warden went his way, a sadly puzzled man. Ballard sat at his cell door until daylight, his face, drawn and white with terror, pressed against the bars, and looking out into the prison with wide, staring eyes.

That day, the fourth since the incarceration of The Thinking Machine, was enlivened considerably by the volunteer prisoner, who spent most of his time at the little window of his cell. He began proceedings by throwing another piece of linen down to the guard, who picked it up dutifully and took it to the warden. On it was written:

'Only three days more.'

The warden was in no way surprised at what he read; he understood that The Thinking Machine meant only three days more of his imprisonment, and he regarded the note as a boast. But how was the thing written? Where had The Thinking Machine found this new piece of linen? Where? How? He carefully examined the linen. It was white, of fine texture, shirting material. He took the shirt which he had taken and carefully fitted the two original pieces of the linen to the torn places. This third piece was entirely superfluous; it didn't fit anywhere, and yet it was unmistakably the same goods.

'And where—where does he get anything to write with?' demanded the warden of the world at large.

Still later on the fourth day The Thinking Machine, through the window of his cell, spoke to the armed guard outside.

'What day of the month is it?' he asked.

'The fifteenth,' was the answer.

The Thinking Machine made a mental astronomical calculation and satisfied himself that the moon would not rise until after nine o'clock that night. Then he asked another question:

'Who attends to those arc lights?'

'Man from the company.'

'You have no electricians in the building?'

'No.'

'I should think you could save money if you had your own man.'

'None of my business,' replied the guard.

The guard noticed The Thinking Machine at the cell window frequently during that day, but always the face seemed listless and there was a certain wistfulness in the squint eyes behind the glasses. After a while he accepted the presence of the leonine head as a matter of course. He had seen other prisoners do the same thing; it was the longing for the outside world.

That afternoon, just before the day guard was relieved, the head appeared at the window again, and The Thinking Machine's hand held something out between the bars. It fluttered to the ground and the guard picked it up. It was a five-dollar bill.

'That's for you,' called the prisoner.

As usual, the guard took it to the warden. That gentleman looked at it suspiciously; he looked at everything that came from Cell 13 with suspicion.

'He said it was for me,' explained the guard.

'It's a sort of tip, I suppose,' said the warden. I see no particular reason why you shouldn't accept—'

Suddenly he stopped. He had remembered that The Thinking Machine had gone into Cell 13 with one five-dollar bill and two ten-dollar bills; twenty-five dollars in all. Now a five-dollar bill had been tied around the first pieces of linen that came from the cell. The warden still had it, and to convince himself he took it out and looked at it. It was five dollars; yet here was another five dollars, and The Thinking Machine had only had ten-dollar bills.

'Perhaps somebody changed one of the bills for him,' he thought at last, with a sigh of relief.

But then and there he made up his mind. He would search Cell 13 as a cell was never before searched in this world. When a man could write at will, and change money, and do other wholly inexplicable things, there was something radically wrong with his prison. He planned to enter the cell at night—three o'clock would be an excellent time. The Thinking Machine must do all the weird things he did sometime. Night seemed the most reasonable.

Thus it happened that the warden stealthily descended upon Cell 13 that night at three o'clock. He paused at the door and listened. There was no sound save the steady, regular breathing of the prisoner. The keys unfastened the double locks with scarcely a clank, and the warden entered, locking the door behind him. Suddenly he flashed his dark-lantern in the face of the recumbent figure.

If the warden had planned to startle The Thinking Machine he was mistaken, for that individual merely opened his eyes quietly, reached for his glasses and inquired, in a most matter-of-fact tone:

'Who is it?'

It would be useless to describe the search that the warden made. It was minute. Not one inch of the cell or the bed was overlooked. He found the round hole in the floor, and with a flash of inspiration thrust his thick fingers into it. After a moment of fumbling there he drew up something and looked at it in the light of his lantern.

'Ugh!' he exclaimed.

The thing he had taken out was a rat—a dead rat. His inspiration fled as a mist before the sun. But he continued the search. The Thinking Machine, without a word, arose and kicked the rat out of the cell into the corridor.

The warden climbed on the bed and tried the steel bars on the tiny window. They were perfectly rigid; every bar of the door was the same.

Then the warden searched the prisoner's clothing, beginning at the shoes. Nothing hidden in them! Then the trousers' waist band. Still nothing! Then the pockets of the trousers. From one side he drew out some paper money and examined it.

'Five one-dollar bills,' he gasped.

'That's right,' said the prisoner.

'But the—you had two tens and a five—what the—how do you do it?'

'That's my business,' said The Thinking Machine.

'Did any of my men change this money for you—on your word of honour?'

The Thinking Machine paused just a fraction of a second.

'No,' he said.

'Well, do you make it?' asked the warden. He was prepared to believe anything.

'That's my business,' again said the prisoner.

The warden glared at the eminent scientist fiercely. He felt—he knew—that this man was making a fool of him, yet he didn't know how. If he were a real prisoner he would get the truth—but, then, perhaps, those inexplicable things which had happened would not have been brought before him so sharply. Neither of the men spoke for a long time, then suddenly the warden turned fiercely and left the cell, slamming the door behind him. He didn't dare to speak, then.

He glanced at the clock. It was ten minutes to four. He had hardly settled himself in bed when again came that heart-breaking shriek through the prison. With a few muttered words, which, while not elegant, were highly expressive, he relighted his lantern and rushed through the prison again to the cell on the upper floor.

Again Ballard was crushing himself against the steel door, shrieking, shrieking at the top of his voice. He stopped only when the warden flashed his lamp in the cell.

'Take me out, take me out,' he screamed. 'I did it, I did it, I killed her. Take it away.'

'Take what away?' asked the warden.

'I threw the acid in her face—I did it—I confess. Take me out of here.'

Ballard's condition was pitiable; it was only an act of mercy to let him out into the corridor. There he crouched in a corner, like an animal at bay, and clasped his hands to his ears. It took half an hour to calm him sufficiently for him to speak. Then he told incoherently what had happened. On the night before at four o'clock he had heard a voice—a sepulchral voice, muffled and wailing in tone.

'What did it say?' asked the warden, curiously.

'Acid—acid—acid!' gasped the prisoner. 'It accused me. Acid! I threw the acid, and the woman died. Oh!' It was a long shuddering wail of terror.

'Acid?' echoed the warden, puzzled. The case was beyond him.

'Acid. That's all I heard—that one word, repeated several times. There were other things, too, but I didn't hear them.'

'That was last night, eh?' asked the warden. 'What happened to-night—what frightened you just now?'

'It was the same thing,' gasped the prisoner. 'Acid—acid—acid!' He covered his face with his hands and sat shivering. 'It was acid I used on her, but I didn't mean to kill her. I just heard the words. It was something accusing me—accusing me.' He mumbled, and was silent.

'Did you hear anything else?'

'Yes—but I couldn't understand—only a little bit—just a word or two.'

'Well, what was it?'

'I heard "acid" three times, then I heard a long, moaning sound, then—then—I heard "No. 8 hat." I heard that twice.'

'No. 8 hat,' repeated the warden. 'What the devil—No. 8 hat? Accusing voices of conscience have never talked about No. 8 hats, so far as I ever heard.'

'He's insane,' said one of the jailers, with an air of finality.

'I believe you,' said the warden. 'He must be. He probably heard something and got frightened. He's trembling now. No. 8 hat! What the——'

V

When the fifth day of The Thinking Machine's imprisonment rolled around the warden was wearing a hunted look. He was anxious for the end of the thing. He could not help but feel that his distinguished prisoner had been amusing himself. And if this were so, The Thinking Machine had lost none of his sense of humour. For on this fifth day he flung down another linen note to the outside guard, bearing the words; 'Only two days more.' Also he flung down half a dollar.

Now the warden knew—he *knew*—that the man in Cell 13 didn't have any half dollars—he *couldn't* have any half dollars, no more than he could have pen and ink and linen, and yet he did have them. It was a condition, not a theory; that is one reason why the warden was wearing a hunted look.

That ghastly, uncanny thing, too, about 'Acid' and 'No. 8 hat' clung to him tenaciously. They didn't mean anything, of course, merely the ravings of an insane murderer who had been driven by fear to confess his crime, still there were so many things that 'didn't mean anything' happening in the prison now since The Thinking Machine was there.

On the sixth day the warden received a postal stating that Dr Ransome and Mr Fielding would be at Chisholm Prison on the following evening, Thursday, and in the event Professor Van Dusen had not yet escaped—

and they presumed he had not because they had not heard from him—they would meet him there.

'In the event he had not yet escaped!' The warden smiled grimly. Escaped!

The Thinking Machine enlivened this day for the warden with three notes. They were on the usual linen and bore generally on the appointment at half-past eight o'clock Thursday night, which appointment the scientist had made at the time of his imprisonment.

On the afternoon of the seventh day the warden passed Cell 13 and glanced in. The Thinking Machine was lying on the iron bed, apparently sleeping lightly. The cell appeared precisely as it always did from a casual glance. The warden would swear that no man was going to leave it between that hour—it was then four o'clock—and half-past eight o'clock that evening.

On his way back past the cell the warden heard the steady breathing again, and coming close to the door looked in. He wouldn't have done so if The Thinking Machine had been looking, but now—well, it was different.

A ray of light came through the high window and fell on the face of the sleeping man. It occurred to the warden for the first time that his prisoner appeared haggard and weary. Just then The Thinking Machine stirred slightly and the warden hurried on up the corridor guiltily. That evening after six o'clock he saw the jailer.

'Everything all right in Cell 13?' he asked.

'Yes, sir,' replied the jailer. 'He didn't eat much, though.'

It was with a feeling of having done his duty that the warden received Dr Ransome and Mr Fielding shortly after seven o'clock. He intended to show them the linen notes and lay before them the full story of his woes, which was a long one. But before this came to pass the guard from the river side of the prison yard entered the office.

'The arc light on my side of the yard won't light,' he informed the warden.

'Confound it, that man's a hoodoo,' thundered the official. 'Everything has happened since he's been here.'

The guard went back to his post in the darkness, and the warden 'phoned to the electric light company.

'This is Chisholm Prison,' he said through the 'phone. 'Send three or four men down here quick, to fix an arc light.'

The reply was evidently satisfactory, for the warden hung up the receiver and passed out into the yard. While Dr Ransome and Mr Fielding sat waiting the guard at the outer gate came in with a special delivery letter. Dr Ransome happened to notice the address, and, when the guard went out, looked at the letter more closely.

'By George!' he exclaimed.

'What is it?' asked Mr Fielding.

Silently the doctor offered the letter. Mr Fielding examined it closely. 'Coincidence,' he said. 'It must be.'

It was nearly eight o'clock when the warden returned to his office. The electricians had arrived in a wagon, and were now at work. The warden pressed the buzz-button communicating with the man at the outer gate in the wall.

'How many electricians came in?' he asked, over the short 'phone. 'Four? Three workmen in jumpers and overall and the manager? Frock coat and silk hat? All right. Be certain that only four go out. That's all.'

He turned to Dr Ransome and Mr Fielding.

'We have to be careful here—particularly,' and there was broad sarcasm in his tone, 'since we have scientists locked up.'

The warden picked up the special delivery letter carelessly, and then began to open it.

'When I have read this I want to tell you gentlemen something about how—Great Caesar!' he ended, suddenly, as he glanced at the letter. He sat with mouth open, motionless, from astonishment.

'What is it?' asked Mr Fielding.

'A special delivery letter from Cell 13,' gasped the warden. 'An invitation to supper.'

'What?' and the two others arose, unanimously.

The warden sat dazed, staring at the letter for a moment, then called sharply to a guard outside in the corridor.

'Run down to Cell 13 and see if that man's in there.'

The guard went as directed, while Dr Ransome and Mr Fielding examined the letter.

'It's Van Dusen's handwriting; there's no question of that,' said Dr Ransome. 'I've seen too much of it.'

Just then the buzz on the telephone from the outer gate sounded, and the warden, in a semi-trance, picked up the receiver.

'Hello! Two reporters, eh? Let 'em come in.' He turned suddenly to the doctor and Mr Fielding. 'Why, the man *can't* be out. He must be in his cell.'

Just at that moment the guard returned.

'He's still in his cell, sir,' he reported. 'I saw him. He's lying down.'

'There, I told you so,' said the warden, and he breathed freely again. 'But how did he mail that letter?'

There was a rap on the steel door which led from the jail yard into the warden's office.

'It's the reporters,' said the warden. 'Let them in,' he instructed the guard; then to the other two gentlemen: 'Don't say anything about this before them, because I'd never hear the last of it.'

The door opened, and the two men from the front gate entered.

'Good-evening, gentlemen,' said one. That was Hutchinson Hatch; the warden knew him well.

'Well?' demanded the other, irritably, 'I'm here.'

That was The Thinking Machine.

He squinted belligerently at the warden, who sat with mouth agape. For the moment that official had nothing to say. Dr Ransome and Mr Fielding were amazed, but they didn't know what the warden knew. They were only amazed; he was paralyzed. Hutchinson Hatch, the reporter, took in the scene with greedy eyes.

'How—how—how did you do it?' gasped the warden, finally.

'Come back to the cell,' said The Thinking Machine, in the irritated voice which his scientific associates knew so well.

The warden, still in a condition bordering on trance, led the way.

'Flash your light in there,' directed The Thinking Machine.

The warden did so. There was nothing unusual in the appearance of the cell, and there—there on the bed lay the figure of The Thinking Machine. Certainly! There was the yellow hair! Again the warden looked at the man beside him and wondered at the strangeness of his own dreams.

With trembling hands he unlocked the cell door and The Thinking Machine passed inside.

'See here,' he said.

He kicked at the steel bars in the bottom of the cell door and three of them were pushed out of place. A fourth broke off and rolled away in the corridor.

'And here, too,' directed the erstwhile prisoner as he stood on the bed to reach the small window. He swept his hand across the opening and every bar came out.

'What's this in the bed?' demanded the warden, who was slowly recovering.

'A wig,' was the reply. 'Turn down the cover.'

The warden did so. Beneath it lay a large coil of strong rope, thirty feet or more, a dagger, three files, ten feet of electric wire, a thin, powerful pair of steel pliers, a small tack hammer with its handle, and—and a Derringer pistol.

'How did you do it?' demanded the warden.

'You gentlemen have an engagement to supper with me at half-past nine o'clock,' said The Thinking Machine. 'Come on, or we shall be late.'

'But how did you do it?' insisted the warden.

'Don't ever think you can hold any man who can use his brain,' said The Thinking Machine. 'Come on; we shall be late.'

VI

It was an impatient supper party in the rooms of Professor Van Dusen and a somewhat silent one. The guests were Dr Ransome, Albert

Fielding, the warden, and Hutchinson Hatch, reporter. The meal was served to the minute, in accordance with Professor Van Dusen's instructions of one week before; Dr Ransome found the artichokes delicious. At last the supper was finished and The Thinking Machine turned full on Dr Ransome and squinted at him fiercely.

'Do you believe it now?' he demanded.

'I do,' replied Dr Ransome.

'Do you admit that it was a fair test?'

'I do.'

With the others, particularly the warden, he was waiting anxiously for the explanation.

'Suppose you tell us how—' began Mr Fielding.

'Yes, tell us how,' said the warden.

The Thinking Machine readjusted his glasses, took a couple of preparatory squints at his audience, and began the story. He told it from the beginning logically; and no man ever talked to more interested listeners.

'My agreement was,' he began, 'to go into a cell, carrying nothing except what was necessary to wear, and to leave that cell within a week. I had never seen Chisholm Prison. When I went into the cell I asked for tooth powder, two ten and one five-dollar bills, and also to have my shoes blacked. Even if these requests had been refused it would not have mattered seriously. But you agreed to them.

'I knew there would be nothing in the cell which you thought I might use to advantage. So when the warden locked the door on me I was apparently helpless, unless I could turn three seemingly innocent things to use. They were things which would have been permitted any prisoner under sentence of death, were they not, warden?'

'Tooth powder and polished shoes, but not money,' replied the warden.

'Anything is dangerous in the hands of a man who knows how to use it,' went on The Thinking Machine. 'I did nothing that first night but sleep and chase rats.' He glared at the warden. 'When the matter was broached I knew I could do nothing that night, so suggested next day. You gentlemen thought I wanted time to arrange an escape with outside assistance, but this was not true. I knew I could communicate with whom I pleased, when I pleased.'

The warden stared at him a moment, then went on smoking solemnly.

'I was aroused next morning at six o'clock by the jailer with my breakfast,' continued the scientist. 'He told me dinner was at twelve and supper at six. Between these times, I gathered I would be pretty much to myself. So immediately after breakfast I examined my outside surroundings from my cell window. One look told me it would be useless to try to scale the wall, even should I decide to leave my cell by the window, for my purpose was to leave not only the cell, but the prison. Of course, I could have gone over the wall, but it would have taken me longer to lay my plans that way. Therefore, for the moment, I dismissed all idea of that.

'From this first observation I knew the river was on that side of the prison, and that there was also a playground there. Subsequently these surmises were verified by a keeper. I knew then one important thing—that anyone might approach the prison wall from that side if necessary without attracting any particular attention. That was well to remember. I remembered it.

'But the outside thing which most attracted my attention was the feed wire to the arc light which ran within a few feet—probably three or four—of my cell window. I knew that would be valuable in the event I found it necessary to cut off that arc light.'

'Oh, you shut it off tonight, then?' asked the warden.

'Having learned all I could from that window,' resumed The Thinking Machine, without heeding the interruption, 'I considered the idea of escaping through the prison proper. I recalled just how I had come into the cell, which I knew would be the only way. Seven doors lay between me and the outside. So, also for the time being, I gave up the idea of escaping that way. And I couldn't go through the solid granite walls of the cell.'

The Thinking Machine paused for a moment and Dr Ransome lighted a new cigar. For several minutes there was silence, then the scientific jail-breaker went on:

'While I was thinking about these things a rat ran across my foot. It suggested a new line of thought. There were at least half a dozen rats in the cell—I could see their beady eyes. Yet I had noticed none come under the cell door. I frightened them purposely and watched the cell door to see if they went out that way. They did not, but they were gone. Obviously they went another way. Another way meant another opening.

'I searched for this opening and found it. It was an old drain pipe, long unused and partly choked with dirt and dust. But this was the way the rats had come. They came from somewhere. Where? Drain pipes usually lead outside prison grounds. This one probably led to the river, or near it. The rats must therefore come from that direction. If they came a part of the way, I reasoned that they came all the way, because it was extremely unlikely that a solid iron or lead pipe would have any hole in it except at the exit.

'When the jailer came with my luncheon he told me two important things, although he didn't know it. One was that a new system of plumbing had been put in the prison seven years before; another that the river was only three hundred feet away. Then I knew positively that the pipe was a part of an old system; I knew, too, that it slanted generally toward the river. But did the pipe end in the water or on land?

'This was the next question to be decided. I decided it by catching several of the rats in the cell. My jailer was surprised to see me engaged in this work. I examined at least a dozen of them. They were perfectly dry; they had come through the pipe, and, most important of all, they were *not house rats, but field rats.* The other end of the pipe was on land, then, outside the prison walls. So far, so good.

'Then I knew that if I worked freely from this point I must attract the warden's attention in another direction. You see, by telling the warden that I had come there to escape you made the test more severe, because I had to trick him by false scents.'

The warden looked up with a sad expression in his eyes.

'The first thing was to make him think I was trying to communicate with you, Dr Ransome. So I wrote a note on a piece of linen I tore from my shirt, addressed it to Dr Ransome, tied a five-dollar bill around it and threw it out of the window. I knew the guard would take it to the warden but I rather hoped the warden would send it as addressed. Have you that first linen note, warden?'

The warden produced the cipher.

'What the deuce does it mean, anyhow?' he asked.

'Read it backwards, beginning with the "T" signature and disregard the division into words,' instructed The Thinking Machine.

The warden did so.

'T-h-i-s, this,' he spelled, studied it a moment, then read it off, grinning:

'This is not the way I intend to escape.'

'Well, now what do you think o' that?' he demanded, still grinning.

'I knew that would attract your attention, just as it did,' said The Thinking Machine, 'and if you really found out what it was it would be a sort of gentle rebuke.'

'What did you write it with?' asked Dr Ransome, after he had examined the linen and passed it to Mr Fielding.

'This,' said the erstwhile prisoner, and he extended his foot. On it was the shoe he had worn in prison, though the polish was gone—scraped off clean. 'The shoe blacking, moistened with water, was my ink; the metal tip of the shoe lace made a fairly good pen.'

The warden looked up and suddenly burst into a laugh, half of relief, half of amusement.

'You're a wonder,' he said, admiringly. 'Go on.'

'That precipitated a search of my cell by the warden, as I had intended,' continued The Thinking Machine. 'I was anxious to get the warden into the habit of searching my cell, so that finally, constantly finding nothing, he would get disgusted and quit. This at last happened, practically.'

The warden blushed.

'He then took my white shirt away and gave me a prison shirt. He was satisfied that those two pieces of the shirt were all that was missing. But while he was searching my cell I had another piece of that same shirt, about nine inches square, rolled up into a small ball in my mouth.'

'Nine inches of that shirt?' demanded the warden. 'Where did it come from?'

'The bosoms of all stiff white shirts are of triple thickness,' was the explanation. 'I tore out the inside thickness, leaving the bosom only two thicknesses. I knew you wouldn't see it. So much for that.'

There was a little pause, and the warden looked from one to another of the men with a sheepish grin.

'Having disposed of the warden for the time being by giving him something else to think about, I took my first serious step toward freedom,' said Professor Van Dusen. 'I knew, within reason, that the pipe led somewhere to the playground outside; I knew a great many boys played there; I knew that rats came into my cell from out there. Could I communicate with some one outside with these things at hand?

'First was necessary, I saw, a long and fairly reliable thread, so—but here,' he pulled up his trouser legs and showed that the tops of both stockings, of fine, strong lisle, were gone. 'I unravelled those—after I got them started it wasn't difficult—and I had easily a quarter of a mile of thread I could depend on.

'Then on half of my remaining linen I wrote, laboriously enough I assure you, a letter explaining my situation to this gentleman here,' and he indicated Hutchinson Hatch. 'I knew he would assist me—for the value of the newspaper story. I tied firmly to this linen letter a ten-dollar bill—there is no surer way of attracting the eye of anyone—and wrote on the linen: "Finder of this deliver to Hutchinson Hatch, *Daily American*, who will give another ten dollars for the information."

'The next thing was to get this note outside on that playground where a boy might find it. There were two ways, but I chose the best. I took one of the rats—I became adept in catching them—tied the linen and money firmly to one leg, fastened my lisle thread to another, and turned him loose in the drain pipe. I reasoned that the natural fright of the rodent would make him run until he was outside the pipe and then out on earth he would probably stop to gnaw off the linen and money.

'From the moment the rat disappeared into that dusty pipe I became anxious. I was taking so many chances. The rat might gnaw the string, of which I held one end; other rats might gnaw it; the rat might run out of the pipe and leave the linen and money where they would never be found; a thousand other things might have happened. So began some nervous hours, but the fact that the rat ran on until only a few feet of the string remained in my cell made me think he was outside the pipe. I had carefully instructed Mr Hatch what to do in case the note reached him. The question was: would it reach him?

'This done, I could only wait and make other plans in case this one failed. I openly attempted to bribe my jailer, and learned from him that he held the keys to only two of seven doors between me and freedom. Then I did something else to make the warden nervous. I took the steel supports out of the heels of my shoes and made a pretence of sawing the bars of my cell window. The warden raised a pretty row about that. He developed, too, the habit of shaking the bars of my cell window to see if they were solid. They were—then.'

Again the warden grinned. He had ceased being astonished.

'With this one plan I had done all I could and could only wait to see what happened,' the scientist went on. 'I couldn't know whether my note had been delivered or even found, or whether the rat had gnawed it up. And I didn't dare to draw back through the pipe that one slender thread which connected me with the outside.

'When I went to bed that night I didn't sleep, for fear there would come the slight signal twitch at the thread which was to tell me that Mr Hatch had received the note. At half-past three o'clock, I judge, I felt this twitch, and no prisoner actually under sentence of death ever welcomed a thing more heartily.'

The Thinking Machine stopped and turned to the reporter.

'You'd better explain just what you did,' he said.

'The linen note was brought to me by a small boy who had been playing baseball,' said Mr Hatch. 'I immediately saw a big story in it, so I gave the boy another ten dollars, and got several spools of silk, some twine, and a roll of light, pliable wire. The professor's note suggested that I have the finder of the note show me just where it was picked up, and told me to make my search from there, beginning at two o'clock in the morning. If I found the other end of the thread I was to twitch it gently three times, then a fourth.

'I began the search with a small bulb electric light. It was an hour and twenty minutes before I found the end of the drain pipe, half hidden in weeds. The pipe was very large there, say twelve inches across. Then I found the end of the lisle thread, twitched it as directed and immediately I got an answering twitch.

'Then I fastened the silk to this and Professor Van Dusen began to pull it into his cell. I nearly had heart disease for fear the string would break. To the end of the silk I fastened the twine, and when that had been pulled in I tied on the wire. Then that was drawn into the pipe and we had a substantial line, which rats couldn't gnaw, from the mouth of the drain into the cell.'

The Thinking Machine raised his hand and Hatch stopped.

'All this was done in absolute silence,' said the scientist. 'But when the wire reached my hand I could have shouted. Then we tried another experiment, which Mr Hatch was prepared for. I tested the pipe as a speaking tube. Neither of us could hear very clearly, but I dared not speak loud for fear of attracting attention in the prison. At last I made him understand what I wanted immediately. He seemed to have great difficulty in understanding when I asked for nitric acid, and I repeated the word "acid" several times.

'Then I heard a shriek from a cell above me. I knew instantly that some one had overheard, and when I heard you coming, Mr Warden, I feigned sleep. If you had entered my cell at that moment the whole plan of escape would have ended there. But you passed on. That was the nearest I ever came to being caught.

'Having established this improvised trolley it is easy to see how I got things in the cell and made them disappear at will. I merely dropped them back into the pipe. You, Mr Warden, could not have reached the connecting wire with your fingers; they are too large. My fingers, you see, are longer and more slender. In addition I guarded the top of that pipe with a rat—you remember how.'

'I remember,' said the warden, with a grimace.

'I thought that if any one were tempted to investigate that hole the rat would dampen his ardour. Mr Hatch could not send me anything useful through the pipe until next night, although he did send me change for ten dollars as a test, so I proceeded with other parts of my plan. Then I evolved the method of escape, which I finally employed.

'In order to carry this out successfully it was necessary for the guard in the yard to get accustomed to seeing me at the cell window. I arranged this by dropping linen notes to him, boastful in tone, to make the warden believe, if possible, one of his assistants was communicating with the outside for me. I would stand at my window for hours gazing out, so the guard could see, and occasionally I spoke to him. In that way I learned that the prison had no electricians of its own, but was dependent upon the lighting company if anything should go wrong.

'That cleared the way to freedom perfectly. Early in the evening of the last day of my imprisonment, when it was dark, I planned to cut the feed wire which was only a few feet from my window, reaching it with an acid-tipped wire I had. That would make that side of the prison perfectly dark while the electricians were searching for the break. That would also bring Mr Hatch into the prison yard.

'There was only one more thing to do before I actually began the work of setting myself free. This was to arrange final details with Mr Hatch through our speaking tube. I did this within half an hour after the warden left my cell on the fourth night of my imprisonment. Mr Hatch again had serious difficulty in understanding me, and I repeated the word "acid" to him several times, and later the words: "Number eight hat"—that's my size—and these were the things which made a prisoner upstairs confess to murder, so one of the jailers told me next day. This prisoner heard our voices, confused of course, through the pipe, which also went to his cell. The cell directly over me was not occupied, hence no one else heard.

'Of course the actual work of cutting the steel bars out of the window and door was comparatively easy with nitric acid, which I got through the pipe in thin bottles, but it took time. Hour after hour on the fifth and sixth and seventh days the guard below was looking at me as I worked on the bars of the window with the acid on a piece of wire. I used the tooth powder to prevent the acid spreading. I looked away abstractedly as I worked and each minute the acid cut deeper into the metal. I noticed that the jailers always tried the door by shaking the upper part, never the lower bars, therefore I cut the lower bars, leaving them hanging in place by thin strips of metal. But that was a bit of dare-devilry. I could not have gone that way so easily.'

The Thinking Machine sat silently for several minutes.

'I think that makes everything clear,' he went on. 'Whatever points I have not explained were merely to confuse the warden and jailers. These things in my bed I brought in to please Mr Hatch, who wanted to improve the story. Of course, the wig was necessary in my plan. The special delivery letter I wrote and directed in my cell with Mr Hatch's fountain pen, then sent it out to him and he mailed it. That's all, I think.'

'But your actually leaving the prison grounds and then coming in through the outer gate to my office?' asked the warden.

'Perfectly simple,' said the scientist. 'I cut the electric light wire with acid, as I said, when the current was off. Therefore when the current was turned on the arc didn't light. I knew it would take some time to find out what was the matter and make repairs. When the guard went to report to you the yard was dark, I crept out the window—it was a tight fit, too—replaced the bars by standing on a narrow ledge and remained in a shadow until the force of electricians arrived. Mr Hatch was one of them.

'When I saw him I spoke and he handed me a cap, a jumper and overalls, which I put on within ten feet of you, Mr Warden, while you were in the yard. Later Mr Hatch called me, presumably as a workman, and together we went out the gate to get something out of the wagon. The gate guard let us pass out readily as two workmen who had just passed in. We changed our clothing and reappeared, asking to see you. We saw you. That's all.'

There was silence for several minutes. Dr Ransome was first to speak.

'Wonderful!' he exclaimed. 'Perfectly amazing.'

'How did Mr Hatch happen to come with the electricians?' asked Mr Fielding.

'His father is manager of the company,' replied The Thinking Machine.

'But what if there had been no Mr Hatch outside to help?'

'Every prisoner has one friend outside who would help him escape if he could.'

'Suppose—just suppose—there had been no old plumbing system there?' asked the warden, curiously.

'There were two other ways out,' said The Thinking Machine, enigmatically.

Ten minutes later the telephone bell rang. It was a request for the warden.

'Light all right, eh?' the warden asked, through the 'phone. 'Good. Wire cut beside Cell 13? Yes, I know. One electrician too many? What's that? Two came out?'

The warden turned to the others with a puzzled expression.

'He only let in four electricians, he has let out two and says there are three left.'

'I was the odd one,' said The Thinking Machine.

'Oh,' said the warden. 'I see.' Then through the 'phone: 'Let the fifth man go. He's all right.'

QUESTIONS

1. Compare the character of the "Thinking Machine" with that of C. Auguste Dupin and Sherlock Holmes.

2. Discuss the role of humor in stories of this type.

3. One of the conventions of the traditional detective story is the quite patiently explained solution, which can often take up as much as one-third of the story. What, aside from the obvious desire to learn the solution, keeps you interested in this sort of writing?

4. While you read this story, did you find points where you *almost* grasped the main solutions? Thinking back, what prevented you from going on to the full solution before you heard Van Dusen's explanation?

5. Discuss the element of false leads and false clues in detective fiction. Does a story like "The Problem of Cell 13" train us to distrust our first explanations? Is the most apparent solution almost always wrong because it is too easy? Does the detective story increase our tolerance for complexity?

6. Trace the ironic elements in the story. If a writer does not use irony consistently, is he in any way cheating his reader?

The Blue Cross

G. K. Chesterton

Between the silver ribbon of morning and the green glittering ribbon of sea, the boat touched Harwich and let loose a swarm of folk like flies, among whom the man we must follow was by no means conspicuous—nor wished to be. There was nothing notable about him, except a slight contrast between the holiday gayety of his clothes and the official gravity of his face. His clothes included a slight, pale gray jacket, a white waistcoat, and a silver straw hat with a gray-blue ribbon. His lean face was dark by contrast, and ended in a curt black beard that looked Spanish and suggested an Elizabethan ruff. He was smoking a cigarette with the seriousness of an idler. There was nothing about him to indicate the fact that the gray jacket covered a loaded revolver, that the white waistcoat covered a police card, or that the straw hat covered one of the most powerful intellects in Europe. For this was Valentin himself, the head of the Paris police and the most famous investigator of the world; and he was coming from Brussels to London to make the greatest arrest of the century.

Flambeau was in England. The police of three countries had tracked the great criminal at last from Ghent to Brussels, from Brussels to the Hook of Holland; and it was conjectured that he would take some advantage of the unfamiliarity and confusion of the Eucharistic Congress, then taking place in London. Probably he would travel as some minor clerk or secretary connected with it; but, of course, Valentin could not be certain; nobody could be certain about Flambeau.

It is many years now since this colossus of crime suddenly ceased keeping the world in a turmoil; and when he ceased, as they said after the death of Roland, there was a great quiet upon the earth. But in his best days (I mean, of course, his worst) Flambeau was a figure as statuesque and international as the Kaiser. Almost every morning the daily paper announced that he had escaped the consequences of one extraordinary crime by committing another. He was a Gascon of gigantic stature and bodily daring; and the wildest tales were told of his outburst of athletic humor; how he turned the *juge d'instruction* upside down and stood him on his head, "to clear his mind"; how he ran down the Rue de Rivoli with a policeman under each arm. It is due to him to say that his fantastic physical strength was generally employed in such bloodless though undignified scenes; his real crimes were chiefly those of ingenious and wholesale robbery. But each of his thefts was almost a new sin, and would make a story by itself. It was he who ran the great Tyrolean Dairy Company in London, with no dairies, no cows, no carts, no milk, but with some thousand subscribers. These he served by the simple operation of moving the little milk cans outside people's doors to the doors of his own customers. It was he who had kept up an unaccountable and close correspondence with a young lady whose whole letter-bag was intercepted, by the extraordinary trick of photographing his messages infinitesimally small upon the slides of a microscope. A sweeping simplicity, however, marked many of his experiments. It is said that he once repainted all the numbers in a street in the dead of night merely to divert one traveler into a trap. It is quite certain that he invented a portable pillar-box, which he put up at corners in quiet suburbs on the chance of strangers dropping postal orders into it. Lastly, he was known to be a startling acrobat; despite his huge figure, he could leap like a grasshopper and melt into the tree-tops like a monkey. Hence the great Valentin, when he set out to find Flambeau, was perfectly aware that his adventures would not end when he had found him.

But how was he to find him? On this the great Valentin's ideas were still in process of settlement.

There was one thing which Flambeau, with all his dexterity of disguise, could not cover, and that was his singular height. If Valentin's quick eye had caught a tall apple-woman, a tall grenadier, or even a tolerably tall duchess, he might have arrested them on the spot. But all along his train there was nobody that could be a disguised Flambeau, any more than a cat could be a disguised giraffe. About the people on the boat he had already satisfied himself; and the people picked up at Harwich or on the journey limited themselves with certainty to six. There was a short railway official traveling up to the terminus, three fairly short market gardeners picked up two stations afterwards, one very short widow lady going up from a small Essex town, and a very short Roman Catholic priest going up from a small Essex village. When it came to the last case, Valentin gave it up and almost laughed. The little priest was so much the essence of those Eastern flats; he had a face as round and dull as a Norfolk dumpling; he had eyes as empty as the North Sea; he had several brown paper parcels, which he was quite incapable of collecting. The Eucharistic Congress had doubtless sucked out of their local stagnation many such creatures, blind and helpless, like moles disinterred. Valentin was a skeptic in the severe style of France, and could have no love for priests. But he could have pity for them, and this one might have provoked pity in anybody. He had a large, shabby umbrella, which constantly fell on the floor. He did not seem to know which was the right end of his return ticket. He explained with a moon-calf simplicity to everybody in the carriage that he had to be careful, because he had something made of real silver "with blue stones" in one of his brown-paper parcels. His quaint blending of Essex flatness with saintly simplicity continuously amused the Frenchman till the priest arrived (somehow) at Tottenham with all his parcels, and came back for his umbrella. When he did the last, Valentin even had the good nature to warn him not to take care of the silver by telling everybody about it. But to whomever he talked, Valentin kept his eye open for some one else; he looked out steadily for any one, rich or poor, male or female, who was well up to six feet; for Flambeau was four inches above it.

He alighted at Liverpool Street, however, quite conscientiously secure that he had not missed the criminal so far. He then went to Scotland Yard to regularize his position and arrange for help in case of need; he then lit another cigarette and went for a long stroll in the streets of London. As he was walking in the streets and squares beyond Victoria, he paused suddenly and stood. It was a quaint, quiet square, very typical of London, full of an accidental stillness. The tall, flat houses round looked at once prosperous and uninhabited; the square of shrubbery in the center looked as deserted as a green Pacific islet. One of the four sides was much higher than the rest, like a dais; and the line of this side was broken by one of London's admirable accidents—a restaurant that looked as if it had strayed from Soho. It was an unreasonably attractive object, with dwarf plants in pots and long, striped blinds of lemon yellow and white. It stood specially high above the street, and in the usual patchwork way of London, a flight of steps from the street ran up to meet the front door almost as a fire-escape might run up to a first-floor window. Valentin stood and smoked in front of the yellow-white blinds and considered them long.

The most incredible thing about miracles is that they happen. A few clouds in heaven do come together into the staring shape of one human eye. A tree does stand up in the landscape of a doubtful journey in the exact and elaborate shape of a note of interrogation. I have seen both these things myself within the last few days. Nelson does die in the instant of victory; and a man named Williams does quite accidentally murder a man named Williamson; it sounds like a sort of infanticide. In short, there is in life an element of elfin coincidence which people reckoning on the prosaic may perpetually miss. As it has been well expressed in the paradox of Poe, wisdom should reckon on the unforeseen.

Aristide Valentin was unfathomably French; and the French intelligence is intelligence specially and solely. He was not "a thinking machine"; for that is a brainless phrase of modern fatalism and materialism. A machine only *is* a machine because it cannot think. But he was a thinking man, and a plain man at the same time. All his wonderful successes, that looked like conjuring, had been gained by plodding logic, by clear and commonplace French thought. The French electrify the world not by starting any paradox, they electrify it by carrying out a truism. They carry a truism so far—as in the French Revolution. But exactly because Valentin understood reason, he understood the limits of reason. Only a man who knows nothing of motors talks of motoring without petrol; only a man who knows nothing of reason talks of reasoning without strong, undisputed first principles. Here he had no strong first principles. Flambeau had been missed at Harwich; and if he was in London at all, he might be anything from a tall tramp on Wimbledon Common to a tall toastmaster at the Hôtel Métropole. In such a naked state of nescience, Valentin had a view and a method of his own.

In such cases he reckoned on the unforeseen. In such cases, when he could not follow the train of the reasonable, he coldly and carefully followed the train of the unreasonable. Instead of going to the right places—banks, police stations, rendezvous—he systematically went to the wrong places; knocked at every empty house, turned down every *cul de sac*, went up every lane blocked with rubbish, went round every crescent that led him uselessly out of the way. He defended this crazy course quite logically. He said that if one had a clue this was the worst way; but if one had no clue at all it was the best, because there was just the chance that any oddity that caught the eye of the pursuer might be the same that had caught the eye of the pursued. Somewhere a man must begin, and it had better be just where another man might stop. Something about that flight of steps up to the shop, something about the quietude and quaintness of the restaurant, roused all the detective's rare romantic fancy and made him resolve to strike at random. He went up the steps, and sitting down at a table by the window, asked for a cup of black coffee.

It was half-way through the morning, and he had not breakfasted; the slight litter of other breakfasts stood about on the table to remind him of his hunger; and adding a poached egg to his order, he proceeded musingly to shake some white sugar into his coffee, thinking all the time about Flambeau. He remembered how Flambeau had escaped, once by a pair of nail scissors, and once by a house on fire; once by having to pay for an unstamped letter, and once by getting people to look through a telescope at a comet that might destroy the world. He thought his detective brain as good as the criminal's, which was true. But he fully realized the disadvantage. "The criminal is the creative artist; the detective only the critic," he said with a sour smile, and lifted his coffee cup to his lips slowly, and put it down very quickly. He had put salt in it.

He looked at the vessel from which the silvery powder had come; it was certainly a sugar-basin; as unmistakably meant for sugar as a champagne bottle for champagne. He wondered why they should keep salt in it. He looked to see if there were any more orthodox vessels. Yes;

there were two salt-cellars quite full. Perhaps there was some specialty in the condiment in the salt-cellars. He tasted it; it was sugar. Then he looked round at the restaurant with a refreshed air of interest, to see if there were any other traces of that singular artistic taste which puts the sugar in the salt-cellars and the salt in the sugar-basin. Except for an odd splash of some dark fluid on one of the white-papered walls, the whole place appeared neat, cheeful and ordinary. He rang the bell for the waiter.

When that official hurried up, fuzzy-haired and somewhat blear-eyed at that early hour, the detective (who was not without an appreciation of the simpler forms of humor) asked him to taste the sugar and see if it was up to the high reputation of the hotel. The result was that the waiter yawned suddenly and woke up.

"Do you play this delicate joke on your customers every morning?" inquired Valentin. "Does changing the salt and sugar never pall on you as a jest?"

The waiter, when this irony grew clearer, stammeringly assured him that the establishment had certainly no such intention; it must be a most curious mistake. He picked up the sugar-basin and looked at it; he picked up the salt-cellar and looked at that, his face growing more and more bewildered. At last he abruptly excused himself, and hurrying away, returned in a few seconds with the proprietor. The proprietor also examined the sugar-basin and then the salt-cellar; the proprietor also looked bewildered.

Suddenly the waiter seemed to grow inarticulate with a rush of words.

"I zink," he stuttered eagerly, "I zink it is those two clergymen."

"What two clergymen?"

"The two clergymen," said the waiter, "that threw soup at the wall."

"Threw soup at the wall?" repeated Valentin, feeling sure this must be some singular Italian metaphor.

"Yes, yes," said the attendant excitedly, and pointing at the dark splash on the white paper; "threw it over there on the wall."

Valentin looked his query at the proprietor, who came to his rescue with fuller reports.

"Yes, sir," he said, "it's quite true, though I don't suppose it has anything to do with the sugar and salt. Two clergymen came in and drank soup here very early, as soon as the shutters were taken down. They were both very quiet, respectable people; one of them paid the bill and went out; the other, who seemed a slower coach altogether, was some minutes longer getting his things together. But he went at last. Only, the instant before he stepped into the street he deliberately picked up his cup, which he had only half emptied, and threw the soup slap on the wall. I was in the back room myself, and so was the waiter; so I could only rush out in time to find the wall splashed and the shop empty. It don't do any particular damage, but it was confounded cheek; and I tried

to catch the men in the street. They were too far off though; I only
noticed they went round the next corner into Carstairs Street."

The detective was on his feet, hat settled and stick in his hand. He had
already decided that in the universal darkness of his mind he could only
follow the first odd finger that pointed; and this finger was odd enough.
Paying his bill and clashing the glass doors behind him, he was soon
swinging round into the other street.

It was fortunate that even in such fevered moments his eye was cool
and quick. Something in a shop-front went by him like a mere flash; yet
he went back to look at it. The shop was a popular greengrocer and
fruiterer's, an array of goods set out in the open air and plainly ticketed
with their names and prices. In the two most prominent compartments
were two heaps, of oranges and of nuts respectively. On the heap of nuts
lay a scrap of cardboard, on which was written in bold, blue chalk, "Best
tangerine oranges, two a penny." On the oranges was the equally clear
and exact description, "Finest Brazil nuts, 4d. a lb." M. Valentin looked
at these two placards and fancied he had met this highly subtle form of
humor before, and that somewhat recently. He drew the attention of the
red-faced fruiterer, who was looking rather sullenly up and down the
street, to this inaccuracy in his advertisements. The fruiterer said
nothing, but sharply put each card into its proper place. The detective,
leaning elegantly on his walking-cane, continued to scrutinize the shop.
At last he said, "Pray excuse my apparent irrelevance, my good sir, but I
should like to ask you a question in experimental psychology and the
association of ideas."

The red-faced shopman regarded him with an eye of menace; but he
continued gayly, swinging his cane. "Why," he pursued, "why are two
tickets wrongly placed in a greengrocer's shop like a shovel hat that has
come to London for a holiday? Or, in case I do not make myself clear,
what is the mystical association which connects the idea of nuts marked
as oranges with the idea of two clergymen, one tall and the other short?"

The eyes of the tradesman stood out of his head like a snail's; he really
seemed for an instant likely to fling himself upon the stranger. At last he
stammered angrily: "I don't know what you 'ave to do with it, but if
you're one of their friends, you can tell 'em from me that I'll knock their
silly 'eads off, parsons or no parsons, if they upset my apples again."

"Indeed," asked the detective, with great sympathy. "Did they upset
your apples?"

"One of 'em did," said the heated shopman; "rolled 'em all over the
street. I'd 'ave caught the fool but for havin' to pick 'em up."

"Which way did these parsons go?" asked Valentin.

"Up that second road on the left-hand side, and then across the
square," said the other promptly.

"Thanks," replied Valentin, and vanished like a fairy. On the other side of the second square he found a policeman, and said: "This is urgent, constable; have you seen two clergymen in shovel hats?"

The policeman began to chuckle heavily. "I 'ave, sir; and if you arst me, one of 'em was drunk. He stood in the middle of the road that bewildered that—"

"Which way did they go?" snapped Valentin.

"They took one of them yellow buses over there," answered the man; "them that go to Hampstead."

Valentin produced his official card and said very rapidly: "Call up two of your men to come with me in pursuit," and crossed the road with such contagious energy that the ponderous policeman was moved to almost agile obedience. In a minute and a half the French detective was joined on the opposite pavement by an inspector and a man in plain clothes.

"Well, sir," began the former, with smiling importance, "and what may—?"

Valentin pointed suddenly with his cane. "I'll tell you on the top of that omnibus," he said, and was darting and dodging across the tangle of the traffic. When all three sank panting on the top seats of the yellow vehicle, the inspector said: "We could go four times as quick in a taxi."

"Quite true," replied their leader placidly, "if we only had an idea of where we were going."

"Well, where *are* you going?" asked the other, staring.

Valentin smoked frowningly for a few seconds; then, removing his cigarette, he said: "If you *know* what a man's doing, get in front of him; but if you want to guess what he's doing, keep behind him. Stray when he strays; stop when he stops; travel as slowly as he. Then you may see what he saw and may act as he acted. All we can do is to keep our eyes skinned for a queer thing."

"What sort of queer thing do you mean?" asked the inspector.

"Any sort of queer thing," answered Valentin, and relapsed into obstinate silence.

The yellow omnibus crawled up the northern roads for what seemed like hours on end; the great detective would not explain further, and perhaps his assistants felt a silent and growing doubt of his errand. Perhaps, also, they felt a silent and growing desire for lunch, for the hours crept long past the normal luncheon hour, and the long roads of the North London suburbs seemed to shoot out into length after length like an infernal telescope. It was one of those journeys on which a man perpetually feels that now at last he must have come to the end of the universe, and then finds he has only come to the beginning of Tufnell Park. London died away in draggled taverns and dreary scrubs, and then was unaccountably born again in blazing high streets and blatant hotels. It was like passing through thirteen separate vulgar cities all just touching each other. But though the winter twilight was already threatening the road ahead of them, the Parisian detective still sat silent and watchful, eyeing the frontage of the streets that slid by on either side. By the time they had left Camden Town behind, the policemen were nearly asleep; at least, they gave something like a jump as Valentin leaped erect, struck a hand on each man's shoulder, and shouted to the driver to stop.

They tumbled down the steps into the road without realizing why they had been dislodged; when they looked round for enlightenment they found Valentin triumphantly pointing his finger towards a window on the left side of the road. It was a large window, forming part of the long façade of a gilt and palatial public-house; it was the part reserved for respectable dining, and labeled "Restaurant." This window, like all the rest along the frontage of the hotel, was of frosted and figured glass; but in the middle of it was a big, black smash, like a star in the ice.

"Our cue at last," cried Valentin, waving his stick: "the place with the broken window."

"What window? What cue?" asked his principal assistant. "Why, what proof is there that this has anything to do with them?"

Valentin almost broke his bamboo stick with rage.

"Proof!" he cried. "Good God! the man is looking for proof! Why, of course, the chances are twenty to one that it has *nothing* to do with them. But what else can we do? Don't you see we must either follow one wild possibility or else go home to bed?" He banged his way into the restaurant, followed by his companions, and they were soon seated at a late luncheon at a little table, and looking at the star of smashed glass from the inside. Not that it was very informative to them even then.

"Got your window broken, I see," said Valentin to the waiter as he paid the bill.

"Yes, sir," answered the attendant, bending busily over the change, to which Valentin silently added an enormous tip. The waiter straightened himself with mild but unmistakable animation.

"Ah, yes, sir," he said. "Very odd thing, that, sir."

"Indeed?" Tell us about it," said the detective with careless curiosity.

"Well, two gents in black came in," said the waiter; "two of those foreign parsons that are running about. They had a cheap and quiet little lunch, and one of them paid for it and went out. The other was just going out to join him when I looked at my change again and found he'd paid me more than three times too much. 'Here,' I says to the chap who was nearly out of the door, 'you've paid too much.' 'Oh,' he says, very cool, 'have we?' 'Yes,' I says, and picks up the bill to show him. Well, that was a knockout."

"What do you mean?" asked his interlocutor.

"Well, I'd have sworn on seven Bibles that I'd put 4s. on that bill. But now I saw I'd put 14s., as plain as paint."

"Well?" cried Valentin, moving slowly, but with burning eyes, "and then?"

"The parson at the door he says all serene, "Sorry to confuse your accounts, but it'll pay for the window." 'What window?' I says. 'The one I'm going to break,' he says, and smashed that blessed pane with his umbrella."

All three inquirers made an explanation; and the inspector said under his breath, "Are we after escaped lunatics?" The waiter went on with some relish for the ridiculous story:

"I was so knocked silly for a second, I couldn't do anything. The man marched out of the place and joined his friend just round the corner. Then they went so quick up Bullock Street that I couldn't catch them, though I ran round the bars to do it."

"Bullock Street," said the detective, and shot up that thoroughfare as quickly as the strange couple he pursued.

Their journey now took them through bare brick ways like tunnels; streets with few lights and even with few windows; streets that seemed built out of the blank backs of everything and everywhere. Dusk was deepening, and it was not easy even for the London policemen to guess in what exact direction they were treading. The inspector, however, was pretty certain that they would eventually strike some part of Hampstead Heath. Abruptly one bulging gas-lit window broke the blue twilight like a bull's-eye lantern; and Valentin stopped an instant before a little garish sweetstuff shop. After an instant's hesitation he went in; he stood amid the gaudy colors of the confectionery with entire gravity and brought thirteen chocolate cigars with a certain care. He was clearly preparing an opening, but he did not need one.

An angular, elderly young woman in the shop had regarded his elegant appearance with a merely automatic inquiry; but when she saw the door behind him blocked with the blue uniform of the inspector, her eyes seemed to wake up.

"Oh," she said, "if you've come about that parcel, I've sent it off already."

"Parcel!" repeated Valentin; and it was his turn to look inquiring.

"I mean the parcel the gentleman left—the clergyman gentleman."

"For goodness' sake," said Valentin, leaning forward with his first real confession of eagerness, "for Heaven's sake tell us what happened exactly."

"Well," said the woman a little doubtfully, "the clergymen came in about half an hour ago and bought some peppermints and talked a bit, and then went off towards the Heath. But a second after, one of them runs back into the shop and says, 'Have I left a parcel?' Well, I looked everywhere and couldn't see one; so he says, 'Never mind; but if it should turn up, please post it to this address,' and he left me the address and a shilling for my trouble. And sure enough, though I thought I'd looked everywhere, I found he'd left a brown paper parcel, so I posted it to the place he said. I can't remember the address now; it was somewhere in

Westminster. But as the thing seemed so important, I thought perhaps the police had come about it."

"So they have," said Valentin shortly. "Is Hampstead Heath near here?"

"Straight on for fifteen minutes," said the woman, "and you'll come right out on the open." Valentin sprang out of the shop and began to run. The other detectives followed him at a reluctant trot.

The street they threaded was so narrow and shut in by shadows that when they came out unexpectedly into the void common and vast sky they were startled to find the evening still so light and clear. A perfect dome of peacock-green sank into gold amid the blackening trees and the dark violet distances. The glowing green tint was just deep enough to pick out in points of crystal one or two stars. All that was left of the daylight lay in a golden glitter across the edge of Hampstead and that popular hollow which is called the Vale of Health. The holiday makers who roam this region had not wholly dispersed; a few couples sat shapelessly on benches; and here and there a distant girl still shrieked in one of the swings. The glory of heaven deepened and darkened around the sublime vulgarity of man; and standing on the slope and looking across the valley, Valentin beheld the thing which he sought.

Among the black and breaking groups in that distance was one especially black which did not break—a group of two figures clerically clad. Though they seemed as small as insects, Valentin could see that one of them was much smaller than the other. Though the other had a student's stoop and an inconspicuous manner, he could see that the man was well over six feet high. He shut his teeth and went forward, whirling his stick impatiently. By the time he had substantially diminished the distance and magnified the two black figures as in a vast microscope, he had perceived something else; something which startled him, and yet which he had somehow expected. Whoever was the tall priest, there could be no doubt about the identity of the short one. It was his friend of the Harwich train, the stumpy little *curé* of Essex whom he had warned about his brown paper parcels.

Now, so far as this went, everything fitted in finally and rationally enough. Valentin had learned by his inquiries that morning that a Father Brown from Essex was bringing up a silver cross with sapphires, a relic of considerable value, to show some of the foreign priests at the congress. This undoubtedly was the "silver with blue stones"; and Father Brown undoubtedly was the little greenhorn in the train. Now there was nothing wonderful about the fact that what Valentin had found out Flambeau had also found out; Flambeau found out everything. Also there was nothing wonderful in the fact that when Flambeau heard of a sapphire cross he should try to steal it; that was the most natural thing in all natural history. And most certainly there was nothing wonderful about the fact that Flambeau should have it all his own way with such a silly sheep as the man with the umbrella and the parcels. He was the sort of man whom anybody could lead on a string to the North Pole; it was not surprising that an actor like Flambeau, dressed as another priest, could lead him to Hampstead Heath. So far the crime seemed clear enough; and while the detective pitied the priest for his helplessness, he almost despised Flambeau for condescending to so gullible a victim. But when Valentin thought of all that had happened in between, of all that had led him to his triumph, he racked his brains for the smallest rhyme or reason in it. What had the stealing of a blue-and-silver cross from a priest from Essex to do with chucking soup at wall paper? What had it to do with calling nuts oranges, or with paying for windows first and breaking them afterwards? He had come to the end of his chase; yet somehow he had missed the middle of it. When he failed (which was seldom), he had usually grasped the clue, but nevertheless missed the criminal. Here he had grasped the criminal, but still he could not grasp the clue.

The two figures that they followed were crawling like black flies across the huge green contour of a hill. They were evidently sunk in conversation, and perhaps did not notice where they were going; but they were certainly going to the wilder and more silent heights of the Heath. As their pursuers gained on them, the latter had to use the undignified attitudes of the deer-stalker, to crouch behind clumps of trees and even to crawl prostrate in deep grass. By these ungainly ingenuities the hunters even came close enough to the quarry to hear the murmur of the discussion, but no word could be distinguished except the word "reason" recurring frequently in a high and almost childish voice. Once over an abrupt dip of land and a dense tangle of thickets, the detectives actually lost the two figures they were following. They did not find the trail again for an agonizing ten minutes, and then it led round the brow of a great dome of hill overlooking an amphitheater of rich and desolate sunset scenery. Under a tree in this commanding yet neglected spot was an old ramshackle wooden seat. On this seat sat the two priests still in serious speech together. The gorgeous green and gold still clung to the darkening horizon; but the dome above was turning slowly from peacock-green to peacock-blue, and the stars detached themselves more and more like solid jewels. Mutely motioning to his followers, Valentin contrived to creep up behind the big branching tree, and, standing there in deathly silence, heard the words of the strange priests for the first time.

After he had listened for a minute and a half, he was gripped by a devilish doubt. Perhaps he had dragged the two English policemen to the wastes of a nocturnal heath on an errand no saner than seeking figs on its thistles. For the two priests were talking exactly like priests, piously, with learning and leisure, about the most aerial enigmas of theology. The little Essex priest spoke the more simply, with his round face turned to the strengthening stars; the other talked with his head bowed, as if he were not even worthy to look at them. But no more innocently clerical conversation could have been heard in any white Italian cloister or black Spanish cathedral.

The first he heard was the tail of one of Father Brown's sentences, which ended: ". . . what they really meant in the Middle Ages by the heavens being incorruptible."

The taller priest nodded his bowed head and said:

"Ah, yes, these modern infidels appeal to their reason; but who can look at those millions of worlds and not feel that there may well be wonderful universes above us where reason is utterly unreasonable?"

"No," said the other priest: "reason is always reasonable, even in the last limbo, in the lost borderland of things. I know that people charge the Church with lowering reason, but it is just the other way. Alone on earth, the Church makes reason really supreme. Alone on earth, the Church affirms that God himself is bound by reason."

The other priest raised his austere face to the spangled sky and said:

"Yet who knows if in that infinite universe—?"

"Only infinite physically," said the little priest, turning sharply in his seat, "not infinite in the sense of escaping from the laws of truth."

Valentin behind his tree was tearing his finger-nails with silent fury. He seemed almost to hear the sniggers of the English detectives whom he had brought so far on a fantastic guess only to listen to the metaphysical gossip of two mild old parsons. In his impatience he lost the equally elaborate answer of the tall cleric, and when he listened again it was Father Brown who was speaking:

"Reason and justice grip the remotest and loneliest star. Look at those stars. Don't they look as if they were single diamonds and sapphires? Well, you can imagine any mad botany or geology you please. Think of forests of adamant with leaves of brilliants. Think the moon is a blue moon, a single elephantine sapphire. But don't fancy that all that frantic astronomy would make the smallest difference to the reason and justice of conduct. On plains of opal, under cliffs cut out of pearl, you would still find a notice-board, 'Thou shalt not steal.' "

Valentin was just in the act of rising from his rigid and crouching attitude and creeping away as softly as might be, felled by the one great folly of his life. But something in the very silence of the tall priest made him stop until the latter spoke. When at last he did speak, he said simply, his head bowed and his hands on his knees:

"Well, I still think that other worlds may perhaps rise higher than our reason. The mystery of heaven is unfathomable, and I for one can only bow my head."

Then, with brow yet bent and without changing by the faintest shade his attitude or voice, he added:

"Just hand over that sapphire cross of yours, will you? We're all alone here, and I could pull you to pieces like a straw doll."

The utterly unaltered voice and attitude added a strange violence to that shocking change of speech. But the guarder of the relic only seemed to turn his head by the smallest section of the compass. He seemed still to have a somewhat foolish face turned to the stars. Perhaps he had not understood. Or, perhaps, he had understood and sat rigid with terror.

"Yes," said the tall priest, in the same low voice and in the same still posture, "yes, I am Flambeau."

Then, after a pause, he said:

"Come, will you give me that cross?"

"No," said the other, and the monosyllable had an odd sound.

Flambeau suddenly flung off all his pontifical pretensions. The great robber leaned back in his seat and laughed low but long.

"No," he cried, "you won't give it me, you proud prelate. You won't give it me, you little celibate simpleton. Shall I tell you why you won't give it me? Because I've got it already in my own breast-pocket."

The small man from Essex turned what seemed to be a dazed face in the dusk, and said, with the timid eagerness of "The Private Secretary":

"Are—are you sure?"

Flambeau yelled with delight.

"Really, you're as good as a three-act farce," he cried. "Yes, you turnip, I am quite sure. I had the sense to make a duplicate of the right parcel, and now, my friend, you've got the duplicate and I've got the jewels. An old dodge, Father Brown—a very old dodge."

"Yes," said Father Brown, and passed his hand through his hair with the same strange vagueness of manner. "Yes, I've heard of it before."

The colossus of crime leaned over to the little rustic priest with a sort of sudden interest.

"*You* have heard of it?" he asked. "Where have *you* heard of it?"

"Well, I mustn't tell you his name, of course," said the little man simply. "He was a penitent, you know. He had lived prosperously for about twenty years entirely on duplicate brown paper parcels. And so, you see, when I began to suspect you, I thought of this poor chap's way of doing it at once."

"Began to suspect me?" repeated the outlaw with increased intensity. "Did you really have the gumption to suspect me just because I brought you up to this bare part of the heath?"

"No, no," said Father Brown with an air of apology. "You see, I suspected you when we first met. It's that little bulge up the sleeve where you people have the spiked bracelet."

"How in Tartarus," cried Flambeau, "did you ever hear of the spiked bracelet?"

"Oh, one's little flock, you know!" said Father Brown, arching his eyebrows rather blankly. "When I was a curate in Hartlepool, there were three of them with spiked bracelets. So, as I suspected you from the first, don't you see, I made sure that the cross should go safe, anyhow. I'm afraid I watched you, you know. So at last I saw you change the parcels. Then, don't you see, I changed them back again. And then I left the right one behind."

"Left it behind?" repeated Flambeau, and for the first time there was another note in his voice beside his triumph.

"Well, it was like this," said the little priest, speaking in the same unaffected way. "I went back to that sweetshop and asked if I'd left a parcel, and gave them a particular address if it turned up. Well, I knew I hadn't; but when I went away again I did. So, instead of running after me with that valuable parcel, they have sent it flying to a friend of mine in Westminster." Then he added rather sadly: "I learnt that, too, from a poor fellow in Hartlepool. He used to do it with handbags he stole at railway stations, but he's in a monastery now. Oh, one gets to know, you know," he added, rubbing his head again with the same sort of desperate apology. "We can't help it being priests. People come and tell us these things."

Flambeau tore a brown paper parcel out of his inner pocket and rent it in pieces. There was nothing but paper and sticks of lead inside it. He sprang to his feet with a gigantic gesture, and cried:

"I don't believe you. I don't believe a bumpkin like you could manage all that. I believe you've still got the stuff on you, and if you don't give it up—why, we're all alone, and I'll take it by force!"

"No," said Father Brown simply, and stood up also, "you won't take it by force. First, because I really haven't still got it. And, second, because we are not alone."

Flambeau stopped in his stride forward.

"Behind that tree," said Father Brown, pointing, "are two strong policemen and the greatest detective alive. How did they come here, do you ask? Why, I brought them, of course! How did I do it? Why, I'll tell you if you like! Lord bless you, we have to know twenty such things when we work among the criminal classes! Well, I wasn't sure you were a thief, and it would never do to make a scandal against one of our own clergy. So I just tested you to see if anything would make you show yourself. A man generally makes a small scene if he finds salt in his coffee; if he doesn't, he has some reason for keeping quiet. I changed the salt and sugar, and *you* kept quiet. A man generally objects if his bill is three times too big. If he pays it, he has some motive for passing unnoticed. I altered your bill, and *you* paid it."

The world seemed waiting for Flambeau to leap like a tiger. But he was held back as by a spell; he was stunned with the utmost curiosity.

"Well," went on Father Brown, with lumbering lucidity, "as you wouldn't leave any tracks for the police, of course somebody had to. At every place we went to, I took care to do something that would get us talked about for the rest of the day. I didn't do much harm—a splashed wall, spilt apples, a broken window; but I saved the cross, as the cross will always be saved. It is at Westminster by now. I rather wonder you didn't stop it with the Donkey's Whistle."

"With the what?" asked Flambeau.

"I'm glad you've never heard of it," said the priest, making a face. "It's a foul thing. I'm sure you're too good a man for a Whistler. I couldn't have countered it even with the Spots myself; I'm not strong enough in the legs."

"What on earth are you talking about?" asked the other.

"Well, I did think you'd know the Spots," said Father Brown, agreeably surprised. "Oh, you can't have gone so very wrong yet!"

"How in blazes do you know all these horrors?" cried Flambeau.

The shadow of a smile crossed the round, simple face of his clerical opponent.

"Oh, by being a celibate simpleton, I suppose," he said. "Has it never struck you that a man who does next to nothing but hear men's real sins is not likely to be wholly unaware of human evil? But, as a matter of fact, another part of my trade, too, made me sure you weren't a priest."

"What?" asked the thief, almost gaping.

"You attacked reason," said Father Brown. "It's bad theology."

And even as he turned away to collect his property, the three policemen came out from under the twilight trees. Flambeau was an artist and a sportsman. He stepped back and swept Valentin a great bow.

"Do not bow to me, *mon ami*," said Valentin with silver clearness. "Let us both bow to our master."

And they both stood an instant uncovered while the little Essex priest blinked about for his umbrella.

QUESTIONS

1. Read G. K. Chesterton's essay in the "Theories" section below and discuss how this story illustrates the ideas he sets forth.

2. Father Brown is, of course, a priest. But "The Blue Cross" contains a much more significant religious element than may be immediately recognized. Trace the religious elements of this story, especially as they relate to theme. Particularly examine Father Brown's discussion of religion and reason.

3. Valentin says, "The criminal is the creative artist; the detective only the critic." Explore the accuracy of this observation in relation to this and other stories in the sourcebook.

4. Three "masterminds" of a sort are present in this story. Two are almost legendary as a result of their past deeds. Their attitudes

toward each other reveal a kind of mutual respect. Discuss this respect, connecting it to the "understanding" between criminal and law enforcement figures so often seen in detective fiction.

5. What is a "paradox"? What role does the idea of paradox play in the story?

Fly Paper

Dashiell Hammett

It was a wandering daughter job.

The Hambletons had been for several generations a wealthy and decently prominent New York family. There was nothing in the Hambleton history to account for Sue, the youngest member of the clan. She grew out of childhood with a kink that made her dislike the polished side of life, like the rough. By the time she was twenty-one, in 1926, she definitely preferred Tenth Avenue to Fifth, grifters to bankers, and Hymie the Riveter to the Honorable Cecil Windown, who had asked her to marry him.

The Hambletons tried to make Sue behave, but it was too late for that. She was legally of age. When she finally told them to go to hell and walked out on them there wasn't much they could do about it. Her father, Major Waldo Hambleton, had given up all the hopes he ever had of salvaging her, but he didn't want her to run into any grief that could be avoided. So he came into the Continental Detective Agency's New York office and asked to have an eye kept on her.

Hymie the Riveter was a Philadelphia racketeer who had moved north to the big city, carrying a Thompson submachine gun wrapped in blue-checkered oil cloth, after a disagreement with his partners. New York wasn't so good a field as Philadelphia for machine gun work. The Thompson lay idle for a year or so while Hymie made expenses with an automatic, preying on small-time crap games in Harlem.

Three or four months after Sue went to live with Hymie he made what looked like a promising connection with the first of the crew that came into New York from Chicago to organize the city on the western scale. But the boys from Chi didn't want Hymie; they wanted the Thompson. When he showed it to them, as the big item in his application for employment, they shot holes in the top of Hymie's head and went away with the gun.

Sue Hambleton buried Hymie, had a couple of lonely weeks in which she hocked a ring to eat, and then got a job as hostess in a speakeasy run by a Greek named Vassos.

One of Vassos' customers was Babe McCloor, two hundred and fifty pounds of hard Scotch-Irish-Indian bone and muscle, a black-haired, blue-eyed, swarthy giant who was resting up after doing a fifteen-year hitch in Leavenworth for ruining most of the smaller post offices between New Orleans and Omaha. Babe was keeping himself in drinking money while he rested by playing with pedestrians in dark streets.

Babe liked Sue. Vassos liked Sue. Sue liked Babe. Vassos didn't like that. Jealousy spoiled the Greek's judgment. He kept the speakeasy door locked one night when Babe wanted to come in. Babe came in, bringing pieces of the door with him. Vassos got his gun out, but couldn't shake Sue off his arm. He stopped trying when Babe hit him with the part of the door that had the brass knob on it. Babe and Sue went away from Vassos' together.

Up to that time the New York office had managed to keep in touch with Sue. She hadn't been kept under constant surveillance. Her father hadn't wanted that. It was simply a matter of sending a man around every week or so to see that she was still alive, to pick up whatever information he could from her friends and neighbors, without, of course, letting her know she was being tabbed. All that had been easy enough, but when she and Babe went away after wrecking the gin mill, they dropped completely out of sight.

After turning the city upside-down, the New York office sent a journal on the job to the other Continental branches throughout the country, giving the information above and enclosing photographs and descriptions of Sue and her new playmate. That was late in 1927.

We had enough copies of the photographs to go around, and for the next month or so whoever had a little idle time on his hands spent it looking through San Francisco and Oakland for the missing pair. We didn't find them. Operatives in other cities, doing the same thing, had the same luck.

Then, nearly a year later, a telegram came to us from the New York office. Decoded, it read:

> Major Hambleton today received telegram from daughter in San Francisco quote Please wire me thousand dollars care apartment two hundred six number six hundred one Eddis Street stop I will come home if you will let me stop Please tell me if I can come but please please wire money anyway unquote Hambleton authorizes payment of money to her immediately stop Detail competent operative to call on her with money and to arrange for her return home stop If possible have man and woman operative accompany her here stop Hambleton wiring her stop Report immediately by wire.

The Old Man gave me the telegram and a check, saying, "You know the situation. You'll know how to handle it."

I pretended I agreed with him, went down to the bank, swapped the check for a bundle of bills of several sizes, caught a streetcar, and went up to 601 Eddis Street, a fairly large apartment building on the corner of Larkin.

The name on Apartment 206's vestibule mail box was J. M. Wales.

I pushed 206's button. When the locked door buzzed off I went into the building, past the elevator to the stairs, and up a flight. 206 was just around the corner from the stairs.

The apartment door was opened by a tall, slim man of thirty-something in neat dark clothes. He had narrow dark eyes set in a long pale face. There was some gray in the dark hair brushed flat to his scalp.

"Miss Hambleton," I said.

"Uh—what about her?" His voice was smooth, but not too smooth to be agreeable.

"I'd like to see her."

His upper eyelids came down a little and the brows over them came a little closer together. He asked, "Is it—?" and stopped, watching me steadily.

I didn't say anything. Presently he finished his question, "Something to do with a telegram?"

"Yeah."

His long face brightened immediately. He asked, "You're from her father?"

"Yeah."

He stepped back and swung the door wide open, saying, "Come in. Major Hambleton's wire came to her only a few minutes ago. He said someone would call."

We went through a small passageway into a sunny living room that was cheaply furnished, but neat and clean enough.

"Sit down," the man said, pointing at a brown rocking chair.

I sat down. He sat on the burlap-covered sofa facing me. I looked around the room. I didn't see anything to show that a woman was living there.

He rubbed the long bridge of his nose with a longer forefinger and asked slowly, "You brought the money?"

I said I'd feel more like talking with her there.

He looked at the finger with which he had been rubbing his nose, and then up at me, saying softly, "But I'm her friend."

I said, "Yeah?" to that.

"Yes," he repeated. He frowned slightly, drawing back the corners of his thin-lipped mouth. "I've only asked whether you've brought the money."

I didn't say anything.

"The point is," he said quite reasonably, "that if you brought the money she doesn't expect you to hand it over to anybody except her. If you didn't bring it she doesn't want to see you. I don't think her mind can be changed about that. That's why I asked if you had brought it."

"I brought it."

He looked doubtfully at me. I showed him the money I had got from the bank. He jumped up briskly from the sofa.

"I'll have her here in a minute or two," he said over his shoulder as his long legs moved him toward the door. At the door he stopped to ask, "Do you know her?" Or shall I have her bring means of identifying herself?"

"That would be best," I told him.

He went out, leaving the corridor door open.

In five minutes he was back with a slender blonde girl of twenty-three in pale green silk. The looseness of her small mouth and the puffiness around her blue eyes weren't yet pronounced enough to spoil her prettiness.

I stood up.

"This is Miss Hambleton," he said.

She gave me a swift glance and then lowered her eyes again, nervously playing with the strap of a handbag she held.

"You can identify yourself?" I asked.

"Sure," the man said. "Show them to him, Sue."

She opened the bag, brought out some papers and things, and held them up for me to take.

"Sit down, sit down," the man said as I took them.

They sat on the sofa. I sat in the rocking chair again and examined the things she had given me. There were two letters addressed to Sue Hambleton here, her father's telegram welcoming her home, a couple of receipted department store bills, an automobile driver's license, and a savings account pass book that showed a balance of less than ten dollars.

By the time I had finished my examination the girl's embarrassment was gone. She looked levelly at me, as did the man beside her. I felt in my pocket, found my copy of the photograph New York had sent us at the beginning of the hunt, and looked from it to her.

"Your mouth could have shrunk, maybe," I said, "but how could your nose have got that much longer?"

"If you don't like my nose," she said, "how'd you like to go to hell?" Her face had turned red.

"That's not the point. It's a swell nose, but it's not Sue's. I held the photograph out to her. "See for yourself."

She glared at the photograph and then at the man.

"What a smart guy you are," she told him.

He was watching me with dark eyes that had a brittle shine to them between narrow-drawn eyelids. He kept on watching me while he spoke to her out the side of his mouth, crisply. "Pipe down."

She piped down. He sat and watched me. I sat and watched him. A clock ticked seconds away behind me. His eyes began shifting their focus from one of my eyes to the other. The girl sighed.

He said in a low voice, "Well?"

I said, "You're in a hole."

"What can you make out of it?" he asked casually.

"Conspiracy to defraud."

The girl jumped up and hit one of his shoulders angrily with the back of a hand, crying, "What a smart guy you are, to get me in a jam like this. It was going to be duck soup—yeh! Eggs in the coffee—yeh! Now look at you. You haven't even got guts enough to tell this guy to go chase himself." She spun around to face me, pushing her red face down at me—I was still sitting in the rocker—snarling, "Well, what are you waiting for? Waiting to be kissed goodbye? We don't owe you anything, do we? We didn't get any of your lousy money, did we? Outside, then. Take the air. Dangle."

"Stop it, sister," I growled. "You'll bust something."

The man said, "For God's sake stop that bawling, Peggy, and give somebody else a chance." He addressed me, "Well, what do you want?"

"How'd you get into this?" I asked.

He spoke quickly, eagerly, "A fellow named Kenny gave me that stuff and told me about this Sue Hambleton, and her old man having plenty. I thought I'd give it a whirl. I figured the old man would either wire the dough right off the reel or wouldn't send it at all. I didn't figure on this send-a-man stuff. Then when his wire came, saying he was sending a man to see her, I ought to have dropped it.

"But hell! Here was a man coming with a grand in cash. That was too good to let go of without a try. It looked like there still might be a chance of copping, so I got Peggy to do Sue for me. If the man was coming today, it was a cinch he belonged out here on the Coast, and it was an even bet he wouldn't know Sue, would only have a description of her. From what Kenny had told me about her, I knew Peggy would come pretty close to fitting her description. I still don't see how you got that photograph. I only wired the old man yesterday. I mailed a couple of letters to Sue, here, yesterday, so we'd have them with the other identification stuff to get the money from the telegraph company on."

"Kenny gave you the old man's address?"

"Sure he did."

"Did he give you Sue's?"

"No."

"How'd Kenny get hold of the stuff?"

"He didn't say."

"Where's Kenny now?"

"I don't know. He was on his way east, with something else on the fire, and couldn't fool with this. That's why he passed it on to me."

"Big-hearted Kenny," I said. "You know Sue Hambleton?"

"No," emphatically. "I'd never even heard of her till Kenny told me."

"I don't like this Kenny," I said, "though without him your story's got some good points. Could you tell it leaving him out?"

He shook his head slowly from side to side, saying, "It wouldn't be the way it happened."

"That's too bad. Conspiracies to defraud don't mean as much to me as finding Sue. I might have made a deal with you."

He shook his head again, but his eyes were thoughtful, and his lower lip moved up to overlap the upper a little.

The girl had stepped back so she could see both of us as we talked, turning her face, which showed she didn't like us, from one to the other as we spoke our pieces. Now she fastened her gaze on the man, and her eyes were growing angry again.

I got up on my feet, telling him, "Suit yourself. But if you want to play it that way I'll have to take you both in."

He smiled with indrawn lips and stood up.

The girl thrust herself in between us, facing him.

"This is a swell time to be dummying up," she spit at him. "Pop off, you lightweight, or I will. You're crazy if you think I'm going to take the fall with you."

"Shut up," he said in his throat.

"Shut me up," she cried.

He tried to, with both hands. I reached over her shoulders and caught one of his wrists, knocked the other hand up.

She slid out from between us and ran around behind me, screaming, "Joe does know her. He got the things from her. She's at the St. Martin on O'Farrell Street—her and Babe McCloor."

While I listened to this I had to pull my head aside to let Joe's right hook miss me, had got his left arm twisted behind him, had turned my hip to catch his knee, and had got the palm of my left hand under his chin. I was ready to give his chin the Japanese tilt when he stopped wrestling and grunted, "Let me tell it."

"Hop to it," I consented, taking my hands away from him and stepping back.

He rubbed the wrist I had wrenched, scowling past me at the girl. He called her four unlovely names, the mildest of which was "a dumb twist," and told her, "He was bluffing about throwing us in the can. You don't think old man Hambleton's hunting for newspaper space, do you?" That wasn't a bad guess.

He sat on the sofa again, still rubbing his wrist. The girl stayed on the other side of the room, laughing at him through her teeth.

I said, "All right, roll it out, one of you."

"You've got it all," he muttered. "I glaumed that stuff last week when I was visiting Babe, knowing the story and hating to see a promising layout like that go to waste."

"What's Babe doing now?" I asked.

"I don't know."

"Is he still puffing them?"

"I don't know."

"Like hell you don't."

"I don't," he insisted. "If you know Babe you know you can't get anything out of him about what he's doing."

"How long have he and Sue been here?"

"About six months that I know of."

"Who's he mobbed up with?"

"I don't know. Any time Babe works with a mob he picks them up on the road and leaves them on the road."

"How's he fixed?"

"I don't know. There's always enough grub and liquor in the joint."

Half an hour of this convinced me that I wasn't going to get much information about my people here.

I went to the phone in the passageway and called the Agency. The boy on the switchboard told me MacMan was in the operative's room. I asked to have him sent up to me, and went back to the living room. Joe and Peggy took their heads apart when I came in.

MacMan arrived in less than ten minutes. I let him in and told him, "This fellow says his name's Joe Wales, and the girl's supposed to be Peggy Carroll who lives upstairs in 421. We've got them cold for conspiracy to defraud, but I've made a deal with them. I'm going out to look at it now. Stay here with them, in this room. Nobody goes in or out, and nobody but you gets to the phone. There's a fire escape in front of the window. The window's locked now. I'd keep it that way. If the deal turns out O.K. we'll let them go, but if they cut up on you while I'm gone there's no reason why you can't knock them around as much as you want."

MacMan nodded his hard round head and pulled a chair out between them and the door. I picked up my hat.

Joe Wales called, "Hey, you're not going to uncover me to Babe, are you? That's got to be part of the deal."

"Not unless I have to."

"I'd just as leave stand the rap," he said. "I'd be safer in jail."

"I'll give you the best break I can," I promised, "but you'll have to take what's dealt you."

Walking over to the St. Martin—only half a dozen blocks from Wales's place—I decided to go up against McCloor and the girl as a Continental op who suspected Babe of being in on a branch bank stick-up in Alameda the previous week. He hadn't been in on it—if the bank people had described half-correctly the men who had robbed them—so it wasn't likely my supposed suspicions would frighten him much. Clearing himself, he might give me some information I could use. The chief thing I wanted, of course, was a look at the girl, so I could report to her father that I had seen her. There was no reason for supposing that she and Babe knew her father was trying to keep an eye on her. Babe had a record. It was natural enough for sleuths to drop in now and then and try to hang something on him.

The St. Martin was a small three-story apartment house of red brick between two taller hotels. The vestibule register showed R. K. McCloor, 313, as Wales and Peggy had told me.

I pushed the bell button. Nothing happened. Nothing happened any of the four times I pushed it. I pushed the button labeled *Manager*.

The door clicked open. I went indoors. A beefy woman in a pink-striped cotton dress that needed pressing stood in an apartment doorway just inside the street door.

"Some people named McCloor live here?" I asked.

"Three-thirteen," she said.

"Been living here long?"

She pursed her fat mouth, looked intently at me, hesitated, but finally said, "Since last June."

"What do you know about them?"

She balked at that, raising her chin and her eyebrows.

I gave her my card. That was safe enough; it fit in with the pretext I intended using upstairs.

Her face, when she raised it from reading the card, was oily with curiosity.

"Come in here," she said in a husky whisper, backing through the doorway.

I followed her into her apartment. We sat on a chesterfield and she whispered, "What is it?"

"Maybe nothing." I kept my voice low, playing up to her theatricals. "He's done time for safe burglary. I'm trying to get a line on him now, on the off chance that he might have been tied up in a recent job. I don't know that he was. He may be going straight for all I know." I took his photograph—front and profile, taken at Leavenworth—out of my pocket. "This him?"

She seized it eagerly, nodded, said, "Yes, that's him, all right," turned it over to read the description on the back, and repeated, "Yes, that's him, all right."

"His wife is here with him?" I asked.

She nodded vigorously.

"I don't know her," I said. "What sort of looking girl is she?"

She described a girl who could have been Sue Hambleton. I couldn't show Sue's picture; that would have uncovered me if she and Babe heard about it.

I asked the woman what she knew about the McCloors. What she knew wasn't a great deal: paid their rent on time, kept irregular hours, had occasional drinking parties, quarreled a lot.

"Think they're in now?" I asked. "I got no answer on the bell."

"I don't know," she whispered. "I haven't seen either of them since night before last, when they had a fight."

"Much of a fight?"

"Not much worse than usual."

"Could you find out if they're in?" I asked.

She looked at me out of the ends of her eyes.

"I'm not going to make any trouble for you," I assured her. "But if they've blown I'd like to know it, and I reckon you would too."

"All right, I'll find out." She got up, patting a pocket in which keys jingled. "You wait here."

"I'll go as far as the third floor with you," I said, "and wait out of sight there."

"All right," she said reluctantly.

On the third floor, I remained by the elevator. She disappeared around a corner of the dim corridor, and presently a muffled electric bell rang. It rang three times. I heard her keys jingle and one of them grate in a lock. The lock clicked. I heard the doorknob rattle as she turned it.

Then a long moment of silence was ended by a scream that filled the corridor from wall to wall.

I jumped for the corner, swung around it, saw an open door ahead, went through it, and slammed the door shut behind me.

The scream stopped.

I was in a small dark vestibule with three doors beside the one I had come through. One door was shut. One opened into a bathroom. I went to the other.

The fat manager stood just inside it, her round back to me. I pushed past her and saw what she was looking at.

Sue Hambleton, in pale yellow pajamas trimmed with black lace, was lying across the bed. She lay on her back. Her arms were stretched out over her head. One leg was bent under her, one stretched out so that its bare foot rested on the floor. That bare foot was whiter than a live foot could be. Her face was white as her foot, except for a mottled swollen area from the right eyebrow to the right cheek-bone and dark bruises on her throat.

Phone the police," I told the woman, and began poking into corners, closets and drawers.

It was late afternoon when I returned to the Agency. I asked the file clerk to see if we had anything on Joe Wales and Peggy Carroll, and then went into the Old Man's office.

He put down some reports he had been reading, gave me a nodded invitation to sit down, and asked, "You've seen her?"

"Yeah. She's dead."

The Old Man said, "Indeed," as if I had said it was raining, and smiled with polite attentiveness while I told him about it—from the time I had rung Wales's bell until I had joined the fat manager in the dead girl's apartment.

"She had been knocked around some, was bruised on the face and neck," I wound up. "But that didn't kill her."

"You think she was murdered?" he asked, still smiling gently.

"I don't know. Doc Jordan says he thinks it could have been arsenic. He's hunting for it in her now. We found a funny thing in the joint. Some thick sheets of dark gray paper were stuck in a book—*The Count of Monte Cristo*—wrapped in a month-old newspaper and wedged into a dark corner between the stove and the kitchen wall."

"Ah, arsenical fly paper," the Old Man murmured. "The Maybrick-Seddons trick. Mashed in water, four to six grains of arsenic can be soaked out of a sheet—enough to kill two people."

I nodded, saying, "I worked on one in Louisville in 1916. The mulatto janitor saw McCloor leaving at half-past nine yesterday morning. She was probably dead before that. Nobody's seen him since. Earlier in the morning the people in the next apartment had heard them talking, her groaning. But they had too many fights for the neighbors to pay much attention to that. The landlady told me they had a fight the night before that. The police are hunting for him."

"Did you tell the police who she was?"

"No. What do we do on that angle? We can't tell them about Wales without telling them all."

"I dare say the whole thing will have to come out," he said thoughtfully. "I'll wire New York."

I went out of his office. The file clerk gave me a couple of newspaper clippings. The first told me that fifteen months ago Joseph Wales, alias Holy Joe, had been arrested on the complaint of a farmer named Toomey that he had been taken for twenty-five hundred dollars on a phony "business opportunity" by Wales and three other men. The second clipping said the case had been dropped when Toomey failed to appear against Wales in court—bought off in the customary manner by the return of part or all of his money. That was all our files held on Wales, and they had nothing on Peggy Carroll.

*   *   *

MacMan opened the door for me when I returned to Wales's apartment.

"Anything doing?" I asked him.

"Nothing—except they've been belly-aching a lot." Wales came forward, asking eagerly, "Satisfied now?"

The girl stood by the window, looking at me with anxious eyes.

I didn't say anything.

"Did you find her?" Wales asked, frowning. "She was where I told you?"

"Yeah," I said.

"Well, then." Part of his frown went away. "That lets Peggy and me out, doesn't—" He broke off, ran his tongue over his lower lip, put a hand to his chin, asked sharply, "You didn't give them the tip-off on me, did you?"

I shook my head, no.

He took his hand from his chin and asked irritably, "What's the matter with you, then? What are you looking like that for?"

Behind him the girl spoke bitterly. "I knew damned well it would be like this," she said. "I knew damned well we weren't going to get out of it. Oh, what a smart guy you are!"

"Take Peggy into the kitchen, and shut both doors," I told MacMan. "Holy Joe and I are going to have a real heart-to-heart talk."

The girl went out willingly, but when MacMan was closing the door she put her head in again to tell Wales, "I hope he busts you in the nose if you try to hold out on him."

MacMan shut the door.

"Your playmate seems to think you know something," I said.

Wales scowled at the door and grumbled, "She's more help to me than a broken leg." He turned his face to me, trying to make it look frank and friendly. "What do you want? I came clean with you before. What's the matter now?"

"What do you guess?"

He pulled his lips in between his teeth. "What do you want to make me guess for?" he demanded. "I'm willing to play ball with you. But what can I do if you won't tell me what you want? I can't see inside your head."

"You'd get a kick out of it if you could."

He shook his head wearily and walked back to the sofa, sitting down bent forward, his hands together between his knees. "All right," he sighed. "Take your time about asking me. I'll wait for you."

I went over and stood in front of him. I took his chin between my left thumb and fingers, raising his head and bending my own down until our noses were almost touching. I said, "Where you stumbled, Joe, was in sending the telegram right after the murder."

"He's dead?" It popped out before his eyes had even had time to grow round and wide.

The question threw me off balance. I had to wrestle with my forehead to keep it from wrinkling, and I put too much calmness in my voice when I asked, "Is who dead?"

"Who? How do I know? Who do you mean?"

"Who did you think I meant?" I insisted.

"How do I know? Oh, all right! Old man Hambleton, Sue's father."

"That's right," I said, and took my hand away from his chin.

"And he was murdered, you say?" He hadn't moved his face an inch from the position into which I had lifted it. "How?"

"Arsenic fly paper."

"Arsenic fly paper." He looked thoughtful. "That's a funny one."

"Yeah, very funny. Where'd you go about buying some if you wanted it?"

"Buying it? I don't know. I haven't seen any since I was a kid. Nobody uses fly paper here in San Francisco anyway. There aren't enough flies."

"Somebody used some here," I said, "on Sue."

"Sue?" He jumped so that the sofa squeaked under him.

"Yeah. Murdered yesterday morning—arsenical fly paper."

"Both of them?" he asked incredulously.

"Both of who?"

"Her and her father."

"Yeah."

He put his chin far down on his chest and rubbed the back of one hand with the palm of the other. "Then I am in a hole," he said slowly.

"That's what," I cheerfully agreed. "Want to try talking yourself out of it?"

"Let me think."

I let him think, listening to the tick of the clock while he thought. Thinking brought drops of sweat out on his gray-white face. Presently he sat up straight, wiping his face with a fancily colored handkerchief. "I'll talk," he said. "I've got to talk now. Sue was getting ready to ditch Babe. She and I were going away. She— Here, I'll show you."

He put his hand in his pocket and held out a folded sheet of thick note paper to me. I took it and read:

Dear Joe:—

I can't stand this much longer—we've simply got to go soon. Babe beat me again tonight. Please, if you really love me, let's make it soon.

Sue

The handwriting was a nervous woman's, tall, angular, and piled up.

"That's why I made the play for Hambleton's grand," he said. "I've been shatting on my uppers for a couple of months, and when that letter came yesterday I just had to raise dough somehow to get her away. She wouldn't have stood for tapping her father though, so I tried to swing it without her knowing."

"When did you see her last?"

"Day before yesterday, the day she mailed that letter. Only I saw her in the afternoon—she was here—and she wrote it that night."

"Babe suspect what you were up to?"

"We didn't think he did. I don't know. He was jealous as hell all the time, whether he had any reason to be or not."

"How much reason did he have?"

Wales looked me straight in the eye and said, "Sue was a good kid."

I said, "Well, she's been murdered."

He didn't say anything.

Day was darkening into evening. I went to the door and pressed the light button. I didn't lose sight of Holy Joe Wales while I was doing it.

As I took my finger away from the button, something clicked at the window. The click was loud and sharp.

I looked at the window.

A man crouched there on the fire escape, looking in through the glass and lace curtain. He was a thick-featured dark man whose size identified him as Babe McCloor. The muzzle of a big black automatic was touching the glass in front of him. He had tapped the glass with it to catch our attention.

He had our attention.

There wasn't anything for me to do just then. I stood there and looked at him. I couldn't tell whether he was looking at me or at Wales. I could see him clearly enough, but the lace curtain spoiled my view of details like that. I imagined he wasn't neglecting either of us, and I didn't imagine the lace curtain hid much from him. He was closer to the curtain than we, and I had turned on the room's lights.

Wales, sitting dead-still on the sofa, was looking at McCloor. Wales's face wore a peculiar, stiffly sullen expression. His eyes were sullen. He wasn't breathing.

McCloor flicked the nose of his pistol against the pane, and a triangular piece of glass fell out, tinkling apart on the floor. It didn't, I was afraid, make enough noise to alarm MacMan in the kitchen. There were two closed doors between here and there.

Wales looked at the broken pane and closed his eyes. He closed them slowly, little by little, exactly as if he were falling asleep. He kept his stiffly sullen blank face turned straight to the window.

McCloor shot him three times.

The bullets knocked Wales down on the sofa, back against the wall. Wales's eyes popped open, bulging. His lips crawled back over his teeth, leaving them naked to the gums. His tongue came out. Then his head fell down and he didn't move any more.

When McCloor jumped away from the window I jumped to it. While I was pushing the curtain aside, unlocking the window and raising it, I heard his feet land on the cement paving below.

MacMan flung the door open and came in, the girl at his heels.

"Take care of this," I ordered as I scrambled over the sill. "McCloor shot him."

Wales's apartment was on the second floor. The fire escape ended there with a counter-weighted iron ladder that a man's weight would swing down into a cement-paved court.

I went down as Babe McCloor had gone, swinging down on the ladder till within dropping distance of the court, and then letting go.

There was only one street exit to the court. I took it.

A startled looking, smallish man was standing in the middle of the sidewalk close to the court, gaping at me as I dashed out.

I caught his arm, shook it. "A big guy running." Maybe I yelled. "Where?"

He tried to say something, couldn't, and waved his arm at billboards standing across the front of a vacant lot on the other side of the street.

I forgot to say, "Thank you," in my hurry to get over there.

I got behind the billboards by crawling under them instead of going to either end, where there were openings. The lot was large enough and weedy enough to give cover to anybody who wanted to lie down and bushwhack a pursuer—even anybody as large as Babe McCloor.

While I considered that, I heard a dog barking at one corner of the lot. He could have been barking at a man who had run by. I ran to that corner of the lot. The dog was in a board-fenced backyard, at the corner of a narrow alley that ran from the lot to a street.

I chinned myself on the board fence, saw a wire-haired terrier alone in the yard, and ran down the alley while he was charging my part of the fence.

I put my gun back in my pocket before I left the alley for the street.

A small touring car was parked at the curb in front of a cigar store some fifteen feet from the alley. A policeman was talking to a slim dark-faced man in the cigar store doorway.

"The big fellow that come out of the alley a minute ago," I said. "Which way did he go?"

The policeman looked dumb. The slim man nodded his head down the street, said, "Down that way," and went on with his conversation.

I said, "Thanks," and went on down the corner. There was a taxi phone there and two idle taxis. A block and a half below, a streetcar was going away. "Did the big fellow who came down here a minute ago take a taxi or the streetcar?" I asked the two taxi chauffeurs who were leaning against one of the taxis.

The rattier-looking one said, "He didn't take a taxi."

I said, "I'll take one. Catch that streetcar for me."

The streetcar was three blocks away before we got going. The street wasn't clear enough for me to see who got on and off it. We caught it when it stopped at Market Street.

"Follow along," I told the driver as I jumped out.

On the rear platform of the streetcar I looked through the glass. There were only eight or ten people aboard.

"There was a great big fellow got on at Hyde Street," I said to the conductor. "Where'd he get off?"

The conductor looked at the silver dollar I was turning over in my fingers and remembered that the big man got off at Taylor Street. That won the silver dollar.

I dropped off as the streetcar turned into Market Street. The taxi, close behind, slowed down, and its door swung open. "Sixth and Mission," I said as I hopped in.

McCloor could have gone in any direction from Taylor Street. I had to guess. The best guess seemed to be that he would make for the other side of Market Street.

It was fairly dark by now. We had to go down to Fifth Street to get off Market, then over to Mission, and back up to Sixth. We got to Sixth Street without seeing McCloor. I couldn't see him on Sixth Street— either way from the crossing.

"On up to Ninth," I ordered, and while we rode told the driver what kind of man I was looking for.

We arrived at Ninth Street. No McCloor. I cursed and pushed my brains around.

The big man was a yegg. San Francisco was on fire for him. The yegg instinct would be to use a rattler to get away from trouble. The freight yards were in this end of town. Maybe he would be shifty enough to lie low instead of trying to powder. In that case, he probably hadn't crossed Market Street at all. If he stuck, there would still be a chance of picking him up tomorrow. If he was high-tailing, it was catch him now or not at all.

"Down to Harrison," I told the driver.

We went down to Harrison Street, and down Harrison to Third, up Bryant to Eighth, down Brannan to Third again, and over to Townsend —and we didn't see Babe McCloor.

"That's tough, that is," the driver sympathized as we stopped across the street from the Southern Pacific passenger station.

"I'm going over and look around in the station," I said. "Keep your eyes open while I'm gone."

When I told the copper in the station my trouble he introduced me to a couple of plain-clothes men who had been planted there to watch for McCloor. That had been done after Sue Hambleton's body was found. The shooting of Holy Joe Wales was news to them.

I went outside again and found my taxi in front of the door, its horn working overtime, but too asthmatically to be heard indoors. The ratty driver was excited.

"A guy like you said come up out of King Street just now and swung on a Number 16 car as it pulled away," he said.

"Going which way?"

"Thataway," pointing southeast.

"Catch him," I said, jumping in.

The streetcar was out of sight around a bend in Third Street two blocks below. When we rounded the bend, the streetcar was slowing up, four blocks ahead. It hadn't slowed up very much when a man leaned far out and stepped off. He was a tall man, but didn't look tall on account of his shoulder spread. He didn't check his momentum, but used it to carry him across the sidewalk and out of sight.

We stopped where the man had left the car.

I gave the driver too much money and told him, "Go back to Townsend Street and tell the copper in the station that I've chased Babe McCloor into the S. P. yards."

I thought I was moving silently down between two strings of box cars, but I had gone less than twenty feet when a light flashed in my face and a sharp voice ordered, "Stand still, you."

I stood still. Men came from between cars. One of them spoke my name, adding, "What are you doing here? Lost?" It was Harry Pebble, a police detective.

I stopped holding my breath and said, "Hello, Harry. Looking for Babe?"

"Yes. We've been going over the rattlers."

"He's here. I just tailed him in from the street."

Pebble swore and snapped the light off.

"Watch, Harry," I advised. "Don't play with him. He's packing plenty of gun and he's cut down one boy tonight."

"I'll play with him," Pebble promised, and told one of the men with him to go over and warn those on the other side of the yard that McCloor was in, and then to ring for reinforcements.

"We'll just sit on the edge and hold him in till they come," he said.

That seemed a sensible way to play it. We spread out and waited. Once Pebble and I turned back a lanky bum who tried to slip into the yard between us, and one of the men below us picked up a shivering kid who was trying to slip out. Otherwise nothing happened until Lieutenant Duff arrived with a couple of carloads of coppers.

Most of our force went into a cordon around the yard. The rest of us went through the yard in small groups, working it over car by car. We picked up a few hoboes that Pebble and his men had missed earlier, but we didn't find McCloor.

We didn't find any trace of him until somebody stumbled over a railroad bum huddled in the shadow of a gondola. It took a couple of minutes to bring him to, and he couldn't talk then. His jaw was broken. But when we asked if McCloor had slugged him, he nodded, and when we asked in which direction McCloor had been headed, he moved a feeble hand to the east.

We went over and searched the Santa Fe yards.

We didn't find McCloor.

I rode up to the Hall of Justice with Duff. MacMan was in the captain of detectives' office with three or four police sleuths.

"Wales die?" I asked.

"Yep."

"Say anything before he went?"

"He was gone before you were through the window."

"You held on to the girl?"

"She's here."

"She say anything?"

"We were waiting for you before we tapped her," detective-sergeant O'Gar said, "not knowing the angle on her."

"Let's have her in. I haven't had any dinner yet. How about the autopsy on Sue Hambleton?"

"Chronic arsenic poisoning."

"Chronic? That means it was fed to her little by little, and not in a lump?"

"Uh-huh. From what he found in her kidneys, intestines, liver, stomach and blood, Jordan figures there was less than a grain of it in her. That wouldn't be enough to knock her off. But he says he found arsenic in the tips of her hair, and she'd have to be given some at least a month ago for it to have worked out that far."

"Any chance that it wasn't arsenic that killed her?"

"Not unless Jordan's a bum doctor."

A policewoman came in with Peggy Carroll.

The blonde girl was tired. Her eyelids, mouth corners and body drooped, and when I pushed a chair out toward her she sagged down in it.

O'Gar ducked his grizzled bullet head at me.

"Now, Peggy," I said, "tell us where you fit into this mess."

"I don't fit into it." She didn't look up. Her voice was tired. "Joe dragged me into it. He told you."

"You his girl?"

"If you want to call it that," she admitted.

"You jealous?"

"What," she asked, looking up at me, her face puzzled, "has that got to do with it?"

"Sue Hambleton was getting ready to go away with him when she was murdered."

The girl sat up straight in the chair and said deliberately, "I swear to God I didn't know she was murdered."

"But you did know she was dead," I said positively.

"I didn't," she replied just as positively.

I nudged O'Gar with my elbow. He pushed his undershot jaw at her and barked, "What are you trying to give us? You knew she was dead. How could you kill her without knowing it?"

While she looked at him I waved the others in. They crowded close around her and took up the chorus of the sergeant's song. She was barked, roared, and snarled at plenty in the next few minutes.

The instant she stopped trying to talk back to them I cut in again. "Wait," I said, very earnestly. "Maybe she didn't kill her."

"The hell she didn't," O'Gar stormed, holding the center of the stage so the others could move away from the girl without their retreat seeming too artificial. "Do you mean to tell me this baby—"

"I didn't say she didn't," I remonstrated. "I said maybe she didn't."

"Then who did?"

I passed the question to the girl. "Who did?"

"Babe," she said immediately.

O'Gar snorted to make her think he didn't believe her.

I asked, as if I were honestly perplexed, "How do you know that if you didn't know she was dead?"

"It stands to reason he did," she said. "Anybody can see that. He found out she was going away with Joe, so he killed her and then came to Joe's and killed him. That's just exactly what Babe would do when he found it out."

"Yeah? How long have *you* known they were going away together?"

"Since they decided to. Joe told me a month or two ago."

"And you didn't mind?"

"You've got this all wrong," she said. "Of course I didn't mind. I was being cut in on it. You know her father had the bees. That's what Joe was after. She didn't mean anything to him but an in to the old man's pockets. And I was to get my dib. And you needn't think I was crazy enough about Joe or anybody else to step off in the air for them. Babe got next and fixed the pair of them. That's a cinch."

"Yeah? How do you figure Babe would kill her?"

"That guy? You don't think he'd—"

"I mean how would he go about killing her?"

"Oh!" She shrugged. "With his hands, likely as not."

"Once he'd made up his mind to do it, he'd do it quick and violent?" I suggested.

"That would be Babe," she agreed.

"But you can't see him slow-poisoning her—spreading it out over a month?"

Worry came into the girl's blue eyes. She put her lower lip between her teeth, then said slowly, "No, I can't see him doing it that way. Not Babe."

"Who can you see doing it that way?"

She opened her eyes wide, asking, "You mean Joe?"

I didn't say anything.

"Joe might have," she said persuasively. "God only knows what he'd want to do it for, why he'd want to get rid of the kind of meal ticket she was going to be. But you couldn't always guess what he was getting at. He pulled plenty of dumb ones. He was too slick without being smart. If he was going to kill her, though, that would be about the way he'd go about it."

"Were he and Babe friendly?"

"No."

"Did he go to Babe's much?"

"Not at all that I know about. He was too leery of Babe to take a chance on being caught there. That's why I moved upstairs, so Sue could come over to our place to see him."

"Then how could Joe have hidden the fly paper he poisoned her with in her apartment?"

"Fly paper!" Her bewilderment seemed honest enough.

"Show it to her," I told O'Gar.

He got a sheet from the desk and held it close to the girl's face.

She stared at it for a moment and then jumped up and grabbed my arm with both hands.

"I didn't know what it was," she said excitedly. "Joe had some a couple of months ago. He was looking at it when I came in. I asked him what it was for, and he smiled that wisenheimer smile of his and said, 'You make angles out of it,' and wrapped it up again and put it in his pocket. I didn't pay much attention to him; he was always fooling with some kind of tricks that were supposed to make him wealthy, but never did."

"Ever see it again?"

"No."

"Did you know Sue very well?"

"I didn't know her at all. I never even saw her. I used to keep out of the way so I wouldn't gum Joe's play with her."

"But you know Babe?"

"Yes, I've been on a couple of parties where he was. That's all I know him."

"Who killed Sue?"

"Joe," she said. "Didn't he have that paper you say she was killed with?"

"Why did he kill her?"

"I don't know. He pulled some awful dumb tricks sometimes."

"You didn't kill her?"

"No, no, no!"

I jerked the corner of my mouth at O'Gar.

"You're a liar," he bawled, shaking the fly paper in her face. "You killed her." The rest of the team closed in, throwing accusations at her. They kept it up until she was groggy and the policewoman beginning to look worried.

Then I said angrily, "All right. Throw her in a cell and let her think it over." To her, "You know what you told Joe this afternoon: this is no time to dummy up. Do a lot of thinking tonight."

"Honest to God I didn't kill her," she said.

I turned my back to her. The policewoman took her away.

"Ho-hum," O'Gar yawned. "We gave her a pretty good ride at that, for a short one."

"Not bad," I agreed. "If anybody else looked likely, I'd say she didn't kill Sue. But if she's telling the truth, then Holy Joe did it. And why should he poison the goose that was going to lay nice yellow eggs for him? And how and why did he cache the poison in their apartment? Babe had the motive, but damned if he looks like a slow-poisoner to me. You can't tell, though; he and Holy Joe could even have been working together on it."

"Could," Duff said. "But it takes a lot of imagination to get that one down. Anyway you twist it, Peggy's our best bet so far. Go up against her again, hard, in the morning?"

"Yeah," I said. "And we've got to find Babe."

The others had had dinner. MacMan and I went out and got ours. When we returned to the detective bureau an hour later it was practically deserted of the regular operatives.

"All gone to Pier 42 on a tip that McCloor's there," Steve Ward told us.

"How long ago?"

"Ten minutes."

MacMan and I got a taxi and set out for Pier 42. We didn't get to Pier 42.

On First Street, half a block from the Embarcadero, the taxi suddenly shrieked and slid to a halt.

"What—?" I began, and saw a man standing in front of the machine. He was a big man with a big gun. "Babe," I grunted, and put my hand on MacMan's arm to keep him from getting his gun out.

"Take me to—" McCloor was saying to the frightened driver when he saw us. He came around to my side and pulled the door open, holding the gun on us.

He had no hat. His hair was wet, plastered to his head. Little streams of water trickled down from it. His clothes were dripping wet.

He looked surprised at us and ordered, "Get out."

As we got out he growled at the driver, "What the hell you got your flag up for if you had fares?"

The driver wasn't there. He had hopped out the other side and was scooting away down the street. McCloor cursed him and poked his gun at me, growling, "Go on, beat it."

Apparently he hadn't recognized me. The light here wasn't good, and I had a hat on now. He had seen me for only a few seconds in Wales's room.

I stepped aside. MacMan moved to the other side.

McCloor took a backward step to keep us from getting him between us and started an angry word.

MacMan threw himself on McCloor's gun arm.

I socked McCloor's jaw with my fist. I might just as well have hit somebody else for all it seemed to bother him.

He swept me out of his way and pasted MacMan in the mouth. MacMan fell back till the taxi stopped him, spit out a tooth, and came back for more.

I was trying to climb up McCloor's left side.

MacMan came in on his right, failed to dodge a chop of the gun, caught it square on the top of the noodle, and went down hard. He stayed down.

I kicked McCloor's ankle, but couldn't get his foot from under him. I rammed my right fist into the small of his back and got a left-handful of his wet hair, swinging on it. He shook his head, dragging me off my feet.

He punched me in the side and I could feel my ribs and guts flattening together like leaves in a book.

I swung my fist against the back of his neck. That bothered him. He made a rumbling noise down in his chest, crunched my shoulder in his left hand, and chopped at me with the gun in his right.

I kicked him somewhere and punched his neck again.

Down the street, at the Embarcadero, a police whistle was blowing. Men were running up First Street toward us.

McCloor snorted like a locomotive and threw me away from him. I didn't want to go. I tried to hang on. He threw me away from him and ran up the street.

I scrambled up and ran after him, dragging my gun out.

At the first corner he stopped to squirt metal at me—three shots. I squirted one at him. None of the four connected.

He disappeared around the corner. I swung wide around it, to make him miss if he were flattened to the wall waiting for me. He wasn't. He was a hundred feet ahead, going into a space between two warehouses. I went in after him, and out after him at the other end, making better time with my hundred and ninety pounds than he was making with his two-fifty.

He crossed a street, turning up, away from the waterfront. There was a light on the corner. When I came into its glare he wheeled and leveled his gun at me. I didn't hear it click, but I knew it had when he threw it at me. The gun went past with a couple of feet to spare and raised hell against a door behind me.

McCloor turned and ran up the street. I ran up the street after him.

I put a bullet past him to let the others know where we were. At the next corner he started to turn to the left, changed his mind, and went straight on.

I sprinted, cutting the distance between us to forty or fifty feet, and yelped, "Stop or I'll drop you."

He jumped sidewise into a narrow alley.

I passed it on the jump, saw he wasn't waiting for me, and went in. Enough light came in from the street to let us see each other and our surroundings. The alley was blind—walled on each side and at the other end by tall concrete buildings with steel-shuttered windows and doors.

McCloor faced me, less than twenty feet away. His jaw stuck out. His arms curved down free of his sides. His shoulders were bunched.

"Put them up," I ordered, holding my gun level.

"Get out of my way, little man," he grumbled, taking a stiff-legged step toward me. "I'll eat you up."

"Keep coming," I said, "and I'll put you down."

"Try it." He took another step, crouching a little. "I can still get to you *with* slugs in me."

"Not where I'll put them." I was wordy, trying to talk him into waiting till the others came up. I didn't want to have to kill him. We could have done that from the taxi. "I'm no Annie Oakley, but if I can't pop your kneecaps with two shots at this distance, you're welcome to me. And if you think smashed kneecaps are a lot of fun, give it a whirl."

"Hell with that," he said and charged.

I shot his right knee.

He lurched toward me.

I shot his left knee.

He tumbled down.

"You would have it," I complained.

He twisted around, and with his arms pushed himself into a sitting position facing me.

"I didn't think you had sense enough to do it," he said through his teeth.

I talked to McCloor in the hospital. He lay on his back in bed with a couple of pillows slanting his head up. The skin was pale and tight around his mouth and eyes, but there was nothing else to show he was in pain.

"You sure devastated me, bo," he said when I came in.

"Sorry," I said, "but—"

"I ain't beefing. I asked for it."

"Why'd you kill Holy Joe?" I asked, off-hand, as I pulled a chair up beside the bed.

"Uh-uh—you're tooting the wrong ringer."

I laughed and told him I was the man in the room with Joe when it happened.

McCloor grinned and said, "I thought I'd seen you somewheres before. So that's where it was. I didn't pay no attention to your mug, just so your hands didn't move."

"Why'd you kill him?"

He pursed his lips, screwed up his eyes at me, thought something over, and said, "He killed a broad I knew."

"He killed Sue Hambleton?" I asked.

He studied my face a while before he replied, "Yep."

"How do you figure that out?"

"Hell," he said, "I don't have to. Sue told me. Give me a butt."

I gave him a cigarette, held a lighter under it, and objected. "That doesn't exactly fit in with other things I know. Just what happened and what did she say? You might start back with the night you gave her the goog."

He looked thoughtful, letting smoke sneak slowly out of his nose, then said, "I hadn't ought to hit her in the eye, that's a fact. But, see, she had been out all afternoon and wouldn't tell me where she'd been, and we had a row about it. What's this—Thursday morning? That was Monday, then. After the row I went out and spent the night in a dump over on Army Street. I got home about seven the next morning. Sue was sick as hell, but she wouldn't let me get a croaker for her. That was kind of funny, because she was scared stiff."

McCloor scratched his head meditatively and suddenly drew in a great lungful of smoke, practically eating up the rest of the cigarette. He let the smoke leak out of mouth and nose together, looking dully through the cloud at me. Then he said brusquely, "Well, she went under. But before she went she told me she'd been poisoned by Holy Joe."

"She say how he'd given it to her?"

McCloor shook his head.

"I'd been asking her what was the matter, and not getting anything out of her. Then she starts whining that she's poisoned. 'I'm poisoned, Babe,' she whines. 'Arsenic. That damned Holy Joe,' she says. Then she won't say anything else, and it's not a hell of a while after that that she kicks off."

"Yeah? Then what'd you do?"

"I went gunning for Holy Joe. I knew him but didn't know where he jungled up, and didn't find out till yesterday. You was there when I came. You know about that. I had picked up a boiler and parked it over on Turk Street, for the getaway. When I got back to it, there was a copper standing close to it. I figured he might have spotted it as a hot one and was waiting to see who came for it, so I let it alone, and caught a streetcar instead, and cut for the yards. Down there I ran into a whole flock of hammer and saws and had to go overboard in China Basin, swimming up to a pier, being ranked again by a watchman there, swimming off to another, and finally getting through the line only to run into another bad break. I wouldn't of flagged that taxi if the *For Hire* flag hadn't been up."

"You knew Sue was planning to take a run-out on you with Joe?"

"I don't know it yet," he said. "I knew damned well she was cheating on me, but I didn't know who with."

"What would you have done if you had known that?" I asked.

"Me?" He grinned wolfishly. "Just what I did."

"Killed the pair of them," I said.

He rubbed his lower lip with a thumb and asked calmly, "You think I killed Sue?"

"You did."

"Serves me right," he said. "I must be getting simple in my old age. What the hell am I doing barbering with a lousy dick? That never got nobody nothing but grief. Well, you might just as well take it on the heel and toe now, my lad. I'm through spitting."

And he was. I couldn't get another word out of him.

The Old Man sat listening to me, tapping his desk lightly with the point of a long yellow pencil, staring past me with mild blue rimless-spectacled eyes. When I had brought my story up to date, he asked pleasantly, "How is MacMan?"

"He lost two teeth, but his skull wasn't cracked. He'll be out in a couple of days."

The Old Man nodded and asked, "What remains to be done?"

"Nothing. We can put Peggy Carroll on the mat again, but it's not likely we'll squeeze much more out of her. Outside of that, the returns are pretty well all in."

"And what do you make of it?"

I squirmed in my chair and said, "Suicide."

The Old Man smiled at me, politely but skeptically.

"I don't like it either," I grumbled. "And I'm not ready to write in a report yet. But that's the only total that what we've got will add up to. That fly paper was hidden behind the kitchen stove. Nobody would be crazy enough to try to hide something from a woman in her own kitchen like that. But the woman might hide it there.

"According to Peggy, Holy Joe had the fly paper. If Sue hid it, she got it from him. For what? They were planning to go away together, and were only waiting till Joe, who was on the nut, raised enough dough. Maybe they were afraid of Babe, and had the poison there to slip him if he tumbled to their plan before they went. Maybe they meant to slip it to him before they went anyway.

"When I started talking to Holy Joe about murder, he thought Babe was the one who had been bumped off. He was surprised, maybe, but as if he was surprised that it had happened so soon. He was more surprised when he heard that Sue had died too, but even then he wasn't so surprised as when he saw McCloor alive at the window.

"She died cursing Holy Joe, and she knew she was poisoned, and she wouldn't let McCloor get a doctor. Can't that mean that she had turned against Joe, and had taken the poison herself instead of feeding it to Babe? The poison was hidden from Babe. But even if he found it, I can't figure him as a poisoner. He's too rough. Unless he caught her trying to poison him and made her swallow the stuff. But that doesn't account for the month-old arsenic in her hair."

"Does your suicide hypothesis take care of that?" the Old Man asked.

"It could," I said. "Don't be kicking holes in my theory. It's got enough as it stands. But, if she committed suicide this time, there's no reason why she couldn't have tried it once before—say after a quarrel with Joe a month ago—and failed to bring it off. That would have put the arsenic in her. There's no real proof that she took any between a month ago and day before yesterday."

"No real proof," the Old Man protested mildly, "except the autopsy's finding—chronic poisoning."

I was never one to let experts' guesses stand in my way. I said, "They base that on the small amount of arsenic they found in her remains—less than a fatal dose. And the amount they find in your stomach after you're dead depends on how much you vomit before you die."

The Old Man smiled benevolently at me and asked, "But you're not, you say, ready to write this theory into a report? Meanwhile, what do you propose doing?"

"If there's nothing else on tap, I'm going home, fumigate my brains with Fatimas, and try to get this thing straightened out in my head. I think I'll get a copy of *The Count of Monte Cristo* and run through it. I haven't read it since I was a kid. It looks like the book was wrapped up with the fly paper to make a bundle large enough to wedge tightly between the wall and stove, so it wouldn't fall down. But there might be something in the book. I'll see anyway."

"I did that last night," the Old Man murmured.

I asked, "And?"

He took a book from his desk drawer, opened it where a slip of paper marked a place, and held it out to me, one pink finger marking a paragraph.

"Suppose you were to take a milligramme of this poison the first day, two milligrammes the second day, and so on. Well, at the end of ten days you would have taken a centigramme: at the end of twenty days increasing another milligramme, you would have taken three hundred centigrammes; that is to say, a dose you would support without inconvenience, and which would be very dangerous for any other person who had not taken the same precautions as yourself. Well, then, at the end of the month, when drinking water from the same carafe, you would kill the person who had drunk this water, without your perceiving otherwise than from slight inconvenience that there was any poisonous substance mingled with the water."

"That does it," I said. "That does it. They were afraid to go away without killing Babe, too certain he'd come after them. She tried to make herself immune from arsenic poisoning by getting her body accustomed to it, taking steadily increasing doses, so when she slipped the big shot in Babe's food she could eat it with him without danger. She'd be taken sick, but wouldn't die, and the police couldn't hang his death on her because she too had eaten the poisoned food.

"That clicks. After the row Monday night, when she wrote Joe the note urging him to make the getaway soon, she tried to hurry up her immunity, and increased her preparatory doses too quickly, took too large a shot. That's why she cursed Joe at the end; it was his plan."

"Possibly she overdosed herself in an attempt to speed it along," the Old Man agreed, "but not necessarily. There are people who can cultivate an ability to take large doses of arsenic without trouble, but it seems to be a sort of natural gift with them, a matter of some constitutional peculiarity. Ordinarily, anyone who tried it would do what Sue Hambleton did—slowly poison themselves until the cumulative effect was strong enough to cause death."

Babe McCloor was hanged, for killing Holy Joe Wales, six months later.

Questions

1. The story originally appeared in a pulp magazine, appealing to the kind of readers who might prefer "escape" to "quality" fiction. What techniques does Hammet use to gain and keep their interest in the story?

2. Discuss the detective's "acceptance" of crime and murder, his constant lack of surprise.

3. Note Hammett's use of character names. Do they help increase the reader's sense of familiarity with the story's people?

4. Can you justify the use of explicit violence in the story? Is this an "exciting" story? What do you mean by "exciting"? Relate particularly to the chases and to the kneecap-shooting scene.

5. There is a certain amount of police harassment here. This sort of backroom questioning is, in present times, illegal (i.e., the Supreme

Court's *Miranda* decision). Do you feel that present laws protecting the suspect are justified, necessary?

6. Describe Hammett's prose style. How does he keep the story moving so quickly? What major effects are gained by his use of dialogue and description? Does the use of slang hinder your understanding? Does the context "explain" the meaning of the slang?

7. In what way does the title serve as a central metaphor as well as the central plot device in the story? Note the next-to-the-last paragraph.

8. The first sentence ("It was a wandering daughter job.") sends the plot into motion. The rich runaway daughter is a very familiar feature in detective stories. There are obvious plot advantages in using her, but what other advantages are afforded by the device?

9. On page 168 Hammett writes that ". . . the New York office sent a journal on the job to the other Continental branches throughout the country, giving the information above. . . ." If the agency actually had written the first page and a half of "Fly Paper," how would it have differed from Hammett's presentation of the background material?

The Curtain

Raymond Chandler

I

The first time I ever saw Larry Batzel he was drunk outside Sardi's in a secondhand Rolls-Royce. There was a tall blonde with him who had eyes you wouldn't forget. I helped her argue him out from under the wheel so that she could drive.

The second time I saw him he didn't have any Rolls-Royce or any blonde or any job in pictures. All he had was the jitters and a suit that needed pressing. He remembered me. He was that kind of drunk.

I bought him enough drinks to do him some good and gave him half my cigarettes. I used to see him from time to time "between pictures." I got to lending him money. I don't know just why. He was a big, handsome brute with eyes like a cow and something innocent and honest in them. Something I don't get much of in my business.

The funny part was he had been a liquor runner for a pretty hard mob before Repeal. He never got anywhere in pictures, and after a while I didn't see him around any more.

Then one day out of the clear blue I got a check for all he owed me and a note that he was working on the tables—gambling not dining—at the Dardanella Club, and to come out and look him up. So I knew he was back in the rackets.

I didn't go to see him, but I found out somehow or other that Joe Mesarvey owned the place, and that Joe Mesarvey was married to the blonde with the eyes, the one Larry Batzel had been with in the Rolls that time. I still didn't go out there.

Then very early one morning there was a dim figure standing by my bed, between me and the windows. The blinds had been pulled down. That must have been what wakened me. The figure was large and had a gun.

I rolled over and rubbed my eyes.

"Okay," I said sourly. "There's twelve bucks in my pants and my wrist watch cost twenty-seven fifty. You couldn't get anything on that."

The figure went over to the window and pulled a blind aside an inch

194

and looked down at the street. When he turned again I saw that it was
Larry Batzel.

His face was drawn and tired and he needed a shave. He had dinner
clothes on still and a dark double-breasted overcoat with a dwarf rose
drooping in the lapel.

He sat down and held the gun on his knee for a moment before he put
it away, with a puzzled frown, as if he didn't know how it got into his
hand.

"You're going to drive me to Berdoo," he said. "I've got to get out of
town. They've put the pencil on me."

"Okay," I said. "Tell me about it."

I sat up and felt the carpet with my toes and lit a cigarette. It was a
little after five-thirty.

"I jimmied your lock with a piece of celluloid," he said. "You ought to
use your night latch once in a while. I wasn't sure which was your flop
and I didn't want to rouse the house."

"Try the mailboxes next time," I said. "But go ahead. You're not
drunk, are you?"

"I'd like to be, but I've got to get away first. I'm just rattled. I'm not so
tough as I used to be. You read about the O'Mara disappearance of
course."

"Yeah."

"Listen, anyway. If I keep talking I won't blow up. I don't think I'm
spotted here."

"One drink won't hurt either of us," I said. "The Scotch is on the table
there."

He poured a couple of drinks quickly and handed me one. I put on a
bathrobe and slippers. The glass rattled against his teeth when he drank.

He put his empty glass down and held his hands tight together.

"I used to know Dud O'Mara pretty well. We used to run stuff
together down from Hueneme Point. We even carried the torch for the
same girl. She's married to Joe Mesarvey now. Dud married five million
dollars. He married General Dade Winslow's rickety-rackety divorcée
daughter."

"I know all that," I said.

"Yeah. Just listen. She picked him out of a speak, just like I'd pick up a
cafeteria tray. But he didn't like the life. I guess he used to see Mona. He
got wise Joe Mesarvey and Lash Yeager had a hot car racket on the side.
They knocked him off."

"The hell they did," I said. "Have another drink."

"No. Just listen. There's just two points. The night O'Mara pulled
down the curtain—no, the night the papers got it—Mona Mesarvey
disappeared too. Only she didn't. They hid her out in a shack a couple of
miles beyond Realito in the orange belt. Next door to a garage run by a

heel named Art Huck, a hot car drop. I found out. I trailed Joe there."

"What made it your business?" I asked.

"I'm still soft on her. I'm telling you this because you were pretty swell to me once. You can make something of it after I blow. They hid her out there so it would look as if Dud had blown with her. Naturally the cops were not too dumb to see Joe after the disappearance. But they didn't find Mona. They have a system on disappearances and they play the system."

He got up and went over to the window again, looked through the side of the blind.

"There's a blue sedan down there I think I've seen before," he said. "But maybe not. There's a lot like it."

He sat down again. I didn't speak.

"This place beyond Realito is on the first side road north from the Foothill Boulevard. You can't miss it. It stands all alone, the garage and the house next door. There's an old cyanide plant up above there. I'm telling you this—"

"That's point one," I said. "What was the second point?"

"The punk that used to drive for Lash Yeager lit out a couple of weeks back and went East. I lent him fifty bucks. He was broke. He told me Yeager was out to the Winslow estate the night Dud O'Mara disappeared."

I stared at him. "It's interesting, Larry. But not enough to break eggs over. After all we do have a police department."

"Yeah. Add this. I got drunk last night and told Yeager what I knew. Then I quit the job at the Dardanella. So somebody shot at me outside where I live when I got home. I've been on the dodge ever since. Now, will you drive me to Berdoo?"

I stood up. It was May but I felt cold. Larry Batzel looked cold, even with his overcoat on.

"Absolutely," I said. "But take it easy. Later will be much safer than now. Have another drink. You don't *know* they knocked O'Mara off."

"If he found out about the hot car racket, with Mona married to Joe Mesarvey, they'd have to knock him off. He was that kind of guy."

I stood up and went towards the bathroom. Larry went over to the window again.

"It's still there," he said over his shoulder. "You might get shot at riding with me."

"I'd hate that," I said.

"You're a good sort of heel, Carmady. It's going to rain. I'd hate like hell to be buried in the rain, wouldn't you?"

"You talk too damn much," I said, and went into the bathroom.

It was the last time I ever spoke to him.

II

I heard him moving around while I was shaving, but not after I got under the shower, of course. When I came out he was gone. I padded over and looked into the kitchenette. He wasn't in there. I grabbed a bathrobe and peeked out into the hall. It was empty except for a milkman starting down the back stairs with his wiry tray of bottles, and the fresh folded papers leaning against the shut doors.

"Hey," I called out to the milkman, "did a guy just come out of here and go by you?"

He looked back at me from the corner of the wall and opened his mouth to answer. He was a nice-looking boy with fine large white teeth. I remember his teeth well, because I was looking at them when I heard the shots.

They were not very near or very far. Out back of the apartment house, by the garages, or in the alley, I thought. There were two quick, hard shots and then the riveting machine. A burst of five or six, all a good chopper should ever need. Then the roar of the car going away.

The milkman shut his mouth as if a winch controlled it. His eyes were huge and empty looking at me. Then he very carefully set his bottles down on the top step and leaned against the wall.

"That sounded like shots," he said.

All this took a couple of seconds and felt like half an hour. I went back into my place and threw clothes on, grabbed odds and ends off the bureau, barged out into the hall. It was still empty, even of the milkman. A siren was dying somewhere near. A bald head with a hangover under it poked out of a door and made a snuffling noise.

I went down the back stairs.

There were two or three people out in the lower hall. I went out back. The garages were in two rows facing each other across a cement space, then two more at the end, leaving a space to go out to the alley. A couple of kids were coming over a fence three houses away.

Larry Batzel lay on his face, with his hat a yard away from his head, and one hand flung out to within a foot of a big black automatic. His ankles were crossed, as if he had spun as he fell. Blood was thick on the side of his face, on his blond hair, especially on his neck. It was also thick on the cement yard.

Two radio cops and the milk driver and a man in a brown sweater and bibless overalls were bending over him. The man in overalls was our janitor.

I went up to them, about the same time the two kids from over the fence hit the yard. The milk driver looked at me with a queer, strained expression. One of the cops straightened up and said: "Either of you guys know him? He's still got half his face."

He wasn't talking to me. The milk driver shook his head and kept on looking at me from the corner of his eyes. The janitor said: "He ain't a tenant here. He might of been a visitor. Kind of early for visitors, though, ain't it?"

"He's got party clothes on. You know your flophouse better'n I do," the cop said heavily. He got out a notebook.

The other cop straightened up too and shook his head and went towards the house, with the janitor trotting beside him.

The cop with the notebook jerked a thumb at me and said harshly: "You was here first after these two guys. Anything from you?"

I looked at the milkman. Larry Batzel wouldn't care, and a man has a living to earn. It wasn't a story for a prowl car anyway.

"I just heard the shots and came running," I said.

The cop took that for an answer. The milk driver looked up at the lowering gray sky and said nothing.

After a while I got back into my apartment and finished my dressing. When I picked my hat up off the window table by the Scotch bottle there was a small rosebud lying on a piece of scrawled paper.

The note said: "You're a good guy, but I think I'll go it alone. Give the rose to Mona, if you ever should get a chance. Larry."

I put those things in my wallet, and braced myself with a drink.

III

About three o'clock that afternoon I stood in the main hallway of the Winslow place and waited for the butler to come back. I had spent most of the day not going near my office or apartment, and not meeting any homicide men. It was only a question of time until I had to come through, but I wanted to see General Dade Winslow first. He was hard to see.

Oil paintings hung all around me, mostly portraits. There were a couple of statues and several suits of time-darkened armor on pedestals of dark wood. High over the huge marble fireplace hung two bullet-torn —or moth-eaten—cavalry pennants crossed in a glass case, and below them the painted likeness of a thin, spry-looking man with a black beard and mustachios and full regimentals of about the time of the Mexican War. This might be General Dade Winslow's father. The general himself, though pretty ancient, couldn't be quite that old.

Then the butler came back and said General Winslow was in the orchid house and would I follow him, please.

We went out of the french doors at the back and across the lawns to a big glass pavilion well beyond the garages. The butler opened the door into a sort of vestibule and shut it when I was inside, and it was already hot. Then he opened the inner door and it was really hot.

The air steamed. The walls and ceiling of the greenhouse dripped. In the half light enormous tropical plants spread their blooms and branches all over the place, and the smell of them was almost as overpowering as the smell of boiling alcohol.

The butler, who was old and thin and very straight and white-haired, held branches of the plants back for me to pass, and we came to an opening in the middle of the place. A large reddish Turkish rug was spread down on the hexagonal flagstones. In the middle of the rug, in a wheel chair, a very old man sat with a traveling rug around his body and watched us come.

Nothing lived in his face but the eyes. Black eyes, deepset, shining, untouchable. The rest of his face was the leaden mask of death, sunken temples, a sharp nose, outward-turning ear lobes, a mouth that was a thin white slit. He was wrapped partly in a reddish and very shabby bathrobe and partly in the rug. His hands had purple fingernails and were clasped loosely, motionless on the rug. He had a few scattered wisps of white hair on his skull.

The butler said: "This is Mr. Carmady, General."

The old man stared at me. After a while a sharp, shrewish voice said: "Place a chair for Mr. Carmady."

The butler dragged a wicker chair out and I sat down. I put my hat on the floor. The butler picked it up.

"Brandy," the general said. "How do you like your brandy, sir?"

"Any way at all," I said.

He snorted. The butler went away. The general stared at me with his unblinking eyes. He snorted again.

"I always take champagne with mine," he said. "A third of a glass of brandy under the champagne, and the champagne as cold as Valley Forge. Colder, if you can get it colder."

A noise that might have been a chuckle came out of him.

"Not that I was at Valley Forge," he said. "Not quite that bad. You may smoke, sir."

I thanked him and said I was tired of smoking for a while. I got a handkerchief out and mopped my face.

"Take your coat off, sir. Dud always did. Orchids require heat, Mr. Carmady—like sick old men."

I took my coat off, a raincoat I had brought along. It looked like rain. Larry Batzel had said it was going to rain.

"Dud is my son-in-law. Dudley O'Mara. I believe you had something to tell me about him."

"Just hearsay," I said. "I wouldn't want to go into it, unless I had your O.K., General Winslow."

The basilisk eyes stared at me. "You are a private detective. You want to be paid, I suppose."

"I'm in that line of business," I said. "But that doesn't mean I have to be paid for every breath I draw. It's just something I heard. You might like to pass it on yourself to the Missing Persons Bureau."

"I see," he said quietly. "A scandal of some sort."

The butler came back before I could answer. He wheeled a tea wagon in through the jungle, set it at my elbow and mixed me a brandy and soda. He went away.

I sipped the drink. "It seems there was a girl," I said. "He knew her before he knew your daughter. She's married to a racketeer now. It seems—"

"I've heard all that," he said. "I don't give a damn. What I want to know is where he is and if he's all right. If he's happy."

I stared at him popeyed. After a moment I said weakly: "Maybe I could find the girl, or the boys downtown could, with what I could tell them."

He plucked at the edge of his rug and moved his head about an inch. I think he was nodding. Then he said very slowly: "Probably I'm talking too much for my health, but I want to make something clear. I'm a cripple. I have two ruined legs and half my lower belly. I don't eat much or sleep much. I'm a bore to myself and a damn nuisance to everybody else. So I miss Dud. He used to spend a lot of time with me. Why, God only knows."

"Well—" I began.

"Shut up. You're a young man to me, so I can be rude to you. Dud left without saying goodbye to me. That wasn't like him. He drove his car away one evening and nobody has heard from him since. If he got tired of my fool daughter and her brat, if he wanted some other woman, that's all right. He got a brainstorm and left without saying goodbye to me, and now he's sorry. That's why I don't hear from him. Find him and tell him I understand. That's all—unless he needs money. If he does, he can have all he wants."

His leaden cheeks almost had a pink tinge now. His black eyes were brighter, if possible. He leaned back very slowly and closed his eyes.

I drank a lot of my drink in one long swallow. I said: "Suppose he's in a jam. Say, on account of the girl's husband. This Joe Mesarvey."

He opened his eyes and winked. "Not an O'Mara," he said. "It's the other fellow would be in a jam."

"Okay. Shall I just pass on to the Bureau where I heard this girl was?"

"Certainly not. They've done nothing. Let them go on doing it. Find him yourself. I'll pay you a thousand dollars—even if you only have to walk across the street. Tell him everything is all right here. The old man's doing fine and sends his love. That's all."

I couldn't tell him. Suddenly I couldn't tell him anything Larry Batzel had told me, or what had happened to Larry, or anything about it. I finished my drink and stood up and put my coat back on. I said: "That's too much money for the job, General Winslow. We can talk about that later. Have I your authority to represent you in my own way?"

He pressed a bell on his wheel chair. "Just tell him," he said. "I want to know he's all right and I want him to know I'm all right. That's all—unless he needs money. Now you'll have to excuse me. I'm tired."

He closed his eyes. I went back through the jungle and the butler met me at the door with my hat.

I breathed in some cool air and said: "The general wants me to see Mrs. O'Mara."

IV

This room had a white carpet from wall to wall. Ivory drapes of immense height lay tumbled casually on the white carpet inside the many windows. The windows stared towards the dark foothills, and the air beyond the glass was dark too. It hadn't started to rain yet, but there was a feeling of pressure in the atmosphere.

Mrs. O'Mara was stretched out on a white chaise longue with both her slippers off and her feet in the net stockings they don't wear any more. She was tall and dark, with a sulky mouth. Handsome, but this side of beautiful.

She said: "What in the world can *I* do for you? It's all known. Too damn known. Except that I don't know you, do I?"

"Well, hardly," I said. "I'm just a private copper in a small way of business."

She reached for a glass I hadn't noticed but would have looked for in a moment, on account of her way of talking and the fact she had her slippers off. She drank languidly, flashing a ring.

"I met him in a speakeasy," she said with a sharp laugh. "A very handsome bootlegger, with thick curly hair and an Irish grin. So I married him. Out of boredom. As for him, the bootlegging business was even then uncertain—if there were no other attractions."

She waited for me to say there were, but not as if she cared a lot whether I came through. I just said: "You didn't see him leave on the day he disappeared?"

"No. I seldom saw him leave, or come back. It was like that." She drank some more of her drink.

"Huh," I grunted. "But, of course, you didn't quarrel." They never do.

"There are so many ways of quarreling, Mr. Carmady."

"Yeah. I like your saying that. Of course you knew about the girl."

"I'm glad I'm being properly frank to an old family detective. Yes, I knew about the girl." She curled a tendril of inky hair behind her ear.

"Did you know about her before he disappeared?" I asked politely.

"Certainly."

"How?"

"You're pretty direct, aren't you? Connections, as they say. I'm an old speak fancier. Or didn't you know that?"

"Did you know the bunch at the Dardanella?"

"I've been there." She didn't look startled, or even surprised. "In fact I practically lived there for a week. That's where I met Dudley O'Mara."

"Yeah. Your father married pretty late in life, didn't he?"

I watched color fade in her cheeks. I wanted her mad, but there was nothing doing. She smiled and the color came back and she rang a push bell on a cord down in the swansdown cushions of the chaise longue.

"Very late," she said, "if it's any of your business."

"It's not," I said.

A coy-looking maid came in and mixed a couple of drinks at a side table. She gave one to Mrs. O'Mara, put one down beside me. She went away again, showing a nice pair of legs under a short skirt.

Mrs. O'Mara watched the door shut and then said: "The whole thing has got Father into a mood. I wish Dud would wire or write or something."

I said slowly: "He's an old, old man, crippled, half buried already. One thin thread of interest held him to life. The thread snapped and nobody gives a damn. He tries to act as if he didn't give a damn himself. I don't call that a mood. I call that a pretty swell display of intestinal fortitude."

"Gallant," she said, and her eyes were daggers. "But you haven't touched your drink."

"I have to go," I said. "Thanks all the same."

She held a slim, tinted hand out and I went over and touched it. The thunder burst suddenly behind the hills and she jumped. A gust of air shook the windows.

I went down a tiled staircase to the hallway and the butler appeared out of a shadow and opened the door for me.

I looked down a succession of terraces decorated with flower beds and imported trees. At the bottom a high metal railing with gilded spearheads and a six-foot hedge inside. A sunken driveway crawled down to the main gates and a lodge inside them.

Beyond the estate the hill sloped down to the city and the old oil wells of La Brea, now partly a park, partly a deserted stretch of fenced-in wild land. Some of the wooden derricks still stood. These had made the wealth of the Winslow family and then the family had run away from them up the hill, far enough to get away from the smell of the sumps, not too far for them to look out of the front windows and see what made them rich.

I walked down brick steps between the terraced lawns. On one of them a dark-haired, pale-faced kid of ten or eleven was throwing darts at a target hung on a tree. I went along near him.

"You young O'Mara?" I asked.

He leaned against a stone bench with four darts in his hand and looked at me with cold, slaty eyes, old eyes.

"I'm Dade Winslow Trevillyan," he said grimly.

"Oh, then Dudley O'Mara's not your dad."

"Of course not." His voice was full of scorn. "Who are you?"

"I'm a detective. I'm going to find your—I mean, Mr. O'Mara."

That didn't bring us any closer. Detectives were nothing to him. The thunder was tumbling about in the hills like a bunch of elephants playing tag. I had another idea.

"Bet you can't put four out of five into the gold at thirty feet."

He livened up sharply. "With these?"

"Uh-huh."

"How much you bet?" he snapped.

"Oh, a dollar."

He ran to the target and cleaned darts off it, came back and took a stance by the bench.

"That's not thirty feet," I said.

He gave me a sour look and went a few feet behind the bench. I grinned, then I stopped grinning.

His small hand darted so swiftly I could hardly follow it. Five darts hung in the gold center of the target in less than that many seconds. He stared at me triumphantly.

"Gosh, you're pretty good, Master Trevillyan," I grunted, and got my dollar out.

His small hand snapped at it like a trout taking the fly. He had it out of sight like a flash.

"That's nothing," he chuckled. "You ought to see me on our target range back of the garages. Want to go over there and bet some more?"

I looked back up the hill and saw part of a low white building backed up to a bank.

"Well, not today," I said. "Next time I visit here maybe. So Dud O'Mara is not your dad. If I find him anyway, will it be all right with you?"

He shrugged his thin, sharp shoulders in a maroon sweater. "Sure. But what can you do the police can't do?"

"It's a thought," I said, and left him.

I went on down the brick walk to the bottom of the lawns and along inside the hedge towards the gatehouse. I could see glimpses of the street through the hedge. When I was halfway to the lodge I saw the blue sedan outside. It was a small neat car, low-slung, very clean, lighter than a police car, but about the same size. Over beyond it I could see my roadster waiting under the pepper tree.

I stood looking at the sedan through the hedge. I could see the drift of somebody's cigarette smoke against the windshield inside the car. I turned my back to the lodge and looked up the hill. The Trevillyan kid had gone somewhere out of sight, to salt his dollar down maybe, though a dollar shouldn't have meant much to him.

I bent over and unsheathed the 7.65 Lugar I was wearing that day and stuck it nose-down inside my left sock, inside my shoe. I could walk that way, if I didn't walk too fast. I went on to the gates.

They kept them locked and nobody got in without identification from the house. The lodge keeper, a big husky with a gun under his arm, came out and let me through a small postern at the side of the gates. I stood talking to him through the bars for a minute, watching the sedan.

It looked all right. There seemed to be two men in it. It was about a hundred feet along in the shadow of the high wall on the other side. It was a very narrow street, without sidewalks. I didn't have far to go to my roadster.

I walked a little stiffly across the dark pavement and got in, grabbed quickly down into a small compartment in the front part of the seat where I kept a spare gun. It was a police Colt. I slid it inside my under-arm holster and started the car.

I eased the brake off and pulled away. Suddenly the rain let go in big splashing drops and the sky was as black as Carrie Nation's bonnet. Not so black but that I saw the sedan wheel away from the curb behind me.

I started the windshield wiper and built up to forty miles an hour in a hurry. I had gone about eight blocks when they gave me the siren. That fooled me. It was a quiet street, deadly quiet. I slowed down and pulled over to the curb. The sedan slid up beside me and I was looking at the black snout of a submachine gun over the sill of the rear door.

Behind it a narrow face with reddened eyes, a fixed mouth. A voice above the sound of the rain and the windshield wiper and the noise of the two motors said: "Get in here with us. Be nice, if you know what I mean."

They were not cops. It didn't matter now. I shut off the ignition, dropped my car keys on the floor and got out on the running board. The man behind the wheel of the sedan didn't look at me. The one behind kicked a door open and slid away along the seat, holding the tommy gun nicely.

I got into the sedan.

"Okay, Louie. The frisk."

The driver came out from under his wheel and got behind me. He got the Colt from under my arm, tapped my hips and pockets, my belt line.

"Clean," he said, and got back into the front of the car.

The man with the tommy reached forward with his left hand and took my Colt from the driver, then lowered the tommy to the floor of the car and draped a brown rug over it. He leaned back in the corner again, smooth and relaxed, holding the Colt on his knee.

"Okay, Louie. Now let's ride."

V

We rode—idly, gently, the rain drumming on the roof and streaming down the windows on one side. We wound along curving hill streets, among estates that covered acres, whose houses were distant clusters of wet gables beyond blurred trees.

A tang of cigarette smoke floated under my nose and the red-eyed man said: "What did he tell you?"

"Little enough," I said. "That Mona blew town the night the papers got it. Old Winslow knew it already."

"He wouldn't have to dig very deep for that," Red-eyes said. "The buttons didn't. What else?"

"He said he'd been shot at. He wanted me to ride him out of town. At the last moment he ran off alone. I don't know why."

"Loosen up, peeper," Red-eyes said dryly. "It's your only way out."

"That's all there is," I said, and looked out of the window at the driving rain.

"You on the case for the old guy?"

"No. He's tight."

Red-eyes laughed. The gun in my shoe felt heavy and unsteady, and very far away. I said: "That might be all there is to know about O'Mara."

The man in the front seat turned his head a little and growled: "Where the hell did you say that street was?"

"Top of Beverly Glen, stupid. Mulholland Drive."

"Oh, that. Jeeze, that ain't paved worth a damn."

"We'll pave it with the peeper," Red-eyes said.

The estates thinned out and scrub oak took possession of the hillsides.

"You ain't a bad guy," Red-eyes said. "You're just tight, like the old man. Don't you get the idea? We want to know *everything* he said, so we'll know whether we got to blot you or no."

"Go to hell," I said. "You wouldn't believe me anyway."

"Try us. This is just a job to us. We just do it and pass on."

"It must be nice work," I said. "While it lasts."

"You'll crack wise once too often, guy."

"I did—long ago, while you were still in Reform School. I'm still getting myself disliked."

Red-eyes laughed again. There seemed to be very little bluster about him.

"Far as we know you're clean with the law. Didn't make no cracks this morning. That right?"

"If I say yes, you can blot me right now. Okay."

"How about a grand pin money and forget the whole thing?"

"You wouldn't believe that either."

"Yeah, we would. Here's the idea. We do the job and pass on. We're an organization. But you live here, you got goodwill and a business. You'd play ball."

"Sure," I said. "I'd play ball."

"We don't," Red-eyes said softly, "never knock off a legit. Bad for the trade."

He leaned back in the corner, the gun on his right knee, and reached into an inner pocket. He spread a large tan wallet on his knee and fished two bills out of it, slid them folded along the seat. The wallet went back into his pocket.

"Yours," he said gravely. "You won't last twenty-four hours if you slip your cable."

I picked the bills up. Two five hundreds. I tucked them in my vest. "Right," I said. "I wouldn't be a legit any more then, would I?"

"Think that over, dick."

We grinned at each other, a couple of nice lads getting along in a harsh, unfriendly world. Then Red-eyes turned his head sharply.

"Okay, Louie. Forget the Mulholland stuff. Pull up."

The car was halfway up a long bleak twist of hill. The rain drove in gray curtains down the slope. There was no ceiling, no horizon. I could see a quarter of a mile and I could see nothing outside our car that lived.

The driver edged over to the side of the bank and shut his motor off. He lit a cigarette and draped an arm on the back seat.

He smiled at me. He had a nice smile—like an alligator.

"We'll have a drink on it," Red-eyes said. "I wish I could make me a grand that easy. Just tyin' my nose to my chin."

"You ain't got no chin," Louie said, and went on smiling.

Red-eyes put the Colt down on the seat and drew a flat half-pint out of his side pocket. It looked like good stuff, green stamp, bottled in bond. He unscrewed the top with his teeth, sniffed at the liquor and smacked his lips.

"No Crow McGee in this," he said. "This is the company spread. Tilt her."

He reached along the seat and gave me the bottle. I could have had his wrist, but there was Louie, and I was too far from my ankle.

I breathed shallowly from the top of my lungs and held the bottle near my lips, sniffed carefully. Behind the charred smell of the bourbon there was something else, very faint, a fruity odor that would have meant nothing to me in another place. Suddenly and for no reason at all I remembered something Larry Batzel had said, something like: "East of Realito, towards the mountains, near the old cyanide plant." Cyanide. .That was the word.

There was a swift tightness in my temples as I put the bottle to my mouth. I could feel my skin crawling, and the air was suddenly cold on it. I held the bottle high up around the liquor level and took a long gurgling drag at it. Very hearty and relaxing. About half a teaspoonful went into my mouth and none of that stayed there.

I coughed sharply and lurched forward gagging. Red-eyes laughed.

"Don't say you're sick from just one drink, pal."

I dropped the bottle and sagged far down in the seat, gagging violently. My legs slid away to the left, the left one underneath. I sprawled down on top of them, my arms limp. I had the gun.

I shot him under my left arm, almost without looking. He never touched the Colt except to knock it off the seat. The one shot was enough. I heard him lurch. I snapped a shot upward towards where Louie would be.

Louie wasn't there. He was down behind the front seat. He was silent. The whole car, the whole landscape was silent. Even the rain seemed for a moment to be utterly silent rain.

I still didn't have time to look at Red-eyes, but he wasn't doing anything. I dropped the Luger and yanked the tommy gun out from under the rug, got my left hand on the front grip, got it set against my shoulder low down. Louie hadn't made a sound.

"Listen, Louie," I said softly, "I've got the stutter gun. How's about it?"

A shot came through the seat, a shot that Louie knew wasn't going to do any good. It starred a frame of unbreakable glass. There was more silence. Louie said thickly: "I got a pineapple here. Want it?"

"Pull the pin and hold it," I said. "It will take care of both of us."

"Hell!" Louie said violently. "Is he croaked? I ain't got no pineapple."

I looked at Red-eyes then. He looked very comfortable in the corner of the seat, leaning back. He seemed to have three eyes, one of them redder even than the other two. For under-arm shooting that was something to be almost bashful about. It was too good.

"Yeah, Louie, he's croaked," I said. "How do we get together?"

I could hear his hard breathing now, and the rain had stopped being silent. "Get out of the heap," he growled. "I'll blow."

"You get out, Louie. I'll blow."

"Jeeze, I can't walk home from here, pal."

"You won't have to, Louie. I'll send a car for you."

"Jeeze, I ain't done nothing. All I done was drive."

"Then reckless driving will be the charge, Louie. You can fix that—you and your organization. Get out before I uncork this popgun."

A door latch clicked and feet thumped on the running board, then on the roadway. I straightened up suddenly with the chopper. Louie was in the road in the rain, his hands empty and the alligator smile still on his face.

I got out past the dead man's neatly shod feet, got my Colt and the Luger off the floor, laid the heavy twelve-pound tommy gun back on the car floor. I got handcuffs off my hip, motioned to Louie. He turned around sulkily and put his hands behind him.

"You got nothing on me," he complained. "I got protection."

I clicked the cuffs on him and went over him for guns, much more carefully than he had gone over me. He had one besides the one he had left in the car.

I dragged Red-eyes out of the car and let him arrange himself on the wet roadway. He began to bleed again, but he was quite dead. Louie eyed him bitterly.

"He was a smart guy," he said. "Different. He liked tricks. Hello, smart guy."

I got my handcuff key out and unlocked one cuff, dragged it down and locked it to the dead man's lifted wrist.

Louie's eyes got round and horrified and at last his smile went away.

"Jeeze," he whined. "Holy—! Jeeze. You ain't going to leave me like this, pal?"

"Goodbye, Louie," I said. "That was a friend of mine you cut down this morning."

"Holy—!" Louie whined.

I got into the sedan and started it, drove on to a place where I could turn, drove back down the hill past him. He stood stiffly as a scorched tree, his face as white as snow, with the dead man at his feet, one linked hand reaching up to Louie's hand. There was the horror of a thousand nightmares in his eyes.

I left him there in the rain.

It was getting dark early. I left the sedan a couple of blocks from my own car and locked it up, put the keys in the oil strainer. I walked back to my roadster and drove downtown.

I called the homicide detail from a phone booth, asked for a man named Grinnell, told him quickly what had happened and where to find Louie and the sedan. I told him I thought they were the thugs that machine-gunned Larry Batzel. I didn't tell him anything about Dud O'Mara.

"Nice work," Grinnell said in a queer voice. "But you better come in fast. There's a tag out for you, account of what some milk driver phoned in an hour ago."

"I'm all in," I said. "I've got to eat. Keep me off the air and I'll come in after a while."

"You better come in, boy. I'm sorry, but you better."

"Well, okay," I said.

I hung up and left the neighborhood without hanging around. I had to break it now. I had to, or get broken myself.

I had a meal down near the Plaza and started for Realito.

VI

At about eight o'clock two yellow vapor lamps glowed high up in the rain and a dim stencil sign strung across the highway read: "Welcome to Realito."

Frame houses on the main street, a sudden knot of stores, the lights of the corner drugstore behind fogged glass, a flying-cluster of cars in front of a tiny movie palace, and a dark bank on another corner, with a knot of men standing in front of it in the rain. That was Realito. I went on. Empty fields closed in again.

This was past the orange country; nothing but the empty fields and the crouched foothills, and the rain.

It was a smart mile, more like three, before I spotted a side road and a faint light on it, as if from behind drawn blinds in a house. Just at that moment my left front tire let go with an angry hiss. That was cute. Then the right rear let go the same way.

I stopped almost exactly at the intersection. Very cute indeed. I got out, turned my raincoat up a little higher, unshipped a flash, and looked at a flock of heavy galvanized tacks with heads as big as dimes. The flat shiny butt of one of them blinked at me from my tire.

Two flats and one spare. I tucked my chin down and started towards the faint light up the side road.

It was the place all right. The light came from the tilted skylight on the garage roof. Big double doors in front were shut tight, but light showed at the cracks, strong white light. I tossed the beam of the flash up and read: "Art Huck—Auto Repairs and Refinishing."

Beyond the garage a house sat back from the muddy road behind a thin clump of trees. That had light too. I saw a small buttoned-up coupé in front of the wooden porch.

The first thing was the tires, if it could be worked, and they didn't know me. It was a wet night for walking.

I snapped the flash out and rapped on the doors with it. The light inside went out. I stood there licking rain off my upper lip, the flash in my left hand, my right inside my coat. I had the Luger back under my arm again.

A voice spoke through the door, and didn't sound pleased.

"What you want? Who are you?"

"Open up," I said. "I've got two flat tires on the highway and only one spare. I need help."

"We're closed up, mister. Realito's a mile west of here."

I started to kick the door. There was swearing inside, then another, much softer voice.

"A wise guy, huh? Open up, Art."

A bolt squealed and half of the door sagged inward. I snapped the flash again and it hit a gaunt face. Then an arm swept and knocked it out of my hand. A gun had just peeked at me from the flailing hand.

I dropped low, felt around for the flash and was still. I just didn't pull a gun.

"Kill the spot, mister. Guys get hurt that way."

The flash was burning down in the mud. I snapped it off, stood up with it. Light went on inside the garage, outlined a tall man in coveralls. He backed inward and his gun held on me.

"Come on in and shut the door."

I did that. "Tacks all over the end of your street," I said. "I thought you wanted the business."

"Ain't you got any sense? A bank job was pulled at Realito this afternoon."

"I'm a stranger here," I said, remembering the knot of men in front of the bank in the rain.

"Okay, okay. Well there was and the punks are hid out somewhere in the hills, they say. You stepped on their tacks, huh?"

"So it seems." I looked at the other man in the garage.

He was short, heavy-set, with a cool brown face and cool brown eyes. He wore a belted raincoat of brown leather. His brown hat had the usual rakish tilt and was dry. His hands were in his pockets and he looked bored.

There was a hot sweetish smell of pyroxylin paint on the air. A big sedan over in the corner had a paint gun lying on its fender. It was a Buick, almost new. It didn't need the paint it was getting.

The man in coveralls tucked his gun out of sight through a flap in the side of his clothes. He looked at the brown man. The brown man looked at me and said gently: "Where you from, stranger?"

"Seattle," I said.

"Going west—to the big city?" He had a soft voice, soft and dry, like the rustle of well-worn leather.

"Yes. How far is it?"

"About forty miles. Seems farther in this weather. Come the long way, didn't you? By Tahoe and Lone Pine?"

"Not Tahoe," I said. "Reno and Carson City."

"Still the long way." A fleeting smile touched the brown lips.

"Take a jack and get his flats, Art."

"Now, listen, Lash—" the man in the coveralls growled, and stopped as though his throat had been cut from ear to ear.

I could have sworn that he shivered. There was dead silence. The brown man didn't move a muscle. Something looked out of his eyes, and then his eyes lowered, almost shyly. His voice was the same soft, dry rustle of sound.

"Take two jacks, Art. He's got two flats."

The gaunt man swallowed. Then he went over to a corner and put a coat on, and a cap. He grabbed up a socket wrench and a handjack and wheeled a dolly jack over to the doors.

"Back on the highway, is it?" he asked me almost tenderly.

"Yeah. You can use the spare for one spot, if you're busy," I said.

"He's not busy," the brown man said and looked at his fingernails.

Art went out with his tools. The door shut again. I looked at the Buick. I didn't look at Lash Yeager. I knew it was Lash Yeager. There wouldn't be two men called Lash that came to that garage. I didn't look at him because I would be looking across the sprawled body of Larry Batzel, and it would show in my face. For a moment, anyway.

He glanced towards the Buick himself. "Just a panel job to start with," he drawled. "But the guy that owns it has dough and his driver needed a few bucks. You know the racket."

"Sure," I said.

The minutes passed on tiptoe. Long, sluggish minutes. Then feet crunched outside and the door was pushed open. The light hit pencils of rain and made silver wires of them. Art trundled two muddy flats in sulkily, kicked the door shut, let one of the flats fall on its side. The rain and fresh air had given him his nerve back. He looked at me savagely.

"Seattle," he snarled. "Seattle, my eye!"

The brown man lit a cigarette as if he hadn't heard. Art peeled his coat off and yanked my tire up on a rim spreader, tore it loose viciously, had the tube out and cold-patched in nothing flat. He strode scowling over to the wall near me and grabbed an air hose, let enough air into the tube to give it body, and hefted it in both hands to dip it in a washtub of water.

I was a sap, but their teamwork was very good. Neither had looked at the other since Art came back with my tires.

Art tossed the air-stiffened tube up casually, caught it with both hands wide, looked it over sourly beside the washtub of water, took one short easy step and slammed it down over my head and shoulders.

He jumped behind me in a flash, leaned his weight down on the rubber, dragged it tight against my chest and arms. I could move my hands, but I couldn't get near my gun.

The brown man brought his right hand out of his pocket and tossed a wrapped cylinder of nickels up and down on his palm as he stepped lithely across the floor.

I heaved back hard, then suddenly threw all my weight forward. Just as suddenly Art let go of the tube, and kneed me from behind.

I sprawled, but I never knew when I reached the floor. The fist with the weighted tube of nickels met me in mid-flight. Perfectly timed, perfectly weighted, and with my own weight to help it out.

I went out like a puff of dust in a draft.

VII

It seemed there was a woman and she was sitting beside a lamp. Light shone on my face, so I shut my eyes again and tried to look at her through my eyelashes. She was so platinumed that her head shone like a silver fruit bowl.

She wore a green traveling dress with a mannish cut to it and a broad white collar falling over the lapels. A sharp-angled glossy bag stood at her feet. She was smoking, and a drink was tall and pale at her elbow.

I opened my eye wider and said: "Hello there."

Her eyes were the eyes I remembered, outside Sardi's in a secondhand Rolls-Royce. Very blue eyes, very soft and lovely. Not the eyes of a hustler around the fast money boys.

"How do you feel?" Her voice was soft and lovely too.

"Great," I said. "Except somebody built a filling station on my jaw."

"What did you expect, Mr. Carmady? Orchids?"

"So you know my name."

"You slept well. They had plenty of time to go through your pockets. They did everything but embalm you."

"Right," I said.

I could move a little, not very much. My wrists were behind my back, handcuffed. There was a little poetic justice in that. From the cuffs a cord ran to my ankles, and tied them, and then dropped down out of sight over the end of the davenport and was tied somewhere else. I was almost as helpless as if I had been screwed up in a coffin.

"What time is it?"

She looked sideways down at her wrist, beyond the spiral of her cigarette smoke.

"Ten-seventeen. Got a date?"

"Is this the house next the garage? Where are the boys—digging a grave?"

"You wouldn't care, Carmady. They'll be back."

"Unless you have the key to these bracelets you might spare me a little of that drink."

She rose all in one piece and came over to me, with the tall amber glass in her hand. She bent over me. Her breath was delicate. I gulped from the glass craning my neck up.

"I hope they don't hurt you," she said distantly, stepping back. "I hate killing."

"And you Joe Mesarvey's wife. Shame on you. Gimme some more of the hooch."

She gave me some more. Blood began to move in my stiffened body.

"I kind of like you," she said. "Even if your face does look like a collision mat."

"Make the most of it," I said. "It won't last long even this good."

She looked around swiftly and seemed to listen. One of the two doors was ajar. She looked towards that. Her face seemed pale. But the sounds were only the rain.

She sat down by the lamp again.

"Why did you come here and stick your neck out?" she asked slowly, looking at the floor.

The carpet was made of red and tan squares. There were bright green pine trees on the wallpaper and the curtains were blue. The furniture, what I could see of it, looked as if it came from one of those places that advertise on bus benches.

"I had a rose for you," I said. "From Larry Batzel."

She lifted something off the table and twirled it slowly, the dwarf rose he had left for her.

"I got it," she said quietly. "There was a note, but they didn't show me that. Was it for me?"

"No, for me. He left it on my table before he went out and got shot."

Her face fell apart like something you see in a nightmare. Her mouth and eyes were black hollows. She didn't make a sound. And after a moment her face settled back into the same calmly beautiful lines.

"They didn't tell me that either," she said softly.

"He got shot," I said carefully, "because he found out what Joe and Lash Yeager did to Dud O'Mara. Bumped him off."

That one didn't faze her at all. "Joe didn't do anything to Dud O'Mara," she said quietly. "I haven't seen Dud in two years. That was just newspaper hooey, about me seeing him."

"It wasn't in the papers," I said.

"Well, it was hooey wherever it was. Joe is in Chicago. He went yesterday by plane to sell out. If the deal goes through, Lash and I are to follow him. Joe is no killer."

I stared at her.

Her eyes got haunted again. "Is Larry—is he—?"

"He's dead," I said. "It was a professional job, with a tommy gun. I didn't mean they did it personally."

She took hold of her lip and held it for a moment tight between her teeth. I could hear her slow, hard breathing. She jammed her cigarette in an ashtray and stood up.

"Joe didn't do it!" she stormed. "I know damn well he didn't. He—" She stopped cold, glared at me, touched her hair, then suddenly yanked it off. It was a wig. Underneath her own hair was short like a boy's, and streaked yellow and whitish brown, with darker tints at the roots. It couldn't make her ugly.

I managed a sort of laugh. "You just came out here to molt, didn't you, Silver-Wig? And I thought they were hiding you out—so it would look as if you had skipped with Dud O'Mara."

She kept on staring at me. As if she hadn't heard a word I said. Then she strode over to a wall mirror and put the wig back on, straightened it, turned and faced me.

"Joe didn't kill anybody," she said again, in a low, tight voice. "He's a heel—but not that kind of heel. He doesn't know anything more about where Dud O'Mara went than I do. And I don't know anything."

"He just got tired of the rich lady and scrammed," I said dully.

She stood near me now, her white fingers down at her sides, shining in the lamplight. Her head above me was almost in shadow. The rain drummed and my jaw felt large and hot and the nerve along the jawbone ached, ached.

"Lash has the only car that was here," she said softly. "Can you walk to Realito, if I cut the ropes?"

"Sure. Then what?"

"I've never been mixed up in a murder. I won't now. I won't ever."

She went out of the room very quickly, and came back with a long kitchen knife and sawed the cord that tied my ankles, pulled it off, cut the place where it was tied to the handcuffs. She stopped once to listen, but it was just the rain again.

I rolled up to a sitting position and stood up. My feet were numb, but that would pass. I could walk. I could run, if I had to.

"Lash has the key of the cuffs," she said dully.

"Let's go," I said. "Got a gun?"

"No. I'm not going. You beat it. He may be back any minute. They were just moving stuff out of the garage."

I went over close to her. "You're going to stay here after turning me loose? Wait for that killer? You're nuts. Come on, Silver-Wig, you're going with me."

"No."

"Suppose," I said, "he did kill O'Mara? Then he also killed Larry. It's got to be that way."

"Joe never killed anybody," she almost snarled at me.

"Well, suppose Yeager did."

"You're lying, Carmady. Just to scare me. Get out. I'm not afraid of Lash Yeager. I'm his boss's wife."

"Joe Mesarvey is a handful of mush," I snarled back. "The only time a girl like you goes for a wrong gee is when he's a handful of mush. Let's drift."

"Get out!" she said hoarsely.

"Okay." I turned away from her and went through the door.

She almost ran past me into the hallway and opened the front door, looked out into the black wetness. She motioned me forward.

"Goodbye," she whispered. "I hope you find Dud. I hope you find who killed Larry. But it wasn't Joe."

I stepped close to her, almost pushed her against the wall with my body.

"You're still crazy, Silver-Wig. Goodbye."

She raised her hands quickly and put them on my face. Cold hands, icy cold. She kissed me swiftly on the mouth with cold lips.

"Beat it, strong guy. I'll be seeing you some more. Maybe in heaven."

I went through the door and down the dark slithery wooden steps of the porch, across gravel to the round grass plot and the clump of thin trees. I came past them to the roadway, went back along it towards Foothill Boulevard. The rain touched my face with fingers of ice that were no colder than her fingers.

The curtained roadster stood just where I had left it, leaned over, the left front axle on the tarred shoulder of the highway. My spare and one stripped rim were thrown in the ditch.

They had probably searched it, but I still hoped. I crawled in backwards and banged my head on the steering post and rolled over to get the manacled hands into my little secret gun pocket. They touched the barrel. It was still there.

I got it out, got myself out of the car, got hold of the gun by the right end and looked it over.

I held it tight against my back to protect it a little from the rain and started back towards the house.

VIII

I was halfway there when he came back. His lights turning quickly off the highway almost caught me. I flopped into the ditch and put my nose in the mud and prayed.

The car hummed past. I heard the wet rasp of its tires shouldering the gravel in front of the house. The motor died and lights went off. The door slammed. I didn't hear the house door shut, but I caught a feeble fringe of light through the trees as it opened.

I got up on my feet and went on. I came up beside the car, a small coupé, rather old. The gun was down at my side, pulled around my hip as far as the cuffs would let it come.

The coupé was empty. Water gurgled in the radiator. I listened and heard nothing from the house. No loud voices, no quarrel. Only the heavy bong-bong-bong of the raindrops hitting the elbows at the bottom of rain gutters.

Yeager was in the house. She had let me go and Yeager was in there with her. Probably she wouldn't tell him anything. She would just stand and look at him. She was his boss's wife. That would scare Yeager to death.

He wouldn't stay long, but he wouldn't leave her behind, alive or dead. He would be on his way and take her with him. What happened to her later on was something else.

All I had to do was wait for him to come out. I didn't do it.

I shifted the gun into my left hand and leaned down to scoop up some gravel. I threw it against the front window. It was a weak effort. Very little even reached the glass.

I ran back behind the coupé and got its door open and saw the keys in the ignition lock. I crouched down on the running board, holding on to the door post.

The house had already gone dark, but that was all. There wasn't any sound from it. No soap. Yeager was too cagy.

I reached in with my foot and found the starter, then strained back with one hand and turned the ignition key. The warm motor caught at once, throbbed gently against the pounding rain.

I got back to the ground and slid along to the rear of the car, crouched down.

The sound of the motor got him. He couldn't be left there without a car.

A darkened window slid up an inch, only some shifting of light on the glass showing it moved. Flame spouted from it, the racket of three quick shots. Glass broke in the coupé.

I screamed and let the scream die into a gurgling groan. I was getting good at that sort of thing. I let the groan die in a choked gasp. I was through, finished. He had got me. Nice shooting, Yeager.

Inside the house a man laughed. Then silence again, except for the rain and the quietly throbbing motor of the coupé.

Then the house door inched open. A figure showed in it. She came out on the porch, stiffly, the white showing at her collar, the wig showing a little but not so much. She came down the steps like a wooden woman. I saw Yeager crouched behind her.

She started across the gravel. Her voice said slowly, without any tone at all:

"I can't see a thing, Lash. The windows are all misted."

She jerked a little, as if a gun had prodded her, and came on. Yeager didn't speak. I could see him now past her shoulder, his hat, part of his face. But no kind of a shot for a man with cuffs on his wrists.

She stopped again, and her voice was suddenly horrified.

"He's behind the wheel!" she yelled. "Slumped over!"

He fell for it. He knocked her to one side and started to blast again. More glass jumped around. A bullet hit a tree on my side of the car. A cricket whined somewhere. The motor kept right on humming.

He was low, crouched against the black, his face a grayness without form that seemed to come back very slowly after the glare of the shots. His own fire had blinded him too—for a second. That was enough.

I shot him four times, straining the pulsing Colt against my ribs.

He tried to turn and the gun slipped away from his hand. He half snatched for it in the air, before both his hands suddenly went against his stomach and stayed there. He sat down on the wet gravel and his harsh panting dominated every other sound of the wet night.

I watched him lie down on his side, very slowly, without taking his hands away from his stomach. The panting stopped.

It seemed like an age before Silver-Wig called out to me. Then she was beside me, grabbing my arm.

"Shut the motor off!" I yelled at her. "And get the key of these damn irons out of his pocket."

"You d-darn fool," she babbled. "W-what did you come back for?"

IX

Captain Al Roof of the Missing Persons Bureau swung in his chair and looked at the sunny window. This was another day, and the rain had stopped long since.

He said gruffly: "You're making a lot of mistakes, brother. Dud O'Mara just pulled down the curtain. None of those people knocked him off. The Batzel killing had nothing to do with it. They've got Mesarvey in Chicago and he looks clean. The Heeb you anchored to the dead guy don't even know who they were pulling the job for. Our boys asked him enough to be sure of that."

"I'll bet they did," I said. "I've been in the same bucket all night and I couldn't tell them much either."

He looked at me slowly, with large, bleak, tired eyes. "Killing Yeager was all right, I guess. And the chopper. In the circumstances. Besides I'm not homicide. I couldn't link any of that to O'Mara—unless you could."

I could, but I hadn't. Not yet. "No," I said. "I guess not." I stuffed and lit my pipe. After a sleepless night it tasted better.

"That all that's worrying you?"

"I wondered why you didn't find the girl, at Realito. It couldn't have been very hard—for you."

"We just didn't. We should have. I admit it. We didn't. Anything else?"

I blew smoke across his desk. "I'm looking for O'Mara because the general told me to. It wasn't any use my telling him you would do everything that could be done. He could afford a man with all his time on it. I suppose you resent that."

He wasn't amused. "Not at all, if he wants to waste money. The people that resent you are behind a door marked Homicide Bureau."

He planted his feet with a slap and elbowed his desk.

"O'Mara had fifteen grand in his clothes. That's a lot of jack but O'Mara would be the boy to have it. So he could take it out and have his old pals see him with it. Only they wouldn't think it was fifteen grand of real dough. His wife says it was. Now with any other guy but an ex-legger in the gravy that might indicate an intention to disappear. But not O'Mara. He packed it all the time."

He bit a cigar and put a match to it. He waved a large finger. "See?"

I said I saw.

"Okay. O'Mara had fifteen grand, and a guy that pulls down the curtain can keep it down only so long as his wad lasts. Fifteen grand is a good wad. I might disappear myself, if I had that much. But after it's gone we get him. He cashes a check, lays down a marker, hits a hotel or store for credit, gives a reference, writes a letter or gets one. He's in a new town and he's got a new name, but he's got the same old appetite. He has to get back into the fiscal system one way or another. A guy can't have friends everywhere, and if he had, they wouldn't all stay clammed forever. Would they?"

"No, they wouldn't," I said.

"He went far," Roof said. "But the fifteen grand was all the preparation he made. No baggage, no boat or rail or plane reservation, no taxi or private rental hack to a point out of town. That's all checked. His own car was found a dozen blocks from where he lived. But that means nothing. He knew people who would ferry him several hundred miles and keep quiet about it, even in the face of a reward. Here, but not everywhere. Not new friends."

"But you'll get him," I said.

"When he gets hungry."

"That could take a year or two. General Winslow may not live a year. That is a matter of sentiment, not whether you have an open file when you retire."

"You attend to the sentiment, brother." His eyes moved and bushy reddish eyebrows moved with them. He didn't like me. Nobody did, in the police department, that day.

"I'd like to," I said and stood up. "Maybe I'd go pretty far to attend to that sentiment."

"Sure," Roof said, suddenly thoughtful. "Well, Winslow is a big man. Anything I can do let me know."

"You could find out who had Larry Batzel gunned," I said. "Even if there isn't any connection."

"We'll do that. Glad to," he guffawed and flicked ash all over his desk. "You just knock off the guys who can talk and we'll do the rest. We like to work that way."

"It was self-defense," I growled. "I couldn't help myself."

"Sure. Take the air, brother. I'm busy."

But his large bleak eyes twinkled at me as I went out.

X

The morning was all blue and gold and the birds in the ornamental trees of the Winslow estate were crazy with song after the rain.

The gatekeeper let me in through the postern and I walked up the driveway and along the top terrace to the huge carved Italian front door. Before I rang the bell I looked down the hill and saw the Trevillyan kid sitting on his stone bench with his head cupped in his hands, staring at nothing.

I went down the brick path to him. "No darts today, son?"

He looked up at me with his lean, slaty, sunken eyes.

"No. Did you find him?"

"Your dad? No, sonny, not yet."

He jerked his head. His nostrils flared angrily. "He's not my dad I told you. And don't talk to me as if I was four years old. My dad he's—he's in Florida or somewhere."

"Well, I haven't found him yet, whoever's dad he is," I said.

"Who smacked your jaw?" he asked, staring at me.

"Oh, a fellow with a roll of nickels in his hand."

"Nickels?"

"Yeah. That's as good as brass knuckles. Try it sometime, but not on me." I grinned.

"You won't find him," he said bitterly, staring at my jaw. "Him, I mean. My mother's husband."

"I bet I do."

"How much you bet?"

"More money than even you've got in your pants."

He kicked viciously at the edge of a red brick in the walk. His voice was still sulky, but more smooth. His eyes speculated.

"Want to bet on something else? C'mon over to the range. I bet you a dollar I can knock down eight out of ten pipes in ten shots."

I looked back towards the house. Nobody seemed impatient to receive me.

"Well," I said, "we'll have to make it snappy. Let's go."

We went along the side of the house under the windows. The orchid green-house showed over the tops of some bushy trees far back. A man in neat whipcord was polishing the chromium on a big car in front of the garages. We went past there to the low white building against the bank.

The boy took a key out and unlocked the door and we went into close air that still held traces of cordite fumes. The boy clicked a spring lock on the door.

"Me first," he snapped.

The place looked something like a small beach shooting gallery. There was a counter with a .22 repeating rifle on it and a long, slim target pistol.

Both well oiled but dusty. About thirty feet beyond the counter was a waist-high, solid-looking partition across the building, and behind that a simple layout of clay pipes and ducks and two round white targets marked off with black rings and stained by lead bullets.

The clay pipes ran in an even line across the middle, and there was a big skylight, and a row of hooded overhead lights.

The boy pulled a cord on the wall and a thick canvas blind slid across the skylight. He turned on the hooded lights and then the place really looked like a beach shooting gallery.

He picked up the .22 rifle and loaded it quickly from a cardboard box of shells, .22 shorts.

"A dollar I get eight out of ten pipes?"

"Blast away," I said, and put my money on the counter.

He took aim almost casually, fired too fast, showing off. He missed three pipes. It was pretty fancy shooting at that. He threw the rifle down on the counter.

"Gee, go set up some more. Let's not count that one. I wasn't set."

"You don't aim to lose any money, do you, son? Go set 'em up yourself. It's your range."

His narrow face got angry and his voice got shrill. "You do it! I've got to relax, see. I've got to relax."

I shrugged at him, lifted a flap in the counter and went along the whitewashed side wall, squeezed past the end of the low partition. The boy clicked his reloaded rifle shut behind me.

"Put that down," I growled back at him. "Never touch a gun when there's anyone in front of you."

He put it down, looking hurt.

I bent down and grabbed a handful of clay pipes out of the sawdust in a big wooden box on the floor. I shook the yellow grains of wood off them and started to straighten up.

I stopped with my hat above the barrier, just the top of my hat. I never knew why I stopped. Blind instinct.

The .22 cracked and the lead bullet bonged into the target in front of my head. My hat stirred lazily on my head, as though a blackbird had swooped at it during the nesting season.

A nice kid. He was full of tricks, like Red-eyes. I dropped the pipes and took hold of my hat by the brim, lifted it straight up off my head a few inches. The gun cracked again. Another metallic bong on the target.

I let myself fall heavily to the wooden flooring, among the pipes.

A door opened and shut. That was all. Nothing else. The hard glare from the hooded lights beat down on me. The sun peeked in at the edges of the skylight blind. There were two bright new splashes on the nearest target, and there were four small round holes in my hat, two and two, on each side.

I crawled to the end of the barrier and peeked around it. The boy was gone. I could see the small muzzles of the two guns on the counter.

I stood up and went back along the wall, switched the lights off, turned the knob of the spring lock and went out. The Winslow chauffeur whistled at his polish job around in front of the garages.

I crushed my hat in my hand and went back along the side of the house, looking for the kid. I didn't see him. I rang the front door bell.

I asked for Mrs. O'Mara. I didn't let the butler take my hat.

XI

She was in an oyster-white something, with white fur at the cuffs and collar and around the bottom. A breakfast table on wheels was pushed to one side of her chair and she was flicking ashes among the silver.

The coy-looking maid with the nice legs came and took the table out and shut the tall white door. I sat down.

Mrs. O'Mara leaned her head back against a cushion and looked tired. The line of her throat was distant, cold. She stared at me with a cool, hard look, in which there was plenty of dislike.

"You seemed rather human yesterday," she said. "But I see you are just a brute like the rest of them. Just a brutal cop."

"I came to ask you about Lash Yeager," I said.

She didn't even pretend to be amused. "And why should you think of asking me?"

"Well—if you lived a week at the Dardanella Club—" I waved my crunched-together hat.

She looked at her cigarette fixedly. "Well, I did meet him, I believe. I remember the rather unusual name."

"They all have names like that, those animals," I said. "It seems that Larry Batzel—I guess you read in your paper about him too—was a friend of Dud O'Mara's once. I didn't tell you about him yesterday. Maybe that was a mistake."

A pulse began to throb in her throat. She said softly: "I have a suspicion you are about to become very insolent, that I may even have to have you thrown out."

"Not before I've said my piece," I said. "It seems that Mr. Yeager's driver—they have drivers as well as unusual names, those animals—told Larry Batzel that Mr. Yeager was out this way the night O'Mara disappeared."

The old army blood had to be good for something in her. She didn't move a muscle. She just froze solid.

I got up and took the cigarette from between her frozen fingers and killed it in a white jade ashtray. I laid my hat carefully on her white satin knee. I sat down again.

Her eyes moved after a while. They moved down and looked at the hat. Her face flushed very slowly, in two vivid patches over the cheekbones. She fought around with her tongue and lips.

"I know," I said. "It's not much of a hat. I'm not making you a present of it. But just look at the bullet holes in it once."

Her hand became alive and snatched at the hat. Her eyes became flames.

She spread the crown out, looked at the holes, and shuddered.

"Yeager?" she asked, very faintly. It was a wisp of a voice, an old voice.

I said very slowly: "Yeager wouldn't use a .22 target rifle, Mrs. O'Mara."

The flame died in her eyes. They were pools of darkness, much emptier than darkness.

"You're his mother," I said. "What do you want to do about it?"

"Merciful God! Dade! He . . . shot at you!"

"Twice," I said.

"But why? . . . Oh, why?"

"You think I'm a wise guy, Mrs. O'Mara. Just another hard-eyed boy from the other side of the tracks. It would be easy in this spot, if I was. But I'm not that at all, really. Do I have to tell why he shot at me!"

She didn't speak. She nodded slowly. Her face was a mask now.

"I'd say he probably can't help it," I said. "He didn't want me to find his stepfather, for one thing. Then he's a little lad that likes money. That seems small, but it's part of the picture. He almost lost a dollar to me on his shooting. It seems small, but he lives in a small world. Most of all, of course, he's a crazy little sadist with an itchy trigger finger."

"How dare you!" she flared. It didn't mean anything. She forgot it herself instantly.

"How dare I? I do dare. Let's not bother figuring why he shot at *me*. I'm not the first, am I? You wouldn't have known what I was talking about, you wouldn't have assumed he did it on purpose."

She didn't move or speak. I took a deep breath.

"So let's talk about why he shot Dud O'Mara," I said.

If I thought she would yell even this time, I fooled myself. The old man in the orchid house had put more into her than her tallness and her dark hair and her reckless eyes.

She pulled her lips back and tried to lick them, and it made her look like a scared little girl, for a second. The lines of her cheeks sharpened and her hand went up like an artificial hand moved by wires and took hold of the white fur at her throat and pulled it tight and squeezed it until her knuckles looked like bleached bone. Then she just stared at me.

Then my hat slid off her knee on to the floor, without her moving. The sound it made falling was one of the loudest sounds I had ever heard.

"Money," she said in a dry croak. "Of course you want money."

"How much money do I want?"

"Fifteen thousand dollars."

I nodded, stiff-necked as a floor walker trying to see with his back.

"That would be about right. That would be the established retainer. That would be about what he had in his pockets and what Yeager got for getting rid of him."

"You're too—damned smart," she said horribly. "I could kill you myself and like it."

I tried to grin. "That's right. Smart and without a feeling in the world. It happened something like this. The boy got O'Mara where he got me, by the same simple ruse. I don't think it was a plan. He hated his stepfather, but he wouldn't exactly plan to kill him."

"He hated him," she said.

"So they're in the little shooting gallery and O'Mara is dead on the floor, behind the barrier, out of sight. The shots, of course, meant nothing there. And very little blood, with a head shot, small caliber. So the boy goes out and locks the door and hides. But after a while he has to tell somebody. He has to. He tells you. You're his mother. You're the one to tell."

"Yes," she breathed. "He did just that." Her eyes had stopped hating me.

"You think about calling it an accident, which is okay, except for one thing. The boy's not a normal boy, and you know it. The general knows it, the servants know. There must be other people that know it. And the law, dumb as you think they are, are pretty smart with subnormal types. They get to handle so many of them. And I think he would have talked. I think, after a while, he would even have bragged."

"Go on," she said.

"You wouldn't risk that," I said. "Not for your son and not for the sick old man in the orchid house. You'd do any awful criminal callous thing rather than risk that. You did it. You knew Yeager and you hired him to get rid of the body. That's all—except that hiding the girl, Mona Mesarvey, helped to make it look like a deliberate disappearance."

"He took him away after dark, in Dud's own car," she said hollowly.

I reached down and picked my hat off the floor. "How about the servants?"

"Norris knows. The butler. He'd die on the rack before he told."

"Yeah. Now you know why Larry Batzel was knocked off and why I was taken for a ride, don't you?"

"Blackmail," she said. "It hadn't come yet, but I was waiting for it. I would have paid anything, and he would know that."

"Bit by bit, year by year, there was a quarter of a million in it for him, easy. I don't think Joe Mesarvey was in it at all. I know the girl wasn't."

She didn't say anything. She just kept her eyes on my face.

"Why in hell," I groaned, "didn't you take the guns away from him?"

"He's worse than you think. That would have started something worse. I'm—I'm almost afraid of him myself."

"Take him away," I said. "From here. From the old man. He's young enough to be cured, by the right handling. Take him to Europe. Far away. Take him now. It would kill the general out of hand to know his blood was in that."

She got up draggingly and dragged herself across to the windows. She stood motionless, almost blending into the heavy white drapes. Her hands hung at her sides, very motionless also. After a while she turned and walked past me. When she was behind me she caught her breath and sobbed just once.

"It was very vile. It was the vilest thing I ever heard of. Yet I would do it again. Father would not have done it. He would have spoken right out. It would, as you say, have killed him."

"Take him away," I pounded on. "He's hiding out there now. He thinks he got me. He's hiding somewhere like an animal. Get him. He can't help it."

"I offered you money," she said, still behind me. "That's nasty. I wasn't in love with Dudley O'Mara. That's nasty too. I can't thank you. I don't know what to say."

"Forget it," I said. "I'm just an old workhorse. Put *your* work on the boy."

"I promise. Goodbye, Mr. Carmady."

We didn't shake hands. I went back down the stairs and the butler was at the front door as usual. Nothing in his face but politeness.

"You will not want to see the general today, sir?"

"Not today, Norris."

I didn't see the boy outside. I went through the postern and got into my rented Ford and drove on down the hill, past where the old oil wells were.

Around some of them, not visible from the street, there were still sumps in which waste water lay and festered with a scum of oil on top.

They would be ten or twelve feet deep, maybe more. There would be dark things in them. Perhaps in one of them—

I was glad I had killed Yeager.

On the way back downtown I stopped at a bar and had a couple of drinks. They didn't do me any good.

All they did was make me think of Silver-Wig, and I never saw her again.

Philip Durham, in his introduction to *Killer in the Rain* (Houghton Mifflin, 1964; Ballantine Books, 1972), writes, "When Raymond Chandler published *The Big Sleep*, his first of seven novels, in 1939, he did what multitudes of writers had done before him: he reused some of his earlier material. Unlike most writers, however, reusing previously published stories left him with an uneasy feeling. Once a story was used in a novel it became—to use his word—cannibalized. Therefore he could justify this writing method only by leaving such stories buried, virtually unknown in the pages of the rapidly disappearing pulp magazines. The stories in this volume [The volume includes "The Curtain."—Eds.], then, were not collected during the author's lifetime. Since his death, however, there have been very many requests that they should be reprinted and there no longer seems any good reason why, provided their origin is clearly explained, they should be denied to the many thousands of Chandler's readers. Apart from the pleasure Chandler's audience will derive from the stories themselves, it is further hoped that his readers will realize that only a skilled craftsman could turn eight separately conceived short stories into three excellent novels." Readers are referred to this introduction and to the entire *Killer in the Rain* for detailed commentary and examples of Chandler's writing methods. These particularly regard Chandler's extreme skill in, as Durham notes, "combining and enlarging plots, maintaining a thematic consistency, blowing up scenes, and adapting, fusing, and adding characters." Durham continues, "In each of these stories the hero is 'a man fit for adventure.' He is a knight whose mission in life is to protect the weak and to make sure justice is done. It was in the stories in this volume that Chandler developed his detective-hero, the man he wrote about so eloquently in his essay 'The Simple Art of Murder.' "

QUESTIONS

1. Compare Carmady with the detective in "Fly Paper."
2. Discuss the use of violence in this story. Is it disgusting, distasteful, exciting, necessary? What is added to the story by the explicitness of the violent scenes?
3. Describe Chandler's use of description, especially in such paragraphs as the first in section IV. There is often little time for description in popular detective stories. It must be done quickly, create the desired atmosphere, and not delay the forward push of the narrative. How are some of the same results gained in Chandler's method of characterization, especially of the General?
4. How convincing are the actions of the 11-year-old in "The Curtain"? Of his mother?
5. At the end of the story, Carmady says, "I was glad I had killed Yeager." Compare a similar statement made by Sherlock Holmes regarding the death of the stepfather in "The Adventure of the Speckled Band." What does the phrasing of the two statements reveal about the attitudes conveyed?
6. Examine the use of dialogue and short sentences in this story. What effects are gained and lost in this sort of style? Compare Chandler's style to Hammett's.
7. What is your opinion of Carmady's morality? Do you believe his refusal of so much money would take place in an actual situation? What gives Carmady the right to keep to himself what he has discovered?
8. Much of this story was later incorporated into Chandler's novel *The Big Sleep*. Read the novel and then compare it with this short story. Does Chandler's "cannibalization" lend insight into the workings of the two different forms? If you can, compare the story and novel with the film version of *The Big Sleep* (often on late-night TV). Note the changes. Can you detect the hand of one of the co-authors of the screenplay, William Faulkner?

Find the Woman

Ross Macdonald

I sat in my brand-new office with the odor of paint in my nostrils and waited for something to happen. I had been back on the Boulevard for one day. This was the beginning of the second day. Below the window, flashing in the morning sun, the traffic raced and roared with a noise like battle. It made me nervous. It made me want to move. I was all dressed up in civilian clothes with no place to go and nobody to go with.

Till Millicent Dreen came in.

I had seen her before, on the Strip with various escorts, and knew who she was: publicity director for Tele-Pictures. Mrs. Dreen was over forty and looked it, but there was electricity in her, plugged in to a secret source that time could never wear out. Look how high and tight I carry my body, her movements said. My hair is hennaed but comely, said her coiffure, inviting not to conviction but to suspension of disbelief. Her eyes were green and inconstant like the sea. They said what the hell.

She sat down by my desk and told me that her daughter had disappeared the day before, which was September the seventh.

"I was in Hollywood all day. We keep an apartment here, and there was some work I had to get out fast. Una isn't working, so I left her at the beach house by herself."

"Where is it?"

"A few miles above Santa Barbara."

"That's a long way to commute."

"It's worth it to me. When I can maneuver a weekend away from this town, I like to get *really* away."

"Maybe your daughter feels the same, only more so. When did she leave?"

"Sometime yesterday. When I drove home to the beach house last night she was gone."

"Did you call the police?"

"Hardly. She's twenty-two and knows what she's doing. I hope. Anyway, apron strings don't become me." She smiled like a cat and moved her scarlet-taloned fingers in her narrow lap. "It was very late and I was—tired. I went to bed. But when I woke up this morning it occurred to me that she might have drowned. I objected to it because she wasn't a strong swimmer, but she went in for solitary swimming. I think of the most dreadful things when I wake up in the morning."

"*Went* in for solitary swimming, Mrs. Dreen?"

" 'Went' slipped out, didn't it? I told you I think of dreadful things when I wake up in the morning."

"If she drowned you should be talking to the police. They can arrange for dragging and such things. All I can give you is my sympathy."

As if to estimate the value of that commodity, her eyes flickered from my shoulders to my waist and up again to my face. "Frankly, I don't know about the police. I do know about you, Mr. Archer. You just got out of the army, didn't you?"

"Last week." I failed to add that she was my first postwar client.

"And you don't belong to anybody, I've heard. You've never been bought. Is that right?"

"Not outright. You can take an option on a piece of me, though. A hundred dollars would do for a starter."

She nodded briskly. From a bright black bag she gave me five twenties. "Naturally, I'm conscious of publicity angles. My daughter retired a year ago when she married—"

"Twenty-one is a good age to retire."

"From pictures, maybe you're right. But she could want to go back if her marriage breaks up. And I have to look out for myself. It isn't true that there's no such thing as bad publicity. *I* don't know why Una went away."

"Is your daughter Una Sand?"

"Of course. I assumed you knew." My ignorance of the details of her life seemed to cause her pain. She didn't have to tell me that she had a feeling for publicity angles.

Though Una Sand meant less to me than Hecuba, I remembered the name and with it a glazed blonde who had had a year or two in the sun, but who'd made a better pin-up than an actress.

"Wasn't her marriage happy? I mean, isn't it?"

"You see how easy it is to slip into the past tense?" Mrs. Dreen smiled another fierce and purring smile, and her fingers fluttered in glee before her immobile body. "I suppose her marriage is happy enough. Her Ensign's quite a personable young man—handsome in a masculine way, and passionate she tells me, and naive enough."

"Naive enough for what?"

"To marry Una. Jack Rossiter was quite a catch in this woman's town. He was runner-up at Forest Hills the last year he played tennis. And now of course he's a flier. Una did right well by herself, even if it doesn't last."

What do you expect of a war marriage? she seemed to be saying. Permanence? Fidelity? The works?

"As a matter of fact," she went on, "it was thinking about Jack, more than anything else, that brought me here to you. He's due back this week, and naturally"—like many unnatural people, she overused that adverb—"he'll expect her to be waiting for him. It'll be rather embarrassing for me if he comes home and I can't tell him where she's gone, or why, or with whom. You'd really think she'd leave a note."

"I can't keep up with you," I said. "A minute ago Una was in the clutches of the cruel crawling foam. Now she's taken off with a romantic stranger."

"I consider possibilities, is all. When I was Una's age, married to Dreen, I had quite a time settling down. I still do."

Our gazes, mine as impassive as hers I hoped, met, struck no spark, and disengaged. The female spider who eats her mate held no attraction for me.

"I'm getting to know you pretty well," I said with the necessary smile, "but not the missing girl. Who's she been knocking around with?"

"I don't think we need to go into that. She doesn't confide in me, in any case."

"Whatever you say. Shall we look at the scene of the crime?"

"There isn't any *crime*."

"The scene of the accident, then, or the departure. Maybe the beach house will give me something to go on."

She glanced at the wafer-thin watch on her brown wrist. Its diamonds glittered coldly. "Do I have to drive all the way back?"

"If you can spare the time, it might help. We'll take my car."

She rose decisively but gracefully, as though she had practiced the movement in front of a mirror. An expert bitch, I thought as I followed her high slim shoulders and tight-sheathed hips down the stairs to the bright street. I felt a little sorry for the army of men who had warmed themselves, or been burned, at that secret electricity. And I wondered if her daughter Una was like her.

When I did get to see Una, the current had been cut off; I learned about it only by the marks it left. It left marks.

We drove down Sunset to the sea and north on 101 Alternate. All the way to Santa Barbara, she read a typescript whose manila cover was marked: "Temporary— This script is not final and is given to you for advance information only." It occurred to me that the warning might apply to Mrs. Dreen's own story.

As we left the Santa Barbara city limits, she tossed the script over her shoulder into the back seat. "It *really* smells. It's going to be a smash."

A few miles north of the city, a dirt road branched off to the left beside a filling station. It wound for a mile or more through broken country to her private beach. The beach house was set well back from the sea at the convergence of brown bluffs which huddled over it like scarred shoulders. To reach it we had to drive along the beach for a quarter of a mile, detouring to the very edge of the sea around the southern bluff.

The blue-white dazzle of sun, sand, and surf was like an arc-furnace. But I felt some breeze from the water when we got out of the car. A few languid clouds moved inland over our heads. A little high plane was gamboling among them like a terrier in a henyard.

"You have privacy," I said to Mrs. Dreen.

She stretched, and touched her varnished hair with her fingers. "One tires of the goldfish role. When I lie out there in the afternoons I—forget I have a name." She pointed to the middle of the cove beyond the breakers, where a white raft moved gently in the swells. "I simply take off my clothes and revert to protoplasm. *All* my clothes."

I looked up at the plane whose pilot was doodling in the sky. It dropped, turning like an early falling leaf, swooped like a hawk, climbed like an aspiration.

She said with a laugh: "If they come too low I cover my face, of course."

We had been moving away from the house towards the water. Nothing could have looked more innocent than the quiet cove held in the curve of the white beach like a benign blue eye in a tranquil brow. Then its colors shifted as a cloud passed over the sun. Cruel green and violent purple ran in the blue. I felt the old primitive terror and fascination. Mrs. Dreen shared the feeling and put it into words:

"It's got queer moods. I hate it sometimes as much as I love it." For an instant she looked old and uncertain. "I hope she isn't in there."

The tide had turned and was coming in, all the way from Hawaii and beyond, all the way from the shattered islands where bodies lay unburied in the burnt-out caves. The waves came up towards us, fumbling and gnawing at the beach like an immense soft mouth.

"Are there bad currents here, or anything like that?"

"No. It's deep, though. It must be twenty feet under the raft. I could never bottom it."

"I'd like to look at her room," I said. "It might tell us where she went, and even with whom. You'd know what clothes were missing?"

She laughed a little apologetically as she opened the door. "I used to dress my daughter, naturally. Not any more. Besides, more than half of her things must be in the Hollywood apartment. I'll try to help you, though."

It was good to step out of the vibrating brightness of the beach into shadowy stillness behind Venetian blinds. "I noticed that you unlocked the door," I said. "It's a big house with a lot of furniture in it. No servants?"

"I occasionally have to knuckle under to producers. But I won't to my employees. They'll be easier to get along with soon, now that the plane plants are shutting down."

We went to Una's room, which was light and airy in both atmosphere and furnishings. But it showed the lack of servants. Stockings, shoes, underwear, dresses, bathing suits, lipstick-smeared tissue littered the chairs and the floor. The bed was unmade. The framed photograph on the night table was obscured by two empty glasses which smelt of highball, and flanked by overflowing ash trays.

I moved the glasses and looked at the young man with the wings on his chest. Naive, handsome, passionate were words which suited the strong blunt nose, the full lips and square jaw, the wide proud eyes. For Mrs. Dreen he would have made a single healthy meal, and I wondered again if her daughter was a carnivore. At least the photograph of Jack Rossiter was the only sign of a man in her room. The two glasses could easily have been from separate nights. Or separate weeks, to judge by the condition of the room. Not that it wasn't an attractive room. It was like a pretty girl in disarray. But disarray.

We examined the room, the closets, the bathroom, and found nothing of importance, either positive or negative. When we had waded through the brilliant and muddled wardrobe which Una had shed, I turned to Mrs. Dreen.

"I guess I'll have to go back to Hollywood. It would help me if you'd come along. It would help me more if you'd tell me who your daughter knew. Or rather who she liked—I suppose she knew everybody. Remember, you suggested yourself that there's a man in this."

"I take it you haven't found anything?"

"One thing I'm pretty sure of. She didn't intentionally go away for long. Her toilet articles and pills are still in her bathroom. She's got quite a collection of pills."

"Yes, Una's always been a hypochondriac. Also she left Jack's picture. She only had the one, because she liked it best."

"That isn't so conclusive," I said. "I don't suppose you'd know whether there's a bathing suit missing?"

"I really couldn't say, she had so many. She was at her best in them."

"Still *was?*"

"I guess so, as a working hypothesis. Unless you can find me evidence to the contrary."

"You didn't like your daughter much, did you?"

"No. I didn't like her father. And she was prettier than I."

"But not so intelligent?"

"Not as bitchy, you mean? She was bitchy enough. But I'm still worried about Jack. He loved her. Even if I didn't."

The telephone in the hall took the cue and began to ring. "This is Millicent Dreen," she said into it. "Yes, you may read it to me." A pause. 'Kill the fatted calf, ice the champagne, turn down the sheets and break out the black silk nightie. Am coming home tomorrow.' Is that right?"

Then she said, "Hold it a minute. I wish to send an answer. To Ensign

Jack Rossiter, USS *Guam*, CVE 173, Naval Air Station, Alameda—is that Ensign Rossiter's correct address? The text is: 'Dear Jack join me at the Hollywood apartment there is no one at the beach house. Millicent.' Repeat it, please. . . . Right. Thank you."

She turned from the phone and collapsed in the nearest chair, not forgetting to arrange her legs symmetrically.

"So Jack is coming home tomorrow?" I said. "All I had before was no evidence. Now I have no evidence and until tomorrow."

She leaned forward to look at me. "I've been wondering how far can I trust you."

"Not so far. But I'm not a blackmailer. I'm not a mindreader, either, and it's sort of hard to play tennis with the invisible man."

"The invisible man has nothing to do with this. I called him when Una didn't come home. Just before I came to your office."

"All right," I said. "You're the one that wants to find Una. You'll get around to telling me. In the meantime, who else did you call?"

"Hilda Karp, Una's best friend—her *only* female friend."

"Where can I get hold of her?"

"She married Gray Karp, the agent. They live in Beverly Hills."

Their house, set high on a plateau of rolling lawn, was huge and fashionably grotesque: Spanish Mission with a dash of Paranoia. The room where I waited for Mrs. Karp was as big as a small barn and full of blue furniture. The bar had a brass rail.

Hilda Karp was a Dresden blonde with an athletic body and brains. By appearing in it, she made the room seem more real. "Mr. Archer, I believe?" She had my card in her hand, the one with "Private Investigator" on it.

"Una Sand disappeared yesterday. Her mother said you were her best friend."

"Millicent—Mrs. Dreen—called me early this morning. But, as I said then, I haven't seen Una for several days."

"Why would she go away?"

Hilda Karp sat down on the arm of a chair, and looked thoughtful. "I can't understand why her mother should be worried. She can take care of herself, and she's gone away before. I don't know why this time. I know her well enough to know that she's unpredictable."

"Why did she go away before?"

"Why do girls leave home, Mr. Archer?"

"She picked a queer time to leave home. Her husband's coming home tomorrow."

"That's right, she told me he sent her a cable from Pearl. He's a nice boy."

"Did Una think so?"

She looked at me frigidly as only a pale blonde can look, and said nothing.

"Look," I said. "I'm trying to do a job for Mrs. Dreen. My job is laying skeletons to rest, not teaching them the choreography of the *Danse Macabre*."

"Nicely put," she said. "Actually there's no skeleton. Una has played around, in a perfectly casual way I mean, with two or three men in the last year."

"Simultaneously, or one at a time?"

"One at a time. She's monandrous to that extent. The latest is Terry Neville."

"I thought he was married."

"In an interlocutory way only. For God's sake don't bring my name into it. My husband's in business in this town."

"He seems to be prosperous," I said, looking more at her than at the house. "Thank you very much, Mrs. Karp. Your name will never pass my lips."

"Hideous, isn't it? The name, I mean. But I couldn't help falling in love with the guy. I hope you find her. Jack will be terribly disappointed if you don't."

I had begun to turn towards the door, but turned back. "It couldn't be anything like this, could it? She heard he was coming home, she felt unworthy of him, unable to face him, so she decided to lam out?"

"Millicent said she didn't leave a letter. Women don't go in for all such drama and pathos without leaving a letter. Or at least a marked copy of Tolstoi's *Resurrection*."

"I'll take your word for it." Her blue eyes were very bright in the great dim room. "How about this? She didn't like Jack at all. She went away for the sole purpose of letting him know that. A little sadism, maybe?"

"But she did like Jack. It's just that he was away for over a year. Whenever the subject came up in a mixed gathering, she always insisted that he was a wonderful lover."

"Like that, eh? Did Mrs. Dreen say you were Una's best friend?"

Her eyes were brighter and her thin, pretty mouth twisted in amusement. "Certainly. You should have heard her talk about me."

"Maybe I will. Thanks. Good-bye."

A telephone call to a screen writer I knew, the suit for which I had paid a hundred and fifty dollars of separation money in a moment of euphoria, and a false air of assurance got me past the studio guards and as far as the door of Terry Neville's dressing room. He had a bungalow to himself, which meant that he was as important as the publicity claimed. I didn't know what I was going to say to him, but I knocked on the door and, when someone said, "Who is it?" showed him.

Only the blind had not seen Terry Neville. He was over six feet, colorful, shapely, and fragrant like a distant garden of flowers. For a minute he went on reading and smoking in his brocaded armchair, carefully refraining from raising his eyes to look at me. He even turned a page of his book.

"Who are you?" he said finally. "I don't know you."

"Una Sand—"

"I don't know her, either." Grammatical solecisms had been weeded out of his speech, but nothing had been put in their place. His voice was impersonal and lifeless.

"Millicent Dreen's daughter," I said, humoring him. "Una Rossiter."

"Naturally I know Millicent Dreen. But you haven't said anything. Good day."

"Una disappeared yesterday. I thought you might be willing to help me find out why."

"You still haven't said anything." He got up and took a step towards me, very tall and wide. "What I said was *good day.*"

But not tall and wide enough. I've always had an idea, probably incorrect, that I could handle any man who wears a scarlet silk bathrobe. He saw that idea on my face and changed his tune: "If you don't get out of here, my man, I'll call a guard."

"In the meantime I'd straighten out that marcel of yours. I might even be able to make a little trouble for you." I said that on the assumption that any man with his face and sexual opportunities would be on the brink of trouble most of the time.

It worked. "What do you mean by saying that?" he said. A sudden pallor made his carefully plucked black eyebrows stand out starkly. "You could get into a very great deal of hot water by standing there talking like that."

"What happened to Una?"

"I don't know. Get out of here."

"You're a liar."

Like one of the clean-cut young men in one of his own movies, he threw a punch at me. I let it go over my shoulder and while he was off balance placed the heel of my hand against his very flat solar plexus and pushed him down into his chair. Then I shut the door and walked fast to the front gate. I'd just as soon have gone on playing tennis with the invisible man.

"No luck, I take it?" Mrs. Dreen said when she opened the door of her apartment to me.

"I've got nothing to go on. If you really want to find your daughter you'd better go to Missing Persons. They've got the organization and the connections."

"I suppose Jack will be going to them. He's home already."

"I thought he was coming tomorrow."

"That telegram was sent yesterday. It was delayed somehow. His ship got in yesterday afternoon."

"Where is he now?"

"At the beach house by now, I guess. He flew down from Alameda in a Navy plane and called me from Santa Barbara."

"What did you tell him?"

"What could I tell him? That Una was gone. He's frantic. He thinks she may have drowned." It was late afternoon, and in spite of the whiskey which she was absorbing steadily, like an alcohol lamp, Mrs. Dreen's fires were burning low. Her hands and eyes were limp, and her voice was weary.

"Well," I said, "I might as well go back to Santa Barbara. I talked to Hilda Karp but she couldn't help me. Are you coming along?"

"Not again. I have to go to the studio tomorrow. Anyway, I don't want to see Jack just now. I'll stay here."

The sun was low over the sea, gold-leafing the water and bloodying the sky, when I got through Santa Barbara and back onto the coast highway. Not thinking it would do any good but by way of doing something or other to earn my keep, I stopped at the filling station where the road turned off to Mrs. Dreen's beach house.

"Fill her up," I said to the woman attendant. I needed gas anyway.

"I've got some friends who live around here," I said when she held out her hand for her money. "Do you know where Mrs. Dreen lives?"

She looked at me from behind disapproving spectacles. "You should know. You were down there with her today, weren't you?"

I covered my confusion by handing her a five and telling her: "Keep the change."

"No, thank you."

"Don't misunderstand me. All I want you to do is tell me who was there yesterday. You see all. Tell a little."

"Who are you?"

I showed her my card.

"Oh." Her lips moved unconsciously, computing the size of the tip. "There was a guy in a green convert, I think it was a Chrysler. He went down around noon and drove out again around four, I guess it was, like a bat out of hell."

"That's what I wanted to hear. You're wonderful. What did he look like?"

"Sort of dark and pretty good-looking. It's kind of hard to describe. Like the guy that took the part of the pilot in that picture last week—*you* know—only not so good-looking."

"Terry Neville."

"That's right, only not so good-looking. I've seen him go down there plenty of times."

"I don't know who that would be," I said, "but thanks anyway. There wasn't anybody with him, was there?"

"Not that I could see."

I went down the road to the beach house like a bat into hell. The sun, huge and angry red, was horizontal now, half-eclipsed by the sea and almost perceptibly sinking. It spread a red glow over the shore like a soft and creeping fire. After a long time, I thought, the cliffs would crumble, the sea would dry up, the whole earth would burn out. There'd be nothing left but bone-white cratered ashes like the moon.

When I rounded the bluff and came within sight of the beach I saw a man coming out of the sea. In the creeping fire which the sun shed he, too, seemed to be burning. The diving mask over his face made him look strange and inhuman. He walked out of the water as if he had never set foot on land before.

I walked towards him. "Mr. Rossiter?"

"Yes." He raised the glass mask from his face and with it the illusion of strangeness lifted. He was just a handsome young man, well-set-up, tanned, and worried-looking.

"My name is Archer."

He held out his hand, which was wet, after wiping it on his bathing trunks, which were also wet. "Oh, yes, Mr. Archer. My mother-in-law mentioned you over the phone."

"Are you enjoying your swim?"

"I am looking for the body of my wife." It sounded as if he meant it. I looked at him more closely. He was big and husky, but he was just a kid, twenty-two or -three at most. Out of school into the air, I thought. Probably met Una Sand at a party, fell hard for all that glamour, married her the week before he shipped out, and had dreamed bright dreams ever since. I remembered the brash telegram he had sent, as if life was like the people in slick magazine advertisements.

"What makes you think she drowned?"

"She wouldn't go away like this. She knew I was coming home this week. I cabled her from Pearl."

"Maybe she never got the cable."

After a pause he said: "Excuse me." He turned towards the waves which were breaking almost at his feet. The sun had disappeared, and the sea was turning gray and cold-looking, an antihuman element.

"Wait a minute. If she's in there, which I doubt, you should call the police. This is no way to look for her."

"If I don't find her before dark, I'll call them then," he said. "But if she's here, I want to find her myself." I could never have guessed his reason for that, but when I found it out it made sense. So far as anything in the situation made sense.

He walked a few steps into the surf, which was heavier now that the tide was coming in, plunged forward, and swam slowly towards the raft with his masked face under the water. His arms and legs beat the rhythm of the crawl as if his muscles took pleasure in it, but his face was downcast, searching the darkening sea floor. He swam in widening circles about the raft, raising his head about twice a minute for air.

He had completed several circles and I was beginning to feel that he wasn't really looking for anything, but expressing his sorrow, dancing a futile ritualistic water dance, when suddenly he took air and dived. For what seemed a long time but was probably about twenty seconds, the surface of the sea was empty except for the white raft. Then the masked head broke water, and Rossiter began to swim towards shore. He swam a laborious side stroke, with both arms submerged. It was twilight now, and I couldn't see him very well, but I could see that he was swimming very slowly. When he came nearer I saw a swirl of yellow hair.

He stood up, tore off his mask, and threw it away into the sea. He looked at me angrily, one arm holding the body of his wife against him. The white body half-floating in the shifting water was nude, a strange bright glistening catch from the sea floor.

"Go away," he said in a choked voice.

I went to get a blanket out of the car, and brought it to him where he laid her out on the beach. He huddled over her as if to protect her body from my gaze. He covered her and stroked her wet hair back from her face. Her face was not pretty. He covered that, too.

I said: "You'll have to call the police now."

After a time he answered: "I guess you're right. Will you help me carry her into the house?"

I helped him. Then I called the police in Santa Barbara, and told them that a woman had been drowned and where to find her. I left Jack Rossiter shivering in his wet trunks beside her blanketed body, and drove back to Hollywood for the second time.

Millicent Dreen was in her apartment in the Park-Wilshire. In the afternoon there had been a nearly full decanter of Scotch on her buffet. At ten o'clock it was on the coffee table beside her chair, and nearly empty. Her face and body had sagged. I wondered if every day she aged so many years, and every morning recreated herself through the power of her will.

She said: "I thought you were going back to Santa Barbara. I was just going to go to bed."

"I did go. Didn't Jack phone you?"

"No." She looked at me, and her green eyes were suddenly very much alive, almost fluorescent. "You found her," she said.

"Jack found her in the sea. She was drowned."

"I was afraid of that." But there was something like relief in her voice. As if worse things might have happened. As if at least she had lost no weapons and gained no foes in the daily battle to hold her position in the world's most competitive city.

"You hired me to find her," I said. "She's found, though I had nothing to do with finding her—and that's that. Unless you want me to find out who drowned her."

"What do you mean?"

"What I said. Perhaps it wasn't an accident. Or perhaps somebody stood by and watched her drown."

I had given her plenty of reason to be angry with me before, but for the first time that day she was angry. "I gave you a hundred dollars for doing nothing. Isn't that enough for you? Are you trying to drum up extra business?"

"I did one thing. I found out that Una wasn't by herself yesterday."

"Who was with her?" She stood up and walked quickly back and forth across the rug. As she walked her body was remolding itself into the forms of youth and vigor. She recreated herself before my eyes.

"The invisible man," I said. "My tennis partner."

Still she wouldn't speak the name. She was like the priestess of a cult whose tongue was forbidden to pronounce a secret word. But she said quickly and harshly: "If my daughter was killed I want to know who did it. I don't care who it was. But if you're giving me a line and if you make trouble for me and nothing comes of it, I'll have you kicked out of Southern California. I could do that."

Her eyes flashed, her breath came fast, and her sharp breast rose and fell with many of the appearances of genuine feeling. I liked her very much at that moment. So I went away, and instead of making trouble for her I made trouble for myself.

I found a booth in a drugstore on Wilshire and confirmed what I knew, that Terry Neville would have an unlisted number. I called a girl I knew who fed gossip to a movie columnist, and found out that Neville lived in Beverly Hills but spent most of his evenings around town. At this time of night he was usually at Ronald's or Chasen's, a little later at Ciro's. I went to Ronald's because it was nearer, and Terry Neville was there.

He was sitting in a booth for two in the long, low, smoke-filled room, eating smoked salmon and drinking stout. Across from him there was a sharp-faced terrier-like man who looked like his business manager and was drinking milk. Some Hollywood actors spend a lot of time with their managers, because they have a common interest.

I avoided the headwaiter and stepped up to Neville's table. He saw me and stood up, saying: "I warned you this afternoon. If you don't get out of here I'll call the police."

I said quietly: "I sort of am the police. Una is dead." He didn't answer and I went on: "This isn't a good place to talk. If you'll step outside for a minute I'd like to mention a couple of facts to you."

"You say you're a policeman," the sharp-faced man snapped, but quietly. "Where's your identification? Don't pay any attention to him, Terry."

Terry didn't say anything. I said: "I'm a private detective. I'm investigating the death of Una Rossiter. Shall we step outside, gentlemen?"

"We'll go out to the car," Terry Neville said tonelessly. "Come on, Ed," he added to the terrier-like man.

The car was not a green Chrysler convertible, but a black Packard limousine equipped with a uniformed chauffeur. When we entered the parking lot he got out of the car and opened the door. He was big and battered-looking.

I said: "I don't think I'll get in. I listen better standing up. I always stand up at concerts and confessions.

"You're not going to listen to anything," Ed said.

The parking lot was deserted and far back from the street, and I forgot to keep my eye on the chauffeur. He rabbit-punched me and a gush of pain surged into my head. He rabbit-punched me again and my eyes rattled in their sockets and my body became invertebrate. Two men moving in a maze of lights took hold of my upper arms and lifted me into the car. Unconsciousness was a big black limousine with a swiftly purring motor and the blinds down.

Though it leaves the neck sore for days, the effect of a rabbit punch on the centers of consciousness is sudden and brief. In two or three minutes I came out of it, to the sound of Ed's voice saying:

"We don't like hurting people and we aren't going to hurt you. But you've got to learn to understand, whatever your name is—"

"Sacher-Masoch," I said.

"A bright boy," said Ed. "But a bright boy can be too bright for his own good. You've got to learn to understand that you can't go around annoying people, especially very important people like Mr. Neville here."

Terry Neville was sitting in the far corner of the back seat, looking worried. Ed was between us. The car was in motion, and I could see lights moving beyond the chauffeur's shoulders hunched over the wheel. The blinds were down over the back windows.

"Mr. Neville should keep out of my cases," I said. "At the moment you'd better let me out of this car or I'll have you arrested for kidnapping."

Ed laughed, but not cheerfully. "You don't seem to realize what's happening to you. You're on your way to the police station, where Mr. Neville and I are going to charge you with attempted blackmail."

"Mr. Neville is a very brave little man," I said. "Inasmuch as he was seen leaving Una Sand's house shortly after she was killed. He was seen leaving in a great hurry and a green convertible."

"My God, Ed," Terry Neville said, "you're getting me in a frightful mess. You don't know what a frightful mess you're getting me in." His voice was high, with a ragged edge of hysteria.

"For God's sake, you're not afraid of this bum, are you?" Ed said in a terrier yap.

"You get out of here, Ed. This is a terrible thing, and you don't know how to handle it. I've got to talk to this man. Get out of this car."

He leaned forward to take the speaking tube, but Ed put a hand on his shoulder. "Play it your way, then, Terry. I still think I had the right play, but you spoiled it."

"Where are we going?" I said. I suspected that we were headed for Beverly Hills, where the police know who pays them their wages.

Neville said into the speaking tube: "Turn down a side street and park. Then take a walk around the block."

"That's better," I said when we had parked. Terry Neville looked frightened. Ed looked sulky and worried. For no good reason, I felt complacent.

"Spill it," I said to Terry Neville. "Did you kill the girl? Or did she accidentally drown—and you ran away so you wouldn't get mixed up in it? Or have you thought of a better one than that?"

"I'll tell you the truth," he said. "I didn't kill her. I didn't even know she was dead. But I was there yesterday afternoon. We were sunning ourselves on the raft, when a plane came over flying very low. I went away, because I didn't want to be seen there with her—"

"You mean you weren't exactly sunning yourselves?"

"Yes. That's right. This plane came over high at first, then he circled back and came down very low. I thought maybe he recognized me, and might be trying to take pictures or something."

"What kind of a plane was it?"

"I don't know. A military plane, I guess. A fighter plane. It was a single-seater painted blue. I don't know military planes."

"What did Una Sand do when you went away?"

"I don't know. I swam to shore, put on some clothes, and drove away. She stayed on the raft, I guess. But she was certainly all right when I left her. It would be a terrible thing for me if I was dragged into this thing, Mr.—"

"Archer."

"Mr. Archer. I'm terribly sorry if we hurt you. If I could make it right with you—" He pulled out a wallet.

His steady pallid whine bored me. Even his sheaf of bills bored me. The situation bored me.

I said: "I have no interest in messing up your brilliant career, Mr. Neville. I'd like to mess up your brilliant pan sometime, but that can wait. Until I have some reason to believe that you haven't told me the truth, I'll keep what you said under my hat. In the meantime, I want to hear what the coroner has to say."

They took me back to Ronald's, where my car was, and left me with many protestations of good fellowship. I said good night to them, rubbing the back of my neck with an exaggerated gesture. Certain other gestures occurred to me.

When I got back to Santa Barbara the coroner was working over Una. He said that there were no marks of violence on her body, and very little water in her lungs and stomach, but this condition was characteristic of about one drowning in ten.

I hadn't known that before, so I asked him to put it into sixty-four-dollar words. He was glad to.

"Sudden inhalation of water may result in a severe reflex spasm of the larynx, followed swiftly by asphyxia. Such a laryngeal spasm is more likely to occur if the victim's face is upward, allowing water to rush into the nostrils, and would be likely to be facilitated by emotional or nervous shock. It may have happened like that or it may not."

"Hell," I said, "she may not even be dead."

He gave me a sour look. "Thirty-six hours ago she wasn't."

I figured it out as I got in my car. Una couldn't have drowned much later than four o'clock in the afternoon on September the seventh.

It was three in the morning when I checked in at the Barbara Hotel. I got up at seven, had breakfast in a restaurant, and went to the beach house to talk to Jack Rossiter. It was only about eight o'clock when I got there, but Rossiter was sitting on the beach in a canvas chair watching the sea.

"You again?" he said when he saw me.

"I'd think you'd have had enough of the sea for a while. How long were you out?"

"A year." He seemed unwilling to talk.

"I hate bothering people," I said, "but my business is always making a nuisance out of me."

"Evidently. What exactly is your business?"

"I'm currently working for your mother-in-law. I'm still trying to find out what happened to her daughter."

"Are you trying to needle me?" He put his hands on the arms of the chair as if to get up. For a moment his knuckles were white. Then he relaxed. "You saw what happened, didn't you?"

"Yes. But do you mind my asking what time your ship got into San Francisco on September the seventh?"

"No. Four o'clock. Four o'clock in the afternoon."

"I suppose that could be checked?"

He didn't answer. There was a newspaper on the sand beside his chair and he leaned over and handed it to me. It was the Late Night Final of a San Francisco newspaper for the seventh.

"Turn to page four," he said.

I turned to page four and found an article describing the arrival of the

USS *Guam* at the Golden Gate, at four o'clock in the afternoon. A contingent of Waves had greeted the returning heroes, and a band had played "California, Here I Come."

"If you want to see Mrs. Dreen, she's in the house," Jack Rossiter said. "But it looks to me as if your job is finished."

"Thanks," I said.

"And if I don't see you again, good-bye."

"Are you leaving?"

"A friend is coming out from Santa Barbara to pick me up in a few minutes. I'm flying up to Alameda with him to see about getting leave. I just had a forty-eight, and I've got to be here for the inquest tomorrow. And the funeral." His voice was hard. His whole personality had hardened overnight. The evening before his nature had been wide open. Now it was closed and invulnerable.

"Good-bye," I said, and plodded through the soft sand to the house. On the way I thought of something, and walked faster.

When I knocked, Mrs. Dreen came to the door holding a cup of coffee, not very steadily. She was wearing a heavy wool dressing robe with a silk rope around the waist, and a silk cap on her head. Her eyes were bleary.

"Hello," she said. "I came back last night after all. I couldn't work today anyway. And I didn't think Jack should be by himself."

"He seems to be doing all right."

"I'm glad you think so. Will you come in?"

I stepped inside. "You said last night that you wanted to know who killed Una no matter who it was."

"Well?"

"Does that still go?"

"Yes. Why? Did you find out something?"

"Not exactly. I thought of something, that's all."

"The coroner believes it was an accident. I talked to him on the phone this morning." She sipped her black coffee. Her hand vibrated steadily, like a leaf in the wind.

"He may be right," I said. "He may be wrong."

There was the sound of a car outside, and I moved to the window and looked out. A station wagon stopped on the beach, and a Navy officer got out and walked towards Jack Rossiter. Rossiter got up and they shook hands.

"Will you call Jack, Mrs. Dreen, and tell him to come into the house for a minute?"

"If you wish." She went to the door and called him.

Rossiter came to the door and said a little impatiently: "What is it?"

"Come in," I said. "And tell me what time you left the ship the day before yesterday."

"Let's see. We got in at four—"

"No, you didn't. The ship did, but not you. Am I right?"

"I don't know what you mean."

"You know what I mean. It's so simple that it couldn't fool anybody for a minute, not if he knew anything about carriers. You flew your plane off the ship a couple of hours before she got into port. My guess is that you gave that telegram to a buddy to send for you before you left the ship. You flew down here, caught your wife being made love to by another man, landed on the beach—and drowned her."

"You're insane!" After a moment he said less violently: "I admit I flew off the ship. You could easily find that out anyway. I flew around for a couple of hours, getting in some flying time—"

"Where did you fly?"

"Along the coast. I don't get down this far. I landed at Alameda at five-thirty, and I can prove it."

"Who's your friend?" I pointed through the open door to the other officer, who was standing on the beach looking out to sea.

"Lieutenant Harris. I'm going to fly up to Alameda with him. I warn you, don't make any ridiculous accusations in his presence, or you'll suffer for it."

"I want to ask him a question," I said. "What sort of plane were you flying?"

"FM-3."

I went out of the house and down the slope to Lieutenant Harris. He turned towards me and I saw the wings on his blouse.

"Good morning, Lieutenant," I said. "You've done a good deal of flying, I suppose?"

"Thirty-two months. Why?"

"I want to settle a bet. Could a plane land on this beach and take off again?"

"I think maybe a Piper Cub could. I'd try it anyway. Does that settle the bet?"

"It was a fighter I had in mind. An FM-3."

"Not an FM-3," he said. "Not possibly. It might just conceivably be able to land but it'd never get off again. Not enough room, and very poor surface. Ask Jack, he'll tell you the same."

I went back to the house and said to Jack: "I was wrong. I'm sorry. As you said, I guess I'm all washed up with this case."

"Good-bye, Millicent," Jack said, and kissed her cheek. "If I'm not back tonight I'll be back first thing in the morning. Keep a stiff upper lip."

"You do, too, Jack."

He went away without looking at me again. So the case was ending as it had begun, with me and Mrs. Dreen alone in a room wondering what had happened to her daughter.

"You shouldn't have said what you did to him," she said. "He's had enough to bear."

My mind was working very fast. I wondered whether it was producing anything. "I suppose Lieutenant Harris knows what he's talking about. He says a fighter couldn't land and take off from this beach. There's no other place around here he could have landed without being seen. So he didn't land."

"But I still don't believe that he wasn't here. No young husband flying along the coast within range of the house where his wife was—well, he'd fly low and dip his wings to her, wouldn't he? Terry Neville saw the plane come down."

"Terry Neville?"

"I talked to him last night. He was with Una before she died. The two of them were out on the raft together when Jack's plane came down. Jack saw them, and saw what they were doing. They saw him. Terry Neville went away. Then what?"

"You're making this up," Mrs. Dreen said, but her green eyes were intent on my face.

"I'm making it up, of course. I wasn't here. After Terry Neville ran away, there was no one here but Una, and Jack in a plane circling over her head. I'm trying to figure out why Una died. I *have* to make it up. But I think she died of fright. I think Jack dived at her and forced her into the water. I think he kept on diving at her until she was gone. Then he flew back to Alameda and chalked up his flying time."

"Fantasy," she said. "And very ugly. I don't believe it."

"You should. You've got that cable, haven't you?"

"I don't know what you're talking about."

"Jack sent Una a cable from Pearl, telling her what day he was arriving. Una mentioned it to Hilda Karp. Hilda Karp mentioned it to me. It's funny you didn't say anything about it."

"I didn't know about it," Millicent Dreen said. Her eyes were blank.

I went on, paying no attention to her denial: "My guess is that the cable said not only that Jack's ship was coming in on the seventh, but that he'd fly over the beach house that afternoon. Fortunately, I don't have to depend on guesswork. The cable will be on file at Western Union, and the police will be able to look at it. I'm going into town now."

"Wait," she said. "Don't go to the police about it. You'll only get Jack in trouble. I destroyed the cable to protect him, but I'll tell you what was in it. Your guess was right. He said he'd fly over on the seventh."

"When did you destroy it?"

"Yesterday, before I came to you. I was afraid it would implicate Jack."

"Why did you come to me at all, if you wanted to protect Jack? It seems that you knew what happened."

"I wasn't sure. I didn't know what had happened to her, and until I found out I didn't know what to do."

"You're still not sure," I said. "But I'm beginning to be. For one thing, it's certain that Una never got her cable, at least not as it was sent. Otherwise she wouldn't have been doing what she was doing on the afternoon that her husband was going to fly over and say hello. You changed the date on it, perhaps? So that Una expected Jack a day later? Then you arranged to be in Hollywood on the seventh, so that Una could spend a final afternoon with Terry Neville."

"Perhaps." Her face was completely alive, controlled but full of dangerous energy, like a cobra listening to music.

"Perhaps you wanted Jack for yourself," I said. "Perhaps you had another reason, I don't know. I think even a psychoanalyst would have a hard time working through your motivations, Mrs. Dreen, and I'm not one. All I know is that you precipitated a murder. Your plan worked even better than you expected."

"It was accidental death," she said hoarsely. "If you go to the police you'll only make a fool of yourself, and cause trouble for Jack."

"You care about Jack, don't you?"

"Why shouldn't I?" she said. "He was mine before he ever saw Una. She took him away from me."

"And now you think you've got him back." I got up to go. "I hope for your sake he doesn't figure out for himself what I've just figured out."

"Do you think he will?" Sudden terror had jerked her face apart.

I didn't answer her.

QUESTIONS

1. Note the use of simile and metaphor throughout this story. How effective do you think it is?

2. What do you think of Macdonald's style, especially the repetition of phrases such as "I learned about it only by the marks it left. It left marks." Compare Macdonald's style to that of the other "hard-boiled" writers, Hammett and Chandler.

3. More often than not, the hard-boiled detective is employed by the wealthy. Discuss the detective's attitude toward wealth and wealthy people revealed in this story.

4. Why are older people so often main characters in detective fiction? Compare the general in "The Curtain."

5. The method of murder used in this story is one among many examples of the grotesque. Why do you think so many famous crime and detective stories feature macabre rather than "usual" murders?

6. In many detective stories, members of the same family plot against each other, their actions revealing disturbed minds. Why do you think authors are so often drawn toward writing about situations of this sort?

7. Compare the descriptions of the sea with the various descriptions of Millicent Dreen. Does the same "current" drive each? What is Macdonald trying to suggest? You might also note the scene where Jack Rossiter emerges from the sea.

Inspector Maigret Pursues

Georges Simenon

The four men were packed in the taxi. It was freezing all over Paris. At half-past seven in the morning the city looked wan; the wind was whipping the powdery frost along the ground. The thinnest of the four men, on one of the flap seats, had a cigaret stuck to his lower lip and handcuffs on his wrists. The most important one, clothed in a thick overcoat, heavy-jawed, a bowler hat on his head, was smoking his pipe and watching the railings of the Bois de Boulogne file past.

"You want me to put on a big dramatic scene?" the handcuffed man suggested politely. "With struggling, frothing at the mouth, insults, and all?"

Taking the cigaret from between the man's lips and opening the door, for they had arrived at the Porte de Bagatelle, Inspector Maigret growled, "Don't overdo it."

The pathways in the Bois were deserted, white as limestone, and as hard. A dozen or so people were standing around at the corner of a bridle path, and a photographer prepared to go into action on the group as it approached.

But, as instructed, P'tit Louis raised his arms in front of his face.

Maigret, looking surly, swung his head from side to side like a bear, taking everything in—the new blocks of flats on the Boulevard Richard-Wallace, their shutters still closed, a few workmen on bikes coming from Puteaux, a lighted tram, two concierges approaching, their hands blue with cold.

"Is this it?" he asked.

The day before he had arranged for the following information to appear in the newspapers:

BAGATELLE MURDER

This time the police will not have been long in clearing up an affair that looked as if it presented insurmountable difficulties. It will be remembered that on Monday morning a park-keeper in the Bois de Boulogne discovered along one of the pathways a hundred yards or so from the Porte de Bagatelle a corpse it was possible to identify on the spot.

It was Ernest Borms, a well-known Viennese doctor who had been in practice in Neuilly for several years. Borms was wearing evening clothes. He must have been attacked during the night of Sunday/Monday, while returning to his flat on the Boulevard Richard-Wallace.

A bullet fired at point-blank range from a small-caliber revolver struck him full in the heart.

Borms, still young and handsome and well turned-out, led a fairly social life.

Scarcely forty-eight hours after the murder Police Headquarters have just made an arrest. Tomorrow morning, between seven and eight o'clock, the man concerned will be conducted to the scene for the purpose of a reconstruction of the crime.

As things turned out, this case was to be referred to at Headquarters as the one perhaps most characteristically Maigret; but when they spoke of it in his hearing, he had a curious way of turning his head away with a groan.

To proceed, everything was ready. Hardly any gaping onlookers, as planned. It was not for nothing that Maigret had chosen this early hour of the morning. Moreover, among the ten or twelve people who were hanging about, could be spotted some plainclothesmen wearing their most innocent air. One of them, Torrence, who loved disguises, was dressed as a milkman. At the sight of him his chief shrugged eloquently. If only P'tit Louis didn't overact. An old customer of theirs who had been picked up the day before for picking pockets in the Métro. . . .

"You give us a hand tomorrow morning and we'll see that we aren't too hard on you this time. . . ." They had fetched him up from the cells.

"Now, then," growled Maigret, "when you heard the footsteps you were hiding in this corner here, weren't you?"

"As you say, Chief Inspector. I was famished. Stony broke. . . . I said to myself, a gent on his way home all dressed up like that must be carrying a walletful. 'Your money or your life!' was what I whispered right into his ear. And I swear it wasn't my fault that the thing went off. I'm quite sure it was the cold made me squeeze the trigger."

11:00 A.M. Maigret was pacing round his office at Headquarters, smoking solidly and constantly fiddling with the phone.

"Is that you, Chief? Lucas here. I followed the old man who seemed so interested in the reconstruction. Nothing doing there—he's just a lunatic who takes a stroll every morning in the Bois."

"All right, you can come back."

11:15 A.M. "Hullo, is that you, Chief? Torrence. I shadowed the young man you tipped me the wink on. He always hangs round when the plainclothes boys are called in. He's an assistant in a shop on the Champs Elysées. Shall I come back?"

From Janvier no call till 11:55.

"I've got to be quick, Chief. I'm afraid he'll give me the slip. I'm keeping an eye on him in the mirror of the booth. I'm at the Yellow Dwarf Bar, Boulevard Rochechouart. . . . Yes, he spotted me. He's got something on his mind. Crossing the Seine, he threw something in the river. He's tried over and over to shake me off. Will you be coming?"

So began a chase that was to last five days and nights. Among the hurrying crowds, across an unsuspecting Paris, from bar to bar, bistro to bistro, a lone man on the one hand, and on the other Maigret and his detectives, taking it in turn and, in the long run, just as harassed as the man they were following.

Maigret got out of his taxi opposite the Yellow Dwarf at the busy time just before lunch, and found Janvier leaning on the bar. He wasn't troubling to put on any façade of innocence. Quite the opposite.

"Which one is it?"

The detective motioned with his jaw toward a man sitting in the corner at a small table. The man was watching them; his eyes, which were a light blue-gray, gave a foreign cast to his face. Nordic? Slav? More likely a Slav. He was wearing a gray overcoat, a well-cut suit, a soft felt hat. About thirty-five years old, so far as one could judge. He was pale, close-shaven.

"What're you having, Chief? A hot toddy?"

"Toddy let it be. What's *he* drinking?"

"Brandy. It's his fifth this morning. You mustn't mind if I sound slurred, but I've had to follow him round all the bistros. He's tough, you know. Look at him—it's been like that all morning. He wouldn't lower his eyes for all the kingdoms of the earth."

It was true. And it was strange. You couldn't call it arrogance or defiance. The man was just looking at them. If he felt any anxiety, it was concealed. It was sadness rather that his face expressed, but a calm, reflective sadness.

"At Bagatelle, when he noticed you were watching him, he went off straight away and I fell into step behind him. He hadn't gone a hundred yards before he turned round. Then instead of leaving the Bois, as he apparently meant to do, he strode off down the first path he came to. He turned round again. He recognized me. He sat down on a bench, despite the cold, and I stopped. More than once I had the impression he wanted to speak to me, but in the end he only shrugged and set off again.

"At the Porte Dauphine I almost lost him. He jumped into a taxi and it was just luck that I found one almost immediately. He got out at the Place de l'Opéra, and rushed into the Métro. One behind the other, we changed trains five times before he began to realize he wouldn't shake me off that way. . . .

"We went up again into the street. We were at Place Clichy. Since then we have been going from bar to bar. I was waiting for one with a telephone booth where I could keep him in sight. When he saw me phoning, he gave a bitter little laugh. Honestly, you'd have sworn after that he was waiting for you."

"Ring up H.Q. Lucas and Torrence are to hold themselves ready to join me as soon as they're called. And a photographer, too, from the technical branch, with a miniature camera."

"Waiter!" the man called out. "What do I owe you?"

"Three-fifty."

"I bet he's a Pole," Maigret breathed to Janvier. "On our way. . . ."

They didn't get far. At Place Blanche they followed the man into a restaurant, sat down at the next table. It was an Italian place, and they ate pasta.

At three, Lucas came to take over from Janvier, who was with Maigret at a *brasserie* opposite the Gare du Nord.

"The photographer?" Maigret asked.

"He's waiting outside to get him as he leaves."

And sure enough, when the Pole left the place, having finished reading the papers, a detective hurried up. At less than three feet he took a shot of him. The man raised his hand quickly to his face, but it was already too late. Then, proving that he knew what was going on, he cast a reproachful look at Maigret.

Aha, my little man, Maigret said to himself, you have some good reason for not revealing where you live. Well, you may be patient, but so am I.

By evening a few snowflakes were fluttering down in the street, the stranger walked on, hands in pocket, waiting for bedtime.

"I'll take over for the night, Chief?" Lucas suggested.

"No. I'd rather you coped with the photograph. Look at the hotel registrations first. Then see what you can find out in the foreign quarters. That fellow knows his Paris. He didn't arrive yesterday. There must be people who know him."

"How about putting his picture in the papers?"

Maigret eyed his subordinate with scorn. How could Lucas, who had been working for him for so many years, fail to understand? Had the police one single clue? Nothing. Not one piece of evidence. A man killed during the night in the Bois de Boulogne. No weapon is found. No prints. Dr. Borms lives alone, and his only servant doesn't know where he spent the previous evening. "Do as I say. Get going. . . ."

Finally at midnight the man decides to go into a hotel. Maigret follows him in. It is a second- or even third-class hotel.

"I want a room."

"Will you register here, please?"

He registers hesitantly, his fingers stiff with cold. He looks Maigret up and down as if to say, "If you think that's any problem—I can write any name that comes."

And, in fact, he has done so. Nicolas Slaatkovitch, resident of Cracow, arrived the day before in Paris. It is all false, obviously.

Maigret telephones to Headquarters. They hunt through the files of furnished lodgings, the registers of foreigners, they get in touch with the frontier posts. No Nicolas Slaatkovitch.

"And a room for you?" the proprietor asks with distaste, for he senses the presence of a policeman.

"No, thank you. I'll spend the night on the stairs."

It's safer that way. He sits down on a step in front of the door of Room 7. Twice the door opens. The man peers through the gloom, makes out Maigret's silhouette, and ends up by going to bed. In the morning his face is rough with stubble. He hasn't been able to change his shirt. He hasn't even got a comb, and his hair is rumpled.

Lucas has just arrived. "I'll do the next shift, Chief?"

Maigret refuses to leave his stranger. He has watched him pay the bill. He has seen him grow pale. He guesses his thoughts. . . .

And a little later, in a bar where, almost side by side, they are breakfasting on white coffee and croissants, the man openly counts up his fortune. One hundred-franc note, two twenty-franc pieces, one of ten, and some small change. He makes a bitter grimace.

Well, he won't get far on that. When he arrived at the Bois de Boulogne, he had come straight from home, for he was freshly shaved, not a speck of dust, not a crease in his clothes. He hadn't even looked to see how much money he had on him.

What he threw in the Seine, Maigret guesses, were his identification papers, perhaps visiting cards. At all costs he wants to prevent their finding out his address.

And so the round of the homeless begins again: the loitering in front of shops or round street traders, the bars one has to go into from time to time, even if it's only to sit down, especially when it's cold outside, the papers one reads in the *brasseries*. . . .

One hundred and fifty francs. No more lunchtime restaurant. The man makes do with hard-boiled eggs, which he eats, along with his pint, standing up at the bar counter, while Maigret gulps down sandwiches.

For a long time the man has been thinking about going into a movie, his hand fingering the small change in his pocket. Better to stick it out. He walks . . . and walks. . . .

There is, incidentally, one detail that strikes Maigret. It is always in the same districts that this exhausting stroll takes place: from the Trinité to Place Clichy, from Place Clichy to Barbès, by way of Rue Caulaincourt . . . from Barbès to the Gare du Nord and Rue Lafayette. Besides, the man's afraid of being recognized, isn't he? Of course he's chosen the districts farthest from his home or hotel, those he didn't usually frequent. . . .

Does he, like many foreigners, haunt Montparnasse? The parts around the Panthéon?

His clothes indicate he is reasonably well off. They are comfortable, sober, and well cut. A professional man, no doubt. What's more, he wears a ring, so he's married.

Maigret has had to agree to hand over to Torrence, and has dashed home. Madame Maigret is displeased: her sister has come up from Orléans, she has taken a lot of trouble over the dinner, and her husband, after a shave and a change of clothes, is already off again, and doesn't know when he'll be back.

He drives off to the Quai des Orfèvres. "Lucas hasn't left anything for me?"

Yes, he has. There's a note from the sergeant. He's been round several of the Polish and Russian quarters showing the photograph. Nobody knows the man. Nothing from the political circles, either. As a last resource he has had a large number of copies made of the photograph, and police are now going from door to door in all the districts of Paris, from concierge to concierge, showing the document to bar owners and waiters.

"Hello, is that Chief Inspector Maigret? This is one of the usherettes at the newsreel theater on the Boulevard de Strasbourg. It's a gentleman —Monsieur Torrence. He's asked me to call you to say he's here, but he didn't want to leave his place in the theater."

Not so stupid, on the stranger's part. He has worked out that it's the best heated place to pass a few hours cheaply—two francs to get in, and you can see the program several times.

A curious intimacy has sprung up between follower and followed, between the man, whose face is now dark with stubble and whose clothes are crumpled, and Maigret, who never for a moment stops trailing him. There is even one rather comic point: they've both caught colds. Their noses are red; they pull out their handkerchiefs almost in time with one another. Once, in spite of himself, the stranger had to smile as he saw Maigret going off into a series of sneezes.

After five consecutive newsreel programs, a dirty hotel on the boulevard de la Chapelle. Same name on the register. And again Maigret installs himself on the stairs. But as this is a hotel with a casual trade, he is disturbed every ten minutes by couples going up and down; they stare at him curiously, and the women don't find him a reassuring sight.

When he's at the end of his tether, or at the breaking point, will the man decide to go home? In one of the *brasseries*, where he stays long enough to take off his gray coat, Maigret without more ado seizes the garment and looks inside the collar. The coat comes from Old England, the shop on the Boulevard des Italiens. It is a ready-made coat, and the shop must have sold dozens of others like it. One clue, however: it is last year's model, so the stranger has been in Paris for a year at least. And in a year must have found somewhere to hang out. . . .

Maigret has started drinking grog to cure his cold. The other now pays out his money drop by drop. He drinks his coffee straight; he lives on croissants and hard-boiled eggs.

The news from the office is always the same: nothing to report. Nobody recognizes the photograph of the Pole. No one has heard of any missing person.

As to the dead man, nothing there, either. A good practice, he made a lot of money, wasn't interested in politics, went out a lot, and, as he dealt with nervous diseases, most of his patients were women.

There was one experiment Maigret had not yet had the chance of seeing through to the end: how long it would take for a well-bred, well-cared-for, well-dressed man to lose his outward polish.

Four days. As he now knew. To begin with, the unshavenness. The first morning the man looked like a lawyer, or doctor, or an architect, or a businessman; you could picture him leaving his cosy flat. A four-day growth transformed him to such an extent that if one had now put his picture in the papers and referred to the Bois de Boulogne affair, everyone would have said, "You can see he's a murderer."

The bitter weather and lack of sleep had reddened his eyelids, and his cheeks were feverish from his cold. His shoes, which were no longer polished, seemed to have lost their shape. His coat weighed on him, and his trousers were baggy round the knees.

Even his walk was no longer the same. He sidled along the wall, he lowered his eyes when people looked at him. Another thing: he turned his head away when he passed a restaurant where one could see people sitting down to large meals. . . .

"Your last twenty francs," Maigret worked out, "poor wretch. What now?"

Lucas, Torrence, and Janvier took over from him from time to time, but he left his post as little as possible. He would burst into the Quai des Orfèvres, would see his Chief.

"You'd be well advised to take a rest, Maigret."

It was a peevish Maigret, touchy as if he were torn between contradictory emotions. "Am I or am I not supposed to be finding the murderer?"

"Of course."

"Well then, back to my post." As if resentfully, he would sigh. "I wonder where we'll sleep tonight."

Only twenty francs left. Not even that—when he got back, Torrence said the man had eaten three hard-boiled eggs and drunk two rum coffees in a bar on the corner of the Rue Montmartre.

"Eight francs, fifty. That leaves eleven francs fifty."

Maigret admired him. Far from hiding himself, Maigret now tailed him quite openly, sometimes walking right next to him, and he had some difficulty to refrain from speaking to him. "Come now, don't you think it's time to have a proper meal? Somewhere there's a warm home where you're expected. A bed, slippers, a razor. Eh? And a good dinner."

But the man continued to prowl under the arc lamps of Les Halles, like one who no longer knows where to turn. In and out among the heaps of cabbages and carrots, stepping out of the way at the whistle of the train or when the farmers' trucks passed.

"Hasn't even the price of a hotel room."

That evening the National Meteorological Office registered a temperature of eight degrees below zero. The man treated himself to hot sausages from a stall in the streets. Now he would reek of garlic and fat the whole night through.

Once he tried to slip into a shelter and stretch out in the corner. A policeman, whom Maigret wasn't able to stop in time, moved him on. He was hobbling now. Along the quais. The Pont des Arts. As long as he didn't take it into his head to throw himself into the Seine. Maigret didn't feel he had the courage to jump in after him into the black water that was beginning to fill with drift ice.

The man was walking along the towpath level, where the tramps lay grumbling and, under the bridges, all the good places were taken.

In a small street close to the Place Maubert, through the windows of a strange bistro, old men could be seen sleeping with their heads on the tables. Twenty sous, wine included. The man stared in through the gloom. Then, with a fatalistic shrug, he pushed open the door.

Before it closed behind him. Maigret had time to be sickened by the smelly gust that struck him in the face. He preferred to stay outside. He called a policeman, posted him in his place on the pavement while he went to telephone Lucas to take over for the night.

"I've been trying to get you for the last hour, Chief. We've found him! Thanks to a concierge. The fellow's called Stefan Strevzki, an architect, thirty-four years old, born in Warsaw, been in France for three years. Works for a firm in the Faubourg Saint-Honoré. Married to a Hungarian, a magnificent creature named Dora. Living at Passy, Rue de la Pompe, in a twelve-thousand-franc flat. No political interests. The concierge has never seen the dead man. Stefan left the house earlier than usual on Monday morning. She was surprised not to see him return, but she wasn't worried, having ascertained—"

"What time is it?"

"Half-past three. I'm alone at Headquarters. I've had some beer brought up, but it's too cold."

"Listen, Lucas, you're going—yes, I know, too late for the morning ones. But the evening ones . . . understand?"

That morning the man's clothing gave off a muffled odor of poverty. His eyes were sunken. The look he cast at Maigret in the pale morning contained the deepest pathos and reproach.

Had he not been driven, little by little, but for all that at a dizzy pace, to the very lowest depths? He turned up the collar of his overcoat. He didn't leave the neighborhood, but he rushed into a bistro that had just opened and downed four quick drinks, as if to rid himself of the appalling aftertaste the night had left in his throat and chest.

So much the worse for him. From now on he no longer had anything. Nothing was left for him but to walk up and down the streets the frost was making slippery. He must be stiff all over. He was limping with his left leg. From time to time he stopped and looked around despairingly.

As soon as he stopped going into cafés where there was a telephone, Maigret could no longer summon a relief. Back again along the quais. Then that mechanical gesture of flipping through the book bargains, turning the pages, pausing to check the authenticity of an engraving or a print.

A freezing wind was sweeping across the Seine. The water tinkled as the barges moved through it, as tiny fragments of ice glittered and jostled against one another. From a distance Maigret caught sight of the windows of his own office. His sister-in-law had gone back to Orléans. As long as Lucas had. . . .

He didn't know yet that this dreadful trail was to become a classic, and that for years the older generation of detectives would recount the details to new colleagues. The silliest thing about it all was that it was a ridiculous detail that upset him most: the man had a pimple on his forehead, a pimple that, on close inspection, turned out to be a boil, which was changing from red to purple.

As long as Lucas . . .

At midday the man, who certainly knew his Paris, made for the free soup kitchen that is situated at the end of the Boulevard Saint-Germain. He took his place in the queue of down-and-outers. An old man spoke to him, but he pretended not to understand. Then another, with a pock-marked face, spoke to him in Russian.

Maigret crossed over to the opposite pavement, and paused. When he was driven to have sandwiches in a bistro, he half turned so that the other should not see him eating them through the windows.

The poor wretches moved forward slowly, went in, four or maybe six at a time, to the room where bowls of hot soup were being served. The queue grew longer. From time to time there was a shove from the back, which aroused protests from some of the others.

One o'clock. A newsboy appeared at the far end of the street; he was running, his body sloping forward. "L'Intransigeant! Get your Intran—" He, too, was in a hurry to get there before the others. He could tell his customers from far off, and he paid no attention to the queue of down-and-outers. "Get your—"

"Pst!" Timidly, the man raised his hand to attract the boy's attention. The others stared at him. So he had still a few sous left to spend on a paper?

Maigret, too, summoned the boy, unfolded the paper, and to his relief, found what he was looking for—the photograph of a beautiful young woman smiling out of the front page.

STRANGE DISAPPEARANCE

A young Polish woman, Madame Dora Strevzki, who disappeared four days ago from her home in Passy, 17 Rue de la Pompe, has now been reported missing. Her husband, Monsieur Stefan Strevzki, has also been missing from his home since the previous day—i.e., Monday—and the concierge, who reported the disappearance to the police, states. . . .

The man had only five or six yards more to go in the queue before he could claim his bowl of steaming soup, when he left his place in the line and was almost run over by a bus. He reached the opposite pavement just as Maigret drew level.

"I'm ready," he said simply. "Take me away. I'll answer all your questions. . . ."

They were all standing in the corridor of Headquarters—Lucas, Janvier, Torrence, and others who had not been in on the case but knew about it. As they passed, Lucas made a triumphant signal to Maigret.

A door opened and shut. Beer and sandwiches on the table.

"Take something to eat first."

Not so easy. Mouthfuls stuck in his throat. Then, at last, "Now that she's gone and is somewhere safe. . . ."

Maigret couldn't face him: he had to turn away and poke the stove.

"When I read the accounts of the murder in the papers I had already suspected Dora of deceiving me with that man. I knew, too, she wasn't his only mistress. Knowing Dora and her impetuous nature. . . . You understand? If he wanted to get rid of her, I knew she was capable of. . . . And she always carried an ivory-handled gun in her handbag. When the papers reported that an arrest had been made and there was to be a reconstruction of the crime, I wanted to see. . . ."

Maigret would have liked to be able to say to him, as the British police do, "I must warn you that anything you say may be used in evidence against you."

He had kept his coat on and he was still wearing his hat. "Now that she's safe. . . . For I suppose. . . ." He looked about him anxiously. A suspicion crossed his mind.

"She must have understood when I didn't come home. I knew it would end like that—that Borms wasn't the man for her, that she wouldn't accept the role of a mere plaything, and that she'd come back to me. She went out alone that Sunday evening, as she had been doing recently. She must have killed him then."

Maigret blew his nose. He took a long time over it. A ray of sunlight—the harsh winter sunlight that goes with sharp frost—came in the window. The pimple or boil gleamed on the forehead of the man—as Maigret found he had to go on calling him.

"So your wife killed him. When she found out he had never really cared for her. And you, you realized she had done it. And you didn't want. . . ."

He suddenly went up to the Pole. "I'm sorry, old man," he grunted, as if he was talking to an old friend. "I had to find out the truth, hadn't I? It was my duty."

Then he opened the door. "Bring in Madame Dora Strevzki. Lucas, you can carry on. I—"

And for the next two days nobody saw him again at Headquarters. His chief telephoned him at home. "Well now, Maigret. You know she's confessed, and—by the way, how's your cold? They tell me—"

"It's nothing, Chief. It's getting better. Another day. How is he?"

"What? Who?"

"He—the man."

"Oh, I see. He's got hold of the best lawyer in Paris. He has hopes—you know, *crimes passionnels*. . . ."

Maigret went back to bed and sank into a grog-and-aspirin stupor. When, later on, he was asked about the investigation, his grumbled "What investigation?" was enough to discourage further questions.

As for the man, he came to see him once or twice a week, and kept him informed of the hopes the defense were holding out.

It wasn't a straightforward acquittal: one year's imprisonment, with sentence suspended.

And the man—it was he who taught Maigret to play chess.

QUESTIONS

1. Inspector Maigret says, "I'm sorry, old man. I had to find out the truth, hadn't I? It was my duty." Do you think the duty justified the means he used?

2. Georges Simenon is famous for his writing style. Even though this story is a translation, the main elements of the style come through. How would you describe the style? Could it in any way be called "classic"?

3. Folk wisdom says that a "criminal always returns to the scene

of his crime." Certainly the story uses this assumption, but with a twist. Are you happy that the man Maigret pursued was not the murderer? Why or why not?

4. Discuss the use of setting and atmosphere in the story.

5. "A curious intimacy has sprung up between follower and followed. . . ." Relate this to other detective stories and connections made in them between the criminal and the detective.

6. Note the story's final sentence. Is it excellent, appropriate, symbolic, weak?

7. How is time used in the story? Note the points where tenses switch. What is accomplished by the switching? Do you find the changes obtrusive?

The Cold Winds of Adesta

Thomas Flanagan

"There are the headlights," the young lieutenant said. "He is coming." The lieutenant, in his fur-collared greatcoat, was standing by the dirt-streaked window, looking across the pass.

"How long does the trip take?" Major Tennente asked.

"It is five minutes from the border of the Republic, and he is under observation all that time. We can watch his lights."

Tennente drew a thin twisted cigar from his pocket and lit it. The wind hurled itself against the hut, shaking the single window. He looked up from the chair in which he was sitting, and in the light of the flickering gasoline lamp he seemed old to the lieutenant. The yellow light caught his hollowed-out cheeks, his thin hooked nose, but left his eyes in shadow.

"Is it always like this here?" he asked.

"This is a bad night and the bad season," Lieutenant Bonares said. "It is the wind cutting down the pass between the mountains. They speak of the cold winds of Adesta."

Tennente did not reply. He held the cigar between his teeth, his hands thrust deep into his pockets. He watched the young lieutenant at the window place his hand nervously on his automatic, then drop it to his side. A whistle blew shrilly.

"He has passed the roadblock," Bonares said. "The men outside will stop him now."

When the lieutenant had left the hut, Tennente stood up, a thin bent man, and, limping slightly, walked to the window. The heavy, closed truck had been halted before the hut, and by the light of the full moon Tennente could see Bonares speaking to the driver, who was gesturing angrily. Bonares turned to the two slouching troopers and they walked toward the truck. The driver climbed down then and went with Bonares to the hut.

He knows his work, that young man, Tennente thought. He continued to stare out the window when he heard the door open behind him. The moon illuminated the mountainsides and the winding road between them, and he could see, far off, the lighted windows of the Republic frontier post across the border. Then he turned.

The driver was a soft fleshy man, incongruously dressed in cap and windbreaker. There was a dead cigarette in the corner of his strangely thin mouth, which gave him a puckish, age-denying quality.

"This is Gomar," the lieutenant said. "We are old friends by now, aren't we, Gomar?"

Gomar smiled amusedly at Tennente, whom he had been watching through half-closed eyes, and shrugged.

"You transport wines?" Tennente asked.

"Anything but wines. Ask the lieutenant here. I carry guns, drugs, women. Whatever you say I carry."

"He brings wine from the Republic," Bonares said.

Tennente stepped away from the window and walked across the loose planking to the center of the room. His eyes, the eyes of a tired, watchful hawk, were no longer in shadow. "Listen to me, Gomar. I will give you a wise thought. When I speak to you, answer me properly. Answer me clearly and plainly."

"Yes," Gomar said. "I transport wine."

"We produce much wine in this country," Tennente said. He removed the cigar from his strong, discolored teeth. "You can't make money by bringing more in."

"That is my affair. If I don't use this pass, I will use one far to the south. If you close all the passes to me, I will ship by boat and then go bankrupt. That is your affair."

"Yes," Tennente said. "It is. But the pass of Adesta is almost never used. Why did you choose it?"

Gomar shrugged. "It was convenient. I carry wine from the Republic. I am licensed in both countries. It is my own concern what pass I use."

"How did you manage to get an importing license?"

"I bribed an official in the capital."

The lieutenant walked toward him stiffly, but Gomar reached in his pocket for a box of matches and re-lit his cigarette.

Tennente chuckled appreciatively. "You are an unusual merchant, Gomar. How is it that you drive your own truck?"

"Perhaps it is because my profits are small. Perhaps it is because I like the night air." Gomar drew in on his cigarette. "And I am tired of questions. My truck is open for inspection."

Tennente looked at him a moment, then said, "Thank you." He jerked his head and the others followed him outside. The wind thrust him back against the door for a moment, but he shook off Bonares' hand. "Show me how you search," he said.

At Bonares' order the troopers opened the truck and removed the casks, placing them on the hard, snow-covered ground in front of the headlights. They shook each cask. They went over the truck carefully. Bonares had trained them well, or perhaps they were particularly zealous in the presence of an official from the capital. Then they stood before the major, working their numb, cold-clumsy fingers.

"Open one of the casks," Tennente said.

"That isn't necessary," Gomar said in sudden anger. "You can tell what is in a cask by shaking it. At least, you can tell whether it is wine or guns."

"Why do you think we are looking for guns?" Tennente asked.

"Because I am not a fool. Only gunrunning would bring a major of police to the pass of Adesta in winter."

"Open a cask," Tennente said to the soldiers.

"I am not sure we have orders for that," Bonares said. "You must take the responsibility, Major."

Tennente reached out suddenly and drew the lieutenant's automatic from its holster, flicked off the safety catch, and emptied the gun into one of the casks. The wine ran blood-red on the snow. He handed the gun, butt first, to Bonares, who received it in stunned admiration.

"That wine cost me a great deal of money," Gomar said evenly. "You are a violent man, Major—"

"Tennente."

He saw Gomar's eyes widen imperceptibly. "I understand your violence now, Major. You have that reputation."

Tennente threw down his cigar. "I am not violent, but my temper is short. When you return to town, file a report. It will be buried with a pile of other complaints." He turned to the soldiers, who had been watching him with quiet, frightened eyes. "Load his truck carefully. Wine should not be mistreated."

Tennente watched them, and then watched Gomar's truck begin to move down the twisting, dangerous road toward the lights of the town of Adesta. Then he walked back into the hut, with the lieutenant following him.

Tennente stood wordlessly at the window while Bonares heated coffee on the alcohol stove. When Bonares brought the coffee to him, he wrapped his hands gratefully about the hot white cup and held it without drinking.

"How often does he make the trip?" Tennente asked.

"Every night."

"So? For wine, every night. And how long has he been doing this?"

"He began two weeks ago."

"Where does he go now?"

"There is only one place to go—the town of Adesta. And he does not stop on the road. They have watched his lights. From the terrace of the hotel you can see the road clear up to the hut here." Bonares hesitated, then said, "It is guns we are looking for, isn't it?"

Tennente looked at him. The lieutenant was a slim man and very young. His eyes were clear and dark against his olive skin. "Yes," Tennente said. "It is guns."

"It does not seem possible," Bonares said. "But of course in the capital they understand these things better."

"Why does it not seem possible, Lieutenant?" Tennente asked. He lifted the white cup to his lips and drank from it.

Bonares looked at him perplexedly. "Because we would find them when we search. Unless, of course, Gomar is a ghost."

Tennente turned away from the window and walked to the table where he set down the coffee cup gently. "No, Gomar is not a ghost. But in a sense the guns are. They are dead men's guns."

Bonares began to question him, then changed his mind, and finally asked, "You know how he does it?"

Tennente shook his head. "You can phone to the town for my car, Lieutenant."

The young man hesitated again, then spoke. "Major?"

"Yes?"

"If I can be of help to you while you are here, will you use me?"

"Why are you so anxious to be of use?"

Bonares smiled with engaging candor. "I am a junior lieutenant on a border post. If I am able to help you, in twenty years I may be a senior lieutenant. Why do you ask?"

"In this country everyone is patriotic for a reason," Tennente said. "I like to collect those reasons. It is a hobby of mine. Phone now, Lieutenant."

Colonel Jarel felt that he had reason to be troubled, for Tennente was a troublesome person. Tennente was a rash man and an insolent one. It was said that he was insolent even to the General.

From his office window Jarel could see Tennente crossing the square toward him. The major was carrying the canvas-wrapped package which he had brought with him yesterday, when he first came to Adesta. The colonel, who knew what the package contained, shuddered slightly. The sun still fell in a golden wash on the white buildings and suffused the plaza, and the armed and solitary patrol still moved untroubled among the villagers. But Jarel had only to look again at the hungry, predatory figure approaching his office to lose once more his lightly held ease.

The major had not shaved and his uniform was unpressed; cigars bulged from his tunic pocket, and his garrison cap was pushed back from the high creased forehead. That is how officers looked before the days of the General, Jarel thought. Tennente limped into the room, put the bundle on the desk, and then sat down. The colonel turned away from the window and looked at him. "You saw Gomar last night?" the colonel asked.

"I saw Gomar. I saw his wine."

"But no guns?"

Tennente shook his head. "No, no guns."

"Because he carries no guns," Jarel said. "Because there are no guns. Not in this region."

"Gomar drives his truck up the pass and into the Republic. When he comes back, he carries guns as well as wine."

Jarel groaned to himself: all that business of yesterday over again, and even after Tennente had made his own inspection. "How?" he asked with constrained politeness.

"I don't know that. Yet."

Jarel walked to the desk and sat behind it facing Tennente, hating the major's drawn, tired face, the watchful eyes. "You have checked the truck. I have checked the truck. Bonares has checked it. The casks are examined. The truck itself is examined. There is only wine."

"Guns come down from the pass," Tennente said, with his maddening, calm indifference. "It is my job to discover how it is done. Your disbelief does not interest me."

You must match this man's calm, Jarel told himself. Tennente is a dangerous man. "It is the disbelief of the commandant of the town of Adesta, Major. It is my duty to see that the public welfare is maintained in this region. I would hardly be so remiss in that duty as to allow a man to enter the country once a night in a truck filled with contraband arms."

Tennente shrugged, and the shrug seemed to imply many things, all of them unflattering. Jarel felt anger working in his mind like a strong liquor. Tennente placed his hand on the canvas bundle which yesterday he had opened for the colonel. "This is one of the guns. Last week the police shot the man who carried it. But there will be many guns and many men carrying them, unless Gomar is shot."

"Shot!" Jarel echoed, but not incredulously; like Gomar, he knew the major by reputation. "You can't shoot a man for transporting wine under license."

"Gomar is not a wine merchant. He is a gunrunner, and that is a capital offense."

Jarel pushed back his chair, stood up, and walked to the wall map. He put a short plump finger on the town of Adesta, and then, by stretching himself, placed the other arm across the border into the Republic. "This is Gomar's route," he said. "He is first searched by the border guards of the Republic, and then, with his truck visible at all times to Bonares, he moves down the mountain road to our hut. There he is searched a second time. Then he continues down into the town, always under the eyes of Bonares and anyone in the valley who cares to look up toward the mountains."

"Young Bonares," Tennente interrupted. "Do you trust him?"

"I trust him," Jarel said. "He is a bright lad. But I trust no one that much. I have made surprise checks. You have made one yourself. For that matter, the Republic guards have offered to let us assist them in their search."

"Yes," Tennente said. "If we give them sufficient warning."

Jarel, ignoring the major's qualification, turned away from the map. "You must see my position, Major. I have the greatest respect for the secret police, but I will not arrest a man without evidence."

Tennente stroked the shrouded rifle. "Here is your evidence, Colonel. It could only have come from this region. And only Gomar has used the pass."

"You believe the story of the arms cache," Jarel said. "An old wives' tale fifteen years old. A story told in cafés by idlers."

"It is not merely a café story. It is a fact of history. The gun cache exists, and in the mountains of Adesta." Tennente's eyes were veiled by their heavy hoods. "In the final days of the General's revolution—"

"War of liberation," Jarel corrected him automatically.

"Thank you. War of liberation. A Government army, the only one to remain intact, moved to this region and crossed to the Republic. They were turned back, and so they returned to this region and into the power of the General. But they returned without their arms. Their arms were buried, either on this side of the pass or the other. And now Gomar has found a way of removing them." Tennente threw the rifle onto the desk. "Do you think I cannot recognize those arms, Colonel?"

"You should be able to," Jarel said. "You were in one of the armies which fought the General."

"Just so," Tennente said courteously. Jarel had noticed that Tennente's infamous temper was his servant; it exploded only when he chose. "And this gun came from the mountains of Adesta."

"Then the guns come either from our side or from the Republic side. If from the Republic side, then Gomar must carry them past the Republic border patrol."

"That might not be difficult to do."

"And then he would have to get them past our guards, and that *is* difficult to do." Jarel stood with his back against the map. There was no reason why he should hold his temper; Tennente was hardly a man in political favor.

"Perhaps they come from our side," Tennente said.

Jarel tugged at the map cord, and the mountains of Adesta shot upward and vanished. "Really, Major Tennente. I am not as ignorant of the details of my command as you suggest." He walked to a steel filing cabinet, rummaged through its disorder, and pulled out a wrinkled document. "I have read the report of the military commission, and I presume that you have, as well. Immediately after the revolution—"

"The war of liberation," Tennente said, his face bland.

"—the General sent a commission here. They built a border hut and then searched our side of the border." Jarel untied the red tape, opened the dossier, and extracted a map. It was similar to the one which Tennente had just seen disappear, save in one detail. Jarel placed his short blunt finger on the border post. "Here is the hut they built," he said, "and here is how they searched. Inch by inch. Do you see these circles in red ink? Each circle represents a stage of search. They would have found a single pistol, had it been buried there."

Jarel looked up at Tennente, who had been following him closely. "And now, if the guns exist at all, they are carried down the mountain in a truck which contains only wine. Does that make sense to you?"

"No, but it does not have to make sense, because it happens. You are like the mathematician who confronts the runner at the end of his race and proves to him that he could not have run as fast as he did." Tennente picked up the map, folded it, and slipped it in his tunic pocket.

"Major Tennente—"

"Colonel Jarel." Tennente stood up stiffly. "I did not come here to discuss the niceties of logical demonstration with you."

"Nevertheless, you will have a demonstration. Would you like to have Gomar arrested when he reaches the town tonight?"

"By no means. I am not interested in one load of arms. I am interested in discovering his source of supply and his means of transportation. And then, too, it might develop that tonight he will not be carrying arms."

Jarel walked up to him. "And why not, Major? Because he will be warned—is that what you mean?"

"I mean only that I will tell you when he is to be arrested and shot. Only that."

"And when that time comes, and if you are mistaken, I will press for a court-martial. I am not a man without friends."

"And I am a man without friends," Tennente said, "in your government." He pushed back his garrison cap and looked at Jarel. "You will not arrest without evidence, Colonel. That is rare in the General's country. I like that." He picked up the rifle, raised his hand in a sketchy parody of the General's salute, and left the room.

From the window Jarel watched as Tennente walked painfully to his staff car, across the plaza. There is a man one could follow, he thought, and then corrected himself. There is a man one could have followed. Perhaps twenty years ago. Before Jarel's wife had given birth to the two daughters who were now in a convent school at the capital. Before Jarel's body had run to fat and his mind to caution. He looked at a photograph of the General which hung on the opposite wall. Like himself, a plump man. A man who knew how to be safe, how to twist and turn. . . .

"You see," Lieutenant Bonares said, "on a clear afternoon like this you can see the frontier post of the Republic clearly, and the people moving there in front of it. We could wave to each other if we wanted to, but we never do."

"No," Tennente said, as he stood beside the young man outside the border hut. "I can see that." He looked upward. "It will snow."

"It often does, up here, although it always remains warm in the town below. Here it is always quiet."

"Myself, I like it."

"I am not your age, sir."

"No. That is so. It will take you many years to learn that life like this can be pleasant, or at least not ugly."

"In the cities," Bonares said, "there it is always pleasant, and promotions come quickly. One could be a colonel at forty, one could—" He caught his tongue and flushed through his olive skin at his bad manners.

"It is all right," Tennente said. "I have been a colonel. And once I was almost a general. When I was young I would not have liked this place. When I was young I was a fool." He walked over to his staff car, and his sergeant handed him a canvas-wrapped bundle. While the two border troopers outside the hut looked at the bundle with idle, bored curiosity, Tennente and the lieutenant went into the hut.

Tennente unwrapped the rifle and placed it on the table near the unwashed coffee cups of the morning.

"You asked if Gomar were smuggling guns," Tennente said. "He is. This is one of them. Pick it up. Examine it."

Bonares looked at it with a vague, professional interest and then replaced it.

Tennente slipped into a chair. "You have never seen a gun like it?"

Bonares shook his head.

"No," Tennente said. "That is because you were too young. This model is no longer used in the army, and it is not a good gun, perhaps, because it lost a war."

"Major," Bonares said. "I have told you what I know, and I will help you if I can."

"Yes," Tennente said. His voice was even, but there was a tired edge to it. "I understand that. Perhaps I have come up here so that you can tell me what you do not know. The route is clear. You know it, and Jarel knows it, and I know it. But something happens on that route which only Gomar knows."

He reached in his pocket, pulled out the map, and unfolded it on the table, beside the rifle. Then he motioned to the lieutenant to sit beside him. He scratched the stubble on his chin. "I wish that I were the kind of officer your colonel is—all logic and crisp argument. When I was at the Academy I was always poor at that. If I were such an officer I could say, 'Don't you see, my dear Colonel, it was done thus-and-so'—telling him exactly how. But instead I know only that it was done."

Bonares shook his head. "I wish I could tell you."

"The map and the rifle," Tennente said. "Logic and violence. What those two cannot do when they are joined! Together they can make a revolution."

"A trickle of guns will not make a revolution," Bonares said self-consciously. He had been taught that politics are not a soldier's concern.

"In the country which the General rules?" Tennente asked. "There were enough guns in that arms cache for a regiment. A gun will never stay buried, Lieutenant—never."

"He brings no guns to this post, Major. I swear it!"

Tennente ran his hand along the dull barrel of the rifle, and now the voice which spoke to the young officer was more quiet. "Once I wished that there were more of these weapons—in the days before this gun was buried, when the General's artillery was rolling across the plains, when towns which contained not a single soldier were bombed and destroyed. You don't remember those days, Lieutenant. You were a little boy in school."

"I have heard the story."

"How proud we were then of the army of Adesta. The army which buried their arms rather than surrender them." He smiled. "And how pleased we were when the report of the commission made it clear that the arms were out of reach of the General."

"If one feels as you do," Bonares said, "why are you not still proud?"

Tennente looked at Bonares who, frightened by his rudeness, dropped his eyes to the map. "Because I have come to hate violence and those who make use of it. I was proud that those guns could be used again. But not by Gomar." Tennente pushed back his chair and stood up. "Not by Gomar. I am not proud that the guns of my old army should be used to destroy my own country." He leaned forward. "Right in this pass, Lieutenant, our country is being betrayed."

"In this pass," Bonares said, his young clear eyes troubled. "I had not thought of it that way."

"And that is why I cannot use the fine logic of your colonel, who shows me circles on maps. Because the one man I hate even more than the General is carrying guns here. And I am going to stop him."

Bonares' hands were pressed so hard against the table that the tips of his fingers were white. "I would help you if I could, Major."

"Though why I should stop this Gomar I do not know," Tennente said. "Nor for whom. For a fat General whose chief virtue is that he is only a little bit better than a totalitarian government? For a fat colonel who is afraid of a bad report? For a lieutenant who wants a pleasant post in the capital?" He walked to the window. "Perhaps I will stop him for the honor of an army whose members are scattered or dead and all betrayed."

It was beginning to snow, and the first flakes were falling slowly and noiselessly. "It must have been snowing that day," he said. "That day fifteen years ago. Over the pass an army moved up and then moved back. An army defeated, and honeycombed by men like Gomar. Now where is your logic, Lieutenant? That quality which Colonel Jarel values so highly. Tell me what you do not know." He glanced momentarily at Bonares, whose eyes were fixed on the map.

"Logic is always helpful," Bonares said sententiously, without raising his eyes. "And ultimately it is always correct."

"Then how does he carry through his guns?" Tennente asked.

"How can I tell you what I do not know?" Bonares said, and then looked up. "I can tell you only that he does not carry guns to this post."

"Yet logic is always correct," Tennente said. "Ultimately." He turned back to the window, and for an instant he saw imprinted on the retina of his imagination the long weary columns of men moving backward, down the long steep road to the General's tribunals and concentration camps, and he felt that if he could sharpen the focus of his vision he would be able to see whether or not they still carried their arms. For Tennente knew that guns will not stay buried, nor violence stay hidden in the earth. He tried to look backward, fifteen years, to the clue which the present did not hold.

The snow was falling more swiftly now, and as it did so, it wiped from Tennente's mind the picture which his tired imagination had conjured up. And in place of that picture was an idea, an implausible, improbable idea. An idea which was against all Jarel's logic, but which was really the only logical answer.

He turned. "Lieutenant, do you still wish to be of service to me?"

"In anything, Major."

"After you have searched Gomar's truck tonight, phone me. I will be at the hotel."

"Of course," Bonares said.

"I want to time him, to see how long it takes him to reach the town." He walked to the door. "If he comes tonight. It is snowing hard."

"He always comes," Bonares said bitterly.

In the years before the first world war an attempt was made to establish Adesta as a resort town. They built a large hotel at the edge of the town, fronting the valley, a hotel with a fine long marbled terrace from which one could look across the brief valley at the mountains. Here, for a few years, ladies from the capital sat with their parasols, sipping ices while the gentlemen strolled up and down, pretending that Adesta was Biarritz or Sorrento or Zurich. They would drive into Adesta in their open touring cars, swathed in dust-coats and mufflers, and stay for weeks.

In those days the neighboring Republic was a friendly land and there were no frontier guards. The visitors, on windless days, would drive up the narrow twisting road and over the pass for picnics on the green warm meadows and then drive back in the cool evening for dancing on the terrace of the hotel. But the cold winds drove them away and the manager went bankrupt and sold the hotel to a native innkeeper. Now it was visibly decaying.

There were few servants now, and the pink stucco walls were unwashed. The expensive walnut bar had been replaced by one of zinc, about which the wine growers and farmers would gather in the evening, discussing prices and the strange things which happened in the city. One wing of the hotel had been destroyed by artillery fire during the revolution and had not been replaced. The marble of the long terrace, which had once been the pride of its owner, was cracked and dirty now, and the tiny tables were unwashed.

It was late in the evening when Colonel Jarel joined Tennente on the terrace, although the major had been sitting there since twilight. Jarel sank into the tiny wicker chair beside Tennente. "There is a roadblock at the foot of the mountain now. Gomar will be stopped when he reaches it. It is all arranged precisely as you suggested."

Tennente nodded. He was smoking, and the tiny glow of his cigar outlined the long creased face.

"You may be right," Jarel said placatingly. "We will find out. It would be much to our credit if you were right."

"It does not matter," Tennente said.

"It matters. Of course it matters—if guns are being supplied."

"Here, there, everywhere. . . . Did you ever have rats in your house, Jarel? You find their hole, plug it up with cement, and sit back. You see no more rats. But they are there, moving delicately behind the woodwork, sounding out the weakness of the wood. They find a section which has been badly joined and they begin to gnaw. And soon there is another hole and you have to plug that one up."

"But you simply keep on plugging up the holes," Jarel said.

"Oh, yes. Unless you build strongly, with good wood."

A wind was beginning to rise, and now it blew gently across the terrace. Jarel, as he watched Tennente's motionless figure, shivered slightly. It is the wind, he thought.

"I can get into a great deal of trouble for what I am doing," Jarel said, "and I have always avoided trouble. But now I am not afraid."

"You will be," Tennente said. "Fear is in this country like malaria in a swamp."

"What are you afraid of?" Jarel asked.

Tennente pointed with his cigar. "There are Gomar's lights," he said. "He is coming to Bonares' hut." *I am afraid of nothing because I am a coward*, he thought; *I am not afraid because I have no hope.*

He drew in on his cigar, and then, to remain calm, he began to talk, while Jarel watched the lights of the truck, crawling like twin, malign insects, toward Bonares. "From the first there has been an impossibility. If the guns were on the Republic side, the guards would have discovered them. If they were on our side, the military commission would have discovered them fifteen years ago."

"Exactly."

"Exactly," Tennente repeated dryly.

"Bonares has stopped the truck," Jarel said. It would be simple, he thought, to phone and have the roadblock removed. He looked nervously at Tennente, remembering what the major had said. *You will be afraid again.*

"And I thought that either the guards have been bribed to pass through the guns or else the commission did not do a good job. But the guards could not have been bribed in that fashion, or they would have been trapped when we made our surprise inspections."

Tennente had been watching the tip of his cigar, but when Jarel said, "He has left Bonares," he looked up and watched the two small headlights move slowly down the mountain.

"And I had the report of the commission. They did not do a haphazard job. Building a hut, moving outward from the hut, inch by inch—this is not the method of bunglers."

The wind brushed across Jarel's face like a soft, impalpable leaf. "Bonares should have phoned."

"He will," Tennente said. "He will phone to tell you that Gomar brought no guns to the hut. And between these two facts I ran back and forth like a squirrel. Then, this afternoon, at the border hut, when I realized that Bonares found it impossible to lie, I had an idea which grew to a certainty." He smiled mirthlessly. "You know it is very cold up there, with only the snow and high winds for your companions."

The wind, cutting down the path, swept across the terrace. It whipped up the dead brown leaves which were scattered on the terrace and pushed them against the tables. The wind shook the doors and windows of the decaying hotel. Somewhere inside there was a sound of rotting wood being torn loose.

"I have never known the wind to be so high," Jarel said. "It makes the terrace dangerous."

"The building was not built strongly," Tennente said. "Pink stucco and cheap marble." That is not the way to build—either a hotel or a nation. One built with honor and integrity, solid stone upon solid stone.

They sat in silence as the lights approached the foot of the mountain. Presently Tennente, with a curious savagery, flung his cigar over the marbeled rail of the terrace and looked up toward the hut. "Something is wrong up there. Something is wrong."

"No," Jarel said. "Bonares phoned me just before I came here."

Suddenly Tennente sat very still, but he said only, "Why?"

"He asked me to tell you that Gomar would carry no more guns down the mountain."

For a moment only the sound of the wind and the driven leaves filled the terrace, and then Tennente said, "You are sure those were his exact words? No more guns will come down the mountain?"

"Quite sure," Jarel said, puzzled and very frightened.

A waiter came out and summoned Jarel to the phone. When he came back, he was sweating in the cold night air. "You were right, Major. Half of Gomar's casks contained guns, when the border troopers at the roadblock searched them."

He looked across at the lights of the stopped car.

"Anything else?" Tennente asked.

"Yes," Jarel said. "The two border troopers rode down with him. The officer in charge of the roadblock has no explanation."

"They were trying to get away," Tennente said quietly. "They had helped Gomar shoot Bonares."

The two men—the one who understood and the one who did not—sat without speaking, until Jarel could no longer stand being alone with the wind and the gaunt man beside him. "Why?" he asked.

"Because honor is so strange and tenuous a thing," Tennente said. "Because it would allow Lieutenant Bonares to do a terrible thing but would not allow him to lie. Bonares was a good young man, but a naive one, and rather weak. We teach our young officers that they should know nothing of politics. It was so in my time too. Perhaps it is a good thing, perhaps a bad. He would have killed himself rather than be a traitor. But a little gunrunning now, a profitable and a dangerously romantic affair for a poor officer with no chance of promotion. And so he and the guards took Gomar's bribes. But he would not lie.

"When I went up to him today, I showed him a gun, and spoke of what that gun would mean in the possession of a traitor. And then we looked together at the map of the military commission. Slowly, I suppose, we realized together: I where the guns were hidden, and he what he had been doing. I noticed, in passing almost, that he would always answer my questions with a kind of formula: 'Gomar brings no guns to the hut.' Never did he say, 'Gomar will take no guns away from the hut.' So, when I began to suspect this afternoon, I hoped, I prayed, that he would speak, but he did not. Now I know why. He planned to stop Gomar or be killed. His men were not so noble." Tennente shook his head. "It does not matter."

But Jarel said, "Where were the guns?"

"In the only place where the commission did *not* search. Buried deep in the earth *under* the hut—the hut built *before* the commission began to search. The guards were not bribed to pass the guns through, but to give them to Gomar. Each night he would drive to the Republic side, pick up some casks of wine, then drive back to the hut, where the arms casks would be carried up from their pit and loaded aboard. Then the floor planks of the hut would be replaced until the next night. Of course, when we came up, Gomar merely drove down with wine." Tennente smiled. "Logical demonstration," he said.

Jarel stood up. "We can't be sure what has happened at the hut. Perhaps they did not kill Bonares. Perhaps they—" But Tennente had closed his eyes.

The colonel stood up and walked across the terrace to the door, and then turned and looked back. Tennente had opened his eyes, but his back was half turned to the decaying hotel. He was looking through the darkness to the mountains.

QUESTIONS

1. How is the disillusioned character of Major Tennente similar to that of other fictional detectives you have encountered? How do you explain the seeming contradiction in his thinking, "*I am afraid of nothing because I am a coward . . . I am not afraid because I have no hope*"?

2. Discuss the character and actions of Bonares in relation to how a "good" man can turn "bad."

3. Jarel and the General are similar ("Like himself, a plump man. A man who knew how to be safe, how to twist and turn"). Why has their kind been so able to subject those who are like Major Tennente, or so he seems once to have been?

4. Define "honor." How does the author's attaching "honor" to a character so often effectively make us admire the character? What prompts our almost automatic response to the value of honor?

5. Tennente repeats, "It does not matter." Does he mean the opposite?

6. Have character, background, ethics become more important in this story than the detection and mystery element? If you think so, explain how Flanagan has accomplished this.

7. What does the hotel symbolize?

The Stolen White Elephant

Mark Twain

I

The following curious history was related to me by a chance railway acquaintance. He was a gentleman more than seventy years of age, and his thoroughly good and gentle face and earnest and sincere manner imprinted the unmistakable stamp of truth upon every statement which fell from his lips. He said:

You know in what reverence the royal white elephant of Siam is held by the people of that country. You know it is sacred to kings, only kings may possess it, and that it is indeed in a measure even superior to kings, since it receives not merely honor but worship. Very well; five years ago, when the troubles concerning the frontier line arose between Great Britain and Siam, it was presently manifest that Siam had been in the wrong. Therefore every reparation was quickly made, and the British representative stated that he was satisfied and the past should be forgotten. This greatly relieved the King of Siam, and partly as a token of gratitude, but partly also, perhaps, to wipe out any little remaining vestige of unpleasantness which England might feel toward him, he wished to send the Queen a present—the sole sure way of propitiating an enemy, according to Oriental ideas. This present ought not only to be a royal one, but transcendently royal. Wherefore, what offering could be so meet as that of a white elephant? My position in the Indian civil service was such that I was deemed peculiarly worthy of the honor of conveying the present to her Majesty. A ship was fitted out for me and my servants and the officers and attendants of the elephant, and in due time I arrived in New York harbor and placed my royal charge in admirable quarters in Jersey City. It was necessary to remain awhile in order to recruit the animal's health before resuming the voyage.

All went well during a fortnight—then my calamities began. The white elephant was stolen! I was called up at dead of night and informed of this fearful misfortune. For some moments I was beside myself with terror and anxiety; I was helpless. Then I grew calmer and collected my faculties. I soon saw my course—for indeed there was but the one course for an intelligent man to pursue. Late as it was, I flew to New York and got a policeman to conduct me to the headquarters of the detective force. Fortunately I arrived in time, though the chief of the force, the celebrated Inspector Blunt, was just on the point of leaving for his home. He was a man of middle size and compact frame, and when he was thinking deeply he had a way of knitting his brows and tapping his forehead reflectively with his finger, which impressed you at once with the conviction that you stood in the presence of a person of no common order. The very sight of him gave me confidence and made me hopeful. I stated my errand. It did not flurry him in the least; it had no more visible effect upon his iron self-possession than if I had told him somebody had stolen my dog. He motioned me to a seat, and said calmly:

"Allow me to think a moment, please."

So saying, he sat down at his office table and leaned his head upon his hand. Several clerks were at work at the other end of the room; the scratching of their pens was all the sound I heard during the next six or seven minutes. Meantime the inspector sat there, buried in thought. Finally he raised his head, and there was that in the firm lines of his face which showed me that his brain had done its work and his plan was made. Said he—and his voice was low and impressive—

"This is no ordinary case. Every step must be warily taken; each step must be made sure before the next is ventured. And secrecy must be observed—secrecy profound and absolute. Speak to no one about the matter, not even the reporters. I will take care of *them*; I will see that they get only what it may suit my ends to let them know." He touched a bell; a youth appeared. "Alaric, tell the reporters to remain for the present." The boy retired. "Now let us proceed to business—and systematically. Nothing can be accomplished in this trade of mine without strict and minute method."

He took a pen and some paper. "Now—name of the elephant?"

"Hassan Ben Ali Ben Selim Abdallah Mohammed Moisé Alhammal Jamsetjejeebhoy Dhuleep Sultain Ebu Bhudpoor."

"Very well. Given name?"

"Jumbo."

"Very well. Place of birth?"

"The capital city of Siam."

"Parents living?"

"No—dead."

"Had they any other issue besides this one?"

"None. He was an only child."

"Very well. These matters are sufficient under that head. Now please describe the elephant, and leave out no particular, however insignificant —that is, insignificant from *your* point of view. To men in my profession there *are* no insignificant particulars; they do not exist."

I described—he wrote. When I was done, he said:

"Now listen. If I have made any mistakes, correct me."

He read as follows:

"Height, 19 feet; length from apex of forehead to insertion of tail, 26 feet; length of trunk, 16 feet; length of tail, 6 feet; total length, including trunk and tail, 48 feet; length of tusks, 9½ feet; ears in keeping with these dimensions; footprint resembles the mark left when one upends a barrel in the snow; color of the elephant, a dull white; has a hole the size of a plate in each ear for the insertion of jewelry, and possesses the habit in a remarkable degree of squirting water upon spectators and of maltreating with his trunk not only such persons as he is acquainted with, but even entire strangers; limps slightly with his right hind leg, and has a small scar in his left armpit caused by a former boil; had on, when stolen, a castle containing seats for fifteen persons, and a gold-cloth saddle-blanket the size of an ordinary carpet."

There were no mistakes. The inspector touched the bell, handed the description to Alaric, and said:

"Have fifty thousand copies of this printed at once and mailed to every detective office and pawnbroker's shop on the continent." Alaric retired. "There—so far, so good. Next, I must have a photograph of the property."

I gave him one. He examined it critically, and said:

"It must do, since we can do no better; but he has his trunk curled up and tucked into his mouth. That is unfortunate, and is calculated to mislead, for of course he does not usually have it in that position." He touched his bell.

"Alaric, have fifty thousand copies of this photograph made, the first thing in the morning, and mail them with the descriptive circulars."

Alaric retired to execute his orders. The inspector said:

"It will be necessary to offer a reward, of course. Now as to the amount?"

"What sum would you suggest?"

"To *begin* with, I should say—well, twenty-five thousand dollars. It is an intricate and difficult business; there are a thousand avenues of escape and opportunities of concealment. These thieves have friends and pals everywhere—"

"Bless me, do you know who they are?"

The wary face, practiced in concealing the thoughts and feelings within, gave me no token, nor yet the replying words, so quietly uttered:

"Never mind about that. I may, and I may not. We generally gather a pretty shrewd inkling of who our man is by the manner of his work and the size of the game he goes after. We are not dealing with a pickpocket or a hall thief, now, make up your mind to that. This property was not 'lifted' by a novice. But, as I was saying, considering the amount of travel which will have to be done, and the diligence with which the thieves will cover up their traces as they move along, twenty-five thousand may be too small a sum to offer, yet I think it worth while to start with that."

So we determined upon that figure, as a beginning. Then this man, whom nothing escaped which could by any possibility be made to serve as a clue, said:

"There are cases in detective history to show that criminals have been detected through peculiarities in their appetites. Now, what does this elephant eat, and how much?"

"Well, as to *what* he eats—he will eat *anything*. He will eat a man, he will eat a Bible—he will eat anything *between* a man and a Bible."

"Good—very good indeed, but too general. Details are necessary—details are the only valuable things in our trade. Very well—as to men. At one meal—or, if you prefer, during one day—how many men will he eat, if fresh?"

"He would not care whether they were fresh or not; at a single meal he could eat five ordinary men."

"Very good; five men; we will put that down. What nationalities would he prefer?"

"He is indifferent about nationalities. He prefers acquaintances, but is not prejudiced against strangers."

"Very good. Now, as to Bible. How many Bibles would he eat at a meal?"

"He would eat an entire edition."

"It is hardly succinct enough. Do you mean an ordinary octavo, or the family illustrated?"

"I think he would be indifferent to illustrations; that is, I think he would not value illustrations above simple letter-press."

"No, you do not get my idea. I refer to bulk. The ordinary octavo Bible weighs about two pounds and a half, while the great quarto with the illustrations weighs ten or twelve. How many Doré Bibles would he eat at a meal?"

"If you knew this elephant, you would not ask. He would take what they had."

"Well, put it in dollars and cents, then. We must get at it somehow. The Doré costs a hundred dollars a copy, Russia leather, bevelled."

"He would require about fifty thousand dollars' worth—say an edition of five hundred copies."

"Now that is more exact. I will put that down. Very well; he likes men and Bibles; so far, so good. What else will he eat? I want particulars."

"He will leave Bibles to eat bricks, he will leave bricks to eat bottles, he will leave bottles to eat clothing, he will leave clothing to eat cats, he will leave cats to eat oysters, he will leave oysters to eat ham, he will leave ham to eat sugar, he will leave sugar to eat pie, he will leave pie to eat potatoes, he will leave potates to eat bran, he will leave bran to eat hay, he will leave hay to eat oats, he will leave oats to eat rice, for he was mainly raised on it. There is nothing whatever that he will not eat but European butter, and he would eat that if he could taste it."

"Very good. General quantity at a meal—say about—"

"Well, anywhere from a quarter to half a ton."

"And he drinks—"

"Everything that is fluid. Milk, water, whiskey, molasses, castor oil, camphene, carbolic acid—it is no use to go into particulars; whatever fluid occurs to you set it down. He will drink anything that is fluid, except European coffee."

"Very good. As to quantity?"

"Put it down five to fifteen barrels—his thirst varies; his other appetites do not."

"These things are unusual. They ought to furnish quite good clues toward tracing him."

He touched the bell.

"Alaric, summon Captain Burns."

Burns appeared. Inspector Blunt unfolded the whole matter to him, detail by detail. Then he said in the clear, decisive tones of a man whose plans are clearly defined in his head, and who is accustomed to command:

"Captain Burns, detail Detectives Jones, Davis, Halsey, Bates and Hackett to shadow the elephant."

"Yes, sir."

"Detail Detectives Moses, Dakin, Murphy, Rogers, Tupper, Higgins, and Bartholomew to shadow the thieves."

"Yes, sir."

"Place a strong guard—a guard of thirty picked men, with a relief of thirty—over the place from whence the elephant was stolen, to keep strict watch there night and day, and allow none to approach—except reporters—without written authority from me."

"Yes, sir."

"Place detectives in plain clothes in the railway, steamship, and ferry depots, and upon all roadways leading out of Jersey City, with orders to search all suspicious persons."

"Yes, sir."

"Furnish all these men with photograph and accompanying description of the elephant, and instruct them to search all trains and outgoing ferry boats and other vessels."

"Yes, sir."

"If the elephant should be found, let him be seized and the information forwarded to me by telegraph."

"Yes, sir."

"Let me be informed at once if any clues should be found—footprints of the animal, or anything of that kind."

"Yes, sir."

"Get an order commanding the harbor police to patrol the frontages vigilantly."

"Yes, sir."

"Dispatch detectives in plain clothes over all the railways, north as far as Canada, west as far as Ohio, south as far as Washington."

"Yes, sir."

"Place experts in all the telegraph offices to listen to all messages; and let them require that all cipher dispatches be interpreted to them."

"Yes, sir."

"Report to me promptly at the usual hour."

"Yes, sir."

"Go!"

"Yes, sir."

He was gone.

Inspector Blunt was silent and thoughtful a moment, while the fire in his eye cooled down and faded out. Then he turned to me and said in a placid voice:

"I am not given to boasting, it is not my habit; but—we shall find the elephant."

I shook him warmly by the hand and thanked him; and I *felt* my thanks, too. The more I had seen of the man the more I liked him, and the more I admired him and marveled over the mysterious wonders of his profession. Then we parted for the night, and I went home with a far happier heart than I had carried with me to his office.

II

Next morning it was all in the newspapers, in the minutest detail. It even had additions—consisting of Detective This, Detective That, and Detective The Other's "Theory" as to how the robbery was done, who the robbers were, and whither they had flown with their booty. There were eleven of these theories, and they covered all the possibilities; and this single fact shows what independent thinkers detectives are. No two theories were alike, or even much resembled each other, save in one striking particular, and in that one all the eleven theories were absolutely agreed. That was, that although the rear of my building was torn out and the only door remained locked, the elephant had not been removed through the rent, but by some other (undiscovered) outlet. All agreed that the robbers had made that rent only to mislead the detectives. That never would have occurred to me or to any other layman, perhaps, but it had not deceived the detectives for a moment. Thus, what I had supposed was the only thing that had no mystery about it was in fact the very thing I had gone further astray in. The eleven theories all named the supposed robbers, but no two named the same robbers; the total number of suspected persons was thirty-seven. The various newspaper accounts all closed with the most important opinion of all—that of Chief Inspector Blunt. A portion of this statement read as follows:

> "The chief knows who the two principals are, namely, 'Brick' Duffy and 'Red' McFadden. Ten days before the robbery was achieved he was already aware that it was to be attempted, and had quietly proceeded to shadow these two noted villains; but unfortunately on the night in question their track was lost, and before it could be found again the bird was flown—that is, the elephant.
>
> "Duffy and McFadden are the boldest scoundrels in the profession; the chief has reasons for believing that they are the men who stole the stove out of the detective headquarters on a bitter night last winter,—in consequence of which the chief and every detective present were in the hands of the physicians before morning, some with frozen feet, others with frozen fingers, ears, and other members."

When I read the first half of that I was more astonished than ever at the wonderful sagacity of this strange man. He not only saw everything in the present with a clear eye, but even the future could not be hidden from him. I was soon at his office, and said I could not help wishing he had had those men arrested, and so prevented the trouble and loss; but his reply was simple and unanswerable:

"It is not our province to prevent crime, but to punish it. We cannot punish it until it is committed."

I remarked that the secrecy which he had begun had been marred by the newspapers; not only all our facts but all our plans had been revealed; even all the suspected persons had been named; these would doubtless disguise themselves now, or go into hiding.

"Let them. They will find that when I am ready for them my hand will descend upon them, in their secret places, as unerringly as the hand of fate. As to the newspapers, we *must* keep in with them. Fame, reputation, constant public mention—these are the detective's bread and butter. He must publish his facts, else he will be supposed to have none; he must publish his theory, for nothing is so strange or striking as a detective's theory, or brings him so much wondering respect; we must publish our plans, for these the journals insist upon having, and we could not deny them without offending. We must constantly show the public what we are doing, or they will believe we are doing nothing. It is much pleasanter to have a newspaper say, 'Inspector Blunt's ingenious and extraordinary theory is as follows,' than to have it say some harsh thing, or, worse still, some sarcastic one."

"I see the force of what you say. But I noticed that in one part of your remarks in the papers this morning you refused to reveal your opinion upon a certain minor point."

"Yes, we always do that; it has a good effect. Besides, I had not formed any opinion on that point, anyway."

I deposited a considerable sum of money with the inspector, to meet current expenses, and sat down to wait for news. We are expecting the telegrams to begin to arrive at any moment now. Meantime I re-read the newspapers and also our descriptive circular, and observed that our $25,000 reward seemed to be offered only to detectives. I said I thought it ought to be offered to anybody who would catch the elephant. The inspector said:

"It is the detectives who will find the elephant, hence the reward will go to the right place. If other people found the animal, it would only be by watching the detectives and taking advantage of clues and indications stolen from them, and that would entitle the detectives to the reward, after all. The proper office of a reward is to stimulate the men who deliver up their time and their trained sagacities to this sort of work, and not to confer benefits upon chance citizens who stumble upon a capture without having earned the benefits by their own merits and labors."

This was reasonable enough, certainly. Now the telegraphic machine in the corner began to click, and the following dispatch was the result:

> Flower Station, N. Y., 7:30 A.M.
>
> Have got a clew. Found a succession of deep tracks across a farm near here. Followed them two miles east without result; think elephant went west. Shall now shadow him in that direction.
>
> Darley, *Detective*

"Darley's one of the best men on the force," said the inspector. "We shall hear from him again before long."

Telegram No. 2 came:—

> Barker's, N. J., 7:40 A.M.
>
> Just arrived. Glass factory broken open here during night and eight hundred bottles taken. Only water in large quantity near here is five miles distant. Shall strike for there. Elephant will be thirsty. Bottles were empty.
>
> Baker, *Detective*

"That promises well, too," said the inspector. "I told you the creature's appetites would not be bad clews."

Telegram No. 3:—

> Taylorville, L. I., 8:15 A.M.
>
> A haystack near here disappeared during the night. Probably eaten. Have got a clew, and am off.
>
> Hubbard, *Detective*

"How he does move around!" said the inspector. "I knew we had a difficult job on hand, but we shall catch him yet."

Flower Station, N. Y., 9 A.M.

Shadowed the tracks three miles westward. Large, deep, and ragged. Have just met a farmer who says they are not elephant tracks. Says they are holes where he dug up saplings for shade-trees when ground was frozen last winter. Give me orders how to proceed.

Darley, *Detective*

"Aha! a confederate of the thieves! The thing grows warm," said the inspector.

He dictated the following telegram to Darley:

Arrest the man and force him to name his pals. Continue to follow the tracks,—to the Pacific, if necessary.

Chief Blunt

Next telegram:—

Coney Point, Pa., 8:45 A.M.

Gas office broken open here during night and three months' unpaid gas bills taken. Have got a clew and am away.

Murphy, *Detective*

"Heavens!" said the inspector; "would he eat gas bills?"

"Through ignorance—yes; but they cannot support life. At least, unassisted."

Now came this exciting telegram:—

Ironville, N. Y., 9:30 A.M.

Just arrived. This village in consternation. Elephant passed through here at five this morning. Some say he went east, some say west, some north, some south—but all say they did not wait to notice particularly. He killed a horse; have secured a piece of it for a clew. Killed it with his trunk; from style of blow, think he struck it left-handed. From position in which horse lies, think elephant traveled northward along line of Berkley railway. Has four and a half hours' start, but I move on his track at once.

Hawes, *Detective*

I uttered exclamations of joy. The inspector was as self-contained as a graven image. He calmly touched his bell.

"Alaric, send Captain Burns here."

Burns appeared.

"How many men are ready for instant orders?"

"Ninety-six, sir."

"Send them north at once. Let them concentrate along the line of the Berkley road north of Ironville."

"Yes, sir."

"Let them conduct their movements with the utmost secrecy. As fast as others are at liberty, hold them for orders."

"Yes, sir."

"Go!"

"Yes, sir."

Presently came another telegram:—

> Sage Corners, N. Y., 10:30
>
> Just arrived. Elephant passed through here at 8:15. All escaped from the town but a policeman. Apparently elephant did not strike at policeman, but at the lamp-post. Got both. I have secured a portion of the policeman as clew.
>
> Stumm, *Detective*

"So the elephant has turned westward," said the inspector. "However, he will not escape, for my men are scattered all over that region."

The next telegram said:—

> Glover's, 11:15
>
> Just arrived. Village deserted, except sick and aged. Elephant passed through three-quarters of an hour ago. The anti-temperance mass meeting was in session; he put his trunk in at a window and washed it out with water from cistern. Some swallowed it—since dead; several drowned. Detectives Cross and O'Shaughnessy were passing through town, but going south,—so missed elephant. Whole region for many miles around in terror,—people flying from their homes. Wherever they turn they meet elephant, and many are killed.
>
> Brant, *Detective*

I could have shed tears, this havoc so distressed me. But the inspector only said,—

"You see,—we are closing in on him. He feels our presence; he has turned eastward again."

Yet further troublous news was in store for us. The telegraph brought this:—

Hoganport, 12:19

Just arrived. Elephant passed through half an hour ago, creating wildest fright and excitement. Elephant raged around streets; two plumbers going by, killed one—other escaped. Regret general.

O'Flaherty, *Detective*

"Now he is right in the midst of my men," said the inspector. "Nothing can save him."

A succession of telegrams came from detectives who were scattered through New Jersey and Pennsylvania, and who were following clews consisting of ravaged barns, factories, and Sunday School libraries, with high hopes,—hopes amounting to certainties, indeed. The inspector said,—

"I wish I could communicate with them and order them north, but that is impossible. A detective only visits a telegraph office to send his report; then he is off again, and you don't know where to put your hand on him."

Now came this despatch:—

Bridgeport, Ct., 12:15

Barnum offers rate of $4,000 a year for exclusive privilege of using elephant as traveling advertising medium from now until detectives find him. Wants to paste circus-posters on him. Desires immediate answer.

Boggs, *Detective*

"That is perfectly absurd!" I exclaimed.

"Of course it is," said the inspector. "Evidently Mr. Barnum, who thinks he is so sharp, does not know me,—but I know him."

Then he dictated this answer to the despatch:

Mr. Barnum's offer declined. Make it $7,000 or nothing.

Chief Blunt

"There. We shall not have to wait long for an answer. Mr. Barnum is not at home; he is in the telegraph office,—it is his way when he has business on hand. Inside of three—"

Done—P. T. Barnum

So interrupted the clicking telegraphic instrument. Before I could make a comment upon this extraordinary episode, the following despatch carried my thoughts into another and very distressing channel:—

Bolivia, N. Y., 12:50

Elephant arrived here from the south and passed through toward the forest at 11:50, dispersing a funeral on the way, and diminishing the mourners by two. Citizens fired some small cannonballs into him, and then fled. Detective Burke and I arrived ten minutes later, from the north, but mistook some excavations for footprints, and so lost a good deal of time; but at last we struck the right trail and followed it to the woods. We then got down on our hands and knees and continued to keep a sharp eye on the track, and so shadowed it into the brush. Burke was in advance. Unfortunately the animal had stopped to rest; therefore, Burke having his head down, intent upon the track, butted up against the elephant's hind legs before he was aware of his vicinity. Burke instantly arose to his feet, seized the tail, and exclaimed joyfully, "I claim the re—" but got no further, for a single blow of the huge trunk laid the brave fellow's fragments low in death. I fled rearward, and the elephant turned and shadowed me to the edge of the wood, making tremendous speed, and I should inevitably have been lost, but the remains of the funeral providentially intervened again and diverted his attention. I have just learned that nothing of that funeral is now left; but this is no loss, for there is an abundance of material for another. Meantime, the elephant has disappeared again.

Mulrooney, *Detective*

We heard no news except from the diligent and confident detectives scattered about New Jersey, Pennsylvania, Delaware and Virginia,—who were all following fresh and encouraging clews,—until shortly after 2 P.M., when this telegram came:—

Baxter Centre, 2:15

Elephant been here, plastered over with circus-bills, and broke up a revival, striking down and damaging many who were on the point of entering upon a better life. Citizens penned him up, and established a guard. When Detective Brown and I arrived, some time after, we entered enclosure and proceeded to identify elephant by photograph and description. All marks tallied exactly except one, which we could not see,—the boil-scar under armpit. To make sure, Brown crept under to look, and was immediately brained,—that is, head crushed and destroyed, though nothing issued from debris. All fled; so did elephant, striking right and left with much effect. Has escaped, but left bold blood-track from cannon-wounds. Rediscovery certain. He broke south-ward, through a dense forest.

Brent, *Detective*

That was the last telegram. At nightfall a fog shut down which was so dense that objects but three feet away could not be discerned. This lasted all night. The ferry-boats and even the omnibuses had to stop running.

III

Next morning the papers were as full of detective theories as before; they had all our tragic facts in detail also, and a great many more which they had received from their telegraphic correspondents. Column after column was occupied, a third of its way down, with glaring head-lines, which it made my heart sick to read. Their general tone was like this:—

"The White Elephant at Large! He Moves Upon His Fatal March! Whole Villages Deserted by Their Fright-Stricken Occupants! Pale Terror Goes Before Him, Death and Devastation Follow After! After these, the detectives. Barns Destroyed, Factories Gutted, Harvests Devoured, Public Assemblages Dispersed, Accompanied by Scenes of Carnage Impossible to Describe! Theories of Thirty-four of the Most Distinguished Detectives on the Force! Theory of Chief Blunt!"

"There!" said Inspector Blunt, almost betrayed into excitement, "this is magnificent! This is the greatest windfall that any detective organiza-tion ever had. The fame of it will travel to the ends of the earth, and endure to the end of time, and my name with it."

But there was no joy for me. I felt as if I had committed all those red crimes, and that the elephant was only my irresponsible agent. And how the list had grown! In one place he had "interfered with an election and killed five repeaters." He had followed this act with the destruction of two poor fellows, named O'Donohue and McFlannigan, who had "found a refuge in the home of the oppressed of all lands only the day before, and were in the act of exercising for the first time the noble right of American citizens at the polls, when stricken down by the relentless hand of the Scourge of Siam." In another, he had "found a crazy sensation-preacher preparing his next season's heroic attacks on the dance, the theatre, and other things which can't strike back, and had stepped on him." And in still another place he had "killed a lightning-rod agent." And so the list went on, growing redder and redder, and more and more heart-breaking. Sixty persons had been killed, and two hundred and forty wounded. All the accounts bore just testimony to the activity and devotion of the detectives, and all closed with the remark that "three hundred thousand citizens and four detectives saw the dread creature, and two of the latter he destroyed."

I dreaded to hear the telegraphic instrument begin to click again. By and by the messages began to pour in, but I was happily disappointed in their nature. It was soon apparent that all trace of the elephant was lost. The fog had enabled him to search out a good hiding-place unobserved. Telegrams from the most absurdly distant points reported that a dim vast mass had been glimpsed there through the fog at such and such an hour, and was "undoubtedly the elephant." This dim vast mass had been glimpsed in New Haven, in New Jersey, in Pennsylvania, in interior New York, in Brooklyn, and even in the city of New York itself! But in all cases the dim vast mass had vanished quickly and left no trace. Every detective of the large force scattered over this huge extent of country sent his hourly report, and each and every one of them had a clew, and was shadowing something, and was hot upon the heels of it.

But the day passed without other result.

The next day the same.

The next just the same.

The newspaper reports began to grow monotonous with facts that amounted to nothing, clews which led to nothing, and theories which had nearly exhausted the elements which surprise and delight and dazzle.

By advice of the inspector I doubled the reward.

Four more dull days followed. Then came a bitter blow to the poor, hard-working detectives,—the journalists declined to print their theories, and coldly said, "Give us a rest."

Two weeks after the elephant's disappearance I raised the reward to $75,000 by the inspector's advice. It was a great sum, but I felt that I would rather sacrifice my whole private fortune than lose my credit with my government. Now that the detectives were in adversity, the newspapers turned upon them, and began to fling the most stinging sarcasms at them. This gave the minstrels an idea, and they dressed themselves as detectives and hunted the elephant on the stage in the most extravagant way. The caricaturists made pictures of detectives scanning the country with spy-glasses, while the elephant, at their backs, stole apples out of their pockets. And they made all sorts of ridiculous pictures of the detective badge,—you have seen that badge printed in gold on the back of detective novels, no doubt,—it is a wide-staring eye, with the legend, "We Never Sleep." When detectives called for a drink, the would-be facetious bar-keeper resurrected an obsolete form of expression and said, "Will you have an eye-opener?" All the air was thick with sarcasms.

But there was one man who moved calm, untouched, unaffected, through it all. It was that heart of oak, the Chief Inspector. His brave eye never dwarfed, his serene confidence never wavered. He always said,—

"Let them rail on; he laughs best who laughs last."

My admiration for the man grew into a species of worship. I was at his side always. His office had become an unpleasant place to me, and now became daily more and more so. Yet if he could endure it I meant to do so also; at least, as long as I could. So I came regularly, and stayed—the only outsider who seemed to be capable of it. Everybody wondered how I could; and often it seemed to me that I must desert, but at such times I looked into that calm and apparently unconscious face, and held my ground.

About three weeks after the elephant's disappearance I was about to say, one morning, that I should *have* to strike my colors and retire, when the great detective arrested the thought by proposing one more superb and masterly move.

This was to compromise with the robbers. The fertility of this man's invention exceeded anything I have ever seen, and I have had a wide intercourse with the world's finest minds. He said he was confident he could compromise for $100,000 and recover the elephant. I said I believed I could scrape the amount together, but what would become of the poor detectives who had worked so faithfully? He said,—

"In compromise they always get half."

This removed my only objection. So the inspector wrote two notes, in this form:—

> Dear Madam,—Your husband can make a large sum of money (and be entirely protected from the law) by making an immediate appointment with me.
>
> *Chief* Blunt

He sent one of these by his confidential messenger to the "reputed wife" of Brick Duffy, and the other to the reputed wife of Red McFadden.

Within the hour these offensive answers came:

> Ye Owld Fool: brick McDuffys bin ded 2 yere.
> Bridget Mahoney

> Chief Bat,—Red McFadden is hung and in heving 18 month. Any Ass but a dective knose that.
> Mary O'Hooligan

"I had long suspected these facts," said the inspector; "this testimony proves the unerring accuracy of my instinct."

The moment one resource failed him he was ready with another. He immediately wrote an advertisement for the morning papers, and I kept a copy of it:—

A.—xwblv. 242 N. Tjnd—fz328wmlg. Ozpo,—; 2 m! ogw. Mum.

He said that if the thief was alive this would bring him to the usual rendezvous. He further explained that the usual rendezvous was a place where all business affairs between detectives and criminals were conducted. This meeting would take place at twelve the next night.

We could do nothing till then, and I lost no time in getting out of the office, and was grateful indeed for the privilege.

At 11 the next night I brought $100,000 in banknotes and put them into the chief's hands, and shortly afterward he took his leave, with the brave old undimmed confidence in his eye. An almost intolerable hour dragged to a close; then I heard his welcome tread, and rose gasping and tottered to meet him. How his fine eyes flamed with triumph! He said,—

"We've compromised! The jokers will sing a different tune tomorrow! Follow me!"

He took a lighted candle and strode down into the vast vaulted basement where sixty detectives always slept, and where a score were now playing cards to while the time. I followed close after him. He walked swiftly down to the dim remote end of the place, and just as I succumbed to the pangs of suffocation and was swooning away he stumbled and fell over the outlying members of a mighty object, and I heard him exclaim as he went down,—

"Our noble profession is vindicated. Here is your elephant!"

I was carried to the office above and restored with carbolic acid. The whole detective force swarmed in, and such another season of triumphant rejoicing ensued as I had never witnessed before. The reporters were called, baskets of champagne were opened, toasts were drunk, the handshakings and congratulations were continuous and enthusiastic. Naturally the chief was the hero of the hour, and his happiness was so complete and had been so patiently and worthily and bravely won that it made me happy to see it, though I stood there a homeless beggar, my priceless charge dead, and my position in my country's service lost to me through what would always seem my fatally careless execution of a great trust. Many an eloquent eye testified its deep admiration for the chief, and many a detective's voice murmured, "Look at him,—just the king of the profession,—only give him a clew, it's all he wants, and there ain't anything hid that he can't find." The dividing of the $50,000 made great pleasure; when it was finished the chief made a little speech while he put his share in his pocket, in which he said, "Enjoy it, boys, for you've earned it; and more than that you've earned for the detective profession undying fame."

A telegram arrived, which read:—

Monroe, Mich., 10 P.M.

First time I've struck a telegraph office in over three weeks. Have followed those footprints, horseback, through the woods, a thousand miles to here, and they get stronger and bigger and fresher every day. Don't worry—inside of another week I'll have the elephant. This is dead sure.

Darley, *Detective*

The chief ordered three cheers for "Darley, one of the finest minds on the force," and then commanded that he be telegraphed to come home and receive his share of the reward.

So ended that marvelous episode of the stolen elephant. The newspapers were pleasant with praises once more, the next day, with one contemptible exception. This sheet said, "Great is the detective! He may be a little slow in finding a little thing like a mislaid elephant,—he may hunt him all day and sleep with his rotting carcass all night for three weeks, but he will find him at last—if he can get the man who mislaid him to show him the place!"

Poor Hassan was lost to me forever. The cannonshots had wounded him fatally, he had crept to that unfriendly place in the fog, and there, surrounded by his enemies and in constant danger of detection, he had wasted away with hunger and suffering till death gave him peace.

The compromise cost me $100,000; my detective expenses were $42,000 more; I never applied for a place under my government; I am a ruined man and a wanderer in the earth,—but my admiration for that man, whom I believe to be the greatest detective the world has ever produced, remains undimmed to this day, and will so remain unto the end.

QUESTIONS

1. Compare this story to "Views of My Father Weeping." Are the styles of the stories really very different?

2. Discuss the humor in the story, focusing on the element of exaggeration.

3. What about the character of the detective? Is he a good parody of literary detectives you have so far encountered?

4. The inspector says, "Details are necessary—details are the only valuable things in our trade." What about details and clues? Has Twain succeeded in making most of them seem absurd?

5. In what way could the story be called "mock epic"? Why is the extent and manner of the killings so funny?

6. Are there any exceedingly bitter and caustic effects of the story? How does "The Stolen White Elephant" reveal Twain's opinion of "the damned human race"?

7. What is the proverbial meaning of *white elephant?*

part 3

The Genre Extended

Minor and popular forms of literature affect the works of major artists, just as stories and styles of major literary figures affect writers of literature who seek primarily to entertain the audience. The basic elements of fiction are, of course, present in all forms, all genres. And if life, as the existential humanists have maintained, is basically a search for meaning, then the detective story is one of the most elemental examples of this search: exposing, often in crude form, the main outlines of how a man seeks answers, if not wisdom.

It is the search for truth itself that characterizes Henry James' short story "The Tree of Knowledge." Peter Brench can usefully be seen as the detective-observing, weighing, questioning. There are secrets. Why have the Mallows stayed so long together? Why does no one in the family know how mediocre Mr. Mallow's art is? What did Lance learn in Paris? James, in his fiction, was constantly concerned with the play of consciousness, the establishment of the knowledge that a psychological insight might often affect a life more than an incident or event in the physical, temporal world. "The Tree of Knowledge" also shows how, when the truth is discovered, its finder can come to realize that he is the one most affected and changed by knowledge.

The same kind of search and discovery plays a role in other stories in this section. In Jorges Luis Borges' "Death and the Compass," clues are put together to lead a learned, devoted detective toward a rendezvous with a murderer. Yet at the rendezvous the story becomes stranger still, and we suddenly realize that the search has been even more metaphysical than we had thought and the outcome the result of a pattern to be repeated. The author has said of this story that the atmosphere is more important than the plot, and in reading it we are asked to seek clues and symbols in suggestiveness as much as in the world of concrete objects and events.

A similar approach to mystery is found in William Burrough's "They Do Not Always Remember." What is the "truth" of the situation? What crime has actually been committed? Who is who? Is it that we are all both criminals and prosecuters? Faces and motives and solutions blur.

"Views of My Father Weeping" is the story of a son seeking clues to how and why his father was killed. Was there criminal intent? Is it all the fault of the "aristocrats"? Did he himself kill his father or did his father commit suicide? Of what use is ratiocination in stories like this?

The two chapters from Ross Macdonald's The Far Side of the Dollar *show how elements of quality fiction blend back into popular forms. Macdonald is concerned with truth and with character, with the hidden secrets freighted with the past. Lew Archer hears stories; he makes judgment; he becomes an aspect of forgotten lives.*

Flitcraft's story, told by Sam Spade in Dashiell Hammett's The Maltese Falcon, *reveals how the detective, almost despite himself, can understand intuitively how closely patterns hold us. It is the patterns, perhaps—the knowledge of patterns, learned through much experience—that enable the detective to solve the larger mysteries or the human to grow wise. We cannot help but endlessly repeat ourselves, relive aspects of our lives over and over, year to year. The writer, the detective, the philosopher finds the pattern, and he begins to understand what we are up to, what we are about.*

The Tree of Knowledge

Henry James

It was one of the secret opinions, such as we all have, of Peter Brench that his main success in life would have consisted in his never having committed himself about the work, as it was called, of his friend Morgan Mallow. This was a subject on which it was, to the best of his belief, impossible with veracity to quote him, and it was nowhere on record that he had, in the connexion, on any occasion and in any embarrassment, either lied or spoken the truth. Such a triumph had its honour even for a man of other triumphs—a man who had reached fifty, who had escaped marriage, who had lived within his means, who had been in love with Mrs. Mallow for years without breathing it, and who, last but not least, had judged himself once for all. He had so judged himself in fact that he felt an extreme and general humility to be his proper portion; yet there was nothing that made him think so well of his parts as the course he had steered so often through the shallows just mentioned. It became thus a real wonder that the friends in whom he had most confidence were just those with whom he had most reserves. He couldn't tell Mrs. Mallow—or at least he supposed, excellent man, he couldn't—that she was the one beautiful reason he had never married; any more than he could tell her husband that the sight of the multiplied marbles in that gentleman's studio was an affliction of which even time had never blunted the edge. His victory, however, as I have intimated, in regard to these productions, was not simply in his not having let it out that he deplored them; it was, remarkably, in his not having kept it in by anything else.

The whole situation, among these good people, was verily a marvel, and there was probably not such another for a long way from the spot that engages us—the point at which the soft declivity of Hampstead began at that time to confess in broken accents to Saint John's Wood. He despised Mallow's statues and adored Mallow's wife, and yet was distinctly fond of Mallow, to whom, in turn, he was equally dear. Mrs. Mallow rejoiced in the statues—though she preferred, when pressed, the busts; and if she was visibly attached to Peter Brench it was because of his affection for Morgan. Each loved the other moreover for the love borne in each case to Lancelot, whom the Mallows respectively cherished as their only child and whom the friend of their fireside identified as the third—but decidedly the handsomest—of his godsons. Already in the old years it had come to that—that no one, for such a relation, could possibly have occurred to any of them, even to the baby itself, but Peter. There was luckily a certain independence, of the pecuniary sort, all round: the Master could never otherwise have spent his solemn *Wanderjahre* in Florence and Rome, and continued by the Thames as well as by the Arno and the Tiber to add unpurchased group to group and model, for what was too apt to prove in the event mere love, fancy-heads of celebrities either too busy or too buried—too much of the age or too little of it—to sit. Neither could Peter, lounging in almost daily, have found time to keep the whole complicated tradition so alive by his presence. He was massive but mild, the depositary of these mysteries—large and loose and ruddy and curly, with deep tones, deep eyes, deep pockets, to say nothing of the habit of long pipes, soft hats and brownish greyish weather-faded clothes, apparently always the same.

He had "written," it was known, but had never spoken, never spoken in particular of that; and he had the air (since, as was believed, he continued to write) of keeping it up in order to have something more—as if he hadn't at the worst enough—to be silent about. Whatever his air, at any rate, Peter's occasional unmentioned prose and verse were quite truly the result of an impulse to maintain the purity of his taste by establishing still more firmly the right relation of fame to feebleness. The little green door of his domain was in a garden-wall on which the discoloured stucco made patches, and in the small detached villa behind it everything was old, the furniture, the servants, the books, the prints, the immemorial habits and the new improvements. The Mallows, at Carrara Lodge, were within ten minutes, and the studio there was on their little land, to which they had added, in their happy faith, for building it. This was the good fortune, if it was not the ill, of her having brought him in marriage a portion that put them in a manner at their ease and enabled them thus, on their side, to keep it up. And they did keep it up—they always had—the infatuated sculptor and his wife, for whom nature had refined on the impossible by relieving them of the sense of the difficult. Morgan had at all events everything of the sculptor but the spirit of Phidias—the brown velvet, the becoming *beretto*, the "plastic" presence, the fine fingers, the beautiful accent in Italian and the old Italian factotum. He seemed to make up for everything when he addressed Egidio with the "tu" and waved him to turn one of the rotary pedestals of which the place was full. They were tremendous Italians at Carrara Lodge, and the secret of the part played by this fact in Peter's life was in a large degree that it gave him, sturdy Briton as he was, just the amount of "going abroad" he could bear. The Mallows were all his Italy, but it was in a measure for Italy he liked them. His one worry was that Lance—to which they had shortened his godson—was, in spite of a public school, perhaps a shade too Italian. Morgan meanwhile looked like somebody's flattering idea of somebody's own person as expressed in the great room provided at the Uffizi Museum for the general illustration of that idea by eminent hands. The Master's sole regret that he hadn't been born rather to the brush than to the chisel sprang from his wish that he might have contributed to that collection.

It appeared with time at any rate to be to the brush that Lance had been born; for Mrs. Mallow, one day when the boy was turning twenty, broke it to their friend, who shared, to the last delicate morsel, their problems and pains, that it seemed as if nothing would really do but that he should embrace the career. It had been impossible longer to remain blind to the fact that he was gaining no glory at Cambridge, where Brench's own college had for a year tempered its tone to him as for Brench's own sake. Therefore why renew the vain form of preparing him for the impossible? The impossible—it had become clear—was that he should be anything but an artist.

"Oh dear, dear!" said poor Peter.

"Don't you believe in it?" asked Mrs. Mallow, who still, at more than forty, had her violet velvet eyes, her creamy satin skin and her silken chestnut hair.

"Believe in what?"

"Why in Lance's passion."

"I don't know what you mean by 'believing in it.' I've never been unaware, certainly, of his disposition, from his earliest time, to daub and draw; but I confess I've hoped it would burn out."

"But why should it," she sweetly smiled, "with his wonderful heredity? Passion is passion—though of course indeed *you*, dear Peter, know nothing of that. Has the Master's ever burned out?"

Peter looked off a little and, in his familiar formless way, kept up for a moment, a sound between a smothered whistle and a subdued hum. "Do you think he's going to be another Master?"

She seemed scarce prepared to go that length, yet she had on the whole a marvellous trust. "I know what you mean by that. Will it be a career to incur the jealousies and provoke the machinations that have been at times almost too much for his father? Well—say it may be, since nothing but clap-trap, in these dreadful days, *can*, it would seem, make its way, and since, with the curse of refinement and distinction, one may easily find one's self begging one's bread. Put it at the worst—say he *has* the misfortune to wing his flight further than the vulgar taste of his stupid countrymen can follow. Think, all the same, of the happiness— the same the Master has had. He'll *know*."

Peter looked rueful. "Ah but *what* will he know?"

"Quiet joy!" cried Mrs. Mallow, quite impatient and turning away.

II

He had of course before long to meet the boy himself on it and to hear that practically everything was settled. Lance was not to go up again, but to go instead to Paris where, since the die was cast, he would find the best advantages. Peter had always felt he must be taken as he was, but had never perhaps found him so much of that pattern as on this occasion. "You chuck Cambridge then altogether? Doesn't that seem rather a pity?"

Lance would have been like his father, to his friend's sense, had he had less humour, and like his mother had he had more beauty. Yet it was a good middle way for Peter that, in the modern manner, he was, to the eye, rather the young stockbroker than the young artist. The youth reasoned that it was a question of time—there was such a mill to go through, such an awful lot to learn. He had talked with fellows and had judged. "One has got, today," he said, "don't you see? to know."

His interlocutor, at this, gave a groan. "Oh hang it, *don't* know!"

Lance wondered. " 'Don't'? Then what's the use—?"

"The use of what?"

"Why of anything. Don't you think I've talent?"

Peter smoked away for a little in silence; then went on: "It isn't knowledge, it's ignorance that—as we've been beautifully told—is bliss."

"Don't you think I've talent?" Lance repeated.

Peter, with his trick of queer kind demonstrations, passed his arm round his godson and held him a moment. "How do I know?"

"Oh," said the boy, "if it's your own ignorance you're defending—!"

Again, for a pause, on the sofa, his godfather smoked. "It isn't. I've the misfortune to be omniscient."

"Oh well," Lance laughed again, "if you know *too* much—!"

"That's what I do, and it's why I'm so wretched."

Lance's gaiety grew. "Wretched? Come, I say!"

"But I forgot," his companion went on—"you're not to know about that. It would indeed for you too make the too much. Only I'll tell you what I'll do." And Peter got up from the sofa. "If you'll go up again I'll pay your way at Cambridge."

Lance stared, a little rueful in spite of being still more amused. "Oh Peter! You disapprove so of Paris?"

"Well, I'm afraid of it."

"Ah I see!"

"No, you don't see—yet. But you will—that is you would. And you mustn't."

The young man thought more gravely. "But one's innocence, already—!"

"Is considerably damaged? Ah that won't matter," Peter persisted—"we'll patch it up here."

"Here? Then you want me to stay at home?"

Peter almost confessed to it. "Well, we're so right—we four together—just as we are. We're so safe. Come, don't spoil it."

The boy, who had turned to gravity, turned from this, on the real pressure in his friend's tone, to consternation. "Then what's a fellow to be?"

"My particular care. Come, old man"—and Peter now fairly pleaded—"*I'll* look out for you."

Lance, who had remained on the sofa with his legs out and his hands in his pockets, watched him with eyes that showed suspicion. Then he got up. "You think there's something the matter with me—that I can't make a success."

"Well, what do you call a success?"

Lance thought again. "Why the best sort, I suppose, is to please one's self. Isn't that the sort that, in spite of cabals and things, is—in his own peculiar line—the Master's?"

There were so much too many things in this question to be answered at once that they practically checked the discussion, which became particularly difficult in the light of such renewed proof that, though the young man's innocence might, in the course of his studies, as he contended, somewhat have shrunken, the finer essence of it still remained. That was indeed exactly what Peter had assumed and what above all he desired; yet perversely enough it gave him a chill. The boy believed in the cabals and things, believed in the peculiar line, believed, to be brief, in the Master. What happened a month or two later wasn't that he went up again at the expense of his godfather, but that a fortnight after he had got settled in Paris this personage sent him fifty pounds.

He had meanwhile at home, this personage, made up his mind to the worst; and what that might be had never yet grown quite so vivid to him as when, on his presenting himself one Sunday night, as he never failed to do, for supper, the mistress of Carrara Lodge met him with an appeal as to—of all things in the world—the wealth of the Canadians. She was earnest, she was even excited. "Are many of them *really* rich?"

He had to confess he knew nothing about them, but he often thought afterwards of that evening. The room in which they sat was adorned with sundry specimens of the Master's genius, which had the merit of being, as Mrs. Mallow herself frequently suggested, of an unusually convenient size. They were indeed of dimensions not customary in the products of the chisel, and they had the singularity that, if the objects and features intended to be small looked too large, the objects and features intended to be large looked too small. The Master's idea, either in respect to this matter or to any other, had in almost any case, even after years, remained undiscoverable to Peter Brench. The creations that so failed to reveal it stood about on pedestals and brackets, on tables and shelves, a little staring white population, heroic, idyllic, allegoric, mythic, symbolic, in which "scale" had so strayed and lost itself that the public square and the chimney-piece seemed to have changed places, the monumental being all diminutive and the diminutive all monumental; branches at any rate, markedly, of a family in which stature was rather oddly irrespective of function, age and sex. They formed, like the Mallows themselves, poor Brench's own family—having at least to such a degree the note of familiarity. The occasion was one of those he had long ago learnt to know and to name—short flickers of the faint flame, soft gusts of a kinder air. Twice a year regularly the Master believed in his fortune, in addition to believing all the year round in his genius. This time it was to be made by a bereaved couple from Toronto, who had given him the handsomest order for a tomb to three lost children, each of whom they desired to see, in the composition, emblematically and characteristically represented.

Such was naturally the moral of Mrs. Mallow's question: if their wealth was to be assumed, it was clear, from the nature of their admiration, as well as from mysterious hints thrown out (they were a little odd!) as to other possibilities of the same mortuary sort, that their further patronage might be; and not less evident that should the Master become at all known in those climes nothing would be more inevitable than a run of Canadian custom. Peter had been present before at runs of custom, colonial and domestic—present at each of those of which the aggregation had left so few gaps in the marble company round him; but it was his habit never at these junctures to prick the bubble in advance. The fond illusion, while it lasted, eased the wound of elections never won, the long ache of medals and diplomas carried off, on every chance, by every one but the Master; it moreover lighted the lamp that would glimmer through the next eclipse. They lived, however, after all—as it was always beautiful to see—at a height scarce susceptible of ups and downs. They strained a point at times charmingly, strained it to admit that the public was here and there not too bad to buy; but they would have been nowhere without their attitude that the Master was always too good to sell. They were at all events deliciously formed, Peter often said to himself, for their fate; the Master had a vanity, his wife had a loyalty, of which success, depriving these things of innocence, would have diminished the merit and the grace. Any one could be charming under a charm, and as he looked about him at a world of prosperity more void of proportion even than the Master's museum he wondered if he knew another pair that so completely escaped vulgarity.

"What a pity Lance isn't with us to rejoice!" Mrs. Mallow on this occasion sighed at supper.

"We'll drink to the health of the absent," her husband replied, filling his friend's glass and his own and giving a drop to their companion; "but we must hope he's preparing himself for a happiness much less like this of ours this evening—excusable as I grant it to be!—than like the comfort we have always (whatever has happened or has not happened) been able to trust ourselves to enjoy. The comfort," the Master explained, leaning back in the pleasant lamplight and firelight, holding up his glass and looking round at his marble family, quartered more or less, a monstrous brood, in every room—"the comfort of art in itself!"

Peter looked a little shyly at his wine. "Well—I don't care what you may call it when a fellow doesn't—but Lance must learn to *sell*, you know. I drink to his acquisition of the secret of a base popularity!"

"Oh, yes, *he* must sell," the boy's mother, who was still more, however, this seemed to give out, the Master's wife, rather artlessly allowed.

"Ah," the sculptor after a moment confidently pronounced, "Lance *will*. Don't be afraid. He'll have learnt."

"Which is exactly what Peter," Mrs. Mallow gaily returned—"why in the world were you so perverse, Peter?—wouldn't when he told him hear of."

Peter, when this lady looked at him with accusatory affection—a grace on her part not infrequent—could never find a word; but the Master, who was always all amenity and tact, helped him out now as he had often helped him before. "That's his old idea, you know—on which we've so often differed: his theory that the artist should be all impulse and instinct. *I* go in of course for a certain amount of school. Not too much—but a due proportion. There's where his protest came in," he continued to explain to his wife, "as against what *might*, don't you see? be in question for Lance."

"Ah well"—and Mrs. Mallow turned the violet eyes across the table at the subject of this discourse—"he's sure to have meant of course nothing but good. Only that wouldn't have prevented him, if Lance *had* taken his advice, from being in effect horribly cruel."

They had a sociable way of talking of him to his face as if he had been in the clay or—at most—in the plaster, and the Master was unfailingly generous. He might have been waving Egidio to make him revolve. "Ah but poor Peter wasn't so wrong as to what it may after all come to that he *will* learn."

"Oh but nothing artistically bad," she urged—still, for poor Peter, arch and dewy.

"Why just the little French tricks," said the Master: on which their friend had to pretend to admit, when pressed by Mrs. Mallow, that these aesthetic vices had been the objects of his dread.

III

"I know now," Lance said to him the next year, "why you were so much against it." He had come back supposedly for a mere interval and was looking about him at Carrara Lodge, where indeed he had already on two or three occasions since his expatriation briefly reappeared. This had the air of a longer holiday. "Something rather awful has happened to me. It *isn't* so very good to know."

"I'm bound to say high spirits don't show in your face," Peter was rather ruefully forced to confess. "Still, are you very sure you do know?"

"Well, I at least know about as much as I can bear." These remarks were exchanged in Peter's den, and the young man, smoking cigarettes, stood before the fire with his back against the mantel. Something of his bloom seemed really to have left him.

Poor Peter wondered. "You're clear then as to what in particular I wanted you not to go for?"

"In particular?" Lance thought. "It seems to me that in particular there can have been only one thing."

They stood for a little sounding each other. "Are you quite sure?"

"Quite sure I'm a beastly duffer? Quite—by this time."

"Oh!"—and Peter turned away as if almost with relief.

"It's *that* that isn't pleasant to find out."

"Oh I don't care for 'that,' " said Peter, presently coming round again. "I mean I personally don't."

"Yet I hope you can understand a little that I myself should!"

"Well, what do you mean by it?" Peter sceptically asked.

And on this Lance had to explain—how the upshot of his studies in Paris had inexorably proved a mere deep doubt of his means. These studies had so waked him up that a new light was in his eyes; but what the new light did was really to show him too much. "Do you know what's the matter with me? I'm too horribly intelligent. Paris was really the last place for me. I've learnt what I can't do."

Poor Peter stared—it was a staggerer; but even after they had had, on the subject, a longish talk in which the boy brought out to the full the hard truth of his lesson, his friend betrayed less pleasure than usually breaks into a face to the happy tune of "I told you so!" Poor Peter himself made now indeed so little a point of having told him so that Lance broke ground in a different place a day or two after. "What was it then that—before I went—you were afraid I should find out?" This, however, Peter refused to tell him—on the ground that if he hadn't yet guessed perhaps he never would, and that in any case nothing at all for either of them was to be gained by giving the thing a name. Lance eyed him on this an instant with the bold curiosity of youth—with the air indeed of having in his mind two or three names, of which one or other would be right. Peter nevertheless, turning his back again, offered no encouragement, and when they parted afresh it was with some show of impatience on the side of the boy. Accordingly on their next encounter Peter saw at a glance that he had now, in the interval, divined and that, to sound his note, he was only waiting till they should find themselves alone. This he had soon arranged and he then broke straight out. "Do you know your conundrum has been keeping me awake? But in the watches of the night the answer came over me—so that, upon my honour, I quite laughed out. Had you been supposing I had to go to Paris to learn *that?*" Even now, to see him still so sublimely on his guard, Peter's young friend had to laugh afresh. "You won't give a sign till you're sure? Beautiful old Peter!" But Lance at last produced it. "Why, hang it, the truth about the Master."

It made between them for some minutes a lively passage, full of wonder for each at the wonder of the other. "Then how long have you understood—"

"The true value of his work? I understood it," Lance recalled, "as soon as I began to understand anything. But I didn't begin fully to do that, I admit, till I got *là-bas.*"

"Dear, dear!"—Peter gasped with retrospective dread.

"But for what have you taken me? I'm a hopeless muff—that I *had* to have rubbed in. But I'm not such a muff as the Master!" Lance declared.

"Then why did you never tell me—?"

"That I hadn't, after all"—the boy took him up—"remained such an idiot? Just because I never dreamed *you* knew. But I beg your pardon. I only wanted to spare you. And what I don't now understand is how the deuce then for so long you've managed to keep bottled."

Peter produced his explanation, but only after some delay and with a gravity not void of embarrassment. "It was for your mother."

"Oh!" said Lance.

"And that's the great thing now—since the murder *is* out. I want a promise from you. I mean"—and Peter almost feverishly followed it up—"a vow from you, solemn and such as you owe me here on the spot, that you'll sacrifice anything rather than let her ever guess—"

"That *I've* guessed?"—Lance took it in. "I see." He evidently after a moment had taken in much. "But what is it you've in mind that I may have a chance to sacrifice?"

"Oh one has always something."

Lance looked at him hard. "Do you mean that *you've* had—?" The look he received back, however, so put the question by that he found soon enough another. "Are you really sure my mother doesn't know?"

Peter, after renewed reflexion, was really sure. "If she does she's too wonderful."

"But aren't we all too wonderful?"

"Yes," Peter granted—"but in different ways. The thing's so desperately important because your father's little public consists only, as you know then," Peter developed—"well, of how many?"

"First of all," the Master's son risked, "of himself. And last of all too. I don't quite see of whom else."

Peter had an approach to impatience. "Of your mother, I say—*always.*"

Lance cast it all up. "You absolutely feel that?"

"Absolutely."

"Well then with yourself that makes three."

"Oh *me!*"—and Peter, with a wag of his kind old head, modestly excused himself. "The number's at any rate small enough for any individual dropping out to be too dreadfully missed. Therefore, to put it in a nutshell, take care, my boy—that's all—that *you're* not!"

"I've got to keep on humbugging?" Lance wailed.

"It's just to warn you of the danger of your failing of that that I've seized this opportunity."

"And what do you regard in particular," the young man asked, "as the danger?"

"Why this certainty: that the moment your mother, who feels so strongly, should suspect your secret—well," said Peter desperately, "the fat would be on the fire."

Lance for a moment seemed to stare at the blaze. "She'd throw me over?"

"She'd throw *him* over."

"And come round to us?"

Peter, before he answered, turned away. "Come round to *you.*" But he had said enough to indicate—and, as he evidently trusted, to avert—the horrid contingency.

IV

Within six months again, none the less, his fear was on more occasions than one all before him. Lance had returned to Paris for another trial; then had reappeared at home and had had, with his father, for the first time in his life, one of the scenes that strike sparks. He described it with much expression to Peter, touching whom (since they had never done so before) it was the sign of a new reserve on the part of the pair at Carrara Lodge that they at present failed, on a matter of intimate interest, to open themselves—if not in joy then in sorrow—to their good friend. This produced perhaps practically between the parties a shade of alienation and a slight intermission of commerce—marked mainly indeed by the fact that to talk at his ease with his old playmate Lance had in general to come to see him. The closest if not quite the gayest relation they had yet known together was thus ushered in. The difficulty for poor Lance was a tension at home—begotten by the fact that his father wished him to be at least the sort of success he himself had been. He hadn't "chucked" Paris—though nothing appeared more vivid to him than that Paris had chucked him: he would go back again because of the fascination in trying, in seeing, in sounding the depths—in learning one's lesson, briefly, even if the lesson were simply that of one's impotence in the presence of one's larger vision. But what did the Master, all aloft in his senseless fluency, know of impotence, and what vision—to be called such—had he in all his blind life ever had? Lance, heated and indignant, frankly appealed to his godparent on this score.

His father, it appeared, had come down on him for having, after so long, nothing to show, and hoped that on his next return this deficiency would be repaired. *The* thing, the Master complacently set forth was—for any artist, however inferior to himself—at least to "do" something. "What can you do? That's all I ask!" *He* had certainly done enough, and there was no mistake about what he had to show. Lance had tears in his eyes when it came thus to letting his old friend know how great the strain might be on the "sacrifice" asked of him. It wasn't so easy to continue humbugging—as from son to parent—after feeling one's self despised for not grovelling in mediocrity. Yet a noble duplicity was what, as they intimately faced the situation, Peter went on requiring; and it was still for a time what his young friend, bitter and sore, managed loyally to comfort him with. Fifty pounds more than once again, it was true, rewarded both in London and in Paris the young friend's loyalty; none the less sensibly, doubtless, at the moment, that the money was a direct advance on a decent sum for which Peter had long since privately prearranged an ultimate function. Whether by these arts or others, at all events, Lance's just resentment was kept for a season—but only for a season—at bay. The day arrived when he warned his companion that he could hold out—or hold in—no longer. Carrara Lodge had had to listen to another lecture delivered from a great height—an infliction really heavier at last than, without striking back or in some way letting the Master have the truth, flesh and blood could bear.

"And what I don't see is," Lance observed with a certain irritated eye for what was after all, if it came to that, owing to himself too; "what I don't see is, upon my honour, how *you*, as things are going, can keep the game up."

"Oh the game for me is only to hold my tongue," said placid Peter. "And I have my reason."

"Still my mother?"

Peter showed a queer face as he had often shown it before—that is by turning it straight away. "What will you have? I haven't ceased to like her."

"She's beautiful—she's a dear of course," Lance allowed; "but what is she to you, after all, and what is it to you that, as to anything whatever, she should or she shouldn't?"

Peter, who had turned red, hung fire a little. "Well—it's all simply what I make of it."

There was now, however, in his young friend a strange, an adopted insistence. "What are you after all to *her?*"

"Oh nothing. But that's another matter."

"She cares only for my father," said Lance the Parisian.

"Naturally—and that's just why."

"Why you've wished to spare her?"

"Because she cares so tremendously much."

Lance took a turn about the room, but with his eyes still on his host. "How awfully—always—you must have liked her!"

"Awfully. Always," said Peter Brench.

The young man continued for a moment to muse—then stopped again in front of him. "Do you know how much she cares?" Their eyes met on it, but Peter, as if his own found something new in Lance's, appeared to hesitate, for the first time in an age, to say he did know. "*I've* only just found out," said Lance. "She came to my room last night, after being present, in silence and only with her eyes on me, at what I had had to take from him; she came—and she was with me an extraordinary hour."

He had paused again and they had again for a while sounded each other. Then something—and it made him suddenly turn pale—came to Peter. "She *does* know?"

"She does know. She let it all out to me—so as to demand of me no more than 'that,' as she said, of which she herself had been capable. She has always, always known," said Lance without pity.

Peter was silent a long time; during which his companion might have heard him gently breathe, and on touching him might have felt within him the vibration of a long low sound suppressed. By the time he spoke at last he had taken everything in. "Then I do see how tremendously much."

"Isn't it wonderful?" Lance asked.

"Wonderful," Peter mused.

"So that if your original effort to keep me from Paris was to keep me from knowledge—!" Lance exclaimed as if with a sufficient indication of this futility.

It might have been at the futility. Peter appeared for a little to gaze. "I think it must have been—without my quite at the time knowing it—to keep *me!*" he replied at last as he turned away.

QUESTIONS

1. How does Peter Brench's search compare and contrast with the detective's search?

2. Discuss the use of symbolism in the story, particularly in the names of the characters and in the title.

3. How does James *mislead* you through the story? What clues does he provide?

4. Do you think most "truth" about one's own life situation is really subconsciously known?

5. Why does such an actual *short* story seem so long? How does James' style compare with the style of other writers, both in this section and in *The Detective* section?

Death and the Compass

Jorges Luis Borges

Of the many problems which exercised the daring perspicacity of Lönnrot none was so strange—so harshly strange, we may say—as the staggered series of bloody acts which culminated at the villa of Triste-le-Roy, amid the boundless odor of the eucalypti. It is true that Erik Lönnrot did not succeed in preventing the last crime, but it is indisputable that he foresaw it. Nor did he, of course, guess the identity of Yarmolinsky's unfortunate assassin, but he did divine the secret morphology of the vicious series as well as the participation of Red Scharlach, whose alias is Scharlach the Dandy. This criminal (as so many others) had sworn on his honor to kill Lönnrot, but the latter had never allowed himself to be intimidated. Lönnrot thought of himself as a pure thinker, an Auguste Dupin, but there was something of the adventurer in him, and even of the gamester.

The first crime occurred at the Hôtel du Nord—that high prism that dominates the estuary whose waters are the colors of the desert. To this tower (which most manifestly unites the hateful whiteness of a sanitorium, the numbered divisibility of a prison, and the general appearance of a bawdy house) on the third day of December came the delegate from Podolsk to the Third Talmudic Congress, Doctor Marcel Yarmolinsky, a man of gray beard and gray eyes. We shall never know whether the Hôtel du Nord pleased him: he accepted it with the ancient resignation which had allowed him to endure three years of war in the Carpathians and three thousand years of oppression and pogroms. He was given a sleeping room on floor R, in front of the suite which the Tetrarch of Galilee occupied not without some splendor. Yarmolinsky supped, postponed until the following day an investigation of the unknown city, arranged upon a cupboard his many books and his few possessions, and before midnight turned off the light. (Thus declared the Tetrarch's chauffeur, who slept in an adjoining room.) On the fourth, at 11:03 A.M., there was a telephone call for him from the editor of the *Yiddische Zeitung*; Doctor Yarmolinsky did not reply; he was found in his room, his face already a little dark, and his body, almost nude, beneath a large anachronistic cape. He was lying not far from the door which gave onto the corridor; a deep stab wound had split open his breast. In the same room, a couple of hours later, in the midst of journalists, photographers, and police, Commissioner Treviranus and Lönnrot were discussing the problem with equanimity.

"There's no need to look for a Chimera, or a cat with three legs," Treviranus was saying as he brandished an imperious cigar. "We all know that the Tetrarch of Galilee is the possessor of the finest sapphires in the world. Someone, intending to steal them, came in here by mistake. Yarmolinsky got up; the robber had to kill him. What do you think?"

"It's possible, but not interesting," Lönnrot answered. "You will reply that reality hasn't the slightest need to be of interest. And I'll answer you that reality may avoid the obligation to be interesting, but that hypotheses may not. In the hypothesis you have postulated, chance intervenes largely. Here lies a dead rabbi; I should prefer a purely rabbinical explanation; not the imaginary mischances of an imaginary robber."

Treviranus answered ill-humoredly:

"I am not interested in rabbinical explanations; I am interested in the capture of the man who stabbed this unknown person."

"Not so unknown," corrected Lönnrot. "Here are his complete works." He indicated a line of tall volumes: A *Vindication of the Cabala*; *An Examination of the Philosophy of Robert Fludd*) a literal translation of the *Sepher Yezirah*; a *Biography of the Baal Shem*; a *History of the Sect of the Hasidim*; a monograph (in German) on the Tetragrammaton; another, on the divine nomenclature of the Pentateuch. The Commissioner gazed at them with suspicion, almost with revulsion. Then he fell to laughing.

"I'm only a poor Christian," he replied. "Carry off all these moth-eaten classics if you like; I haven't got time to lose in Jewish superstitions."

"Maybe this crime belongs to the history of Jewish superstitions," murmured Lönnrot.

"Like Christianity," the editor of the *Yiddische Zeitung* dared to put in. He was a myope, an atheist, and very timid.

No one answered him. One of the agents had found inserted in the small typewriter a piece of paper on which was written the following inconclusive sentence.

The first letter of the Name has been spoken

Lönnrot abstained from smiling. Suddenly become a bibliophile—or Hebraist—he directed that the dead man's books be made into a parcel, and he carried them to his office. Indifferent to the police investigation, he dedicated himself to studying them. A large octavo volume revealed to him the teachings of Israel Baal Shem-Tob, founder of the sect of the Pious; another volume, the virtues and terrors of the Tetragrammaton, which is the ineffable name of God; another, the thesis that God has a secret name, in which is epitomized (as in the crystal sphere which the Persians attribute to Alexander of Macedon) his ninth attribute, eternity—that is to say, the immediate knowledge of everything that will exist, exists, and has existed in the universe. Tradition numbers ninety-nine names of God; the Hebraists attribute this imperfect number to the magical fear of even numbers; the Hasidim reason that this hiatus indicates a hundredth name—the Absolute Name.

From this erudition he was distracted, within a few days, by the appearance of the editor of the *Yiddische Zeitung*. This man wished to talk of the assassination; Lönnrot preferred to speak of the diverse names of God. The journalist declared, in three columns, that the investigator Erik Lönnrot had dedicated himself to studying the names of God in order to "come up with" the name of the assassin. Lönnrot, habituated to the simplifications of journalism, did not become indignant. One of those shopkeepers who have found that there are buyers for every book came out with a popular edition of the *History of the Sect of the Hasidim*.

The second crime occurred on the night of the third of January, in the most deserted and empty corner of the capital's western suburbs. Toward dawn, one of the gendarmes who patrol these lonely places on horseback detected a man in a cape, lying prone in the shadow of an ancient paint shop. The hard visage seemed bathed in blood; a deep stab wound had split open his breast. On the wall, upon the yellow and red rhombs, there were some words written in chalk. The gendarme spelled them out. . . .

That afternoon Treviranus and Lönnrot made their way toward the remote scene of the crime. To the left and right of the automobile, the city disintegrated; the firmament grew larger and the houses meant less and less and a brick kiln or a poplar grove more and more. They reached their miserable destination: a final alley of rose-colored mud walls which in some way seemed to reflect the disordered setting of the sun. The dead man had already been identified. He was Daniel Simon Azevedo, a man of some fame in the ancient northern suburbs, who had risen from wagoner to political tough, only to degenerate later into a thief and even an informer. (The singular style of his death struck them as appropriate: Azevedo was the last representative of a generation of bandits who knew how to handle a dagger, but not a revolver.) The words in chalk were the following:

The second letter of the Name has been spoken

The third crime occurred on the night of the third of February. A little before one o'clock, the telephone rang in the office of Commissioner Treviranus. In avid secretiveness a man with a guttural voice spoke: he said his name was Ginzberg (or Ginsburg) and that he was disposed to communicate, for a reasonable remuneration, an explanation of the two sacrifices of Azevedo and Yarmolinsky. The discordant sound of whistles and horns drowned out the voice of the informer. Then the connection was cut off. Without rejecting the possibility of a hoax (it was carnival time), Treviranus checked and found he had been called from Liverpool House, a tavern on the Rue de Toulon—that dirty street where cheek by jowl are the peepshow and the milk store, the bordello and the women selling Bibles. Treviranus called back and spoke to the owner. This personage (Black Finnegan by name, an old Irish criminal who was crushed, annihilated almost, by respectability) told him that the last person to use the establishment's phone had been a lodger, a certain Gryphius, who had just gone out with some friends. Treviranus immediately went to Liverpool House, where Finnegan related the following facts. Eight days previously, Gryphius had taken a room above the saloon. He was a man of sharp features, a nebulous gray beard, shabbily clothed in black; Finnegan (who put the room to a use which Treviranus guessed) demanded a rent which was undoubtedly excessive; Gryphius immediately paid the stipulated sum. He scarcely ever went out; he dined and lunched in his room; his face was hardly known in the bar. On this particular night, he came down to telephone from Finnegan's office. A closed coupe stopped in front of the tavern. The driver did not move from his seat; several of the patrons recalled that he was wearing a bear mask. Two harlequins descended from the coupe; they were short in stature, and no one could fail to observe that they were very drunk. With a tooting of horns they burst into Finnegan's office; they embraced Gryphius, who seemed to recognize them but who replied to them coldly; they exchanged a few words in Yiddish—he, in a low guttural voice; they, in shrill, falsetto tones—and then the party climbed to the upstairs room. Within a quarter hour the three descended, very joyous; Gryphius, staggering, seemed as drunk as the others. He walked—tall, dazed—in the middle, between the masked harlequins. (One of the women in the bar remembered the yellow, red and green rhombs, the diamond designs.) Twice he stumbled; twice he was held up by the harlequins. Alongside the adjoining dock basin, whose water was rectangular, the trio got into the coupe and disappeared. From the running board, the last of the harlequins had scrawled an obscene figure and a sentence on one of the slates of the outdoor shed.

Treviranus gazed upon the sentence. It was nearly foreknowable. It read:

The last of the letters of the Name has been spoken

He examined, then, the small room of Gryphius-Ginzberg. On the floor was a violent star of blood; in the corners, the remains of some Hungarian-brand cigarettes; in a cabinet, a book in Latin—the *Philologus Hebraeo-Graecus* (1739) of Leusden—along with various manuscript notes. Treviranus studied the book with indignation and had Lönnrot summoned. The latter, without taking off his hat, began to read while the Commissioner questioned the contradictory witnesses to the possible kidnapping. At four in the morning they came out. In the tortuous Rue de Toulon, as they stepped on the dead serpentines of the dawn, Treviranus said:

"And supposing the story of this night were a sham?"

Erik Lönnrot smiled and read him with due gravity a passage (underlined) of the thirty-third dissertation of the *Philologus*:

> *Dies Judaeorum incipit a solis occasu*
> *usque ad solis occasum diei sequentis.*

"This means," he added, "that *the Hebrew day begins at sundown and lasts until the following sundown.*"

Treviranus attempted an irony.

"Is this fact the most worthwhile you've picked up tonight?"

"No. Of even greater value is a word Ginzberg used."

The afternoon dailies did not neglect this series of disappearances. *The Cross and the Sword* contrasted them with the admirable discipline and order of the last Eremitical Congress; Ernest Palast, writing in *The Martyr*, spoke out against "the intolerable delays in this clandestine and frugal pogrom, which has taken three months to liquidate three Jews"; the *Yiddische Zeitung* rejected the terrible hypothesis of an anti-Semitic plot, "even though many discerning intellects do not admit of any other solution to the triple mystery"; the most illustrious gunman in the South, Dandy Red Scharlach, swore that in his district such crimes as these would never occur, and he accused Commissioner Franz Treviranus of criminal negligence.

On the night of March first, the Commissioner received an imposing-looking, sealed envelope. He opened it: the envelope contained a letter signed Baruj Spinoza, and a detailed plan of the city, obviously torn from a Baedeker. The letter prophesied that on the third of March there would *not* be a fourth crime, inasmuch as the paint shop in the West, the Tavern on the Rue de Toulon and the Hôtel du Nord were the "perfect vertices of an equilateral and mystic triangle"; the regularity of this triangle was made clear on the map with red ink. This argument, *more geometrico*, Treviranus read with resignation, and sent the letter and map on to Lönnrot—who deserved such a piece of insanity.

Erik Lönnrot studied the documents. The three sites were in fact equidistant. Symmetry in time (the third of December, the third of

January, the third of February); symmetry in space as well. . . . Of a sudden he sensed he was about to decipher the mystery. A set of calipers and a compass completed his sudden intuition. He smiled, pronounced the word "Tetragrammaton" (of recent acquisition), and called the Commissioner on the telephone. He told him:

"Thank you for the equilateral triangle you sent me last night. It has enabled me to solve the problem. Tomorrow, Friday, the criminals will be in jail, we can rest assured."

"In that case, they're not planning a fourth crime?"

"Precisely because they *are* planning a fourth crime can we rest assured."

Lönnrot hung up. An hour later he was traveling in one of the trains of the Southern Railways, en route to the abandoned villa of Triste-le-Roy. South of the city of our story there flows a blind little river filled with muddy water made disgraceful by floating scraps and garbage. On the further side is a manufacturing suburb where, under the protection of a chief from Barcelona, gunmen flourish. Lönnrot smiled to himself to think that the most famous of them—Red Scharlach—would have given anything to know of this clandestine visit. Azevedo had been a comrade of Scharlach's; Lönnrot considered the remote possibility that the fourth victim might be Scharlach himself. Then, he put aside the thought. . . . He had virtually deciphered the problem; the mere circumstances, or the reality (names, prison records, faces, judicial and penal proceedings), scarcely interested him now. Most of all he wanted to take a stroll, to relax from three months of sedentary investigation. He reflected on how the explanation of the crimes lay in an anonymous triangle and a dust-laden Greek word. The mystery seemed to him almost crystalline now; he was mortified to have dedicated a hundred days to it.

The train stopped at a silent loading platform. Lönnrot descended. It was one of those deserted afternoons which seem like dawn. The air over the muddy plain was damp and cold. Lönnrot set off across the fields. He saw dogs, he saw a wagon on a dead road, he saw the horizon, he saw a silvery horse drinking the crapulous water of a puddle. Dusk was falling when he saw the rectangular belvedere of the villa of Triste-le-Roy, almost as tall as the black eucalypti which surrounded it. He thought of the fact that only one more dawn and one more nightfall (an ancient splendor in the east, and another in the west) separated him from the hour so much desired by the seekers of the Name.

A rust colored wrought-iron fence defined the irregular perimeter of the villa. The main gate was closed. Without much expectation of entering, Lönnrot made a complete circuit. In front of the insurmountable gate once again, he put his hand between the bars almost mechanically and chanced upon the bolt. The creaking of the iron surprised him. With laborious passivity the entire gate gave way. Lönnrot advanced among the eucalypti, stepping amidst confused generations of rigid, broken leaves. Close up, the house on the estate of Triste-le-Roy was seen to abound in superfluous symmetries and in maniacal repetitions: a glacial Diana in one lugubrious niche was complemented by another Diana in another niche; one balcony was repeated by another balcony; double steps of stairs opened into a double balustrade. A two-faced Hermes cast a monstrous shadow. Lönnrot circled the house as he had the estate. He examined everything; beneath the level of the terrace he noticed a narrow shutter door.

He pushed against it: some marble steps descended to a vault. Versed now in the architect's preferences, Lönnrot divined that there would be a set of stairs on the opposite wall. He found them, ascended, raised his hands, and pushed up a trap door.

The diffusion of light guided him to a window. He opened it: a round, yellow moon outlined two stopped-up fountains in the melancholy garden. Lönnrot explored the house. He traveled through antechambers and galleries to emerge upon duplicate patios; several times he emerged upon the same patio. He ascended dust-covered stairways and came out into circular antechambers; he was infinitely reflected in opposing mirrors; he grew weary of opening or half-opening windows which revealed the same desolate garden outside, from various heights and various angles; inside, the furniture was wrapped in yellow covers and the chandeliers bound up with cretonne. A bedroom detained him; in the bedroom, a single rose in a porcelain vase—at the first touch the ancient petals fell apart. On the second floor, on the top story, the house seemed to be infinite and growing. *The house is not this large*, he thought. *It is only made larger by the penumbra, the symmetry, the mirrors, the years, my ignorance, the solitude.*

Going up a spiral staircase he arrived at the observatory. The evening moon shone through the rhomboid diamonds of the windows, which were yellow, red and green. He was brought to a halt by a stunning and dizzying recollection.

Two men of short stature, ferocious and stocky, hurled themselves upon him and took his weapon. Another man, very tall, saluted him gravely, and said:

"You are very thoughtful. You've saved us a night and a day."

It was Red Scharlach. His men manacled Lönnrot's hands. Lönnrot at length found his voice.

"Are you looking for the Secret Name, Scharlach?"

Scharlach remained standing, indifferent. He had not participated in the short struggle; he scarcely stretched out his hand to receive Lönnrot's revolver. He spoke; in his voice Lönnrot detected a fatigued triumph, a hatred the size of the universe, a sadness no smaller than that hatred.

"No," answered Scharlach. "I am looking for something more ephemeral and slippery, I am looking for Erik Lönnrot. Three years ago, in a gambling house on the Rue de Toulon, you arrested my brother and had him sent to prison. In the exchange of shots that night my men got me away in a coupe, with a police bullet in my chest. Nine days and nine nights I lay dying in this desolate, symmetrical villa; I was racked with fever, and the odious double-faced Janus who gazes toward the twilights of dusk and dawn terrorized my dreams and my waking. I learned to abominate my body, I came to feel that two eyes, two hands, two lungs are as monstrous as two faces. An Irishman attempted to convert me to the faith of Jesus; he repeated to me that famous axiom of the *goyim*: All roads lead to Rome. At night, my delirium nurtured itself on this metaphor: I sensed that the world was a labyrinth, from which it was impossible to flee, for all paths, whether they seemed to lead north or south, actually led to Rome, which was also the quadrilateral jail where my brother was dying and the villa of Triste-le-Roy. During those nights I swore by the god who sees from two faces, and by all the gods of fever and of mirrors, to weave a labyrinth around the man who had imprisoned my brother. I have woven it, and it holds: the materials are a dead writer on heresies, a compass, an eighteenth-century sect, a Greek word, a dagger, the rhombs of a paint shop.

"The first objective in the sequence was given me by chance. I had made plans with some colleagues—among them, Daniel Azevedo—to take the Tetrarch's sapphires. Azevedo betrayed us; with the money we advanced him he got himself inebriated and started on the job a day early. In the vastness of the hotel he got lost; at two in the morning he blundered into Yarmolinsky's room. The latter, harassed by insomnia, had set himself to writing. He was editing some notes, apparently, or writing an article on the Name of God; he had just written the words *The first letter of the Name has been spoken.* Azevedo enjoined him to be quiet; Yarmolinsky reached out his hand for the bell which would arouse all the hotel's forces; Azevedo at once stabbed him in the chest. It was almost a reflex action: half a century of violence had taught him that it was easiest and surest to kill. . . . Ten days later, I learned through the *Yiddische Zeitung* that you were perusing the writings of Yarmolinsky for the key to his death. For my part I read the *History of the Sect of the Hasidim*; I learned that the reverent fear of pronouncing the Name of God had given rise to the doctrine that this Name is all-powerful and mystic. I learned that some Hasidim, in search of this secret Name, had gone as far as to offer human sacrifices. . . . I knew you would conjecture that the Hasidim had sacrificed the rabbi; I set myself to justifying this conjecture.

"Marcel Yarmolinsky died on the night of December third; for the second sacrifice I selected the night of January third. Yarmolinsky died in the North; for the second sacrifice a place in the West was preferable. Daniel Azevedo was the inevitable victim. He deserved death: he was an impulsive person, a traitor; his capture could destroy the entire plan. One of our men stabbed him; in order to link his corpse to the other one

I wrote on the paint shop diamonds *The second letter of the Name has been spoken.*

"The third 'crime' was produced on the third of February. It was as Treviranus must have guessed, a mere mockery, a simulacrum. I am Gryphius-Ginzberg-Ginsburg; I endured an interminable week (filled out with a tenuous false beard) in that perverse cubicle on the Rue de Toulon, until my friends spirited me away. From the running board one of them wrote on a pillar *The last of the letters of the Name has been spoken.* This sentence revealed that the series of crimes was *triple.* And the public thus understood it; nevertheless, I interspersed repeated signs that would allow you, Erik Lönnrot, the reasoner, to understand that it is *quadruple.* A portent in the North, others in the East and West, demand a fourth portent in the South; the Tetragrammaton—the name of God, JHVH—is made up of *four* letters; the harlequins and the paint shop sign suggested four points. In the manual of Leusden I underlined a certain passage: it manifested that the Hebrews calculate a day counting from dusk to dusk and that therefore the deaths occurred on the *fourth* day of each month. To Treviranus I sent the equilateral triangle. I sensed that you would supply the missing point. The point which would form a perfect rhomb, the point which fixes where death, exactly, awaits you. In order to attract you I have premeditated everything. Erik Lönnrot, so as to draw you to the solitude of Triste-le-Roy."

Lönnrot avoided Scharlach's eyes. He was looking at the trees and the sky divided into rhombs of turbid yellow, green and red. He felt a little cold, and felt, too, an impersonal, almost anonymous sadness. It was already night; from the dusty garden arose the useless cry of a bird. For the last time, Lönnrot considered the problem of symmetrical and periodic death.

"In your labyrinth there are three lines too many," he said at last. "I know of a Greek labyrinth which is a single straight line. Along this line so many philosophers have lost themselves that a mere detective might well do so too. Scharlach, when, in some other incarnation you hunt me, feign to commit (or do commit) a crime at A, then a second crime at B, eight kilometers from A, then a third crime at C, four kilometers from A and B, halfway enroute between the two. Wait for me later at D, two kilometers from A and C, halfway, once again, between both. Kill me at D, as you are now going to kill me at Triste-le-Roy."

"The next time I kill you," said Scharlach, "I promise you the labyrinth made of the single straight line which is invisible and everlasting."

He stepped back a few paces. Then, very carefully, he fired.

1942
—*Translated by* Anthony Kerrigan

QUESTIONS

1. Trace as much of the imagery and symbolism as you can, as it creates a pattern through the story. Note, especially, the use of the color red.

2. Does the difficulty of the story, and particularly its references, make you stop trying to "detect" before the detective? Does the story demand a second reading? Is a writer justified in employing elaborate symbolism and a multiplicity of meanings? What do you think of the writer who deliberately risks the loss of a popular audience?

3. Could this story in any way be called a parody of the traditional detective story? Is the use of details and clues similar to that in "The Stolen White Elephant"?

4. Much of the "plot" of the story follows a traditional pattern (crime, complication, solution, explanation). How do you account for the different *effect* of the plot, however?

5. Explain the meaning of the concluding speeches of Lönnrot and Scharlach.

They Do Not Always Remember

William Burroughs

It was in Monterrey Mexico . . . a square a fountain a café. I had stopped by the fountain to make an entry in my notebook: "dry fountain empty square silver paper in the wind frayed sounds of a distant city."

"What have you written there?" I looked up. A man was standing in front of me barring the way. He was corpulent but hard-looking with a scared red face and pale grey eyes. He held out his hand as if presenting a badge but the hand was empty. In the same movement he took the notebook out of my hands.

"You have no right to do that. What I write in a notebook is my business. Besides I don't believe you are a police officer."

Several yards away I saw a uniformed policeman thumbs hooked in his belt. "Let's see what he has to say about this."

We walked over to the policeman. The man who had stopped me spoke rapidly in Spanish and handed him the notebook. The policeman leafed through it. I was about to renew my protests but the policeman's manner was calm and reassuring. He handed the notebook back to me said something to the other man who went back and stood by the fountain.

"You have time for a coffee *señor?*" the policeman asked. "I will tell you a story. Years ago in this city there were two policemen who were friends and shared the same lodgings. One was Rodriguez. He was content to be a simple *agente* as you see me now. The other was Alfaro. He was brilliant, ambitious and rose rapidly in the force until he was second in command. He introduced new methods . . . tape recorders . . . speech prints. He even studied telepathy and took a drug once which he thought would enable him to detect the criminal mind. He did not hesitate to take action where more discreet officials preferred to look the other way . . . the opium fields . . . the management of public funds . . . bribery in the police force . . . the behavior of policemen off-duty. *Señor* he put through a rule that any police officer drunk and carrying a pistol would have his pistol permit canceled for one flat year and what is more he enforced the rule. Needless to say he made enemies. One night he received a phone call and left the apartment he still shared with

Rodriguez . . . he had never married and preferred to live simply you understand . . . just there by the fountain he was struck by a car . . . an accident? perhaps . . . for months he lay in a coma between life and death . . . he recovered finally . . . perhaps it would have been better if he had not." The policeman tapped his forehead "You see the brain was damaged . . . a small pension . . . he is a major of police and sometimes the old Alfaro is there. I recall an American tourist, cameras slung all over him like great tits, protesting, waving his passport. There he made a mistake. I looked at the passport and did not like what I saw. So I took him along to the *comisaría* where it came to light the passport was forged; the American tourist was a Dane wanted for passing worthless checks in twenty-three countries including Mexico. A female impersonator from East St. Louis turned out to be an atomic scientist wanted by the F.B.I. for selling secrets to the Chinese. Yes thanks to Alfaro I have made important arrests. More often I must tell to some tourist once again the story of Rodriguez and Alfaro." He took a toothpick out of his mouth and looked meditatively at the end of it, "Yes?"

"I think Rodriguez has his Alfaro and for every Alfaro there is always a Rodriguez. They do not always remember." He tapped his forehead. "You will pay the coffee."

I put a note down on the table. Rodriguez snatched it up. "This note is counterfeit *señor*. You are under arrest." "But I got it from American Express two hours ago!" "*Mentiras!* You think we Mexicans are so stupid? No doubt you have a suitcase full of this filth in your hotel room." Alfaro was standing by the table smiling. He showed a police badge. "I am the F.B.I. *señor* . . . the Federal Police of Mexico. Allow me." He took the note and held it up to the light smiling he handed it back to me. He said something to Rodriguez who walked out and stood by the fountain. I noticed for the first time that he was not carrying a pistol. Alfaro looked after him shaking his head sadly. "You have time for a coffee *señor*? I will tell you a story." "That's enough!" I pulled a card out of my wallet and snapped crisply, "I am District Supervisor Lee of the American Narcotics Department and I am arresting you and your accomplice Rodriguez for acting in concert to promote the sale of narcotics . . . caffeine among other drugs. . . ."

A hand touched my shoulder. I looked up. A grey-haired Irishman was standing there with calm authority, the face portentous and distant as if I were recovering consciousness after a blow on the head. They do not always remember. "Go over there by the fountain, Bill. I'll look into this." I could feel his eyes on my back see the sad head shake hear him order two coffees in excellent Spanish . . . dry fountain empty square silver paper in the wind frayed sounds of distant city . . . everything grey and fuzzy . . . my mind isn't working right . . . who are you over there telling the story of Harry and Bill? . . . The square clicked back into focus. My mind cleared. I walked toward the café with calm authority.

QUESTIONS

1. Both this story and the Borges story have been called "science fiction" by some critics. Why? How do SF and detective fiction compare, especially as the genres merge in stories like "Death and the Compass" and "They Do Not Always Remember"?

2. What crime has actually been committed?

3. Look up the definition of "paranoid." Is this story an example of paranoia?

4. Discuss the story in terms of the writer and his approach to observation and the rendering of his art. Note the only striking simile used in the story.

5. Does every person contain within himself a Rodriguez and Alfaro, a Puritan and a libertine?

6. Is caffeine a dangerous drug? Is some sort of folly implied in the control of drugs that are "dangerous"?

Views of My Father Weeping

Donald Barthelme

An aristocrat was riding down the street in his carriage. He ran over my father.

*　*　*

After the ceremony I walked back to the city. I was trying to think of the reason my father had died. Then I remembered: he was run over by a carriage.

*　*　*

I telephoned my mother and told her of my father's death. She said she supposed it was the best thing. I too supposed it was the best thing. His enjoyment was diminishing. I wondered if I should attempt to trace the aristocrat whose carriage had run him down. There were said to have been one or two witnesses.

*　*　*

Yes it is possible that it is not my father who sits there in the center of the bed weeping. It may be someone else, the mailman, the man who delivers the groceries, an insurance salesman or tax collector, who knows. However, I must say, it resembles my father. The resemblance is very strong. He is not smiling through his tears but frowning through them. I remember once we were out on the ranch shooting peccadillos (result of a meeting, on the plains of the West, of the collared peccary and the nine-banded armadillo). My father shot and missed. He wept. This weeping resembles that weeping.

*　*　*

"Did you see it?" "Yes but only part of it. Part of the time I had my back turned." The witness was a little girl, eleven or twelve. She lived in a very poor quarter and I could not imagine that, were she to testify, anyone would credit her. "Can you recall what the man in the carriage looked like?" "Like an aristocrat," she said.

*　*　*

The first witness declares that the man in the carriage looked "like an aristocrat." But that might be simply the carriage itself. Any man sitting in a handsome carriage with a driver on the box and perhaps one or two footmen up behind tends to look like an aristocrat. I wrote down her name and asked her to call me if she remembered anything else. I gave her some candy.

*   *   *

I stood in the square where my father was killed and asked people passing by if they had seen, or knew of anyone who had seen, the incident. At the same time I felt the effort was wasted. Even if I found the man whose carriage had done the job, what would I say to him? "You killed my father." "Yes," the aristocrat would say, "but he ran right in under the legs of the horses. My man tried to stop but it happened too quickly. There was nothing anyone could do." Then perhaps he would offer me a purse full of money.

*   *   *

The man sitting in the center of the bed looks very much like my father. He is weeping, tears coursing down his cheeks. One can see that he is upset about something. Looking at him I see that something is wrong. He is spewing like a fire hydrant with its lock knocked off. His yammer darts in and out of all the rooms. In a melting mood I lay my paw on my breast and say, "Father." This does not distract him from his plaint, which rises to a shriek, sinks to a pule. His range is great, his ambition commensurate. I say again, "Father," but he ignores me. I don't know whether it is time to flee or will not be time to flee until later. He may suddenly stop, assume a sternness. I have kept the door open and nothing between me and the door, and moreover the screen unlatched, and on top of that the motor running, in the Mustang. But perhaps it is not my father weeping there, but another father: Tom's father, Phil's father, Pat's father, Pete's father, Paul's father. Apply some sort of test, voiceprint reading or

*   *   *

My father throws his ball of knitting up in the air. The orange wool hangs there.

*   *   *

My father regards the tray of pink cupcakes. Then he jams his thumb into each cupcake, into the top. Cupcake by cupcake. A thick smile spreads over the face of each cupcake.

*   *   *

Then a man volunteered that he had heard two other men talking about the accident in a shop. "What shop?" The man pointed it out to me, a draper's shop on the south side of the square. I entered the shop and made inquiries. "It was your father, eh? He was bloody clumsy if you ask me." This was the clerk behind the counter. But another man standing nearby, well-dressed, even elegant, a gold watchchain stretched across his vest, disagreed. "It was the fault of the driver," the second man said. "He could have stopped them if he had cared to." "Nonsense," the clerk said, "not a chance in the world. If your father hadn't been drunk—" "He wasn't drunk," I said. "I arrived on the scene soon after it happened and I smelled no liquor."

✻   ✻   ✻

This was true. I had been notified by the police, who came to my room and fetched me to the scene of the accident. I bent over my father, whose chest was crushed, and laid my cheek against his. His cheek was cold. I smelled no liquor but blood from his mouth stained the collar of my coat. I asked the people standing there how it had happened. "Run down by a carriage," they said. "Did the driver stop?" "No, he whipped up the horses and went off down the street and then around the corner at the end of the street, toward King's New Square." "You have no idea as to whose carriage. . . ." "None." Then I made the arrangements for the burial. It was not until several days later that the idea of seeking the aristocrat in the carriage came to me.

✻   ✻   ✻

I had had in my life nothing to do with aristocrats, did not even know in what part of the city they lived, in their great houses. So that even if I located someone who had seen the incident and could identify the particular aristocrat involved, I would be faced with the further task of finding his house and gaining admittance (and even then, might he not be abroad?). "No, the driver was at fault," the man with the gold watchchain said. "Even if your father was drunk—and I can't say about that, one way or another, I have no opinion—even if your father was drunk, the driver could have done more to avoid the accident. He was dragged, you know. The carriage dragged him about forty feet." I had noticed that my father's clothes were torn in a peculiar way. "There was one thing," the clerk said, "don't tell anyone I told you, but I can give you one hint. The driver's livery was blue and green."

✻   ✻   ✻

It is someone's father. That much is clear. He is fatherly. The gray in the head. The puff in the face. The droop in the shoulders. The flab on the gut. Tears falling. Tears falling. Tears falling. Tears falling. More tears. It seems that he intends to go further along this salty path. The facts suggest that this is his program, weeping. He has something in mind, more weeping. O lud lud! But why remain? Why watch it? Why tarry? Why not fly? Why subject myself? I could be somewhere else, reading a book, watching the telly, stuffing a big ship into a little bottle, dancing the Pig. I could be out in the streets feeling up eleven-year-old girls in their soldier drag, there are thousands, as alike as pennies, and I could be— Why doesn't he stand up, arrange his clothes, dry his face? He's trying to embarrass us. He wants attention. He's trying to make himself interesting. He wants his brow wrapped in cold cloths perhaps, his hands held perhaps, his back rubbed, his neck kneaded, his wrists patted, his elbows anointed with rare oils, his toenails painted with tiny scenes representing God blessing America. I won't do it.

*   *   *

My father has a red bandana tied around his face covering the nose and mouth. He extends his right hand in which there is a water pistol. "Stick 'em up!" he says.

*   *   *

But blue and green livery is not unusual. A blue coat with green trousers, or the reverse, if I saw a coachman wearing such livery I would take no particular notice. It is true that most livery tends to be blue and buff, or blue and white, or blue and a sort of darker blue (for the trousers). But in these days one often finds a servant aping the more exquisite color combinations affected by his masters. I have even seen them in red trousers although red trousers used to be reserved, by unspoken agreement, for the aristocracy. So that the colors of the driver's livery were not of much consequence. Still it was something. I could now go about in the city, especially in stables and gin shops and such places, keeping a weather eye for the livery of the lackeys who gathered there. It was possible that more than one of the gentry dressed his servants in this blue and green livery, but on the other hand, unlikely that there were as many as half a dozen. So that in fact the draper's clerk had offered a very good clue indeed, had one the energy to pursue it vigorously.

*   *   *

There is my father, standing alongside an extremely large dog, a dog ten hands high at the very least. My father leaps on the dog's back, straddles him. My father kicks the large dog in the ribs with his heels. "Giddyap!"

*   *   *

My father has written on the white wall with his crayons.

*   *   *

I was stretched out on my bed when someone knocked at the door. It was the small girl to whom I had given candy when I had first begun searching for the aristocrat. She looked frightened, yet resolute; I could see that she had some information for me. "I know who it was," she said. "I know his name." "What is it?" "First you must give me five crowns." Luckily I had five crowns in my pocket; had she come later in the day, after I had eaten, I would have had nothing to give her. I handed over the money and she said, "Lars Bang." I looked at her in some surprise. "What sort of name is that for an aristocrat?" "His coachman," she said. "The coachman's name is Lars Bang." Then she fled.

*   *   *

When I heard this name, which in its sound and appearance is rude, vulgar, not unlike my own name, I was seized with repugnance, thought of dropping the whole business, although the piece of information she had brought had just cost me five crowns. When I was seeking him and he was yet nameless, the aristocrat and, by extension, his servants, seemed vulnerable: they had, after all, been responsible for a crime, or a sort of crime. My father was dead and they were responsible, or at least involved; and even though they were of the aristocracy or servants of the aristocracy, still common justice might be sought for; they might be required to make reparation, in some measure, for what they had done. Now, having the name of the coachman, and being thus much closer to his master than when I merely had the clue of the blue and green livery, I became afraid. For, after all, the unknown aristocrat must be a very powerful man, not at all accustomed to being called to account by people like me; indeed, his contempt for people like me was so great that, when one of us was so foolish as to stray into the path of his carriage, the aristocrat dashed him down, or permitted his coachman to do so, dragged him along the cobblestones for as much as forty feet, and then went gaily on his way, toward King's New Square. Such a man, I reasoned, was not very likely to take kindly to what I had to say to him. Very possibly there would be no purse of money at all, not a crown, not an öre; but rather he would, with an abrupt, impatient nod of his head, set his servants upon me. I would be beaten, perhaps killed. Like my father.

*   *   *

But if it is not my father sitting there in the bed weeping, why am I standing before the bed, in an attitude of supplication? Why do I desire with all my heart that this man, my father, cease what he is doing, which is so painful to me? Is it only that my position is a familiar one? That I remember, before, desiring with all my heart that this man, my father, cease what he is doing?

*   *   *

Why! . . . there's my father! . . . sitting in the bed there! . . . and he's *weeping!* . . . as though his heart would burst! . . . Father! . . . how is this? . . . who has wounded you? . . . name the man! . . . why I'll . . . I'll . . . here, Father, take this handkerchief! . . . and this handkerchief! . . . and this handkerchief! . . . I'll run for a towel . . . for a doctor . . . for a priest . . . for a good fairy . . . is there . . . can you . . . can I . . . a cup of hot tea? . . . bowl of steaming soup? . . . shot of Calvados? . . . a joint? . . . a red jacket? . . . a blue jacket? . . . Father, please! . . . look at me, Father . . . who has insulted you? . . . are you, then, compromised? . . . ruined? . . . a slander is going around? . . . an obloquy? . . . a traducement? . . . 'sdeath! . . . I won't permit it! . . . I won't abide it! . . . I'll . . . move every mountain . . . climb . . . every river . . . etc.

*   *   *

My father is playing with the salt and pepper shakers, and with the sugar bowl. He lifts the cover off the sugar bowl, and shakes pepper into it.

*   *   *

Or: My father thrusts his hand through a window of the doll's house.

His hand knocks over the doll's chair, knocks over the doll's chest of drawers, knocks over the doll's bed.

*   *   *

The next day, just before noon, Lars Bang himself came to my room. "I understand that you are looking for me." He was very much of a surprise. I had expected a rather burly, heavy man, of a piece with all of the other coachmen one saw sitting up on the box; Lars Bang was, instead, slight, almost feminine-looking, more the type of the secretary or valet than the coachman. He was not threatening at all, contrary to my fears; he was almost helpful, albeit with the slightest hint of malice in his helpfulness. I stammeringly explained that my father, a good man although subject to certain weaknesses, including a love of the bottle, had been run down by an aristocrat's coach, in the vicinity of King's New Square, not very many days previously; that I had information that the coach had dragged him some forty feet; and that I was eager to establish certain facts about the case. "Well then," Lars Bang said, with a helpful nod, "I'm your man, for it was my coach that was involved. A sorry business! Unfortunately I haven't the time right now to give you the full particulars, but if you will call round at the address written on this card, at six o'clock in the evening, I believe I will be able to satisfy you." So saying, he took himself off, leaving me with the card in my hand.

*   *   *

I spoke to Miranda, quickly sketching what had happened. She asked to see the white card; I gave it to her, for the address meant nothing to me. "Oh my," she said. "17 rue du Bac, that's over by the Vixen Gate—a very special quarter. Only aristocrats of the highest rank live there, and common people are not even allowed into the great park that lies between the houses and the river. If you are found wandering about there at night, you are apt to earn yourself a very severe beating." "But I have an appointment," I said. "An appointment with a coachman!" Miranda cried, "how foolish you are! Do you think the men of the watch will believe that, or even if they believe it (you have an honest enough face) will allow you to prowl that rich quarter, where so many thieves would dearly love to be set free for an hour or so, after dark? Go to!" Then she advised me that I must carry something with me, a pannier of beef or some dozen bottles of wine, so that if apprehended by the watch, I could say that I was delivering to such and such a house, and thus be judged an honest man on an honest errand, and escape a beating. I saw that she was right; and going out, I purchased at the wine merchant's a dozen bottles of a rather good claret (for it would never do to be delivering wine no aristocrat would drink); this cost me thirty crowns, which I had borrowed from Miranda. The bottles we wrapped round with straw, to prevent them banging into one another, and the whole we arranged in a sack, which I could carry on my back. I remember thinking,

how they rhymed, fitted together, *sack* and *back*. In this fashion I set off
across the city.

✻   ✻   ✻

There is my father's bed. In it, my father. Attitude of dejection.
Graceful as a mule deer once, the same large ears. For a nanosecond,
there is a nanosmile. Is he having me on? I remember once we went out
on the ups and downs of the West (out past Vulture's Roost) to shoot.
First we shot up a lot of old beer cans, then we shot up a lot of old
whiskey bottles, better because they shattered. Then we shot up some
mesquite bushes and some parts of a Ford pickup somebody'd left lying
around. But no animals came to our party (it was noisy, I admit it). A
long list of animals failed to arrive, no deer, quail, rabbit, seals, sea lions,
condylarths. It was pretty boring shooting up mesquite bushes, so we
hunkered down behind some rocks, Father and I, he hunkered down
behind his rocks and I hunkered down behind my rocks, and we
commenced to shooting at each other. That was interesting.

✻   ✻   ✻

My father is looking at himself in a mirror. He is wearing a large hat
(straw) on which there are a number of blue and yellow plastic jonquils.
He says: "How do I look?"

✻   ✻   ✻

Lars Bang took the sack from me and without asking permission
reached inside, withdrawing one of the straw-wrapped bottles of claret.
"Here's something!" he exclaimed, reading the label. "A gift for the
master, I don't doubt!" Then, regarding me steadily all the while, he
took up an awl and lifted the cork. There were two other men seated at
the pantry table, dressed in the blue-and-green livery, and with them a
dark-haired, beautiful girl, quite young, who said nothing and looked at
no one. Lars Bang obtained glasses, kicked a chair in my direction, and
poured drinks all round. "To your health!" he said (with what I thought
an ironical overtone) and we drank. "This young man," Lars Bang said,
nodding at me, "is here seeking our advice on a very complicated
business. A murder, I believe you said? "I said nothing of the kind. I seek
information about an accident." The claret was soon exhausted.
Without looking at me, Lars Bang opened a second bottle and set it in
the center of the table. The beautiful dark-haired girl ignored me along
with all the others. For my part, I felt I had conducted myself rather well
thus far. I had not protested when the wine was made free of (after all,
they would be accustomed to levying a sort of tax on anything entering
through the back door). But also I had not permitted his word "murder"
to be used, but instead specified the use of the word "accident."
Therefore I was, in general, comfortable sitting at the table drinking the
wine, for which I have no better head than had my father. "Well," said
Lars Bang, at length, "I will relate the circumstances of the accident, and

you may judge for yourself as to whether myself and my master, the Lensgreve Aklefeldt, were at fault." I absorbed this news with a slight shock. A count! I had selected a man of very high rank indeed to put my question to. In a moment my accumulated self-confidence drained away. A count! Mother of God, have mercy on me.

*   *   *

There is my father, peering through an open door into an empty house. He is accompanied by a dog (small dog; not the same dog as before). He looks into the empty room. He says: "Anybody home?"

*   *   *

There is my father, sitting in his bed, weeping.

*   *   *

"It was a Friday," Lars Bang began, as if he were telling a tavern story. "The hour was close upon noon and my master directed me to drive him to King's New Square, where he had some business. We were proceeding there at a modest easy pace, for he was in no great hurry. Judge of my astonishment when, passing through the drapers' quarter, we found ourselves set upon by an elderly man, thoroughly drunk, who flung himself at my lead pair and began cutting at their legs with a switch, in the most vicious manner imaginable. The poor dumb brutes reared, of course, in fright and fear, for," Lars Bang said piously, "they are accustomed to the best of care, and never a blow do they receive from me, or from the other coachman, Rik, for the count is especially severe upon this point, that his animals be well-treated. The horses, then, were rearing and plunging; it was all I could do to hold them; I shouted at the man, who fell back for an instant. The count stuck his head out of the window, to inquire as to the nature of the trouble; and I told him that a drunken man had attacked our horses. Your father, in his blindness, being not content with the mischief he had already worked, ran back in again, close to the animals, and began madly cutting at their legs with his stick. At this renewed attack the horses, frightened out of their wits, jerked the reins from my hands, and ran headlong over your father, who fell beneath their hooves. The heavy wheels of the carriage passed over him (I felt two quite distinct thumps), his body caught upon a projection under the boot, and he was dragged some forty feet, over the cobblestones. I was attempting, with all my might, merely to hang on to the box, for, having taken the bit between their teeth, the horses were in no mood to tarry; nor could any human agency have stopped them. We flew down the street . . ."

*   *   *

My father is attending a class in good behavior.

"Do the men rise when friends greet us while we are sitting in a booth?"

"The men do not rise when they are seated in a booth," he answers, "although they may half-rise and make apologies for not fully rising."

* * *

". . . the horses turning into the way that leads to King's New Square; and it was not until we reached that place that they stopped and allowed me to quiet them. I wanted to go back and see what had become of the madman, your father, who had attacked us; but my master, vastly angry and shaken up, forbade it. I have never seen him in so fearful a temper as that day; if your father had survived, and my master got his hands on him, it would have gone ill with your father, that's a certainty. And so, you are now in possession of all the facts. I trust you are satisfied, and will drink another bottle of this quite fair claret you have brought us, and be on your way." Before I had time to frame a reply, the dark-haired girl spoke. "Bang is an absolute bloody liar," she said.

* * *

Etc.

QUESTIONS

1. What do you think of the style of this story? Why does it conclude with the word "Etc."?

2. Who do the "aristocrats" symbolize?

3. Is this story humorous? Is it a satire? An absurd comedy? Discuss.

4. Discuss the element of sorrow in the story. What does the man feel most deeply about his father? Does the main character act absurdly in order to avoid becoming, himself, overly sentimental, or are his actions otherwise motivated?

5. Notice the time sense, particularly in relation to plot, used in this story and in the stories by Borges and Burroughs. Describe how the sense of time is altered in both stories.

6. Is the main character "in possession of all the facts"? What are "facts," anyway? Is Bang, indeed, "an absolute bloody liar"? Does it make any difference?

from The Far Side
of the Dollar

Ross Macdonald

CHAPTER 16

Their farm, green and golden in the slanting light, lay in a curve of the river. I drove down a dusty lane to the farmhouse. It was built of white brick, without ornament of any kind. The barn, unpainted, was weathered gray and in poor repair.

The late afternoon was windless. The trees surrounding the fenced yard were as still as watercolors. The heat was oppressive, in spite of the river nearby, even worse than it had been in Vegas.

It was a far cry from Vegas to here, and difficult to believe that Harley had come home, or ever would. But the possibility had to be checked out.

A black and white farm collie with just one eye barked at me through the yard fence when I stepped out of the car. I tried to calm him down by talking to him, but he was afraid of me and he wouldn't be calmed. Eventually an old woman wearing an apron came out of the house and silenced the dog with a word. She called to me:

"Mr. Harley's in the barn."

I let myself in through the wire gate. "May I talk to you?"

"That depends what the talk's about."

"Family matters."

"If that's another way to sell insurance, Mr. Harley doesn't believe in insurance."

"I'm not selling anything. Are you Mrs. Harley?"

"I am."

She was a gaunt woman of seventy, square-shouldered in a long-sleeved, striped shirtwaist. Her gray hair was drawn back severely from her face. I liked her face, in spite of the brokenness in and around the eyes. There was humor in it, and suffering half transformed into understanding.

"Who are you?" she said.

"A friend of your son Harold's. My name is Archer."

"Isn't that nice? We're going to sit down to supper as soon as Mr.

Harley finishes up the milking. Why don't you stay and have some supper with us?"

"You're very kind." But I didn't want to eat with them.

"How is Harold?" she said. "We don't hear from him so often since he married his wife, Lila."

Evidently she hadn't heard the trouble her sons were in. I hesitated to tell her, and she noticed my hesitation.

"Is something the matter with Harold?" she said sharply.

"The matter is with Mike. Have you seen him?"

Her large rough hands began to wipe themselves over and over on the front of her apron. "We haven't seen Mike in twenty years. We don't expect to see him again in this life."

"You may, though. He told a man he was coming home."

"This is not his home. It hasn't been since he was a boy. He turned his back on us then. He went off to Pocatello to live with a man named Brown, and that was his downfall."

"How so?"

"That daughter of Brown was a Jezebel. She ruined my son. She taught him all the filthy ways of the world."

Her voice had changed. It sounded as if the voice of somebody slightly crazy was ranting ventriloquially through her. I said with deliberate intent to stop it:

"Carol's been paid back for whatever she did to him. She was murdered in California on Monday."

Her hands stopped wiping themselves and flew up in front of her. She looked at their raw ugliness with her broken eyes.

"Did Mike do it to her?"

"We think so. We're not sure."

"And you're a policeman," she stated.

"More or less."

"Why do you come to us? We did our best, but we couldn't control him. He passed out of our control long ago." Her hands dropped to her sides.

"If he gets desperate enough, he may head this way."

"No, he never will. Mr. Harley said he would kill him if he ever set foot on our property again. That was twenty years ago, when he ran away from the Navy. Mr. Harley meant it, too. Mr. Harley never could abide a lawbreaker. It isn't true that Mr. Harley treated him cruelly. Mr. Harley was only trying to save him from the Devil."

The ranting, ventriloquial note had entered her voice again. Apparently she knew nothing about her son, and if she did she couldn't talk about him in realistic terms. It was beginning to look like a dry run.

I left her and went to the barn to find her husband. He was in the stable under the barn, sitting on a milking stool with his forehead against the black and white flank of a Holstein cow. His hands were busy at her teats, and her milk surged in the pail between his knees. Its sweet fresh smell penetrated the smell of dung that hung like corruption in the heated air.

"Mr. Harley?"

"I'm busy," he said morosely. "This is the last one, if you want to wait."

I backed away and looked at the other cows. There were ten or twelve of them, moving uneasily in their stanchions as I moved. Somewhere out of sight a horse blew and stamped.

"You're disturbing the livestock," Mr. Harley said. "Stand still if you want to stay."

I stood still for about five minutes. The one-eyed collie drifted into the stable and did a thorough job of smelling my shoes. But he still wouldn't let me touch him. When I reached down, he moved back.

Mr. Harley got up and emptied his pail into a ten-gallon can; the foaming milk almost overflowed. He was a tall old man wearing overalls and a straw hat which almost brushed the low rafters. His eyes were as flat and angry and his mouth as sternly righteous as in Harold's portrait of him. The dog retreated whining as he came near.

"You're not from around here. Are you on the road?"

"No." I told him who I was. "And I'll get to the point right away. Your son Mike's in very serious trouble."

"Mike is not my son," he intoned solemnly, "and I have no wish to hear about him or his trouble."

"But he may be coming here. He said he was. If he does, you'll have to inform the police."

"You don't have to instruct me in what I ought to do. I get my instructions from a higher power. He gives me my instructions direct in my heart." He thumped his chest with a gnarled fist.

"That must be convenient."

"Don't blaspheme or make mock, or you'll regret it. I can call down the punishment."

He reached for a pitchfork leaning against the wall. The dog ran out of the stable with his tail down. I became aware suddenly that my shirt was sticking to my back and I was intensely uncomfortable. The three tines of the pitchfork were sharp and gleaming, and they were pointed at my stomach.

"Get out of here," the old man said. "I've been fighting the Devil all my life, and I know one of his cohorts when I see one."

So do I, I said, but not out loud. I backed as far as the door, stumbled on the high threshold, and went out. Mrs. Harley was standing near my car, just inside the wire gate. Her hands were quiet on her meager breast.

"I'm sorry," she said to me. "I'm sorry for Carol Brown. She wasn't a bad little girl, but I hardened my heart against her."

"It doesn't matter now. She's dead."

"It matters in the sight of heaven."

She raised her eyes to the arching sky as if she imagined a literal heaven like a second story above it. Just now it was easier for me to imagine a literal hell, just over the horizon, where the sunset fires were burning.

"I've done so many wrong things," she said, "and closed my eyes to so many others. But don't you see, I had to make a choice."

"I don't understand you."

"A choice between Mr. Harley and my sons. I knew that he was a hard man. A cruel man, maybe not quite right in the head. But what could I do? I had to stick with my husband. And I wasn't strong enough to stand up to him. Nobody is. I had to stand by while he drove our sons out of our home. Harold was the soft one, he forgave us in the end. But Mike never did. He's like his father. I never even got to see my grandson."

Tears ran in the gullies of her face. Her husband came out of the barn carrying the ten-gallon can in his left hand and the pitchfork in his right.

"Go in the house, Martha. This man is a cohort of the Devil. I won't allow you to talk to him."

"Don't hurt him. Please."

"Go in the house," he repeated.

She went, with her gray head down and her feet dragging.

"As for you, cohort," he said, "you get off my farm or I'll call down the punishment on you."

He shook his pitchfork at the reddening sky. I was already in the car and turning up the windows.

I turned them down again as soon as I got a few hundred yards up the lane. My shirt was wet through now, and I could feel sweat running down my legs. Looking back, I caught a glimpse of the river, flowing sleek and solid in the failing light, and it refreshed me.

CHAPTER 17

Before driving out to the Harley farm, I had made an evening appointment with Robert Brown and his wife. They already knew what had happened to their daughter. I didn't have to tell them.

I found their house in the north end of the city, on a pleasant, tree-lined street parallel to Arthur Street. Night had fallen almost completely, and the street lights were shining under the clotted masses of the trees. It was still very warm. The earth itself seemed to exude heat like a hot-blooded animal.

Robert Brown had been watching for me. He hailed me from his front porch and came out to the curb. A big man with short gray hair, vigorous in his movements, he still seemed to be wading in some invisible substance, age or sorrow. We shook hands solemnly.

He spoke with more apparent gentleness than force: "I was planning to fly out to California tomorrow. It might have saved you a trip if you had known."

"I wanted to talk to the Harleys, anyway."

"I see." He cocked his head on one side in a birdlike movement which seemed odd in such a big man. "Did you get any sense out of them?"

"Mrs. Harley made a good deal of sense. Harley didn't."

"I'm not surprised. He's a pretty good farmer, they say, but he's been in and out of the mental hospital. I took—my wife and I took care of his son Mike during one of his bouts. We took him into our home." He sounded ashamed of the act.

"That was a generous thing to do."

"I'm afraid it was misguided generosity. But who can prophesy the future? Anyway, it's over now. All over." He forgot about me completely for a moment, then came to himself with a start. "Come in, Mr. Archer. My wife will want to talk to you."

He took me into the living room. It had group and family photos on the walls, and a claustrophobic wallpaper, which lent it some of the stuffiness of an old-fashioned country parlor. The room was sedately furnished with well-cared-for maple pieces. Across the mantel marched a phalanx of sports trophies gleaming gold and silver in the harsh overhead light.

Mrs. Brown was sitting in an armchair under the light. She was a strikingly handsome woman a few years younger than her husband, maybe fifty-five. She had chosen to disguise herself in a stiff and rather dowdy black dress. Her too precisely marcelled brown hair had specks of gray in it. Her fine eyes were confused, and surrounded by dark patches. When she gave me her hand, the gesture seemed less like a greeting than a bid for help.

She made me sit down on a footstool near her. "Tell us all about poor Carol, Mr. Archer."

All about Carol. I glanced around the safe, middle-class room, with the pictures of Carol's ancestors on the walls, and back at her parents' living faces. Where did Carol come in? I could see the source of her beauty in her mother's undisguisable good looks. But I couldn't see how one life led to the other, or why Carol's life had ended as it had.

Brown said: "We know she's dead, murdered, and that Mike probably did it, and that's about all." His face was like a Roman general's, a late Roman general's, after a long series of defeats by barbarian hordes.

"It's about all I know. Mike seems to have been using her as a decoy in an extortion attempt. You know about the Hillman boy?"

He nodded. "I read about it before I knew that my daughter—" His voice receded.

"They say he may be dead, too," his wife said.

"He may be, Mrs. Brown."

"And Mike did these things? I knew he was far gone, but I didn't know he was a monster."

"He's not a monster," Brown said wearily. "He's a sick man. His father was a sick man. He still is, after all the mental hospital could do for him."

"If Mike was so sick, why did you bring him into this house and expose your daughter to him?"

"She's your daughter, too."

"I know that. I'm not allowed to forget it. But I'm not the one that ruined her for life."

"You certainly had a hand in it. You were the one, for instance, who encouraged her to enter that beauty contest."

"She didn't win, did she?"

"That was the trouble."

"Was it? The trouble was the way you felt about that Harley boy."

"I wanted to help him. He needed help, and he had talent."

"Talent?"

"As an athlete. I thought I could develop him."

"You developed him all right."

They were talking across me, not really oblivious of me, using me as a fulcrum for leverage, or a kind of stand-in for reality. I guessed that the argument had been going on for twenty years.

"I wanted a son," Brown said.

"Well, you got a son. A fine upstanding son."

He looked as if he was about to strike her. He didn't, though. He turned to me:

"Forgive us. We shouldn't do this. It's embarrassing."

His wife stared at him in unforgiving silence. I tried to think of something that would break or at least soften the tension between them:

"I didn't come here to start a quarrel."

"You didn't start it, let me assure you." Brown snickered remorsefully. "It started the day Carol ran off with Mike. It was something I didn't foresee—"

His wife's bitter voice cut in: "It started when she was born, Rob. You wanted a son. You didn't want a daughter. You rejected her and you rejected me."

"I did nothing of the sort."

"He doesn't remember," she said to me. "He has one of these convenient memories that men have. You blot out anything that doesn't suit your upright idea of yourself. My husband is a very dishonest man." She had a peculiar angry gnawing smile.

"That's nonsense," he protested. "I've been faithful to you all my life."

"Except in ways I couldn't cope with. Like when you brought the Harley boy into our home. The great altruist. The noble counselor."

"You have no right to jeer at me," he said. "I wanted to help him. I had no way of knowing that he couldn't be reached."

"Go on. You wanted a son any way you could get one."

He said stubbornly: "You don't understand. A man gets natural pleasure from raising a boy, teaching him what he knows."

"All you succeeded in teaching Mike was your dishonesty."

He turned to me with a helpless gesture, his hands swinging out. "She blames me for everything." Walking rather aimlessly, he went out to the back part of the house.

I felt as if I'd been left alone with a far from toothless lioness. She stirred in her chair:

"I blame myself as well for being a fool. I married a man who has the feelings of a little boy. He still gets excited about his high-school football teams. The boys adore him. Everybody adores him. They talk about him as if he was some kind of a plaster saint. And he couldn't even keep his own daughter out of trouble."

"You and your husband should be pulling together."

"It's a little late to start, isn't it?"

Her glance came up to my face, probed at it for a moment, moved restlessly from side to side.

"It may be that you'll kill him if you go on like this."

"No. He'll live to be eighty, like his father."

She jerked her marcelled head toward one of the pictures on the wall. Seen from varying angles, her head was such a handsome object I could hardly take my eyes off it. It was hard to believe that such a finely shaped container could be full of cold boiling trouble.

I said, partly because I wanted to, and partly to appease her: "You must have been a very beautiful girl."

"Yes. I was."

She seemed to take no pleasure even from her vanity. I began to suspect that she didn't relate to men. It happened sometimes to girls who were too good-looking. They were treated as beautiful objects until they felt like that and nothing more.

"I could have married anybody," she said, "any man I went to college with. Some of them are bank presidents and big corporation executives now. But I had to fall in love with a football player."

"Your husband is a little more than that."

"Don't *sell* him to me," she said. "I know what he is, and I know what my life has been. I've been defrauded. I gave everything I had to marriage and motherhood, and what have I got to show for it? Do you know I never even saw my grandson?"

Mrs. Harley had said the same thing. I didn't mention the coincidence.

"What happened to your grandson?"

"Carol put him out for adoption, can you imagine? Actually I know why she did it. She didn't trust her husband not to harm the baby. That's the kind of a man she married."

"Did she tell you this?"

"More or less. Mike is a sadist, among other things. He used to swing cats by their tails. He lived in this house for over a year and all the time I was afraid of him. He was terribly strong, and I never was certain what he was going to do."

"Did he ever attack you?"

"No. He never dared to."

"How old was he when he left?"

"Let me see, Carol was fifteen at the time. That would make him seventeen or eighteen."

"And he left to join the Navy, is that correct?"

"He didn't go into the Navy right away. He left town with an older man, a policeman who used to be on the local force. I forgot his name. Anyway, this man lost his position on the force through bribery, and left town, taking Mike with him. He said he was going to make a boxer out of him. They went out to the west coast. I think Mike joined the Navy a few months later. Carol could—" She stopped in dismay.

"What about Carol?"

"I was going to say that Carol could tell you." The angry smile twisted and insulted her mouth. "I must be losing my mind."

"I doubt that, Mrs. Brown. It takes time to get used to these shocks and changes."

"More time than I have. More time than I'll ever have." She rose impatiently and went to the mantelpiece. One of the trophies standing on it was out of line with the others. She reached up and adjusted its position. "I wonder what Rob thinks he's doing in the kitchen."

She didn't go and find out what he was doing. She stood in an awkward position, one hip out, in front of the empty fireplace. Under her dowdy black dress, the slopes and masses of her body were angry. But nothing that she could do with her body, or her face, could change the essential beauty of the structure. She was trapped in it, as her daughter had been.

"I wish you'd go on with your story, Mrs. Brown."

"It hardly qualifies as a story."

"Whatever you want to call it, then. I'm very grateful for the chance to talk to you. It's the first decent chance I've had to get any information about the background of this case."

"The background hardly matters now, or the foreground either."

"It does, though. You may tell me something that will help me to find Harley. I take it you've seen him and Carol from time to time over the years."

"I saw *him* just once more—after that, I wouldn't give him house room—when he came home from the Navy in the winter of 1944–45. He claimed to be on leave. Actually he was absent without leave. He talked himself back into Rob's good graces. Rob had been terribly let down when he left town with that ex-policeman, the bribery artist. But my gullible husband fell for his line all over again. He even gave him money. Which Mike used to elope with my only daughter."

"Why did Carol go with him?"

She scratched at her forehead, leaving faint weals in the clear skin. "I asked her that, the last time she was home, just a couple of months ago. I asked her why she went and why she stuck with him. She didn't really know. Of course she wanted to get out of Pocatello. She hated Pocatello. She wanted to go out to the coast and break into the movies. I'm afraid my daughter had very childish dreams."

"Girls of fifteen do." With a pang, I thought of Stella. The pang became a vaguely formed idea in an unattended area of my mind. Generation after generation had to start from scratch and learn the world over again. It changed so rapidly that children couldn't learn from their parents or parents from their children. The generations were like alien tribes islanded in time.

"The fact is," I said, "Carol did make it into the movies."

"Really? She told me that once, but I didn't believe her."

"Was she a chronic liar?"

"No. Mike was the chronic liar. I simply didn't believe that she could succeed at anything. She never had."

The woman's bitterness was getting me down. She seemed to have an inexhaustible reservoir of the stuff. If she had been like this twenty years before, I could understand why Carol had left home at the first opportunity, and stayed away.

"You say you saw Carol just a couple of months ago."

"Yes. She rode the bus from Lake Tahoe in June. I hadn't seen her for quite a long time. She was looking pretty bedraggled. God knows what kind of a life he was leading her. She didn't talk much."

"It was a chancy life. Harley seems to have lost his job, and they were on their uppers."

"So she told me. There was the usual plea for money. I guess Rob gave her money. He always did. He tried to pretend afterwards, to me, that he gave her the car, too, but I know better. She took it. Apparently their old car had broken down, and they couldn't live at Tahoe without a car."

"How do you know she took it if your husband says she didn't?"

She showed signs of embarrassment. "It doesn't matter. They were welcome to the car." It was her first generous word. She half-spoiled it: "We needed a new one, anyway, and I'm sure she did it on the spur of the moment. Carol always was a very impulsive girl.

"The point is," she said, "she left without saying goodbye. She took the car to go downtown to the movies and simply never came back. She even left her suitcase in her room."

"Had there been trouble?"

"No more than the usual trouble. We did have an argument at supper."

"What about?"

"My grandson. She had no right to put him out for adoption. She said he was her baby to do with as she pleased. But she had no right. If she couldn't keep him, she should have brought him to us. We could have given him opportunities, an education." She breathed heavily and audibly. "She said an unforgivable thing to me that evening. She said, did I mean the kind of opportunities she had? And she walked out. I never saw her again. Neither did her father." Her head jerked forward in emphatic affirmation: "We *did* give her opportunities. It's not our fault if she didn't take advantage of them. It isn't fair to blame us."

"You blame each other," I said. "You're tearing each other to pieces."

"Don't give me that sort of talk. I've had enough of it from my husband."

"I'm merely calling your attention to an obvious fact. You need some kind of an intermediary, a third party, to help straighten out your thinking."

"And you're electing yourself, are you?"

"Far from it. You need an expert counselor."

"My husband *is* a counselor," she said. "What good has it done him? Anyway, I don't believe in seeking that kind of help. People should be able to handle their own problems."

She composed her face and sat down in the armchair again, with great calm, to show me how well she was handling hers.

"But what if they can't, Mrs. Brown?"

"Then they can't, that's all."

I made one more attempt. "Do you go to church?"

"Naturally I do."

"You could talk these problems over with your minister."

"What problems? I'm not aware of any outstanding problems." She was in despair so deep that she wouldn't even look up toward the light. I think she was afraid it would reveal her to herself.

I turned to other matters. "You mentioned a suitcase that your daughter left behind. Is it still here in the house?"

"It's up in her room. There isn't much in it. I almost threw it out with the trash, but there was always the chance that she would come back for it."

"May I see it?"

"I'll go and get it."

"If you don't mind, I'd sooner go up to her room."

"I don't mind."

We went upstairs together, with Mrs. Brown leading the way. She turned on the light in a rear bedroom and stood back to let me enter.

The room provided the first clear evidence that she had been hit very hard by Carol's running away. It was the bedroom of a high-school girl. The flouncy yellow cover on the French provincial bed matched the yellow flounces on the dressing table, where a pair of Kewpie-doll lamps smiled vacantly at each other. A floppy cloth dog with his red felt tongue hanging out watched me from the yellow lamb's wool rug. A little bookcase, painted white like the bed, was filled with high-school texts and hospital novels and juvenile mysteries. There were college pennants tacked around the walls.

"I kept her room as she left it," Mrs. Brown said behind me.

"Why?"

"I don't know. I guess I always thought that she'd come home in the end. Well, she did a few times. The suitcase is in the closet."

The closet smelled faintly of sachet. It was full of skirts and dresses, the kind girls wore in high school a half-generation before. I began to suspect that the room and its contents had less to do with Carol than with some secret fantasy of her mother's. Her mother said, as if in answer to my thought:

"I spend a lot of time here in this room. I feel very close to her here. We really were quite close at one time. She used to tell me everything, all about the boys she dated and so on. It was like living my own high school days over again."

"Is that good?"

"I don't know." Her lips gnawed at each other. "I guess not, because she suddenly turned against me. Suddenly she closed up completely. I didn't know what went on in her life, but I could see her changing, coarsening. She was such a pretty girl, such a pure-looking girl." Her mouth was wrenched far off center and it remained that way, as if the knowledge of her loss had fallen on her like a cerebral stroke.

The suitcase was an old scuffed cowhide one with Rob Brown's initials on it. I pulled it out into the middle of the floor and opened it. Suddenly I was back in Dack's Auto Court opening Carol's other suitcase. The same sour odor of regret rose from the contents of this one and seemed to permeate the room.

There was the same tangle of clothes, this time all of them women's, skirts and dresses and underthings and stockings, a few cosmetics, a paperback book on the divination of dreams. A hand-scrawled piece of paper was stuck in this as a bookmark. I pulled it out and looked at it. It was signed "Your Brother 'Har.'"

> Dear Mike,
>   I'm sorry you and Carole are haveing a "tough time" and I enclose a money order for fifty which I hope will help out you have to cash it at a

postoffice. I would send more but things are a little "tight" since I got married to Lila shes a good girl but does not believe that blood is thicker than water which it is. You asked me do I like bing married well in some ways I really like it in other ways I dont Lila has very strong ideas of her own. Shes no "sinsational" beauty like Carole is but we get long.

Im sorry you lost your job Mike unskilled jobs are hard to come by in these times I know you are a good bartender and that is a skill you should be able to pick up something in that line even if they are prejudiced like you say. I did look up Mr. Sipe like you asked me to but he is in no position to do anything for anybody hes on the skids himself the Barcelona went bankrupt last winter and now old Sipe is just watchman on the place but he sent his best regards for old time sake he wanted to know if you ever developed a left.

I saw another "freind" of yours last week I mean Captain Hillman I know you bear a grudge there but after all he treated you pretty good he could have sent you to prison for ten years. No Im not rakeing up old recrimations because Hillman could do something for you if he wanted you ought to see the raceing yacht he has thats how I saw him went down to Newport to take some sailing pictures. I bet he has twenty-five thousand in that yacht the guy is loaded. I found out he lives with his wife and boy in Pacific Point if you want to try him for a job hes head of some kind of "smogless industry."

Well thats about all for now if you deside to come out to "sunny Cal" you know where we live and dont worry Lila will make you welcome shes a good soul "at heart."

Sincerely Yours

Mrs. Brown had come out of her trance and moved toward me with a curious look. "What is that?"

"A letter to Mike from his brother Harold. May I have it?"

"You're welcome to it."

"Thank you. I believe it's evidence. It seems to have started Mike thinking about the possibility of bleeding the Hillmans for money." And it explained, I thought, why Harold had blamed himself for instigating the crime.

"May I read it?"

I handed it to her. She held it at arm's length, squinting.

"I'm afraid I need my glasses."

We went downstairs to the living room, where she put on horn-rimmed reading glasses and sat in her armchair with the letter. "Sipe," she said when she finished reading it. "That's the name I was trying to think of before." She raised her voice and called: "Robert! Come in here."

Rob Brown answered from the back of the house: "I was just coming."

He appeared in the doorway carrying a clinking pitcher and three glasses on a tray. He said with a placatory look at his wife: "I thought I'd make some fresh lemonade for the three of us. It's a warm night."

"That was thoughtful, Robert. Put it down on the coffee table. Now, what was the name of the ex-policeman that Mike left town with, the first time?"

"Sipe. Otto Sipe." He flushed slightly. "That man was a bad influence, I can tell you."

I wondered if he still was. The question seemed so urgent that I drove right back to the airport and caught the first plane out, to Salt Lake City. A late jet from Minneapolis rescued me from a night in the Salt Lake City airport and deposited me at Los Angeles International, not many miles from the Barcelona Hotel, where a man named Sipe was watchman.

QUESTIONS

1. Ross Macdonald's novels have, in the 1960's and 1970's, come increasingly to be praised as quality literature. Basing your comments on this section from *The Far Side of the Dollar* and any other works by Macdonald you may have read, show what aspects of his work might make him superior to other writers of detective fiction. You might refer to George Grella's discussion of Macdonald's work (see "Theories" section of this book).

2. What is Macdonald suggesting symbolically about Mr. Harley?

3. In what ways do these two chapters complement each other? In what way are the two families either extremes or archetypes of families in general?

4. At the outset of Chapter 17, Archer "couldn't see how one life led to the other." Does he seem to, later in the chapter?

5. Does a crisis situation always seem to bring out family and friend hatred in detective fiction? Compare these chapters to Macdonald's "Find the Woman."

6. How is the detective more than just a third person? How does he so effortlessly take on the psychiatrist's role?

7. The crimes in Macdonald's work are almost always rooted in the past, seen as results of heredity, upbringing, environment. Do you think Macdonald must literally believe in environmental theories of crime? Might an author choose to use a theory because it will provide him with a strong plot structure? Do you think Macdonald's plots and the motives of his characters are realistic?

8. How does Ross Macdonald, in these two chapters and in the novel as a whole (if you can get a chance to read it), seek to expand the

possibilities of detective literature? Dorothy Sayers says that detective stories "do not show the inner workings of the murderer's mind." Nor does Macdonald often delve into this interior. However, the effort of "detection" can create grounds for interpretation of character through an investigation of the criminal's past. Do these chapters and the novel, literally and symbolically, increase your understanding of the characters and their world?

from The Maltese Falcon

Dashiell Hammett

CHAPTER 7

G in the Air

In his bedroom that was a living-room now the wall-bed was up, Spade
took Brigid O'Shaughnessy's hat and coat, made her comfortable in a
padded rocking chair, and telephoned the Hotel Belvedere. Cairo had
not returned from the theatre. Spade left his telephone-number with the
request that Cairo call him as soon as he came in. Spade sat down in the
armchair beside the table and without any preliminary, without an
introductory remark of any sort, began to tell the girl about a thing that
had happened some years before in the Northwest. He talked in a steady
matter-of-fact voice that was devoid of emphasis or pauses, though now
and then he repeated a sentence slightly rearranged, as if it were
important that each detail be related exactly as it had happened. At the
beginning Brigid O'Shaughnessy listened with only partial attentiveness,
obviously more surprised by his telling the story than interested in it, her
curiosity more engaged with his purpose in telling the story than with the
story he told; but presently, as the story went on, it caught her more and
more fully and she became still and receptive.

A man named Flitcraft had left his real-estate-office, in Tacoma, to go
to luncheon one day and had never returned. He did not keep an
engagement to play golf after four that afternoon, though he had taken
the initiative in making the engagement less than half an hour before he
went out to luncheon. His wife and children never saw him again. His
wife and he were supposed to be on the best of terms. He had two
children, boys, one five and the other three. He owned his house in a
Tacoma suburb, a new Packard, and the rest of the appurtenances of
successful American living.

Flitcraft had inherited seventy thousand dollars from his father, and,
with his success in real estate, was worth something in the neighborhood
of two hundred thousand dollars at the time he vanished. His affairs were
in order, though there were enough loose ends to indicate that he had

not been setting them in order preparatory to vanishing. A deal that would have brought him an attractive profit, for instance, was to have been concluded the day after the one on which he disappeared. There was nothing to suggest that he had more than fifty or sixty dollars in his immediate possession at the time of his going. His habits for months past could be accounted for too thoroughly to justify any suspicion of secret vices, or even of another woman in his life, though either was barely possible. "He went like that," Spade said, "like a fist when you open your hand."

When he had reached this point in his story the telephone-bell rang. "Hello," Spade said into the instrument. "Mr. Cairo? . . . This is Spade. Can you come up to my place—Post Street—now? . . . Yes, I think it is." He looked at the girl, pursed his lips, and then said rapidly: "Miss O'Shaughnessy is here and wants to see you."

Brigid O'Shaughnessy frowned and stirred in her chair, but did not say anything. Spade put the telephone down and told her: "He'll be up in a few minutes. Well, that was in 1942. In 1947 I was with one of the big detective agencies in Seattle. Mrs. Flitcraft came in and told us somebody had seen a man in Spokane who looked a lot like her husband. I went over there. It was Flitcraft, all right. He had been living in Spokane for a couple of years as Charles—that was his first name— Pierce. He had an automobile-business that was netting him twenty or twenty-five thousand a year, a wife, a baby son, owned his home in a Spokane suburb, and usually got away to play golf after four in the afternoon during the season."

Spade had not been told very definitely what to do when he found Flitcraft. They talked in Spade's room at the Davenport. Flitcraft had no feeling of guilt. He had left his first family well provided for, and what he had done seemed to him perfectly reasonable. The only thing that bothered him was a doubt that he could make that reasonableness clear to Spade. He had never told anybody his story before, and thus had not had to attempt to make its reasonableness explicit. He tried now. "I got it all right," Spade told Brigid O'Shaughnessy, "but Mrs. Flitcraft never did. She thought it was silly. Maybe it was. Anyway, it came out all right. She didn't want any scandal, and, after the trick he had played on her—the way she looked at it—she didn't want him. So they were divorced on the quiet and everything was swell.

"Here's what happened to him. Going to lunch he passed an office-building that was being put up—just the skeleton. A beam or something fell eight or ten stories down and smacked the sidewalk alongside him. It brushed pretty close to him, but didn't touch him, though a piece of the sidewalk was chipped off and flew up and hit his cheek. It only took a piece of skin off, but he still had the scar when I saw him. He rubbed it with his finger—well, affectionately—when he told me about it. He was scared stiff of course, he said, but he was more shocked than really frightened. He felt like somebody had taken the lid off life and let him look at the works."

Flitcraft had been a good citizen and a good husband and father, not by any outer compulsion, but simply because he was a man who was most comfortable in step with his surroundings. He had been raised that way. The people he knew were like that. The life he knew was a clean orderly sane responsible affair. Now a falling beam had shown him that life was fundamentally none of these things. He, the good citizen-husband-father, could be wiped out between office and restaurant by the accident of a falling beam. He knew then that men died at haphazard like that, and lived only while blind chance spared them. It was not, primarily, the injustice of it that disturbed him: he accepted that after the first shock. What disturbed him was the discovery that in sensibly ordering his affairs he had got out of step, and not into step, with life. He said he knew before he had gone twenty feet from the fallen beam that he would never know peace again until he had adjusted himself to this new glimpse of life. By the time he had eaten his luncheon he had found his means of adjustment. Life could be ended for him at random by a falling beam: he would change his life at random by simply going away. He loved his family, he said, as much as he supposed was usual, but he knew he was leaving them adequately provided for, and his love for them was not of the sort to make absence painful.

"He went to Seattle that afternoon," Spade said, "and from there by boat to San Francisco. For a couple of years he wandered around and then drifted back to the Northwest, and settled in Spokane and got married. His second wife didn't look like the first, but they were more alike than they were different. You know, the kind of women that play fair games of golf and bridge and like new salad-recipes. He wasn't sorry for what he had done. It seemed reasonable enough to him. I don't think he even knew he had settled back naturally into the same groove he had jumped out of in Tacoma. But that's the part of it I always liked. He adjusted himself to beams falling, and then no more of them fell, and he adjusted himself to them not falling."

"How perfectly fascinating," Brigid O'Shaughnessy said. She left her chair and stood in front of him, close. Her eyes were wide and deep. "I don't have to tell you how utterly at a disadvantage you'll have me, with him here, if you choose."

Spade smiled slightly without separating his lips. "No, you don't have to tell me," he agreed.

"And you know I'd never have placed myself in this position if I hadn't trusted you completely." Her thumb and forefinger twisted a black button on his blue coat.

Spade said, "That again!" with mock resignation.

"But you know it's so," she insisted.

"No, I don't know it." He patted the hand that was twisting the button. "My asking for reasons why I should trust you brought us here. Don't let's confuse things. You don't have to trust me, anyhow, as long as you can persuade me to trust you."

She studied his face. Her nostrils quivered. Spade laughed. He patted her hand again and said: "Don't worry about that now. He'll be here in a moment. Get your business with him over, and then see how we stand."

"And you'll let me go about it—in my own way?"

"Sure."

She turned her hand under his so that her fingers pressed his. She said softly: "You're a God-send."

Spade said: "Don't overdo it."

She looked reproachfully at him, though smiling, and returned to the padded rocker.

QUESTIONS

1. Discuss Flitcraft's feeling that he has "got out of step, and not into step, with life."

2. Flitcraft has been shocked, yet he settles down into a life similar to his previous one. Was this inevitable?

3. Flitcraft "felt like somebody had taken the lid off life and let him look at the works." What are "the works"?

4. How does this story reveal the detective's knowledge of life? Would Spade think Flitcraft's story is a rather typical one?

5. Consider, in this scene, that among other things Sam Spade is making love to Brigid O'Shaughnessy. How much is he telling her about himself by choosing to relate this story?

6. In what way can this tale be considered "existential"? If you've read the novel, in what way would you say that The Maltese Falcon can, as a whole, be considered "existential"?

7. The famous movie version of The Maltese Falcon, although remarkably faithful to the novel, does not include this speech by Spade. Why not? Is it strictly a matter of pace and plot, or might there have been other reasons for the deletion?

part 4

Theories

In 1950 Raymond Chandler wrote that "the average critic never recognizes an achievement when it happens. He explains it after it has become respectable." Chandler spoke of the day when some "literary antiquarian" would search the pulp magazines such as Black Mask, which flourished in the years after the first World War, finding in them the roots and the achievement of the hard-boiled detective writers. More than twenty years have passed since Chandler's prediction. A reading of George Grella's essay "Murder and the Mean Streets: The Hard-Boiled Detective Novel" seems to validate Chandler's foresight. The hard-boiled detective writers, as well as the more formal detective writers, are the subject of critical scrutiny in the "Theories" section. If this scrutiny sometimes lacks the detachment of a debate among scholars, perhaps it is because three of the essays were written by authors who were themselves practitioners of detective fiction. These "Theories" do not lack intelligence or force, and some have the zest of a feud among men and women of varied letters.

For instance, Chandler's essay "The Simple Art of Murder," written in 1944, is among other things an argument against the case brought forward in 1929 by Dorothy Sayers' "Omnibus of Crime." Chandler felt the kind of story praised by Sayers too divorced from his reality. He saw a blessed divide between the "Old Lady" school and the energy of the "hard-boiled" school. Fifteen years later the poet W. H. Auden saw much the same divide, but perceived in different terms. Among other things, his essay "The Guilty Vicarage" attempts to arbitrate the dispute between Sayers and Chandler through classical and theological references. Undoubtedly neither Sayers nor Chandler would be satisfied with Auden's categorizations. Such is the way of arbitration.

Beginning the "Theories" section is Sayers' historical overview of the genre. We may note her prejudices, the way she pats Edgar Allan Poe's head while chiding him. We may also note that her essay shows curiously little sign of being dated. One explanation for this phenomenon is that the kind of story she discusses and lauds survives unchanged. It is the kind of story she herself wrote and the kind Agatha Christie still writes. Christie is still enormously popular and prolific. Among the more ingenious explanations of the popularity of the straight "puzzle" story of detection is Lee Wright's. He maintains that detective fiction "does not fall under the head of fiction in the ordinary sense," that

> *the structure and mechanism of the crossword puzzle and the detective novel are very similar. In each there is a problem to be solved; and the solution depends wholly on mental processes–on analysis, on the fitting together of apparently unrelated parts, on a knowledge of the ingredients, and, in some measure, on guessing. Each is supplied with a series of overlapping clues to guide the solver; and these clues, when fitted into place, blaze the path for future progress. In each, when the final solution is achieved, all the details are found to be woven into a complete, interrelated and closely knitted fabric.*

The *"puzzle"* in the hands of a master such as Sayers or Christie is all-engrossing. The characters may be too eccentric to be taken seriously, and in spite of murder the world they inhabit will be coherent and orderly because that world is fixed in the past—timeless, untimely. Perhaps for this reason many modern British writers of popular fiction have shown a preference for the related but more open and ambiguous milieu of the spy story. We might ungenerously accuse the *"genteel"* school of failing to express *"the poetry of modern life."* In his pioneering essay *"A Defence of Detective Stories,"* G. K. Chesterton cites this sense of poetry as the wellspring of the detective story's appeal and worth. He sees the detective as a *"knight"* in collusion with the forces of civilization, dealing in morality, *"the most dark and daring of conspiracies."* To Chesterton's priest-detective Father Brown, Earth might be called Compromise and the maintenance of civilization a supreme act of compassion.

Raymond Chandler, in *"The Simple Art of Murder,"* similarly envisions the detective as a *"man of honor . . . the best man in his world."* But Chandler's Philip Marlowe bears little resemblance to Chesterton's Father Brown. Marlowe is no advertant defender of the social contract. His world is far too dangerously compromised to permit a defense of any abstraction or to honor any conscience other than his own. In much the same spirit Chandler says the writer of *"realistic"* fiction must know that while craft can be learned, *"honesty is an art."*

In *"The Guilty Vicarage"* a different kind of honesty is asserted as a poet confesses his addiction to detective stories. He examines his conscience in terms of art. Auden sees the genteel detective as a *"representative of the ethical"* and the detective story as *"the dialectic of innocence and guilt."* Murder (*"negative creation"*) prompts investigation; investigation reveals the evil-doer and exorcises the reader's guilt. In the end the reader finds Eden restored, a conclusion Auden suggests no work of art would be likely to permit itself.

George Grella's survey of the major figures of the *"hard-boiled"* school operates on different assumptions. *"Murder and the Mean Streets"* provides historical background as well as some critical apparatus. Grella places the *"realistic"* detectives of Hammett, Chandler, Macdonald, and Spillane against the backdrop of American literary traditions and the pull of social forces. The hard-boiled dick is seen as combining the *"characteristics of the national hero* with those of the knight." Inevitably, as reality clashes with the mythical, shards of the American Dream are crushed underfoot.

After Grella's critical excursion, Robert Daley interposes a disconcerting slice of life. While reading "Police Report on the TV Cop Shows," we may be increasingly willing to see every detective as a figure padded in layers of literary convention. Daley's tone is urgent. He is concerned that elements of unreality in the portrayals of "Cop Shows" have already damaged the practical mechanisms of law enforcement and the courts. He sees harm when "mindless and irrational" evil is presented in coherent and "beautifully constructed" segments. Daley's real-life detective is the average man, who, like all of us, is ruled by procedure and, in violent situations, fear.

A different kind of realism is dealt with in Fred P. Graham's "A Contemporary History of Modern Crime." Perhaps, after much qualification, the graphs and statistics do mean something, as Graham finally suggests. We are looking at the bureaucratic barometers that measure, however imprecisely, the pressures of our lives. We are far from literature here. We are walking quickly, trying to read the obscured numbers on Chandler's mean streets. There is no hero anywhere in sight.

The Omnibus of Crime

Dorothy L. Sayers

The art of self-tormenting is an ancient one, with a long and honourable literary tradition. Man, not satisfied with the mental confusion and unhappiness to be derived from contemplating the cruelties of life and the riddle of the universe, delights to occupy his leisure moments with puzzles and bugaboos. The pages of every magazine and newspaper swarm with cross-words, mathematical tricks, puzzle-pictures, enigmas, acrostics, and detective-stories, as also with stories of the kind called "powerful" (which means unpleasant), and those which make him afraid to go to bed. It may be that in them he finds a sort of catharsis or purging of his fears and self-questionings. These mysteries made only to be solved, these horrors which he knows to be mere figments of the creative brain, comfort him by subtly persuading that life is a mystery which death will solve, and whose horrors will pass away as a tale that is told. Or it may be merely that his animal faculties of fear and inquisitiveness demand more exercise than the daily round affords. Or it may be pure perversity. The fact remains that if you search the second-hand bookstalls for his cast-off literature, you will find fewer mystery stories than any other kind of book. Theology and poetry, philosophy and numismatics, love-stories and biography, he discards as easily as old razor-blades, but Sherlock Holmes and Wilkie Collins are cherished and read and reread, till their covers fall off and their pages crumble to fragments.

Both the detective-story proper and the pure tale of horror are very ancient in origin. All native folk-lore has its ghost tales, while the first four detective-stories in this book hail respectively from the Jewish Apocrypha, Herodotus, and the Æneid. But, whereas the tale of horror has flourished in practically every age and country, the detective-story has had a spasmodic history, appearing here and there in faint, tentative sketches and episodes, until it suddenly burst into magnificent flower in the middle of the last century.

EARLY HISTORY OF DETECTIVE FICTION

Between 1840 and 1845 the wayward genius of Edgar Allan Poe (himself a past-master of the horrible) produced five tales, in which the general principles of the detective-story were laid down for ever. In "The Murders in the Rue Morgue" and, with a certain repulsive facetiousness, in "Thou Art the Man" he achieved the fusion of the two distinct genres and created what we may call the story of mystery, as distinct from pure detection on the one hand and pure horror on the other. In this fused genre, the reader's blood is first curdled by some horrible and apparently inexplicable murder or portent; the machinery of detection is then brought in to solve the mystery and punish the murderer. Since Poe's time all three branches—detection, mystery, and horror—have flourished. We have such pleasant little puzzles as Conan Doyle's "Case of Identity," in which there is nothing to shock or horrify; we have mere fantasies of blood and terror—human, as in Conan Doyle's "The Case of Lady Sannox," [1] or supernatural, as in Marion Crawford's "The Upper Berth;" [2] most satisfactory of all, perhaps, we have such fusions as "The Speckled Band," [3] or "The Hammer of God," [4] in which the ghostly terror is invoked only to be dispelled.

It is rather puzzling that the detective-story should have had to wait so long to find a serious exponent. Having started so well, why did it not develop earlier? The Oriental races, with their keen appreciation of intellectual subtlety, should surely have evolved it. The germ was there. "Why do you not come to pay your respects to me?" says Æsop's lion to the fox. "I beg your Majesty's pardon," says the fox, "but I noticed the track of the animals that have already come to you; and, while I see many hoof-marks going in, I see none coming out. Till the animals that have entered your cave come out again, I prefer to remain in the open air." Sherlock Holmes could not have reasoned more lucidly from the premises.

Cacus the robber, be it noted, was apparently the first criminal to use the device of forged footprints to mislead the pursuer, though it is a long development from his primitive methods to the horses shod with cow-shoes in Conan Doyle's "Adventure of the Priory School." [5] Hercules's methods of investigation, too, were rather of the rough and ready sort, though the reader will not fail to observe that this early detective was accorded divine honours by his grateful clients.

---

[1] Conan Doyle: *Round the Red Lamp.*
[2] Marion Crawford: *Uncanny Tales.*
[3] Conan Doyle: *Adventures of Sherlock Holmes.*
[4] G. K. Chesterton: *The Innocence of Father Brown.*
[5] Conan Doyle: *Return of Sherlock Holmes.*

The Jews, with their strongly moral preoccupation, were, as our two Apocryphal stories show, peculiarly fitted to produce the *roman policier*.[6] The Romans, logical and given to law-making, might have been expected to do something with it, but they did not. In one of the folk-tales collected by the Grimms, twelve maidens disguised as men are set to walk across a floor strewn with peas, in the hope that their shuffling feminine tread will betray them; the maidens are, however, warned, and baffle the detectives by treading firmly. In an Indian folk-tale a similar ruse is more successful. Here a suitor is disguised as a woman, and has to be picked out from the women about him by the wise princess. The princess throws a lemon to each in turn, and the disguised man is detected by his instinctive action in clapping his knees together to catch the lemon, whereas the real women spread their knees to catch it in their skirts. Coming down to later European literature, we find the Bel-and-the-Dragon motif of the ashes spread on the floor reproduced in the story of Tristan. Here the king's spy spreads flour between Tristan's bed and that of Iseult; Tristan defeats the scheme by leaping from one bed to the other. The eighteenth century also contributed at least one outstanding example, in the famous detective chapter of Voltaire's *Zadig*.

It may be, as Mr. E. M. Wrong has suggested in a brilliant little study,[7] that throughout this early period "a faulty law of evidence was to blame, for detectives cannot flourish until the public has an idea of what constitutes proof, and while a common criminal procedure is arrest, torture, confession, and death." One may go further, and say that, though crime stories might, and did, flourish, the detective-story proper could not do so until public sympathy had veered round to the side of law and order. It will be noticed that, on the whole, the tendency in early crime-literature is to admire the cunning and astuteness of the criminal.[8] This must be so while the law is arbitrary, oppressive, and brutally administered.

We may note that, even to-day, the full blossoming of the detective-stories is found among the Anglo-Saxon races. It is notorious that an English crowd tends to side with the policeman in a row. The British legal code, with its tradition of "sportsmanship" and "fair play for the criminal" is particularly favourable to the production of detective

---

[6] In "Bel and the Dragon" the science of deduction from material clues, in the popular Scotland Yard manner, is reduced to its simplest expression. "Susanna," on the other hand, may be taken as foreshadowing the Gallic method of eliciting the truth by the confrontation of witnesses.

[7] Preface to *Tales of Crime and Detection*. World's Classics. (Oxford University Press, 1926.)

[8] e.g. "The Story of Rhampsinitus;" "Jacob and Esau;" "Reynard the Fox;" "Ballads of Robin Hood;" etc.

fiction, allowing, as it does, sufficient rope to the quarry to provide a ding-dong chase, rich in up-and-down incident. In France, also, though the street policeman is less honoured than in England, the detective-force is admirably organised and greatly looked up to. France has a good output of detective-stories, though considerably smaller than that of the English-speaking races. In the Southern States of Europe the law is less loved and the detective story less frequent. We may not unreasonably trace a connection here.

Some further light is thrown on the question by a remark made by Herr Lion Feuchtwanger when broadcasting during his visit to London in 1927. Contrasting the tastes of the English, French, and German publics, he noted the great attention paid by the Englishman to the external details of men and things. The Englishman likes material exactness in the books he reads; the German and the Frenchman, in different degrees, care little for it in comparison with psychological truth. It is hardly surprising, then, that the detective-story, with its insistence on footprints, blood-stains, dates, times, and places, and its reduction of character-drawing to bold, flat outline, should appeal far more strongly to Anglo-Saxon taste than to that of France or Germany.

Taking these two factors together, we begin to see why the detective-story had to wait for its full development for the establishment of an effective police organisation in the Anglo-Saxon countries. This was achieved—in England, at any rate—during the early part of the nineteenth century,[9] and was followed about the middle of that century by the first outstanding examples of the detective-story as we know it to-day.[10]

To this argument we may add another. In the nineteenth century the vast, unexplored limits of the world began to shrink at an amazing and unprecedented rate. The electric telegraph circled the globe; railways brought remote villages into touch with civilisation; photographs made known to the stay-at-homes the marvels of foreign landscapes, customs, and animals; science reduced seeming miracles to mechanical marvels;

---

[9] In a letter to W. Thornbury, dated February 18, 1862, Dickens says: "The Bow Street Runners ceased out of the land soon after the introduction of the new police. I remember them very well. . . . They kept company with thieves and such-like, much more than the detective police do. I don't know what their pay was, but I have no doubt their principal complements were got under the rose. It was a very slack institution, and its head-quarters were the Brown Bear, in Bow Street, a public house of more than doubtful reputation, opposite the police-office." The first "peelers" were established in 1829.

[10] The significance of footprints, and the necessity for scientific care in the checking of alibis, were understood at quite an early date, though, in the absence of an effective detective police, investigations were usually carried out by private persons at the instigation of the coroner. A remarkable case, which reads like a Freeman Wills Crofts novel, was that of R. v. Thornton (1818).

popular education and improved policing made town and country safer for the common man than they had ever been. In place of the adventurer and the knight errant, popular imagination hailed the doctor, the scientist, and the policeman as saviours and protectors. But if one could no longer hunt the manticora, one could still hunt the murderer; if the armed escort had grown less necessary, yet one still needed the analyst to frustrate the wiles of the poisoner; from this point of view, the detective steps into his right place as the protector of the weak—the latest of the popular heroes, the true successor of Roland and Lancelot.

EDGAR ALLAN POE: EVOLUTION OF THE DETECTIVE

Before tracing further the history of detective fiction, let us look a little more closely at those five tales of Poe's, in which so much of the future development is anticipated. Probably the first thing that strikes us is that Poe has struck out at a blow the formal outline on which a large section of detective fiction has been built up. In the three Dupin stories, one of which figures in the present collection, we have the formula of the eccentric and brilliant private detective whose doings are chronicled by an admiring and thick-headed friend. From Dupin and his unnamed chronicler springs a long and distinguished line: Sherlock Holmes and his Watson; Martin Hewitt and his Brett; Raffles and his Bunny (on the criminal side of the business, but of the same breed); Thorndyke and his various Jardines, Ansteys, and Jervises; Hanaud and his Mr. Ricardo; Poirot and his Captain Hastings; Philo Vance and his Van Dine. It is not surprising that this formula should have been used so largely, for it is obviously a very convenient one for the writer. For one thing, the admiring satellite may utter expressions of eulogy which would be unbecoming in the mouth of the author, gaping at his own colossal intellect. Again, the reader, even if he is not, in R. L. Stevenson's phrase, "always a man of such vastly greater ingenuity than the writer," is usually a little more ingenious than Watson. He sees a little further through the brick wall; he pierces, to some extent, the cloud of mystification with which the detective envelops himself. "Aha!" he says to himself, "the average reader is supposed to see no further than Watson. But the author has not reckoned with me. I am one too many for him." He is deluded. It is all a device of the writer's for flattering him and putting him on good terms with himself. For though the reader likes to be mystified, he also likes to say, "I told you so," and "I spotted that." And this leads us to the third great advantage of the Holmes-Watson convention: by describing the clues as presented to the dim eyes and bemused mind of Watson, the author is enabled to preserve a spurious appearance of frankness, while keeping to himself the special knowledge on which the interpretation of those clues depends. This is a question of paramount importance, involving the whole artistic ethic of the detec-, tive-story. We shall return to it later. For the moment, let us consider a few other interesting types and formulæ which make their first appearance in Poe.

The personality of Dupin is eccentric, and for several literary generations eccentricity was highly fashionable among detective heroes. Dupin, we are informed, had a habit of living behind closed shutters, illumined by "a couple of tapers which, strongly perfumed, threw out only the ghastliest and feeblest of rays." From this stronghold he issued by night, to promenade the streets and enjoy the "infinity of mental excitement" afforded by quiet observation. He was also given to startling his friends by analysing their thought-processes, and he had a rooted contempt for the methods of the police.

Sherlock Holmes modelled himself to a large extent upon Dupin, substituting cocaine for candlelight, with accompaniments of shag and fiddle-playing. He is a more human and endearing figure than Dupin, and has earned as his reward the supreme honour which literature has to bestow—the secular equivalent of canonisation. He has passed into the language. He also started a tradition of his own—the hawk-faced tradition, which for many years dominated detective fiction.

So strong, indeed, was this domination that subsequent notable eccentrics have displayed their eccentricities chiefly by escaping from it. "Nothing," we are told, "could have been less like the traditional detective than"—so-and-so. He may be elderly and decrepit, like Baroness Orczy's Old Man in the Corner, whose characteristic habit is the continual knotting of string. Or he may be round and innocent-looking, like Father Brown or Poirot. There is Sax Rohmer's Moris Klaw,[11] with his bald, scholarly forehead; he irrigates his wits with a verbena spray, and carries about with him an "odically-sterilised" cushion to promote psychic intuition. There is the great Dr. Thorndyke, probably the handsomest detective in fiction; he is outwardly bonhomous, but spiritually detached, and his emblem is the green research-case, filled with miniature microscopes and scientific implements. Max Carrados has the distinction of being blind; Old Ebbie wears a rabbit-skin waistcoat; Lord Peter Wimsey (if I may refer to him without immodesty) indulges in the buying of incunabula and has a pretty taste in wines and haberdashery. By a final twist of the tradition, which brings the wheel full circle, there is a strong modern tendency to produce detectives remarkable for their ordinariness; they may be well-bred walking gentlemen, like A. A. Milne's Antony Gillingham, or journalists, like Gaston Leroux's Rouletabille, or they may even be policemen, like

---

[11] Sax Rohmer: *The Dream Detective.*

Freeman Wills Crofts' Inspector French, or the heroes of Mr. A. J. Rees's sound and well-planned stories.[12]

There have also been a few women detectives,[13] but on the whole, they have not been very successful. In order to justify their choice of sex, they are obliged to be so irritatingly intuitive as to destroy that quiet enjoyment of the logical which we look for in our detective reading. Or else they are active and courageous, and insist on walking into physical danger and hampering the men engaged on the job. Marriage, also, looms too large in their view of life; which is not surprising, for they are all young and beautiful. Why these charming creatures should be able to tackle abstruse problems at the age of twenty-one or thereabouts, while the male detectives are usually content to wait till their thirties or forties before setting up as experts, it is hard to say. Where do they pick up their worldly knowledge? Not from personal experience, for they are always immaculate as the driven snow. Presumably it is all intuition.

Better use has been made of women in books where the detecting is strictly amateur—done, that is, by members of the family or house-party themselves, and not by a private consultant. Evelyn Humblethorne[14] is a detective of this kind, and so is Joan Cowper, in *The Brooklyn Murders.*[15] But the really brilliant woman detective has yet to be created.[16]

While on this subject, we must not forget the curious and interesting development of detective fiction which has produced the *Adventures of Sexton Blake,* and other allied cycles. This is the Holmes tradition, adapted for the reading of the board-school boy and crossed with the Buffalo Bill adventure type. The books are written by a syndicate of authors, each one of whom uses a set of characters of his own invention, grouped about a central and traditional group consisting of Sexton Blake and his boy assistant, Tinker, their comic landlady Mrs. Bardell, and their bulldog Pedro. As might be expected, the quality of the writing and the detective methods employed vary considerably from one author to another. The best specimens display extreme ingenuity, and an immense

---

[12] A. J. Rees: *The Shrieking Pit; The Hand in the Dark;* (with J. R. Watson) *The Hampstead Mystery; The Mystery of the Downs,* etc. Messrs. Rees and Watson write of police affairs with the accuracy born of inside knowledge, but commendably avoid the dullness which is apt to result from a too-faithful description of correct official procedure.

[13] e.g. Anna Katharine Green: *The Golden Slipper;* Baroness Orczy: *Lady Molly of Scotland Yard;* G. R. Sims: *Dorcas Dene;* Valentine: *The Adjusters;* Richard Marsh: *Judith Lee;* Arthur B. Reeve: *Constance Dunlap;* etc.

[14] Lord Gorell: *In the Night.*

[15] G. D. H. & M. Cole.

[16] Wilkie Collins—who was curiously fascinated by the "strong-minded" woman—made two attempts at the woman detective in *No Name* and *The Law and the Lady.* The spirit of the time was, however, too powerful to allow these attempts to be altogether successful.

vigour and fertility in plot and incident. Nevertheless, the central types are pretty consistently preserved throughout the series. Blake and Tinker are less intuitive than Holmes, from whom however, they are directly descended, as their address in Baker Street shows. They are more careless and reckless in their methods; more given to displays of personal heroism and pugilism; more simple and human in their emotions. The really interesting point about them is that they present the nearest modern approach to a national folk-lore, conceived as the centre for a cycle of loosely connected romances in the Arthurian manner. Their significance in popular literature and education would richly repay scientific investigation.

EDGAR ALLAN POE: EVOLUTION OF THE PLOT

As regards plot also, Poe laid down a number of sound keels for the use of later adventurers. Putting aside his instructive excursion into the psychology of detection—instructive, because we can trace their influence in so many of Poe's successors down to the present day—putting these aside, and discounting that atmosphere of creepiness which Poe so successfully diffused about nearly all he wrote, we shall probably find that to us, sophisticated and trained on an intensive study of detective fiction, his plots are thin to transparency. But in Poe's day they represented a new technique. As a matter of fact, it is doubtful whether there are more than half a dozen deceptions in the mystery-monger's bag of tricks, and we shall find that Poe has got most of them, at any rate in embryo.

Take, first, the three Dupin stories. In "The Murders in the Rue Morgue," an old woman and her daughter are found horribly murdered in an (apparently) hermetically sealed room. An innocent person is arrested by the police. Dupin proves that the police have failed to discover one mode of entrance to the room, and deduces from a number of observations that the "murder" was committed by a huge ape. Here is, then, a combination of three typical motifs: the wrongly suspected man, to whom all the superficial evidence (motive, access, etc.) points; the hermetically sealed death-chamber (still a favourite central theme); finally, the *solution by the unexpected means.* In addition, we have Dupin drawing deductions, which the police have overlooked, from the evidence of witnesses (superiority in inference), and discovering clues which the police have not thought of looking for owing to obsession by an *idée fixe* (superiority in observation based on inference). In this story also are enunciated for the first time those two great aphorisms of detective science: first, that when you have eliminated all the impossibilities, then, whatever remains, *however improbable*, must be the truth; and, secondly, that the more *outré* a case may appear, the easier it is to solve. Indeed, take it all round, "The Murders in the Rue Morgue" constitutes in itself almost a complete manual of detective theory and practice.

In "The Purloined Letter," we have one of those stolen documents on whose recovery hangs the peace of mind of a distinguished personage. It is not, indeed, one of the sort whose publication would spread consternation among the Chancelleries of Europe, but it is important enough. The police suspect a certain minister of taking it. They ransack every corner of his house, in vain. Dupin, arguing from his knowledge of the minister's character, decides that subtlety must be met by subtlety. He calls on the minister and discovers the letter, turned inside out and stuck in a letter-rack in full view of the casual observer.

Here we have, besides the reiteration, in inverted form,[17] of aphorism No. 2 (above), the method of *psychological deduction* and the solution by the formula of the *most obvious place*. This trick is the forerunner of the diamond concealed in the tumbler of water, the man murdered in the midst of a battle, Chesterton's "Invisible Man" (the postman, so familiar a figure that his presence goes unnoticed)[18] and a whole line of similar ingenuities.

The third Dupin story, "The Mystery of Marie Rogêt," has fewer imitators, but is the most interesting of all to the connoisseur. It consists entirely of a series of newspaper cuttings relative to the disappearance and murder of a shopgirl, with Dupin's comments thereon. The story contains no solution of the problem, and, indeed, no formal ending— and that for a very good reason. The disappearance was a genuine one, its actual heroine being one Mary Cecilia Rogers, and the actual place New York. The newspaper cuttings, were also, *mutatis mutandis*, genuine. The paper which published Poe's article dared not publish his conclusion. Later on it was claimed that his argument was, in substance, correct; and though this claim has, I believe, been challenged of late years, Poe may, nevertheless, be ranked among the small band of

---

[17] "The business is very simple indeed, and I make no doubt that we can manage it sufficiently well ourselves; but then I thought Dupin would like to hear of it because it is so excessively *odd*."

"Simple and odd," said Dupin.

"Why, yes; and not exactly that either. The fact is, we have all been a good deal puzzled because the affair *is* so simple, and yet baffles us altogether."

"Perhaps it is the very simplicity of the thing which puts you at fault," said Dupin.

The psychology of the matter is fully discussed in Poe's characteristic manner a few pages further on.

[18] G. K. Chesterton: *The Innocence of Father Brown.*

mystery-writers who have put their skill in deduction to the acid test of a problem which they had not in the first place invented.[19]

Of the other Poe stories, one, "Thou Art the Man," is very slight in theme and unpleasantly flippant in treatment. A man is murdered; a hearty person, named, with guileless cunning, Goodfellow, is very energetic in fixing the crime on a certain person. The narrator of the story makes a repulsive kind of jack-in-the-box out of the victim's corpse, and extorts a confession of guilt from—Goodfellow! Of course. Nevertheless, we have here two more leading motifs that have done overtime since Poe's day: the trail of false clues laid by the real murderer,[20] and the *solution by way of the most unlikely person.*

The fifth story is "The Gold Bug." In this a man finds a cipher which leads him to the discovery of a hidden treasure. The cipher is of the very simple one-sign-one-letter type, and its solution, of the mark-where-the-shadow-falls-take-three-paces-to-the-east-and-dig variety. In technique this story is the exact opposite of "Marie Rogêt"; the narrator is astonished by the antics of his detective friend, and is kept in entire ignorance of what he is about until *after* the discovery of the treasure; only then is the cipher for the first time either mentioned or explained. Some people think that "The Gold Bug" is Poe's finest mystery-story.

Now, with "The Gold Bug" at the one extreme and "Marie Rogêt" at the other, and the other three stories occupying intermediate places, Poe stands at the parting of the ways for detective fiction. From him go the two great lines of development—the Romantic and the Classic, or, to use terms less abraded by ill-usage, the purely Sensational and the purely Intellectual. In the former, thrill is piled on thrill and mystification on mystification; the reader is led on from bewilderment to bewilderment, till everything is explained in a lump in the last chapter. This school is strong in dramatic incident and atmosphere; its weakness is a tendency to confusion and a dropping of links—its explanations do not always explain; it is never dull, but it is sometimes nonsense. In the other—the purely Intellectual type—the action mostly takes place in the first chapter or so; the detective then follows up quietly from clue to clue till the problem is solved, the reader accompanying the great man in his search and being allowed to try his own teeth on the material provided. The strength of this school is its analytical ingenuity; its weakness is its liability to dullness and pomposity, its mouthing over the infinitely little, and its lack of movement and emotion.

---

[19] Sir Arthur Conan Doyle's successful efforts on behalf of George Edalji and Oscar Slater deserve special mention.

[20] See also "The Story of Susanna."

INTELLECTUAL AND SENSATIONAL
LINES OF DEVELOPMENT

The purely Sensational thriller is not particularly rare—we may find plenty of examples in the work of William Le Queux, Edgar Wallace, and others. The purely Intellectual is rare indeed; few writers have consistently followed the "Marie Rogêt" formula of simply spreading the *whole* evidence before the reader and leaving him to deduce the detective's conclusion from it if he can.

M. P. Shiel, indeed, did so in his trilogy, *Prince Zaleski*, whose curious and elaborate beauty recaptures in every arabesque sentence the very accent of Edgar Allan Poe. Prince Zaleski, "victim of a too importunate, too unfortunate Love, which the fulgor of the throne itself could not abash," sits apart in his ruined tower in "the semi-darkness of the very faint greenish lustre radiated from an open censer-like *lampas* in the centre of the domed encausted roof," surrounded by Flemish sepulchral brasses, runic tablets, miniature paintings, winged bulls, Tamil scriptures on lacquered leaves of the talipot, mediæval reliquaries richly gemmed, Brahmin gods, and Egyptian mummies, and lulled by "the low, liquid tinkling of an invisible musical-box." Like Sherlock Holmes, he indulges in a drug—"the narcotic *cannabis sativa:* the base of the *bhang* of the Mohammedans." A friend brings to him the detective problems of the outside world, which he proceeds to solve from the data given and (except in the final story) without stirring from his couch. He adorns his solutions with philosophical discourses on the social progress of mankind, all delivered with the same melancholy grace and remote intellectual disdain. The reasoning is subtle and lucid, but the crimes themselves are fantastic and incredible—a fault which these tales have in common with those of G. K. Chesterton.

Another writer who uses the "Marie Rogêt" formula is Baroness Orczy. Her *Old Man in the Corner* series is constructed precisely on those lines, and I have seen a French edition in which, when the expository part of the story is done, the reader is exhorted to: "Pause a moment and see if you can arrive at the explanation yourself, before you read the Old Man's solution." This pure puzzle is a formula which obviously has its limitations. Nearest to this among modern writers comes Freeman Wills Crofts, whose painstaking sleuths always "play fair" and display their clues to the reader as soon as they have picked them up. The intellectually minded reader can hardly demand more than this. The aim of the writer of this type of detective-story is to make the reader say at the end, neither: "Oh well, I knew it must be that all along," nor yet: "Dash it all! I couldn't be expected to guess that"; but: "Oh, of course! What a fool I was not to see it! Right under my nose all the time!" Precious tribute! How often striven for! How rarely earned!

On the whole, however, the tendency is for the modern educated public to demand fair play from the writer, and for the Sensational and Intellectual branches of the story to move further apart.

Before going further with this important question, we must look back once more to the middle of the last century, and see what development took place to bridge the gap between Dupin and Sherlock Holmes.

Poe, like a restless child, played with his new toy for a little while, and then, for some reason, wearied of it. He turned his attention to other things, and his formula lay neglected for close on forty years. Meanwhile a somewhat different type of detective-story was developing independently in Europe. In 1848 the elder Dumas, always ready to try his hand at any novel and ingenious thing, suddenly inserted into the romantic body of the *Vicomte de Bragelonne* a passage of pure scientific deduction. This passage is quite unlike anything else in the Musketeer cycle, and looks like the direct outcome of Dumas' keen interest in actual crime.[21]

But there is another literary influence which, though the fact is not generally recognised, must have been powerfully exerted at this date upon writers of mystery fiction. Between 1820 and 1850 the novels of Fenimore Cooper began to enjoy their huge popularity, and were not only widely read in America and England, but translated into most European languages. In *The Pathfinder, The Deerslayer, The Last of the Mohicans,* and the rest of the series, Cooper revealed to the delighted youth of two hemispheres the Red Indian's patient skill in tracking his quarry by footprints, in interrogating a broken twig, a mossy trunk, a fallen leaf. The imagination of childhood was fired; every boy wanted to be an Uncas or a Chingachgook. Novelists, not content with following and imitating Cooper on his own ground, discovered a better way, by transferring the romance of the woodland tracker to the surroundings of their native country. In the 'sixties the generation who had read Fenimore Cooper in boyhood turned, as novelists and readers, to tracing the spoor of the criminal upon their own native heath. The enthusiasm for Cooper combined magnificently with that absorbing interest in crime and detection which better methods of communication and an improved police system had made possible. While, in France, Gaboriau and Fortuné du Boisgobey concentrated upon the police novel pure and simple, English writers, still permeated by the terror and mystery of the romantic movement, and influenced by the "Newgate novel" of Bulwer and Ainsworth, perfected a more varied and imaginative genre, in which the ingenuity of the detective problem allied itself with the sombre terrors of the weird and supernatural.

---

[21] He published a great collection of famous crimes.

THE PRE-DOYLE PERIOD

Of the host of writers who attempted this form of fiction in the 'sixties and 'seventies, three may be picked out for special mention.

That voluminous writer, Mrs. Henry Wood, represents, on the whole, the melodramatic and adventurous development of the crime-story as distinct from the detective problem proper. Through *East Lynne*, crude and sentimental as it is, she exercised an enormous influence on the rank and file of sensational novelists, and at her best, she is a most admirable spinner of plots. Whether her problem concerns a missing will, a vanished heir, a murder, or a family curse, the story spins along without flagging, and, though she is a little too fond of calling in Providence to cut the knot of intrigue with the sword of coincidence, the mystery is fully and properly unravelled, in a workmanlike manner and without any loose ends. She makes frequent use of supernatural thrills. Sometimes these are explained away: a "murdered" person is seen haunting the local churchyard, and turns out never to have been killed at all. Sometimes the supernatural remains supernatural, as, for instance, the coffin-shaped appearance in *The Shadow of Ashlydyat*. Her morality is perhaps a little oppressive, but she is by no means without humour, and at times can produce a shrewd piece of characterisation.

Melodramatic, but a writer of real literary attainment, and gifted with a sombre power which has seldom been equalled in painting the ghastly and the macabre, is Sheridan Le Fanu. Like Poe, he has the gift of investing the most mechanical of plots with an atomosphere of almost unbearable horror. Take, for example, that scene in *Wylder's Hand* where the aged Uncle Lorne appears—phantom or madman? we are not certain which—to confront the villainous Lake in the tapestried room.

" 'Mark Wylder is in evil plight,' said he.

" 'Is he?' said Lake with a sly scoff, though he seemed to me a good deal scared. 'We hear no complaints, however, and fancy he must be tolerably comfortable notwithstanding.'

" 'You know where he is,' said Uncle Lorne.

" 'Aye, in Italy; everyone knows that,' answered Lake.

" 'In Italy,' said the old man reflectively, as if trying to gather up his ideas, 'Italy. . . . He has had a great tour to make. It is nearly accomplished now; when it is done, he will be like me, *humano major*. He has seen the places which you are yet to see.'

" 'Nothing I should like better; particularly Italy,' said Lake.

" 'Yes,' said Uncle Lorne, lifting up slowly a different finger at each name in his catalogue. 'First, Lucus Mortis; then Terra Tenebrosa; next, Tartarus; after that Terra Oblivionis; then Herebus; then Barathrum; then Gehenna, and then Stagnum Ignis.'

" 'Of course,' acquiesced Lake, with an ugly sneer. . . .

" 'Don't be frightened—but he's alive; I think they'll make him mad. It is a frightful plight. Two angels buried him alive in Vallombrosa by night; I saw it, standing among the lotus and hemlocks. A negro came to me, a black clergyman with white eyes, and remained beside me; and the angels imprisoned Mark; they put him on duty forty days and forty nights, with his ear to the river listening for voices; and when it was over we blessed them; and the clergyman walked with me a long while, to-and-fro, to-and-fro upon the earth, telling me the wonders of the abyss.'

" And is it from the abyss, sir, he writes his letters?" enquired the Town Clerk, with a wink at Lake.

" 'Yes, yes, very diligent; it behoves him; and his hair is always standing straight on his head for fear. But he'll be sent up again, at last, a thousand, a hundred, ten and one, black marble steps, and then it will be the other one's turn. So it was prophesied by the black magician.' "

This chapter leads immediately to those in which Larkin, the crooked attorney, discovers, by means of a little sound detective work of a purely practical sort, that Mark Wylder's letters have indeed been written "from the abyss." Mark Wylder has, in fact, been murdered, and the letters are forgeries sent abroad to be despatched by Lake's confederate from various towns in Italy. From this point we gradually learn to expect the ghastly moment when he is "sent up again at last" from the grave, in the Blackberry Dell at Gylingden.

"In the meantime the dogs continued their unaccountable yelling close by.

" 'What the devil's that?' said Wealden.

"Something like a stunted, blackened branch was sticking out of the peat, ending in a set of short, thickish twigs. This is what it seemed. The dogs were barking at it. It was, really, a human hand and arm. . . ."

In this book the detection is done by private persons, and the local police are only brought in at the end to secure the criminal. This is also the case in that extremely interesting book *Checkmate* (1870), in which the plot actually turns upon the complete alteration of the criminal's appearance by a miracle of plastic surgery. It seems amazing that more use has not been made of this device in post-war days, now that the reconstruction of faces has become comparatively common and, with the perfecting of aseptic surgery, infinitely easier than in Le Fanu's day. I can only call to mind two recent examples of this kind: one, Mr. Hopkins Moorhouse's *Gauntlet of Alceste*; the other, a short story called "The

Losing of Jasper Virel," by Beckles Willson.[22] In both stories the alterations include the tattooing of the criminal's eyes from blue to brown.

For sheer grimness and power, there is little in the literature of horror to compare with the trepanning scene in Le Fanu's *The House by the Churchyard*. Nobody who has ever read it could possibly forget that sick chamber, with the stricken man sunk in his deathly stupor; the terrified wife; the local doctor, kindly and absurd—and then the pealing of the bell, and the entry of the brilliant, brutal Dillon "in dingy splendours and a great draggled wig, with a gold-headed cane in his bony hand . . . diffusing a reek of whisky-punch, and with a case of instruments under his arm," to perform the operation. The whole scene is magnificently written, with the surgeon's muttered technicalities heard through the door, the footsteps—then the silence while the trepanning is proceeding, and the wounded Sturk's voice, which no one ever thought to hear again, raised as if from the grave to denounce his murderer. That chapter in itself would entitle Le Fanu to be called a master of mystery and horror.

Most important of all during this period we have Wilkie Collins. An extremely uneven writer, Collins is less appreciated today than his merits and influence deserve.[23] He will not bear comparison with Le Fanu in his treatment of the weird, though he was earnestly ambitious to succeed in this line. His style was too dry and inelastic, his mind too legal. Consider the famous dream in *Armadale*, divided into seventeen separate sections, each elaborately and successively fulfilled in laborious detail! In the curious semi-supernatural rhythm of *The Woman in White* he came nearer to genuine achievement, but, on the whole, his eeriness is wire-drawn and unconvincing. But he greatly excels Le Fanu in humour, in the cunning of his rogues,[24] in character-drawing, and especially in the architecture of his plots. Taking everything into consideration, *The Moonstone* is probably the very finest detective story ever written. By comparison with its wide scope, its dove-tailed completeness and the marvellous variety and soundness of its characterisation, modern mystery fiction looks thin and mechanical. Nothing human is perfect, but *The Moonstone* comes about as near perfection as anything of its kind can be.

---

[22] *Strand Magazine*, July 1909.

[23] In the British Museum catalogue only two critical studies of this celebrated English mystery-monger are listed: one is by an American, the other by a German.

[24] Collins made peculiarly his own the art of plot and counter-plot. Thus we have the magnificent duels of Marion Halcombe and Count Fosco in *The Woman in White*; Captain Wragge and Mrs. Lecount in *No Name*; the Pedgifts and Miss Gwilt in *Armadale*. Move answers to move as though on a chessboard (but very much more briskly), until the villain is manœuvred into the corner where a cunningly contrived legal checkmate has been quietly awaiting him from the beginning of the game.

In *The Moonstone* Collins used the convention of telling the story in a series of narratives from the pens of the various actors concerned. Modern realism—often too closely wedded to externals—is prejudiced against this device. It is true that, for example, Betteredge's narrative is not at all the kind of thing that a butler would be likely to write; nevertheless, it has an ideal truth—it is the kind of thing that Betteredge might think and feel, even if he could not write it. And, granted this convention of the various narratives, how admirably the characters are drawn! The pathetic figure of Rosanna Spearman, with her deformity and her warped devotion, is beautifully handled, with a freedom from sentimentality which is very remarkable. In Rachel Verinder, Collins has achieved one of the novelist's hardest tasks; he has depicted a girl who is virtuous, a gentlewoman, and really interesting, and that without the slightest exaggeration or deviation from naturalness and probability. From his preface to the book it is clear that he took especial pains with this character, and his success was so great as almost to defeat itself. Rachel is so little spectacular that we fail to realise what a singularly fine and truthful piece of work she is.

The detective part of the story is well worth attention. The figure of Sergeant Cuff is drawn with a restraint and sobriety which makes him seem a little colourless beside Holmes and Thorndyke and Carrados, but he is a very living figure. One can believe that he made a success of his rose-growing when he retired; he genuinely loved roses, whereas one can never feel that the great Sherlock possessed quite the right feeling for his bees. Being an official detective, Sergeant Cuff is bound by the etiquette of his calling. He is never really given a free hand with Rachel, and the conclusion he comes to is a wrong one. But he puts in a good piece of detective work in the matter of Rosanna and the stained nightgown; and the scenes in which his shrewdness and knowledge of human nature are contrasted with the blundering stupidity of Superintendent Seagrave read like an essay in the manner of Poe.

It is, of course, a fact that the Dupin stories had been published fifteen years or so when *The Moonstone* appeared. But there is no need to seek in them for the original of Sergeant Cuff. He had his prototype in real life, and the whole nightgown incident was modelled, with some modifications, upon a famous case of the early 'sixties—the murder of little William Kent by his sixteen-year-old sister, Constance. Those who are interested in origins will find an excellent account of the "Road murder," as it is called, in Miss Tennyson Jesse's *Murder and its Motives*, or in Atlay's *Famous Trials of the Nineteenth Century*, and may compare the methods of Sergeant Cuff with those of the real Detective Whicher.

Wilkie Collins himself claimed that nearly all his plots were founded on fact; indeed, this was his invariable answer when the charge of improbability was preferred against him.

" 'I wish,' he cries angrily to a friend, 'before people make such assertions, they would think what they are writing or talking about. I know of very few instances in which fiction exceeds the probability of reality. I'll tell you where I got many of my plots from. I was in Paris, wandering about the streets with Charles Dickens, amusing ourselves by looking into the shops. We came to an old book stall—half-shop and half-store—and I found some dilapidated volumes and records of French crime—a sort of French Newgate Calendar. I said to Dickens "Here is a prize!" So it turned out to be. In them I found some of my best plots.' " [25]

Not that Collins was altogether disingenuous in his claim never to have o'erstepped the modesty of nature. While each one of his astonishing contrivances and coincidences might, taken separately, find its parallel in real life, it remains true that in cramming a whole series of such improbabilities into the course of a single story he does frequently end by staggering all belief. But even so, he was a master craftsman, whom many modern mystery-mongers might imitate to their profit. He never wastes an incident; he never leaves a loose end; no incident, however trivial on the one hand or sensational on the other, is ever introduced for the mere sake of amusement or sensation. Take, for example, the great "sensation-scene" in No Name, where for half an hour Magdalen sits, with the bottle of laudanum in her hand, counting the passing ships. "If, in that time, an even number passed her—the sign given should be a sign to live. If the uneven number prevailed, the end should be—death." Here, you would say, is pure sensationalism; it is a situation invented deliberately to wring tears and anguish from the heart of the reader. But you would be wrong. That bottle of laudanum is brought in because it will be wanted again, later on. In the next section of the story it is found in Magdalen's dressing-case, and this discovery, by leading her husband to suppose that she means to murder him, finally induces him to cut her out of his will, and so becomes one of the most important factors in the plot.

In The Moonstone, which of all his books comes nearest to being a detective-story in the modern sense, Collins uses with great effect the formula of the most unlikely person[26] and the unexpected means in conjunction. Opium is the means in this case—a drug with whose effects

---

[25] Wybert Reeve: "Recollections of Wilkie Collins," Chambers' Journal, Vol IX., p. 458.

[26] Franklin Blake—the actual, though unconscious thief. By an ingenious turn, this discovery does not end the story. The diamond is still missing, and a further chase leads to the really guilty party (Godfrey Ablewhite). The character of this gentleman is enough to betray his villainy to the modern reader, though it may have seemed less repulsive to the readers in the 'sixties. His motive, however, is made less obvious, although it is quite honourably and fairly hinted at for the observant reader to guess.

we are tolerably familiar to-day, but which in Collins's time was still something of an unknown quantity, de Quincey notwithstanding. In the opium of *The Moonstone* and the plastic surgery of *Checkmate* we have the distinguished forebears of a long succession of medical and scientific mysteries which stretches down to the present day.

During the 'seventies and early 'eighties the long novel of marvel and mystery held the field, slowly unrolling its labyrinthine complexity through its three ample volumes crammed with incident and leisurely drawn characters.[27]

SHERLOCK HOLMES AND HIS INFLUENCE

In 1887 *A Study in Scarlet* was flung like a bombshell into the field of detective fiction, to be followed within a few short and brilliant years by the marvellous series of Sherlock Holmes short stories. The effect was electric. Conan Doyle took up the Poe formula and galvanised it into life and popularity. He cut out the elaborate psychological introductions, or restated them in crisp dialogue. He brought into prominence what Poe had only lightly touched upon—the deduction of staggering conclusions from trifling indications in the Dumas-Cooper-Gaboriau manner. He was sparkling, surprising, and short. It was the triumph of the epigram.

A comparison of the Sherlock Holmes tales with the Dupin tales shows clearly how much Doyle owed to Poe, and, at the same time, how greatly he modified Poe's style and formula. Read, for instance, the opening pages of "The Murders in the Rue Morgue," which introduce Dupin, and compare them with the first chapter of *A Study in Scarlet*. Or merely set side by side the two passages which follow and contrast the relations between Dupin and his chronicler on the one hand, and between Holmes and Watson on the other:

> "I was astonished, too, at the vast extent of his reading; and, above all, I felt my soul enkindled within me by the wild fervour, and the vivid freshness of his imagination. Seeking in Paris the objects I then sought, I felt that the society of such a man would be to me a treasure beyond price; and this feeling I frankly confided to him. It was at length arranged that we should live together . . . and as my worldly

---

[27] We must not leave this period without mentioning the stories of Anna Katharine Green, of which the long series begins with *The Leavenworth Case* in 1883, and extends right down to the present day. They are genuine detective-stories, often of considerable ingenuity, but marred by an uncritical sentimentality of style and treatment which makes them difficult reading for the modern student. They are, however, important by their volume and by their influence on other American writers.

circumstances were somewhat less embarrassed than his own, I was permitted to be at the expense of renting, and furnishing in a style which suited the rather fantastic gloom of our common temper, a time-eaten and grotesque mansion . . . in a retired and desolate portion of the Faubourg Saint Germain . . . It was a freak of fancy in my friend (for what else shall I call it?) to be enamoured of the Night for her own sake; and into this *bizarrerie*, as into all his others, I quietly fell, giving myself up to his wild whims with a perfect abandon." [28]

"An anomaly which often struck me in the character of my friend Sherlock Holmes was that, though in his methods of thought he was the neatest and most methodical of mankind, and although also he affected a certain quiet primness of dress, he was none the less in his personal habits one of the most untidy men that ever drove a fellow-lodger to distraction. Not that I am in the least conventional in that respect myself. The rough-and-tumble work in Afghanistan, coming on the top of a natural Bohemianism of disposition, has made me rather more lax than befits a medical man. But with me there is a limit, and when I find a man who keeps his cigars in the coal-scuttle, his tobacco in the toe-end of a Persian slipper, and his unanswered correspondence transfixed by a jack-knife into the very centre of his wooden mantel-piece, then I begin to give myself virtuous airs. I have always held, too, that pistol-practice should distinctly be an open-air pastime; and when Holmes in one of his queer humours would sit in an arm-chair, with his hair-trigger and a hundred Boxer cartridges, and proceed to adorn the opposite wall with a patriotic V.R. done in bullet-pocks, I felt strongly that neither the atmosphere nor the appearance of our room was improved by it." [29]

See how the sturdy independence of Watson adds salt and savour to the eccentricities of Holmes, and how flavourless beside it is the hero-worshipping self-abnegation of Dupin's friend. See, too, how the concrete details of daily life in Baker Street lift the story out of the fantastic and give it a solid reality. The Baker Street ménage has just that touch of humorous commonplace which appeals to British readers.

Another pair of parallel passages will be found in "The Purloined Letter" and "The Naval Treaty." They show the two detectives in dramatic mood, surprising their friends by their solution of the mystery. In "The Adventure of the Priory School," also, a similar situation occurs, though Holmes is here shown in a grimmer vein, rebuking wickedness in high places.

---

[28] "The Murders in the Rue Morgue."
[29] "The Musgrave Ritual."

Compare, also, the conversational styles of Holmes and Dupin, and the reasons for Holmes's popularity become clearer than ever. Holmes has enriched English literature with more than one memorable aphorism and turn of speech.

> " 'You know my methods, Watson.'
> " 'A long shot, Watson—a very long shot.'
> " '—a little monograph on the hundred-and-fourteen varieties of tobacco-ash.'
> " 'These are deep waters, Watson.'
> " 'Excellent!' cried Mr. Acton.—'But very superficial,' said Holmes.
> " 'Excellent!' I cried.—'Elementary,' said he.
> " 'It is of the highest importance in the art of detection to be able to recognise out of a number of facts which are incidental and which vital.'
> " 'You mentioned your name as if I should recognise it, but beyond the obvious fact that you are a bachelor, a solicitor, a Freemason and an asthmatic, I know nothing whatever about you.'
> " 'Every problem becomes very childish when once it is explained to you.' "

Nor must we forget that delightful form of riposto which Father Ronald Knox has wittily christened the "Sherlockismus":

> " 'I would call your attention to the curious incident of the dog in the night-time.'
> " 'The dog did nothing in the night-time.'
> " 'That was the curious incident.' "

So, with Sherlock Holmes, the ball—the original nucleus deposited by Edgar Allan Poe nearly forty years earlier—was at last set rolling. As it went, it swelled into a vast mass—it set off others—it became a spate—a torrent—an avalanche of mystery fiction. It is impossible to keep track of all the detective-stories produced to-day. Book upon book, magazine upon magazine pour out from the Press, crammed with murders, thefts, arsons, frauds, conspiracies, problems, puzzles, mysteries, thrills, maniacs, crooks, poisoners, forgers, garrotters, police, spies, secret-service men, detectives, until it seems that half the world must be engaged in setting riddles for the other half to solve.

THE SCIENTIFIC DETECTIVE

The boom began in the 'nineties, when the detective short story, till then rather neglected, strode suddenly to the front and made the pace rapidly under the ægis of Sherlock Holmes. Of particular interest is the long series which appeared under various titles from the pens of L. T. Meade and her collaborators. These struck out a line—not new, indeed, for, as we have seen, it is as old as Collins and Le Fanu, but important because it was paving the way for great developments in a scientific age—the medical mystery story. Mrs. Meade opened up this fruitful vein with *Stories from the Diary of a Doctor* in 1893,[30] and pursued it in various magazines almost without a break to *The Sorceress of the Strand*[31] in 1902. These tales range from mere records of queer cases to genuine detective-stories in which the solution has a scientific or medical foundation. During this long collaboration, the authors deal with such subjects as hypnotism, catalepsy (so-called—then a favourite disease among fiction-writers), somnambulism, lunacy, murder by the use of X-rays and hydrocyanic acid gas, and a variety of other medical and scientific discoveries and inventions.

More definitely in the Holmes tradition is the sound and excellent work of Arthur Morrison in the "Martin Hewitt" books. Various authors such as John Oxenham and Manville Fenn also tried their hands at the detective-story, before turning to specialise in other work. We get also many lively tales of adventure and roguery, with a strong thread of detective interest, as, for example, the "African Millionaire" series by Grant Allen.

Now in the great roar and rush of enthusiasm which greeted Sherlock Holmes, the detective-story became swept away on a single current of development. We observed, in discussing the Poe tales, that there were three types of story—the Intellectual ("Marie Rogêt"), the Sensational ("The Gold Bug"), and the Mixed ("Murders in the Rue Morgue"). "Sherlock Holmes" tales, as a rule, are of the mixed type. Holmes—I regret to say it—does not always play fair with the reader. He "picks up," or "pounces upon," a "minute object," and draws a brilliant deduction from it, but the reader, however brilliant, cannot himself anticipate that deduction because he is not told what the "small object" is. It is Watson's fault, of course—Holmes, indeed, remonstrated with him on at least one occasion about his unscientific methods of narration.

An outstanding master of this "surprise" method is Melville Davisson Post. His tales are so admirably written, and his ideas so ingenious, that we fail at first reading to realise how strictly sensational they are in their method. Take, for instance, "An Act of God" from *Uncle Abner* (1911). In this tale, Uncle Abner uses the phonetic mis-spelling in a letter supposed to be written by a deaf mute to prove that the letter was not, in fact, written by him. If the text of the letter were placed before the

---

[30] In collaboration with "Clifford Halifax."

[31] In collaboration with Robert Eustace. In these stories the scientific basis was provided by Robert Eustace, and the actual writing done, for the most part, by L. T. Meade.

reader, and he were given a chance to make his deduction for himself, the tale would be a true detective-story of the Intellectual type; but the writer keeps this clue to himself, and springs the detective's conclusions upon us like a bolt from the blue.

THE MODERN "FAIR-PLAY" METHOD

For many years, the newness of the genre and the immense prestige of Holmes blinded readers' eyes to these feats of legerdemain. Gradually, however, as the bedazzlement wore off, the public became more and more exacting. The uncritical are still catered for by the "thriller," in which nothing is explained, but connoisseurs have come, more and more, to call for a story which puts them on an equal footing with the detective himself, as regards all clues and discoveries.[32]

Seeing that the demand for equal opportunities is coupled to-day with an insistence on strict technical accuracy in the smallest details of the story, it is obvious that the job of writing detective-stories is by no means growing easier. The reader must be given every clue—but he must not be told, surely, all the detective's deductions, lest he should see the solution too far ahead. Worse still, supposing, even without the detective's help, he interprets all the clues accurately on his own account, what becomes of the surprise? How can we at the same time show the reader everything and yet legitimately obfuscate him as to its meaning?

Various devices are used to get over the difficulty. Frequently the detective, while apparently displaying his clues openly, will keep up his sleeve some bit of special knowledge which the reader does not possess. Thus, Thorndyke can cheerfully show you all his finds. You will be none the wiser, unless you happen to have an intimate acquaintance with the fauna of local ponds; the effect of belladonna on rabbits; the physical and chemical properties of blood; optics; tropical diseases; metallurgy; hieroglyphics, and a few other trifles. Another method of misleading is to tell the reader what the detective has observed and deduced—but to make the observations and deductions turn out to be incorrect, thus leading up to a carefully manufactured surprise-packet in the last chapter.[33]

Some writers, like Mrs. Agatha Christie, still cling to the Watson

---

[32] Yet even to-day the naughty tradition persists. In *The Crime at Diana's Pool*, for instance (1927), V. L. Whitechurch sins notably, twice over, in this respect, in the course of an otherwise excellent tale. But such crimes bring their own punishment, for the modern reader is quick to detect and resent unfairness, and a stern, though kindly letter of rebuke is presently despatched to the erring author!

[33] E. C. Bentley: *Trent's Last Case*; Lord Gorell: *In the Night*; George Pleydell: *The Ware Case*; etc.

formula. The story is told through the mouth, or at least through the eyes, of a Watson.[34] Others, like A. A. Milne in his *Red House Mystery*, adopt a mixed method. Mr. Milne begins by telling his tale from the position of a detached spectator; later on, we find that he has shifted round, and is telling it through the personality of Bill Beverley (a simple-minded but not unintelligent Watson); at another moment we find ourselves actually looking out through the eyes of Antony Gillingham, the detective himself.

IMPORTANCE OF THE VIEWPOINT

The skill of a modern detective novelist is largely shown by the play he makes with these various viewpoints.[35] Let us see how it is done in an acknowledged masterpiece of the genre. We will examine for the purpose a page of Mr. E. C. Bentley's *Trent's Last Case*. Viewpoint No. 1 is what we may call the Watson viewpoint; the detective's external actions only are seen by the reader. Viewpoint No. 2 is the middle viewpoint; we see what the detective sees, but are not told what he observes. Viewpoint No. 3 is that of close intimacy with the detective; we see all he sees, and are at once told his conclusions.
We begin from Viewpoint No. 2.

> "Two bedroom doors faced him on the other side of the passage. He opened that which was immediately opposite, and entered a bedroom by no means austerely tidy. Some sticks and fishing-rods stood confusedly in one corner, a pile of books in another. The housemaid's hand had failed to give a look of order to the jumble of heterogeneous objects left on the dressing-table and on the mantel-shelf—pipes, penknives, pencils, keys, golf-balls, old letters, photographs, small boxes, tins, and bottles. Two fine etchings and some water-colour sketches hung on the walls; leaning against the end of the wardrobe, unhung, were a few framed engravings."

---

[34] An exceptional handling of the Watson theme is found in Agatha Christie's *Murder of Roger Ackroyd*, which is a *tour de force*. Some critics, as, for instance, Mr. W. H. Wright in his introduction to *The Great Detective Stories* (Scribner's, 1927), consider the solution illegitimate. I fancy, however, that this opinion merely represents a natural resentment at having been ingeniously bamboozled. All the necessary data are given. The reader ought to be able to guess the criminal, if he is sharp enough, and nobody can ask for more than this. It is, after all, the reader's job to keep his wits about him, and, like the perfect detective, to suspect *everybody.*

[35] For a most fascinating and illuminating discussion of this question of viewpoint in fiction, see Mr. Percy Lubbock: *The Craft of Fiction.*

First Shift: Viewpoint No. 1.

> "A row of shoes and boots were ranged beneath the window. Trent crossed the room and studied them intently; then he measured some of them with his tape, whistling very softly. This done, he sat on the side of the bed, and his eyes roamed gloomily about the room."

Here we observe Trent walking, studying, measuring, whistling, looking gloomy; but we do not know what was peculiar about the boots, nor what the measurements were. From our knowledge of Trent's character we may suppose that his conclusions are unfavourable to the amiable suspect, Marlowe, but we are not ourselves allowed to handle the material evidence.

Second Shift: Back to Viewpoint No. 2.

> "The photographs on the mantel-shelf attracted him presently. He rose and examined one representing Marlowe and Manderson on horseback. Two others were views of famous peaks in the Alps. There was a faded print of three youths—one of them unmistakably his acquaintance of the haggard blue eyes [i.e. Marlowe]—clothed in tatterdemalion soldier's gear of the sixteenth century. Another was a portrait of a majestic old lady, slightly resembling Marlowe. Trent, mechanically taking a cigarette from an open box on the mantel-shelf, lit it and stared at the photographs."

Here, as at the opening of the paragraph, we are promoted to a more privileged position. We see all the evidence, and have an equal opportunity with Trent of singling out the significant detail—the fancy-costume portrait—and deducting from it that Marlowe was an active member of the O.U.D.S., and, by inference, capable of acting a part at a pinch.

Third Shift: Viewpoint No. 3.

> "Next he turned his attention to a flat leathern case that lay by the cigarette-box. It opened easily. A small and light revolver, of beautiful workmanship, was disclosed, with a score or so of loose cartridges. On the stock were engraved the initials 'J.M.' . . .
>
> "With the pistol in its case between them, Trent and the Inspector looked into each other's eyes for some moments. Trent was the first to speak. 'This mystery is all wrong,' he observed. 'It is insanity. The symptoms of mania are very marked. Let us see how we stand.'"

Throughout the rest of this scene we are taken into Trent's confidence. The revolver is described, we learn what Trent thinks about it from his own lips.

Thus, in a single page, the viewpoint is completely shifted three times, but so delicately that, unless we are looking for it, we do not notice the change.

In a later chapter, we get the final shift to a fourth viewpoint—that of complete mental identification with the detective:

> "Mrs. Manderson had talked herself into a more emotional mood than she had yet shown to Trent. Her words flowed freely, and her voice had begun to ring and give play to a natural expressiveness that must hitherto have been dulled, he thought, by the shock and self-restraint of the past few days."

Here the words "had yet shown to Trent" clinch the identification of viewpoint. Throughout the book, we always, in fact, see Mrs. Manderson through Trent's emotions, and the whole second half of the story, when Trent has abandoned his own enquiries and is receiving the true explanation from Marlowe and Cupples, is told from Viewpoint No. 4.

The modern evolution in the direction of "fair play" [36] is to a great extent a revolution. It is a recoil from the Holmes influence and a turning back to *The Moonstone* and its contemporaries. There is no mystification about *The Moonstone*—no mystification of the reader, that is. With such scrupulous care has Collins laid the clues that the "ideal reasoner" might guess the entire outline of the story at the end of the first ten chapters of Betteredge's first narrative.[37]

---

[36] It is needless to add that the detectives must be given fair play, too. Once they are embarked upon an investigation, no episode must ever be described which does not come within their cognisance. It is artistically shocking that the reader should be taken into the author's confidence behind the investigator's back. Thus, the reader's interest in *The Deductions of Colonel Gore* (Lynn Brock) is sensibly diminished by the fact of his knowing (as Gore does not) that it was Cecil Arndale who witnessed the scene between Mrs. Melhuish and Barrington near the beginning of the book. Those tales in which the action is frequently punctuated by eavesdropping of this kind on the reader's part belong to the merely Sensational class of detective-story, and rapidly decline into melodrama.

[37] Poe performed a similar feat in the case of *Barnaby Rudge*, of which he correctly prognosticated the whole development after reading the first serial part. Unhappily, he was not alive to perform the same office for *Edwin Drood*! Dickens came more and more to hanker after plot and mystery. His early efforts in this style are crude, and the mystery as a rule pretty transparent. In *Edwin Drood* he hoped that the "story would turn upon an interest suspended until the end," and the hope was only too thoroughly fulfilled. Undoubtedly his close friendship with Collins helped to influence him in the direction of mystery fiction; in the previous year (1867) he had pronounced *The Moonstone*: "Much better than anything he [Collins] has done."

ARTISTIC STATUS OF THE
DETECTIVE-STORY

As the detective ceases to be impenetrable and infallible and becomes a man touched with the feeling of our infirmities, so the rigid technique of the art necessarily expands a little. In its severest form, the mystery-story is a pure analytical exercise, and, as such, may be a highly finished work of art, within its highly artificial limits. There is one respect, at least, in which the detective-story has an advantage over every other kind of novel. It possesses an Aristotelian perfection of beginning, middle, and end. A definite and single problem is set, worked out, and solved; its conclusion is not arbitrarily conditioned by marriage or death.[38] It has the rounded (though limited) perfection of a triolet. The farther it escapes from pure analysis, the more difficulty it has in achieving artistic unity.

It does not, and by hypothesis never can, attain the loftiest level of literary achievement. Though it deals with the most desperate effects of rage, jealousy, and revenge, it rarely touches the heights and depths of human passion. It presents us only with the *fait accompli*, and looks upon death and mutilation with a dispassionate eye. It does not show us the inner workings of the murderer's mind—it must not; for the identity of the murderer is hidden until the end of the book.[39] The victim is shown rather as a subject for the dissecting-table than as a husband and father. A too violent emotion flung into the glittering mechanism of the detective-story jars the movement by disturbing its delicate balance. The most successful writers are those who contrive to keep the story running from beginning to end upon the same emotional level, and it is better to err in the direction of too little feeling than too much. Here, the writer whose detective is a member of the official force has an advantage: from

---

[38] This should appeal to Mr. E. M. Forster, who is troubled by the irrational structure of the novel from this point of view. Unhappily, he has openly avowed himself "too priggish" to enjoy detective-stories. This is bad luck, indeed.

[39] An almost unique example of the detective-story told from the point of view of the hunted instead of the hunter is *Ashes to Ashes* by Isabel Ostrander. This shows the clues being left by the murderer, who is then compelled to look on while they are picked up, one after the other, by the detectives, despite all his desperate efforts to cover them. It is a very excellent piece of work which, in the hands of a writer of a little more distinction, might have been a powerful masterpiece. Isabel Ostrander, who also wrote under the name of Robert Orr Chipperfield and other pseudonyms, was a particularly competent spinner of yarns. Her straightforward police-detective, McCarty, is always confounding the conclusions of Terhune—a "scientific" private detective, who believes in modern psycho-analytical detective apparatus.

him a detached attitude is correct; he can suitably retain the impersonal attitude of the surgeon. The sprightly amateur must not be sprightly all the time, lest at some point we should be reminded that this is, after all, a question of somebody's being foully murdered, and that flippancy is indecent. To make the transition from the detached to the human point of view is one of the writer's hardest tasks. It is especially hard when the murderer has been made human and sympathetic. A real person has then to be brought to the gallows, and this must not be done too lightheartedly. Mr. G. K. Chesterton deals with this problem by merely refusing to face it. His Father Brown (who looks at sin and crime from the religious point of view) retires from the problem before the arrest is reached. He is satisfied with a confession. The sordid details take place "off." Other authors permit sympathetic villains to commit suicide. Thus, Mr. Milne's Gillingham, whose attitude starts by being flippant and ends by being rather sentimental, warns Cayley of his approaching arrest, and Cayley shoots himself, leaving a written confession. Monsters of villainy can, of course, be brought to a bad end without compunction; but modern taste rejects monsters, therefore the modern detective-story is compelled to achieve a higher level of writing, and a more competent delineation of character. As the villain is allowed more good streaks in his composition, so the detective must achieve a tenderer human feeling beneath his frivolity or machine-like efficiency.

LOVE INTEREST

One fettering convention, from which detective fiction is only very slowly freeing itself, is that of the "love interest." Publishers and editors still labour under the delusion that all stories must have a nice young man and woman who have to be united in the last chapter. As a result, some of the finest detective-stories are marred by a conventional love-story, irrelevant to the action and perfunctorily worked in. The most harmless form of this disease is that taken, for example, in the works of Mr. Austin Freeman. His secondary characters fall in love with distressing regularity, and perform a number of conventional antics suitable to persons in their condition, but they do not interfere with the course of the story. You can skip the love-passages if you like, and nothing is lost. Far more blameworthy are the heroes who insist on fooling about after young women when they ought to be putting their minds on the job of detection. Just at the critical moment when the trap is set to catch the villain, the sleuth learns that his best girl has been spirited away. Heedlessly he drops everything, and rushes off to Chinatown or to the lonely house on the marshes or wherever it is, without even leaving a note to say where he is going. Here he is promptly sandbagged or entrapped or otherwise made a fool of, and the whole story is impeded and its logical development ruined.

The instances in which the love-story is an integral part of the plot are extremely rare. One very beautiful example occurs in *The Moonstone.* Here the entire plot hangs on the love of two women for Franklin Blake. Both Rachel Verinder and Rosanna Spearman know that he took the diamond, and the whole mystery arises from their efforts to shield him. Their conduct is, in both cases, completely natural and right, and the characters are so finely conceived as to be entirely convincing. E. C. Bentley, in *Trent's Last Case,* has dealt finely with the still harder problem of the detective in love. Trent's love for Mrs. Manderson is a legitimate part of the plot; while it does not prevent him from drawing the proper conclusion from the evidence before him, it does prevent him from acting upon his conclusions, and so prepares the way for the real explanation. Incidentally, the love-story is handled artistically and with persuasive emotion.

In *The House of the Arrow* and, still more strikingly, in *No Other Tiger,* A. E. W. Mason has written stories of strong detective interest which at the same time have the convincing psychological structure of the novel of character. The characters are presented as a novelist presents them—romantically, it is true, but without that stark insistence on classifying and explaining which turns the persons of the ordinary detective-story into a collection of museum exhibits.

Apart from such unusual instances as these, the less love in a detective-story, the better. *"L'amour au théâtre,"* says Racine, *"ne peut pas être en seconde place,"* and this holds good of detective fiction. A casual and perfunctory love-story is worse than no love-story at all, and, since the mystery must, by hypothesis, take the first place, the love is better left out.

Lynn Brock's *The Deductions of Colonel Gore* affords a curious illustration of this truth. Gore sets out, animated by an unselfish devotion to a woman, to recover some compromising letters for her, and, in so doing, becomes involved in unravelling an intricate murder plot. As the story goes on, the references to the beloved woman become chillier and more perfunctory; not only does the author seem to have lost interest, but so does Colonel Gore. At length the author notices this, and explains it in a paragraph:

> "There were moments when Gore accused himself—or, rather, felt that he ought to accuse himself—of an undue coldbloodedness in these speculations of his. The business was a horrible business. One ought to have been decently shocked by it. One ought to have been horrified by the thought that three old friends were involved in such a business.
>
> "But the truth was—and his apologies to himself for that truth became feebler and feebler—that the thing had now so caught hold of

him that he had come to regard the actors in it as merely pieces of a puzzle baffling and engrossing to the verge of monomania."

There is the whole difficulty about allowing real human beings into a detective-story. At some point or other, either their emotions make hay of the detective interest, or the detective interest gets hold of them and makes their emotions look like pasteboard. It is, of course, a fact that we all adopt a detached attitude towards "a good murder" in the newspaper. Like Betteredge in *The Moonstone*, we get "detective fever," and forget the victim in the fun of tracking the criminal. For this reason, it is better not to pitch the emotional key too high at the start; the inevitable drop is thus made less jarring.

FUTURE DEVELOPMENTS: FASHIONS AND FORMULÆ

Just at present, therefore, the fashion in detective fiction is to have characters credible and lively; not conventional, but, on the other hand, not too profoundly studied—people who live more or less on the *Punch* level of emotion. A little more psychological complexity is allowed than formerly; the villain may not be a villain from every point of view; the heroine, if there is one, is not necessarily pure; the falsely accused innocent need not be a sympathetic character.[40] The automata —the embodied vices and virtues—the weeping fair-haired girl—the stupid but manly young man with the biceps—even the colossally evil scientist with the hypnotic eyes—are all disappearing from the intellectual branch of the art, to be replaced by figures having more in common with humanity.

An interesting symptom of this tendency is the arrival of a number of books and stories which recast, under the guise of fiction, actual murder cases drawn from real life. Thus, Mrs. Belloc Lowndes and Mrs. Victor Rickard have both dealt with the Bravo Poisoning Mystery. Anthony Berkeley has retold the Maybrick case; Mr. E. H. W. Meyerstein has published a play based on the Seddon poisoning case, and Mr. Aldous Huxley, in "The Gioconda Smile," has reinterpreted in his own manner another famous case of recent years.[41]

We are now in a position to ask ourselves the favourite question of

---

[40] e.g. in J. J. Connington's *The Tragedy at Ravensthorpe*, where the agoraphobic Maurice is by no means an agreeable person to have about the house.

[41] *What Really Happened,* by Mrs. Belloc Lowndes; *Not Sufficient Evidence,* by Mrs. Victor Rickard; *The Wychford Poisoning Drama* by the Author of *The Layton Court Mystery; Heddon,* by E. H. W. Meyerstein; *Mortal Coils,* by Aldous Huxley.

modern times: What next? Where is the detective-story going? Has it a future? Or will the present boom see the end of it?

THE MOST UNLIKELY PERSON

In early mystery fiction, the problem tends to be, *who* did the crime? At first, while readers were still unsophisticated, the formula of the Most Unlikely Person had a good run. But the reader soon learned to see through this. If there was a single person in the story who appeared to have no motive for the crime and who was allowed to amble through to the penultimate chapter free from any shadow of suspicion, that character became a marked man or woman. "I knew he must be guilty because nothing was said about him," said the cunning reader. Thus we come to a new axiom, laid down by Mr. G. K. Chesterton in a brilliant essay in the *New Statesman:* the real criminal must be suspected at least once in the course of the story. Once he is suspected, and then (apparently) cleared, he is made safe from future suspicion. This is the principle behind Mr. Wills Crofts' impregnable alibis, which are eventually broken down by painstaking enquiry. Probably the most baffling form of detective-story is still that in which suspicion is distributed equally among a number of candidates, one of whom turns out to be guilty. Other developments of the Most Unlikely Person formula make the guilty person a juror at the inquest or trial;[42] the detective himself;[43] the counsel for the prosecution;[44] and, as a supreme effort of unlikeness, the actual narrator of the story.[45] Finally, resort has been made to the doublecross, and the person originally suspected turns out to be the right person after all.[46]

THE UNEXPECTED MEANS

There are signs, however, that the possibilities of the formula are becoming exhausted, and of late years much has been done in exploring the solution by the unexpected means. With recent discoveries in medical and chemical science, this field has become exceedingly fruitful, particularly in the provision of new methods of murder. It is fortunate for the mystery-monger that, whereas, up to the present, there is only one

---

[42] Robert Orr Chipperfield: *The Man in the Jury-Box.*
[43] Bernard Capes: *The Skeleton Key;* Gaston Leroux: *Mystère de la Chambre Jaune;* etc.
[44] G. K. Chesterton: "The Mirror of the Magistrate" (*Innocence of Father Brown*).
[45] Agatha Christie: *The Murder of Roger Ackroyd.*
[46] Father R. Knox: *The Viaduct Murder,* and others.

known way of getting born, there are endless ways of getting killed. Here is a brief selection of handy short cuts to the grave: Poisoned tooth-stoppings; licking poisoned stamps; shaving-brushes inoculated with dread diseases; poisoned boiled eggs (a bright thought); poison-gas; a cat with poisoned claws; poisoned mattresses; knives dropped through the ceiling; stabbing with a sharp icicle; electrocution by telephone; biting by plague-rats and typhoid-carrying lice; boiling lead in the ears (much more effective than cursed hebanon in a vial): air-bubbles injected into the arteries; explosion of a gigantic "Prince Rupert's drop"; frightening to death; hanging head-downwards; freezing to atoms in liquid air; hypodermic injections shot from air-guns; exposure, while insensible, to extreme cold; guns concealed in cameras; a thermometer which explodes a bomb when the temperature of the room reaches a certain height; and so forth.

The methods of disposing of inconvenient corpses are also varied and peculiar; burial under a false certificate obtained in a number of ways; substitution of one corpse for another (very common in fiction, though rare in real life); mummification; reduction to bone-dust; electro-plating; arson; "planting" (not in the church-yard, but on innocent parties)—a method first made famous by R. L. Stevenson.[47] Thus, of the three questions, "Who?" "How?" and "Why?" "How" is at present the one which offers most scope for surprise and ingenuity, and is capable of sustaining an entire book on its own, though a combination of all three naturally provides the best entertainment.[48]

The mystery-monger's principal difficulty is that of varying his surprises. "You know my methods, Watson," says the detective, and it is only too painfully true. The beauty of Watson was, of course, that after thirty years he still did not know Holmes's methods; but the average reader is sharper-witted. After reading half a dozen stories by one author, he is sufficiently advanced in Dupin's psychological method[49] to see with the author's eyes. He knows that, when Mr. Austin Freeman drowns somebody in a pond full of water-snails, there will be something odd and localised about those snails; he knows that, when one of Mr. Wills Crofts's characters has a cast-iron alibi, the alibi will turn out to have holes in it; he knows that if Father Knox casts suspicion on a Papist, the Papist will turn out to be innocent; instead of detecting the murderer, he is engaged in detecting the writer. That is why he gets the impression

---

[47] *The Wrong Box.*

[48] Mr. Austin Freeman has specialised in a detective-story which rejects all three questions. He tells the story of the crime first, and relies for his interest on the pleasure afforded by following the ingenious methods of the investigator. *The Singing Bone* contains several tales of this type. Mr. Freeman has had few followers, and appears to have himself abandoned the formula, which is rather a pity.

[49] As outlined in "The Purloined Letter."

that the writer's later books are seldom or never "up to" his earlier efforts. He has become married to the writer's muse, and marriage has destroyed the mystery.

There certainly does seem a possibility that the detective-story will some time come to an end, simply because the public will have learnt all the tricks. But it has probably many years to go yet, and in the meantime a new and less rigid formula will probably have developed, linking it more closely to the novel of manners and separating it more widely from the novel of adventure. The latter will, no doubt, last as long as humanity, and while crime exists, the crime thriller will hold its place. It is, as always, the higher type that is threatened with extinction.

At the time of writing (1928) the detective-story is profiting by a reaction against novels of the static type. Mr. E. M. Forster is indeed left murmuring regretfully, "Yes, ah! yes—the novel tells a story"; but the majority of the public are rediscovering that fact with cries of triumph. Sexual abnormalities are suffering a slight slump at the moment; the novel of passion still holds the first place, especially among women, but even women seem to be growing out of the simple love-story. Probably the cheerful cynicism of the detective-tale suits better with the spirit of the times than the sentimentality which ends in wedding bells. For, make no mistake about it, the detective-story is part of the literature of escape, and not of expression. We read tales of domestic unhappiness because that is the kind of thing which happens to us; but when these things gall too close to the sore, we fly to mystery and adventure because they do not, as a rule, happen to us. "The detective-story," says Philip Guedalla, "is the normal recreation of noble minds." And it is remarkable how strong is the fascination of the higher type of detective-story for the intellectually-minded, among writers as well as readers. The average detective-novel to-day is extremely well written, and there are few good living writers who have not tried their hand at it at one time or another.[50]

QUESTIONS

1. Sayers writes that early crime literature expressed an admiration for the "cunning and astuteness of the criminal." Does a significant

---

[50] Among men of letters distinguished in other lines who have turned their attention to the detective-story may be mentioned A. E. W. Mason, Eden Phillpotts, "Lynn Brock" (whose pseudonym protects the personality of a well-known writer), Somerset Maugham, Rudyard Kipling, A. A. Milne, Father R. Knox, J. D. Beresford.

It is owing to the work of such men as these that the detective-novel reaches a much higher artistic level in England than in any other country. At every turn the quality of the writing and the attention to beauty of form and structure betray the hand of the practised novelist.

amount of contemporary crime literature do the same thing? Think especially of recent movies in which the criminal escapes scot-free. Would this in some way indicate that many now feel contemporary law is "arbitrary, oppressive, and brutally administered"?

2. Why are there so few fictional detectives under thirty or forty? Do traditional detective stories naturally feature older characters and appeal primarily to older readers?

3. Do you agree that "it is doubtful whether there are more than half a dozen deceptions in the mystery-monger's bag of tricks"?

4. Categorize the stories in this book in line with Sayers' classifications of the "Romantic" and the "Classic," the "Sensational" and the "Intellectual." Do they fit easily? How do these classifications apply to the stories in "The Genre Extended"?

5. Sayers mentions many authors who are doubtless unknown to the readers of this sourcebook. Why do so few detective story writers achieve lasting fame, despite their popularity in their own times?

6. What do you think of Sayers' discussion of point of view? Explain your reaction.

7. Discuss Sayers' thoughts about "detached attitudes," "lack of feeling," "real human beings." How do they apply to writers of the hard-boiled school? Do the cautions apply heavily to contemporary detective story writers, or has a gain in "art" been made?

A Defence of
Detective Stories

G. K. Chesterton

In attempting to reach the genuine psychological reason for the popularity of detective stories, it is necessary to rid ourselves of many mere phrases. It is not true, for example, that the populace prefer bad literature to good, and accept detective stories because they are bad literature. The mere absence of artistic subtlety does not make a book popular. Bradshaw's Railway Guide contains few gleams of psychological comedy, yet it is not read aloud unroariously on winter evenings. If detective stories are read with more exuberance than railway guides, it is certainly because they are more artistic. Many good books have fortunately been popular; many bad books, still more fortunately, have been unpopular. A good detective story would probably be even more popular than a bad one. The trouble in this matter is that many people do not realize that there is such a thing as a good detective story; it is to them like speaking of a good devil. To write a story about a burglary is, in their eyes, a sort of spiritual manner of committing it. To persons of somewhat weak sensibility this is natural enough; it must be confessed that many detective stories are as full of sensational crime as one of Shakespeare's plays.

There is, however, between a good detective story and a bad detective story as much, or, rather more, difference than there is between a good epic and a bad one. Not only is a detective story a perfectly legitimate form of art, but it has certain definite and real advantages as an agent of the public weal.

The first essential value of the detective story lies in this, that it is the earliest and only form of popular literature in which is expressed some sense of the poetry of modern life. Men lived among mighty mountains and eternal forests for ages before they realized that they were poetical; it may reasonably be inferred that some of our descendants may see the chimney-pots as rich a purple as the mountain-peaks, and find the lamp-posts as old and natural as the trees. Of this realization of a great city itself as something wild and obvious the detective story is certainly the 'Iliad.' No one can have failed to notice that in these stories the hero or the investigator crosses London with something of the loneliness and liberty of a prince in a tale of elfland, that in the course of that incalculable journey the casual omnibus assumes the primal colours of a fairy ship. The lights of the city begin to glow like innumerable goblin eyes, since they are the guardians of some secret, however crude, which the writer knows and the reader does not. Every twist of the road is like a finger pointing to it; every fantastic skyline of chimney-pots seems wildly and derisively signalling the meaning of the mystery.

This realization of the poetry of London is not a small thing. A city is, properly speaking, more poetic even than a countryside, for while Nature is a chaos of unconscious forces, a city is a chaos of conscious ones. The crest of the flower or the pattern of the lichen may or may not be significant symbols. But there is no stone in the street and no brick in the wall that is not actually a deliberate symbol—a message from some man, as much as if it were a telegram or a post-card. The narrowest street possesses, in every crook and twist its intention, the soul of the man who built it, perhaps long in his grave. Every brick has as human a hieroglyph as if it were a graven brick of Babylon; every slate on the roof is as educational a document as if it were a slate covered with addition and subtraction sums. Anything which tends, even under the fantastic form of the minutiæ of Sherlock Holmes, to assert this romance of detail in civilization, to emphasize this unfathomably human character in flints and tiles, is a good thing. It is good that the average man should fall into the habit of looking imaginatively at ten men in the street even if it is only on the chance that the eleventh might be a notorious thief. We may dream, perhaps, that it might be possible to have another and higher romance of London, that men's souls have stranger adventures than their bodies, and that it would be harder and more exciting to hunt their virtues than to hunt their crimes. But since our great authors (with the admirable exception of Stevenson) decline to write of that thrilling mood and moment when the eyes of the great city, like the eyes of a cat, begin to flame in the dark, we must give fair credit to the popular literature which, amid a babble of pedantry and preciosity, declines to regard the present as prosaic or the common as commonplace. Popular art in all ages has been interested in contemporary manners and costume; it dressed the groups around the Crucifixion in the garb of Florentine gentlefolk or Flemish burghers. In the last century it was the custom for distinguished actors to present Macbeth in a powdered wig and ruffles. How far we are ourselves in this age from such conviction of the poetry of our own life and manners may easily be conceived by anyone who chooses to imagine a picture of Alfred the Great toasting the cakes dressed in tourist's knickerbockers, or a performance of 'Hamlet' in which the Prince appeared in a frock-coat, with a crape band round his hat. But this instinct of the age to look back, like Lot's wife, could not go on for ever. A rude, popular literature of the romantic possibilities of the modern city was bound to arise. It has arisen in the popular detective stories, as rough and refreshing as the ballads of Robin Hood.

There is, however, another good work that is done by detective stories. While it is the constant tendency of the Old Adam to rebel against so universal and automatic a thing as civilization, to preach departure and rebellion, the romance of police activity keeps in some sense before the mind the fact that civilization itself is the most sensational of departures and the most romantic of rebellions. By dealing with the unsleeping sentinels who guard the outposts of society, it tends to remind us that we live in an armed camp, making war with a chaotic world, and that the criminals, the children of chaos, are nothing but the traitors within our gates. When the detective in a police romance stands alone, and somewhat fatuously fearless amid the knives and fists of a thieves' kitchen, it does certainly serve to make us remember that it is the agent of social justice who is the original and poetic figure, while the burglars and footpads are merely placid old cosmic conservatives, happy in the immemorial respectability of apes and wolves. The romance of the police force is thus the whole romance of man. It is based on the fact that morality is the most dark and daring of conspiracies. It reminds us that the whole noiseless and unnoticeable police management by which we are ruled and protected is only a successful knight-errantry.

QUESTIONS

1. Do you agree that "it is not true . . . that the populace prefer bad literature to good"?

2. Chesterton says "we must give fair credit to the popular literature which . . . declines to regard the present as prosaic or the common as commonplace." Does his statement apply to many types of contemporary literature?

3. Are criminals "children of chaos . . . nothing but the traitors within our gates"?

4. What do you think of the statement: "The romance of the police force is . . . the whole romance of man"?

5. Why do so many detective stories take place in an urban environment? Are your reasons in addition to those mentioned by Sayers and Chesterton?

6. Do you prefer to regard the majority of detective stories as "realistic" or "romantic"? Why?

The Simple Art of Murder

Raymond Chandler

Fiction in any form has always intended to be realistic. Old-fashioned novels which now seem stilted and artificial to the point of burlesque did not appear that way to the people who first read them. Writers like Fielding and Smollett could seem realistic in the modern sense because they dealt largely with uninhibited characters, many of whom were about two jumps ahead of the police, but Jane Austen's chronicles of highly inhibited people against a background of rural gentility seem real enough psychologically. There is plenty of that kind of social and emotional hypocrisy around today. Add to it a liberal dose of intellectual pretentiousness and you get the tone of the book page in your daily paper and the earnest and fatuous atmosphere breathed by discussion groups in little clubs. These are the people who make best-sellers, which are promotional jobs based on a sort of indirect snob-appeal, carefully escorted by the trained seals of the critical fraternity, and lovingly tended and watered by certain much too powerful pressure groups whose business is selling books, although they would like you to think they are fostering culture. Just get a little behind in your payments and you will find out how idealistic they are.

The detective story for a variety of reasons can seldom be promoted. It is usually about murder and hence lacks the element of uplift. Murder, which is a frustration of the individual and hence a frustration of the race, may, and in fact has, a good deal of sociological implication. But it has been going on too long for it to be news. If the mystery novel is at all realistic (which it very seldom is) it is written in a certain spirit of detachment; otherwise nobody but a psychopath would want to write it or read it. The murder novel has also a depressing way of minding its own business, solving its own problems and answering its own questions. There is nothing left to discuss, except whether it was well enough written to be good fiction, and the people who make up the half-million sales wouldn't know that anyway. The detection of quality in writing is difficult enough even for those who make a career of the job, without paying too much attention to the matter of advance sales.

The detective story (perhaps I had better call it that, since the English formula still dominates the trade) has to find its public by a slow process of distillation. That it does do this, and holds on thereafter with such tenacity, is a fact; the reasons for it are a study for more patient minds than mine. Nor is it any part of my thesis to maintain that it is a vital and significant form of art. There are no vital and significant forms of art; there is only art, and precious little of that. The growth of populations has in no way increased the amount; it has merely increased the adeptness with which substitutes can be produced and packaged.

Yet the detective story, even in its most conventional form, is difficult to write well. Good specimens of the art are much rarer than good serious novels. Rather second-rate items outlast most of the high velocity fiction, and a great many that should never have been born simply refuse to die at all. They are as durable as the statues in public parks and just about that dull. This is very annoying to people of what is called discernment. They do not like it that penetrating and important works of fiction of a few years back stand on their special shelf in the library marked "Best-Sellers of Yesteryear," and nobody goes near them but an occasional shortsighted customer who bends down, peers briefly and hurries away; while old ladies jostle each other at the mystery shelf to grab off some item of the same vintage with a title like *The Triple Petunia Murder Case*, or *Inspector Pinchbottle to the Rescue*. They do not like it that "really important books" get dusty on the reprint counter, while *Death Wears Yellow Garters* is put out in editions of fifty or one hundred thousand copies on the news-stands of the country, and is obviously not there just to say goodbye.

To tell you the truth, I do not like it very much myself. In my less stilted moments I too write detective stories, and all this immortality makes just a little too much competition. Even Einstein couldn't get very far if three hundred treatises of the higher physics were published every year, and several thousand others in some form or other were hanging around in excellent condition, and being read too. Hemingway says somewhere that the good writer competes only with the dead. The good detective story writer (there must after all be a few) competes not only with all the unburied dead but with all the hosts of the living as well. And on almost equal terms; for it is one of the qualities of this kind of writing that the thing that makes people read it never goes out of style. The hero's tie may be a little off the mode and the good gray inspector may arrive in a dogcart instead of a streamlined sedan with siren screaming, but what he does when he gets there is the same old futzing around with timetables and bits of charred paper and who trampled the jolly old flowering arbutus under the library window.

I have, however, a less sordid interest in the matter. It seems to me that production of detective stories on so large a scale, and by writers whose immediate reward is small and whose need of critical praise is almost nil, would not be possible at all if the job took any talent. In that sense the raised eyebrow of the critic and the shoddy merchandizing of the publisher are perfectly logical. The average detective story is probably no worse than the average novel, but you never see the average novel. It doesn't get published. The average—or only slightly above average—detective story does. Not only is it published but it is sold in small quantities to rental libraries, and it is read. There are even a few optimists who buy it at the full retail price of two dollars, because it looks so fresh and new, and there is a picture of a corpse on the cover. And the strange thing is that this average, more than middling dull, pooped-out piece of utterly unreal and mechanical fiction is not terribly different from what are called the masterpieces of the art. It drags on a little more slowly, the dialogue is a little grayer, the cardboard out of which the characters are cut is a shade thinner, and the cheating is a little more obvious; but it is the same kind of book. Whereas the good novel is not at all the same kind of book as the bad novel. It is about entirely different things. But the good detective story and the bad detective story are about exactly the same things, and they are about them in very much the same way. There are reasons for this too, and reasons for the reasons; there always are.

I suppose the principal dilemma of the traditional or classic or straight-deductive or logic—and—deduction novel of detection is that for any approach to perfection it demands a combination of qualities not found in the same mind. The cool-headed constructionist does not also come across with lively characters, sharp dialogue, a sense of pace and an acute use of observed detail. The grim logician has as much atmosphere as a drawing-board. The scientific sleuth has a nice new shiny laboratory, but I'm sorry I can't remember the face. The fellow who can write you a vivid and colorful prose simply won't be bothered with the coolie labor of breaking down unbreakable alibis. The master of rare knowledge is living psychologically in the age of the hoop skirt. If you know all you should know about ceramics and Egyptian needlework, you don't know anything at all about the police. If you know that platinum won't melt under about 2800 degrees F. by itself, but will melt at the glance of a pair of deep blue eyes when put close to a bar of lead, then you don't know how men make love in the twentieth century. And if you know enough about the elegant flânerie of the pre-war French Riviera to lay your story in that locale, you don't know that a couple of capsules of barbital small enough to be swallowed will not only not kill a man—they will not even put him to sleep, if he fights against them.

Every detective story writer makes mistakes, and none will ever know as much as he should. Conan Doyle made mistakes which completely invalidated some of his stories, but he was a pioneer, and Sherlock Holmes after all is mostly an attitude and a few dozen lines of unforgettable dialogue. It is the ladies and gentlemen of what Mr. Howard Haycraft (in his book *Murder for Pleasure*) calls the Golden Age of detective fiction that really get me down. This age is not remote. For

Mr. Haycraft's purpose it starts after the first World War and lasts up to about 1930. For all practical purposes it is still here. Two-thirds or three-quarters of all the detective stories published still adhere to the formula the giants of this era created, perfected, polished and sold to the world as problems in logic and deduction. These are stern words, but be not alarmed. They are only words. Let us glance at one of the glories of the literature, an acknowledged masterpiece of the art of fooling the reader without cheating him. It is called *The Red House Mystery*, was written by A. A. Milne, and has been named by Alexander Woollcott (rather a fast man with a superlative) "one of the three best mystery stories of all time." Words of that size are not spoken lightly. The book was published in 1922, but is quite timeless, and might as easily have been published in July 1939, or, with a few slight changes, last week. It ran thirteen editions and seems to have been in print, in the original format, for about sixteen years. That happens to few books of any kind. It is an agreeable book, light, amusing in the *Punch* style, written with a deceptive smoothness that is not as easy as it looks.

It concerns Mark Ablett's impersonation of his brother Robert, as a hoax on his friends. Mark is the owner of the Red House, a typical laburnum-and-lodge-gate English country house, and he has a secretary who encourages him and abets him in this impersonation, because the secretary is going to murder him, if he pulls it off. Nobody around the Red House has ever seen Robert, fifteen years absent in Australia, known to them by repute as a no-good. A letter from Robert is talked about, but never shown. It announces his arrival, and Mark hints it will not be a pleasant occasion. One afternoon, then, the supposed Robert arrives, identifies himself to a couple of servants, is shown into the study, and Mark (according to testimony at the inquest) goes in after him. Robert is then found dead on the floor with a bullet hole in his face, and of course Mark has vanished into thin air. Arrive the police, suspect Mark must be the murderer, remove the debris and proceed with the investigation, and in due course, with the inquest.

Milne is aware of one very difficult hurdle and tries as well as he can to get over it. Since the secretary is going to murder Mark once he has established himself as Robert, the impersonation has to continue on and fool the police. Since, also, everybody around the Red House knows Mark intimately, disguise is necessary. This is achieved by shaving off Mark's beard, roughening his hands ("not the hands of a manicured gentleman"—testimony) and the use of a gruff voice and rough manner. But this is not enough. The cops are going to have the body and the clothes on it and whatever is in the pockets. Therefore none of this must suggest Mark. Milne therefore works like a switch engine to put over the motivation that Mark is such a thoroughly conceited performer that he dresses the part down to the socks and underwear (from all of which the secretary has removed the maker's labels), like a ham blacking himself all over to play Othello. If the reader will buy this (and the sales record shows he must have) Milne figures he is solid. Yet, however light in texture the story may be, it is offered as a problem of logic and deduction. If it is not that, it is nothing at all. There is nothing else for it to be. If the situation is false, you cannot even accept it as a light novel, for there is no story for the light novel to be about. If the problem does not contain the elements of truth and plausibility, it is no problem; if the logic is an illusion, there is nothing to deduce. If the impersonation is impossible once the reader is told the conditions it must fulfill, then the whole thing is a fraud. Not a deliberate fraud, because Milne would not have written the story if he had known what he was up against. He is up against a number of deadly things, none of which he even considers. Nor, apparently, does the casual reader, who wants to like the story, hence takes it at its face value. But the reader is not called upon to know the facts of life; it is the author who is the expert in the case. Here is what this author ignores:

1. The coroner holds formal jury inquest on a body for which no competent legal identification is offered. A coroner, usually in a big city, will sometimes hold inquest on a body that *cannot* be identified, if the record of such an inquest has or may have a value (fire, disaster, evidence of murder, etc.). No such reason exists here, and there is no one to identify the body. A couple of witnesses said the man said he was Robert Ablett. This is mere presumption, and has weight only if nothing conflicts with it. Identification is a condition precedent to an inquest. Even in death a man has a right to his own identity. The coroner will, wherever humanly possible, enforce that right. To neglect it would be a violation of his office.

2. Since Mark Ablett, missing and suspected of the murder, cannot defend himself, all evidence of his movements before and after the murder is vital (as also whether he has money to run away on); yet all such evidence is given by the man closest to the murder, and is without corroboration. It is automatically suspect until proved true.

3. The police find by direct investigation that Robert Ablett was not well thought of in his native village. Somebody there must have known him. No such person was brought to the inquest. (The story couldn't stand it.)

4. The police know there is an element of threat in Robert's supposed visit, and that it is connected with the murder must be obvious to them. Yet they make no attempt to check Robert in Australia, or find out what character he had there, or what associates, or even if he actually came to England, and with whom. (If they had, they would have found out he had been dead three years.)

5. The police surgeon examines the body with a recently shaved beard (exposing unweathered skin), artificially roughened hands, yet the body of a wealthy, soft-living man, long resident in a cool climate. Robert was

a rough individual and had lived fifteen years in Australia. That is the surgeon's information. It is impossible he would have noticed nothing to conflict with it.

6. The clothes are nameless, empty, and have had the labels removed. Yet the man wearing them asserted an identity. The presumption that he was not what he said he was is overpowering. Nothing whatever is done about this peculiar circumstance. It is never even mentioned as being peculiar.

7. A man is missing, a well-known local man, and a body in the morgue closely resembles him. It is impossible that the police should not at once eliminate the chance that the missing man *is* the dead man. Nothing would be easier than to prove it. Not even to think of it is incredible. It makes idiots of the police, so that a brash amateur may startle the world with a fake solution.

The detective in the case is an insouciant gent named Antony Gillingham, a nice lad with a cheery eye, a cozy little flat in London, and that airy manner. He is not making any money on the assignment, but is always available when the local gendarmerie loses its notebook. The English police seem to endure him with their customary stoicism; but I shudder to think of what the boys down at the Homicide Bureau in my city would do to him.

There are less plausible examples of the art than this. In *Trent's Last Case* (often called "the perfect detective story") you have to accept the premise that a giant of international finance, whose lightest frown makes Wall Street quiver like a chihuahua, will plot his own death so as to hang his secretary, and that the secretary when pinched will maintain an aristocratic silence; the old Etonian in him maybe. I have known relatively few international financiers, but I rather think the author of this novel has (if possible) known fewer. There is one by Freeman Wills Crofts (the soundest builder of them all when he doesn't get too fancy) wherein a murderer by the aid of makeup, split second timing, and some very sweet evasive action, impersonates the man he has just killed and thereby gets him alive and distant from the place of the crime. There is one of Dorothy Sayers' in which a man is murdered alone at night in his house by a mechanically released weight which works because he always turns the radio on at just such a moment, always stands in just such a position in front of it, and always bends over just so far. A couple of inches either way and the customers would get a rain check. This is what is vulgarly known as having God sit in your lap; a murderer who needs that much help from Providence must be in the wrong business. And there is a scheme of Agatha Christie's featuring M. Hercule Poirot, that ingenious Belgian who talks in a literal translation of school-boy French, wherein, by duly messing around with his "little gray cells," M. Poirot decides that nobody on a certain through sleeper could have done the murder alone, therefore everybody did it together, breaking the process down into a series of simple operations, like assembling an egg-beater. This is the type that is guaranteed to knock the keenest mind for a loop. Only a halfwit could guess it.

There are much better plots by these same writers and by others of their school. There may be one somewhere that would really stand up under close scrutiny. It would be fun to read it, even if I did have to go back to page 47 and refresh my memory about exactly what time the second gardener potted the prize-winning tearose begonia. There is nothing new about these stories and nothing old. The ones I mentioned are all English only because the authorities (such as they are) seem to feel the English writers had an edge in this dreary routine, and that the Americans, (even the creator of Philo Vance—probably the most asinine character in detective fiction) only made the Junior Varsity.

This, the classic detective story, has learned nothing and forgotten nothing. It is the story you will find almost any week in the big shiny magazines, handsomely illustrated, and paying due deference to virginal love and the right kind of luxury goods. Perhaps the tempo has become a trifle faster, and the dialogue a little more glib. There are more frozen daiquiris and stingers ordered, and fewer glasses of crusty old port; more clothes by *Vogue*, and décors by the *House Beautiful*, more chic, but not more truth. We spend more time in Miami hotels and Cape Cod summer colonies and go not so often down by the old gray sundial in the Elizabethan garden. But fundamentally it is the same careful grouping of suspects, the same utterly incomprehensible trick of how somebody stabbed Mrs. Pottington Postlethwaite III with the solid platinum poignard just as she flatted on the top note of the Bell Song from *Lakmé* in the presence of fifteen ill-assorted guests; the same ingenue in fur-trimmed pajamas screaming in the night to make the company pop in and out of doors and ball up the timetable; the same moody silence next day as they sit around sipping Singapore slings and sneering at each other, while the flat-feet crawl to and fro under the Persian rugs, with their derby hats on.

Personally I like the English style better. It is not quite so brittle, and the people as a rule, just wear clothes and drink drinks. There is more sense of background, as if Cheesecake Manor really existed all around and not just the part the camera sees; there are more long walks over the Downs and the characters don't all try to behave as if they had just been tested by MGM. The English may not always be the best writers in the world, but they are incomparably the best dull writers.

There is a very simple statement to be made about all these stories: they do not really come off intellectually as problems, and they do not come off artistically as fiction. They are too contrived, and too little aware of what goes on in the world. They try to be honest, but honesty is an art. The poor writer is dishonest without knowing it, and the fairly good one can be dishonest because he doesn't know what to be honest about. He thinks a complicated murder scheme which baffles the lazy reader, who won't be bothered itemizing the details, will also baffle the police, whose business is with details. The boys with their feet on the desks know that the easiest murder case in the world to break is the one somebody tried to get very cute with; the one that really bothers them is the murder somebody only thought of two minutes before he pulled it off. But if the writers of this fiction wrote about the kind of murders that happen, they would also have to write about the authentic flavor of life as it is lived. And since they cannot do that, they pretend that what they do is what should be done. Which is begging the question—and the best of them know it.

In her introduction to the first *Omnibus of Crime*, Dorothy Sayers wrote: "It (the detective story) does not, and by hypothesis never can, attain the loftiest level of literary achievement." And she suggested somewhere else that this is because it is a "literature of escape" and not "a literature of expression." I do not know what the loftiest level of literary achievement is: neither did Aeschylus or Shakespeare; neither does Miss Sayers. Other things being equal, which they never are, a more powerful theme will provoke a more powerful performance. Yet some very dull books have been written about God, and some very fine ones about how to make a living and stay fairly honest. It is always a matter of who writes the stuff, and what he has in him to write it with. As for literature of expression and literature of escape, this is critics' jargon, a use of abstract words as if they had absolute meanings. Everything written with vitality expresses that vitality; there are no dull subjects, only dull minds. All men who read escape from something else into what lies behind the printed page; the quality of the dream may be argued, but its release has become a functional necessity. All men must escape at times from the deadly rhythm of their private thoughts. It is part of the process of life among thinking beings. It is one of the things that distinguish them from the three-toed sloth; he apparently—one can never be quite sure—is perfectly content hanging upside down on a branch, and not even reading Walter Lippmann. I hold no particular brief for the detective story as the ideal escape. I merely say that *all* reading for pleasure is escape, whether it be Greek, mathematics, astronomy, Benedetto Croce, or *The Diary of the Forgotten Man*. To say otherwise is to be an intellectual snob, and a juvenile at the art of living.

I do not think such considerations moved Miss Dorothy Sayers to her essay in critical futility.

I think what was really gnawing at her mind was the slow realization that her kind of detective story was an arid formula which could not even satisfy its own implications. It was second-grade literature because it was not about the things that could make first-grade literature. If it started out to be about real people (and she could write about them—her minor characters show that), they must very soon do unreal things in order to form the artificial pattern required by the plot. When they did unreal things, they ceased to be real themselves. They became puppets and cardboard lovers and papier mâché villains and detectives of exquisite and impossible gentility. The only kind of writer who could be happy with these properties was the one who did not know what reality was. Dorothy Sayers' own stories show that she was annoyed by this triteness; the weakest element in them is the part that makes them detective stories, the strongest the part which could be removed without touching the "problem of logic and deduction." Yet she could not or would not give her characters their heads and let them make their own mystery. It took a much simpler and more direct mind than hers to do that.

In the *Long Week-End*, which is a drastically competent account of English life and manners in the decade following the first World War, Robert Graves and Alan Hodge gave some attention to the detective story. They were just as traditionally English as the ornaments of the Golden Age, and they wrote of the time in which these writers were almost as well-known as any writers in the world. Their books in one form or another sold into the millions, and in a dozen languages. These were the people who fixed the form and established the rules and founded the famous Detection Club, which is a Parnassus of English writers of mystery. Its roster includes practically every important writer of detective fiction since Conan Doyle. But Graves and Hodge decided that during this whole period only one first-class writer had written detective stories at all. An American, Dashiell Hammett. Traditional or not, Graves and Hodge were not fuddy-duddy connoisseurs of the second rate; they could see what went on in the world and that the detective story of their time didn't; and they were aware that writers who have the vision and the ability to produce real fiction do not produce unreal fiction.

How original a writer Hammett really was, it isn't easy to decide now, even if it mattered. He was one of a group, the only one who achieved critical recognition, but not the only one who wrote or tried to write realistic mystery fiction. All literary movements are like this; some one individual is picked out to represent the whole movement; he is usually the culmination of the movement. Hammett was the ace performer, but there is nothing in his work that is not implicit in the early novels and short stories of Hemingway. Yet for all I know, Hemingway may have learned something from Hammett, as well as from writers like Dreiser, Ring Lardner, Carl Sandburg, Sherwood Anderson and himself. A rather revolutionary debunking of both the language and material of fiction had been going on for some time. It probably started in poetry; almost everything does. You can take it clear back to Walt Whitman, if you like. But Hammett applied it to the detective story, and this, because of its heavy crust of English gentility and American psuedo-gentility, was pretty hard to get moving. I doubt that Hammett had any deliberate artistic aims whatever; he was trying to make a living by writing something he had first hand information about. He made some of it up; all writers do; but it had a basis in fact; it was made up out of real things. The only reality the English detection writers knew was the conversational accent of Surbiton and Bognor Regis. If they wrote about dukes and Venetian vases, they knew no more about them out of their own experience than the well-heeled Hollywood character knows about the French Modernists that hang in his Bel-Air château or the semi-antique Chippendale-cum-cobbler's bench that he uses for a coffee table. Hammett took murder out of the Venetian vase and dropped it into the alley; it doesn't have to stay there forever, but it was a good idea to begin by getting as far as possible from Emily Post's idea of how a well-bred debutante gnaws a chicken wing. He wrote at first (and almost to the end) for people with a sharp, aggressive attitude to life. They were not afraid of the seamy side of things; they lived there. Violence did not dismay them; it was right down their street.

Hammett gave murder back to the kind of people that commit it for reasons, not just to provide a corpse; and with the means at hand, not with hand-wrought duelling pistols, curare, and tropical fish. He put these people down on paper as they are, and he made them talk and think in the language they customarily used for these purposes. He had style, but his audience didn't know it, because it was in a language not supposed to be capable of such refinements. They thought they were getting a good meaty melodrama written in the kind of lingo they imagined they spoke themselves. It was, in a sense, but it was much more. All language begins with speech, and the speech of common men at that, but when it develops to the point of becoming a literary medium it only looks like speech. Hammett's style at its worst was almost as formalized as a page of Marius the Epicurean; at its best it could say almost anything. I believe this style, which does not belong to Hammett or to anybody, but is the American language (and not even exclusively that any more), can say things he did not know how to say or feel the need of saying. In his hands it had no overtones, left no echo, evoked no image beyond a distant hill. He is said to have lacked heart, yet the story he thought most of himself is the record of a man's devotion to a friend. He was spare, frugal, hardboiled, but he did over and over again what only the best writers can ever do at all. He wrote scenes that seemed never to have been written before.

With all this he did not wreck the formal detective story. Nobody can; production demands a form that can be produced. Realism takes too much talent, too much knowledge, too much awareness. Hammett may have loosened it up a little here, and sharpened it a little there. Certainly all but the stupidest and most meretricious writers are more conscious of their artificiality than they used to be. And he demonstrated that the detective story can be important writing. *The Maltese Falcon* may or may not be a work of genius, but an art which is capable of it is not "by hypothesis" incapable of anything. Once a detective story can be as good as this, only the pedants will deny that it *could* be even better. Hammett did something else, he made the detective story fun to write, not an exhausting concatenation of insignificant clues. Without him there might not have been a regional mystery as clever as Percival Wilde's *Inquest*, or an ironic study as able as Raymond Postgate's *Verdict of Twelve*, or a savage piece of intellectual double-talk like Kenneth Fearing's *The Dagger of the Mind*, or a tragi-comic idealization of the murderer as in Donald Henderson's *Mr. Bowling Buys a Newspaper*, or even a gay and intriguing Hollywoodian gambol like Richard Sale's *Lazarus No. 7*.

The realistic style is easy to abuse: from haste, from lack of awareness, from inability to bridge the chasm that lies between what a writer would like to be able to say and what he actually knows how to say. It is easy to fake; brutality is not strength, flipness is not wit, edge-of-the-chair writing can be as boring as flat writing; dalliance with promiscuous blondes can be very dull stuff when described by goaty young men with no other purpose in mind than to describe dalliance with promiscuous blondes. There has been so much of this sort of thing that if a character in a detective story says, "Yeah," the author is automatically a Hammett imitator.

And there are still quite a few people around who say that Hammett did not write detective stories at all, merely hard-boiled chronicles of mean streets with a perfunctory mystery element dropped in like the olive in a martini. These are the flustered old ladies—of both sexes (or no sex) and almost all ages—who like their murders scented with magnolia blossoms and do not care to be reminded that murder is an act of infinite cruelty, even if the perpetrators sometimes look like playboys or college professors or nice motherly women with softly graying hair. There are also a few badly-scared champions of the formal or the classic mystery who think no story is a detective story which does not pose a formal and exact problem and arrange the clues around it with neat labels on them. Such would point out, for example, that in reading *The Maltese Falcon* no one concerns himself with who killed Spade's partner, Archer (which is the only formal problem of the story) because the reader is kept thinking about something else. Yet in *The Glass Key* the reader is constantly reminded that the question is who killed Taylor Henry, and exactly the same effect is obtained; an effect of movement, intrigue, cross-purposes and the gradual elucidation of character, which is all the detective story has any right to be about anyway. The rest is spillikins in the parlor.

But all this (and Hammett too) is for me not quite enough. The realist in murder writes of a world in which gangsters can rule nations and almost rule cities, in which hotels and apartment houses and celebrated restaurants are owned by men who made their money out of brothels, in which a screen star can be the fingerman for a mob, and the nice man down the hall is a boss of the numbers racket; a world where a judge with a cellar full of bootleg liquor can send a man to jail for having a pint in his pocket, where the mayor of your town may have condoned murder as an instrument of money-making, where no man can walk down a dark street in safety because law and order are things we talk about but refrain from practising; a world where you may witness a hold-up in broad daylight and see who did it, but you will fade quickly back into the crowd rather than tell anyone, because the hold-up men may have friends with long guns, or the police may not like your testimony, and in any case the shyster for the defense will be allowed to abuse and vilify you in open court, before a jury of selected morons, without any but the most perfunctory interference from a political judge.

It is not a very fragrant world, but it is the world you live in, and certain writers with tough minds and a cool spirit of detachment can make very interesting and even amusing patterns out of it. It is not funny that a man should be killed, but it is sometimes funny that he should be killed for so little, and that his death should be the coin of what we call civilization. All this still is not quite enough.

In everything that can be called art there is a quality of redemption. It may be pure tragedy, if it is high tragedy, and it may be pity and irony, and it may be the raucous laughter of the strong man. But down these mean streets a man must go who is not himself mean, who is neither tarnished nor afraid. The detective in this kind of story must be such a man. He is the hero, he is everything. He must be a complete man and a common man and yet an unusual man. He must be, to use a rather weathered phrase, a man of honor, by instinct, by inevitability, without thought of it, and certainly without saying it. He must be the best man in his world and a good enough man for any world. I do not care much about his private life; he is neither a eunuch nor a satyr; I think he might seduce a duchess and I am quite sure he would not spoil a virgin; if he is a man of honor in one thing, he is that in all things. He is a relatively poor man, or he would not be a detective at all. He is a common man, or he could not go among common people. He has a sense of character, or he would not know his job. He will take no man's money dishonestly and no man's insolence without a due and dispassionate revenge. He is a lonely man and his pride is that you will treat him as a proud man or be very sorry you ever saw him. He talks as the man of his age talks, that is, with rude wit, a lively sense of the grotesque, a disgust for sham, and a contempt for pettiness. The story is his adventure in search of a hidden truth, and it would be no adventure if it did not happen to a man fit for adventure. He has a range of awareness that startles you, but it belongs to him by right, because it belongs to the world he lives in.

If there were enough like him, I think the world would be a very safe place to live in, and yet not too dull to be worth living in.

QUESTIONS

1. Chandler writes: "If the mystery novel is at all realistic (which it very seldom is) it is written in a certain spirit of detachment; otherwise nobody but a psychopath would want to write it or read it." Do you agree? Discuss, especially in comparison with Dorothy Sayers' ideas on this subject.

2. Do you agree that "there are no vital and significant forms of art; there is only art, and precious little of that"?

3. Is Chandler right when he says that the "average detective story is probably no worse than the average novel"? Discuss the implications of this statement.

4. Chandler seriously criticizes several noted detective novels, saying, "They are too contrived, and too little aware of what goes on in the world. They try to be honest, but honesty is an art." Discuss, basing your discussion especially on the stories in the sourcebook.

5. How does Chandler's "The Curtain" reflect the theories presented in this essay?

6. "All men . . . must escape at times from the deadly rhythm of their private thoughts," writes Chandler. But do you agree with him when he says that *all* reading for pleasure is escape? What do you think of the person who reads, say, four or five detective novels to every one "literary" novel? How might escape reading be harmful? (You might refer to the Daley essay for discussion material concerning this question.)

7. Is Chandler fair to Sayers?

8. Consider Chandler's praise for Hammett's style. Read over "Fly Paper," and see if you agree with Chandler. Compare the style to that of Hemingway in "The Killers."

9. Must, as Chandler implies, the best of detective stories contain a detective who is "everything . . . a man of honor . . . the best man in his world"?

The Guilty Vicarage

W. H. Auden

I had not known sin, but by the law.

ROMANS: VII, 7

A CONFESSION

For me, as for many others, the reading of detective stories is an addiction like tobacco or alcohol. The symptoms of this are: firstly, the intensity of the craving—if I have any work to do, I must be careful not to get hold of a detective story for, once I begin one, I cannot work or sleep till I have finished it. Secondly, its specificity—the story must conform to certain formulas (I find it very difficult, for example, to read one that is not set in rural England). And, thirdly, its immediacy. I forget the story as soon as I have finished it, and have no wish to read it again. If, as sometimes happens, I start reading one and find after a few pages that I have read it before, I cannot go on.

Such reactions convince me that, in my case at least, detective stories have nothing to do with works of art. It is possible, however, that an analysis of the detective story, i.e., of the kind of detective story I enjoy, may throw light, not only on its magical function, but also, by contrast, on the function of art.

DEFINITION

The vulgar definition, "a Whodunit," is correct. The basic formula is this: a murder occurs; many are suspected; all but one suspect, who is the murderer, are eliminated; the murderer is arrested or dies.

This definition excludes:

1) Studies of murderers whose guilt is known, e.g., *Malice Afore-thought*. There are borderline cases in which the murderer is known and there are no false suspects, but the proof is lacking, e.g., many of the stories of Freeman Wills Crofts. Most of these are permissible.

2) Thrillers, spy stories, stories of master crooks, etc., when the identification of the criminal is subordinate to the defeat of his criminal designs.

The interest in the thriller is the ethical and characteristic conflict between good and evil, between Us and Them. The interest in the study of a murderer is the observation, by the innocent many, of the sufferings of the guilty one. The interest in the detective story is the dialectic of innocence and guilt.

As in the Aristotelian description of tragedy, there is Concealment (the innocent seem guilty and the guilty seem innocent) and Manifestation (the real guilt is brought to consciousness). There is also peripeteia, in this case not a reversal of fortune but a double reversal from apparent guilt to innocence and from apparent innocence to guilt. The formula may be diagrammed as follows:

Peaceful state before
    murder

False clues, secondary
    murder, etc.

Solution

Arrest of murderer

Peaceful state after
    arrest

False innocence

Revelation of presence
    of guilt

False location of guilt

Location of real guilt

Catharsis

True innocence

In Greek tragedy the audience knows the truth; the actors do not, but discover or bring to pass the inevitable. In modern, e.g., Elizabethan, tragedy the audience knows neither less nor more than the most knowing of the actors. In the detective story the audience does not know the truth at all; one of the actors—the murderer—does; and the detective, of his own free will, discovers and reveals what the murderer, of his own free will, tries to conceal.

Greek tragedy and the detective story have one characteristic in common in which they both differ from modern tragedy, namely, the characters are not changed in or by their actions: in Greek tragedy because their actions are fated, in the detective story because the decisive event, the murder, has already occurred. Time and space therefore are simply the when and where of revealing either what has to happen or what has actually happened. In consequence, the detective story probably should, and usually does, obey the classical unities, whereas modern tragedy, in which the characters develop with time, can only do so by a technical tour de force; and the thriller, like the picaresque novel, even demands frequent changes of time and place.

WHY MURDER?

There are three classes of crime: (A) offenses against God and one's neighbor or neighbors; (B) offenses against God and society; (C) offenses against God. (All crimes, of course, are offenses against oneself.)

Murder is a member and the only member of Class B. The character common to all crimes in Class A is that it is possible, at least theoretically, either that restitution can be made to the injured party (e.g., stolen goods can be returned), or that the injured party can forgive the criminal (e.g., in the case of rape). Consequently, society as a whole is only indirectly involved; its representatives (the police, etc.) act in the interests of the injured party.

Murder is unique in that it abolishes the party it injures, so that society has to take the place of the victim and on his behalf demand restitution or grant forgiveness; it is the one crime in which society has a direct interest.

Many detective stories begin with a death that appears to be suicide and is later discovered to have been murder. Suicide is a crime belonging to Class C in which neither the criminal's neighbors nor society has any interest, direct or indirect. As long as a death is believed to be suicide, even private curiosity is improper; as soon as it is proved to be murder, public inquiry becomes a duty.

The detective story has five elements—the milieu, the victim, the murderer, the suspects, the detectives.

THE MILIEU (HUMAN)

The detective story requires:

1) A closed society so that the possibility of an outside murderer (and hence of the society being totally innocent) is excluded; and a closely related society so that all its members are potentially suspect (cf. the thriller, which requires an open society in which any stranger may be a friend or enemy in disguise).

Such conditions are met by: a) the group of blood relatives (the Christmas dinner in the country house); b) the closely knit geographical group (the old world village); c) the occupational group (the theatrical company); d) the group isolated by the neutral place (the Pullman car).

In this last type the concealment-manifestation formula applies not only to the murder but also to the relations between the members of the group who first appear to be strangers to each other, but are later found to be related.

2) It must appear to be an innocent society in a state of grace, i.e., a society where there is no need of the law, no contradiction between the aesthetic individual and the ethical universal, and where murder, therefore, is the unheard-of act which precipitates a crisis (for it reveals that some member has fallen and is no longer in a state of grace). The law becomes a reality and for a time all must live in its shadow, till the fallen one is identified. With his arrest, innocence is restored, and the law retires forever.

The characters in a detective story should, therefore, be eccentric (aesthetically interesting individuals) and good (instinctively ethical)—good, that is, either in appearance, later shown to be false, or in reality, first concealed by an appearance of bad.

It is a sound instinct that has made so many detective story writers choose a college as a setting. The ruling passion of the ideal professor is the pursuit of knowledge for its own sake so that he is related to other human beings only indirectly through their common relation to the truth; and those passions, like lust and avarice and envy, which relate individuals directly and may lead to murder are, in his case, ideally excluded. If a murder occurs in a college, therefore, it is a sign that some colleague is not only a bad man but also a bad professor. Further, as the basic premise of academic life is that truth is universal and to be shared with all, the *gnosis* of a concrete crime and the *gnosis* of abstract ideas nicely parallel and parody each other.

(The even more ideal contradiction of a murder in a monastery is excluded by the fact that monks go regularly to confession and, while the murderer might well not confess his crime, the suspects who are innocent of murder but guilty of lesser sins cannot be supposed to conceal them without making the monastery absurd. Incidentally, is it an accident that the detective story has flourished most in predominantly Protestant countries?)

The detective story writer is also wise to choose a society with an elaborate ritual and to describe this in detail. A ritual is a sign of harmony between the aesthetic and the ethical in which body and mind, individual will and general laws, are not in conflict. The murderer uses his knowledge of the ritual to commit the crime and can be caught only by someone who acquires an equal or superior familiarity with it.

THE MILIEU (NATURAL)

In the detective story, as in its mirror image, the Quest for the Grail, maps (the ritual of space) and timetables (the ritual of time) are desirable. Nature should reflect its human inhabitants, i.e., it should be the Great Good Place; for the more Eden-like it is, the greater the contradiction of murder. The country is preferable to the town, a well-to-do neighborhood (but not too well-to-do—or there will be a suspicion of ill-gotten gains) better than a slum. The corpse must shock not only because it is a corpse but also because, even for a corpse, it is shockingly out of place, as when a dog makes a mess on a drawing room carpet.

Mr. Raymond Chandler has written that he intends to take the body out of the vicarage garden and give the murder back to those who are good at it. If he wishes to write detective stories, i.e., stories where the reader's principal interest is to learn who did it, he could not be more mistaken, for in a society of professional criminals, the only possible motives for desiring to identify the murderer are blackmail or revenge, which both apply to individuals, not to the group as a whole, and can equally well inspire murder. Actually, whatever he may say, I think Mr. Chandler is interested in writing, not detective stories, but serious studies of a criminal milieu, the Great Wrong Place, and his powerful but extremely depressing books should be read and judged, not as escape literature, but as works of art.

THE VICTIM

The victim has to try to satisfy two contradictory requirements. He has to involve everyone in suspicion, which requires that he be a bad character; and he has to make everyone feel guilty, which requires that he be a good character. He cannot be a criminal because he could then be dealt with by the law and murder would be unnecessary. (Blackmail is the only exception.) The more general the temptation to murder he arouses, the better; e.g., the desire for freedom is a better motive than money alone or sex alone. On the whole, the best victim is the negative Father or Mother Image.

If there is more than one murder, the subsequent victims should be more innocent than the initial victim, i.e., the murderer should start with a real grievance and, as a consequence of righting it by illegitimate means, be forced to murder against his will where he has no grievances but his own guilt.

THE MURDERER

Murder is negative creation, and every murderer is therefore the rebel who claims the right to be omnipotent. His pathos is his refusal to suffer. The problem for the writer is to conceal his demonic pride from the other characters and from the reader, since, if a person has this pride, it tends to appear in everything he says and does. To surprise the reader when the identity of the murderer is revealed, yet at the same time to convince him that everything he has previously been told about the murderer is consistent with his being a murderer, is the test of a good detective story.

As to the murderer's end, of the three alternatives—execution, suicide, and madness—the first is preferable; for if he commits suicide he refuses to repent, and if he goes mad he cannot repent, but if he does not repent society cannot forgive. Execution on the other hand, is the act of atonement by which the murderer is forgiven by society. In real life I disapprove of capital punishment, but in a detective story the murderer must have no future.

(*A Suggestion for Mr. Chandler:* Among a group of efficient professional killers who murder for strictly professional reasons, there is one to whom, like Leopold and Loeb, murder is an *acte gratuite*. Presently murders begin to occur which have not been commissioned. The group is morally outraged and bewildered; it has to call in the police to detect the amateur murderer, rescue the professionals from a mutual suspicion which threatens to disrupt their organization, and restore their capacity to murder.)

THE SUSPECTS

The detective-story society is a society consisting of apparently innocent individuals, i.e., their aesthetic interest as individuals does not conflict with their ethical obligations to the universal. The murder is the act of disruption by which innocence is lost, and the individual and the law become opposed to each other. In the case of the murderer this opposition is completely real (till he is arrested and consents to be punished); in the case of the suspects it is mostly apparent.

But in order for the appearance to exist, there must be some element of reality; e.g., it is unsatisfactory if the suspicion is caused by chance or the murderer's malice alone. The suspects must be guilty of something, because, now that the aesthetic and the ethical are in opposition, if they are completely innocent (obedient to the ethical) they lose their aesthetic interest and the reader will ignore them.

For suspects, the principal causes of guilt are:

1) the wish or even the intention to murder;

2) crimes of Class A or vices of Class C (e.g., illicit amours) which the suspect is afraid or ashamed to reveal;

3) a *hubris* of intellect which tries to solve the crime itself and despises

the official police (assertion of the supremacy of the aesthetic over the ethical). If great enough, this *hubris* leads to its subject getting murdered;

4) a *hubris* of innocence which refuses to cooperate with the investigation;

5) a lack of faith in another loved suspect, which leads its subject to hide or confuse clues.

THE DETECTIVE

Completely satisfactory detectives are extremely rare. Indeed, I only know of three: Sherlock Holmes (Conan Doyle), Inspector French (Freeman Wills Crofts), and Father Brown (Chesterton).

The job of detective is to restore the state of grace in which the aesthetic and the ethical are as one. Since the murderer who caused their disjunction is the aesthetically defiant individual, his opponent, the detective, must be either the official representative of the ethical or the exceptional individual who is himself in a state of grace. If he is the former, he is a professional; if he is the latter, he is an amateur. In either case, the detective must be the total stranger who cannot possibly be involved in the crime; this excludes the local police and should, I think, exclude the detective who is a friend of one of the suspects. The professional detective has the advantage that, since he is not an individual but a representative of the ethical, he does not need a motive for investigating the crime; but for the same reason he has the disadvantage of being unable to overlook the minor ethical violations of the suspects, and therefore it is harder for him to gain their confidence.

Most amateur detectives, on the other hand, are unsatisfactory either because they are priggish supermen, like Lord Peter Wimsey and Philo Vance, who have no motive for being detectives except caprice, or because, like the detectives of the hard-boiled school, they are motivated by avarice or ambition and might just as well be murderers.

The amateur detective genius may have weaknesses to give him aesthetic interest, but they must not be of a kind which outrage ethics. The most satisfactory weaknesses are the solitary oral vices of eating and drinking or childish boasting. In his sexual life, the detective must be either celibate or happily married.

Between the amateur detective and the professional policeman stands the criminal lawyer whose *telos* is, not to discover who is guilty, but to prove that his client is innocent. His ethical justification is that human law is ethically imperfect, i.e., not an absolute manifestation of the universe and divine, and subject to chance aesthetic limitations, e.g., the intelligence or stupidity of individual policemen and juries (in consequence of which an innocent man may sometimes be judged guilty).

To correct this imperfection, the decision is arrived at through an aesthetic combat, i.e., the intellectual gifts of the defense versus those of the prosecution, just as in earlier days doubtful cases were solved by physical combat between the accused and the accuser.

The lawyer-detective (e.g., Joshua Clunk) is never quite satisfactory, therefore, because of his commitment to his client, whom he cannot desert, even if he should really be the guilty party, without ceasing to be a lawyer.

SHERLOCK HOLMES

Holmes is the exceptional individual who is in a state of grace because he is a genius in whom scientific curiosity is raised to the status of a heroic passion. He is erudite but his knowledge is absolutely specialized (e.g., his ignorance of the Copernican system), he is in all matters outside his field as helpless as a child (e.g., his untidiness), and he pays the price for his scientific detachment (his neglect of feeling) by being the victim of melancholia which attacks him whenever he is unoccupied with a case (e.g., his violin playing and cocaine taking).

His motive for being a detective is, positively, a love of the neutral truth (he has no interest in the feelings of the guilty or the innocent), and negatively, a need to escape from his own feelings of melancholy. His attitude towards people and his technique of observation and deduction are those of the chemist or physicist. If he chooses human beings rather than inanimate matter as his material, it is because investigating the inanimate is unheroically easy since it cannot tell lies, which human beings can and do, so that in dealing with them, observation must be twice as sharp and logic twice as rigorous.

INSPECTOR FRENCH

His class and culture are those natural to a Scotland Yard inspector. (The old Oxonian Inspector is insufferable.) His motive is love of duty. Holmes detects for his own sake and shows the maximum indifference to all feelings except a negative fear of his own. French detects for the sake of the innocent members of society, and is indifferent only to his own feelings and those of the murderer. (He would much rather stay at home with his wife.) He is exceptional only in his exceptional love of duty which makes him take exceptional pains; he does only what all could do as well if they had the same patient industry (his checking of alibis for tiny flaws which careless hurry had missed). He outwits the murderer, partly because the latter is not quite so painstaking as he, and partly because the murderer must act alone, while he has the help of all the innocent people in the world who are doing their duty, e.g., the postmen, railway clerks, milkmen, etc., who become, accidentally, witnesses to the truth.

FATHER BROWN

Like Holmes, an amateur; yet, like French, not an individual genius. His activities as a detective are an incidental part of his activities as a priest who cares for souls. His prime motive is compassion, of which the guilty are in greater need than the innocent, and he investigates murders, not for his own sake, nor even for the sake of the innocent, but for the sake of the murderer who can save his soul if he will confess and repent. He solves his cases, not by approaching them objectively like a scientist or a policeman, but by subjectively imagining himself to be the murderer, a process which is good not only for the murderer but for Father Brown himself because, as he says, "it gives a man his remorse beforehand."

Holmes and French can only help the murderer as teachers, i.e., they can teach him that murder will out and does not pay. More they cannot do since neither is tempted to murder; Holmes is too gifted, French too well trained in the habit of virtue. Father Brown can go further and help the murderer as an example, i.e., as a man who is also tempted to murder, but is able by faith to resist temptation.

THE READER

The most curious fact about the detective story is that it makes its greatest appeal precisely to those classes of people who are most immune to other forms of daydream literature. The typical detective story addict is a doctor or clergyman or scientist or artist, i.e., a fairly successful professional man with intellectual interests and well-read in his own field, who could never stomach the *Saturday Evening Post* or *True Confessions* or movie magazines or comics. If I ask myself why I cannot enjoy stories about strong silent men and lovely girls who make love in a beautiful landscape and come into millions of dollars, I cannot answer that I have no fantasies of being handsome and loved and rich, because of course I have (though my life is, perhaps, sufficiently fortunate to make me less envious in a naïve way than some). No, I can only say that I am too conscious of the absurdity of such wishes to enjoy seeing them reflected in print.

I can, to some degree, resist yielding to these or similar desires which tempt me, but I cannot prevent myself from having them to resist; and it is the fact that I have them which makes me feel guilty, so that instead of dreaming about indulging my desires, I dream about the removal of the guilt which I feel at their existence. This I still do, and must do, because guilt is a subjective feeling where any further step is only a reduplication —feeling guilty about guilt. I suspect that the typical reader of detective stories is, like myself, a person who suffers from a sense of sin. From the point of view of ethics, desires and acts are good and bad, and I must choose the good and reject the bad, but the I which makes this choice is ethically neutral; it only becomes good or bad in its choice. To have a sense of sin means to feel guilty at there being an ethical choice to make, a guilt which, however "good" I may become, remains unchanged. It is sometimes said that detective stories are read by respectable law-abiding citizens in order to gratify in fantasy the violent or murderous wishes they dare not, or are ashamed to, translate into action. This may be true for the reader of thrillers (which I rarely enjoy), but it is quite false for the reader of detective stories. On the contrary, the magical satisfaction the latter provide (which makes them escape literature, not works of art) is the illusion of being dissociated from the murderer.

The magic formula is an innocence which is discovered to contain guilt; then a suspicion of being the guilty one; and finally a real innocence from which the guilty other has been expelled, a cure effected, not by me or my neighbors, but by the miraculous intervention of a genius from outside who removes guilt by giving knowledge of guilt. (The detective story subscribes, in fact, to the Socratic daydream: "Sin is ignorance.")

If one thinks of a work of art which deals with murder, *Crime and Punishment* for example, its effect on the reader is to compel an identification with the murderer which he would prefer not to recognize. The identification of fantasy is always an attempt to avoid one's own suffering: the identification of art is a sharing in the suffering of another. Kafka's *The Trial* is another instructive example of the difference between a work of art and the detective story. In the latter it is certain that a crime has been committed and, temporarily, uncertain to whom the guilt should be attached; as soon as this is known, the innocence of everyone else is certain. (Should it turn out that after all no crime has been committed, then all would be innocent.) In *The Trial*, on the other hand, it is the guilt that is certain and the crime that is uncertain; the aim of the hero's investigation is not to prove his innocence (which would be impossible for he knows he is guilty), but to discover what, if anything, he has done to make himself guilty. K, the hero, is, in fact, a portrait of the kind of person who reads detective stories for escape.

The fantasy, then, which the detective story addict indulges is the fantasy of being restored to the Garden of Eden, to a state of innocence, where he may know love as love and not as the law. The driving force behind this daydream is the feeling of guilt, the cause of which is unknown to the dreamer. The fantasy of escape is the same, whether one explains the guilt in Christian, Freudian, or any other terms. One's way of trying to face the reality, on the other hand, will, of course, depend very much on one's creed.

QUESTIONS

1. Do you agree with Auden that "detective stories have nothing to do with works of art"? Judging from what you have read by Raymond Chandler, would you feel he would mainly agree that his "books should be read and judged, not as escape literature, but as works of art"?

2. What stories in this sourcebook would you classify as "thrillers"? Has Auden's system of classification reflected your understanding?

3. Are you satisfied with Auden's statement that "there are three classes of crime"? In your own definitions and classifications, would you pay this much attention to religious attitudes?

4. Discuss this essay as it relates to the differences in British and American detective fiction.

5. Auden says, "the best victim is the negative Father or Mother Image." What does this mean? Can you find stories in this sourcebook in which the victim fits this category?

6. Discuss the idea that the murderer's "pathos is his refusal to suffer."

7. Explain why you agree or disagree that "the detective must be either celibate or happily married."

8. Auden feels "that the typical reader of detective stories . . . suffers from a sense of sin." Explain this further, especially as it relates to the educated audience.

Murder and the Mean Streets:
The Hard-Boiled Detective Novel

George Grella

In America the formal detective novel has never found a proper home. Though read widely, and practiced by such authors as S. S. Van Dine, Rex Stout, and Ellery Queen, the form has never really flourished here. Conditions do not favor the comedy of manners. Where in England a society with recognizable class distinctions provides a propitious background for isolating a select number of privileged characters, American society is vast, polyglot, and heterogeneous, difficult to capsulize. In a culture characterized by diversity rather than homogeneity, microcosms demand at least platoon strength. The United States still lacks the traditions and institutions that Cooper, Hawthorne, and James envied: a ruling class, a landed gentry, an Established Church, the great gentleman-producing public schools and universities, in short, all the developed structures of a venerable history. Where the English are fond of eccentrics, Americans regard the Great Detective as more fatuous than acute. Nero Wolfe's massive misanthropy and misogyny seem more psychopathic than endearing. The gentleman amateur is even more incongruous in a society where "gentleman" connotes far less than in England, and where languid, airy-mannered young men seldom play heroic roles. Ellery Queen and Philo Vance appear prissy, unmasculine, and at times, insufferable. (Ogden Nash's comment, "Philo Vance needs a kick in the pance," is a typical, healthy American reaction.) Finally, where the formal detective novel displays the charm and manner, the generally polished and solid techniques of English fiction, American attempts at the whodunit usually lack style and distinction. As Raymond Chandler remarked, "The English may not always be the best writers in the world, but they are incomparably the best dull writers."

The form that dominates American practice is the "hard-boiled" detective story, radically different from the classic whodunit. Rejecting the established patterns, it drew its materials from the indigenous life of America, including its major literary tradition. If the dominant American novel is, as has been maintained, a romance, so is the American detective story, and for the same reasons. Where the English novel is notable for its mental, moral, and spiritual health, and as Richard Chase points out, "gives the impression of absorbing all extremes into a normative view of life," the American novel has a "penchant for the marvelous, the sensational, the legendary, and in general, the heightened effect." The American novel is "less interested in incarnation and reconciliation than in alienation and disorder." Since the American novel derives from a mixed tradition, encompassing folk tales, medieval literature, Gothic novels, and the works of writers like Scott and Cooper, it reflects a variety of romance elements—pastoral, melodrama, legend, and myth. Influenced by the Puritan imagination, it tends to see life as a Manichean struggle between good and evil; its vision, moreover, is usually obsessed with sin. Energized by the self-reliance of the frontier, it customarily establishes its moral norm within the consciousness of an individual man. The quest motif often supplies its structure, as in the medieval and mythic romance. The hard-boiled detective novel thus employs a characteristically American hero and world view, which it translates into the framework of a twentieth century mystery story. Its central problem is a version of the quest, both a search for truth and an attempt to eradicate evil.

The American detective novel, paradoxically, combines its romance themes and structures with a tough, realistic surface and a highly sensational content, both in part a heritage of its origin in popular cheap magazines. The hard-boiled stories appeared soon after World War I in the "action" pulps, where they shared space with Westerns, hunting and fishing yarns, war stories, and adventure fiction of all kinds. Constrained by the limited education of their audience and performing in the bloody arena of a lowbrow medium, the hard-boiled writers rejected the sometimes constricting formulas of the formal detective novel. Abandoning the static calm, the intricate puzzle, the ingenious deductions, they wrote an entirely different detective story, characterized by rapid action, colloquial language, emotional impact, and the violence that pervades American fiction. The most important magazine, the famous *Black Mask*, rose to prominence under the gifted editorship of Joseph T. Shaw, who outlined his requirements for detective fiction. "We wanted simplicity for the sake of clarity, plausibility, and belief," Shaw wrote. "We wanted action, but held that action is meaningless unless it involves recognizable human character in three-dimensional form." This credo, which appealed to a great many writers and readers, inspired such successful competitors as *Dime Detective, Thrilling Detective, Detective Fiction Weekly*, and *Action Detective. Black Mask*, however, was the acknowledged leader in its field, attracting a specific group of writers— among them Dashiell Hammett, Carroll John Daly, Lester Dent, Raoul Whitfield, Peter Ruric, Thomas Walsh, Reuben Jennings Shay—most of whom are now remembered only by nostalgic buffs. But for two decades the pulps prospered, providing cheap, easily available entertainment when comparatively few popular media existed. *Black Mask*, which outlived its era, finally succumbed in 1953; copies of the magazine are now highly prized collectors' items.

Postwar America provided the hard-boiled school with an abundance of subjects. Undergoing the disorder that accompanies explosive social change, the nation coped unsuccessfully with a variety of problems—the Boom of the twenties, Prohibition, the national spiritual hangover of the Depression, and gangsterism on a spectacular scale. In an era of scandalous municipal and federal corruption, crime flourished in the mean streets of America's great cities. Criminals like Al Capone, John Dillinger, Prettyboy Floyd, Babyface Nelson, and (as we have been recently reminded) Clyde Barrow and Bonnie Parker achieved national notoriety. The country was suffering through a period of turmoil and savagery, a chaotic violence which the hard-boiled writers mirrored in their work. Populated by real criminals and real policemen, reflecting some of the tensions of the time, endowed with considerable narrative urgency, and imbued with the disenchantment peculiar to postwar American writing, the hard-boiled stories were considered by their writers and readers honest, accurate portraits of American life.

In reality, however, the pulp detective stories were often crudely and naively written, as an examination of Joseph T. Shaw's *The Hard-Boiled Omnibus* and Ron Goulart's *The Hardboiled Dicks* demonstrates. A kind of realistic melodrama, they attest to the power of a variety of literary influences. Since the magazines inherited much of the spirit as well as the audience of the nineteenth century Dime Novels, they seldom strayed very far from the primitive manner and matter of their ancestors: the Wild West flavored a great many supposedly urban mystery stories. The tough stance—a blend of sentiment and cynicism—and scrupulously unadorned prose style of the hard-boiled writers stemmed most directly from Ernest Hemingway; both formed part of the standard literary equipment of the 1920's and '30's. In addition, like most of their contemporaries, the *Black Mask* writers were indebted to naturalism, from which, Matthew Bruccoli says, they acquired their interest in "documentary verisimilitude, social stratification, sexual force, and the unpretty aspects of American life."

Today the hard-boiled school is largely forgotten. Only one member of the original *Black Mask* group survived the transition from the pulp story to the novel and outlived his era—Dashiell Hammett, the most important American detective story writer since Poe. In fact, Hammett, who published his five novels and several dozen short stories from 1922 to 1934, made the form internationally famous; he is often given credit for inventing it. Raymond Chandler, perhaps the most distinguished practitioner of the genre, belongs to the second generation of hard-boiled novelists. Chandler began publishing in *Black Mask* and similar magazines in 1933; his first novel, *The Big Sleep*, appeared in 1939, his last, *Playback*, in 1959. The most significant inheritor of the hard-boiled tradition is Ross Macdonald (Kenneth Millar), whose first Lew Archer novel was published in 1949; his latest appeared in 1969. A fourth figure, roughly contemporaneous with Macdonald, Mickey Spillane, grows out of the hard-boiled tradition but represents the perversion it has undergone in the hands of the inept and the unthinking. Hammett, Chandler, and Macdonald constitute a continuum of achievement from the beginning of the hard-boiled school to the present. This solid tradition is the enduring accomplishment of the American detective story.

In addition to founding a truly American detective story, the hard-boiled writers created an appropriate hero, the private eye. They took the professional investigator of real life—usually considered a seedy voyeur—and transformed him into a familiar figure of the popular media, inspiring countless books, magazines, movies, and radio and television shows. Though superficially an altogether new kind of folk hero, the private detective is actually another avatar of that prototypical American hero, Natty Bumppo, also called Leatherstocking, Hawkeye, Deerslayer, and Pathfinder. As Henry Bamford Parkes has noticed, the Leatherstocking archetype possesses qualities which fit the requirements of detective fiction:

> Technical skill, along with physical courage and endurance; simplicity of character, with a distrust of intellectualism; an innate sense of justice; freedom from all social or family ties except those of loyalty to male comrades; and above all a claustrophobic compulsion to escape from civilization, supported by a belief that social organization destroys natural virtue and by a generally critical attitude toward all established institutions.

The American detective hero has his archetype's pronounced physical ability, dealing out and absorbing great quantities of punishment. Like Hawkeye, he is proficient with his gun and seldom goes anywhere without it. Like the lonely man of the forests, he works outside the established social code, preferring his own instinctive justice to the often tarnished justice of civilization. The private detective always finds the police incompetent, brutal, or corrupt, and therefore works alone. He replaces the subtleties of the deductive method with a sure knowledge of his world and a keen moral sense. Finding the social contract vicious and debilitating, he generally isolates himself from normal human relationships. His characteristic toughness and his redeeming moral strength conflict with the values of his civilization and cause him, like Natty Bumppo or Huckleberry Finn, to flee the society which menaces his personal integrity and spiritual freedom.

The three great writers of the hard-boiled tradition employ the

Leatherstocking archetype, but treat him in significantly different ways. Hammett's best known detectives, the nameless Continental Op (i.e., an operative for the Continental Detective Agency) and Sam Spade, are the least complex, basically the sleuths of the pulps. The Op is tough, unemotional, a thorough professional. Spade, younger and more attractive, is a cold, almost cruel man whose code of loyalty redeems him from an otherwise total amorality. Raymond Chandler embellishes the toughness of his Philip Marlowe with compassion, honesty, and wit, and a dimension of nobility that Spade and the laconic Op lack. Lew Archer, named for Spade's partner and modeled on Marlowe, is distinguished, beyond the others, for natural goodness. Perhaps the most sympathetic of the hard-boiled dicks, his forte is neither cynicism nor toughness, but a limitless capacity for pity. The central archetype of the frontiersman remains in all three writers but it evolves from the simple Op into the almost Christ-like Archer, paralleling the development of another Leatherstocking hero, the movie cowboy, from inarticulate roughneck to the smooth and stylized knight of the plains.

Living in a lawless world, the private eye, like the frontier hero, requires physical rather than intellectual ability. The short, fat Op is tough enough to tame a lawless city virtually singlehanded (*Red Harvest*) and tough enough to shoot a woman when he must, though he regrets it: "I had never shot a woman before. I felt queer about it" ("The Gutting of Couffignal"). Handy with both fists and firearms, in *The Maltese Falcon*, Sam Spade holds his own against experienced gunmen and international gangsters. Chandler and Macdonald relate their detectives even more closely to their archetype. Philip Marlowe and Lew Archer occasionally shoot and brawl, but more often absorb alarming physical punishment, being variously slugged, beaten, and battered by criminals and police, invariably recovering to continue their investigation. They display the stoic resistance to physical suffering which typifies Leatherstocking. Their insults and wisecracks are the badge of their courage; refusing to show pain or fear, they answer punishment with flippancy. After Captain Gregorius beats him in *The Long Goodbye*, Marlowe refuses to break: " 'I wouldn't betray an enemy into your hands. You're not only a gorilla, you're an incompetent' " (ch. vii). After a sheriff pistol-whips him in *The Doomsters*, Archer answers, " 'It takes more than a Colt revolver to change a Keystone Kop into an officer' " (ch. xvi).

An almost painful honesty accompanies the private eye's toughness and stamina; however imperfect or limited he may be, he acts according to his apprehension of the truth. No matter what it may cost him, the detective follows his moral code. For Hammett, the code is chiefly professional. Turning down a tempting bribe in "The Gutting of Couffignal," the Continental Op explains, ". . . I like being a detective, like the work. And liking work makes you want to do it as well as you can. Otherwise there'd be no sense to it." In fact, the Op has little interest in anything else. Unconcerned with moral judgments, he cares only about completing his task; as Frederick Garner points out, "to the Op each case is just a job, not a moral crusade." Sam Spade is even less concerned with questions of morality. In *The Maltese Falcon* he carries on affairs with his partner's wife and his client and even participates temporarily in the criminal schemes of Caspar Gutman and Joel Cairo. But Spade also has a code; he turns in Brigid O'Shaughnessy, with whom he has fallen in love, because he owes a certain loyalty to his partner, his profession, and his organization:

> "When one of your organization gets killed it's bad business to let the killer get away with it . . . bad for that one organization, bad for detectives everywhere . . . I'm a detective and expecting me to run criminals down and then let them go free is like asking a dog to catch a rabbit and let it go. It can be done, all right, . . . but it's not the natural thing" (ch. xx).

Philip Marlowe fuses personal integrity with professional ethics. He often endures the third-degree tactics of the police rather than reveal a client's business or, as in *The Long Goodbye*, betray a friend. Above all, he is honorable; he doesn't do all kinds of detection, " 'Only the fairly honest kinds' " (*The Lady in the Lake*, ch. i). His personal code prevents his accepting tainted money, even for doing the right thing: " 'I've got a five-thousand dollar bill in my safe but I'll never spend a nickel of it. Because there was something wrong with the way I got it.' " (*The Long Goodbye*, ch. xxxix). Similarly, because he is loyal, Lew Archer suffers for his clients, whether they deserve it or not. Like Marlowe, he refuses tainted money: offered a thousand dollars to gather information for a gambler, he replies, " 'I wasn't planning to hire myself out as a finger' " (*Black Money*, ch. xxvi).

The detective's code is developed even further in Marlowe and Archer. In addition to a sense of duty, compassion motivates them. Marlowe tells a friend:

> "I'm a romantic, Bernie. I hear voices crying in the night and I go see what's the matter. You don't make a dime that way. You got sense, you shut your windows and turn up more sound on the TV set . . . Stay out of other people's troubles. All it can get you is the smear . . . You don't make a dime that way" (*The Long Goodbye*, ch. xxxix).

Morally concerned, Marlowe and Archer are drawn to the outcast, the vulnerable, the miserable, often working only for what they conceive as justice. Archer is often fired by his clients, yet feels compelled to carry the investigation through to its end. He sees his job in almost Christ-like terms:

> The problem was to love people, to serve them, without wanting anything from them. I was a long way from solving that one (*The Barbarous Coast*, ch. xvi).

Unlike the Op, unlike Spade, he often hates being a detective because of the evil in which he finds himself immersed. And, unlike Spade, he can let the murderer go, as in *The Drowning Pool*, where the criminal is a victim of circumstances. From the Op through Archer, the detective's moral code develops from the simple notion of professionalism to the complex realization of the depth of human need.

The moral code often exacts severe personal sacrifice. The detective generally finds that the beautiful and available girl is also the source of guilt; consequently, he is compelled to arrest a woman he desires or even loves. The particular terms of this sacrifice suggest the marked tendency of American fiction to depict women as potentially destructive, and demonstrate the detective's ambivalence toward them. The Op rejects Princess Zhukovski in "The Gutting of Couffignal." Spade refuses to yield to the entreaties of Brigid O'Shaughnessy in *The Maltese Falcon*, though he suffers for it (" 'I'll have some rotten nights' "). Philip Marlowe and Lew Archer ironically discover that the desirable woman is corrupt, a bitch or a murderess, too evil to deserve their compassion. Chandler's *The Little Sister* most fully develops the hero's ambiguous attitudes. Marlowe rejects three women in the book; two of them, Mavis Weld and Dolores Gonzales, always appear together and are paired like Scott's Rowena and Rebecca or Hawthorne's Priscilla and Zenobia, as the Perfect Blonde and the Seductive Brunette. Marlowe refuses the blonde because she has the movie star's professional unreality. "In a little while she will drift off into a haze of glamor and expensive clothes and muted sex." He resists the brunette because she is "utterly beyond the moral laws of this or any world I could imagine" (ch. xxiv). He rejects the little sister of the title because, though she appears to be an innocent virgin from Kansas, she is a blackmailer and an accessory to murder. The conception of a detective surrounded by pliant females is a latter-day perversion of a major motif in the hard-boiled novel. Even the familiar ideal of masculine companionship, implicit in Cooper, Melville, and Whitman, is denied the detective; a good friend often is the criminal, like Albert Graves in Macdonald's *The Moving Target*. Terry Lennox, with whom Marlowe shares an inarticulate homoerotic friendship, turns out to be unworthy of the detective's devotion. Marlowe rejects him for his innate amorality:

> ". . . You had standards and you lived up to them, but they were personal. They had no relation to any kind of ethics or scruples. You were a nice guy because you had a nice nature. But you were just as

happy with mugs or hoodlums as with honest men . . . You're a moral defeatist" (*The Long Goodbye*, ch. liii).

This loss of a friend, a girl, a colleague, intensifies the private eye's essential loneliness. His successful investigation becomes a kind of defeat. As John Paterson points out:

> There is always at the end of the hard-boiled novel a moment of depression when the mission is completed, the enterprise ended, as if this little victory had cost too much in terms of human suffering.

More than a defeat of the spirit, the moment of depression is a symptom of the detective's personal sacrifice, the sadness that accompanies his adherence to his code. His loneliness is characteristic of the Leatherstocking hero, who must proceed through moral entanglements unencumbered by the impedimenta of social or sexual alliances. Nothing, not even love, must prevent the detective from finishing his quest. Without antecedents, unmarried, childless, he is totally alone. Archer's symbolic maladjustment as a divorced man emphasizes this alienation from human beings and human institutions. The physical exhaustion at the end of the hard-boiled novel is a sign of *accidie*, which even the Op experiences: "I felt tired, washed out" ("106,000 Blood Money"), an eloquent speech, for him, about the demands of his profession.

The detective is finally alone, not only because the romantic hero is doomed to solitude, but because he is too good for the society he inhabits. Although not a perfect man, he is the best man in his world. The hard-boiled novel's vision usually approximates the prevailing vision of American fiction. Its world, implied in Hammett's works, and fully articulated in Chandler and Macdonald, is an urban chaos, devoid of spiritual and moral values, pervaded by viciousness and random savagery. Because its laws and regulations endanger the integrity of the hero, this world resembles the settlements of the Leatherstocking novels and the "civilization" of *Huckleberry Finn*. Because its customs are often evil and its denizens degraded, it is allied with the dreary towns along Huck Finn's Mississippi and the joyless civilization symbolized in *The Great Gatsby's* Valley of Ashes. No one is immune to its pernicious influence. The initial crime of murder has a way of proliferating in the hard-boiled novel, entrapping everyone by association. The complicated plots of Ross Macdonald, with their intricate blood and marital relationships, often symbolize the extent of complicity, a universal guilt which spares no one.

> The circuit of guilty time was too much like a snake with its tail in its mouth, consuming itself. If you looked too long, there'd be nothing left

of it, or you. We were all guilty. We had to learn to live with it (*The Doomsters*, ch. xxxv).

Symbolic sins infest the American thriller. The homosexual gunman, since Joel Cairo of *The Maltese Falcon*, has been a conventional character. Rape, incest, and fratricide further indicate the perversion of all normal human connections. Though the detective is compelled to work in this chaotic and sinful society, he does not share its values; instead, he is always in conflict with or in flight from civilization. He finds no fruitful human relationship possible; his condemnation or rejection of other human beings unites him with the alienated and the lost of American fiction—Ahab, Huck Finn, Nick Adams, Joe Christmas, Holden Caulfield. The private eye observes a moral wasteland and, with no "territory" to flee to (unlike Huck Finn), he retreats into himself.

In the devastated society of the hard-boiled novel, crime is not a temporary aberration, but a ubiquitous fact. In *Red Harvest* the Continental Op fights a small war against an unholy coalition of gangsters, policemen, and politicians. The city of Personville—Poisonville to the *cognoscenti*—even begins to infect the Op, who feels himself "going blood-simple like the natives" (ch. xx). Where the police of the classic whodunit are frequently stupid or incompetent, the American police are brutal and degraded. The detectives of *The Maltese Falcon* continually harass and intimidate Spade, in Chandler's novels they bully and beat the detective. Captain Gregorius of *The Long Goodbye* "solves crimes with the bright light, the soft sap, the kick to the kidneys, the knee to the groin, the fist to the solar plexus, the night stick to the base of the spine" (ch. vii). The detective must work outside the law since its representatives demonstrate the decay of order. He works alone because he cannot compromise as the official detectives must; his faith lies in his own values. Marlowe tells the policemen in *The High Window*, " 'Until you guys own your own souls you don't own mine . . . Until you guys can be trusted every time . . . to seek the truth out . . . I have a right to listen to my own conscience' " (ch. xv).

Criminals and policemen are not the only moral offenders; culpability often begins at the highest social levels. In Poisonville, for example, the source of disorder is the wealthy and powerful Elihu Wison, who owns "a United States senator, a couple of representatives, the governor, the mayor, and most of the state legislature" (ch. i). The affluent are so often responsible for social problems that a quasi-Marxist distrust of the wealthy becomes a minor motif; the rich are merely gangsters who have managed to escape punishment. A character in *The Long Goodbye* voices the common condemnation:

> "There ain't no clean way to make a hundred million bucks . . .
> Somewhere along the line guys got pushed to the wall, nice little

businesses got the ground cut out from under them . . . decent people
lost their jobs . . . Big money is big power and big power gets used
wrong. It's the system" (ch. xxxix).

In Ross Macdonald's novels the rich seem particularly culpable, perhaps
because of this prevailing belief that there is no clean way to make a lot
of money. In *The Barbarous Coast* Lew Archer discovers that a wealthy
movie producer owes his success to a notorious gangster; in *Black Money*
that underworld profits link the honored rich with the hoodlums and
gamblers of Las Vegas.

Even the ordinary bourgeois, including the respected professional
man, is not immune to the general taint. Because the doctor epitomizes
bourgeois values he is suspect; in addition, his education is a target of the
Leatherstocking hero's anti-intellectual antipathy. In Chandler's novels
there are the crooked Dr. Verringer of *The Long Goodbye* (merely one
of three shady doctors in that book), Dr. Sonderborg of *Farewell, My
Lovely*, Dr. Almore of *The Lady in the Lake*, Dr. Lagardie of *The Little
Sister*. Macdonald's novels are full of corrupt doctors; in addition he
attacks the college professor who, like the doctor, has misused his
position. In *The Chill*, Lew Archer discovers the academic community
can conceal scandal, and in *The Far Side of the Dollar* unmasks a
professor-murderer. Crime spreads a general *malaise* through every level
of society:

> We've got the big money, the sharp shooters, the percentage workers,
> the fast-dollar boys, the hoodlums out of New York and Chicago and
> Detroit—and Cleveland. We've got the flash restaurants and night
> clubs they run, and the grifters and con men and female bandits that
> live in them. The luxury trades, the pansy decorators, the Lesbian dress
> designers, the riff-raff . . . Out in the fancy suburbs dear old Dad is
> reading the sports page in front of a picture window, with his shoes off,
> thinking he is high class because he has a three-car garage. Mom is in
> front of her princess dresser trying to paint the suitcases out from under
> her eyes. And Junior is clamped onto the telephone calling up a
> succession of high school girls that talk pigeon English and carry
> contraceptives in their make-up kit (*The Little Sister*, ch. xxvi).

All hard-boiled novels depict a tawdry world which conceals a shabby
and depressing reality beneath its painted facade. Respectable Bay City
hides a dreary criminality, "the pick-pockets and grifters and con men
and drunk rollers and pimps and queens on the board walk" (*The Lady
in the Lake*, ch. xxvi). The general shabbiness is another symptom of
society's debilitating influence; wherever human beings gather, evil
results. The social contract breeds not happiness but culpability.

The general tawdriness characterizes the urban locale of all hard-boiled fiction; in keeping with the American agrarian bias, the city is a place of wickedness. Unlike most American heroes, however, the detective has no other place to go. A man of the wilderness, he finds the wilderness destroyed, replaced by the urban jungle. The novels of Hammett, Chandler, and Macdonald all take place in California, where the frontier has finally disappeared. The private eye has responded to the national urge; he has completed the Westward trek. The detective novel concerns itself with what happens to the national hero once that trip is over, with what happens to Huck Finn when he runs out of "territory."

He does not find the Edenic land of his dreams, the Great Good Place of the American imagination, but the Great Bad Place. He finds, in short, "California, the department-store state" (*The Little Sister*, ch. xiii), a green and golden land raped of its fecundity and beauty. Where he had expected innocence and love, he finds the pervasive blight of sin, a society fallen from grace, an endless struggle against evil. Instead of a fertile valley, he discovers a cultural cesspool, containing the dregs of a neon-and-plastic civilization. He finds the American Dream metamorphosed into the American Nightmare. Its true capital is not the luminous city or the New Jerusalem, but Hollywood, a place devoted to illusions:

> Hollywood started as a meaningless dream, invented for money. But its colors ran, out through the holes in people's heads, spread across the landscape and solidified. North and south along the coast, east across the desert, across the continent. Now we were stuck with the dream without a meaning. It had become the nightmare we live in (*The Barbarous Coast*, ch. xiii).

Natty Bumppo has come to the end of his journey.

Intensifying this dark vision and enriching the romantic associations of the hero, Raymond Chandler and Ross Macdonald employ the conventions and structures of other kinds of romance, giving their novels a further mythic dimension. Philip Durham has characterized Chandler's hero as a knight. In fact, the detectives of both Chandler and Macdonald combine the characteristics of the national hero with those of the knight. Chandler acknowledged that Marlowe's name is an anagram on Malory, and Archer also has medieval connotations. Their loneliness is not only the normal condition of the Leatherstocking hero, but also the celibacy of the pure knight. Chandler and Macdonald scatter numerous romance references throughout their novels to identify their heroes' task with the chivalric quest. Both, for example, employ allusive names. The beautiful Helen Grayle of *Farewell, My Lovely* temporarily distracts the detective from his pursuit of the true Grail. Orfamay Quest initiates the search of *The Little Sister*; another false maiden, her name suggests an association both with the quest and Morgan le Fay. Macdonald, who has a literary background, alludes frequently to medieval romance—he names a character Francis Martel (*Black Money*) and another, who appears at a moment of total disaster in *The Way Some People Die*, Runceyvall. The elegiac tone of the novels, reflected in some of the titles—*The Big Sleep, Farewell, My Lovely, The Long Goodbye, The Way Some People Die*—echoes the autumnal overtones of the Arthurian legends. In *The Lady in the Lake*, Chandler's title refers both to a murder victim and to another important figure from romance.

Chivalric romance serves a more than incidental function, providing not only the hero, but narrative structure and moral judgment as well. The initial omen of *The Big Sleep* capsulizes the action of the novel. Visiting the Sternwood mansion, Marlowe notices a stained glass panel

> . . . showing a knight in dark armor rescuing a lady who was tied to a tree and didn't have any clothes on . . . I stood there and thought that if I lived in the house, I would sooner or later have to climb up there and help him (ch. i).

Marlowe, "the shop-soiled Galahad" (*The High Window*, ch. xxviii), does in fact become the knight of the novel. Hired by the incredibly old, incredibly feeble General Sternwood, an impotent Fisher King, to save his daughter from the Gorgon of blackmail, Marlowe finds the beautiful, depraved girl naked, and saves her, only to discover she is a murderess, the Loathly Lady instead of the fair damsel, the Dark Sister of romance. The detective realizes "It wasn't a game for knights" (*The Big Sleep*, ch. xxiv). His quest is ironic since the hidden truth he discovers is a source of further evil.

One of the most frequently repeated devices of the American thriller is the motif of the magical quack. The detective's investigations lead him to a practitioner of some sort of pseudoscientific or pseudoreligious fakery. Most often, this figure presides over a cult of some kind, practicing faith healing, holding seances, fleecing the credulous. Like many others, the convention seems to begin in Hammett: in *The Dain Curse* the Continental Op encounters apparently supernatural terrors at the Temple of the Holy Grail. Philip Marlowe is temporarily vanquished by the "psychic consultant" Jules Amthor in *Farewell, My Lovely*. In *The Moving Target* Lew Archer visits a self-styled prophet at the Temple of the Clouds, "slipping off the edge of a case into a fairy tale" (ch. xiv). The quackery begins as a reasonable representation of the Southern California setting, where in a richly, though inadvertently, symbolic landscape zany religions proliferate like the orange trees. The device also implies the emptiness of the modern American spiritual condition, enriching the dark vision of the private eye novels by demonstrating the extents to which the faithless will go to find significance in a bleakly dispirited world. Perhaps most important, the bizarre cults and temples lend a quasi-magical element of the Grail romance to the hard-boiled thriller—the detective-knight must journey to a Perilous Chapel where an ambivalent Merlin figure, a mad or evil false priest, presides. His eventual triumph over the charlatan becomes a ritual feat, a besting of the powers of darkness.

Macdonald often demonstrates a sophisticated fusion of myth and legend. He employs variations on the classic identity quests in several books, most notably in *The Far Side of the Dollar*, where a hunt for a runaway boy becomes a multiple search for identity; the boy runs off to find his real parents, his real name, while Archer seeks not only the boy, but also a murderer, an answer to a puzzling series of events in the past, and the son he himself never had. Even Archer's vision of the world and his task employs a familiar romance convention, the visit to the underworld. In *The Moving Target* he imagines "an underground river of filth that ran under the city. There was no turning back. I had to wade the excremental river" (ch. xix). The task of the detective, in chivalric terms, becomes the knight's battle against evil as well as his quest for truth. Because the dragon seems to encompass all society, the detective must accept only partial victories. There is no redemption in the hard-boiled novels because guilt and crime are general and diffuse; the hero cannot simply locate a single source. He sees evil everywhere and can only deal with a small part of it. He wades the excremental river, but is incapable of releasing the wasteland from its blight. In search of the City of the Angels and the Holy Wood, he finds, instead, Los Angeles and Hollywood.

In *Anatomy of Criticism* Northrop Frye characterizes romance as "a sequential and processional form," limiting itself to "a sequence of minor adventures leading up to a major or climacteric adventure." This description, coupled with Richard Chase's statement that the American novel in general "tends to carve out of experience brilliant, highly wrought fragments rather than massive unities," explains the sometimes uncertain plotting of the American thriller. It generally is more preoccupied with the character of its hero, the society he investigates, and the adventures he encounters, than with the central mystery, which gets pushed aside by individual scenes and situations. The detective of the hard-boiled novel generally solves his mystery in a hurried, disordered fashion in the last few pages of his book, with little effort to clear up all points or tie up all loose threads. That the progress of the quest is more interesting than its completion further distinguishes the hard-boiled thriller from the formal detective novel. Because he does not suit his society and its rules and because his quest once again fails to achieve the Grail, the American detective experiences none of the admiration or satisfaction that accompanies the transcendent sleuth's success. He has solved little, he has cured nothing. As Chandler writes of his hero, "I see him always in a lonely street, in lonely rooms, puzzled but never quite defeated." Like Philip Marlowe, he seeks refuge in playing solitary chess against the great masters, where the knights have value and power, and the medieval order of the game has a logic all its own: "beautiful cold remorseless chess, almost creepy in its silent implacability" (*The High Window*, ch. xxxvi). Or like Lew Archer, he is left guilty and alone, contemplating old failures and new disasters.

In the chaotic world of the hard-boiled novel, neither an elegant young man nor a benevolent Prospero can succeed. Its society is too coarse and violent for a languid dilettante of crime; and Prospero's magic is valueless in a civilization governed by Caliban. As Chandler put it, "Down these mean streets a man must go who is not himself mean, who is neither tarnished nor afraid. The detective . . . must be such a man. He is the hero; he is everything." Though many hard-boiled writers thought their hero a "realistic" detective, his is an imaginative realism, summarizing the subconscious vision of his country, as contained in the conventions of its art. In his relationship to the heroes of the past, the private eye, paradoxically, resembles such types as Lord Peter Wimsey and Gideon Fell, who owe more to literary archetypes than to real life or the conventions of the thriller. As a literary hero he fulfills wishful desires, of his own time and of all times, for courage, competence, and goodness; part fairy tale hero, part culture hero, part national hero. His popular appeal demonstrates the extent of literary penetration into subliterary forms: for people who do not read the classics of American literature, he is a classic American hero. D. H. Lawrence, who probably never read a thriller, could have been describing the hard-boiled detective in his discussion of Cooper's novels:

> True myth concerns itself centrally with the onward adventure of the integral soul. And this, for America, is Deerslayer. A man who turns his back on white society. A man who keeps his moral integrity intact. An isolate, almost selfless, stoic, enduring man, who lives by death, by killing, but who is pure white.

The hard-boiled novel inverts the conventions of both whodunit and romance. Where the formal detective story contains a bucolic setting, an integrated and harmonious social order, and a ritual of absolution, the private eye novel employs an urban locale, a disordered society, and a final dissolution. The city of stone and sterility opposes the fertile garden, the general guilt reverses the establishment of innocence, and incest and homosexuality become demonic parodies of normal human relationships. Its nightmare vision reverses normal wish fulfillment, frustrating rather than gratifying human desires. Romance, generally speaking, is also a wish fulfillment form, but the hard-boiled novel transforms the romance conventions. Though the hero succeeds in his quest for a murderer, his victory is Pyrrhic, costing a great price in the coin of the spirit. The fair maidens turn out to be Loathly Ladies in disguise. And the closer the detective approaches to the Grail, the further away it recedes. In the hard-boiled novel the blessed desires of normally wish-fulfilling literature are all ironically altered; the daydream has given way to nightmare.

Only one writer remains to be discussed, the man who represents the perversion of the American detective novel, Mickey Spillane. In Spillane the wisecrack, the wit, the repartee, the rapid action and pace, the inevitable urgency of event, as well as the stylistic grace and gusto of a Chandler or Macdonald, are absent. What remains of the essence of the American thriller is the toughness, the sexuality, the violence, and a distorted version of its themes, motifs, and values. The detective's solipsistic belief in himself, his unerring rightness, his intensely lonely virtue, all become a vivid argument for a totalitarian moral policeman whose code, no matter how vicious, must be forced upon every man. Mike Hammer is convinced he is the hammer of God, free to torture, maim, or kill all who get in his way. The whodunit's implicit endorsement of a system of justice and the hard-boiled novel's explicit sense of morality are transformed in Spillane into dictatorial apologetics, advance propaganda for the police state. A thug and a brute, Hammer would have been the villain of most mysteries, but in Spillane he is the new superman, a plainclothes Nazi. The titles indicate his character: *My Gun Is Quick, I, the Jury, Vengeance Is Mine.*

Where the knight of the romantic thriller usually finds himself torn between two polar ideals—the etherealized spirit of the Perfect Blonde and the sensual earthiness of the Seductive Brunette—finally settling for neither, Mike Hammer usually manages to sleep with both women, then kills the evil one (sometimes both are guilty; often the innocent one is killed by the enemy), having and eating his cake at the same time. The sexual candor of the American thriller, a departure from the British form, becomes in Spillane a nearly pornographic treatment of lust. The common American literary theme of hostility to women resolves itself into a psychotic destructiveness; Spillane's detective has a pathological fear of women and takes his revenge on them in the most repellent manner. He is not content to turn the guilty woman over to the police, but instead invariably shoots the girl (who is in the final episodes always naked and at her most seductive) with a very large gun, as bloodily and painfully as possible. Perhaps the most revelatory of the Mike Hammer novels, *Vengeance Is Mine* ends in the usual woman-shooting scene, but with a rather unusual twist; Juno, the statuesque beauty who has aroused Hammer's lust throughout the book, turns out to be a male homosexual. The plausibility of such a device is itself questionable, but the inherent brutal homosexuality of Mike Hammer seems transparently obvious.

The sexuality itself is not all that makes the Spillane thriller a perverted version of the romantic thriller; perhaps his novels' most salient characteristic is their sadistic scenes. Not only does Mike Hammer have an unfortunate penchant for shooting women in the belly, but he also finds himself engaging in physical struggles against hoodlums and gangsters, which, like the killings, achieve either the zenith or the nadir of American tough-guy brutality.

> . . . I snapped the side of the rod across his jaw and laid the flesh open to the bone. He dropped the sap and staggered into the big boy with a scream starting to come up out of his throat only to get it cut off in the middle as I pounded his teeth back into his mouth with the end of the barrel. The big guy tried to shove him out of the way. He got so mad he came right at me with his head down and I took my own damn time about kicking him in the face. He smashed into the door and lay there bubbling. So I kicked him again and he stopped bubbling. I pulled the knucks off his hand then went over and picked up the sap. The punk was vomiting on the floor, trying to crawl his way under the sink. For laughs I gave him a taste of his own sap on the back of his hand and felt the bones go into splinters. He wasn't going to be using any tools for a long time (*The Big Kill*, ch. iii).

Spillane makes the toughness of Hammett, the insight of Chandler, and the compassion of Macdonald seem like sissified and effeminate stuff indeed.

It is important to remember that Spillane's work flourished in the McCarthyite fifties. His political philosophy—an inversion of the hard-boiled thriller's compassionate identification with liberal political and social thought—smacks strongly of right-wing totalitarianism, of a rabid hatred of anything leftist ("pinko" is his term), of an almost insane fear of "Commies," which parallels his apparent fear of women. The world Spillane describes has no vestige of the failed American Dream or the redemptive hero in it; his streets don't seem particularly mean—except for the fact that they are inhabited by men who resemble Mike Hammer—and his hero is in no way a man of honor. If the private detective of the hard-boiled thriller is yet another version of the cowboy who symbolizes the pastoral dream of America, then in Spillane the death of the good sheriff has finally taken place, and the bad guys walk the streets unhampered by a hero who can rise above his society and exterminate at least a portion of the evil flourishing around him. The private detective story, the romantic thriller, the typically American version of the detective novel, reaches a kind of end in Spillane; though a scant few writers still maintain the form, they are all—except for Ross Macdonald—without the skill, insight, or awareness of the best hard-boiled writers. The private detective has had his day—the shamus, the dick, the peeper, the snooper, who became a powerful American hero in

Hammett and Chandler, has descended to the bully, the sadist, the voyeur, no longer a hero at all, but merely a villain who claims the right always to be right.

Although the hard-boiled writers set out to write tough, contemporary mysteries in modern colloquial language, they ultimately wrote romantic rather than realistic fiction. Virtually every major attempt at accurate reporting became a literary device. Their rendering of contemporary reality—Prohibition, gangsterism, corruption—became an expanding metaphor for universal sinfulness, a modern expression of the American Puritan preoccupation with innate depravity. The private detective, born as a plausible substitute for the conventional sleuths of the whodunit and apparently appropriate to his time and place, evolved into a literary hero, nearer to his archetype's imaginative reality than to an actual detective. The prevalence of booze, blondes, and blood, frequently noted by unfriendly critics, not only lent new energy to the detective story, but also entirely suited the romance form: condemnations of the American thriller's violence and depravity recall Roger Ascham's dismissal of *Morte D'Arthur* for its "open manslaughter and bold bawdry" (*The Schoolmaster*, Book I). Even the clipped, slangy style and the first-person objective point of view, which helped justify the adjective, "hard-boiled," were transformed into a literary medium. Hammett's terse, taut style descends from the American tradition of understatement connecting Emily Dickinson, Mark Twain, and Ernest Hemingway. Indeed, Hammett is the detective story's Hemingway, with a comparable influence on his peers. Chandler, on the other hand, seems the Faulkner of the thriller: his prose, richer and more resonant than Hammett's, demonstrates the considerable power and versatility of the hard-boiled style. His vision, too, broadens and intensifies the bleakly vicious world of his predecessor. In Ross Macdonald hard-boiled writing reaches a high point of stylization, full of learned allusions and rich in un-Bumppoish metaphorical flights. This development of hard-boiled prose from the terseness of Hammett to the rococo conceits of Macdonald parallels the evolution of the American detective thriller from the tough action story of the pulps to the very literary novel of the American romance tradition.

The wide success of the American hard-boiled thriller reveals a hitherto unrealized aesthetic sense in the reading public. Though many writers have attempted hard-boiled novels, none has achieved the popularity or longevity of the great practitioners of the romantic tradition. A. A. Fair, Thomas B. Dewey, Brett Halliday, and Richard S. Prather have won only ephemeral success; like the early writers of the hard-boiled school, in all probability they will be forgotten long before Hammett, Chandler, or Macdonald. The very fact that the ordinary public, as well as a few literary critics, seems to prefer the major practitioners to the minor, the skilled writers to the unskilled, the thoughtful and conscious authors to the superficial and imitative, is significant. The best examples of a particular kind, however questionable that kind may seem to some, retain their popular appeal long after inferior works have disappeared; in the hard-boiled novel, literary and commercial success coincide.

Finally, the literary tradition which informs the American romance thriller nullifies the argument that such works serve merely trivial ends. With their American penchant for dissolution, alienation, and despair, the hard-boiled novels, however tough or exciting on the surface, cannot justly be called wish fulfilling. In fact, they do not even deserve to be termed escapist except in the sense that all art represents escape; as Chandler puts it, "All men who read escape from something else into what lies beyond the printed page; the quality of the dream may be argued, but its release has become a functional necessity." The quality of the American thriller's dream corresponds with the traditional visions of the national literature and life; not a fantasy of human gratification, but an hallucinated vision. The chronicles of the mean streets seem as true as, say, Dickens's murky portraits of London or Fitzgerald's and Hemingway's pictures of a decadent and corrupting society. And the private detective, a "man of honor in all things," seems as appropriate to his fiction as Natty Bumppo or the Arthurian knight. The hard-boiled detective novel, the romance thriller, clearly demonstrates a significant and meaningful relationship with some of the most important American literature; at its best, moreover, it possesses the thoughtfulness and artfulness of serious literary work. A valuable and interesting form, it presents a worthy alternative to the thriller of manners, and indicates the potency and durability of the national cultural vision, the American Dream, as it constantly metamorphoses into nightmare.

QUESTIONS

1. Would you agree that "American attempts at the whodunit usually lack style and distinction"?

2. Discuss the "individualism" of the American detective's basic approach to life, as well as his "loner" qualities. Why are these so appealing to Americans?

3. How strongly do you think the *Zeitgeist* ("Spirit of the Times") affects most writers? Discuss in terms of specific authors.

4. Do you agree with Grella's main claims? Does Grella's essay convince you that in American detective fiction "the detective's moral code develops from the simple notion of professionalism to the complex realization of the depths of human need"?

5. How are women treated in American detective fiction? Discuss.

6. Is it necessarily true that "wherever human beings gather,

evil results. The social contract breeds not happiness but culpability"?

7. Explore the idea that "the detective must accept only partial victories."

8. How strongly would you emphasize the quest motif in American detective fiction? As strongly as Grella?

9. Compare the ideas in this story with those presented by Robert Daley in his "Police Report on the TV Cop Shows," particularly as regards the need for myth and the use of wish-fulfillment.

10. Is Mike Hammer the inevitable end product of the hard-boiled school of writing? Has "the private detective . . . had his day"? What about his portrayal on TV shows? Have there been any significant new developments in the way the detective is portrayed? What about his use of new modes of transportation and methods of information gathering?

11. What does Grella mean by "hallucinated vision"?

12. Saul Bellow has written: "Someone had said that in Los Angeles all the loose objects in the country were collected, as if America had been tilted and everything that wasn't tightly screwed down had slid into Southern California." Discuss the "idea" of California in American detective fiction. Why do so many stories take place there?

Police Report on
the TV Cop Shows

Robert Daley

This is the season of the cop shows. There are dozens of them. They are all around us. The only thing they all share is heroes carrying shields and guns. That plus an incredible collection of prime-time half-truths, illusions, stupidities and outright lies.

Are our police departments important to us? If they are, is it not important that we know who our policemen are and how they conduct themselves? Should we really go on watching actors impersonating the way other actors have always impersonated policemen? Are we in the process of fabricating a police myth via TV that will last for decades to come?

There are so many cop shows that they strike the brain like the Chinese water torture. They are numbing. They do not demand any sort of judgment from the viewer; they make no demands upon his intellect; they do not require his participation in any way. And yet, in real life the police departments all around him are in need of help. The entire criminal justice system is in desperate need of help.

Now help comes principally from tax dollars and from the decisions of a few enlightened men. But as long as our police ideas and opinions are formed principally by TV cop shows, not to mention the occasional incredible book or movie such as "Report to the Commissioner," such as "The French Connection," very little intelligent help can be forthcoming. How could the country at large suspect that help is even needed with so many invincible cops already on hand? How could anybody believe that real evil is loose in the land—or that evil basically is mindless and irrational—when such evil as exists on the TV screen is so neat, so comfortable to watch, so beautifully constructed and motivated? The average citizen, after all, meets a cop only when caught exceeding the speed limit. And on such occasions both parties usually are surly. On such occasional glimpses of the law in action, plus these TV shows, rests the entire police knowledge of the average citizen.

Like 30 million or 40 million or however many millions of Americans, I have sat glued to my TV set for the last several weeks. I watched one cop show after another, taking notes. Here is how the notes read:

MONDAY NIGHT

"The Rookies." Put a young black actor and a young white actor inside cops' suits and seat them in a radio car. Then dab whipped cream all over the plot. In this one, two very bad white guys (eventually caught by the rookies) force a decent black man (eventually saved by the rookies) to serve as driver of their getaway car. This amounts to about three preposterous ideas at once. Crooks are racists, too, and tend to keep the color line. Certainly only the very stupidest white crooks would trust an unreliable, chicken-hearted black man to wait for them with engine running outside the store they were about to stick up.

But more important, no patrolman—and especially no rookie patrolman—ever follows a case through from beginning to end. The patrolman makes his arrest or writes a summons for a traffic violation, and then he goes off in some other direction. He does not get involved in the suspect's life. A patrolman is assigned a sector. He may patrol 10 blocks or 10 miles of road, but he doesn't roam all over the city pursuing a single case. He doesn't decide that he is going to solve this one personally and ask permission from his genial lieutenant. While he's off solving the crime, who is minding his sector? Who is handling the stuck elevators and the heart-attack victims? Who is going up onto the rooftops after prowlers? In the denouement—I believe that's the word Hollywood uses—one of the rookie heroes pulls out his 100-shot pistol and eventually shoots the bad guy dead. His pain at having done so shows in his face, and he lays the weapon upon the fence and walks away. Lovely. If a real cop did that, he'd be up on charges. No cop treats a gun lightly. No one leaves a gun lying around. A cop who has shot and/or killed his first gunman is no doubt shaken up about it. But his principal emotion is terror that he has been in a shoot-out and survived. Of course, maybe if we equipped our New York cops with those 100-shot revolvers they wouldn't get scared either.

One other thing. There are some nice shots of the lieutenant's office back in the station house. Above his desk are shelves with lots of books on them. I have never seen books on anybody's shelf in the Police Department in New York.

On the whole, police offices are among the shabbiest that exist in our world. They are manned 24 hours a day. They are the personal office of nobody. In most cases, the only permanent decorations are wanted posters and maps of sectors or precincts or divisions. Police offices are manned almost exclusively by men; they are not used to impress anybody; no outsider sees what they look like except suspects, who are usually too scared to notice. If such offices are often badly cleaned, this is partly because the men who man them don't complain and partly because they're in use so much of each day. There are no rugs on the floor, and there are no books on the walls. This is a small point perhaps, but it might help the viewing public to realize how shabby crime is and how shabby are the offices from which crime is fought.

WEDNESDAY NIGHT

"Police Surgeon." The New York Police Department lists 26 surgeons. There are a number of other honorary surgeons, and the city is full of doctors who would like to be police surgeons, because they think it will make them immune to traffic and parking violations. Police surgeons treat policemen for illnesses and injuries incurred in the line of duty. They do this in their own offices as part of their lucrative general practices. Some of these surgeons are specialists, and some of them do respond to hospital emergency rooms when a cop is shot. One or two of them are brave men, and I once watched a police surgeon enter a building knowing that at least one stickup man was still at large in there, but believing also that someone had been shot and needed a doctor at once. When Patrolmen Gregory Foster and Rocco Laurie were assassinated in the East Village last January, one police surgeon responded at once to Bellevue Hospital, where he waited in the hall outside the operating room. From time to time, he would peer through the small window in the operating room door. He could see Patrolman Laurie naked on a table with a team of doctors trying to save his life. Occasionally, the door would swing open, and an intern or surgeon would dash out and run down the hall in search of equipment or something. Once or twice the police surgeon attempted to question one of these men. "How is he doing?" The answer would come back over the shoulder of the other doctor's blood-spattered gown: "We're doing all we can for him." The official police surgeon had to wait in the hall for someone to come out who would talk to him.

However, the police surgeon who stars in the TV show of the same name is really more of a detective than a medical man. He accompanies a detective who goes to serve a search warrant at an apartment and actually helps search the apartment. Believe me, police surgeons, like most doctors today, are extremely reluctant even to make house calls, much less engage in the searches of suspects' apartments.

Wednesday this year is one of two big nights for cop shows, the other being Sunday. After watching "Police Surgeon" as attentively as I could, I tuned in on "Adam-12." "Adam-12" purports to show the adventures of two young Los Angeles cops in a radio car. It claims to be an authentic portrayal of police at work, and it is produced by Mark VII Ltd., which is Jack Webb's company. It appears to be a uniformed version of "Dragnet." The two cops handle routine calls as well as the major case of each particular show. Tonight they are flagged down by a girl on a horse, who informs them that a light plane has just landed in a nearby, nearly inaccessible valley. They go bounding over the ground and immediately come to the conclusion that they have fallen upon a marijuana-smuggling operation. But they're not sure, and there's nothing they can do about it now. They are forced to let the plane take off.

Now, there is real mystery in police work. Every time a cop knocks on a door, he has no idea what is waiting for him on the other side—it could be anything from an abandoned baby to a psychopath about to blow the cop's head off. It could be nothing at all. No cop ever knows. A cop must make his judgment and take action on very little evidence. Sometimes the cop takes the wrong action. Sometimes he fails to take any action because he isn't sure, when in fact he has the drop on a desperate and dangerous fugitive.

On TV, the audience almost always knows who the suspect is and whether or not the suspect is guilty, having most likely seen the crime take place. In fact, TV cops are so successful precisely because they appear to have already seen the earliest scenes of the TV play themselves—they know with absolute certitude who's guilty and who is not. And unerringly, they go straight for whatever evidence or witnesses are needed to complete the case.

The best thing about "Adam-12" is that the audience never knows any more than the cops know. Webb constructed the "Dragnet" series this way too, which is perhaps the reason that "Dragnet" reruns are still being seen in New York.

"Adam-12" is not perfect. Apparently the patrol car's radio can't transmit while the car is moving (which is ridiculous), all detectives wear shirts and ties (ditto) and all the radio cars are brand-new and shiny, unlike real ones, which are driven 24 hours a day by a variety of drivers and which look exactly as beat-up as taxicabs in a very short time. Nonetheless, it is a pleasure to watch cops coping with they don't know what.

THURSDAY NIGHT

"Ironside." Before the opening billboards of this program even begin to flash upon the screen, I had already sat through—in a rather stunned silence—60 minutes of "Mod Squad." The story was about a girl who needed plastic surgery because her face was disfigured. Pete, one of the cops, fell in love with her. The police captain, whose primary responsibility, apparently, is to give free rein to the Mod Squad, was also willing to give all this time and thought to this girl. Now I ask you, which police captain or police anything can afford to get personally involved? The police are out there holding the line. They can barely do it. Perhaps they can't do it at all. They certainly do not have the energy or the time or freedom to get personally involved every week at 8 P.M. But this show has already been on TV four seasons and is starting its fifth, and if it still rings true to anyone out there, then nothing I might say could possibly make any difference.

Now on comes Ironside (Chief Ironside, that is), beginning his sixth season in a wheelchair, from which he personally solves nearly all of San Francisco's interesting crimes. During this particular show, Chief Ironside goes on a TV program with other so-called experts to explain the mentality of an unknown murderer who has left them an unexplained body. Chief Ironside is allowed to monopolize the panel show. I've been on a lot of panel shows in my time, all of them distinguished principally by the efforts of everyone on the panel to monopolize the available air time. However, Ironside is a man of such genius or something that the other panel guests allow him to do all the talking and never so much as try to squeeze an opinion in edgewise.

I offer this item in the interest of truth. It has nothing to do with police work. What does have to do with police work is the simple fact that no chief would put his prestige on the line by attempting to solve a murder during a TV broadcast, which is what Ironside here proposes to do. The murderer, obviously, is listening, and, just as obviously, he will crack during the ensuing hour from the relentless pressure of Ironside's cool power of reason and persuasion. Several times Ironside remarks, "The murderer is an amateur."

In New York last year we had 1,466 murders and many attempted murders. We in the police hierarchy took a personal interest in a few of these: the murder of cops, the Joe Colombo hit and one or two rape-murders distinguished by the youth and beauty of the victim. That was all. There are simply too many murders these days. Most of them are committed out of passion or jealousy, or during the commission of some other crime. Cops are interested in murders, but in a detached way, as if they were chess problems.

Unlike ol' Ironside.

Ironside is about to make the murderer, who is safe in his own apartment, crack.

Murderers don't crack. I have never seen a defendant in a murder trial break down on the stand; hardened criminals often become like gifted athletes, who know how to perform under pressure. Nobody cracks, except on TV.

I attended a recent murder trial in which the prosecutor subjected the defendant to one of the most scathing personal attacks that any man has ever had to endure. The jury watched the defendant, and I watched the jury. It seemed to me that I had seen this scene before, and indeed I had, dozens of times, on TV. On TV the murderer always cracks. At length he can take no more. He suddenly breaks down blubbering and admits his guilt.

But this defendant did not break down. He did not admit his guilt. He did not blubber. It seemed to me that I could see the jury conclude before my eyes: Ergo, he cannot be guilty, and the trial ended in a hung jury.

Now I watch this stupid program, and then at last I can't take it anymore, and I walk out of the room. At five minutes to 10 I happen by the TV set en route to bed. My wife and my children watch with the same expressionless faces as the killer rushes onto the TV stage setting, attempts to kill Ironside, but gets caught. The commercials and the closing billboards flash onto the screen, and the sign-off is punctual.

Later, I lie in bed in the dark and brood about the trial I had attended. If TV shows such as this one had never existed, might the jury have found the defendant guilty, even though he didn't crack?

Raymond Burr, who plays Chief Ironside, is just an actor with piercing eyes, trying to make a living. The producers of "Ironside," like the earlier producers of "Perry Mason," are just men trying to make money. But what is the idiocy of programs such as this doing to our country?

SATURDAY NIGHT

"The Streets of San Francisco." This week Janice Rule portrays a prostitute, the terrified target of some psychopath who has already murdered three other prostitutes.

There is good whore dialogue. Obviously, whoever wrote this show knows more about whores than about cops. Perhaps I should add: why have none of us concerned citizens ever thought to become concerned about cops? The best of us seem to have passed our whole lifetimes asking no more questions about the policemen who safeguard our cities than about our garbage collectors.

Karl Malden, a splendid actor no matter how poor his material, is the star of this show. Michael Douglas, son of Kirk, plays his young assistant. Since Janice Rule is likely to be killed before this show is over, they hide her out in a fleabag hotel that has a phone only at the top of the stairs.

In the New York Police Department, we were often obliged to hide out witnesses. We kept them at the Commodore Hotel, or the Howard Johnson's Motor Lodge or such. But tonight we are asked to believe the San Francisco Police Department so poor in finances or so stupid in terms of security as to stash a potential murder victim in a hotel as dumpy as this one.

I also suspect that they, like us, would assign two detectives to watch a prostitute all night. One simply isn't enough. It's not enough should the murderer show up, and it's not enough should the prostitute try anything on the detective. I mean anything.

This is also the first show that I've seen in a number of years wherein a detective shoots the lock out of a door. Anybody with half a brain ought to know that ricocheting bullets are dangerous, and also that if you send a bullet into a lock, you may never get it open.

Young Detective Douglas sits up all night alone in a hotel room with a prostitute but is still on duty all the next day. As well as having a 100-shot revolver in his belt, he doesn't need sleep. Why have we come this far in police dramas without equipping our hero cops with basic human frailties, such as the need for sleep, such as fear when they are getting shot at?

Another point: A cop on the street—almost any cop, even me, and I had not previously been a cop by profession—is all eyeballs. A cop watches everything. A cop sees things other people don't see. A criminal can spot a cop anywhere—not by noting the length of the cop's sideburns, but by watching the cop's eyeballs. Any man eyeballing the street is a cop. Ordinary people don't do that. Ordinary people use their eyes to find a path in whatever direction they're heading. Cops watch windows, doorways, passing cars, and their eyes are constantly getting caught by something that is not exactly the way it should be. All actors who play cops ought to be taught this, but none of them are, not in this show, nor any other. A real cop's eyes are always darting about.

In this particular show, the psychopath is eventually trapped on a rooftop, where the young detective has a conversation with him instead of grabbing him. If you think cops are rough toward speeders, you should see them behave towards felony suspects. The guy would be grabbed, frisked and cuffed faster than it takes a fullback to plunge into the line. But in this show, the psychopath doesn't even get handcuffed after his arrest.

In a number of shows, the prisoner didn't get handcuffed at all, and in others he got handcuffed with his hands in front of him, which is inconceivable. Handcuffs clamped on that way are a deadly weapon in themselves. All the suspect has to do is bring them down on the head of the cop who is attempting to arrest him. That is why suspects are handcuffed behind. Everywhere except on television. This may sound like a small point and not worth mentioning, but it has to do with danger; it has to do with the aura of fear and risk surrounding every cop. If the cop who stops you for a traffic violation seems surly, consider the encounter from his point of view. Perhaps you are armed. Perhaps you will shoot him. It has happened often enough. Perhaps you are a fugitive. Perhaps you are a maniac. A cop on patrol encounters fellow citizens perhaps 10 or a dozen times on each tour. I never heard a cop admit to operating in a state of perpetual fear, but in truth every cop is on his nerves every time he stops a motorist, or investigates a reported prowler or crime, or knocks on the door to somebody's flat. A television show that ignores danger and the natural fear of cops is, it seems to me, an important lie in the lives of all of us.

This is the show in which Janice Rule, the hooker, becomes an honest waitress in the end—every cop show on TV ends up tied with a big red bow. I'm sick of murders by psychopaths. I don't want to be told that all murderers are psychopaths. I don't want to believe that I'm in danger only from psychopaths. That isn't the way life is. How about a murder by someone who meant only to "tap" someone else on the head? How about murders by junkies and accidental murders by stickup men who get frightened, or political murders by organizations such as the Black Liberation Army? One can't cope with lunatics. But there's more out there than lunatics. TV is destroying not only our understanding of cops, but also our understanding of evil.

Not to mention our understanding of the court system. Each crime is treated as if it begins and ends as a police problem, and this is not true. Every cop worries about his arrest getting through the court system intact. Why is this never shown on TV?

SUNDAY NIGHT

Lucky us. The "N.B.C. Mystery Movie" presents "McMillan and Wife." This one starts out with Police Commissioner McMillan himself chasing the suspect up and down Nob Hill on cable cars. When somehow the suspect transfers from an uphill to a downhill car, so does the Police Commissioner, leaping across at the risk of his life. This occurs several times, and eventually the Police Commissioner grabs the suspect, dusts off his hands and remarks: "That closes up the something case." I didn't catch the name of whatever case it closed. I was ready to walk out at once. Police Commissioners do not catch suspects with their bare hands, any more than presidents of General Motors build cars with their bare hands, and for exactly the same reasons. There is too much other work to do—administrative work—which is perhaps not as much fun as catching crooks, but which is absolutely essential if the machine is to work at all.

I suggest that hardly anybody in this country knows what a Police Commissioner does. One thing he does not do is move through the police world accompanied by his wife, as McMillan does. The police world is an all-male world. Even a good many of the police department's social functions—communion breakfasts and the like—are stag. It is true that most police departments contain a few policewomen. In New York, the number is about 350 out of a force of 30,000. The sight of a luscious dish such as Mrs. McMillan hanging about all the time would distract the cops. No work would get done while she was around, and eventually her presence would become downright annoying. The Police Commissioner in a city is not an elected official. He is appointed by the Mayor. He holds one of the most politically sensitive jobs in the city. He must be on his guard always, or he will get toppled. Any sort of political pressure can topple him—pressure from district attorneys, or borough presidents, or community groups. If any of these lean on the Mayor just a little, the Police Commissioner is out of a job. So how can he afford to float through his job with his wife at his side?

WEDNESDAY NIGHT AGAIN

Of all the shows that I watched, the one that upset me most was a TV movie called "Lieutenant Schuster's Wife." About 15 minutes into this show Lieutenant Schuster is shot and killed. Suddenly, evidence turns up to the effect that Lieutenant Schuster was a corrupt cop, and because of this no investigation goes forward, neither to prove that he was corrupt, nor to find out who killed him. The only available savior of the situation is Mrs. Schuster, who's very good looking, extraordinarily brave, and a hell of a detective herself, though her only previous experience was in the housewifery department. One can overlook a number of technical mistakes—all cops in this show seem to have been furnished with brand-new equipment, for example. As was pointed out above, very little new equipment reaches a police department and once it does come in, it is overused so quickly that it becomes old equipment all too soon. If the public realized this, perhaps there would be a little bit more money, and a little more new equipment would make its appearance. A second minor point: Lieutenant Schuster is shot dead from a great distance by a handgun. Handguns are not very reliable at any distance at all, and nearly all police shoot-outs every year take place within a distance of seven yards. Incredible as it may seem, there has never been a cop killed by a handgun in New York over that distance. Still, a lucky shot could have got Schuster or anybody. I waive this point.

However, I would like to point out once and for all that investigations into cop killings are total. There is no more emotional situation within any police department anywhere than the assassination of a policeman. When it happened in New York in my time, some cops cried. They flooded into the station houses of the dead cops in the middle of the night wearing all their guns, with their shields safety-pinned to their lumber jackets. They wanted to help. There is such an emotional pressure behind the investigation into the murder of a cop that there is simply no way for any human hand to stop it.

Except in this TV show. In it, a sergeant says: "This is a high-crime precinct; I'm understaffed; I have to do it all myself."

This line is tragic. When a cop is killed, everything else stops until his murderer is caught. Former Chief of Detectives Albert Seedman once tried to calculate how many millions of dollars the investigations into the assassinations of four cops in New York during the previous 18 months had cost taxpayers. Seedman could come to no conclusion. But Commissioner Patrick Murphy did announce publicly at one point, "We will not conduct business as usual while a would-be cop killer is loose."

Most professional criminals know better than to kill a cop. They're not afraid of getting beaten to a pulp once caught. They're afraid of provoking an investigation of such magnitude that they could not possibly escape it. Nor does anyone attempt to stop an investigation on the grounds that the cop in question was corrupt. It's better to find out that he was corrupt, if such was the case. This reduces the emotional pressure from the other cops and allows the investigation to proceed coolly.

Eventually, in the course of this show, we are told that the "crime commission" has agreed to drop the charges against the murdered cop, provided the police department drops the investigation into his murder. Now I ask you: Do you know who the murderer turns out to be? You won't believe it. At least I hope you won't believe it. The murderer turns out to be the sergeant who was Lieutenant Schuster's partner and best friend.

Now, there are corrupt cops. There always were, and no doubt there always will be. If the struggle against the corrupt cop is less effective than it should be, there is one principal reason: Cops who are honest themselves refuse to turn in brother cops whom they know to be corrupt. Over and over again you can hear them say: "I won't turn in another cop." Cops feel alienated from the rest of society. They feel themselves an army betrayed by the population that has hired and armed them. On duty, they mix only with one another, and some of them mix only with one another off duty as well. The single fact that impressed me most when I was Deputy Police Commissioner was the love that cops feel for one another. They love one another the way members of a football team love one another, and this love is proved every time a signal 10:13 comes over the police radio. When that happens you can hear the sirens for miles, and the radio cars choke the streets for blocks around. If another cop is in trouble, everyone who is reasonably close speeds to the scene. During a recent four month period 61 policemen were hurt, some seriously, in car collisions while racing to respond to a signal 10:13.

But in the course of this show, the sergeant, partner and best friend, had murdered Lieutenant Schuster. He did this, he explained, because he owed the mob $65,000, and they had ordered him to do it.

Cops get into brawls in barrooms and sometimes kill each other. Occasionally they kill each other in fights over girls. They are all armed; they have human passions like everybody else, and some of them are not that brilliant. But I never heard of one who accepted that kind of contract to kill another cop. If you're willing to believe that such a crime could take place, then we had best abolish all our police departments and try something else. The struggle against corruption is real, and it is important that the public understand what corruption we are talking about if we are to have any hope of ridding ourselves of it. We are not talking about corruption wherein one cop accepts a contract to assassinate another cop. This has never happened to my knowledge and I don't expect it to happen in my lifetime. To put such a thing on television is to warp the perception of millions of people about who a cop is and about corruption problems that do exist.

SUNDAY NIGHT AGAIN

By this time, I had reached the point where I was not able to watch TV cop shows more than once a week. They usually left me wanting to scream. But this week's "N.B.C. Mystery Movie" is not really a bad one. It stars Dennis Weaver as McCloud, a deputy marshal from Taos, N. M., who is attached to the Police Department in New York City. He wears a cowboy hat and carries a .45-caliber revolver, which New York cops make fun of.

Well, New York cops would make fun of such a gun. They all carry .38's, and most of them feel this isn't big enough for the game they are asked to bring down all too often. They'd like to have a .45, and they would make jokes about anyone authorized to carry such an enviable piece.

The Chief of Detectives in this program shows training films to his men at times. Chiefs of Detectives do not show training films. Sergeants are usually considered qualified to run projectors. Again, this is only a small point, but wouldn't it help to have some understanding of who and what a Chief of Detectives is? He also does not ride around in a white-top radio car in civilian clothes, his driver also wearing civilian clothes. Only uniformed cops drive radio cars. The Chief of Detectives has his own unmarked car, loaded with radios operating on confidential frequencies.

At a certain point in this show, McCloud cons a sergeant into working late by saying to him that this will help him make lieutenant "when the board meets." One makes lieutenant in the New York Police Department by acquiring the necessary seniority and by passing the civil-service examination. There are no other requirements. This is true of all the civil-service ranks: sergeant, lieutenant and captain. There is no board. If the people realized that promotions were based entirely upon civil-service exams and seniority, perhaps there would be some pressure to change these regulations to make it possible for a conscientious, hard-working, especially able sergeant to make lieutenant when you needed him, possibly well in advance of less qualified individuals who merely happened to do well on the test.

This show ends with McCloud making an arrest in a midtown street on the top of an imitation stagecoach that is owned by The Cattleman restaurant. Please understand that I do not object to such scenes as this, which are good-humored and not in any way meant to reflect reality. I am not against humor, and not against high-flown imagination. But I am very much against attempts by these television shows to pass off as reality that which is misleading and false.

The following Sunday in the same time slot appears a film called "Hec Ramsey," which character is played by Richard Boone. The time is the early nineteen-hundreds, and Boone is a former gunslinger turned deputy police chief. As such he introduces scientific criminology to a Western town.

Though oversimplified, this is not such a bad show. Much is made of Hec's weighing bullets to prove that they came from the same gun. The weight of bullets has nothing to do with whether or not they come from the same gun. After that, Hec peers at them through his microscope and pronounces them identical.

Now, a bullet that has gone into a man looks like a mushroom when it is dug out. It is deformed, and there are bits of flesh attached to it that apparently cannot be scrubbed off, and after a very short time it stinks out of all proportion to its size, though not to its potency. Shooting somebody is never a neat business, and it seems to me that the understanding of all of us would be helped if we could see a few deformed bullets, rather than the perfect specimens we are shown on TV. It might also help to show Hec holding his nose while he works on them.

Similarly, Hec finds fingerprints on guns. Movie and TV cops have always found fingerprints on guns, whereas in actual fact there are almost never fingerprints on guns. A gun has very few surfaces that will hold a print, and to find a usable fingerprint at any crime scene on any surface is extremely difficult, and even rare. What has happened in this country is that juries tend to believe so-called scientific evidence, and more and more they tend to disregard all other evidence. Too often, if the prosecution can't show that prints were found on the murder weapon, the jury will refuse to believe that the accused could possibly have used it to commit the crime. TV viewers are potential jurors, and errors such as this have been perpetuated for so long that in the minds of most of us they have turned into prejudices.

In another scene, Hec is ambushed in the night. He calmly goes to a tree that one bullet has struck, finds it in the bark, and digs it out. It is, of course, an undamaged slug, but beyond that, it is often extremely difficult to find bullets at crime scenes.

One night my television screen stayed dark. Choosing to miss God knows how many cop shows on TV, I went to the movies to see a film called "The New Centurions." This started as a novel by a Los Angeles police sergeant named Joseph Wambaugh, which, though somewhat artless, was an absolutely true book about cops in Los Angeles. In addition, it stuck near the top of the fiction best seller list for half a year or more, proving perhaps that the public appreciates fiction that is real and true. The only reviews of the film which I read praised George C. Scott and panned nearly everything else, and I was not prepared for a movie that was as faithful to truth and as accurate as the book had been.

Now, "The French Connection" was a far more profitable movie, although it purported to tell in blood-stained terms the "true" story of a real narcotics operation. In real life, none of the actual participants was ever so much as scratched by a nail. "The French Connection" was full of preposterous scenes, whereas "The New Centurions," with screenplay by Stirling Silliphant, stuck to scenes that were true to the lives of the men who ride radio cars in Los Angeles and in every other city in this country. The feeling of danger behind every door is in this picture, but the real danger comes when the hero is not prepared for it in any way. Twice he is shot by guns he doesn't know are there. There is only one shoot-out, and for the first time in my memory we are allowed to see the faces of every cop afterwards—and every single face shows terror.

Most New York cops never in their careers ever fire their guns. In this film on numerous occasions the cops in fact don't shoot, knowing that there are bystanders all over the place. The far more normal violence of cops frisking suspects and clamping on handcuffs is in this film. So are scenes of cops getting mauled and bitten by citizens they have come to help. I left the theater totally satisfied, but in the car my wife said: "It didn't seem believable to me when George C. Scott killed himself."

I said: "Anybody who knows anything about cops would accept that scene as absolutely believable." Cops kill themselves all the time. I can think of three police suicides within a few months that I knew about personally. Inevitably, with every cop owning at least two guns, there are going to be suicides.

But in my heart I felt dismay. The American public has been force-fed so much claptrap in movies and TV that hardly anyone anymore is able to recognize truth, or to tell the real from the fraudulent. And if it is this bad on the level of cop films and shows, how can we expect it to be better on any other level—politics, for instance?

All this time I had been hearing that the best of the new cop shows was "Madigan" starring Richard Widmark. Madigan began as a detective in a novel called "The Commissioner" by Richard Dougherty, one of my predecessors as Deputy Police Commissioner. That was quite a true book, and at the end of it Madigan was killed. TV has not only resurrected him, it has promoted him to sergeant, and all around me were reviews and reports to the effect that this show at least was accurate and realistic.

So I arranged to see the first two episodes all alone in a screening room at N.B.C. Inside of five minutes, I had learned that Madigan "always works alone." But no detective works alone, not Madigan, not anybody. If he is at all close to the guilty person, it is too dangerous. It would be all too easy to make him disappear. The second reason is that detectives are forced each working day to go out into the unknown to piece together bits of a mystery, to ask information from people they don't know, and it is simply easier and more practical to do this as a pair than as one man alone.

In any case, in this first episode, Madigan is provided with a partner whom he doesn't want, a chap who has passed some course in social psychology, and has therefore been made a detective on the spot. No one gets made a detective on the spot; only patrolmen can be made detectives. You must pass the civil-service exam first, put in months on probation, and after that you must force your way through the thousands of other patrolmen who also want to become detectives.

Now Madigan and the social psychologist go after a pair of ridiculous whistling muggers, whose crimes are known to everyone: to the audience, which has watched them commit the crimes, and to Madigan who must be psychic. Madigan's radio speaks. The dispatcher in this case is a female—the last time I looked there were no female dispatchers in the New York Police Department. The dispatcher gives him information on which informant he is to meet where. Except for the confidential frequencies used by the Police Commissioner to communicate with his own office, and by one or two other members of the hierarchy, all radio transmissions are conducted in code signals. No conversations take place legally on police radio. Certainly no information about informants ever goes over police radios, because these frequencies can be monitored by anybody with the proper equipment.

On and on the stupidities come. Madigan catches a suspect, and gives him a few soft pats for a frisk. The guy could have been wearing weapons all over him and Madigan wouldn't have found them. It seems to me that Madigan's audiences of millions ought to realize that tossing a suspect is done hard and fast, multiple smacks covering every square inch of the suspect's body. A toss is no funny business, and the risks for a cop are enormous at all times, and for this reason he has mastered some extremely impressive techniques. The audience ought to see these techniques done properly, rather than the way Madigan does them.

At another point, Madigan-Widmark reads the Miranda warning to a suspect before tossing him for weapons. Is Madigan attempting to commit suicide, or what? There isn't a cop in New York who doesn't know enough to start with a quick, brutal toss, followed by pinioning the prisoner's arms behind his back; on go the handcuffs, and after that perhaps the Miranda warning. It's legal that way. And also much safer.

In the next "Madigan," which immediately followed this one, a thousand dollars gets stolen from a dinner party, and when Madigan recaptures the money, he goes back to the principal victim and gives the money back. Did Madigan never hear of the rules of evidence? Is there no property clerk in Madigan's police department?

Again there are radio messages, whole conversations going out over the air. Radio messages are done this way: "Car No. 9, 10:1 your command, acknowledge," the dispatcher might say. Since Car No. 9 was mine, I would pick up the microphone, press the button, and say: "Car No. 9, 10:4." The 10:1 call meant call your command. The 10:4 call meant signal acknowledged. We would then stop at the nearest telephone, and I would call in for whatever my message might be.

This particular show ended with Madigan giving orders to patrolmen regarding a prisoner: "Take him downtown." Downtown where? New York is a big city, and prisoners go to the nearest precinct and are booked there. So I quit making notes, and eventually this second Madigan ended.

It is impossible to stay outraged over a three- or four-week period. When the screen went dark, I got up and went out and ate lunch.

QUESTIONS

1. What causes us to suspend our disbelief and desire for accuracy when we watch detective shows? Or do we believe that what we are viewing is accurate?

2. Do we give up unrealism of the hero so long as we get "hard" reality of dialogue and experience? What does this say about our need for a belief in the individual hero, our dependence on what might be called the "myth" of individuality? If there is such a dependence, does it exist because there *is* such a myth?

3. Discuss Daley's essay as necessary propaganda. List the things Daley wishes the public to accept and do.

4. Over and over Daley stresses the concept that the portrayal of crime and the police on television is literally dangerous to our national health. He asks, "What is the idiocy of [detective programs] doing to our country?" Is "our understanding of evil" being eroded? As you discuss, you might concentrate especially on Daley's remarks about juries.

5. Does the "hard-boiled" school of detective writing meet Daley's wish for realism in detective stories? Could there be more realism if television was not such a restricted family medium? Are realism and accuracy the same as "truth"?

6. Does this article make you value detective fiction less than you did before you read it?

7. What kind of humor does Daley use in his writing? Discuss the tone of this essay.

8. How well do you think fear has been portrayed in detective fiction? Use specific examples to illustrate your answers.

9. Why have TV and movie detective shows not significantly reduced the readership of detective books? Do these shows feed similar, the same, or different audiences than do detective books?

10. Daley says there is "so much claptrap in movies and TV that hardly anyone anymore is able to recognize truth, or tell the real from the fraudulent." He goes on to ask, "if it is this bad on the level of cop films and shows, how can we expect it to be better on any other level—politics, for instance?" Discuss relationships between "popular" perceptions and the "politics" of law enforcement.

A Contemporary History
of American Crime

Fred P. Graham

The land is full of bloody crime and the city is full of violence.

Ezekiel VII:23

On a rainy night last June a "frost notice"—a word-of-mouth warning system used by the U.S. Marines to inform personnel of emergency situations—went out to all Marines in and around the Washington, D.C., area. It concerned the fashionable Georgetown section of residential Washington, a stately neighborhood of tree-lined streets and expensive townhouses where such citizens as Allen Dulles, Averell Harriman, Dean Acheson, and Abe Fortas have their homes.

"It would be inadvisable to frequent the Georgetown area currently," the frost notice warned the Marines, "and in general exercise caution and restraint in Washington." The reason for the warning was that in the early hours of that morning, June 5, two young Marine lieutenants had stopped in Georgetown for coffee in an all-night hamburger shop, had exchanged remarks with a trio of black militants who had come from California for the Poor Peoples' Campaign, and had been shot dead. Only 3 nights earlier an 18-year-old high school senior had been shot to death after a bumping incident with a stranger outside a pharmacy two blocks away. In the 6 weeks before that, the area had been plagued by a series of vicious muggings.

The spectacle of Marines being warned away from Washington's most prestigious neighborhood (all the crimes were within shouting distance of the familiar townhouse from which John F. Kennedy had announced his Cabinet appointments in 1960) was only one of a number of bizarre incidents that seemed to show that violence had become more prevalent and threatening than before. Bus drivers in Washington and Baltimore had gone on strike in protest against being required to carry change, because a number had been beaten and one had been killed by robbers. An all-night grocery chain in Cleveland had issued free food vouchers to policemen so that their comings and goings would frighten away potential robbers. Pistol practice had displaced ladies' bridge clubs as the center of social activity in some suburban communities. A book by a former Ice Follies performer on judo and self-defense for ladies was selling briskly, along with such titles as "How To Avoid Burglary,

Housebreaking, and Other Crimes," and "How To Defend Yourself, Your Family, and Your Home."

Small wonder that in the summer of 1968 the Harris poll found 81 percent of the people believing that law and order had broken down, and that all of the presidential candidates were promising to do something about it.

"Crime is rising nine times faster than the population" was a stock punch line of Richard M. Nixon's all-purpose campaign speech. Vice President Humphrey noted that the annual number of homicides was lower than it was in 1930, but he, too, campaigned from the assumption that the crime rate is getting out of hand. George Wallace never failed to warn his listeners that they might get hit on the head on the way home by a thug who would probably be out of jail before they got out of the hospital.

With most Americans from the President down believing that crime has risen to emergency proportions, there has emerged a puzzling paradox: many of those who have given the subject the most study have, until recently, concluded that it is not so.

Attorney General Ramsey Clark became the whipping boy of the 1968 political campaign because he had expressed the belief in an unguarded moment that "there is no wave of crime in this country." In 1968 Robert M. Cipes, a lawyer and consultant to the President's Commission on Crime in the District of Columbia, published a book, "The Crime War," which proceeded from the thesis that "in fact there is no crime wave," but rather that "current statistics simply reflect the fact that we are digging into the reservoir of unreported crimes." Intellectuals who were not specialists in the field also tended to accept this view. Dr. Karl Menninger, founder of the famed Menninger Clinic of psychiatry, concluded after writing a book on crime and punishment that—

> No crime statistics are dependable: most crime is not reported. Most violent crime takes place in the home. Most nonviolent crime takes place in department stores. My own belief is that there is less violence today than there was 100 years ago, but that we have a much better press and communications to report it.

The President's Commission on Law Enforcement and Administration of Justice, reporting in 1967, could not say after an 18-month study if the crime rate is higher than it has been before, or if Americans have become more criminal than their counterparts in earlier times.

At the center of this controversy had been the ever-rising crime index of the Federal Bureau of Investigation. This index, which has been widely accepted by politicians, policemen, and editorial writers as the official barometer of crime, has also been described by Harvard crime expert Lloyd E. Ohlin as "almost worthless—but it is the only thing there is." Thornstein Sellin, the dean of American criminal statisticians, has been quoted in *Life* magazine as saying that the United States "has the worst crime statistics of any major country in the Western world." The *New York Times* quoted Sophia M. Robinson of the Columbia School of Social Work as saying that "the FBI's figures are not worth the paper they are printed on." Other experts were quoted to the same effect in the press.

Until the last few years, it was fashionable for criminologists to debunk the crime index in this vein when periodic flaps over the FBI's figures erupted and the news media solicited the academicians' views. However, their quoted statements were decidedly more critical than the articles that these same experts were writing for their fellow professionals. Whether they were being quoted out of context (as some claimed) or whether they were victims of betrayed innocence by reporters who did not bother to cushion the professors' true opinions in qualifying padding, the outcome was that the academicians' criticisms of the FBI's statistics were overstated in the mass media. The result was that while the general public tended erroneously to accept the crime index as gospel, the sophisticated readers who delved far enough into news articles to find the scholars' comments were usually persuaded that the statistical proof of rapidly increasing crime was almost certainly wrong. Most of the academic experts did not intend to go that far—but the most respected ones agreed, at least until 1967 or 1968, that the FBI had not proved its case.

This division of opinion was most pronounced with regard to violent crimes. The President's Crime Commission stressed repeatedly that while thefts and other property crimes were rising rapidly, the increase in the type of violent crime that most people fear was lagging far behind. All of this doubt and division cast an aura of unreality about the political dialogue over such suggested reforms as Nixon's demand for changes in the Supreme Court's confessions decisions, Humphrey's call for a ten-fold increase in law enforcement spending, and Wallace's suggestion that Federal judges' lifetime tenures be ended.

So long as some of the most thoughtful crime specialists in the country questioned whether violent crime was rising at an unusual or unexpected rate, there was every reason to hold back on any institutional changes, and especially such drastic ones. But since the President's Crime Commission issued its report in February 1967, events have occurred which have convinced most of the previously skeptical experts that violent crime is rising dangerously, and that the increase can be expected to continue for a decade, at least. The exact nature and extent of this rise is still blurred. But that it is occurring—that the dark prophecy of the crime statisticians and the politicians is coming true—is no longer disputed by the experts.

This has come about in a curious way. In the early 1960's, the academicians could see that a crime scare was being launched on the basis of questionable conclusions drawn from unreliable statistics. Many of them committed themselves publicly then to the proposition that the statistical "crime rise" was overblown. The Crime Commission hinted as much, although it stopped short of laying the blame at the doorstep of J. Edgar Hoover and the FBI, where most of it belonged. Yet after the Commission issued its report in early 1967, crime reports from around the country and special studies in key urban areas have satisfied the most serious doubts of the academic skeptics. In effect, these data have confirmed the conclusions about rising violence that Mr. Hoover had been drawing all along—unjustifiably, the experts thought—from the earlier data.

Despite the circumstances, the justification of J. Edgar Hoover and his crime statistics is certain to have a profound impact on the future of the law-and-order controversy, and possibly of the Supreme Court. The controversy over the mathematics of crime will continue over the meaning of the statistics and the manipulations and distortions to which they are subjected, but the frame of reference has shifted in a dramatic way. Crime—violent crime—is increasing rapidly, and few criminologists will now deny it.

There were three good reasons why, prior to release of the 1967 statistics, thoughtful crime experts bridled at the assumption that violent crime was in a dangerous spiral. First, history shows that there has been a rhythm to criminal violence in the United States, and that its rate has probably been higher at times in the past than it is now. Second, the crime scare had been generated by crime statistics that were so questionable that some critics considered them unworthy of belief, and by distortions and exaggerations of those statistics. Finally, even those statistics did not show an alarming rise in violent crime until 1967.

Attempting to put the recent spurt of lawlessness in perspective, the Crime Commission said:

> There has always been too much crime. Virtually every generation since the founding of the Nation and before has felt itself threatened by the spectre of rising crime and violence.
>
> A hundred years ago contemporary accounts of San Francisco told of extensive areas where "no decent man was in safety to walk the street after dark; while at all hours, both night and day, his property was jeopardized by incendiarism and burglary." Teenage gangs gave rise to the word "hoodlum"; while in one central New York City area, near Broadway, the police entered "only in pairs, and never unarmed." A noted chronicler of the period declared that "municipal law is a failure . . . we must soon fall back on the law of self preservation." "Alarming" increases in robbery and violent crimes were reported

throughout the country prior to the Revolution. And in 1910 one author declared that "crime, especially its more violent forms, and among the young is increasing steadily and is threatening to bankrupt the Nation."

Crime and violence in the past took many forms. During the great railway strike of 1877 hundreds were killed across the country and almost 2 miles of railroad cars and buildings were burned in Pittsburgh in clashes between strikers and company police and the militia. It was nearly a half century later, after pitched battles in the steel industry in the late thirties, that the Nation's long history of labor violence subsided. The looting and takeover of New York for 3 days by mobs in the 1863 draft riots rivaled the violence of Watts, while racial disturbances in Atlanta in 1907, in Chicago, Washington, and East St. Louis in 1919, Detroit in 1943 and New York in 1900, 1935, and 1943 marred big city life in the first half of the 20th century. Lynchings took the lives of more than 4,500 persons throughout the country between 1882 and 1930. And the violence of Al Capone and Jesse James was so striking that they have left their marks permanently on our understanding of the eras in which they lived.

No comprehensive crime figures were collected prior to 1933, but studies of individual cities have been made, and they show that crime characteristically has its ups and downs, rather than a steady growth along with the population. James Q. Wilson, a crime expert at Harvard, has said that the early studies "agree that during the period immediately after the Civil War the rate of violent crime in the big cities was higher than at any other time in our history." Almost all of the available data also indicate that the crime rate rose rapidly during the post-World War I period and the economic boom of the twenties, and that it nosedived within a year or so after the bust in 1929. Although no national figures were collated prior to 1933, figures were available for many cities for 1930–32, and they all show that the downward trend had begun from a crime rise that peaked before 1930. Studies in Boston, Chicago, New York, and other individual cities have shown that the rates were higher in the World War I years and the twenties than they were in the forties, and a detailed analysis of crime in Buffalo, N.Y., showed that crime peaked in the 1870's and at the end of World War I, then dipped in the 1940's.

These studies differ in the timing of the crime peaks, but they all show the steep downswing in crime in the forties. The only available national crime statistics that predate 1933, homicide figures collected by the Department of Health, Education, and Welfare, confirm this slump in the forties. (See Fig. 1.) Although the FBI's figures cannot indicate the height of the peak prior to 1933, they suggest the same pattern as shown

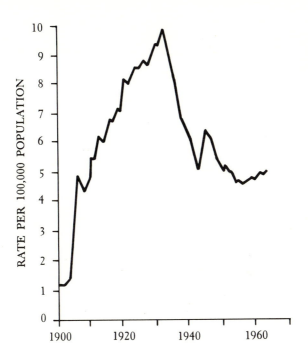

Figure 1.—Homicide rates, 1900–64.

by graphs drawn by the Crime Commission from FBI data, and bear out the impression that crime rates, like women's skirts, go up in periods of prosperity. (See Fig. 2.) However, when the FBI publishes its own crime charts, it always slices off the downward years, showing only the upward side, which seems to bear out its claim of "record highs" in crime, even in mild years. One reason for this is that the FBI's statistical system was overhauled in 1958, and the Bureau doesn't consider the pre- and post-1958 figures to be entirely fungible. Yet as a result of slicing off the earlier years, the FBI gets this skyrocket effect. (See Fig. 3.)

The crime index has given "law and order" an important element in common with the other political issues that have stirred the emotions of the modern electorate—the proposition that things are bad and are likely to get worse can be demonstrated by statistics. Figures on paper were not always a *sine qua non* of scare politics. The prosecutions of the Mormons were not supported by statistical evidence that polygamy was deleterious; there were no figures to support the Red scare that led to the Palmer raids in 1919, and nobody thought it necessary to show on paper that the Japanese-Americans were a threat before the Nisei were rounded up after Pearl Harbor. But since World War II, Americans have

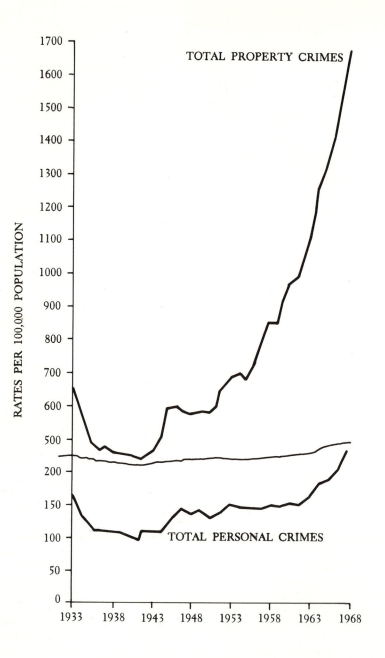

Figure 2.—*Index crime trends, 1933–67.*

not easily been persuaded that evil threatens unless the threat could be reduced to figures on paper. One of the pioneers of statistical politics, Senator Joseph McCarthy, demonstrated that this requirement need not cramp a statesman's style. For so long as the figures are sufficiently obscured that they cannot be absolutely refuted ("I have here in my hand a list of 205 . . . members of the Communist Party . . ."), they usually satisfy the public desire for quantum proof. That this was not some political witchcraft peculiar to Senator McCarthy was later demonstrated by John F. Kennedy during his missile-gap stage and still later by Lyndon B. Johnson, who discovered an alarmingly large category of the "poor" and then substantially reduced its size, all by statistics.

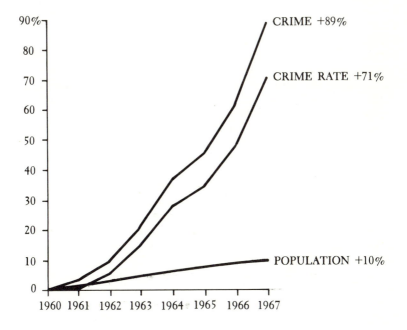

Figure 3.—*Crime and population, 1960–67.*

According to behavioral scientists, the reason why statistics are so willingly swallowed as adequate food for thought on public issues is that society has a gift for accepting and then turning into emotional symbols those statistical indicators that confirm and reinforce existing conceptions. People believe those statistics that tell them what they already believed. This, according to sociologist Albert D. Biderman, is the key to the great prestige of crime statistics in the United States. "The crime index," Professor Biderman says, "shares with many indicators the property of owing much of its credibility and popularity to its being consistent with beliefs formed by everyday experience. . . . [It] serves as a short-hand certifier of beliefs, rather than as a shaper of them."

This once became so galling to Attorney General Nicholas deB. Katzenbach that he is said to have seized a sheet of crime statistics one day, pounded his desk and growled: "It's bad enough to lose the war on crime, but to lose it five times a year is too much!" The offending paper was one of the most predictable of Government documents—the latest report by the Federal Bureau of Investigation on crime. These compilations of crime statistics from local police departments, released to the public in the form of four quarterly reports and a fifth annual recapitulation, are known as Uniform Crime Reports. For the past decade they have been truly uniform in at least one sense—they have invariably declared that crime is rising at a terrifying rate.

By 1966, the year of Mr. Katzenbach's outburst, the periodic crime increase announcement had become a familiar Hoover's Comet that burst upon the national scene at regular intervals, always followed by a trail of indignant editorials and congressional speeches deploring rising crime. In 1968—a typical year—the reports produced these headlines in the *New York Times*: "Major Crimes up 16 percent in '67," "First-quarter Rate of Crime in U.S. Rise 16%," and "Crime Rise of 19% Reported by FBI." After a decade of this steady drumbeat of crime rises, many, if not most, Americans have become conditioned to feel that as a function of the law of averages, their chances of escaping rape, murder, or mugging much longer must be about to run out.

As the federal official primarily responsible for contending with the problem of crime, Mr. Katzenbach had good reason to be irked, for the FBI's stewardship of the nation's crime statistics has resulted in a hysteria that seems more beneficial to the FBI as a crime-fighting public agency than to the public's enlightenment. Three elements appear to have combined to puff the crime picture out of shape, and the FBI could at least have ameliorated two of them.

First, the figures themselves are easily the most suspect statistics published under the imprimatur of the U.S. Government. They are highly susceptible to reporting vagaries, do not allow for built-in increases due to shifting age ratios in the population, and do not clearly separate crimes against property from more serious offenses against people.

These flaws are built into the system and the FBI is not necessarily responsible for them, but in its zest for bearing bad news the Bureau has compounded the mischief that is inherent in the system. The FBI, with its flair for publicity, has managed five times a year to wring the maximum amount of public terror out of a statistical system that was conceived (by the International Association of Chiefs of Police) as a technique for keeping lawmen informed of the trends of their trade. It has consistently emphasized the alarming implications of the statistics (even in good years, such as 1959 and 1961, when crime declined in relation to the population), and has not adequately pointed out their inadequacies.

Finally, the FBI's statistical image of a rising national crime rate has been translated into a personal threat in the minds of many Americans through the instant shared experience of television coverage of a few spectacular crimes and riots. The Crime Commission found that this has created a pervasive "fear of strangers." It noted the interaction between crime statistics and vivid exposure of a few events:

> Many circumstances now conspire to call greater attention to crime as a national, rather than a purely local, problem. Concern with crime is more typically an urban than a rural phenomena and the rural population of the country is declining. At one time, for a majority of the population, reports of crime waves related only to those remote and not quite moral people who inhabited cities.
>
> Now, also, more people are informed by nationally oriented communications media and receive crime reports from a much wider territorial base. In recent years news of the violent and fearful mass killing of eight nurses in a Chicago apartment, five patrons of a beauty shop in Mesa, Arizona, and 13 passersby on the University of Texas campus in Austin received detailed coverage throughout the country. The fear of the people of Boston in 1966 of the brutal attacks of the "Boston Strangler" must have been sympathetically shared and understood in many homes across the land. Some part of the public fear of crime today is undoubtedly due to the fact that the reports of violent crime we receive daily are drawn from a larger pool of crime-incident reports than ever before. But perhaps most important has been the steady stream of reports of rising crime rates in both large and small communities across the Nation. From all this has emerged a sense of crisis in regard to the safety of both persons and property.

The political effects of this have already been profound. During the 1968 Presidential campaign a reporter for the *New York Times* polled the citizens of Webster City, Iowa, which calls itself "Main Street, U.S.A." He found the overriding issue to be "crime in the streets," with particular concern about riots and unruly demonstrations. But when the interviewer inquired about crime in "Main Street, U.S.A.," the complaints were that youngsters were drinking beer, driving fast, and breaking an occasional window. Pressed further, the city fathers complained that trucks hauling turkey feathers through town were unlawfully failing to cover their cargoes to keep from littering Main Street. Another reporter, who found the citizenry of Garnett, Kansas, up in arms over crime, discovered that there hadn't been a rape there for 12 years, nor a murder for 21, and that the only person in jail was a 17-year-old hot-rodder.

To understand how this exaggerated image of "crime" gained currency, long before the academic experts agreed that violence was climbing, it is necessary to comprehend the mechanics of the Uniform Crime Reports. Local police departments voluntarily report to the FBI the volume of crimes known to the police, offenses cleared by arrest, persons held for prosecution, and persons released or found guilty of offenses. Of the 29 different crimes reported, the FBI uses only 7 in its crime index. The "index" crimes, chosen because they are serious and thought to be bellwethers of criminal activity, are murder, forcible rape, robbery (muggings, armed robbery, and theft by threat of force), aggravated assault (assault with intent to kill or seriously injure), burglary (breaking and entering to steal), larceny of $50 or more and auto theft. From this the FBI publishes the famous crime index, which is simply the rate of these offenses per 100,000 people.

The Uniform Crime Reports are naturally suspect because the FBI's crime index reflects only *reported* crime. There is known to be so much crime that is either not reported to the police, or not reported by them to the FBI, that only slight changes in reporting habits could have a yo-yo effect on the crime index. The Crime Commission learned from house-to-house surveys that the volume of unreported crime is far greater than anyone had imagined—double, triple, and even 10 times the volume of offenses that are actually reported, depending on whether the crime involved is the type that shames the victim or whether it is the kind the police are thought likely to solve.

Because there is so much unreported crime, it is theoretically possible to have a "crime wave" on the index charts, when in fact nothing but reporting habits have changed. Thus a crime scare could result from victim sophistication—a realization that only reported thefts can become valid income tax deductions or insurance claims, or a new willingness by nonwhites to report crimes to the police.

The same crime "rise" can occur when the police become more diligent in reporting crime. For years the police of Chicago reported many times more robberies than the city of New York, which has more than twice as many people (in one year, Chicago reported eight times as many robberies). Finally, in 1949, the FBI stopped including New York's statistics because it did not believe them. New York has since been reinstated, but periodically its police have slipped back into their old ways of neglecting to report painful facts.

There seem to be two principal reasons for this tendency by the police to "fudge" on crime reports. One is that much of the crime occurs in Negro neighborhoods, between Negroes, and there has sometimes been an easygoing tolerance of it by the police. It was neither investigated nor reported as carefully as crime was elsewhere. The other reason is that increasing crime is political trouble for city administrations, and they like to give the impression that it is under control. Ambitious police officials realize that their superiors want crime kept down, with the result that complaints sometimes get "lost." The Crime Commission found a secret "file 13" in one city containing a catalog of complaints that were not officially reported, and a single precinct in Philadelphia once had 5,000 more crime reports on file than it had officially recorded.

Some experts suspect that both motives for underreporting are losing their validity, and that a good portion of the crime bulge in certain cities is due to the new official willingness to tell all about crime. In recent years more Negro policemen have been hired and more attention given to ghetto crime. This concern has probably dissipated the feeling that Negro complaints are not worth reporting. Also, with the Supreme Court and not the police being widely blamed for the increase in crime, some resentful policemen are said to be reporting crime with a vengeance. The late Police Chief William Parker of Los Angeles once startled a visiting Federal official by his candid discussion of the huge chart on his wall depicting the rise of crime. Each crime peak was topped with the title of a Supreme Court decision in favor of defendants' rights. Chief Parker explained that the police had seen, years before the Court issued its landmark rulings, that a crime boom was coming despite their best efforts—and that they had been lucky to have the Supreme Court to serve as a lightning rod for the criticism. He said that this was partially responsible for his decision to begin making speeches and writing articles about the connection between crime in the streets and judicial decisions.

Jerome Daunt, the chief of the FBI's crime statistics operation, concedes that some of the index crimes are subject to wide reporting fluctuations, but he points out that some are not. Mr. Daunt, a lean, serious man who learned his crime statistics on the job as an FBI agent, makes the point that certain crimes by their nature are almost always reported: bank robberies, because none is too insignificant to report; assault by gun, because the law requires physicians to file reports; murder, because there is a body to be explained.

Bank robberies have increased even faster than the general index, with a rise of 248 percent from 1960 to 1967. Assault by gun rose 84 percent in the 5 years from 1962 to 1967. Much has been made of the fact that criminal homicide has actually declined by 70 percent since 1933, but Mr. Daunt has an explanation for this: "Police response, ambulance response, and improved medical techniques," he says. "It's like the decline in the relative number of war wounded who die—because they get better, quicker treatment."

"Trends—it is the trends in crime statistics that count," declares Mr. Daunt, "and we have been right on the trends." The FBI has indeed been right on the trends (except that its gloomy projections of future crime levels have invariably fallen short of reality) and this has been due in some part to its painstaking efforts to eliminate error—especially by checking for reporting failures whenever reports began to run suspiciously counter to expectations. But part of this success must also be attributed to the melancholy fact that in dealing with crime, if one predicts disaster long enough, events will finally bear him out.

The most valid complaint against the FBI is not that its figures have been soft, but that the Bureau has not presented them honestly to the public. When the FBI first began to sound the alarm about rising crime a decade ago, the overall increase was small and the violent crime rate was actually frequently in decline. In 1961, for instance, the crime rates for violent offenses decreased across the board. Murder, forcible rape, robbery, and aggravated assault all declined. Yet the overall crime index rate rose by 3 percent because of a modest increase in property crimes. J. Edgar Hoover darkly announced that "major crimes committed in the United States in 1961 have again reached an all-time high," adding that during the year there were "four serious crimes per minute." The reason for the rise was that then, as now, about 9 out of 10 offenses included in the crime index do not involve violence, so that even a modest rise in property offenses can lift the entire crime index. Currently, murders, rapes, and assaults make up only 8 percent of the crimes reported in the index.

If robberies are included as "violent crimes" (about one-fourth of them result in injuries to the victims), it is still true that more than four-fifths of the index crimes are non-violent thefts of property—burglary, larceny of $50 or more, and car theft. Since the crime rates for these offenses were, until recently, consistently higher than the rates for violent crimes, they inflated the overall crime index and gave the impression that violent crime was rising faster than it actually was. This has led to the charge that the FBI's crime index is really a gage of "joyriding" by youngsters in other peoples' cars. In any year the number of auto thefts in the crime index will far outnumber all of the violent crimes taken together, and because 9 out of 10 cars are recovered and returned to their owners, the fearsome "crime rate" is far less a reflection of the pain of victims of rape and assault than the temporary aggravation of those who left their keys in their cars.

Another complaint about the FBI's crime-reporting system is its tendency to tempt exaggeration, oversimplification, and even manipulation of the crime increase. By taking the population increase (1½ percent per year) over a given stretch of years and dividing it into the percentage of crime increase, it can be said that crime is growing many times faster than the population. For instance, if the population increased by approximately 10 percent over a 7-year period, but the number of reported index offenses grew by 88 percent, it could be said that "crime outpaced the population growth by almost nine to one"—J. Edgar

Hoover's latest assessment of the recent crime rise. Once announced, this slightly exaggerated calculation from the highly suspect crime index can be cited as government proof that "crime is growing nine times faster than the population." And when the public recalls that only 1 year earlier Mr. Hoover used the multiple of 7 to describe the increase, and that 2 years before that he used the figure 5, it is given an avalanche impression of "crime"—the threat of attack by strangers—that is puffed out of any relation to the actual threat that any individual will become a victim of violent crime.

An even more warped impression is given by the "crime clocks" that the FBI publishes each year. This baffling presentation, year after year, of the shrinking average interval between the commission of various offenses across the country, seems to have no purpose other than sheer terror. Because the population is growing, the interval between crimes would necessarily narrow each year, even if the crime rate was not increasing. Thus the hands of the FBI's "crime clocks" invariably show fewer minutes between crimes than for the previous year. The "crime clock" device lends itself to shocking conclusions that mean nothing, as a published interpretation of the 1966 figures show: "An American woman is raped every 12 minutes. A house in the United States is burglarized every 27 seconds. Someone is robbed every 4½ minutes in this nation."

By reducing crime to these terms, the "fear of strangers" syndrome is justified in a way that is not borne out by the risks of everyday life. Statistically, the risk of attack by strangers is one of the least likely hazards that the average person encounters. The risk of death from willful homicide in any given year is about 1 in 20,000, and almost three out of four murders are committed by family members or friends. The result is that a person's likelihood of being killed in a car crash is almost 15 times the chances that he will be murdered by a stranger. His risk in any given year of being attacked by a stranger and hurt badly enough to require any degree of hospitalization is about 1 in 4,500—and this is an average possibility: If he lives away from high-crime areas his risk is much lower. As Ramsey Clark used to put it, the average individual's chance of being a victim of a crime of violence is once in 400 years, and Clark always added that if one wished to improve his odds he could avoid his relatives and associates—since they are statistically the most likely to do him harm.

What this shows is that extremely subjective conclusions can be drawn from the basic crime data in this country and that the FBI has consistently presented it in a way that tends to make little old ladies stay indoors and strong men look over their shoulders. As one observer pointed out, rather than publishing the fact that some unfortunate individual is murdered every 48 minutes, the FBI could have told the country that the average citizen's chances of becoming a murder victim on any given day are about 1 in 2 million, and that then he might well be willing to brave those odds without hedging on personal freedom of movement or the country's traditional scheme of personal rights.

As slippery as these figures can be in the hands of crime experts, politicians can turn them to quicksilver. During the 1968 Presidential campaign, Richard Nixon observed that crime had increased 88 percent under the Democratic administration. Attorney General Clark went on television with the reply that crime had risen 98 percent during the Eisenhower period. Aghast, the Republican Task Force on Crime fired back with this statement:

> . . . crime in the 8 Eisenhower years between 1953 and 1960 did not increase by 98 percent. That charge is simply inaccurate.
>
> Crime reported in 1960, the last year of the Eisenhower administration, was 63 percent greater than in 1952, the last year of the Truman administration.
>
> This, of course, covers 8 years. If the experience of 1967 holds true this year, the 8-year Kennedy-Johnson record will show a whopping 118 percent increase for the comparable period, or almost double the rate under a Republican administration. Parenthetically, if only a 7-year frame of reference is used, they fare even worse. During the first 7 years of the Eisenhower administration the crime increase was 43 percent, less than half of the 88 percent recorded during the 7 years thus far under Kennedy and Johnson.

Vice President Humphrey said he deplored this crime numbers game— and added that if he were inclined to play it he could point out that the eight States with the highest crime rates all had Republican Governors.

Because the FBI's crime index was so frequently abused, because its figures were suspect, because even those figures showed the crimes of violence lagging far behind, and possibly because they were liberals indulging in wishful thinking, the academicians refused throughout most of the sixties to admit that serious criminal-violence problem had been proved.

The first break in the familiar statistical pattern came when the 1967 crime reports from across the country were tabulated by the FBI. The usual pattern of relatively low violent-crime rates and high property offenses was shattered by a 16-percent overall increase, composed of a 16-percent rise in violent crimes and a 17-percent increase in property offenses.

But most startling to crime experts was the 28-percent jump in the crime of robbery, which many criminologists consider the bellwether offense in the crime index. Since robbery always involves a threat of force, if not its use, it gives an indication of the public's proclivity toward violence. And since the offender and the victim are usually strangers, the family-quarrel element does not distort the picture. For that reason, criminologists were shocked to see robbery suddenly increasing as rapidly as the property crimes (Fig. 4). Preliminary figures for the first 6 months in 1968 confirmed the trend: robbery increased another 29 percent over the high 1967 level.

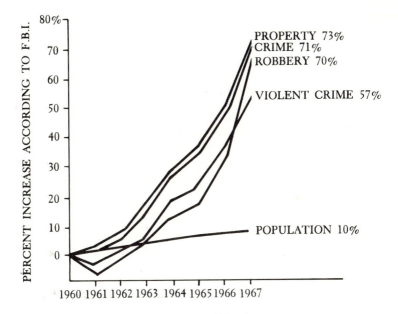

Figure 4.—*The rising U.S. crime rate.*

Meanwhile, new studies showed what Professor Ohlin termed "a pronounced increase in the readiness in people to resort to armed attack." In Philadelphia, where the volume of robberies fluctuated up and down after 1960, the rate of persons injured in robberies began to rise in 1962 and climbed steadily. "Perhaps it is because the robbers tend to be younger, and the young are more likely to use violence," concluded criminologist Marvin E. Wolfgang; "but there has been a considerable increase in the level of violence in robberies."

Ronald H. Beattie, chief of California's Bureau of Criminal Statistics, who had declared as late as 1966 that the available crime statistics "indicate no substantial increase in aggressive crimes during recent years," took another look in 1968 and said that violent crime was growing even faster than crimes against property. Most experts now believe that this rapid surge in crime, with its new heavy component of crimes of violence, will continue and perhaps will accelerate, at least for the next 10 years. The reason is that the types of people who, as one observer put it, are "untamed in the ways of society," and are thus inclined to commit crimes, are increasing in proportion to the population as a whole.

By far the most crime prone of this "untamed" class are young men. More 15-year-olds are arrested for serious crimes than any other group. Yet thanks to the postwar baby boom, there are proportionally more of them around to commit crimes than ever before, and their numbers are growing. Each year since 1961 an additional 1 million youths have reached the age of 15 than did the year before, and already almost one-half of the population is under 25. According to crime experts, almost half of the total increase in arrests in the first half of the 1960's was simply because there were more younger people around.

Another complicating factor is urbanization. Study after study shows that the violent crime rate of Negroes who have moved from the South into the large urban cities is far higher than the national crime rate for Negroes. The same is true, but with less emphasis, for cities as a whole; crime rates invariably rise in proportion to the proximity to an urban center. Concomitant with the anonymity of urban life—where everybody is a stranger to everyone else and the fear of detection and shame of arrest are diminished—a familiar pattern of bold, casual criminality has developed.

There are other indices, all of them pointing upward. Statistics show that communities with large transient populations experience high crime rates, and demographers predict increasing population mobility in the coming years. High crime and narcotics addiction accompany each other, and the narcotics arrests (although heavily weighted with marihuana cases) almost doubled in 1967 over 1966. Some scientists believe that overcrowding alone can cause antisocial behavior, and the decrease in living space is obvious. It is sad but not surprising that Professor Wilson concludes, "We shall be fortunate if we can even slow the rate of increase in crime; we shall be impossibly blessed if we can actually reduce the level of crime."

QUESTIONS

1. Why does Graham imply that it is "the sophisticated readers" who will make the main decisions concerning future social actions?

2. Are you convinced that the crime rate has risen, in your own neighborhood, town or city, in recent years? What explanations can you offer? Do they agree with those presented by Graham in this article?

3. Discuss further why "Americans have become conditioned to feel that as a function of the law of averages, their chances of escaping rape, murder, or mugging much longer must be about to run out."

4. How deeply has television reportage affected your own understanding of crime and law and order?

5. Does the fact "that the average citizen's chances of becoming a murder victim on any given day are about 1 in 2 million" make you feel safer?

6. Before you read this article, did you know that "more 15-year-olds are arrested for serious crime than any other group"? How do you account for this statistic?

7. Explore how anonymity and overcrowding relate to crime.

Topics for Writing and Research

Below, you will find a long list of possible subjects for papers based on this sourcebook. Over two-thirds of the topics can be utilized with only *Detective Fiction: Crime and Compromise* for reference. Other topics will require further reference and reading. At least one hundred more subjects are suggested by the questions that follow each selection and by those raised in the book's preface, introduction, and section introductions. Be sure to check with your instructor for his approval of your topic, for his advice on the paper's type (theme, essay, critical study, research paper, etc.). Ask, too, his advice on length, style, focus, manuscript form.

1. Write a paper in which you attempt a solid definition of detective fiction, showing how it compares and contrasts with mystery fiction, crime fiction, spy fiction, thrillers, suspense fiction. Do you feel that "detective fiction" is the best overall term for the genre?

2. This sourcebook contains stories by many writers not usually praised for their "artistic" achievements. There are also stories by authors commonly regarded as "great" writers. In a paper, compare stories by the two kinds of writer. Decide what elements generally make some stories "interpretive" as opposed to "escape" literature.

3. Do you find your awareness of crime and its meaning to society and the individual sharpened more by your reading of fiction or of nonfiction? Explain. Refer particularly to the articles by Daley and Graham.

4. Analyze a number of the short stories in "The Detective" section with a view toward explaining how plot—especially traditional plot—works in fiction. You might, for instance, compare these stories with ones in "The Genre Extended."

5. Do a study of the "locked room" story. What are its general characteristics? Why is it a particularly popular form of detective fiction? Are "The Adventure of the Speckled Band" and "The Problem of Cell 13" most characteristic of the form?

6. Explore the treatment of women in detective fiction. Is detective fiction mainly a domain of male chauvinism?

7. Compare works of several noted women writers of detective fiction, especially in their treatment of characters, with writings of several male detective fiction writers.

8. Investigate the effect of Prohibition on the genesis of the hard-boiled school, with particular emphasis on the relationship between police corruption and criminal power as circumstances spawning the private eye.

9. Do an analysis of style in traditional detective stories. You might find it valuable to examine differences between the styles of English and American writers or those of writers of any two time periods.

10. Read some critical works on naturalism and realism and write a paper in which you show how the hard-boiled school of detective fiction might reflect these literary philosophies.

11. How well is logic *actually* used in detective fiction? Can you find many examples of valid syllogisms in the detective's speech as he explains how he has solved a crime? Does the detective seem mainly to use deductive or inductive logic?

12. Watch, as did Robert Daley, a number of detective shows on television. Write an essay comparing your observations with his.

13. Is the experience of *reading* detective fiction significantly different from that of *watching* detective movies or television shows? For instance, are your perceptions changed when you sit among people in a theatre and participate in what might well be called a group experience?

14. How heavily does the detective rely on intuition? Write an essay on the use of intuition in detective fiction, perhaps with particular reference to the works of Edgar Allan Poe.

15. Write a paper on the treatment of the wealthy and the role of money in detective fiction. You might look up the word "materialism." Does detective fiction regard most criminal motives as materialistic?

16. Are all writers, including the writers of detective fiction, really "detectives"? Is this why so many writers find the genre so attractive? Write a paper on the writer as detective. It might be most interesting if the writers you take as examples do *not* write detective fiction *per se*.

17. Does detective fiction train the reader to develop not only his reasoning powers but his sense of observation? What dulls the sense of observation in most people?

18. The police are treated as often unfairly as fairly in detective fiction. Examine this treatment, considering what it may reveal about attitudes toward law enforcement.

19. A descriptive and graphic account of modern crime is contained in Gerald Aster's article "What a Waste" (see "Bibliography"). After reading this article about the Boston Homicide Squad, do a short paper concerning your opinion on the amount of exaggerated

violence and gore in detective fiction. Is there such a thing as "the pornography of violence"?

20. One of the detective story writer's main purposes is to keep his readers interested, turning pages. How does he do this? Name particular, commonly used techniques. Is suspense in most detective fiction relatively unsophisticated? How does it differ from the use of suspense techniques in other genres of literature?

21. Many writers of science fiction also write detective fiction, and vice versa. Find and read a number of science fiction stories that use detective story elements. How are the two forms allied? Are the differences only in setting?

22. Do you feel there is a sufficient sense of horror in most detective fiction? (After all, murders have generally been committed.) Is the treatment of horror purposely muted in many stories? Why? When a story does make you feel frightened, how has the writer brought you toward this emotion? How significant is his use of setting?

23. Read several books by such authors as Mickey Spillane, Howard Hunt, Donald Hamilton, Ed McBain. Write a study of these, exploring the philosophies of life implied by their authors. Do you think these philosophies reflect those of most Americans? Of the authors themselves?

24. Detective fiction seemed to exercise real allure for William Faulkner. One of his greatest novels, *Absalom, Absalom!* has been called by Cleanth Brooks "a wonderful detective story." Another volume by Faulkner, *Knight's Gambit*, is devoted exclusively to detective fiction. How well does Faulkner use the conventions of the genre? Does he transcend them? Write a paper on the detection elements in Faulkner's work.

25. Explore the use of the past as it affects characters in detective fiction.

26. How is love interest treated in detective fiction? Why? What about the treatment of sex?

27. Examine the treatment of several minor characters in detective stories—characters such as Watson, the narrator of "The Purloined Letter," Colonel Jarel in "The Cold Winds of Adesta," and the parents in the section from Ross Macdonald's *The Far Side of the Dollar.* How effective, how interesting, how real have these characters been made?

28. Is detective fiction a form of "quest" or "search" literature? Examine the aspects of the search in detective literature. It might be particularly helpful to refer to Northrop Fry's *Anatomy of Criticism* for guidelines in working on this paper. You might also incorporate some of your thoughts into a paper on the detective as hero or as knight figure.

29. What attitude toward free will is generally taken in detective literature? Does the detective story generally presume the existence of

free will? "Markheim" and "Design" might provide good starting points here.

30. Explore the role of revenge in detective fiction. Is it a significant motivation? In a more extensive paper, do a study of Elizabethan and Jacobean "revenge tragedies" as related to modern detective stories.

31. Read several novels in a contemporary detective-hero series and discuss their major elements, their popularity.

32. After you have seen a detective movie, read the novel on which it was based; then explore the differences in the forms. (Be careful to avoid picking a novel based on the screenplay. Or wittingly, choose one based on a screenplay.)

33. Is humor *necessary* in most detective fiction? Why or why not? Find several parodies of detective fiction, in addition to Mark Twain's, and tell what they have revealed about the form. Do some detective stories actually seem to be parodies of themselves, the author unable to take even his own characters very seriously?

34. Write a paper on the pros and cons of prosecution for victimless crimes.

35. Study the correlation between the political sentiments or attitudes expressed in detective novels and main aspects of the general political climate during the time the novels were written.

36. "Evil" might be too strong a word to use in talking about much detective fiction. Do you agree? Can you come up with a definition of "evil" as it is seen in most traditional detective stories?

37. Consider the sense of morality in detective fiction. Is the genre mainly one of "the good" versus "the bad"? Why do people desire to have complex questions simplified to these two elements? Do we really believe that there are characters who are purely bad or good? More important, is there something in us that makes us *need* to believe this?

38. Compare several detective stories with city environments to ones with country environments. Which environment seems to you to be most fitting for detective work? You might find G. K. Chesterton's "A Defence of Detective Stories" most helpful here.

39. How does detective fiction reflect political philosophies? Do you find, for instance, that most detectives would be called "conservative" as opposed to "liberal" in their attitudes toward their work and their lives? Would a steady reading of detective fiction be more apt to make you conservative or liberal?

40. How important is the role of propaganda in detective fiction? Is there almost always an implied desire on the part of the writer for tougher laws and treatment of criminals? Why does the detective so often put himself "above the law," even for the sake of a good cause?

41. Some have said that when television "cleaned up" violence, there was an increase in the popularity of movies where violence was

allowed to be more explicit. Why are humans so eternally attracted to violence? Do you think we regard it as "fantasy," or do we take vicarious satisfaction in it, or do we watch it as an outlet for our own violent tendencies?

42. Find some detective novels or stories written forty or fifty years ago, by authors not mentioned in the "Bibliography" section of this sourcebook. Are there elements in their works that almost automatically date them? How do the works compare to detective fiction that has remained popular, such as A. Conan Doyle's stories and novels?

43. It has been said that the first instance of detective fiction is Sophocles' *Oedipus Rex*. Consider the play as a detective story.

44. Oedipus and other ancient figures, such as Ulysses, have often been used by modern writers to indicate parallels of various types. Find and discuss instances of classical reference in detective stories. You might particularly direct attention to the work of Ross Macdonald.

45. Read a current issue of a detective story magazine and describe and analyze what you have observed about such matters as quality, style, treatment of the detective, attitude toward society.

46. Is a considerable amount of detective literature really "juvenile," appealing to young and unsophisticated readers (contrary to what W. H. Auden supposes)? Explain your opinion. A variation on this paper could explore detective literature as a genre primarily appealing to older readers. Still another might examine the treatment of the "intellectual" in detective fiction.

47. Look up Edmund Wilson's two noted essays attacking detective fiction (see "Bibliography") and write a paper in which you agree or disagree with his criticisms. Support your contentions with direct quotes from Wilson's essays.

48. How heavily does most detective fiction rely on trick or surprise endings? Is their use one of the main reasons why literary critics so seldom have taken the genre as fit for serious academic study?

49. If detective fiction is worthy of study, spy fiction should be also. Many genre writers as well as "serious" authors have written spy fiction. Graham Greene is perhaps most prominent (e.g., *The Third Man, The Quiet American, This Gun for Hire*). Other well-known authors include Joseph Conrad, Somerset Maugham, Anthony Burgess, Eric Ambler, Ian Fleming, John LeCarré, Donald Hamilton, Donald Westlake, Derek Marlowe, and Ivor Drummond. Do a generalized study of the spy fiction genre or a study of a specific spy fiction work.

50. In the introduction to *The Big Knockover*, a collection of Dashiell Hammett's short stories, Lillian Hellman gives a moving and compassionate account of Hammett the man. She comments on his democratic and proletarian sympathies. Can you locate manifestations of this sympathy in Hammett's work? It might be valuable for you to read *Red Harvest*, his first novel.

51. Dashiell Hammett in the 1930's worked at writing "continuing story" cartoons. He created "Secret Agent X-9" to compete with "Dick Tracy." Do you think there is a relationship between the evolution of such cartoons and detective fiction? Is the relationship symbiotic or destructive?

52. Detective novels often deal implicitly with issues of police and political incompetence. Some detective novels deal with these matters in a more explicit way—such as Raymond Chandler's *The Long Goodbye* and, to a lesser extent, Dashiell Hammett's *The Glass Key*. Explore the relationships between the private eye and the "corruption" of the Establishment found in these or other novels.

Suggestions for Further Reading

The following lists will indicate some of the representative published works available to those interested in further materials related to this sourcebook. Many of these works can be obtained in paperback, but the best place to find them will be local public libraries.

The listings are in no way meant to be comprehensive, and the inclusion or exclusion of any particular author or work is not to be construed as a comment on merit. Any fan of the genre would be able to make up his own, quite different listing.

For purposes of space, we have chosen to list mainly anthologies in the *Critical Works* section, rather than the many excellent individual essays and articles collected in these anthologies.

On Aggression, Crime, Police, Spies

Abrahamsen, David. *Our Violent Society*. Funk & Wagnalls, 1970.
———. *The Psychology of Crime*. Columbia University Press, 1960.
Ahern, James F. *Police in Trouble: Our Frightening Crisis in Law Enforcement*. Hawthorn Books, 1972.
Altick, Richard D. *Victorian Studies in Scarlet*. W. W. Norton, 1970.
Ardry, Robert. *African Genesis*. Atheneum, 1961.
———. *The Territorial Imperative*. Atheneum, 1966.
Arendt, Hannah. *On Violence*. Harcourt Brace Jovanovich, 1969.
Astor, Gerald. "What a Waste." *Playboy*. June 1973.
Beccaria, Marchese. *On Crimes and Punishments*. Bobbs-Merrill, 1963.
Becker, Ernest. *The Structure of Evil*. George Braziller, 1968.
Bell, Josephine. *Crime in Our Time*. Nicholas Vane Publishers (London), 1962.
Berkley, George E. *The Democratic Policeman*. Beacon, 1969.
Birkett, Sir Norman. *The Newgate Calendar*. The Folio Society (London), 1951.
Block, Eugene B. *Famous Detectives: True Stories of Great Crime Detection*. Doubleday, 1967.
Blomberg, Abraham S. *Criminal Justice*. Quadrangle Books, 1967.

Bolitho, William. *Murder for Profit*. Time-Life Books, 1954.

Boucher, Anthony, ed. *The Quality of Murder*. Dutton, 1962.

Brophy, John. *The Meaning of Murder*. Whitting and Wheaton (London), 1966.

Caesar, Gene. *Incredible Detective: The Biography of William J. Burns*. Prentice-Hall, 1968.

Caffi, Andrea. *A Critique of Violence*. Bobbs-Merrill, 1970.

Chevigny, Paul. *Cops and Rebels: A Study of Provocation*. Pantheon, 1972.

DeQuincey, Thomas. "Murder Considered as One of the Fine Arts." In numerous editions of his essays.

Dickler, Gerald. *Man on Trial*. Doubleday, 1962.

Dressler, David, ed. *Readings in Criminology and Penology*. Columbia University Press, 1964.

Dulles, Allen. *The Craft of Intelligence*. Harper & Row, 1963.

———, ed. *Great True Spy Stories*. Harper & Row, 1968.

Felix, Christopher. *A Short Course in the Secret War*. Dutton, 1963.

Feshback, Seymour. *Television and Aggression*. Jossey-Bass, 1971.

Fromm, Erich. *Man: Good or Evil*. Collier Books, 1968.

Graham, Hugh Davis and Gurr, Ted Robert, eds. *The History of Violence in America*. Bantam, 1969.

Harris, Richard. *The Fear of Crime*. Praeger, 1968.

Horan, James D. *The Pinkertons: The Detective Dynasty That Made History*. Crown, 1967.

Joyce, James Avery. *Capital Punishment*. Thomas Nelson Sons, 1961.

Kilgallen, Dorothy. *Murder One*. Random House, 1967.

Koestler, Arthur. *Reflections on Hanging*. Macmillan, 1967.

Laurie, Peter. *Scotland Yard*. Holt, Rinehart & Winston, 1970.

Lipsky, Michael, ed. *Police Encounters*. Trans-action Books. Aldine, 1970.

Lorenz, Konrad. *On Aggression*. Bantam, 1967.

Loth, David. *Crime in the Suburbs*. William Morrow, 1967.

May, Rollo. *Power and Innocence*. Delta, 1973.

Menninger, Karl. *Whatever Became of Sin?* Hawthorn, 1973.

Montagu, M. F. Ashley, ed. *Man and Aggression*. Oxford University Press, 1968.

Morris, Norval and Hawkins, Gordon. *The Honest Politician's Guide to Crime Control*. University of Chicago Press, 1970.

Pearson, Edmund. *Murders That Baffled the Experts*. Signet, 1967.

———. *Studies in Murder*. Modern Library, 1938.

Reiss, Albert J., Jr. *The Police and the Public*. Yale University Press, 1971.

Rights in Conflict: The Walker Report to the National Commission on the Causes and Prevention of Violence. Bantam, 1968.

Rumbelow, Donald. *I Spy Blue: The Police and Crime in the City of London from Elizabeth I to Victoria.* St. Martin's Press, 1971.
Savage, Mildred. *A Great Fall.* Simon and Schuster, 1970.
Short, James F., Jr., ed. *Modern Criminals.* Trans-action Books. Aldine, 1970.
Soderman, Harry and O'Connell, John J. *Modern Criminal Investigation.* Funk & Wagnalls, 1945.
Szasz, Thomas S. *Psychiatric Justice.* Macmillan, 1965.
Thorwald, Jürgen. *The Century of the Detective.* Harcourt Brace Jovanovich, 1965.
―――. *Crime and Science: The New Frontier in Criminology.* Harcourt Brace Jovanovich, 1967.
Turner, William W. *The Police Establishment.* Putnam, 1968.
Walker, T. Mike. *Voices from the Bottom of the World; A Policeman's Journal.* Grove Press, 1969.
Whitehouse, Arch. *Espionage and Counterespionage.* Doubleday, 1964.
Wilson, Colin. *A Casebook of Murder: The Changing Patterns of Homicidal Killings.* Cowles, 1969.
Wilson, Colin and Pitman, Patricia, eds. *Encyclopedia of Murder.* Putnam, 1962.
Wilson, James Q. *Varieties of Police Behavior.* Harvard University Press, 1968.

Short Story Collections and Magazines

Anon., ed. *Crime and Detection* (World Classics, Second Series). Oxford University Press, 1930.
Alfred Hitchcock's Mystery Magazine.
Bond, Raymond T., ed. *Famous Stories of Code and Cipher.* Rinehart, 1947.
―――. *Handbook For Poisoners.* Rinehart, 1951.
Bernkopf, Jeanne F., ed. *The Cream of Crime (Tales from Boucher's Choicest).* Dell, 1972.
―――. *The Menace Masters (Tales from Boucher's Choicest).* Dell, 1971.
Boucher, Anthony, ed. *Best Detective Stories of the Year.* Dutton, various years.
―――. *Four and Twenty Bloodhounds.* Simon and Schuster, 1940.
―――. *Great American Detective Stories.* World, 1945.
―――. *The Quintessence of Queen.* Random House, 1962.
Bull, R. C. *Great Tales of Mystery.* Hill & Wang, 1960.
Cartmell, Van H. and Cerf, Bennett, eds. *Famous Plays of Crime and Detection.* Blakiston, 1946.
Charlie Chan's Mystery Magazine.

Daly, Maureen, ed. *My Favorite Mystery Story.* Dodd-Mead, 1966.

Dulles, Allen. *Great Spy Stories from Fiction.* Harper & Row, 1969.

Ellery Queen's Mystery Magazine.

Furman, A. L., ed. *Mystery Companion* (First, Second, etc.). Gold Label, various years.

Greene, Hugh, ed. *Cosmopolitan Crimes.* Penguin, 1972.

———. *The Rivals of Sherlock Holmes.* Penguin, 1971.

Halliday, Brett, ed. *Best Detective Stories of the Year.* Dell, various years.

Haycraft, Howard, ed. *Fourteen Great Detective Stories.* Modern Library, 1949.

Hitchcock, Alfred, ed. *Alfred Hitchcock Presents: Stories That Scared Even Me, Stories Not for the Nervous, Stories My Mother Never Told Me, Stories for Late at Night, My Favorites in Suspense,* etc. Dell, various years.

MacGowan, Kenneth, ed. *Sleuths.* Harcourt Brace Jovanovich, 1931.

Mike Shayne's Mystery Magazine.

Owen, Frank, ed. *Murder for the Millions.* Frederick Fell, 1946.

Queen, Ellery, ed. *Best Bets.* Pyramid, 1972.

———. *Ellery Queen's Minimysteries.* World, 1969.

———. *The Female of the Species.* Little, Brown, 1943.

———. *The Misadventures of Sherlock Holmes.* Little, Brown, 1944.

———. *101 Years' Entertainment.* Little, Brown, 1941.

———. *Poetic Justice.* New American Library, 1967.

———. *The Queen's Awards* (Mystery Annual, Ellery Queen Anthologies). Various publishers, various years.

———. *Rogue's Gallery.* Little, Brown, 1945.

———. *Sporting Blood.* Little, Brown, 1942.

———. *Twentieth Century Detective Stories.* World, 1948.

Rhode, John, ed. *The Avon Book of Detective and Crime Stories.* Avon, 1942.

Sandoe, James, ed. *Murder Plain and Fanciful.* Sheridan House, 1948.

Sayers, Dorothy, ed. *The Omnibus of Crime.* Payson and Clarke, 1929.

———. *The Second Omnibus of Crime.* Coward-McCann, 1932.

———. *The Third Omnibus of Crime.* Coward-McCann, 1935.

Thwing, Eugene, ed. *The World's Best One Hundred Detective Stories.* 10 vol. Funk & Wagnells, 1929.

Van Dine, S. S., ed. *The World's Great Detective Stories.* Blue Ribbon (Doubleday paperback), 1931.

Wright, Lee, ed. *The Pocket Book of Great Detectives.* Pocket Books, 1941.

———. *The Pocket Book of Mystery Stories.* Pocket Books, 1941.

———. *The Pocket Book Mystery Reader.* Pocket Books, 1942.

Wrong, E. M., ed. *Crime and Detection.* Oxford University Press, 1926.

Critical Works

Amis, Kingsley. *The James Bond Dossier*. Jonathan Cape (London), 1965.

Anon, ed. *For Bond Lovers Only*. Dell, 1965.

Barzun, Jacques and Taylor, Wendell Hertig. *A Catalogue of Crime*. Harper & Row, 1971.

Brean, Herbert, ed. *The Mystery Writer's Handbook*. Harper & Row, 1956.

Everson, William K. *The Detective in Film*. Citadel, 1972.

Grella, George. "Murder and Manners." *Novel*, IV, 1970.

Haycraft, Howard, ed. *The Art of the Mystery Story*. Grosset's Universal Library, 1946.

Madden, David, ed. *Tough Guy Writers of the Thirties*. Southern Illinois, 1970.

The Mystery and Detection Annual, Donald K. Adams, ed. Dept. of English, Occidental College, Los Angeles, California.

Nevins, Francis M., Jr., ed. *The Mystery Writer's Art*. Bowling Green University Press, 1971.

Nolan, William F., ed. *Dashiell Hammett, A Casebook*. McNally and Loftin, 1969.

Queen, Ellery. *The Detective Short Story: A Bibliography*. Little, Brown, 1942.

Wilson, Edmund. *Classics and Commercials*. Vintage, 1962.

A Sampling of Crime, Detective, Mystery, Spy Fiction

Allingham, Margery. *The Case Book of Mr. Campion, The Case of the Late Pig, Dancers in Mourning, The Fashion in Shrouds, Mr. Campion: Criminologist, Mr. Campion and Others, Police at the Funeral.*

Ambler, Eric. *A Coffin for Dimitrios, Epitaph for a Spy, The Intercom Conspiracy, State of Siege.*

Armstrong, Charlotte. *A Dram of Poison, A Little Less Than Kind, The Unsuspected.*

Bailey, H. C. *A Clue for Mr. Fortune, Meet Mr. Fortune, Mr. Fortuneer, Mr. Fortune Objects, Mr. Fortune's Practice.*

Bell, Josephine. *Curtain Call for a Corpse, Death at the Medical Board, No Escape.*

Bellairs, George. *Death Before Breakfast, Death in High Provence.*

Belloc, Hilaire. *Shadowed!*

Bentley, E. C. *Trent Intervenes, Trent's Case Book, Trent's Last Case;* (with H. Warner Allen) *Trent's Own Case.*

Berkeley, Anthony. *The Layton Court Mystery, The Second Shot, Top Story Murder, Trial and Error, The Wychford Poisoning Case.*

Biggers, Earl Derr. *The Celebrated Cases of Charlie Chan.*

Blake, Nicholas. *The Corpse in the Snowman, End of Chapter, Head of a Traveller, Minute for Murder, A Penknife in My Heart, The Worm of Death.*

Branson, H. C. *The Case of the Giant Killer, The Fearful Passage, I'll Eat You Last, The Leaden Bubble, The Pricking Thumb.*

Bramah, Ernest. *The Eyes of Max Carrados, Max Carrados, Max Carrados Mysteries.*

Brock, Lynn. *Colonel Gore's Second Case, The Kink, Murder at the Inn, Murder on the Bridge.*

Brown, Fredric. *The Deep End, The Fabulous Clipjoint, The Five-Day Nightmare, The Lenient Beast.*

Bruce, Leo. *The Case Without a Corpse, Death in Albert Park, Furious Old Women.*

Burgess, Anthony. *Tremor of Intent.*

Burton, Miles. *Accidents Do Happen, Bones in the Brickfield, The Cat Jumps, Dark Is the Tunnel, Death at the Club, The Menace on the Downs, The Secret of High Eldersham, Vacation With Corpse, Who Killed the Doctor.*

Cain, James. *Double Indemnity, The Postman Always Rings Twice.*

Cannan, Joanne. *Death at "The Dog," Poisonous Relations, They Rang Up the Police.*

Carmichael, Harry. *Alibi, The Late Unlamented, Requiem for Charles.*

Carr, John Dickson. *The Burning Court, The Case of the Constant Suicides, The Ghost's High Noon, The Nine Wrong Answers.*

Cecil, Henry. *No Bail for the Judge, Settled Out of Court, Unlawful Occasions.*

Chandler, Raymond. *The Big Sleep, Farewell, My Lovely, Five Murders, The High Window, Killer in the Rain, The Lady in the Lake, The Little Sister, The Long Goodbye, Pick-up on Noon Street, Playback, Red Wind, The Simple Art of Murder.*

Charteris, Leslie. *The Saint Versus Scotland Yard,* etc.

Chesterton, G. K. *The Father Brown Omnibus, Four Faultless Felons, The Man Who Knew Too Much, The Man Who Was Thursday.*

Christie, Agatha. *And Then There Were None; Blood Will Tell; The Clocks; Dead Man's Mirror; Double Sin; Easy to Kill; Endless Night; The Labors of Hercules; The Hollow; The Mousetrap; Murder in Retrospect; Murder in the Calais Coach; An Overdose of Death; The Pale Horse; Mr. Parker Pyne, Detective; Partners in Crime; The Passing of Mr. Quin; The Regatta Mystery and Other Stories;*

Thirteen for Luck; The Tuesday Club Murders; Witness for the Prosecution.

Cole, G. D. H. *The Blatchington Tangle, Death in the Quarry, Murder at Crome House.*

Collins, Wilkie, *The Moonstone, The Woman in White.*

Connington, J. J. *The Boathouse Riddle, The Case With Nine Solutions, A Minor Operation, The Sweepstake Murders, Tragedy at Ravensthorpe, The Two-Ticket Puzzle.*

Conrad, Joseph. *The Secret Agent.*

Coryell, John, et al. *Nick Carter, Detective,* etc.

Courtier, S. H. *The Glass Pear, Let the Man Die, Murder's Burning.*

Creasey, John. *The Blind Spot, The Figure in the Dusk, The Toff Goes to Market.*

Crispin, Edmund. *The Long Divorce, Love Lies Bleeding, Obsequies at Oxford.*

Crofts, Freeman Wills. *The Cask, Double Death, Enemy Unseen, The Ponson Case, The Purple Sickle Murders, The Starved Hollow Tragedy.*

Cross, Amanda. *In the Last Analysis, The James Joyce Murder, Poetic Justice.*

Daly, Elizabeth. *Any Shape or Form, Death and Letters, Evidence of Things Seen, Unexpected Night.*

Derleth, August. *Murder Stalks the Wakely Family, No Future for Luana, Sentence Deferred.*

Dickens, Charles. *The Mystery of Edwin Drood.*

Dickson, Carter. *The Department of Queer Complaints, Nine and Death Makes Ten.*

Doyle, Arthur. *The Annotated Sherlock Holmes, The Complete Sherlock Holmes.*

Dürrenmatt, Friedrich. *The Judge and His Hangman.*

Ellin, Stanley. *The Eighth Circle, The Key to Nicholas Street, Mystery Stories, The Valentine Estate.*

Fair, A. A. *The Count of Nine, Double or Quits, Give Em the Ax, Top of the Heap.*

Faulkner, William. *Knight's Gambit.*

Fearing, Kenneth. *The Big Clock, The Dagger of the Mind, The Loneliest Girl in the World.*

Fleming, Ian. *Goldfinger, From Russia With Love, Live and Let Die, On Her Majesty's Secret Service.*

Ford, Leslie. *The Bahamas Murder Case, By the Watchman's Clock, Trial By Ambush, Washington Whispers Murder.*

Francis, Dick. *Blood Sport, Dead Cert, Flying Finish, Forfeit, For Kicks, Nerve, Odds Against.*

Freeman, R. Austin. *As a Thief in the Night; Dr. Thorndyke's Case*

Book; Dr. Thorndyke's Cases; For the Defense: Dr. Thorndyke; The Great Portrait Mystery; The Magic Casket; The Mystery of 31, New Inn; The Red Thumb Mark; The Singing Bone; The Stoneware Monkey.

Futrelle, Jacques. The Diamond Master, The Thinking Machine.

Gardner, Erle Stanley. The Case of the Angry Mourner, The Case of the Crooked Candle, The Case of the Perjured Parrot, The D.A. Draws a Circle.

Gilbert, Michael. Blood and Judgment, Close Quarters, The Danger Within, Death Has Deep Roots, The County-House Burglar, Smallbone Deceased.

Godwin, William. The Adventures of Caleb Williams.

Greene, Graham. A Gun for Sale.

Halliday, Brett. Counterfeit Wife, Die Like a Dog.

Hamilton, Donald. Date With Darkness, The Night Walker, The Steel Mirror.

Hammett, Dashiell. The Adventures of Sam Spade, The Big Knockover, The Dain Curse, Hammett Homicides, The Maltese Falcon, Red Harvest, The Thin Man.

Hare, Cyril. Death Is No Sportsman, Tenant for Death, Tragedy at Law, When the Wind Blows.

Heard, Gerald. A Taste for Honey.

Heyer, Georgette. A Blunt Instrument, Merely Murder, The Unfinished Clue, Why Shoot a Butler.

Household, Geoffrey. Doom's Caravan, Rogue Male, A Rough Shoot, The High Place, The Three Sentences.

Hunt, E. Howard. Festival for Spies, The Venus Probe.

Innes, Michael. The Bloody Wood; Change of Heir; Hamlet, Revenge!; The Man from the Sea; One-Man Show.

Kemelman, Harry. Friday, The Rabbi Slept Late; The Nine-Mile Walk; Saturday, The Rabbi Went Hungry.

Kennedy, Milward. Death in a Deck Chair, Death to the Rescue, The Murderer of Sleep, Poison in the Parish.

Knox, Bill. Blacklight, Figurehead, The Ghost Car, Justice on the Rocks, The Scavengers, Seafire.

Knox, Ronald A. Settled Out of Court, Still Road.

Lathen, Emma. Accounting for Murder, Banking on Death, Come to Dust, Death Shall Overcome, Murder Makes the Wheels Go 'Round, Pick Up Sticks.

Leblanc, Maurice. The Confessions of Arsene Lupin.

Le Carré, John. Call for the Dead, A Murder of Quality, The Spy Who Came In From the Cold.

Lockridge, Richard. Murder Has Its Point, Stand Up and Die, With Option to Die.

Lockridge, Richard and Francis. *Accent on Murder, Catch As Catch Can, The Distant Clue, Think of Death.*

MacDonald, John. *Burnt Orange for the Shroud, Dead Low Tide, The Deep Blue Good-by, Nightmare in Pink, The Quick Red Fox.*

MacDonald, Philip. *Death and Chicanery, The Link, The List of Adrian Messenger, The Rasp.*

Macdonald, Ross. *The Chill, The Doomsters, The Drowning Pool, The Far Side of the Dollar, The Ferguson Affair, The Galton Case, The Instant Enemy, The Ivory Grin, The Moving Target, The Way Some People Die, The Zebra-Striped Hearse.*

MacKenzie, Donald. *The Kyle Contract, Salute From a Dead Man, Sleep Is for the Rich.*

Marric, J. J. *Gideon's Fire, Gideon's Night, Gideon's River, Gideon's Vote.*

Marsh, Ngaio. *Clutch of Constables, Dead Water, Enter a Murderer, Final Curtain, Hand in Glove, Killer Dolphin, Overture to Death, Singing in the Shrouds.*

Maugham, W. Somerset. *Ashenden; or, The British Agent.*

McBain, Ed. *Lady Killer, Killer's Payoff, Killer's Wedge.*

McShane, Marle. *The Crimson Murders of Little Doom, Night's Evil.*

Moffett, Cleveland. *The Sein Mystery, Through the Wall.*

Monteilhet, Hubert. *The Praying Mantises, Return From the Ashes, The Road to Hell.*

Oppenheim, E. Phillips. *The Evil Shepherd, The Great Impersonation, A Maker of History.*

Orczy, Baroness Emmuska. *The Case of Miss Elliott, The Man in the Corner, Skin o' My Tooth.*

Pentecost, Hugh. *Cancelled in Red, The Creeping Hours, The Evil That Men Do, Sniper.*

Phillpotts, Eden. *The Anniversary Murder, "Found Drowned," Monkshood, A Voice From the Dark.*

Poe, Edgar Allan. *Tales of Mystery and Imagination.*

Post, Melville Davisson. *The Bradmoor Murder; The Mystery at the Blue Villa; The Silent Witness; The Sleuth of St. James Square; The Strange Schemes of Randolph Mason; Uncle Abner, Master of Mysteries.*

Proctor, Maurice. *A Body to Spare, The Graveyard Rolls, Man in Ambush, The Ripper, The Pennycross Murders.*

Queen, Ellery. *The Adventures of Ellery Queen, And On the Eighth Day, The Dutch Shoe Mystery, The House of Brass, Q.E.D., Queen's Bureau of Investigation, The Roman Hat Mystery.*

Rhode, John. *The Affair of the Substitute Doctor, The Claverton Affair, Death in Harley Street, Double Indemnities, Dr. Priestley Lays a Trap, Hendon's First Case, The Secret of the Lake House, Shadow of an Alibi; (with Carter Dickson), Fatal Descent.*

Rinehart, Mary Roberts. *The Album, The Door, The Man in the Lower Ten, The Mary Roberts Rinehart Crime Book, Mary Roberts Rinehart's Mystery Book.*

Sayers, Dorothy. *Busman's Honeymoon, Clouds of Witnesses, Gaudy Night, Hangman's Holiday, Have His Carcase, In the Teeth of the Evidence, Lord Peter Views the Body, Murder Must Advertise, The Nine Tailors, Strong Poison, Suspicious Characters, Whose Body?*

Scherf, Margaret. *The Beautiful Birthday Cake, The Corpse in the Flannel Nightgown, The Diplomat and the Gold Piano.*

Shannon, Dell. *Death by Inches, Rain With Violence.*

Simenon, Georges. *The Man Who Watched the Trains Go By, Maigret Hesitates, Maigret in Vichy, Maigret and the Wine Merchant, The Short Cases of Maigret.*

Snow, C. P. *Death Under Sail.*

Spillane, Mickey. *Day of the Guns, Kiss Me Deadly, The Girl Hunters.*

Stout, Rex. *And Be a Villain, And Four to Go, Bad for Business, Champagne for One, Death of a Doxy, A Right to Die, Too Many Crooks, Three Doors to Death, Three Witnesses, Trio for Blunt Instruments, Trouble in Triplicate.*

Thorp, Roderick. *The Detective.*

Underwood, Michael. *Murder Made Absolute, Murder on Trial, The Shadow Game.*

Van Dine, S. S. *The Benson Murder Case, The Canary Murder Case, The Garden Murder Case.*

Van Gulik, Robert. *The Chinese Bell Murders, The Chinese Gold Murders, The Chinese Nail Murders.*

Wayland, Patrick. *Counterstroke, Double Defector, The Waiting Game.*

Waugh, Hillary. *The Con Game, Death and Circumstance, Girl on the Run, 30 Manhattan East.*

Westlake, Donald. *Cops and Robbers, The Fugitive Pigeon, God Save the Mark.*

Whitfield, Raoul. *Green Ice.*

Wolfe, Nero. *Before Midnight.*

Woods, Sarah. *And Shame the Devil, An Improbable Fiction, Tarry and Be Hanged.*

A 4
B 5
C 6
D 7
E 8
F 9
G 0
H 1
I 2
J 3